THE LOEB CLASSICAL LIBRARY

EDITED BY

E. CAPPS, Ph.D., LL.D.   T. E. PAGE, Litt.D.   W. H. D. ROUSE, Litt.D.

PLUTARCH'S LIVES

IV

PLUTARCH'S LIVES

WITH AN ENGLISH TRANSLATION BY

BERNADOTTE PERRIN

IN ELEVEN VOLUMES

IV

ALCIBIADES AND CORIOLANUS
LYSANDER AND SULLA

LONDON : WILLIAM HEINEMANN
NEW YORK : G. P. PUTNAM'S SONS
MCMXVI

PRINTED IN GREAT BRITAIN

PREFATORY NOTE

As in the preceding volumes of this series, agreement between the Sintenis (Teubner, 1873–1875) and Bekker (Tauchnitz, 1855–1857) texts of the *Parallel Lives* has been taken as the basis for the text. Any preference of one to the other where they differ, and any departure from both, have been indicated. None of the *Lives* presented in this volume is contained in the Codex Seitenstettensis (S), the relative value of which is explained in the Introduction to the first volume. A few superior readings have been adopted from the Codex Matritensis (M^a), on the authority of the collations of Charles Graux, as published in *Bursians Jahresbericht* (1884). No attempt has been made, naturally, to furnish either a diplomatic text or a full critical apparatus. The reading which follows the colon in the critical notes is that of the Teubner Sintenis, and also, unless otherwise stated in the note, of the Tauchnitz Bekker.

Some use has been made of the edition of the

PREFATORY NOTE

Sulla by the Rev. Hubert A. Holden, Cambridge, Pitt Press Series, 1886.

The translation of the *Alcibiades* has already appeared in my "Plutarch's Nicias and Alcibiades" (New York, 1912), and is reproduced here (with only slight changes) by the generous consent of the publishers, the Messrs. Charles Scribner's Sons. The translations of the *Coriolanus, Lysander,* and *Sulla* appear here for the first time. All the standard translations of the *Lives* have been carefully compared and utilized, including that of the *Sulla* by Professor Long.

B. PERRIN.

New Haven, Connecticut, U.S.A.
April, 1916.

CONTENTS

ORDER OF THE PARALLEL LIVES IN THIS EDITION IN THE CHRONOLOGICAL SEQUENCE OF THE GREEK LIVES.

THE TRADITIONAL ORDER OF THE PARALLEL LIVES.

(1) Theseus and Romulus.

(2) Lycurgus and Numa.

(3) Solon and Publicola.

(4) Themistocles and Camillus.

5) Pericles and Fabius Maximus.

(6) Alcibiades and Coriolanus.

(7) Timoleon and Aemilius Paulus.

(8) Pelopidas and Marcellus.

(9) Aristides and Cato the Elder.

(10) Philopoemen and Flamininus.

(11) Pyrrhus and Caius Marius.

(12) Lysander and Sulla.

(13) Cimon and Lucullus.

(14) Nicias and Crassus.

(15) Sertorius and Eumenes.

(16) Agesilaus and Pompey.

(17) Alexander and Julius Caesar.

(18) Phocion and Cato the Younger.

(19) Agis and Cleomenes, and Tiberius and Caius Gracchus.

(20) Demosthenes and Cicero.

(21) Demetrius and Antony.

(22) Dion and Brutus.

. . . .

(23) Aratus.

(24) Artaxerxes.

(25) Galba.

(26) Otho.

NOTE.

It has been found necessary to divide Plutarch's Lives into eleven volumes instead of ten as announced in the first four volumes. New title pages and a new "Order of the Parallel Lives" have been printed for the first four volumes, to be substituted for those contained in the copies so far issued, and these will be supplied, on application, to subscribers free of charge.

ALCIBIADES

B

ΑΛΚΙΒΙΑΔΗΣ

Ι. Τὸ Ἀλκιβιάδου γένος ἄνωθεν Εὐρυσάκην τὸν Αἴαντος ἀρχηγὸν ἔχειν δοκεῖ, πρὸς δὲ μητρὸς Ἀλκμαιωνίδης ἦν, ἐκ Δεινομάχης γεγονὼς τῆς Μεγακλέους. ὁ δὲ πατὴρ αὐτοῦ Κλεινίας ἰδιοστόλῳ τριήρει περὶ Ἀρτεμίσιον ἐνδόξως ἐναυμάχησεν, ὕστερον δὲ Βοιωτοῖς μαχόμενος περὶ Κορώνειαν ἀπέθανε. τοῦ δὲ Ἀλκιβιάδου Περικλῆς καὶ Ἀρίφρων οἱ Ξανθίππου, προσήκοντες κατὰ γένος, ἐπετρόπευον.

2 Λέγεται δ' οὐ κακῶς ὅτι τῆς Σωκράτους πρὸς αὐτὸν εὐνοίας καὶ φιλανθρωπίας οὐ μικρὰ πρὸς δόξαν ἀπέλαυσεν, εἴγε Νικίου μὲν καὶ Δημοσθένους καὶ Λαμάχου καὶ Φορμίωνος Θρασυβούλου τε καὶ Θηραμένους, ἐπιφανῶν ἀνδρῶν γενομένων κατ' αὐτόν, οὐδενὸς οὐδ' ἡ μήτηρ ὀνόματος τετύχηκεν, Ἀλκιβιάδου δὲ καὶ τίτθην, γένος Λάκαιναν, Ἀμύκλαν ὄνομα, καὶ Ζώπυρον παιδαγωγὸν ἴσμεν, ὧν τὸ μὲν Ἀντισθένης, τὸ δὲ Πλάτων ἱστόρηκε.

ALCIBIADES

I. THE family of Alcibiades, it is thought, may be traced back to Eurysaces,[1] the son of Aias, as its founder; and on his mother's side he was an Alcmaeonid, being the son of Deinomache, the daughter of Megacles. His father, Cleinias, fitted out a trireme at his own cost and fought it gloriously at Artemisium.[2] He was afterwards slain at Coroneia,[3] fighting the Boeotians, and Alcibiades was therefore reared as the ward of Pericles and Ariphron, the sons of Xanthippus, his near kinsmen.[4]

It is said, and with good reason, that the favour and affection which Socrates showed him contributed not a little to his reputation. Certain it is that Nicias, Demosthenes, Lamachus, Phormio, Thrasybulus, and Theramenes were prominent men, and his contemporaries, and yet we cannot so much as name the mother of any one of them; whereas, in the case of Alcibiades, we even know that his nurse, who was a Spartan woman, was called Amycla, and his tutor Zopyrus. The one fact is mentioned by Antisthenes, the other by Plato.[5]

[1] Plato, *Alcibiades I.* p. 121.   [2] 480 B.C.
[3] 447 B.C.   [4] They were first cousins, once removed.
[5] *Alcibiades I.* p. 122.

3   Περὶ μὲν οὖν τοῦ κάλλους Ἀλκιβιάδου οὐδὲν
ἴσως δεῖ λέγειν, πλὴν ὅτι καὶ παῖδα καὶ μειράκιον
καὶ ἄνδρα πάσῃ συνανθῆσαν τῇ ἡλικίᾳ καὶ ὥρᾳ
τοῦ σώματος ἐράσμιον καὶ ἡδὺν παρέσχεν. οὐ
γάρ, ὡς Εὐριπίδης ἔλεγε, πάντων τῶν καλῶν καὶ
τὸ μετόπωρον καλόν ἐστιν, ἀλλὰ τοῦτο Ἀλκιβιάδῃ μετ᾽ ὀλίγων ἄλλων δι᾽ εὐφυΐαν καὶ
4 ἀρετὴν σώματος ὑπῆρξε.   τῇ δὲ φωνῇ καὶ τὴν
τραυλότητα ἐμπρέψαι λέγουσι καὶ τῷ λάλῳ
πιθανότητα παρασχεῖν χάριν ἐπιτελοῦσαν. μέμνηται δὲ καὶ Ἀριστοφάνης αὐτοῦ τῆς τραυλότητος
ἐν οἷς ἐπισκώπτει Θέωρον·

Εἶτ᾽ Ἀλκιβιάδης εἶπε πρός με τραυλίσας·
" ὁλᾷς Θέωλον; τὴν κεφαλὴν κόλακος ἔχει."
ὀρθῶς γε τοῦτ᾽ Ἀλκιβιάδης ἐτραύλισεν.

καὶ Ἄρχιππος τὸν υἱὸν τοῦ Ἀλκιβιάδου σκώπ-
των· " Βαδίζει," φησί, " διακεχλιδώς, θοἰμάτιον
ἕλκων, ὅπως ἐμφερὴς μάλιστα τῷ πατρὶ δόξειεν
εἶναι,

Κλασαυχενεύεταί τε καὶ τραυλίζεται."

II. Τὸ δ᾽ ἦθος αὐτοῦ πολλὰς μὲν ὕστερον, ὡς
εἰκὸς ἐν πράγμασι μεγάλοις καὶ τύχαις πολυ-
τρόποις, ἀνομοιότητας πρὸς αὐτὸ καὶ μεταβολὰς
ἐπεδείξατο. φύσει δὲ πολλῶν ὄντων καὶ μεγάλων παθῶν ἐν αὐτῷ, τὸ φιλόνεικον ἰσχυρότατον

ALCIBIADES

As regards the beauty of Alcibiades, it is perhaps unnecessary to say aught, except that it flowered out with each successive season of his bodily growth, and made him, alike in boyhood, youth and manhood, lovely and pleasant. The saying of Euripides,[1] that " beauty's autumn, too, is beautiful," is not always true. But it was certainly the case with Alcibiades, as with few besides, because of his excellent natural parts. Even the lisp that he had became his speech, they say, and made his talk persuasive and full of charm. Aristophanes notices this lisp of his in the verses wherein he ridicules Theorus:[2]—

(*Sosias*)   " Then Alcibiades said to me with a lisp, said he,
              ' Cwemahk Theocwus? What a cwaven's head he has !' "
(*Xanthias*) " That lisp of Alcibiades hit the mark for once !"

And Archippus, ridiculing the son of Alcibiades, says : " He walks with utter wantonness, trailing his long robe behind him, that he may be thought the very picture of his father, yes,

He slants his neck awry, and overworks the lisp."[3]

II. His character, in later life, displayed many inconsistencies and marked changes, as was natural amid his vast undertakings and varied fortunes. He was naturally a man of many strong passions, the mightiest of which were the love of rivalry and the love

---

[1] Cf. Aelian, *Var. Hist.* xiii. 4.
[2] *Wasps*, 44 ff. The " lisp" of Alcibiades turned his r's into l's, and the play is on the Greek words κόραξ, *raven*, and κόλαξ, *flatterer* or *craven*.
[3] Kock, *Com. Att. Frag.* i. p. 688.

ἦν καὶ τὸ φιλόπρωτον, ὡς δῆλόν ἐστι τοῖς
παιδικοῖς ἀπομνημονεύμασιν.

2   Ἐν μὲν γὰρ τῷ παλαίειν πιεζούμενος, ὑπὲρ τοῦ
μὴ πεσεῖν ἀναγαγὼν πρὸς τὸ στόμα τὰ ἄμματα
τοῦ πιεζοῦντος, οἷος ἦν διαφαγεῖν τὰς χεῖρας.
ἀφέντος δὲ τὴν λαβὴν ἐκείνου καὶ εἰπόντος·
"Δάκνεις, ὦ Ἀλκιβιάδη, καθάπερ αἱ γυναῖκες,"
"Οὐκ ἔγωγε," εἶπεν, "ἀλλ' ὡς οἱ λέοντες."

Ἔτι δὲ μικρὸς ὢν ἔπαιζεν ἀστραγάλοις ἐν τῷ
στενωπῷ, τῆς δὲ βολῆς καθηκούσης εἰς αὐτὸν
3 ἄμαξα φορτίων ἐπῄει. πρῶτον μὲν οὖν ἐκέλευε
περιμεῖναι τὸν ἄγοντα τὸ ζεῦγος· ὑπέπιπτε γὰρ
ἡ βολὴ τῇ παρόδῳ τῆς ἁμάξης· μὴ πειθομένου δὲ
δι' ἀγροικίαν, ἀλλ' ἐπάγοντος, οἱ μὲν ἄλλοι παῖδες
διέσχον, ὁ δ' Ἀλκιβιάδης καταβαλὼν ἐπὶ στόμα
πρὸ τοῦ ζεύγους καὶ παρατείνας ἑαυτόν, ἐκέλευεν
οὕτως, εἰ βούλεται, διεξελθεῖν, ὥστε τὸν μὲν
ἄνθρωπον ἀνακροῦσαι τὸ ζεῦγος ὀπίσω δείσαντα,
τοὺς δ' ἰδόντας ἐκπλαγῆναι καὶ μετὰ βοῆς συν-
δραμεῖν πρὸς αὐτόν.

4   Ἐπεὶ δὲ εἰς τὸ μανθάνειν ἧκε, τοῖς μὲν ἄλλοις
ὑπήκουε διδασκάλοις ἐπιεικῶς, τὸ δ' αὐλεῖν
ἔφευγεν ὡς ἀγεννὲς καὶ ἀνελεύθερον· πλήκτρου
μὲν γὰρ καὶ λύρας χρῆσιν οὐδὲν οὔτε σχήματος
οὔτε μορφῆς ἐλευθέρῳ πρεπούσης διαφθείρειν,
αὐλοὺς δὲ φυσῶντος ἀνθρώπου στόματι καὶ τοὺς
συνήθεις ἂν πάνυ μόλις διαγνῶναι τὸ πρόσωπον.
5 ἔτι δὲ τὴν μὲν λύραν τῷ χρωμένῳ συμφθέγγε-
σθαι καὶ συνᾴδειν, τὸν δ' αὐλὸν ἐπιστομίζειν καὶ
ἀποφράττειν ἕκαστον τήν τε φωνὴν καὶ τὸν
λόγον ἀφαιρούμενον. "Αὐλείτωσαν οὖν," ἔφη,
"Θηβαίων παῖδες· οὐ γὰρ ἴσασι διαλέγεσθαι·

6

of preëminence. This is clear from the stories recorded of his boyhood.

He was once hard pressed in wrestling, and to save himself from getting a fall, set his teeth in his opponent's arms, where they clutched him, and was like to have bitten through them. His adversary, letting go his hold, cried: "You bite, Alcibiades, as women do!" "Not I," said Alcibiades, "but as lions do."

While still a small boy, he was playing knucklebones in the narrow street, and just as it was his turn to throw, a heavy-laden waggon came along. In the first place, he bade the driver halt, since his cast lay right in the path of the waggon. The driver, however, was a boorish fellow, and paid no heed to him, but drove his team along. Whereupon, while the other boys scattered out of the way, Alcibiades threw himself flat on his face in front of the team, stretched himself out at full length, and bade the driver go on if he pleased. At this the fellow pulled up his beasts sharply, in terror; the spectators, too, were affrighted, and ran with shouts to help the boy.

At school, he usually paid due heed to his teachers, but he refused to play the flute, holding it to be an ignoble and illiberal thing. The use of the plectrum and the lyre, he argued, wrought no havoc with the bearing and appearance which were becoming to a gentleman; but let a man go to blowing on a flute, and even his own kinsmen could scarcely recognize his features. Moreover, the lyre blended its tones with the voice or song of its master; whereas the flute closed and barricaded the mouth, robbing its master both of voice and speech. "Flutes, then," said he, "for the sons of Thebes; they know not

7

ἡμῖν δὲ τοῖς Ἀθηναίοις, ὡς οἱ πατέρες λέγουσιν,
ἀρχηγέτις Ἀθηνᾶ καὶ πατρῷος Ἀπόλλων ἐστίν,
ὧν ἡ μὲν ἔρριψε τὸν αὐλόν, ὁ δὲ καὶ τὸν αὐλητὴν
6 ἐξέδειρεν." τοιαῦτα παίζων ἅμα καὶ σπουδάζων
ὁ Ἀλκιβιάδης αὐτόν τε τοῦ μαθήματος ἀπέστησε
καὶ τοὺς ἄλλους. ταχὺ γὰρ διῆλθε λόγος εἰς
τοὺς παῖδας ὡς εὖ ποιῶν ὁ Ἀλκιβιάδης βδελύτ-
τοιτο τὴν αὐλητικὴν καὶ χλευάζοι τοὺς μανθάν-
οντας. ὅθεν ἐξέπεσε κομιδῇ τῶν ἐλευθέρων
διατριβῶν καὶ προεπηλακίσθη παντάπασιν ὁ
αὐλός.

III. Ἐν δὲ ταῖς Ἀντιφῶντος λοιδορίαις γέγραπται ὅτι παῖς ὤν, ἐκ τῆς οἰκίας ἀπέδρα πρὸς
Δημοκράτη τινὰ τῶν ἐραστῶν· βουλομένου δ᾽ 19
αὐτὸν ἀποκηρύττειν Ἀρίφρονος, Περικλῆς οὐκ
εἴασεν, εἰπών· εἰ μὲν τέθνηκεν, ἡμέρᾳ μιᾷ διὰ τὸ
κήρυγμα φανεῖσθαι πρότερον, εἰ δὲ σῶς ἐστιν,
ἄσωστον αὐτῷ τὸν λοιπὸν βίον ἔσεσθαι· καὶ ὅτι
τῶν ἀκολουθούντων τινὰ κτείνειεν ἐν τῇ Σιβυρ-
τίου παλαίστρᾳ ξύλῳ πατάξας. ἀλλὰ τούτοις
μὲν οὐκ ἄξιον ἴσως πιστεύειν, ἅ γε λοιδορεῖσθαί
τις αὐτῷ δι᾽ ἔχθραν ὁμολογῶν εἶπεν.

IV. Ἤδη δὲ πολλῶν καὶ γενναίων ἀθροιζομένων καὶ περιεπόντων, οἱ μὲν ἄλλοι καταφανεῖς
ἦσαν τὴν λαμπρότητα τῆς ὥρας ἐκπεπληγμένοι
καὶ θεραπεύοντες, ὁ δὲ Σωκράτους ἔρως μέγα

---

¹ Athene threw away the flute because she saw her puffed
and swollen cheeks reflected in the water of a spring.
Marsyas the satyr was vanquished by Apollo in a musical
contest, and was flayed alive.

how to converse. But we Athenians, as our fathers say, have Athene for foundress and Apollo for patron, one of whom cast the flute away in disgust, and the other flayed the presumptuous flute-player. " [1] Thus, half in jest and half in earnest, Alcibiades emancipated himself from this discipline, and the rest of the boys as well. For word soon made its way to them that Alcibiades loathed the art of flute-playing and scoffed at its disciples, and rightly, too. Wherefore the flute was dropped entirely from the programme of a liberal education and was altogether despised.

III. Among the calumnies which Antiphon [2] heaps upon him it is recorded that, when he was a boy, he ran away from home to Democrates, one of his lovers, and that Ariphron was all for having him proclaimed by town crier as a castaway. But Pericles would not suffer it. "If he is dead," said he, "we shall know it only a day the sooner for the proclamation; whereas, if he is alive, he will, in consequence of it, be as good as dead for the rest of his life." Antiphon says also that with a blow of his stick he slew one of his attendants in the palaestra of Sibyrtius. But these things are perhaps unworthy of belief, coming as they do from one who admits that he hated Alcibiades, and abused him accordingly.

IV. It was not long before many men of high birth clustered about him and paid him their attentions. Most of them were plainly smitten with his brilliant youthful beauty and fondly courted him. But it was the love which Socrates had for him that

[2] An abusive oration of Antiphon the Rhamnusian against Alcibiades, cited in Athenaeus, p. 525 b, was probably a fabrication and falsely attributed to him. It is not extant.

μαρτύριον ἦν τῆς ἀρετῆς καὶ εὐφυΐας τοῦ παιδός,
ἣν ἐμφαινομένην τῷ εἴδει καὶ διαλάμπουσαν
ἐνορῶν, φοβούμενος δὲ τὸν πλοῦτον καὶ τὸ ἀξίωμα
καὶ τὸν προκαταλαμβάνοντα κολακείαις καὶ χάρισιν ἀστῶν καὶ ξένων καὶ συμμάχων ὄχλον, οἷος
ἦν ἀμύνειν καὶ μὴ περιορᾶν ὡς φυτὸν ἐν ἄνθει τὸν
2 οἰκεῖον καρπὸν ἀποβάλλον καὶ διαφθεῖρον. οὐδένα γὰρ ἡ τύχη περιέσχεν ἔξωθεν καὶ περιέφραξε
τοῖς λεγομένοις ἀγαθοῖς τοσοῦτον ὥστ' ἄτρωτον
ὑπὸ φιλοσοφίας γενέσθαι, καὶ λόγοις ἀπρόσιτον
παρρησίαν καὶ δηγμὸν ἔχουσιν· ὡς Ἀλκιβιάδης
εὐθὺς ἐξ ἀρχῆς θρυπτόμενος καὶ ἀποκλειόμενος
ὑπὸ τῶν πρὸς χάριν ἐξομιλούντων εἰσακοῦσαι
τοῦ νουθετοῦντος καὶ παιδεύοντος, ὅμως ὑπ' εὐφυΐας ἐγνώρισε Σωκράτη καὶ προσήκατο, διασχὼν
3 τοὺς πλουσίους καὶ ἐνδόξους ἐραστάς. ταχὺ δὲ
ποιησάμενος συνήθη, καὶ λόγων ἀκούσας οὐχ
ἡδονὴν ἄνανδρον ἐραστοῦ θηρεύοντος, οὐδὲ φιλη-
μάτων καὶ ψαύσεως προσαιτοῦντος, ἀλλ' ἐλέγ-
χοντος τὸ σαθρὸν τῆς ψυχῆς αὐτοῦ καὶ πιεζοῦντος
τὸν κενὸν καὶ ἀνόητον τῦφον,

Ἔπτηξ' ἀλέκτωρ δοῦλος ὣς κλίνας πτερόν.

καὶ τὸ μὲν Σωκράτους ἡγήσατο πρᾶγμα τῷ ὄντι
θεῶν ὑπηρεσίαν εἰς νέων ἐπιμέλειαν εἶναι καὶ
4 σωτηρίαν· καταφρονῶν δ' αὐτὸς ἑαυτοῦ, θαυμάζων
δ' ἐκεῖνον, ἀγαπῶν δὲ τὴν φιλοφροσύνην, αἰσχυνό-
μενος δὲ τὴν ἀρετήν, ἐλάνθανεν εἴδωλον ἔρωτος,

bore strong testimony to the boy's native excellence and good parts. These Socrates saw radiantly manifest in his outward person, and, fearful of the influence upon him of wealth and rank and the throng of citizens, foreigners and allies who sought to preëmpt his affections by flattery and favour, he was fain to protect him, and not suffer such a fair flowering plant to cast its native fruit to perdition. For there is no man whom Fortune so envelops and compasses about with the so-called good things of life that he cannot be reached by the bold and caustic reasonings of philosophy, and pierced to the heart. And so it was that Alcibiades, although he was pampered from the very first, and was prevented by the companions who sought only to please him from giving ear to one who would instruct and train him, nevertheless, through the goodness of his parts, at last saw all that was in Socrates, and clave to him, putting away his rich and famous lovers. And speedily, from choosing such an associate, and giving ear to the words of a lover who was in the chase for no unmanly pleasures, and begged no kisses and embraces, but sought to expose the weakness of his soul and rebuke his vain and foolish pride,

" He crouched, though warrior bird, like slave, with drooping wings." [1]

And he came to think that the work of Socrates was really a kind of provision of the gods for the care and salvation of youth. Thus, by despising himself, admiring his friend, loving that friend's kindly solicitude and revering his excellence, he

[1] The iambic trimeter is of unknown authorship.

ὥς φησιν ὁ Πλάτων, ἀντέρωτα κτώμενος, ὥστε
θαυμάζειν ἅπαντας ὁρῶντας αὐτὸν Σωκράτει μὲν
συνδειπνοῦντα καὶ συμπαλαίοντα καὶ συσκη-
νοῦντα, τοῖς δ' ἄλλοις ἐρασταῖς χαλεπὸν ὄντα
καὶ δυσχείρωτον, ἐνίοις δὲ καὶ παντάπασι
σοβαρῶς προσφερόμενον, ὥσπερ Ἀνύτῳ τῷ
Ἀνθεμίωνος.

5   Ἐτύγχανε μὲν γὰρ ἐρῶν τοῦ Ἀλκιβιάδου,
ξένους δέ τινας ἑστιῶν ἐκάλει κἀκεῖνον ἐπὶ τὸ
δεῖπνον. ὁ δὲ τὴν μὲν κλῆσιν ἀπείπατο, μεθυ-
σθεὶς δ' οἴκοι μετὰ τῶν ἑταίρων ἐκώμασε πρὸς
τὸν Ἄνυτον, καὶ ταῖς θύραις ἐπιστὰς τοῦ ἀν-
δρῶνος καὶ θεασάμενος ἀργυρῶν ἐκπωμάτων καὶ
χρυσῶν πλήρεις τὰς τραπέζας, ἐκέλευσε τοὺς
παῖδας τὰ ἡμίση λαβόντας οἴκαδε κομίζειν πρὸς
αὐτόν, εἰσελθεῖν δ' οὐκ ἠξίωσεν, ἀλλὰ ταῦτα
πράξας ἀπῆλθε. τῶν οὖν ξένων δυσχεραινόντων
καὶ λεγόντων ὡς ὑβριστικῶς καὶ ὑπερηφάνως εἴη
τῷ Ἀνύτῳ κεχρημένος ὁ Ἀλκιβιάδης, "Ἐπιεικῶς
μὲν οὖν," ὁ Ἄνυτος ἔφη, "καὶ φιλανθρώπως· ἃ
γὰρ ἐξῆν αὐτῷ λαβεῖν ἅπαντα, τούτων ἡμῖν τὰ
μέρη καταλέλοιπεν."

V. Οὕτω δὲ καὶ τοῖς ἄλλοις ἐρασταῖς ἐχρῆτο·
πλὴν ἕνα μετοικικὸν ἄνθρωπον, ὥς φασιν, οὐ
πολλὰ κεκτημένον, ἀποδόμενον δὲ πάντα καὶ τὸ
συναχθὲν εἰς ἑκατὸν στατῆρας τῷ Ἀλκιβιάδῃ
προσφέροντα καὶ δεόμενον λαβεῖν, γελάσας καὶ
ἡσθεὶς ἐκάλεσεν ἐπὶ δεῖπνον. ἑστιάσας δὲ καὶ
φιλοφρονηθεὶς τό τε χρυσίον ἀπέδωκεν αὐτῷ, καὶ
προσέταξε τῇ ὑστεραίᾳ τοὺς ὠνουμένους τὰ τέλη
τὰ δημόσια ταῖς τιμαῖς ὑπερβάλλειν ἀντωνού-

insensibly acquired an "image of love," as Plato says,[1] "to match love," and all were amazed to see him eating, exercising, and tenting with Socrates,[2] while he was harsh and stubborn with the rest of his lovers. Some of these he actually treated with the greatest insolence, as, for example, Anytus, the son of Anthemion.

This man was a lover of his, who, entertaining some friends, asked Alcibiades also to the dinner. Alcibiades declined the invitation, but after having drunk deep at home with some friends, went in revel rout to the house of Anytus, took his stand at the door of the men's chamber, and, observing the tables full of gold and silver beakers, ordered his slaves to take half of them and carry them home for him. He did not deign to go in, but played this prank and was off. The guests were naturally indignant, and declared that Alcibiades had treated Anytus with gross and overweening insolence. "Not so," said Anytus, "but with moderation and kindness; he might have taken all there were: he has left us half."

V. He treated the rest of his lovers also after this fashion. There was one man, however, a resident alien, as they say, and not possessed of much, who sold all that he had, and brought the hundred staters which he got for it to Alcibiades, begging him to accept them. Alcibiades burst out laughing with delight at this, and invited the man to dinner. After feasting him and showing him every kindness, he gave him back his gold, and charged him on the morrow to compete with the farmers of the public revenues and outbid them all.

[1] *Phaedrus*, p. 255. [2] Cf. Plato, *Symposium*, p. 219 e.

2 μενον. παραιτουμένου δὲ τοῦ ἀνθρώπου διὰ τὸ
πολλῶν ταλάντων εἶναι τὴν ὠνήν, ἠπείλησε
μαστιγώσειν εἰ μὴ ταῦτα πράττοι· καὶ γὰρ 19
ἐτύγχανεν ἐγκαλῶν τι τοῖς τελώναις ἴδιον. ἔωθεν
οὖν προελθὼν[1] ὁ μέτοικος εἰς ἀγορὰν ἐπέθηκε τῇ
ὠνῇ τάλαντον. ἐπεὶ δ' οἱ τελῶναι συστρεφόμενοι
καὶ ἀγανακτοῦντες ἐκέλευον ὀνομάζειν ἐγγυητήν,
ὡς οὐκ ἂν εὑρόντος, θορυβουμένου τοῦ ἀνθρώπου
καὶ ἀναχωροῦντος, ἑστὼς ὁ Ἀλκιβιάδης ἄπωθεν
πρὸς τοὺς ἄρχοντας, "Ἐμὲ γράψατ'," ἔφη, "ἐμὸς
3 φίλος ἐστίν, ἐγγυῶμαι." ταῦτ' ἀκούσαντες οἱ
τελῶναι ἐξηπορήθησαν. εἰωθότες γὰρ ἀεὶ ταῖς
δευτέραις ὠναῖς χρεωλυτεῖν τὰς πρώτας, οὐχ
ἑώρων ἀπαλλαγὴν αὑτοῖς οὖσαν τοῦ πράγματος.
ἐδέοντο δὴ τοῦ ἀνθρώπου ἀργύριον διδόντες· ὁ
δ' Ἀλκιβιάδης οὐκ εἴα λαβεῖν ἔλαττον ταλάντου.
διδόντων δὲ τὸ τάλαντον ἐκέλευσεν ἀποστῆναι
λαβόντα. κἀκεῖνον μὲν οὕτως ὠφέλησεν.

VI. Ὁ δὲ Σωκράτους ἔρως πολλοὺς ἔχων καὶ
μεγάλους ἀνταγωνιστὰς πῇ μὲν ἐκράτει τοῦ
Ἀλκιβιάδου, δι' εὐφυΐαν ἁπτομένων τῶν λόγων
αὐτοῦ καὶ τὴν καρδίαν στρεφόντων καὶ δάκρυα
ἐκχεόντων, ἔστι δ' ὅτε καὶ τοῖς κόλαξι πολλὰς
ἡδονὰς ὑποβάλλουσιν ἐνδιδοὺς ἑαυτόν, ἀπωλί-
σθαινε τοῦ Σωκράτους καὶ δραπετεύων ἀτεχνῶς
ἐκυνηγεῖτο, πρὸς μόνον ἐκεῖνον ἔχων τὸ αἰδεῖσθαι
καὶ τὸ φοβεῖσθαι, τῶν δ' ἄλλων ὑπερορῶν.

2 Ὁ μὲν οὖν Κλεάνθης ἔλεγε τὸν ἐρώμενον ὑφ'

---

[1] προελθὼν Coraës and Bekker, after Reiske: προσελθών

The man protested, because the purchase demanded a capital of many talents ; but Alcibiades threatened to have him scourged if he did not do it, because he cherished some private grudge against the ordinary contractors. In the morning, accordingly, the alien went into the market place and increased the usual bid for the public lands by a talent. The contractors clustered angrily about him and bade him name his surety, supposing that he could find none. The man was confounded and began to draw back, when Alcibiades, standing afar off, cried to the magistrates : " Put my name down ; he is a friend of mine ; I will be his surety." When the contractors heard this, they were at their wit's end, for they were in the habit of paying what they owed on a first purchase with the profits of a second, and saw no way out of their difficulty. Accordingly, they besought the man to withdraw his bid, and offered him money so to do ; but Alcibiades would not suffer him to take less than a talent. On their offering the man the talent, he bade him take it and withdraw. To this lover he was of service in such a way.

VI. But the love of Socrates, though it had many powerful rivals, somehow mastered Alcibiades. For he was of good natural parts, and the words of his teacher took hold of him and wrung his heart and brought tears to his eyes. But sometimes he would surrender himself to the flatterers who tempted him with many pleasures, and slip away from Socrates, and suffer himself to be actually hunted down by him like a runaway slave. And yet he feared and reverenced Socrates alone, and despised the rest of his lovers.

It was Cleanthes who said that any one beloved of

15

ἑαυτοῦ μὲν ἐκ τῶν ὤτων κρατεῖσθαι, τοῖς δ᾽
ἀντερασταῖς πολλὰς λαβὰς παρέχειν ἀθίκτους
ἑαυτῷ, τὴν γαστέρα λέγων καὶ τὰ αἰδοῖα καὶ τὸν
λαιμόν· Ἀλκιβιάδης δ᾽ ἦν μὲν ἀμέλει καὶ πρὸς
ἡδονὰς ἀγώγιμος· ἡ γὰρ ὑπὸ Θουκυδίδου λεγο-
μένη παρανομία εἰς τὸ σῶμα τῆς διαίτης ὑποψίαν
3 τοιαύτην δίδωσιν. οὐ μὴν ἀλλὰ μᾶλλον αὐτοῦ
τῆς φιλοτιμίας ἐπιλαμβανόμενοι καὶ τῆς φιλο-
δοξίας οἱ διαφθείροντες ἐνέβαλλον οὐ καθ᾽ ὥραν
εἰς μεγαλοπραγμοσύνην, ἀναπείθοντες ὡς, ὅταν
πρῶτον ἄρξηται τὰ δημόσια πράττειν, οὐ μόνον
ἀμαυρώσοντα τοὺς ἄλλους στρατηγοὺς καὶ δημαγωγοὺς εὐθύς, ἀλλὰ καὶ τὴν Περικλέους δύναμιν
ἐν τοῖς Ἕλλησι καὶ δόξαν ὑπερβαλούμενον.
4 ὥσπερ οὖν ὁ σίδηρος ἐν τῷ πυρὶ μαλασσόμενος
αὖθις ὑπὸ τοῦ ψυχροῦ πυκνοῦται καὶ σύνεισι
τοῖς μορίοις εἰς αὑτόν, οὕτως ἐκεῖνον ὁ Σωκράτης
θρύψεως διάπλεων καὶ χαυνότητος ὁσάκις ἂν
λάβοι, πιέζων τῷ λόγῳ καὶ συστέλλων ταπεινὸν
ἐποίει καὶ ἄτολμον, ἡλίκων ἐνδεής ἐστι καὶ
ἀτελὴς πρὸς ἀρετὴν μανθάνοντα.

VII. Τὴν δὲ παιδικὴν ἡλικίαν παραλλάσσων
ἐπέστη γραμματοδιδασκάλῳ καὶ βιβλίον ᾔτησεν
Ὁμηρικόν. εἰπόντος δὲ τοῦ διδασκάλου μηδὲν
ἔχειν Ὁμήρου, κονδύλῳ καθικόμενος αὐτοῦ παρῆλθεν. ἑτέρου δὲ φήσαντος ἔχειν Ὅμηρον ὑφ᾽
αὑτοῦ διωρθωμένον, "Εἶτ᾽," ἔφη, "γράμματα
διδάσκεις, Ὅμηρον ἐπανορθοῦν ἱκανὸς ὤν; οὐχὶ
τοὺς νέους παιδεύεις;"
2 Περικλεῖ δὲ βουλόμενος ἐντυχεῖν ἐπὶ θύρας

him must be "downed," as wrestlers say, by the ears alone, though offering to rival lovers many other "holds" which he himself would scorn to take,—meaning the various lusts of the body. And Alcibiades was certainly prone to be led away into pleasure. That "lawless self-indulgence" of his, of which Thucydides speaks,[1] leads one to suspect this. However, it was rather his love of distinction and love of fame to which his corrupters appealed, and thereby plunged him all too soon into ways of presumptuous scheming, persuading him that he had only to enter public life, and he would straightway cast into total eclipse the ordinary generals and public leaders, and not only that, he would even surpass Pericles in power and reputation among the Hellenes. Accordingly, just as iron, which has been softened in the fire, is hardened again by cold water, and has its particles compacted together, so Alcibiades, whenever Socrates found him filled with vanity and wantonness, was reduced to shape by the Master's discourse, and rendered humble and cautious. He learned how great were his deficiencies and how incomplete his excellence.

VII. Once, as he was getting on past boyhood, he accosted a school-teacher, and asked him for a book of Homer. The teacher replied that he had nothing of Homer's, whereupon Alcibiades fetched him a blow with his fist, and went his way. Another teacher said he had a Homer which he had corrected himself. "What!" said Alcibiades, "are you teaching boys to read when you are competent to edit Homer? You should be training young men."

He once wished to see Pericles, and went to his

[1] vi. 15, 4.

ἦλθεν αὐτοῦ. πυθόμενος δὲ μὴ σχολάζειν, ἀλλὰ
σκοπεῖν καθ' ἑαυτὸν ὅπως ἀποδώσει λόγον Ἀθηναίοις, ἀπιὼν ὁ Ἀλκιβιάδης, " Εἶτα," ἔφη, " βέλτιον οὐκ ἦν σκοπεῖν αὐτὸν ὅπως οὐκ ἀποδώσει
λόγον Ἀθηναίοις ; "

Ἔτι δὲ μειράκιον ὢν ἐστρατεύσατο τὴν εἰς
Ποτίδαιαν στρατείαν, καὶ Σωκράτη σύσκηνον
3 εἶχε καὶ παραστάτην ἐν τοῖς ἀγῶσιν. ἰσχυρᾶς
δὲ γενομένης μάχης ἠρίστευσαν μὲν ἀμφότεροι,
τοῦ δ' Ἀλκιβιάδου τραύματι περιπεσόντος ὁ
Σωκράτης προέστη καὶ ἤμυνε καὶ μάλιστα δὴ
προδήλως ἔσωσεν αὐτὸν μετὰ τῶν ὅπλων. ἐγίνετο
μὲν οὖν τῷ δικαιοτάτῳ λόγῳ Σωκράτους τὸ ἀρι-
στεῖον· ἐπεὶ δ' οἱ στρατηγοὶ διὰ τὸ ἀξίωμα τῷ
Ἀλκιβιάδῃ σπουδάζοντες ἐφαίνοντο περιθεῖναι
τὴν δόξαν, ὁ Σωκράτης βουλόμενος αὔξεσθαι τὸ
φιλότιμον ἐν τοῖς καλοῖς αὐτοῦ πρῶτος ἐμαρτύρει
καὶ παρεκάλει στεφανοῦν ἐκεῖνον καὶ διδόναι τὴν
πανοπλίαν.

4 Ἔτι δὲ τῆς ἐπὶ Δηλίῳ μάχης γενομένης καὶ
φευγόντων Ἀθηναίων, ἔχων ἵππον ὁ Ἀλκιβιάδης,
τοῦ δὲ Σωκράτους πεζῇ μετ' ὀλίγων ἀποχωροῦν-
τος, οὐ παρήλασεν ἰδών, ἀλλὰ παρέπεμψε καὶ
περιήμυνεν, ἐπικειμένων τῶν πολεμίων καὶ πολλοὺς ἀναιρούντων. καὶ ταῦτα μὲν ὕστερον
ἐπράχθη.

VIII. Ἱππονίκῳ δὲ τῷ Καλλίου πατρί, καὶ
δόξαν ἔχοντι μεγάλην καὶ δύναμιν ἀπὸ πλούτου
καὶ γένους, ἐνέτριψε κόνδυλον, οὐχ ὑπ' ὀργῆς ἢ
διαφορᾶς τινος προαχθείς, ἀλλ' ἐπὶ γέλωτι,

house. But he was told that Pericles could not see him; he was studying how to render his accounts to the Athenians. "Were it not better for him," said Alcibiades, as he went away, "to study how not to render his accounts to the Athenians?"

While still a stripling, he served as a soldier in the campaign of Potidaea,[1] and had Socrates for his tent-mate and comrade in action. A fierce battle took place, wherein both of them distinguished themselves; but when Alcibiades fell wounded, it was Socrates who stood over him and defended him, and with the most conspicuous bravery saved him, armour and all. The prize of valour fell to Socrates, of course, on the justest calculation; but the generals, owing to the high position of Alcibiades, were manifestly anxious to give him the glory of it. Socrates, therefore, wishing to increase his pupil's honourable ambitions, led all the rest in bearing witness to his bravery, and in begging that the crown and the suit of armour be given to him.

On another occasion, in the rout of the Athenians which followed the battle of Delium,[2] Alcibiades, on horseback, saw Socrates retreating on foot with a small company, and would not pass him by, but rode by his side and defended him, though the enemy were pressing them hard and slaying many. This, however, was a later incident.

VIII. He once gave Hipponicus a blow with his fist —Hipponicus, the father of Callias, a man of great reputation and influence owing to his wealth and family—not that he had any quarrel with him, or was a prey to anger, but simply for the joke of the

[1] 432–431 B.C. Cf. chapter iv. 4.
[2] 424 B.C. Cf. Plato, *Symposium*, p. 221 a.

συνθέμενος πρὸς τοὺς ἑταίρους. περιβοήτου δὲ
τῆς ἀσελγείας ἐν τῇ πόλει γενομένης καὶ συν-
αγανακτούντων, ὥσπερ εἰκός, ἁπάντων, ἅμ᾽ ἡμέρᾳ
παρῆν ὁ Ἀλκιβιάδης ἐπὶ τὴν οἰκίαν τοῦ Ἱππο-
νίκου, καὶ τὴν θύραν κόψας εἰσῆλθε πρὸς αὐτὸν
καὶ θεὶς τὸ ἱμάτιον παρεδίδου τὸ σῶμα, μαστι-
2 γοῦν καὶ κολάζειν κελεύων. ὁ δὲ συνέγνω καὶ
τὴν ὀργὴν ἀφῆκεν, ὕστερον δὲ τῆς θυγατρὸς
Ἱππαρέτης ἐποιήσατο νυμφίον.

Ἔνιοι δέ φασιν, οὐχ Ἱππόνικον, ἀλλὰ Καλλίαν,
τὸν υἱὸν αὐτοῦ, δοῦναι τῷ Ἀλκιβιάδῃ τὴν Ἱππα-
ρέτην ἐπὶ δέκα ταλάντοις· εἶτα μέντοι τεκούσης
ἄλλα πάλιν δέκα προσεισπρᾶξαι τὸν Ἀλκιβιάδην,
ὡς τοῦτο συνθέμενον εἰ γένοιντο παῖδες. ὁ δὲ
Καλλίας ἐπιβουλὴν δεδοικὼς προσῆλθε τῷ δήμῳ
τὰ χρήματα διδοὺς καὶ τὸν οἶκον, ἄνπερ αὐτῷ
συμπέσῃ μὴ καταλιπόντι γενεὰν ἀποθανεῖν.

3 Εὔτακτος δ᾽ οὖσα καὶ φίλανδρος ἡ Ἱππαρέτη,
λυπουμένη δ᾽ ὑπ᾽ αὐτοῦ περὶ τὸν γάμον ἑταίραις
ξέναις καὶ ἀσταῖς συνόντος, ἐκ τῆς οἰκίας ἀπιοῦσα
πρὸς τὸν ἀδελφὸν ᾤχετο. τοῦ δ᾽ Ἀλκιβιάδου μὴ
φροντίζοντος, ἀλλὰ τρυφῶντος, ἔδει τὸ τῆς ἀπο-
λείψεως γράμμα παρὰ τῷ ἄρχοντι θέσθαι, μὴ δι᾽
4 ἑτέρων, ἀλλ᾽ αὐτὴν παροῦσαν. ὡς οὖν παρῆν
τοῦτο πράξουσα κατὰ τὸν νόμον, ἐπελθὼν ὁ
Ἀλκιβιάδης καὶ συναρπάσας αὐτὴν ἀπῆλθε δι᾽
ἀγορᾶς οἴκαδε κομίζων, μηδενὸς ἐναντιωθῆναι
μηδ᾽ ἀφελέσθαι τολμήσαντος. ἔμεινε μέντοι
παρ᾽ αὐτῷ μέχρι τελευτῆς, ἐτελεύτησε δὲ μετ᾽
οὐ πολὺν χρόνον εἰς Ἔφεσον τοῦ Ἀλκιβιάδου
πλεύσαντος.

thing, on a wager with some companions. The wanton deed was soon noised about the city, and everybody was indignant, as was natural. Early the next morning Alcibiades went to the house of Hipponicus, knocked at his door, and on being shown into his presence, laid off the cloak he wore and bade Hipponicus scourge and chastise him as he would. But Hipponicus put away his wrath and forgave him, and afterwards gave him his daughter Hipparete to wife.

Some say, however, that it was not Hipponicus, but Callias, his son, who gave Hipparete to Alcibiades, with a dowry of ten talents; and that afterwards, when she became a mother, Alcibiades exacted other ten talents besides, on the plea that this was the agreement, should children be born. And Callias was so afraid of the scheming of Alcibiades to get his wealth, that he made public proffer to the people of his property and house in case it should befall him to die without lineal heirs.

Hipparete was a decorous and affectionate wife, but being distressed because her husband would consort with courtezans, native and foreign, she left his house and went to live with her brother. Alcibiades did not mind this, but continued his wanton ways, and so she had to put in her plea for divorce to the magistrate, and that not by proxy, but in her own person. On her appearing publicly to do this, as the law required, Alcibiades came up and seized her and carried her off home with him through the market place, no man daring to oppose him or take her from him. She lived with him, moreover, until her death, but she died shortly after this, when Alcibiades was on a voyage to Ephesus.

5   Αὕτη μὲν οὖν οὐ παντελῶς ἔδοξεν ἡ βία παρά-
νομος οὐδ' ἀπάνθρωπος εἶναι· καὶ γὰρ ὁ νόμος
δοκεῖ διὰ τοῦτο προάγειν τὴν ἀπολείπουσαν εἰς
τὸ δημόσιον αὐτήν, ὅπως ἐγγένηται τῷ ἀνδρὶ
συμβῆναι καὶ κατασχεῖν.

IX. Ὄντος δὲ κυνὸς αὐτῷ θαυμαστοῦ τὸ μέγεθος καὶ τὸ εἶδος, ὃν ἑβδομήκοντα μνῶν ἐωνημένος
ἐτύγχανεν, ἀπέκοψε τὴν οὐρὰν πάγκαλον οὖσαν.
ἐπιτιμώντων δὲ τῶν συνήθων καὶ λεγόντων ὅτι
πάντες ἐπὶ τῷ κυνὶ δάκνονται καὶ λοιδοροῦσιν
αὐτόν, ἐπιγελάσας, " Γίνεται τοίνυν," εἶπεν, "ὃ
βούλομαι· βούλομαι γὰρ Ἀθηναίους τοῦτο λαλεῖν,
ἵνα μή τι χεῖρον περὶ ἐμοῦ λέγωσι."

X. Πρώτην δ' αὐτῷ πάροδον εἰς τὸ δημόσιον
γενέσθαι λέγουσι μετὰ χρημάτων ἐπιδόσεως, οὐκ
ἐκ παρασκευῆς, ἀλλὰ παριόντα θορυβούντων
Ἀθηναίων ἐρέσθαι τὴν αἰτίαν τοῦ θορύβου, πυθό-
μενον δὲ χρημάτων ἐπίδοσιν γίνεσθαι παρελθεῖν
καὶ ἐπιδοῦναι· τοῦ δὲ δήμου κροτοῦντος καὶ
βοῶντος ὑφ' ἡδονῆς, ἐπιλαθέσθαι τοῦ ὄρτυγος ὃν
ἐτύγχανεν ἔχων ἐν τῷ ἱματίῳ· πτοηθέντος οὖν
καὶ διαφυγόντος ἔτι μᾶλλον ἐκβοῆσαι τοὺς
Ἀθηναίους, πολλοὺς δὲ συνθηρᾶν ἀναστάντας,
λαβεῖν δ' αὐτὸν Ἀντίοχον τὸν κυβερνήτην καὶ
ἀποδοῦναι· διὸ προσφιλέστατον τῷ Ἀλκιβιάδῃ
γενέσθαι.

2   Μεγάλας δ' αὐτῷ κλεισιάδας ἐπὶ τὴν πολιτείαν

Such violence as this was not thought lawless or cruel at all. Indeed, the law prescribes that the wife who would separate from her husband shall go to court in person, to this very end, it would seem, that the husband may have a chance to meet and gain possession of her.

IX. Possessing a dog of wonderful size and beauty, which had cost him seventy minas,[1] he had its tail cut off, and a beautiful tail it was, too. His comrades chid him for this, and declared that everybody was furious about the dog and abusive of its owner. But Alcibiades burst out laughing and said: "That's just what I want; I want Athens to talk about this, that it may say nothing worse about me."

X. His first entrance into public life, they say, was connected with a contribution of money to the state, and was not of design. He was passing by when the Athenians were applauding in their assembly, and asked the reason for the applause. On being told that a contribution of money to the state was going on, he went forward to the bema and made a contribution himself. The crowd clapped their hands and shouted for joy—so much so that Alcibiades forgot all about the quail which he was carrying in his cloak, and the bird flew away in a fright. Thereupon the Athenians shouted all the more, and many of them sprang to help him hunt the bird. The one who caught it and gave it back to him was Antiochus, the sea captain, who became in consequence a great favourite with Alcibiades.[2]

Though great doors to public service were opened

---

[1] *I.e.* 7000 drachmas, or francs.
[2] Cf. chapter xxxv. 4–6.

ἀνοίγοντος τοῦ τε γένους καὶ τοῦ πλούτου τῆς τε
περὶ τὰς μάχας ἀνδραγαθίας, φίλων τε πολλῶν
καὶ οἰκείων ὑπαρχόντων, ἀπ' οὐδενὸς ἠξίου μᾶλλον ἢ τῆς τοῦ λόγου χάριτος ἰσχύειν ἐν τοῖς 1ͅ
πολλοῖς. καὶ ὅτι μὲν δυνατὸς ἦν εἰπεῖν, οἵ τε
κωμικοὶ μαρτυροῦσι καὶ τῶν ῥητόρων ὁ δυνατώ-
τατος ἐν τῷ κατὰ Μειδίου, λέγων τὸν Ἀλκιβιάδην
καὶ δεινότατον εἰπεῖν γενέσθαι πρὸς τοῖς ἄλλοις.
3 εἰ δὲ Θεοφράστῳ πιστεύομεν, ἀνδρὶ φιληκόῳ
καὶ ἱστορικῷ παρ' ὁντινοῦν τῶν φιλοσόφων,
εὑρεῖν μὲν ἦν τὰ δέοντα καὶ νοῆσαι πάντων
ἱκανώτατος ὁ Ἀλκιβιάδης, ζητῶν δὲ μὴ μόνον ἃ
δεῖ λέγειν, ἀλλὰ καὶ ὡς δεῖ τοῖς ὀνόμασι καὶ τοῖς
ῥήμασιν, οὐκ εὐπορῶν δέ, πολλάκις ἐσφάλλετο
καὶ μεταξὺ λέγων ἀπεσιώπα καὶ διέλειπε, λέξεως
διαφυγούσης αὐτόν, ἀναλαμβάνων καὶ διασκο-
πούμενος.

XI. Αἱ δ' ἱπποτροφίαι περιβόητοι μὲν ἐγένοντο
καὶ τῷ πλήθει τῶν ἁρμάτων· ἑπτὰ γὰρ ἄλλος
οὐδεὶς καθῆκεν Ὀλυμπίασιν ἰδιώτης οὐδὲ βα-
σιλεύς, μόνος δὲ ἐκεῖνος. καὶ τὸ νικῆσαι δὲ καὶ
δεύτερον γενέσθαι καὶ τέταρτον, ὡς Θουκυδίδης
φησίν, ὁ δ' Εὐριπίδης τρίτον, ὑπερβάλλει λαμ-
πρότητι καὶ δόξῃ πᾶσαν τὴν ἐν τούτοις φι-
2 λοτιμίαν. λέγει δ' ὁ Εὐριπίδης ἐν τῷ ᾄσματι
ταῦτα·

24

to him by his birth, his wealth, and his personal bravery in battle; and though he had many friends and followers, he thought that nothing should give him more influence with the people than the charm of his discourse. And that he was a powerful speaker, not only do the comic poets testify, but also the most powerful of orators himself,[1] who says, in his speech "Against Meidias," that Alcibiades was a most able speaker in addition to his other gifts. And if we are to trust Theophrastus, the most versatile and learned of the philosophers, Alcibiades was of all men the most capable of discovering and understanding what was required in a given case. But since he strove to find not only the proper thing to say, but also the proper words and phrases in which to say it; and since in this last regard he was not a man of large resources, he would often stumble in the midst of his speech, come to a stop, and pause a while, a particular phrase eluding him. Then he would resume, and proceed with all the caution in the world.

XI. His breeds of horses were famous the world over, and so was the number of his racing-chariots. No one else ever entered seven of these at the Olympic games—neither commoner nor king—but he alone. And his coming off first, second, and fourth victor (as Thucydides says[2]; third, according to Euripides), transcends in the splendour of its renown all that ambition can aspire to in this field. The ode of Euripides[3] to which I refer runs thus:—

[1] Demosthenes, *Against Meidias*, § 145.
[2] In a speech of Alcibiades, vi. 16. 2.
[3] An *Epinikion*, or hymn of victory, like the extant odes of Pindar.

Σὲ δ᾽ ἀείσομαι, ὦ Κλεινίου παῖ.
καλὸν ἁ νίκα· κάλλιστον δ᾽, ὃ μηδεὶς ἄλλος
'Ελλάνων,
ἅρματι πρῶτα δραμεῖν καὶ δεύτερα καὶ τρίτα,
βῆναί τ᾽ ἀπονητί, Διὸς στεφθέντα τ᾽ ἐλαίᾳ
κάρυκι βοᾶν[1] παραδοῦναι·

XII. Τοῦτο μέντοι τὸ λαμπρὸν ἐπιφανέστερον
ἐποίησεν ἡ τῶν πόλεων φιλοτιμία. σκηνὴν μὲν
γὰρ αὐτῷ κεκοσμημένην διαπρεπῶς ἔστησαν
'Εφέσιοι, τροφὰς δὲ ἵπποις καὶ πλῆθος ἱερείων
παρεῖχεν ἡ Χίων πόλις, οἶνον δὲ Λέσβιοι καὶ τὴν
ἄλλην ὑποδοχὴν ἀφειδῶς ἐστιῶντι πολλούς. οὐ
μὴν ἀλλὰ καὶ διαβολή τις ἢ κακοήθεια γενομένη
περὶ τὴν φιλοτιμίαν ἐκείνην πλείονα λόγον
παρέσχε.

2   Λέγεται γὰρ ὡς ἦν 'Αθήνησι Διομήδης, ἀνὴρ
οὐ πονηρός, 'Αλκιβιάδου φίλος, ἐπιθυμῶν δὲ
νίκην 'Ολυμπικὴν αὐτῷ γενέσθαι· καὶ πυνθανόμενος ἅρμα δημόσιον 'Αργείοις εἶναι, τὸν 'Αλκι-
βιάδην εἰδὼς ἐν "Αργει μέγα δυνάμενον καὶ φίλους
ἔχοντα πολλούς, ἔπεισεν αὐτῷ πρίασθαι τὸ ἅρμα.
3   πριάμενος δὲ ὁ 'Αλκιβιάδης ἴδιον ἀπεγράψατο,
τὸν δὲ Διομήδη χαίρειν εἴασε χαλεπῶς φέροντα
καὶ μαρτυρόμενον θεοὺς καὶ ἀνθρώπους. φαίνεται δὲ καὶ δίκη συστᾶσα περὶ τούτου, καὶ λόγος
'Ισοκράτει γέγραπται περὶ τοῦ ζεύγους ὑπὲρ τοῦ

---

[1] Διὸς στεφθέντα τ᾽ ἐλαίᾳ κάρυκι βοᾶν with Hermann and
Bergk (*Poet. Lyr. Gr.* ii.[4] p. 266): δὶς στεφθέντ᾽ ἐλαίᾳ κάρυκι
βοᾶν (Bekker, βοᾶν).

" Thee will I sing, O child of Cleinias ;
   A fair thing is victory, but fairest is what no other
        Hellene has achieved,
To run first, and second, and third in the contest
        of racing-chariots,
And to come off unwearied, and, wreathed with
        the olive of Zeus,
To furnish theme for herald's proclamation."

XII. Moreover, this splendour of his at Olympia
was made even more conspicuous by the emulous
rivalry of the cities in his behalf. The Ephesians
equipped him with a tent of magnificent adornment ;
the Chians furnished him with provender for his
horses and with innumerable animals for sacrifice ;
the Lesbians with wine and other provisions for his
unstinted entertainment of the multitude. However,
a grave calumny—or malpractice on his part—
connected with this rivalry was even more in the
mouths of men.

It is said, namely, that there was at Athens one
Diomedes, a reputable man, a friend of Alcibiades,
and eagerly desirous of winning a victory at Olympia.
He learned that there was a racing-chariot at Argos
which was the property of that city, and knowing
that Alcibiades had many friends and was very
influential there, got him to buy the chariot.
Alcibiades bought it for his friend, and then entered
it in the racing lists as his own, bidding Diomedes
go hang. Diomedes was full of indignation, and
called on gods and men to witness his wrongs. It
appears also that a law-suit arose over this matter,
and a speech was written by Isocrates [1] for the son of

---

[1] Oration xvi., *De bigis*.

Ἀλκιβιάδου παιδός, ἐν ᾧ Τισίας ἐστίν, οὐ
Διομήδης, ὁ δικασάμενος.

XIII. Ἐπεὶ δ᾽ ἀφῆκεν αὐτὸν εἰς τὴν πολιτείαν
ἔτι μειράκιον ὤν, τοὺς μὲν ἄλλους εὐθὺς ἐτα-
πείνωσε δημαγωγούς, ἀγῶνα δ᾽ εἶχε πρός τε
Φαίακα τὸν Ἐρασιστράτου καὶ Νικίαν τὸν Νικηράτου, τὸν μὲν ἤδη καθ᾽ ἡλικίαν προήκοντα καὶ
στρατηγὸν ἄριστον εἶναι δοκοῦντα, Φαίακα δ᾽
ἀρχόμενον, ὥσπερ αὐτός, αὐξάνεσθαι τότε καὶ
γνωρίμων ὄντα πατέρων, ἐλαττούμενον δὲ τοῖς τε
2 ἄλλοις καὶ περὶ τὸν λόγον. ἐντευκτικὸς γὰρ ἰδίᾳ
καὶ πιθανὸς ἐδόκει μᾶλλον ἢ φέρειν ἀγῶνας ἐν
δήμῳ δυνατός. ἦν γάρ, ὡς Εὔπολίς φησι,

Λαλεῖν ἄριστος, ἀδυνατώτατος λέγειν.

φέρεται δὲ καὶ λόγος τις κατ᾽ Ἀλκιβιάδου ὑπὸ[1]
Φαίακος γεγραμμένος, ἐν ᾧ μετὰ τῶν ἄλλων
γέγραπται καὶ ὅτι τῆς πόλεως πολλὰ πομπεῖα
χρυσᾶ καὶ ἀργυρᾶ κεκτημένης Ἀλκιβιάδης ἐχρῆτο
πᾶσιν αὐτοῖς ὥσπερ ἰδίοις πρὸς τὴν καθ᾽ ἡμέραν
δίαιταν.

3 Ἦν δέ τις Ὑπέρβολος Περιθοΐδης, οὗ μέμνηται
μὲν ὡς ἀνθρώπου πονηροῦ καὶ Θουκυδίδης, τοῖς
δὲ κωμικοῖς ὁμοῦ τι πᾶσι διατριβὴν ἀεὶ σκωπτό-
μενος ἐν τοῖς θεάτροις παρεῖχεν. ἄτρεπτος δὲ
πρὸς τὸ κακῶς ἀκούειν καὶ ἀπαθὴς ὢν ὀλιγωρίᾳ

[1] ὑπὸ with Coraës: καί.

28

Alcibiades "Concerning the Team of Horses." In this speech, however, it is Tisias, not Diomedes, who is the plaintiff.

XIII. On entering public life, though still a mere stripling, he immediately humbled all the other popular leaders except Phaeax, the son of Erasistratus, and Nicias, the son of Niceratus. These men made him fight hard for what he won. Nicias was already of mature years, and had the reputation of being a most excellent general; but Phaeax, like himself, was just beginning his career, and, though of illustrious parentage, was inferior to him in other ways, and particularly as a public speaker. He seemed affable and winning in private conversation rather than capable of conducting public debates. In fact, he was, as Eupolis says,[1]

" A prince of talkers, but in speaking most incapable."

And there is extant a certain speech written by Phaeax [2] " Against Alcibiades," wherein, among other things, it is written that the city's numerous ceremonial utensils of gold and silver were all used by Alcibiades at his regular table as though they were his own.

Now there was a certain Hyperbolus, of the deme Perithoedae, whom Thucydides mentions [3] as a base fellow, and who afforded all the comic poets, without any exception, constant material for jokes in their plays. But he was unmoved by abuse, and insensible

---

[1] In his *Demes* (Kock, *Com. Att. Frag.* i. p. 281).

[2] This has come down to us among the orations of Andocides (Or. iv.). It is clearly a fictitious speech, put by its unknown author into the mouth of Phaeax (cf. §§ 2 and 41).

[3] viii. 73, 3.

δόξης, ἣν ἀναισχυντίαν καὶ ἀπόνοιαν οὖσαν 19
εὐτολμίαν ἔνιοι καὶ ἀνδρείαν καλοῦσιν, οὐδενὶ μὲν
ἤρεσκεν, ἐχρῆτο δ' αὐτῷ πολλάκις ὁ δῆμος ἐπιθυμῶν προπηλακίζειν τοὺς ἐν ἀξιώματι καὶ συκο-
4 φαντεῖν. ἀναπεισθεὶς οὖν ὑπ' αὐτοῦ τότε τὸ
ὄστρακον ἐπιφέρειν ἔμελλεν, ᾧ κολούοντες ἀεὶ τὸν
προὔχοντα δόξῃ καὶ δυνάμει τῶν πολιτῶν ἐλαύνουσι, παραμυθούμενοι τὸν φθόνον μᾶλλον ἢ τὸν
φόβον. ἐπεὶ δὲ δῆλον ἦν ὅτι ἑνὶ τῶν τριῶν τὸ
ὄστρακον ἐποίσουσι, συνήγαγε τὰς στάσεις εἰς
ταὐτὸν ὁ Ἀλκιβιάδης, καὶ διαλεχθεὶς πρὸς τὸν
Νικίαν κατὰ τοῦ Ὑπερβόλου τὴν ὀστρακοφορίαν
ἔτρεψεν.

Ὡς δ' ἔνιοί φασιν, οὐ πρὸς Νικίαν, ἀλλὰ πρὸς
Φαίακα διαλεχθεὶς καὶ τὴν ἐκείνου προσλαβὼν
ἑταιρίαν ἐξήλασε τὸν Ὑπέρβολον οὐδ' ἂν προσ-
5 δοκήσαντα. φαῦλος γὰρ οὐδεὶς ἐνέπιπτεν εἰς
τοῦτον τὸν κολασμὸν οὐδ' ἄδοξος, ὥς που καὶ
Πλάτων ὁ κωμικὸς εἴρηκε τοῦ Ὑπερβόλου μνησ-
θείς,

Καίτοι πέπραχε τῶν προτέρων [1] μὲν ἄξια,
αὑτοῦ δὲ καὶ τῶν στιγμάτων ἀνάξια.
οὐ γὰρ τοιούτων εἵνεκ' ὄστραχ' εὑρέθη.

περὶ μὲν οὖν τούτων ἐν ἑτέροις μᾶλλον εἴρηται τὰ
ἱστορούμενα.

XIV. Τὸν δ' Ἀλκιβιάδην ὁ Νικίας οὐχ ἧττον
ἠνία θαυμαζόμενος ὑπὸ τῶν πολεμίων ἢ τιμώ-

_____
[1] προτέρων with Kock (Com. Att. Frag. i. p. 654): τρόπων
(worthy of his ways).

30

ALCIBIADES

to it, owing to his contempt of public opinion. This feeling some call courage and valour, but it is really mere shamelessness and folly. No one liked him, but the people often made use of him when they were eager to besmirch and calumniate men of rank and station. Accordingly, at the time of which I speak, persuaded by this man, they were about to exercise the vote of ostracism, by which they cripple and banish whatever man from time to time may have too much reputation and influence in the city to please them, assuaging thus their envy rather than their fear. When it was clear that the ostracism would fall on one of three men—Phaeax, Alcibiades, or Nicias—Alcibiades had a conference with Nicias, united their two parties into one and turned the vote of ostracism upon Hyperbolus.

Some say, however, that it was not Nicias, but Phaeax, with whom Alcibiades had the conference which resulted in winning over that leader's party and banishing Hyperbolus, who could have had no inkling of his fate. For no worthless or disreputable fellow had ever before fallen under this condemnation of ostracism. As Plato, the comic poet, has somewhere said, in speaking of Hyperbolus,

" And yet he suffered worthy fate for men of old ;
A fate unworthy though of him and of his brands.
For such as he the ostrakon was ne'er devised."

However, the facts which have been ascertained about this case have been stated more at length elsewhere.[1]

XIV. Alcibiades was sore distressed to see Nicias no less admired by his enemies than honoured by

[1] Cf. *Nicias*, xi.

μενος ὑπὸ τῶν πολιτῶν. πρόξενος μὲν γὰρ ἦν ὁ
Ἀλκιβιάδης τῶν Λακεδαιμονίων, καὶ τοὺς ἁλόν-
τας αὐτῶν περὶ Πύλον ἄνδρας ἐθεράπευσεν·
2 ἐπεὶ δ᾽ ἐκεῖνοί τε διὰ Νικίου μάλιστα τῆς εἰρήνης
τυχόντες καὶ τοὺς ἄνδρας ἀπολαβόντες ὑπερ-
ηγάπων αὐτόν, ἔν τε τοῖς Ἕλλησι λόγος ἦν ὡς
Περικλέους μὲν συνάψαντος αὐτοῖς, Νικίου δὲ
λύσαντος τὸν πόλεμον, οἵ τε πλεῖστοι τὴν εἰρήνην Νικίειον ὠνόμαζον, οὐ μετρίως ἀνιώμενος
ὁ Ἀλκιβιάδης καὶ φθονῶν ἐβούλευε σύγχυσιν
3 ὁρκίων. καὶ πρῶτον μὲν Ἀργείους αἰσθανόμενος
μίσει καὶ φόβῳ τῶν Σπαρτιατῶν ζητοῦντας
ἀποστροφήν, ἐλπίδας αὐτοῖς ἐνεδίδου κρύφα
τῆς Ἀθηναίων συμμαχίας, καὶ παρεθάρρυνε
πέμπων καὶ διαλεγόμενος τοῖς προεστῶσι τοῦ
δήμου μὴ δεδιέναι μηδ᾽ ὑπείκειν Λακεδαιμονίοις,
ἀλλὰ πρὸς Ἀθηναίους τρέπεσθαι καὶ περιμένειν
ὅσον οὐδέπω μεταμελομένους καὶ τὴν εἰρήνην
ἀφιέντας.

4   Ἐπεὶ δὲ Λακεδαιμόνιοι πρός τε τοὺς Βοιωτοὺς
ἐποιήσαντο συμμαχίαν καὶ Πάνακτον οὐχ ἑστός,
ὥσπερ ἔδει, τοῖς Ἀθηναίοις παρέδωκαν, ἀλλὰ
καταλύσαντες, ὀργιζομένους λαβὼν τοὺς Ἀθηναίους ἔτι μᾶλλον ἐξετράχυνε, καὶ τὸν Νικίαν
5 ἐθορύβει καὶ διέβαλλεν εἰκότα κατηγορῶν, ὅτι
τοὺς ἐν Σφακτηρίᾳ τῶν πολεμίων ἀποληφθέντας
αὐτὸς μὲν ἐξελεῖν οὐκ ἠθέλησεν στρατηγῶν,

his fellow-citizens. For although Alcibiades was resident consul for the Lacedaemonians at Athens, and had ministered to their men who had been taken prisoners at Pylos,[1] still, they felt that it was chiefly due to Nicias that they had obtained peace and the final surrender of those men, and so they lavished their regard upon him. And Hellenes everywhere said that it was Pericles who had plunged them into war, but Nicias who had delivered them out of it, and most men called the peace the " Peace of Nicias." [2] Alcibiades was therefore distressed beyond measure, and in his envy planned a violation of the solemn treaty. To begin with, he saw that the Argives hated and feared the Spartans and sought to be rid of them. So he secretly held out hopes to them of an alliance with Athens, and encouraged them, by conferences with the chief men of their popular party, not to fear nor yield to the Lacedaemonians, but to look to Athens and await her action, since she was now all but repentant, and desirous of abandoning the peace which she had made with Sparta.

And again, when the Lacedaemonians made a separate alliance with the Boeotians, and delivered up Panactum to the Athenians not intact, as they were bound to do by the treaty, but dismantled, he took advantage of the Athenians' wrath at this to embitter them yet more. He raised a tumult in the assembly against Nicias, and slandered him with accusations all too plausible. Nicias himself, he said, when he was general, had refused to capture the enemy's men who were cut off on the island of

[1] In 425 B.C. Cf. *Nicias*, vii-viii.
[2] Ratified in 421 B.C. Cf. *Nicias*, ix.

ἑτέρων δ᾽ ἐξελόντων ἀφῆκε καὶ ἀπέδωκε χαριζόμενος Λακεδαιμονίοις· εἶτ᾽ ἐκείνους μὲν οὐκ ἔπεισε
φίλος ὢν Βοιωτοῖς μὴ συνόμνυσθαι μηδὲ Κοριν-
θίοις, Ἀθηναίοις [1] δὲ κωλύει [2] τὸν βουλόμενον
τῶν Ἑλλήνων φίλον εἶναι καὶ σύμμαχον, εἰ μὴ
δόξειε Λακεδαιμονίοις.

6   Ἐκ δὲ τούτου κακῶς φερομένῳ τῷ Νικίᾳ παρῆσαν ὥσπερ κατὰ τύχην πρέσβεις ἀπὸ τῆς Λακεδαίμονος, αὐτόθεν τε λόγους ἐπιεικεῖς ἔχοντες
καὶ πρὸς πᾶν τὸ συμβιβαστικὸν καὶ δίκαιον
αὐτοκράτορες ἥκειν φάσκοντες. ἀποδεξαμένης
δὲ τῆς βουλῆς, τοῦ δὲ δήμου τῇ ὑστεραίᾳ μέλλοντος ἐκκλησιάζειν, δείσας ὁ Ἀλκιβιάδης
διεπράξατο τοὺς πρέσβεις ἐν λόγοις γενέσθαι
7 πρὸς αὐτόν. ὡς δὲ συνῆλθον ἔλεγε· "Τί πεπόν-
θατε, ἄνδρες Σπαρτιᾶται; πῶς ἔλαθεν ὑμᾶς ὅτι
τὰ τῆς βουλῆς ἀεὶ μέτρια καὶ φιλάνθρωπα πρὸς
τοὺς ἐντυγχάνοντάς ἐστιν, ὁ δὲ δῆμος μέγα φρονεῖ
καὶ μεγάλων ὀρέγεται; κἂν φάσκητε κύριοι
πάντων ἀφῖχθαι, προστάττων καὶ βιαζόμενος
ἀγνωμονήσει. φέρε δή, τὴν εὐήθειαν ταύτην
ἀφέντες, εἰ βούλεσθε χρήσασθαι μετρίοις Ἀθηναίοις καὶ μηδὲν ἐκβιασθῆναι παρὰ γνώμην, οὕτω
διαλέγεσθε περὶ τῶν δικαίων ὡς οὐκ ὄντες αὐτο-

---

[1] Ἀθηναίοις Coraës and Bekker, with C : Ἀθηναίους.
[2] κωλύει Coraës, after Reiske : κωλύειν.

Sphacteria, and when others had captured them, he had released and given them back to the Lacedaemonians, whose favour he sought; and then he did not persuade those same Lacedaemonians, tried friend of theirs as he was, not to make separate alliance with the Boeotians or even with the Corinthians, and yet whenever any Hellenes wished to be friends and allies of Athens, he tried to prevent it, unless it were the good pleasure of the Lacedaemonians.

Nicias was reduced to great straits by all this, but just then, by rare good fortune as it were, an embassy came from Sparta, with reasonable proposals to begin on, and with assurances that they came with full powers to adopt any additional terms that were conciliatory and just. The council received them favourably, and the people were to hold an assembly on the following day for their reception. But Alcibiades feared a peaceful outcome, and managed to secure a private conference with the embassy. When they were convened he said to them: "What is the matter with you, men of Sparta? Why are you blind to the fact that the council is always moderate and courteous towards those who have dealings with it, while the people's assembly is haughty and has great ambitions? If you say to them that you are come with unlimited powers, they will lay their commands and compulsions upon you without any feeling. Come now, put away such simplicity as this, and if you wish to get moderate terms from the Athenians, and to suffer no compulsion at their hands which you cannot yourselves approve, then discuss with them what would be a just settlement of your case, assuring them that you have not full powers to act.

κράτορες. συμπράξομεν δ' ἡμεῖς Λακεδαιμονίοις
8 χαριζόμενοι." ταῦτα δ' εἰπὼν ὅρκους ἔδωκεν
αὐτοῖς καὶ μετέστησεν ἀπὸ τοῦ Νικίου, παντάπασι πιστεύοντας αὐτῷ καὶ θαυμάζοντας ἅμα
τὴν δεινότητα καὶ σύνεσιν, ὡς οὐ τοῦ τυχόντος
ἀνδρὸς οὖσαν.

Τῇ δ' ὑστεραίᾳ συνήχθη μὲν ὁ δῆμος, εἰσῆλθον
δ' οἱ πρέσβεις. ἐρωτώμενοι δ' ὑπὸ τοῦ Ἀλκιβιάδου πάνυ φιλανθρώπως ἐφ' οἷς ἀφιγμένοι
τυγχάνουσιν, οὐκ ἔφασαν ἥκειν αὐτοκράτορες.
9 εὐθὺς οὖν ὁ Ἀλκιβιάδης ἐνέκειτο μετὰ κραυγῆς
καὶ ὀργῆς, ὥσπερ οὐκ ἀδικῶν, ἀλλ' ἀδικούμενος,
ἀπίστους καὶ παλιμβόλους ἀποκαλῶν καὶ μηδὲν
ὑγιὲς μήτε πρᾶξαι μήτ' εἰπεῖν ἥκοντας, ἐπη-
γανάκτει δ' ἡ βουλή, καὶ ὁ δῆμος ἐχαλέπαινε,
τὸν δὲ Νικίαν ἔκπληξις εἶχε καὶ κατήφεια τῶν
ἀνδρῶν τῆς μεταβολῆς, ἀγνοοῦντα τὴν ἀπάτην
καὶ τὸν δόλον.

XV. Οὕτω δὲ τῶν Λακεδαιμονίων ἐκπεσόντων,
στρατηγὸς ἀποδειχθεὶς ὁ Ἀλκιβιάδης εὐθὺς
Ἀργείους καὶ Μαντινεῖς καὶ Ἠλείους συμμάχους
ἐποίησε τοῖς Ἀθηναίοις. καὶ τὸν μὲν τρόπον
οὐδεὶς τῆς πράξεως ἐπήνει, μέγα δ' ἦν τὸ πεπραγμένον ὑπ' αὐτοῦ, διαστῆσαι καὶ κραδᾶναι Πελοπόννησον ὀλίγου δεῖν ἅπασαν, καὶ τοσαύτας
ἀσπίδας ἐν ἡμέρᾳ μιᾷ περὶ Μαντίνειαν ἀντιτάξαι
Λακεδαιμονίοις, καὶ πορρωτάτω τῶν Ἀθηνῶν
ἀγῶνα κατασκευάσαι καὶ κίνδυνον αὐτοῖς, ἐν ᾧ
μέγα μὲν οὐδὲν ἡ νίκη προσέθηκε κρατήσασιν, εἰ

I will coöperate with you, out of my regard for the Lacedaemonians." After this speech he gave them his oath, and so seduced them wholly away from the influence of Nicias. They trusted him implicitly, admired his cleverness and sagacity, and thought him no ordinary man.

On the following day the people convened in assembly, and the embassy was introduced to them. On being asked by Alcibiades, in the most courteous tone, with what powers they had come, they replied that they were not come with full and independent powers. At once, then, Alcibiades assailed them with angry shouts, as though he were the injured party, not they, calling them faithless and fickle men, who were come on no sound errand whatever. The council was indignant, the assembly was enraged, and Nicias was filled with consternation and shame at the men's change of front. He was unaware of the deceitful trick which had been played upon him.[1]

XV. After this fiasco on the part of the Lacedaemonians, Alcibiades was appointed general, and straightway brought the Argives, Mantineans, and Eleans into alliance with Athens.[2] The manner of this achievement of his no one approved, but the effect of it was great. It divided and agitated almost all Peloponnesus; it arrayed against the Lacedaemonians at Mantinea[3] so many warlike shields upon a single day; it set at farthest remove from Athens the struggle, with all its risks, in which, when the Lacedaemonians conquered, their victory brought them no great advantage,

---

[1] This parliamentary trick of Alcibiades is related also in *Nicias*, chapter x.   [2] 420 B.C.   [3] 418 B.C.

δ' ἐσφάλησαν, ἔργον ἦν τὴν Λακεδαίμονα περιγενέσθαι.

2   Μετὰ δὲ τὴν μάχην εὐθὺς ἐπέθεντο καταλύειν
ἐν Ἄργει τὸν δῆμον οἱ χίλιοι καὶ τὴν πόλιν
ὑπήκοον ποιεῖν· Λακεδαιμόνιοι δὲ παραγενόμενοι
κατέλυσαν τὴν δημοκρατίαν. αὖθις δὲ τῶν
πολλῶν ἐξενεγκαμένων τὰ ὅπλα καὶ κρατησάν-
των, ἐπελθὼν ὁ Ἀλκιβιάδης τήν τε νίκην ἐβε-
βαίωσε τῷ δήμῳ, καὶ τὰ μακρὰ τείχη συνέπεισε
καθεῖναι καὶ προσμίξαντας τῇ θαλάσσῃ τὴν
πόλιν ἐξάψαι παντάπασι τῆς Ἀθηναίων δυνά-
3   μεως. καὶ τέκτονας καὶ λιθουργοὺς ἐκ τῶν
Ἀθηνῶν ἐκόμισε καὶ πᾶσαν ἐνεδείκνυτο προ-
θυμίαν, οὐχ ἧττον ἑαυτῷ κτώμενος ἢ τῇ πόλει
χάριν καὶ ἰσχύν. ἔπεισε δὲ καὶ Πατρεῖς ὁμοίως
τείχεσι μακροῖς συνάψαι τῇ θαλάσσῃ τὴν πόλιν.
εἰπόντος δέ τινος τοῖς Πατρεῦσιν ὅτι "κατα-
πιοῦνται ὑμᾶς Ἀθηναῖοι·" "Ἴσως," εἶπεν ὁ
Ἀλκιβιάδης, "κατὰ μικρὸν καὶ κατὰ τοὺς πόδας,
Λακεδαιμόνιοι δὲ κατὰ τὴν κεφαλὴν καὶ ἀθρόως."

4   Οὐ μὴν ἀλλὰ καὶ τῆς γῆς συνεβούλευεν ἀντ-
έχεσθαι τοῖς Ἀθηναίοις, καὶ τὸν ἐν Ἀγραύλου
προβαλλόμενον ἀεὶ τοῖς ἐφήβοις ὅρκον ἔργῳ
βεβαιοῦν. ὀμνύουσι γὰρ ὅροις χρήσασθαι τῆς
Ἀττικῆς πυροῖς, κριθαῖς, ἀμπέλοις, ἐλαίαις,
οἰκείαν ποιεῖσθαι διδασκόμενοι τὴν ἥμερον καὶ
καρποφόρον.

XVI. Ἐν δὲ τοιούτοις πολιτεύμασι καὶ λόγοις
καὶ φρονήματι καὶ δεινότητι πολλὴν αὖ πάλιν
τὴν τρυφὴν τῆς διαίτης καὶ περὶ πότους καὶ

whereas, had they been defeated, the very existence of Sparta would have been at stake.

After this battle of Mantinea, the oligarchs of Argos, "The Thousand," set out at once to depose the popular party and make the city subject to themselves; and the Lacedaemonians came and deposed the democracy. But the populace took up arms again and got the upper hand.[1] Then Alcibiades came and made the people's victory secure. He also persuaded them to run long walls down to the sea, and so to attach their city completely to the naval dominion of Athens. He actually brought carpenters and masons from Athens, and displayed all manner of zeal, thus winning favour and power for himself no less than for his city. In like manner he persuaded the people of Patrae to attach their city to the sea by long walls.[2] Thereupon some one said to the Patrensians: "Athens will swallow you up!" "Perhaps so," said Alcibiades, "but you will go slowly, and feet first; whereas Sparta will swallow you head first, and at one gulp."

However, he counselled the Athenians to assert dominion on land also, and to maintain in very deed the oath regularly propounded to their young warriors in the sanctuary of Agraulus. They take oath that they will regard wheat, barley, the vine, and the olive as the natural boundaries of Attica, and they are thus trained to consider as their own all the habitable and fruitful earth.

XVI. But all this statecraft and eloquence and lofty purpose and cleverness was attended with great luxuriousness of life, with wanton drunken-

---

[1] 417 B.C.   [2] 419 B.C.

ἔρωτας ὑβρίσματα, καὶ θηλύτητας ἐσθήτων
ἁλουργῶν ἑλκομένων δι' ἀγορᾶς, καὶ πολυτέλειαν
ὑπερήφανον, ἐκτομάς τε καταστρωμάτων ἐν ταῖς
τριήρεσιν, ὅπως μαλακώτερον ἐγκαθεύδοι, κει-
ρίαις, ἀλλὰ μὴ σανίσι, τῶν στρωμάτων ἐπι-
βαλλομένων, ἀσπίδος τε διαχρύσου ποίησιν οὐδὲν
2 ἐπίσημον τῶν πατρίων ἔχουσαν, ἀλλ' Ἔρωτα
κεραυνοφόρον, ἅπερ[1] ὁρῶντες οἱ μὲν ἔνδοξοι μετὰ
τοῦ βδελύττεσθαι καὶ δυσχεραίνειν ἐφοβοῦντο
τὴν ὀλιγωρίαν αὐτοῦ καὶ παρανομίαν, ὡς τυραννικὰ καὶ ἀλλόκοτα, τοῦ δὲ δήμου τὸ πάθος τὸ   19
πρὸς αὐτὸν οὐ κακῶς ἐξηγούμενος ὁ Ἀριστοφάνης ταῦτ' εἴρηκε·

Ποθεῖ μέν, ἐχθαίρει δέ, βούλεται δ' ἔχειν,

ἔτι δὲ μᾶλλον τῇ ὑπονοίᾳ πιέζων·

Μάλιστα μὲν λέοντα μὴ 'ν πόλει τρέφειν·
ἢν δ' ἐκτρέφῃ τις, τοῖς τρόποις ὑπηρετεῖν.

3 ἐπιδόσεις γὰρ καὶ χορηγίαι καὶ φιλοτιμήματα
πρὸς τὴν πόλιν ὑπερβολὴν μὴ ἀπολείποντα καὶ
δόξα προγόνων καὶ λόγου δύναμις καὶ σώματος
εὐπρέπεια καὶ ῥώμη μετ' ἐμπειρίας τῶν πολεμικῶν καὶ ἀλκῆς πάντα τἆλλα συγχωρεῖν ἐποίει
καὶ φέρειν μετρίως τοὺς Ἀθηναίους, ἀεὶ τὰ πρᾶό-
τατα τῶν ὀνομάτων τοῖς ἁμαρτήμασι τιθεμένους,
παιδιὰς καὶ φιλοτιμίας.

---

[1] ἅπερ. Either some verb is to be supplied from the context
for the preceding accusatives (so Coraës), or ἅπερ is to be
deleted (so Bekker and Sintenis[2]).

ness and lewdness, with effeminacy in dress,—he would trail long purple robes through the market place,—and with prodigal expenditures. He would have the decks of his triremes cut away that he might sleep more softly, his bedding being slung on cords rather than spread on the hard planks. He had a golden shield made for himself, bearing no ancestral device, but an Eros armed with a thunderbolt. The reputable men of the city looked on all these things with loathing and indignation, and feared his contemptuous and lawless spirit. They thought such conduct as his tyrant-like and monstrous. How the common folk felt towards him has been well set forth by Aristophanes [1] in these words :—

" It yearns for him, and hates him too, but wants him
    back ; "

and again, veiling a yet greater severity in his metaphor :—

" A lion is not to be reared within the state ;
  But, once you've reared him up, consult his every
    mood."

And indeed, his voluntary contributions of money, his support of public exhibitions, his unsurpassed munificence towards the city, the glory of his ancestry, the power of his eloquence, the comeliness and vigor of his person, together with his experience and prowess in war, made the Athenians lenient and tolerant towards everything else ; they were forever giving the mildest of names to his transgressions, calling them the product of youthful spirits and ambition.

[1] *Frogs*, 1425 ; 1431–1432.

4 Οἷον ἦν καὶ τὸ Ἀγάθαρχον εἶρξαι τὸν ζωγρά-
φον, εἶτα γράψαντα τὴν οἰκίαν ἀφεῖναι δωρη-
σάμενον· καὶ Ταυρέαν ἀντιχορηγοῦντα ῥαπίσαι
φιλοτιμούμενον ὑπὲρ τῆς νίκης· καὶ τὸ Μηλίαν
γυναῖκα ἐκ τῶν αἰχμαλώτων ἐξελόμενον καὶ
5 συνόντα θρέψαι παιδάριον ἐξ αὐτῆς. καὶ γὰρ
τοῦτο φιλάνθρωπον ἐκάλουν· πλὴν ὅτι τοὺς
Μηλίους ἡβηδὸν ἀποσφαγῆναι τὴν πλείστην
αἰτίαν ἔσχε, τῷ ψηφίσματι συνειπών.

Ἀριστοφῶντος δὲ Νεμέαν γράψαντος ἐν ταῖς
ἀγκάλαις αὑτῆς καθήμενον Ἀλκιβιάδην ἔχουσαν,
ἐθεῶντο καὶ συνέτρεχον χαίροντες. οἱ δὲ πρεσβύτεροι καὶ τούτοις ἐδυσχέραινον ὡς τυραννικοῖς
καὶ παρανόμοις. ἐδόκει δὲ καὶ Ἀρχέστρατος οὐκ
ἀπὸ τρόπου λέγειν ὡς ἡ Ἑλλὰς οὐκ ἂν ἤνεγκε
δύο Ἀλκιβιάδας.

6 Ἐπεὶ δὲ Τίμων ὁ μισάνθρωπος εὐημερήσαντα
τὸν Ἀλκιβιάδην καὶ προπεμπόμενον ἀπὸ τῆς
ἐκκλησίας ἐπιφανῶς οὐ παρῆλθεν οὐδ' ἐξέκλινεν,
ὥσπερ εἰώθει τοὺς ἄλλους, ἀλλ' ἀπαντήσας καὶ
δεξιωσάμενος, "Εὖ γ'," ἔφη, "ποιεῖς αὐξόμενος,
ὦ παῖ· μέγα γὰρ αὔξῃ κακὸν ἅπασι τούτοις," οἱ
μὲν ἐγέλων, οἱ δ' ἐβλασφήμουν, ἐνίους δὲ καὶ πάνυ
τὸ λεχθὲν ἐπέστρεφεν. οὕτως ἄκριτος ἦν ἡ δόξα
περὶ αὐτοῦ διὰ τὴν τῆς φύσεως ἀνωμαλίαν.

XVII. Σικελίας δὲ καὶ Περικλέους ἔτι ζῶντος

For instance, he once imprisoned the painter Agatharchus in his house until he had adorned it with paintings for him, and then dismissed his captive with a handsome present. And when Taureas was supporting a rival exhibition, he gave him a box on the ear, so eager was he for the victory. And he picked out a woman from among the prisoners of Melos to be his mistress, and reared a son she bore him. This was an instance of what they called his kindness of heart, but the execution of all the grown men of Melos[1] was chiefly due to him, since he supported the decree therefor.

Aristophon painted Nemea[2] with Alcibiades seated in her arms; whereat the people were delighted, and ran in crowds to see the picture. But the elders were indignant at this too; they said it smacked of tyranny and lawlessness. And it would seem that Archestratus, in his verdict on the painting, did not go wide of the mark when he said that Hellas couldnot endure more than one Alcibiades.

Timon the misanthrope once saw Alcibiades, after a successful day, being publicly escorted home from the assembly. He did not pass him by nor avoid him, as his custom was with others, but met him and greeted him, saying: "It's well you're growing so, my child; you'll grow big enough to ruin all this rabble." At this some laughed, and some railed, and some gave much heed to the saying. So undecided was public opinion about Alcibiades, by reason of the unevenness of his nature.

XVII. On Sicily the Athenians had cast longing

---

[1] In the summer of 416. Cf. Thuc. v. 116, 2–4.

[2] A personification of the district of Nemea, in the games of which Alcibiades had been victorious. Cf. Pausanias, i. 22, 7, with Frazer's notes.

ἐπεθύμουν Ἀθηναῖοι, καὶ τελευτήσαντος ἥπτοντο,
καὶ τὰς λεγομένας βοηθείας καὶ συμμαχίας
ἔπεμπον ἑκάστοτε τοῖς ἀδικουμένοις ὑπὸ Συρακουσίων ἐπιβάθρας τῆς μείζονος στρατείας τι-
2 θέντες. ὁ δὲ παντάπασι τὸν ἔρωτα τοῦτον
ἀναφλέξας αὐτῶν, καὶ πείσας μὴ κατὰ μέρος
μηδὲ κατὰ μικρόν, ἀλλὰ μεγάλῳ στόλῳ πλεύ-
σαντας ἐπιχειρεῖν καὶ καταστρέφεσθαι τὴν νῆσον,
Ἀλκιβιάδης ἦν, τόν τε δῆμον μεγάλα πείσας
ἐλπίζειν, αὐτός τε μειζόνων ὀρεγόμενος. ἀρχὴν
γὰρ εἶναι, πρὸς ἃ ἤλπίκει, διενοεῖτο τῆς στρατείας,
3 οὐ τέλος, ὥσπερ οἱ λοιποί, Σικελίαν. καὶ Νικίας
μὲν ὡς χαλεπὸν ἔργον ὂν τὰς Συρακούσας ἑλεῖν
ἀπέτρεπε τὸν δῆμον, Ἀλκιβιάδης δὲ Καρχηδόνα
καὶ Λιβύην ὀνειροπολῶν, ἐκ δὲ τούτων προσγενομένων Ἰταλίαν καὶ Πελοπόννησον ἤδη περι-
βαλλόμενος, ὀλίγου δεῖν ἐφόδια τοῦ πολέμου
Σικελίαν ἐποιεῖτο. καὶ τοὺς μὲν νέους αὐτόθεν
εἶχεν ἤδη ταῖς ἐλπίσιν ἐπηρμένους, τῶν δὲ πρεσβυτέρων ἠκροῶντο πολλὰ θαυμάσια περὶ τῆς
στρατείας περαινόντων, ὥστε πολλοὺς ἐν ταῖς
παλαίστραις καὶ τοῖς ἡμικυκλίοις καθέζεσθαι
τῆς τε νήσου τὸ σχῆμα καὶ θέσιν Λιβύης καὶ
Καρχηδόνος ὑπογράφοντας.
4 Σωκράτη μέντοι τὸν φιλόσοφον καὶ Μέτωνα
τὸν ἀστρολόγον οὐδὲν ἐλπίσαι τῇ πόλει χρηστὸν
ἀπὸ τῆς στρατείας ἐκείνης λέγουσιν, ὁ μέν, ὡς
ἔοικε, τοῦ συνήθους δαιμονίου γενομένου καὶ

eyes even while Pericles was living; and after his death they actually tried to lay hands upon it. The lesser expeditions which they sent thither from time to time, ostensibly for the aid and comfort of their allies on the island who were being wronged by the Syracusans, they regarded merely as stepping stones to the greater expedition of conquest. But the man who finally fanned this desire of theirs into flame, and persuaded them not to attempt the island any more in part and little by little, but to sail thither with a great armament and subdue it utterly, was Alcibiades; he persuaded the people to have great hopes, and he himself had greater aspirations still. Such were his hopes that he regarded Sicily as a mere beginning, and not, like the rest, as an end of the expedition. So while Nicias was trying to divert the people from the capture of Syracuse as an undertaking too difficult for them, Alcibiades was dreaming of Carthage and Libya, and, after winning these, of at once encompassing Italy and Peloponnesus. He almost regarded Sicily as the ways and means provided for his greater war. The young men were at once carried away on the wings of such hopes, and their elders kept recounting in their ears many wonderful things about the projected expedition. Many were they who sat in the palaestras and lounging-places mapping out in the sand the shape of Sicily and the position of Libya and Carthage.[1]

Socrates the philosopher, however, and Meton the astrologer, are said to have had no hopes that any good would come to the city from this expedition; Socrates, as it is likely, because he got an inkling of

---

[1] Cf. *Nicias*, xii. 1–2.

προσημαίνοντος, ὁ δὲ Μέτων εἴτε δείσας ἐκ λογισμοῦ τὸ μέλλον εἴτε μαντικῆς τινι τρόπῳ χρησάμενος ἐσκήψατο μεμηνέναι, καὶ λαβὼν δᾷδα   20
καιομένην οἷος ἦν αὐτοῦ τὴν οἰκίαν ὑφάπτειν.
5 ἔνιοι δέ φασι προσποίημα μὲν μανίας μηδὲν
ἐσκευάσθαι τὸν Μέτωνα, καταπρῆσαι δὲ τὴν
οἰκίαν νύκτωρ, εἶθ' ἕωθεν προελθόντα δεῖσθαι καὶ
ἀντιβολεῖν ἐπὶ συμφορᾷ τηλικαύτῃ τὸν υἱὸν
αὑτῷ παρεθῆναι τῆς στρατείας. ἐκεῖνος μὲν οὖν
ἔτυχεν ὧν ἠξίου, παρακρουσάμενος τοὺς πολίτας.

XVIII. Ὁ δὲ Νικίας ἄκων μὲν ᾑρέθη στρατηγός, οὐχ ἥκιστα τὴν ἀρχὴν καὶ διὰ τὸν συνάρ-
χοντα φεύγων· ἐφαίνετο γὰρ τοῖς Ἀθηναίοις τὰ
τοῦ πολέμου βέλτιον ἕξειν μὴ προεμένοις τὸν
Ἀλκιβιάδην ἄκρατον, ἀλλὰ μιχθείσης πρὸς τὴν
τόλμαν αὐτοῦ τῆς Νικίου προνοίας· καὶ γὰρ ὁ
τρίτος στρατηγὸς Λάμαχος ἡλικίᾳ προήκων ὅμως
ἐδόκει μηδὲν ἧττον εἶναι τοῦ Ἀλκιβιάδου διά-
2 πυρος καὶ φιλοκίνδυνος ἐν τοῖς ἀγῶσι· βουλευο-
μένων δὲ περὶ πλήθους καὶ τρόπου παρασκευῆς
ἐπεχείρησεν αὖθις ὁ Νικίας ἐνίστασθαι καὶ κατα-
παύειν τὸν πόλεμον. ἀντειπόντος δὲ τοῦ Ἀλκιβιάδου καὶ κρατήσαντος, ἔγραψε τῶν ῥητόρων
Δημόστρατος καὶ εἶπεν ὡς χρὴ τοὺς στρατηγοὺς
αὐτοκράτορας εἶναι καὶ τῆς παρασκευῆς καὶ τοῦ
πολέμου παντός.

Ἐπιψηφισαμένου δὲ τοῦ δήμου καὶ γενομένων
ἑτοίμων πάντων πρὸς τὸν ἔκπλουν, οὐ χρηστὰ

the future from the divine guide who was his familiar.
Meton—whether his fear of the future arose from
mere calculation or from his use of some sort of
divination—feigned madness, and seizing a blazing
torch, was like to have set fire to his own house. Some
say, however, that Meton made no pretence of
madness, but actually did burn his house down in
the night, and then, in the morning, came before the
people begging and praying that, in view of his
great calamity, his son might be released from the
expedition. At any rate, he succeeded in cheating
his fellow citizens, and obtained his desire.[1]

XVIII. Nicias was elected general against his will,
and he was anxious to avoid the command most of
all because of his fellow commander. For it had
seemed to the Athenians that the war would go on
better if they did not send out Alcibiades unblended,
but rather tempered his rash daring with the
prudent forethought of Nicias. As for the third
general, Lamachus, though advanced in years, he
was thought, age notwithstanding, to be no less
fiery than Alcibiades, and quite as fond of taking
risks in battle. During the deliberations of the
people on the extent and character of the armament,
Nicias again tried to oppose their wishes and put a
stop to the war. But Alcibiades answered all his
arguments and carried the day, and then Demostratus,
the orator, formally moved that the generals have
full and independent powers in the matter of the
armament and of the whole war.[2]

After the people had adopted this motion and all
things were made ready for the departure of the
fleet, there were some unpropitious signs and portents,

---

[1] Cf. *Nicias*, xiii. 5–6.   [2] Cf. *Nicias*, xii. 3–4.

3 παρῆν οὐδὲ τὰ τῆς ἑορτῆς. Ἀδωνίων γὰρ εἰς τὰς
ἡμέρας ἐκείνας καθηκόντων εἴδωλα πολλαχοῦ
νεκροῖς ἐκκομιζομένοις ὅμοια προὔκειντο ταῖς
γυναιξί, καὶ ταφὰς ἐμιμοῦντο κοπτόμεναι, καὶ
θρήνους ᾖδον. ἡ μέντοι τῶν Ἑρμῶν περικοπὴ,
μιᾷ νυκτὶ τῶν πλείστων ἀκρωτηριασθέντων τὰ
πρόσωπα, πολλοὺς καὶ τῶν περιφρονούντων τὰ
τοιαῦτα διετάραξεν. ἐλέχθη μὲν οὖν ὅτι Κορίν-
θιοι διὰ τοὺς Συρακουσίους ἀποίκους ὄντας, ὡς
ἐπισχέσεως ἐσομένης πρὸς τῶν οἰωνῶν ἢ μετα-
4 γνώσεως τοῦ πολέμου, ταῦτα δράσειαν. οὐ μὴν
ἥπτετό γε τῶν πολλῶν οὔθ᾽ οὗτος ὁ λόγος οὔθ᾽ ὁ
τῶν σημείων δεινὸν εἶναι μηδὲν οἰομένων, ἀλλ᾽ οἷα
φιλεῖ φέρειν ἄκρατος ἀκολάστων νέων εἰς ὕβριν
ἐκ παιδιᾶς ὑποφερομένων· ὀργῇ δ᾽ ἅμα καὶ φόβῳ
τὸ γεγονὸς λαμβάνοντες ὡς ἀπὸ συνωμοσίας ἐπὶ
πράγμασι μεγάλοις τετολμημένον, ἅπασαν ἐξή-
ταζον ὑπόνοιαν πικρῶς ἥ τε βουλὴ συνιοῦσα περὶ
τούτων καὶ ὁ δῆμος ἐν ὀλίγαις ἡμέραις πολλάκις.

XIX. Ἐν δὲ τούτῳ δούλους τινὰς καὶ μετοίκους
προήγαγεν Ἀνδροκλῆς ὁ δημαγωγὸς ἄλλων τε
ἀγαλμάτων περικοπὰς καὶ μυστηρίων παρ᾽ οἶνον
ἀπομιμήσεις τοῦ Ἀλκιβιάδου καὶ τῶν φίλων
κατηγοροῦντας. ἔλεγον δὲ Θεόδωρον μέν τινα
δρᾶν τὰ τοῦ κήρυκος, Πουλυτίωνα δὲ τὰ τοῦ
δᾳδούχου, τὰ δὲ τοῦ ἱεροφάντου τὸν Ἀλκιβιάδην,
τοὺς δ᾽ ἄλλους ἑταίρους παρεῖναι καὶ μυεῖσθαι
2 μύστας προσαγορευομένους. ταῦτα γὰρ ἐν τῇ

especially in connection with the festival, namely, the Adonia. This fell at that time, and little images like dead folk carried forth to burial were in many places exposed to view by the women, who mimicked burial rites, beat their breasts, and sang dirges.[1] Moreover, the mutilation of the Hermae, most of which, in a single night, had their faces and forms disfigured, confounded the hearts of many, even among those who usually set small store by such things.[1] It was said, it is true, that Corinthians had done the deed, Syracuse being a colony of theirs, in the hope that such portents would check or stop the war. The multitude, however, were not moved by this reasoning, nor by that of those who thought the affair no terrible sign at all, but rather one of the common effects of strong wine, when dissolute youth, in mere sport, are carried away into wanton acts. They looked on the occurrence with wrath and fear, thinking it the sign of a bold and dangerous conspiracy. They therefore scrutinized keenly every suspicious circumstance, the council and the assembly convening for this purpose many times within a few days.

XIX. During this time Androcles, the popular leader, produced sundry aliens and slaves who accused Alcibiades and his friends of mutilating other sacred images, and of making a parody of the mysteries of Eleusis in a drunken revel. They said that one Theodorus played the part of the Herald, Pulytion that of the Torch-bearer, and Alcibiades that of the High Priest, and that the rest of his companions were there in the rôle of initiates, and were dubbed Mystae. Such indeed was the purport

---

[1] Cf. *Nicias*, xiii. 2, 7.

εἰσαγγελίᾳ γέγραπται Θεσσαλοῦ τοῦ Κίμωνος
εἰσαγγείλαντος Ἀλκιβιάδην ἀσεβεῖν περὶ τὼ
θεώ. τραχυνομένου δὲ τοῦ δήμου καὶ πικρῶς
πρὸς Ἀλκιβιάδην ἔχοντος, καὶ τοῦ Ἀνδροκλέους
(ἦν γὰρ οὗτος ἐχθρὸς ἐν τοῖς μάλιστα τοῦ
Ἀλκιβιάδου) παροξύνοντος, ἐν ἀρχῇ μὲν ἐτα-
3 ράχθησαν οἱ περὶ τὸν Ἀλκιβιάδην. αἰσθόμενοι
δὲ τούς τε ναύτας, ὅσοι πλεῖν ἔμελλον εἰς
Σικελίαν, εὔνους ὄντας αὐτοῖς καὶ τὸ στρατιω-
τικόν, Ἀργείων δὲ καὶ Μαντινέων χιλίων ὄντων
ὁπλιτῶν ἀκούοντες ἀναφανδὸν λεγόντων ὡς δι᾽
Ἀλκιβιάδην στρατεύοιντο διαπόντιον καὶ μακρὰν
στρατείαν, ἐὰν δέ τις ἀγνωμονῇ περὶ τοῦτον,
εὐθὺς ἀποστήσεσθαι, ἀνεθάρρουν καὶ παρίσταντο
τῷ καιρῷ πρὸς τὴν ἀπολογίαν, ὥστε τοὺς ἐχθροὺς
πάλιν ἀθυμεῖν καὶ φοβεῖσθαι μὴ περὶ τὴν κρίσιν
ὁ δῆμος ἀμβλύτερος αὐτῷ γένηται διὰ τὴν
χρείαν.
4   Πρὸς ταῦτ᾽ οὖν τεχνάζουσι τῶν ῥητόρων τοὺς
οὐ δοκοῦντας ἐχθροὺς τοῦ Ἀλκιβιάδου, μισοῦντας
δὲ αὐτὸν οὐχ ἧττον τῶν ὁμολογούντων, ἀνιστα-
μένους ἐν τῷ δήμῳ λέγειν ὡς ἄτοπόν ἐστιν
αὐτοκράτορι στρατηγῷ τηλικαύτης ἀποδεδειγ-
μένῳ δυνάμεως, ἠθροισμένης στρατιᾶς καὶ τῶν
συμμάχων, μεταξὺ κληροῦντας δικαστήριον καὶ
ὕδωρ διαμετροῦντας ἀπολλύναι τὸν καιρόν·
"Ἀλλὰ νῦν μὲν ἀγαθῇ τύχῃ πλεέτω, τοῦ δὲ
πολέμου διαπραχθέντος ἐπὶ τοῖς αὐτοῖς νόμοις
5 ἀπολογείσθω παρών." οὐκ ἐλάνθανε μὲν οὖν
ἡ κακοήθεια τῆς ἀναβολῆς τὸν Ἀλκιβιάδην,
ἀλλ᾽ ἔλεγε παριὼν ὡς δεινόν ἐστιν αἰτίας ἀπο-

of the impeachment which Thessalus, the son of
Cimon, brought in to the assembly, impeaching
Alcibiades for impiety towards the Eleusinian goddesses. The people were exasperated, and felt
bitterly towards Alcibiades, and Androcles, who was
his mortal enemy, egged them on. At first Alcibiades
was confounded. But perceiving that all the seamen
and soldiers who were going to sail for Sicily were
friendly to him, and hearing that the Argive and
Mantinean men-at-arms, a thousand in number, declared plainly that it was all because of Alcibiades that
they were making their long expedition across the
seas, and that if any wrong should be done him they
would at once abandon it, he took courage, and
insisted on an immediate opportunity to defend
himself before the people. His enemies were now
in their turn dejected ; they feared lest the people
should be too lenient in their judgement of him
because they needed him so much.

Accordingly, they devised that certain orators who
were not looked upon as enemies of Alcibiades, but
who really hated him no less than his avowed foes,
should rise in the assembly and say that it was
absurd, when a general had been appointed, with full
powers, over such a vast force, and when his armament
and allies were all assembled, to destroy his beckoning
opportunity by casting lots for jurors and measuring
out time for the case. "Nay," they said, "let him
sail now, and Heaven be with him ! But when
the war is over, then let him come and make his
defence. The laws will be the same then as now."
Of course the malice in this postponement did not
escape Alcibiades. He declared in the assembly
that it was a terrible misfortune to be sent off at the

λιπόντα καθ᾿ ἑαυτοῦ καὶ διαβολὰς ἐκπέμπεσθαι
μετέωρον ἐπὶ τοσαύτης δυνάμεως· ἀποθανεῖν γὰρ
προσήκειν μὴ λύσαντι τὰς κατηγορίας, λύσαντι
δὲ καὶ φανέντι καθαρῷ τρέπεσθαι πρὸς τοὺς
πολεμίους μὴ δεδοικότι τοὺς συκοφάντας.

XX. Ἐπεὶ δ᾿ οὐκ ἔπειθεν, ἀλλὰ πλεῖν ἐκέλευον
αὐτόν, ἀνήχθη μετὰ τῶν συστρατήγων ἔχων
τριήρεις μὲν οὐ πολλῷ τῶν τεσσαράκοντα καὶ
ἑκατὸν ἀποδεούσας, ὁπλίτας δὲ πεντακισχιλίους
καὶ ἑκατόν, τοξότας δὲ καὶ σφενδονήτας καὶ
ψιλοὺς περὶ τριακοσίους καὶ χιλίους, καὶ τὴν
2 ἄλλην παρασκευὴν ἀξιόλογον. προσβαλὼν δ᾿
Ἰταλίᾳ καὶ Ῥήγιον ἑλών, εἰσηγήσατο γνώμην ὅτῳ
τρόπῳ πολεμητέον ἐστί. καὶ Νικίου μὲν ἀντιλέ-
γοντος, Λαμάχου δὲ προσθεμένου, πλεύσας εἰς
Σικελίαν προσηγάγετο Κατάνην, ἄλλο δὲ οὐδὲν
ἔπραξε μετάπεμπτος ὑπὸ τῶν Ἀθηναίων ἐπὶ τὴν
κρίσιν εὐθὺς γενόμενος.

Πρῶτον μὲν γάρ, ὥσπερ εἴρηται, ψυχραί τινες
ὑποψίαι καὶ διαβολαὶ κατὰ τοῦ Ἀλκιβιάδου
3 προσέπιπτον ἀπὸ δούλων καὶ μετοίκων· ἔπειτα
τῶν ἐχθρῶν ἀπόντος αὐτοῦ καθαπτομένων σφο-
δρότερον, καὶ τοῖς περὶ τοὺς Ἑρμᾶς ὑβρίσμασι
καὶ τὰ μυστικὰ συμπλεκόντων, ὡς ἀπὸ μιᾶς
ἐπὶ νεωτερισμῷ συνωμοσίας πεπραγμένα, τοὺς
μὲν ὁπωσοῦν ἐπαιτιαθέντας ἐνέβαλλον ἀκρίτους
εἰς τὸ δεσμωτήριον, ἤχθοντο δὲ τὸν Ἀλκιβιάδην
μὴ λαβόντες ὑπὸ τὰς ψήφους τότε μηδὲ κρίναν-

head of such a vast force with his case still in suspense, leaving behind him vague accusations and slanders ; he ought to be put to death if he did not refute them ; but if he did refute them and prove his innocence, he ought to proceed against the enemy without any fear of the public informers at home.

XX. He could not carry his point, however, but was ordered to set sail. So he put to sea [1] along with his fellow generals, having not much fewer than one hundred and forty triremes ; fifty-one hundred men-at-arms ; about thirteen hundred archers, slingers, and light-armed folk ; and the rest of his equipment to correspond. On reaching Italy and taking Rhegium, he proposed a plan for the conduct of the war.[2] Nicias opposed it, but Lamachus approved it, and so he sailed to Sicily. He secured the allegiance of Catana, but accomplished nothing further, since he was presently summoned home by the Athenians to stand his trial.

At first, as I have said,[3] sundry vague suspicions and calumnies against Alcibiades were advanced by aliens and slaves. Afterwards, during his absence, his enemies went to work more vigorously. They brought the outrage upon the Hermae and upon the Eleusinian mysteries under one and the same design ; both, they said, were fruits of a conspiracy to subvert the government, and so all who were accused of any complicity whatsoever therein were cast into prison without trial. The people were provoked with themselves for not bringing Alcibiades to trial and judgment at the time on such grave charges,

[1] About the middle of the summer of 415 B.C.
[2] Cf. *Nicias*, xiv. 3.   [3] Chapter xix. 1.

4 τες ἐπ᾽ αἰτίαις τηλικαύταις. ὁ δὲ τῇ πρὸς
ἐκεῖνον ὀργῇ παραπεσὼν οἰκεῖος ἢ φίλος ἢ
συνήθης χαλεπωτέροις αὐτοῖς ἐχρήσατο. τοὺς
δὲ μηνύσαντας ὁ μὲν Θουκυδίδης ὀνομάσαι
παρῆκεν, ἄλλοι δ᾽ ὀνομάζουσι Διοκλείδαν καὶ
Τεῦκρον, ὧν καὶ Φρύνιχός ἐστιν ὁ κωμικὸς ταυτὶ
πεποιηκώς·

  Ὦ φίλταθ᾽ Ἑρμῆ, καὶ φυλάσσου, μὴ πεσὼν
  αὑτὸν παρακρούσῃ καὶ παράσχῃς διαβολὴν
  ἑτέρῳ Διοκλείδᾳ βουλομένῳ κακόν τι δρᾶν.

καί·

  Φυλάξομαι· Τεύκρῳ γὰρ οὐχὶ βούλομαι
  μήνυτρα δοῦναι, τῷ παλαμναίῳ ξένῳ.

5   Καίτοι βέβαιον οὐδὲν οὐδ᾽ ἰσχυρὸν οἱ μηνύοντες
ἐδείκνυσαν. εἷς δ᾽ αὐτῶν ἐρωτώμενος ὅπως τὰ
πρόσωπα τῶν Ἑρμοκοπιδῶν γνωρίσειε, καὶ
ἀποκρινάμενος ὅτι πρὸς τὴν σελήνην, ἐσφάλη
τοῦ παντός, ἕνης καὶ νέας οὔσης ὅτε ταῦτ᾽ ἐδρᾶτο·
ὃ [1] θόρυβον μὲν παρέσχε τοῖς νοῦν ἔχουσι, τὸν
δῆμον δ᾽ οὐδὲ τοῦτο μαλακώτερον ἐποίησε πρὸς
τὰς διαβολάς, ἀλλ᾽ ὥσπερ ὥρμησεν ἐξ ἀρχῆς, οὐκ
ἐπαύσατο φέρων καὶ ἐμβάλλων εἰς τὸ δεσμωτήριον
οὗ τις κατείποι.

  XXI. Τῶν οὖν δεθέντων καὶ φυλαττομένων ἐπὶ
κρίσει τότε καὶ Ἀνδοκίδης ἦν ὁ ῥήτωρ, ὃν
Ἑλλάνικος ὁ συγγραφεὺς εἰς τοὺς Ὀδυσσέως
ἀπογόνους ἀνήγαγεν. ἐδόκει δὲ μισόδημος καὶ
ὀλιγαρχικὸς ὁ Ἀνδοκίδης, ὕποπτον δὲ οὐχ

---

[1] ὃ supplied by Coraës and Sint.[2]; Bekker supplies καὶ,
after Bryan.

and any kinsman or friend or comrade of his who fell foul of their wrath against him, found them exceedingly severe. Thucydides neglected to mention [1] the informers by name, but others give their names as Diocleides and Teucer. For instance, Phrynichus the comic poet [2] referred to them thus :—

" Look out too, dearest Hermes, not to get a fall,
  And mar your looks, and so equip with calumny
  Another Diocleides bent on wreaking harm."

And the Hermes replies :—

" I'm on the watch ; there's Teucer, too ; I would not give
  A prize for tattling to an alien of his guilt."

And yet there was nothing sure or steadfast in the statements of the informers. One of them, indeed, was asked how he recognized the faces of the Hermae-defacers, and replied, " By the light of the moon." This vitiated his whole story, since there was no moon at all when the deed was done. Sensible men were troubled thereat, but even this did not soften the people's feeling towards the slanderous stories. As they had set out to do in the beginning, so they continued, haling and casting into prison any one who was denounced.

XXI. Among those thus held in bonds and imprisonment for trial was Andocides the orator, whom Hellanicus the historian included among the descendants of Odysseus. He was held to be a foe to popular government, and an oligarch, but what most made him suspected of the mutilation of the

---

[1] In vi. 53, 2   [2] Kock, *Com. Att. Frag.* i. p. 385.

ἥκιστα τῆς τῶν Ἑρμῶν περικοπῆς ἐποίησεν ὁ
μέγας Ἑρμῆς, ὁ πλησίον αὐτοῦ τῆς οἰκίας
2 ἀνάθημα τῆς Αἰγηΐδος φυλῆς ἱδρυμένος· ἐν γὰρ
ὀλίγοις πάνυ τῶν ἐπιφανῶν μόνος σχεδὸν
ἀκέραιος ἔμεινε· διὸ καὶ νῦν Ἀνδοκίδου καλεῖται,
καὶ πάντες οὕτως ὀνομάζουσι τῆς ἐπιγραφῆς
ἀντιμαρτυρούσης.

Συνέβη δὲ τῷ Ἀνδοκίδῃ μάλιστα τῶν τὴν
αὐτὴν αἰτίαν ἐχόντων ἐν τῷ δεσμωτηρίῳ γενέσθαι
συνήθη καὶ φίλον ἔνδοξον μὲν οὐχ ὁμοίως ἐκείνῳ,
συνέσει δὲ καὶ τόλμῃ περιττόν, ὄνομα Τίμαιον.
3 οὗτος ἀναπείθει τὸν Ἀνδοκίδην ἑαυτοῦ κατήγορον
καὶ τινων ἄλλων γενέσθαι μὴ πολλῶν· ὁμολο-
γήσαντι γὰρ ἄδειαν εἶναι κατὰ ψήφισμα τοῦ
δήμου, τὰ δὲ τῆς κρίσεως ἄδηλα πᾶσι, τοῖς δὲ
δυνατοῖς φοβερώτατα· βέλτιον δὲ σωθῆναι ψευδό-
μενον ἢ μετὰ τῆς αὐτῆς αἰτίας ἀποθανεῖν ἀδόξως,
καὶ τὸ κοινῇ σκοποῦντι συμφέρον ὑπάρχειν,
ὀλίγους καὶ ἀμφιβόλους προέμενον, πολλοὺς
4 καὶ ἀγαθοὺς ἐξελέσθαι τῆς ὀργῆς. ταῦτα τοῦ
Τιμαίου λέγοντος καὶ διδάσκοντος ὁ Ἀνδοκίδης
ἐπείσθη, καὶ γενόμενος μηνυτὴς καθ' αὑτοῦ καὶ
καθ' ἑτέρων ἔσχε τὴν ἐκ τοῦ ψηφίσματος ἄδειαν
αὐτός· οὓς δ' ὠνόμασε πάντες πλὴν τῶν φυγόντων ἀπώλοντο. καὶ πίστεως ἕνεκα προσέθηκεν
αὐτοῖς οἰκέτας ἰδίους ὁ Ἀνδοκίδης.

5 Οὐ μὴν ὅ γε δῆμος τὴν ὀργὴν ἅπασαν ἀφῆκεν

Hermae, was the tall Hermes which stood near his house, a dedication of the Aegeïd tribe. This was almost the only one among the very few statues of like prominence to remain unharmed. For this reason it is called to this day the Hermes of Andocides. Everybody gives it that name, in spite of the adverse testimony of its inscription.

Now it happened that, of all those lying in prison with him under the same charge, Andocides became most intimate and friendly with a man named Timaeus, of less repute than himself, it is true, but of great sagacity and daring. This man persuaded Andocides to turn state's evidence against himself and a few others. If he confessed,—so the man argued,—he would have immunity from punishment by decree of the people ; whereas the result of the trial, while uncertain in all cases, was most to be dreaded in that of influential men like himself. It was better to save his life by a false confession of crime, than to die a shameful death under a false charge of that crime. One who had an eye to the general welfare of the community might well abandon to their fate a few dubious characters, if he could thereby save a multitude of good men from the wrath of the people. By such arguments of Timaeus, Andocides was at last persuaded to bear witness against himself and others. He himself received the immunity from punishment which had been decreed ; but all those whom he named, excepting such as took to flight, were put to death, and Andocides added to their number some of his own household servants, that he might the better be believed.

Still, the people did not lay aside all their wrath

57

ἐνταῦθα, ἀλλὰ μᾶλλον ἀπαλλαγεὶς τῶν Ἑρμοκοπιδῶν ὥσπερ σχολάζοντι τῷ θυμῷ πρὸς τὸν
Ἀλκιβιάδην ὅλος ἐρρύη, καὶ τέλος ἀπέστειλε τὴν
Σαλαμινίαν ἐπ' αὐτόν,[1] οὐ φαύλως αὐτό γε τοῦτο
προστάξας, μὴ βιάζεσθαι μηδ' ἅπτεσθαι τοῦ
σώματος, ἀλλὰ τῷ μετρίῳ λόγῳ χρῆσθαι κελεύ-
οντας ἀκολουθεῖν ἐπὶ κρίσιν καὶ πείθειν τὸν
6 δῆμον. ἐφοβοῦντο γὰρ ταραχὰς τοῦ στρατεύματος ἐν πολεμίᾳ γῇ καὶ στάσιν, ὃ ῥᾳδίως ἂν
ἐξειργάσατο βουληθεὶς ὁ Ἀλκιβιάδης. καὶ γὰρ
ἠθύμουν ἀπιόντος αὐτοῦ, καὶ πολλὴν τριβὴν
προσεδόκων καὶ μῆκος ἀργὸν ἐν τῷ Νικίᾳ τὸν
πόλεμον ἕξειν, καθάπερ μύωπος ἀφῃρημένου τῶν
πράξεων. ὁ γὰρ Λάμαχος ἦν μὲν πολεμικὸς καὶ
ἀνδρώδης, ἀξίωμα δ' οὐ προσῆν οὐδ' ὄγκος αὐτῷ
διὰ πενίαν.

XXII. Εὐθὺς μὲν οὖν ἀποπλέων ὁ Ἀλκιβιάδης
ἀφείλετο Μεσσήνην Ἀθηναίους. ἦσαν γὰρ οἱ
μέλλοντες ἐνδιδόναι τὴν πόλιν, οὓς ἐκεῖνος εἰδὼς
σαφέστατα τοῖς Συρακουσίων φίλοις ἐμήνυσε καὶ
διέφθειρε τὴν πρᾶξιν. ἐν δὲ Θουρίοις γενόμενος
καὶ ἀποβὰς τῆς τριήρους ἔκρυψεν ἑαυτὸν καὶ
2 διέφυγε τοὺς ζητοῦντας. ἐπιγνόντος δέ τινος καὶ
εἰπόντος· "Οὐ πιστεύεις, ὦ Ἀλκιβιάδη, τῇ
πατρίδι;" "Τὰ μὲν ἄλλ'," ἔφη, "πάντα· περὶ δὲ
τῆς ψυχῆς τῆς ἐμῆς οὐδὲ τῇ μητρί, μήπως ἀγνοή-
σασα τὴν μέλαιναν ἀντὶ τῆς λευκῆς ἐπενέγκῃ

[1] ἐπ' αὐτὸν with Mᵃ and Cobet : πρὸς αὐτόν.

at this point, but rather, now that they were done
with the Hermae-defacers, as if their passion had
all the more opportunity to vent itself, they dashed
like a torrent against Alcibiades, and finally dispatched the Salaminian state-galley to fetch him
home. They shrewdly gave its officers explicit
command not to use violence, nor to seize his person,
but with all moderation of speech to bid him accom-
pany them home to stand his trial and satisfy the
people. For they were afraid that their army, in an
enemy's land, would be full of tumult and mutiny
at the summons. And Alcibiades might easily have
effected this had he wished. For the men were
cast down at his departure, and expected that the
war, under the conduct of Nicias, would be drawn
out to a great length by delays and inactivity, now
that their goad to action had been taken away.
Lamachus, it is true, was a good soldier and a brave
man ; but he lacked authority and prestige because
he was poor.

XXII. Alcibiades had no sooner sailed away than
he robbed the Athenians of Messana.[1] There was a
party there who were on the point of surrendering
the city to the Athenians, but Alcibiades knew them,
and gave the clearest information of their design to
the friends of Syracuse in the city, and so brought
the thing to naught. Arrived at Thurii, he left his
trireme and hid himself so as to escape all quest.
When some one recognised him and asked, " Can
you not trust your country, Alcibiades ? " " In all
else," he said, " but in the matter of life I wouldn't
trust even my own mother not to mistake a black
for a white ballot when she cast her vote." And

[1] In September, 415 B.C.

59

ψῆφον." ὕστερον δ' ἀκούσας ὅτι θάνατον αὐτοῦ
κατέγνωκεν ἡ πόλις· "Ἀλλ' ἐγώ," εἶπε, "δείξω
αὐτοῖς ὅτι ζῶ."

3 Τὴν μὲν οὖν εἰσαγγελίαν οὕτως ἔχουσαν ἀνα-
γράφουσι· "Θεσσαλὸς Κίμωνος Λακιάδης Ἀλκιβιάδην Κλεινίου Σκαμβωνίδην εἰσήγγειλεν ἀδικεῖν
περὶ τὼ θεώ, τὴν Δήμητραν καὶ τὴν Κόρην,
ἀπομιμούμενον τὰ μυστήρια καὶ δεικνύοντα τοῖς
αὐτοῦ ἑταίροις ἐν τῇ οἰκίᾳ τῇ ἑαυτοῦ, ἔχοντα
στολὴν οἵανπερ ὁ ἱεροφάντης[1] ἔχων δεικνύει τὰ
ἱερά, καὶ ὀνομάζοντα αὐτὸν μὲν ἱεροφάντην,
Πουλυτίωνα δὲ δᾳδοῦχον, κήρυκα δὲ Θεόδωρον
Φηγαιᾶ, τοὺς δ' ἄλλους ἑταίρους μύστας προσ-
αγορεύοντα καὶ ἐπόπτας παρὰ τὰ νόμιμα καὶ τὰ
καθεστηκότα ὑπό τε Εὐμολπιδῶν καὶ Κηρύκων
4 καὶ τῶν ἱερέων τῶν ἐξ Ἐλευσῖνος." ἐρήμην δ'
αὐτοῦ καταγνόντες καὶ τὰ χρήματα δημεύσαντες
ἔτι καταρᾶσθαι προσεψηφίσαντο πάντας ἱερεῖς
καὶ ἱερείας, ὧν μόνην φασὶ Θεανὼ τὴν Μένωνος
Ἀγραυλῆθεν ἀντειπεῖν πρὸς τὸ ψήφισμα, φάσ-
κουσαν εὐχῶν, οὐ καταρῶν ἱέρειαν γεγονέναι.

XXIII. Τοσούτων δὲ κατεψηφισμένων Ἀλκιβιάδου καὶ κατεγνωσμένων, ἐτύγχανε μὲν ἐν
Ἄργει διατρίβων, ὡς τὸ πρῶτον ἐκ Θουρίων
ἀποδρὰς εἰς Πελοπόννησον διεκομίσθη, φοβούμενος δὲ τοὺς ἐχθροὺς καὶ παντάπασι τῆς πατρίδος ἀπεγνωκὼς ἔπεμψεν εἰς Σπάρτην, ἀξιῶν
ἄδειαν αὐτῷ γενέσθαι καὶ πίστιν ἐπὶ μείζοσι
χρείαις καὶ ὠφελείαις ὧν πρότερον αὐτοὺς ἀμυνό-
2 μενος ἔβλαψε. δόντων δὲ τῶν Σπαρτιατῶν καὶ

---

[1] ὁ ἱεροφάντης with CMᵃ : ἱεροφάντης.

when he afterwards heard that the city had condemned him to death, "I'll show them," he said, "that I'm alive."

His impeachment is on record, and runs as follows: "Thessalus, son of Cimon, of the deme Laciadae, impeaches Alcibiades, son of Cleinias, of the deme Scambonidae, for committing crime against the goddesses of Eleusis, Demeter and Cora, by mimicking the mysteries and showing them forth to his companions in his own house, wearing a robe such as the High Priest wears when he shows forth the sacred secrets to the initiates, and calling himself High Priest, Pulytion Torch-bearer, and Theodorus, of the deme Phegaea, Herald, and hailing the rest of his companions as Mystae and Epoptae, contrary to the laws and institutions of the Eumolpidae, Heralds, and Priests of Eleusis." His case went by default, his property was confiscated, and besides that, it was also decreed that his name should be publicly cursed by all priests and priestesses. Theano, the daughter of Menon, of the deme Agraule, they say, was the only one who refused to obey this decree. She declared that she was a praying, not a cursing priestess.

XXIII. When these great judgments and condemnations were passed upon Alcibiades, he was tarrying in Argos, for as soon as he had made his escape from Thurii, he passed over into Peloponnesus. But fearing his foes there, and renouncing his country altogether, he sent to the Spartans, demanding immunity and confidence, and promising to render them aid and service greater than all the harm he had previously done them as an enemy. The Spartans granted this request and received him

δεξαμένων, παραγενόμενος προθύμως ἐν μὲν εὐθὺς
ἐξειργάσατο, μέλλοντας καὶ ἀναβαλλομένους
βοηθεῖν Συρακουσίοις ἐγείρας καὶ παροξύνας
πέμψαι Γύλιππον ἄρχοντα καὶ θραῦσαι τὴν ἐκεῖ
τῶν Ἀθηναίων δύναμιν· ἕτερον δέ, κινεῖν τὸν
αὐτόθεν πόλεμον ἐπὶ τοὺς Ἀθηναίους· τὸ δὲ
τρίτον καὶ μέγιστον, ἐπιτειχίσαι Δεκέλειαν, οὗ
μᾶλλον οὐδὲν διειργάσατο καὶ κατοικοφθόρησε
τὴν πόλιν.

3   Εὐδοκιμῶν δὲ δημοσίᾳ καὶ θαυμαζόμενος οὐχ
ἧττον ἰδίᾳ τοὺς πολλοὺς κατεδημαγώγει καὶ κατ-
εγοήτευε τῇ διαίτῃ λακωνίζων, ὥσθ' ὁρῶντας ἐν
χρῷ κουριῶντα καὶ ψυχρολουτοῦντα καὶ μάζῃ
συνόντα καὶ ζωμῷ μέλανι χρώμενον ἀπιστεῖν καὶ
διαπορεῖν, εἴ ποτε μάγειρον ἐπὶ τῆς οἰκίας οὗτος
ἀνὴρ ἔσχεν ἢ προσέβλεψε μυρεψὸν ἢ Μιλησίας
4   ἠνέσχετο θιγεῖν χλανίδος. ἦν γάρ, ὥς φασι, μία
δεινότης αὕτη τῶν πολλῶν ἐν αὐτῷ καὶ μηχανὴ
θήρας ἀνθρώπων, συνεξομοιοῦσθαι καὶ συνομο-
παθεῖν τοῖς ἐπιτηδεύμασι καὶ ταῖς διαίταις,
ὀξυτέρας τρεπομένῳ τροπὰς τοῦ χαμαιλέοντος.
πλὴν ἐκεῖνος μέν, ὡς λέγεται, πρὸς ἓν ἐξαδυνατεῖ
χρῶμα τὸ λευκὸν ἀφομοιοῦν ἑαυτόν· Ἀλκιβιάδῃ
δὲ διὰ χρηστῶν ἰόντι καὶ πονηρῶν ὁμοίως οὐδὲν
5   ἦν ἀμίμητον οὐδ' ἀνεπιτήδευτον, ἀλλ' ἐν Σπάρτῃ
γυμναστικός, εὐτελής, σκυθρωπός, ἐν Ἰωνίᾳ χλι-

---

[1] A mountain citadel of Attica, about fourteen miles from
Athens towards Boeotia, commanding the Athenian plain

among them. No sooner was he come than he zealously brought one thing to pass: they had been delaying and postponing assistance to Syracuse; he roused and incited them to send Gylippus thither for a commander, and to crush the force which Athens had there. A second thing he did was to get them to stir up the war against Athens at home; and the third, and most important of all, to induce them to fortify Deceleia.[1] This more than anything else wrought ruin and destruction to his native city.

At Sparta, he was held in high repute publicly, and privately was no less admired. The multitude was brought under his influence, and was actually bewitched, by his assumption of the Spartan mode of life. When they saw him with his hair untrimmed, taking cold baths, on terms of intimacy with their coarse bread, and supping black porridge, they could scarcely trust their eyes, and doubted whether such a man as he now was had ever had a cook in his own house, had even so much as looked upon a perfumer, or endured the touch of Milesian wool. He had, as they say, one power which transcended all others, and proved an implement of his chase for men: that of assimilating and adapting himself to the pursuits and lives of others, thereby assuming more violent changes than the chameleon. That animal, however, as it is said, is utterly unable to assume one colour, namely, white; but Alcibiades could associate with good and bad alike, and found naught that he could not imitate and practice. In Sparta, he was all for bodily training, simplicity of life, and severity of countenance; in Ionia, for

and the shortest routes to Euboea and Boeotia. It was occupied by the Spartans in the spring of 413 B.C.

δανός, ἐπιτερπής, ῥᾴθυμος, ἐν Θρᾴκῃ μεθυστικός,
ἐν Θετταλοῖς ἱππαστικός, Τισαφέρνῃ δὲ τῷ
σατράπῃ συνὼν ὑπερέβαλεν ὄγκῳ καὶ πολυτελείᾳ
τὴν Περσικὴν μεγαλοπρέπειαν, οὐχ αὑτὸν ἐξιστὰς
οὕτω ῥᾳδίως εἰς ἕτερον ἐξ ἑτέρου τρόπον, οὐδὲ
πᾶσαν δεχόμενος τῷ ἤθει μεταβολήν, ἀλλ' ὅτι τῇ
φύσει χρώμενος ἔμελλε λυπεῖν τοὺς ἐντυγχάνον-
τας, εἰς πᾶν ἀεὶ τὸ πρόσφορον ἐκείνοις σχῆμα καὶ
6 πλάσμα κατεδύετο καὶ κατέφευγεν. ἐν γοῦν τῇ
Λακεδαίμονι πρὸς τὰ ἔξωθεν ἦν εἰπεῖν "'Οὐ παῖς
Ἀχιλλέως, ἀλλ' ἐκεῖνος' εἴη ἂν 'αὐτός,' οἷον Λυ-
κοῦργος ἐπαίδευσε·" τοῖς δ' ἀληθινοῖς ἄν τις ἐπε-
φώνησεν αὐτοῦ πάθεσι καὶ πράγμασιν· "'Ἔστιν
ἡ πάλαι γυνή."
7   Τιμαίαν γὰρ τὴν Ἄγιδος γυναῖκα τοῦ βασιλέως
στρατευομένου καὶ ἀποδημοῦντος οὕτω διέφθειρεν
ὥστε καὶ κύειν ἐξ Ἀλκιβιάδου καὶ μὴ ἀρνεῖσθαι,
καὶ τεκούσης παιδάριον ἄρρεν ἔξω μὲν Λεωτυχίδην καλεῖσθαι, τὸ δ' ἐντὸς αὐτοῦ ψιθυριζόμενον
ὄνομα πρὸς τὰς φίλας καὶ τὰς ὀπαδοὺς ὑπὸ τῆς
μητρὸς Ἀλκιβιάδην εἶναι· τοσοῦτος ἔρως κατεῖχε
τὴν ἄνθρωπον. ὁ δ' ἐντρυφῶν ἔλεγεν οὐχ ὕβρει
τοῦτο πράττειν οὐδὲ κρατούμενος ὑφ' ἡδονῆς,
ἀλλ' ὅπως Λακεδαιμονίων βασιλεύσωσιν οἱ ἐξ
8 αὑτοῦ γεγονότες. οὕτω πραττόμενα ταῦτα πολλοὶ κατηγόρουν πρὸς τὸν Ἄγιν. ἐπίστευσε δὲ

---

[1] The first part of the passage in quotation marks is an
adaptation of an iambic trimeter by some unknown poet,

64

luxurious ease and pleasure ; in Thrace, for drinking
deep ; in Thessaly, for riding hard ; and when he
was thrown with Tissaphernes the satrap, he outdid
even Persian magnificence in his pomp and lavishness.
It was not that he could so easily pass entirely from
one manner of man to another, nor that he actually
underwent in every case a change in his real
character ; but when he saw that his natural manners
were likely to be annoying to his associates, he was
quick to assume any counterfeit exterior which
might in each case be suitable for them. At all
events, in Sparta, so far as the outside was concerned,
it was possible to say of him, " ' No child of Achilles
he, but Achilles himself,' [1] such a man as Lycurgus
trained " ; but judging by what he actually felt and
did, one might have cried with the poet, " 'Tis the
selfsame woman still [2] ! "

For while Agis the king was away on his campaigns,
Alcibiades corrupted Timaea his wife, so that she was
with child by him and made no denial of it. When
she had given birth to a male child, it was called
Leotychides in public, but in private the name which
the boy's mother whispered to her friends and
attendants was Alcibiades. Such was the passion
that possessed the woman. But he, in his mocking
way, said he had not done this thing for a wanton
insult, nor at the behest of mere pleasure, but in
order that descendants of his might be kings of the
Lacedaemonians. Such being the state of things,
there were many to tell the tale to Agis, and he believed it, more especially owing to the lapse of time.

which Plutarch uses entire in *Morals*, p. 51 c. Cf. Nauck,
Trag. Graec. Frag.[2] p. 907.

    [2] *Electra*, of Helen, in Euripides, *Orestes*, 129.

τῷ χρόνῳ μάλιστα, ὅτι σεισμοῦ γενομένου φοβηθεὶς ἐξέδραμε τοῦ θαλάμου παρὰ τῆς γυναικός, εἶτα δέκα μηνῶν οὐκέτι συνῆλθεν αὐτῇ, μεθ᾽ οὓς γενόμενον τὸν Λεωτυχίδην ἀπέφησεν ἐξ αὐτοῦ μὴ γεγονέναι. καὶ διὰ τοῦτο τῆς βασιλείας ἐξέπεσεν ὕστερον ὁ Λεωτυχίδης.

XXIV. Μετὰ δὲ τὴν ἐν Σικελίᾳ τῶν Ἀθηναίων δυστυχίαν ἐπρέσβευσαν εἰς Σπάρτην ἅμα Χῖοι καὶ Λέσβιοι καὶ Κυζικηνοὶ περὶ ἀποστάσεως. πραττόντων δὲ Βοιωτῶν μὲν Λεσβίοις, Φαρναβάζου δὲ Κυζικηνοῖς, Ἀλκιβιάδῃ πεισθέντες εἵλοντο Χίοις πρὸ πάντων βοηθεῖν. ἐκπλεύσας 20 δὲ καὶ αὐτὸς ἀπέστησεν ὀλίγου δεῖν ἅπασαν Ἰωνίαν, καὶ πολλὰ συνὼν τοῖς τῶν Λακεδαιμονίων στρατηγοῖς ἔβλαπτε τοὺς Ἀθηναίους.

2 ὁ δ᾽ Ἆγις ἐχθρὸς μὲν ὑπῆρχεν αὐτῷ διὰ τὴν γυναῖκα κακῶς πεπονθώς, ἤχθετο δὲ καὶ τῇ δόξῃ· τὰ γὰρ πλεῖστα γίνεσθαι καὶ προχωρεῖν δι᾽ Ἀλκιβιάδην λόγος ἦν· τῶν δ᾽ ἄλλων Σπαρτιατῶν οἱ δυνατώτατοι καὶ φιλοτιμότατοι τὸν Ἀλκιβιάδην ἤδη ἐβαρύνοντο διὰ φθόνον. ἴσχυσαν οὖν καὶ διεπράξαντο τοὺς οἴκοθεν ἄρχοντας ἐπιστεῖλαι πρὸς Ἰωνίαν ὅπως ἀποκτείνωσιν αὐτόν.

3 Ὁ δ᾽ ἡσυχῇ προγνοὺς καὶ φοβηθεὶς τῶν μὲν πράξεων πασῶν ἐκοινώνει τοῖς Λακεδαιμονίοις, τὸ δ᾽ εἰς χεῖρας ἰέναι παντάπασιν ἔφυγε, Τισαφέρνῃ δέ, τῷ βασιλέως σατράπῃ, δοὺς ἑαυτὸν ὑπὲρ ἀσφαλείας εὐθὺς ἦν παρ᾽ αὐτῷ πρῶτος καὶ 4 μέγιστος. τὸ μὲν γὰρ πολύτροπον καὶ περιττὸν

---

[1] Cf. *Lysander*, xxii. 4–6.

[2] With these words the two years which had elapsed since the flight of Alcibiades (xxii. 1) are passed over, so far as the

There had been an earthquake, and he had run in terror out of his chamber and the arms of his wife, and then for ten months had had no further intercourse with her. And since Leotychides had been born at the end of this period, Agis declared that he was no child of his. For this reason Leotychides was afterwards refused the royal succession.[1]

XXIV. After the Athenian disaster in Sicily,[2] the Chians, Lesbians, and Cyzicenes sent embassies at the same time to Sparta, to discuss a revolt from Athens. But though the Boeotians supported the appeal of the Lesbians, and Pharnabazus that of the Cyzicenes, the Spartans, under the persuasion of Alcibiades, elected to help the Chians first of all. Alcibiades actually set sail in person and brought almost all Ionia to revolt, and, in constant association with the Lacedaemonian generals, wrought injury to the Athenians. But Agis was hostile to him because of the wrong he had suffered as a husband, and he was also vexed at the repute in which Alcibiades stood; for most of the successes won were due to him, as report had it. The most influential and ambitious of the other Spartans also were already envious and tired of him, and soon grew strong enough to induce the magistrates at home to send out orders to Ionia that he be put to death.

His stealthy discovery of this put him on his guard, and while in all their undertakings he took part with the Lacedaemonians, he sedulously avoided coming into their hands. Then, resorting to Tissaphernes, the King's satrap, for safety, he was soon first and foremost in that grandee's favour. For his versatility

Sicilian expedition is concerned. They are covered by the narrative of the *Nicias* (xv.–xxx.).

αὐτοῦ τῆς δεινότητος οὐκ ὢν ἁπλοῦς, ἀλλὰ
κακοήθης καὶ φιλοπόνηρος, ἐθαύμαζεν ὁ βάρβαρος·
ταῖς δὲ καθ᾽ ἡμέραν ἐν τῷ συσχολάζειν καὶ συν-
διαιτᾶσθαι χάρισιν οὐδὲν ἦν ἄτεγκτον ἦθος οὐδὲ
φύσις ἀνάλωτος, ἀλλὰ καὶ δεδιόσι καὶ φθονοῦσιν
ὅμως τὸ συγγενέσθαι καὶ προσιδεῖν ἐκεῖνον ἡδο-
5 νήν τινα καὶ φιλοφροσύνην παρεῖχε. τἆλλ᾽ οὖν
ὢν καὶ μισέλλην ἐν τοῖς μάλιστα Περσῶν ὁ
Τισαφέρνης, οὕτως ἐνεδίδου τῷ Ἀλκιβιάδῃ κολα-
κευόμενος ὥσθ᾽ ὑπερβάλλειν αὐτὸν ἀντικολακεύων
ἐκεῖνος. ὧν γὰρ ἐκέκτητο παραδείσων τὸν κάλλιστον καὶ ὑδάτων καὶ λειμώνων ὑγιεινῶν ἕνεκεν,
διατριβὰς ἔχοντα καὶ καταφυγὰς ἠσκημένας
βασιλικῶς καὶ περιττῶς, Ἀλκιβιάδην καλεῖν
ἔθετο· καὶ πάντες οὕτω καλοῦντες καὶ προσα-
γορεύοντες διετέλουν.

XXV. Ἀπογνοὺς οὖν ὁ Ἀλκιβιάδης τὰ τῶν
Σπαρτιατῶν ὡς ἄπιστα, καὶ φοβούμενος τὸν
Ἆγιν, ἐκάκου καὶ διέβαλλε πρὸς τὸν Τισαφέρνην,
οὐκ ἐῶν βοηθεῖν αὐτοῖς προθύμως οὐδὲ καταλύειν
τοὺς Ἀθηναίους, ἀλλὰ γλίσχρως χορηγοῦντα
θλίβειν καὶ ἀποκναίειν ἀτρέμα καὶ ποιεῖν ἀμφοτέρους βασιλεῖ χειροήθεις καὶ καταπόνους ὑπ᾽
2 ἀλλήλων. ὁ δ᾽ ἐπείθετο ῥᾳδίως καὶ δῆλος ἦν
ἀγαπῶν καὶ θαυμάζων, ὥστ᾽ ἀποβλέπεσθαι τὸν
Ἀλκιβιάδην ἑκατέρωθεν ὑπὸ τῶν Ἑλλήνων, τοὺς
δ᾽ Ἀθηναίους μεταμέλεσθαι τοῖς γνωσθεῖσι περὶ
αὐτοῦ κακῶς πάσχοντας, ἄχθεσθαι δὲ κἀκεῖνον
ἤδη καὶ φοβεῖσθαι μὴ παντάπασι τῆς πόλεως
ἀναιρεθείσης ὑπὸ Λακεδαιμονίοις γένηται μισού-
μενος.

and surpassing cleverness were the admiration of the Barbarian, who was no straightforward man himself, but malicious and fond of evil company. And indeed no disposition could resist and no nature escape Alcibiades, so full of grace was his daily life and conversation. Even those who feared and hated him felt a rare and winning charm in his society and presence. And thus it was that Tissaphernes, though otherwise the most ardent of the Persians in his hatred of the Hellenes, so completely surrendered to the flatteries of Alcibiades as to outdo him in reciprocal flatteries. Indeed, the most beautiful park he had, both for its refreshing waters and grateful lawns, with resorts and retreats decked out in regal and extravagant fashion, he named Alcibiades ; everyone always called it by that name.

XXV. Alcibiades now abandoned the cause of the Spartans, since he distrusted them and feared Agis, and began to malign and slander them to Tissaphernes. He advised him not to aid them very generously, and yet not to put down the Athenians completely, but rather by niggardly assistance to straiten and gradually wear out both, and so make them easy victims for the King when they had weakened and exhausted each other. Tissaphernes was easily persuaded, and all men saw that he loved and admired his new adviser, so that Alcibiades was looked up to by the Hellenes on both sides, and the Athenians repented themselves of the sentence they had passed upon him, now that they were suffering for it. Alcibiades himself also was presently burdened with the fear that if his native city were altogether destroyed, he might come into the power of the Lacedaemonians, who hated him.

3   Ἐν δὲ τῇ Σάμῳ τότε πάντα τὰ πράγματα τοῖς
Ἀθηναίοις σχεδὸν ὑπῆρχε· κἀκεῖθεν ὁρμώμενοι τῇ
ναυτικῇ δυνάμει τὰ μὲν ἀνεκτῶντο τῶν ἀφεστώτων, τὰ δ᾽ ἐφύλαττον ἀμῶς γέ πως ἔτι τοῖς
πολεμίοις κατὰ θάλατταν ὄντες ἀξιόμαχοι, Τισαφέρνην δὲ φοβούμενοι καὶ τὰς λεγομένας ὅσον
οὔπω παρεῖναι Φοινίσσας τριήρεις πεντήκοντα
καὶ ἑκατὸν οὔσας, ὧν ἀφικομένων οὐδεμία σω-
4   τηρίας ἐλπὶς ὑπελείπετο τῇ πόλει.   ταῦτα δ᾽
εἰδὼς Ἀλκιβιάδης ἔπεμπε κρύφα πρὸς τοὺς ἐν
Σάμῳ δυνατοὺς τῶν Ἀθηναίων, ἐλπίδας ἐνδιδοὺς
παρέξειν τὸν Τισαφέρνην φίλον, οὐ τοῖς πολλοῖς
χαριζόμενος οὐδὲ πιστεύων ἐκείνοις, ἀλλὰ τοῖς
ἀρίστοις, εἰ τολμήσειαν ἄνδρες ἀγαθοὶ γενόμενοι
καὶ παύσαντες ὑβρίζοντα τὸν δῆμον αὐτοὶ δι᾽
ἑαυτῶν σῴζειν τὰ πράγματα καὶ τὴν πόλιν.

5   Οἱ μὲν οὖν ἄλλοι σφόδρα προσεῖχον τῷ
Ἀλκιβιάδῃ· τῶν δὲ στρατηγῶν εἷς, Φρύνιχος
ὁ Δειραδιώτης, ὑποπτεύσας, ὅπερ ἦν, τὸν Ἀλκιβιάδην οὐδέν τι μᾶλλον ὀλιγαρχίας ἢ δημοκρα-
τίας δεόμενον, ζητοῦντα δὲ πάντως κατελθεῖν,
ἐκ διαβολῆς τοῦ δήμου προθεραπεύειν καὶ ὑπο-
δύεσθαι τοὺς δυνατούς, ἀνθίστατο.   κρατούμενος
δὲ τῇ γνώμῃ καὶ φανερῶς ἤδη τοῦ Ἀλκιβιάδου
γεγονὼς ἐχθρός, ἐξήγγειλε κρύφα πρὸς Ἀστύοχον   20
τὸν τῶν πολεμίων ναύαρχον, ἐγκελευόμενος
φυλάττεσθαι καὶ συλλαμβάνειν ὡς ἐπαμφοτερί-
6   ζοντα τὸν Ἀλκιβιάδην.   ἐλελήθει δ᾽ ἄρα προδό-

ALCIBIADES

At this time [1] almost all the forces of Athens were at Samos. From this island as their naval base of operations they were trying to win back some of their Ionian allies who had revolted, and were watching others who were disaffected. After a fashion they still managed to cope with their enemies on the sea, but they were afraid of Tissaphernes and of the fleet of one hundred and fifty Phoenician triremes which was said to be all but at hand; if this once came up, no hope of safety was left for their city. Alcibiades was aware of this, and sent secret messages to the influential Athenians at Samos, in which he held out the hope that he might bring Tissaphernes over to be their friend. He did not seek, he said, the favour of the multitude, nor trust them, but rather that of the aristocrats, in case they would venture to show themselves men, put a stop to the insolence of the people, take the direction of affairs into their own hands, and save their cause and city.

Now the rest of the aristocrats were much inclined to Alcibiades. But one of the generals, Phrynichus, of the deme Deirades, suspected (what was really the case) that Alcibiades had no more use for an oligarchy than for a democracy, but merely sought in one way or another a recall from exile, and therefore inveighed against the people merely to court betimes the favour of the aristocrats, and ingratiate himself with them. He therefore opposed him. When his opinion had been overborne and he was now become an open enemy of Alcibiades, he sent a secret message to Astyochus, the enemy's naval commander, bidding him beware of Alcibiades and arrest him, for that he was playing a double game. But without his

[1] During the winter of 412–411 B.C.

τῆς προδότῃ διαλεγόμενος. τὸν γὰρ Τισαφέρνην
ἐκπεπληγμένος ὁ Ἀστύοχος, καὶ τὸν Ἀλκιβιάδην
ὁρῶν παρ' αὐτῷ μέγαν ὄντα, κατεμήνυσε τὰ
τοῦ Φρυνίχου πρὸς αὐτούς. ὁ δ' Ἀλκιβιάδης
εὐθὺς εἰς Σάμον ἔπεμψε τοὺς τοῦ Φρυνίχου
κατηγορήσοντας. ἀγανακτούντων δὲ πάντων καὶ
συνισταμένων ἐπὶ τὸν Φρύνιχον, οὐχ ὁρῶν
ἑτέραν διαφυγὴν ἐκ τῶν παρόντων ἐπεχείρησεν
7 ἰάσασθαι μείζονι κακῷ τὸ κακόν. αὖθις γὰρ
ἔπεμψε πρὸς τὸν Ἀστύοχον, ἐγκαλῶν μὲν ὑπὲρ
τῆς μηνύσεως, ἐπαγγελλόμενος δὲ τὰς ναῦς καὶ
τὸ στρατόπεδον τῶν Ἀθηναίων ὑποχείριον αὐτῷ
παρέξειν.

Οὐ μὴν ἔβλαψέ γε τοὺς Ἀθηναίους ἡ τοῦ
Φρυνίχου προδοσία διὰ τὴν Ἀστυόχου παλιμ-
προδοσίαν. καὶ γὰρ ταῦτα κατεῖπε τοῦ Φρυνίχου
8 πρὸς τοὺς περὶ τὸν Ἀλκιβιάδην. ὁ δὲ Φρύνιχος
προαισθόμενος καὶ προσδεχόμενος δευτέραν κατη-
γορίαν παρὰ τοῦ Ἀλκιβιάδου, φθάσας αὐτὸς
προεῖπε τοῖς Ἀθηναίοις ὅτι μέλλουσιν ἐπιπλεῖν
οἱ πολέμιοι, καὶ παρήνεσε πρὸς ταῖς ναυσὶν
9 εἶναι καὶ περιτειχίσαι τὸ στρατόπεδον. ἐπεὶ
δὲ πραττόντων ταῦτα τῶν Ἀθηναίων ἧκε γράμματα πάλιν παρὰ τοῦ Ἀλκιβιάδου, φυλάττεσθαι
κελεύοντος τὸν Φρύνιχον ὡς προδιδόντα τοῖς
πολεμίοις τὸν ναύσταθμον, ἠπίστησαν οἰόμενοι
τὸν Ἀλκιβιάδην εἰδότα σαφῶς τὴν τῶν πολεμίων
παρασκευὴν καὶ διάνοιαν ἀποχρῆσθαι πρὸς τὴν
10 τοῦ Φρυνίχου διαβολὴν οὐκ ἀληθῶς. ὕστερον

knowing it, it was a case of traitor dealing with traitor. For Astyochus was much in awe of Tissaphernes, and seeing that Alcibiades had great power with the satrap, he disclosed the message of Phrynichus to them both. Alcibiades at once sent men to Samos to denounce Phrynichus. All the Athenians there were incensed and banded themselves together against Phrynichus, who, seeing no other escape from his predicament, attempted to cure one evil by another and a greater. He sent again to Astyochus, chiding him indeed for his disclosure of the former message, but announcing that he stood ready to deliver into his hands the fleet and army of the Athenians.

However, this treachery of Phrynichus did not harm the Athenians at all, because of the fresh treachery of Astyochus. This second message of Phrynichus also he delivered to Alcibiades. But Phrynichus knew all the while that he would do so, and expected a second denunciation from Alcibiades. So he got the start of him by telling the Athenians himself that the enemy were going to attack them, and advising them to have their ships manned and their camp fortified. The Athenians were busy doing this when again a letter came from Alcibiades bidding them beware of Phrynichus, since he had offered to betray their fleet to the enemy. This letter they disbelieved at the time, supposing that Alcibiades, who must know perfectly the equipment and purposes of the enemy, had used his knowledge in order to calumniate Phrynichus falsely. Afterwards, [1]

[1] In the summer of 411 B.C., Phrynichus having been deposed from his command at Samos, and showing himself an ardent supporter of the revolutionary Four Hundred at Athens.

μέντοι τὸν Φρύνιχον ἑνὸς τῶν περιπόλων Ἕρμωνος
ἐν ἀγορᾷ πατάξαντος ἐγχειριδίῳ καὶ διαφθεί-
ραντος, οἱ Ἀθηναῖοι δίκης γενομένης τοῦ μὲν
Φρυνίχου προδοσίαν κατεψηφίσαντο τεθνηκότος,
τὸν δ᾽ Ἕρμωνα καὶ τοὺς μετ᾽ αὐτοῦ συστάντας
ἐστεφάνωσαν.

XXVI. Ἐν δὲ τῇ Σάμῳ τότε κρατήσαντες οἱ
Ἀλκιβιάδου φίλοι πέμπουσι Πείσανδρον εἰς
ἄστυ κινήσοντα τὴν πολιτείαν καὶ παραθαρ-
ρυνοῦντα τοὺς δυνατοὺς τῶν πραγμάτων ἀντιλαμβάνεσθαι καὶ καταλύειν τὸν δῆμον, ὡς ἐπὶ
τούτοις τοῦ Ἀλκιβιάδου Τισαφέρνην αὐτοῖς
φίλον καὶ σύμμαχον παρέξοντος. αὕτη γὰρ
ἦν πρόφασις καὶ τοῦτο πρόσχημα τοῖς καθιστᾶσι
2 τὴν ὀλιγαρχίαν. ἐπεὶ δ᾽ ἴσχυσαν καὶ παρέλαβον
τὰ πράγματα οἱ πεντακισχίλιοι λεγόμενοι,
τετρακόσιοι δὲ ὄντες, ἐλάχιστα τῷ Ἀλκιβιάδῃ
προσεῖχον ἤδη καὶ μαλακώτερον ἥπτοντο τοῦ
πολέμου, τὰ μὲν ἀπιστοῦντες ἔτι πρὸς τὴν
μεταβολὴν ξενοπαθοῦσι τοῖς πολίταις, τὰ δ᾽
οἰόμενοι μᾶλλον ἐνδώσειν αὐτοῖς Λακεδαιμονίους
3 ἀεὶ πρὸς ὀλιγαρχίαν ἐπιτηδείως ἔχοντας. ὁ
μὲν οὖν κατὰ τὴν πόλιν δῆμος ἄκων ὑπὸ δέους
ἡσυχίαν ἦγε· καὶ γὰρ ἀπεσφάγησαν οὐκ ὀλίγοι
τῶν ἐναντιουμένων φανερῶς τοῖς τετρακοσίοις·
οἱ δ᾽ ἐν Σάμῳ ταῦτα πυνθανόμενοι καὶ ἀγανακτοῦντες ὥρμηντο πλεῖν εὐθὺς ἐπὶ τὸν Πειραιᾶ,
καὶ μεταπεμψάμενοι τὸν Ἀλκιβιάδην καὶ στρατηγὸν ἀποδείξαντες ἐκέλευον ἡγεῖσθαι καὶ καταλύειν
τοὺς τυράννους.

4 Ὁ δ᾽ οὐχ οἷον ἄν τις ἐξαίφνης χάριτι τῶν

74

however, when Hermon,[1] one of the frontier guard,
had smitten Phrynichus with a dagger and slain him
in the open market-place, the Athenians tried the
case of the dead man, found him guilty of treachery,
and awarded crowns to Hermon and his accomplices.

XXVI. But at Samos the friends of Alcibiades
soon got the upper hand, and sent Peisander to
Athens to change the form of government. He was
to encourage the leading men to overthrow the democracy and take control of affairs, with the plea
that on these terms alone would Alcibiades make
Tissaphernes their friend and ally. This was the
pretence and this the pretext of those who established the oligarchy at Athens. But as soon as the
so-called Five Thousand (they were really only four
hundred) got the power and took control of affairs,
they at once neglected Alcibiades entirely, and
waged the war with less vigour, partly because they
distrusted the citizens, who still looked askance at
the new form of government, and partly because
they thought that the Lacedaemonians, who always
looked with favour on an oligarchy, would be more
lenient towards them. The popular party in the city
was constrained by fear to keep quiet, because many
of those who openly opposed the Four Hundred had
been slain. But when the army in Samos learned
what had been done at home, they were enraged,
and were eager to sail forthwith to the Piraeus, and
sending for Alcibiades, they appointed him general,
and bade him lead them in putting down the tyrants.

An ordinary man, thus suddenly raised to great

---

[1] The name is wrong, and has crept into the story by an
error which can be traced. Hermon was "commander of the
frontier guard stationed at Munychia" (Thuc. viii. 92, 5).

πολλῶν μέγας γεγονὼς ἔπαθε καὶ ἠγάπησε,
πάντα δεῖν εὐθὺς οἰόμενος χαρίζεσθαι καὶ μηδὲν
ἀντιλέγειν τοῖς ἐκ πλάνητος καὶ φυγάδος αὐτὸν
νεῶν τοσούτων καὶ στρατοπέδου καὶ δυνάμεως
τηλικαύτης ἀποδείξασιν ἡγεμόνα καὶ στρατηγόν,
ἀλλ' ὅπερ ἦν ἄρχοντι μεγάλῳ προσῆκον, ἀνθίστα-
σθαι φερομένοις ὑπ' ὀργῆς, κωλύσας ἐξαμαρτεῖν,
τότε γοῦν τὰ πράγματα τῇ πόλει περιφανῶς
5 ἔσωσεν. εἰ γὰρ ἄραντες ἀπέπλευσαν οἴκαδε,
τοῖς μὲν πολεμίοις εὐθὺς ἔχειν ὑπῆρχεν Ἰωνίαν
ἅπασαν, καὶ τὸν Ἑλλήσποντον[1] ἀμαχεί, καὶ 206
τὰς νήσους, Ἀθηναίοις δὲ πρὸς Ἀθηναίους
μάχεσθαι τὸν πόλεμον εἰς τὴν πόλιν ἐμβαλόντας·
ὃν μόνος μάλιστα μὴ γενέσθαι διεκώλυσεν ὁ
Ἀλκιβιάδης, οὐ μόνον πείθων καὶ διδάσκων τὸ
πλῆθος, ἀλλὰ καὶ καθ' ἕνα τοὺς μὲν ἀντιβολῶν,
6 τῶν δ' ἐπιλαμβανόμενος. συνέπραττε δ' αὐτῷ
καὶ Θρασύβουλος ὁ Στειριεὺς ἅμα παρὼν καὶ
κεκραγώς· ἦν γάρ, ὡς λέγεται, μεγαλοφωνότατος
Ἀθηναίων.

Ἐκεῖνό τε δὴ καλὸν τοῦ Ἀλκιβιάδου καὶ
δεύτερον, ὅτι ὑποσχόμενος τὰς Φοινίσσας ναῦς,
ἃς προσεδέχοντο Λακεδαιμόνιοι βασιλέως πέμψαντος, ἢ μεταστήσειν πρὸς αὐτοὺς ἢ διαπράξε-
σθαι μηδὲ πρὸς ἐκείνους κομισθῆναι, διὰ ταχέων
7 ἐξέπλευσε. καὶ τὰς μὲν ναῦς ἐκφανείσας περὶ
Ἄσπενδον οὐκ ἤγαγεν ὁ Τισαφέρνης, ἀλλ'
ἐψεύσατο τοὺς Λακεδαιμονίους, τὴν δ' αἰτίαν
τοῦ ἀποτρέψαι παρ' ἀμφοτέροις ὁ Ἀλκιβιάδης

---

[1] καὶ τὸν Ἑλλήσποντον Bekker : Ἑλλήσποντον.

power by the favour of the multitude, would have been full of complaisance, thinking that he must at once gratify them in all things and oppose them in nothing, since they had made him, instead of a wandering exile, leader and general of such a fleet and of so large an armed force. But Alcibiades, as became a great leader, felt that he must oppose them in their career of blind fury, and prevented them from making a fatal mistake. Therefore in this instance, at least, he was the manifest salvation of the city. For had they sailed off home, their enemies might at once have occupied all Ionia, the Hellespont without a battle, and the islands, while Athenians were fighting Athenians and making their own city the seat of war. Such a war Alcibiades, more than any other one man, prevented, not only persuading and instructing the multitude together, but also, taking them man by man, supplicating some and constraining others. He had a helper, too, in Thrasybulus of Steiris,[1] who went along with him and did the shouting; for he had, it is said, the biggest voice of all the Athenians.

A second honourable proceeding of Alcibiades was his promising to bring over to their side the Phoenician ships which the King had sent out and the Lacedaemonians were expecting,—or at least to see that those expectations were not realized,—and his sailing off swiftly on this errand. The ships were actually seen off Aspendus, but Tissaphernes did not bring them up, and thereby played the Lacedaemonians false. Alcibiades, however, was

---

[1] This illustrious commander, the son of Lycus, is to be distinguished from Thrasybulus, the son of Thraso (chapter xxxvi. 1).

εἶχε, καὶ μᾶλλον ἔτι παρὰ τοῖς Λακεδαιμονίοις,
ὡς διδάσκων τὸν βάρβαρον αὐτοὺς ὑφ᾽ αὑτῶν
περιορᾶν ἀπολλυμένους τοὺς Ἕλληνας. οὐ γὰρ
ἦν ἄδηλον ὅτι τοῖς ἑτέροις δύναμις τοσαύτη
προσγενομένη τοὺς ἑτέρους ἀφῃρεῖτο κομιδῇ τὸ
κράτος τῆς θαλάττης.

XXVII. Ἐκ τούτου κατελύθησαν μὲν οἱ τετρακόσιοι, τῶν Ἀλκιβιάδου φίλων προθύμως συλ-
λαμβανομένων τοῖς τὰ δήμου φρονοῦσι· βουλομένων δὲ τῶν ἐν ἄστει καὶ κελευόντων κατιέναι
τὸν Ἀλκιβιάδην αὐτὸς ᾤετο δεῖν μὴ κεναῖς χερσὶ
μηδὲ ἀπράκτοις, οἴκτῳ καὶ χάριτι τῶν πολλῶν,
ἀλλ᾽ ἐνδόξως κατελθεῖν. διὸ πρῶτον μὲν ὀλίγαις
ναυσὶν ἐκ Σάμου περιέπλει τὴν Κνιδίων καὶ Κῴων
2 θάλασσαν· ἐκεῖ δ᾽ ἀκούσας Μίνδαρον τὸν Σπαρτιάτην εἰς Ἑλλήσποντον ἀναπλεῖν τῷ στόλῳ
παντὶ καὶ τοὺς Ἀθηναίους ἐπακολουθεῖν, ἠπείγετο
βοηθῆσαι τοῖς στρατηγοῖς. καὶ κατὰ τύχην εἰς
τοῦτο καιροῦ συνήνυσε πλέων ὀκτωκαίδεκα τριήρεσιν, ἐν ᾧ πάσαις ὁμοῦ ταῖς ναυσὶ συμπεσόντες
εἰς τὸ αὐτὸ καὶ διαναυμαχοῦντες περὶ Ἄβυδον
ἀμφότεροι τοῖς μὲν ἡττώμενοι μέρεσι, τοῖς δὲ
νικῶντες ἄχρι δείλης ἀγῶνι μεγάλῳ συνείχοντο.
3 καὶ παρέσχε μὲν ἐναντίαν δόξαν ἀμφοτέροις
ἐπιφανείς, ὥστε θαρρεῖν μὲν τοὺς πολεμίους,
θορυβεῖσθαι δὲ τοὺς Ἀθηναίους. ταχὺ δὲ σημεῖον ἄρας ἀπὸ τῆς ναυαρχίδος φίλιον ὥρμησεν
εὐθὺς ἐπὶ τοὺς κρατοῦντας καὶ διώκοντας τῶν
Πελοποννησίων. τρεψάμενος δ᾽ αὐτοὺς ἐξέωσεν
εἰς τὴν γῆν, καὶ προσκείμενος ἔκοπτε τὰς ναῦς

credited with this diversion of the ships by both parties, and especially by the Lacedaemonians. The charge was that he instructed the Barbarian to suffer the Hellenes to destroy one another. For it was perfectly clear that the side to which such a naval force attached itself would rob the other altogether of the control of the sea.

XXVII. After this the Four Hundred were overthrown,[1] the friends of Alcibiades now zealously assisting the party of the people. Then the city willingly ordered Alcibiades to come back home. But he thought he must not return with empty hands and without achievement, through the pity and favour of the multitude, but rather in a blaze of glory. So, to begin with, he set sail with a small fleet from Samos and cruised off Cnidus and Cos. There he heard that Mindarus the Spartan admiral had sailed off to the Hellespont with his entire fleet, followed by the Athenians, and so he hastened to the assistance of their generals. By chance he came up, with his eighteen triremes, at just that critical point when both parties, having joined battle with all their ships off Abydos, and sharing almost equally in victory and defeat until evening, were locked in a great struggle. The appearance of Alcibiades inspired both sides with a false opinion of his coming : the enemy were emboldened and the Athenians were confounded. But he quickly hoisted Athenian colours on his flagship and darted straight upon the victorious and pursuing Peloponnesians. Routing them, he drove them to land, and following hard after them, rammed and shattered their ships.

[1] They usurped the power in June, of 411 B.C. ; they fell in September of the same year.

καὶ συνετίτρωσκε, τῶν ἀνδρῶν ἐκνεόντων καὶ
Φαρναβάζου πεζῇ προσβοηθοῦντος αὐτοῖς καὶ
μαχομένου παρὰ τὴν θάλατταν ὑπὲρ τῶν νεῶν.
4 τέλος δὲ τῶν μὲν πολεμίων τριάκοντα λαβόντες,
ἀνασώσαντες δὲ τὰς αὑτῶν, τρόπαιον ἔστησαν.

Οὕτω δὲ λαμπρᾷ χρησάμενος εὐτυχίᾳ, καὶ
φιλοτιμούμενος εὐθὺς ἐγκαλλωπίσασθαι τῷ
Τισαφέρνῃ, ξένια καὶ δῶρα παρασκευασάμενος καὶ
θεραπείαν ἔχων ἡγεμονικὴν ἐπορεύετο πρὸς
5 αὐτόν. οὐ μὴν ἔτυχεν ὧν προσεδόκησεν, ἀλλὰ
πάλαι κακῶς ἀκούων ὁ Τισαφέρνης ὑπὸ τῶν
Λακεδαιμονίων, καὶ φοβούμενος αἰτίαν λαβεῖν ἐκ
βασιλέως, ἔδοξεν ἐν καιρῷ τὸν Ἀλκιβιάδην
ἀφῖχθαι, καὶ συλλαβὼν αὐτὸν εἶρξεν ἐν Σάρ-
δεσιν ὡς λύσιν ἐκείνης τῆς διαβολῆς τὴν ἀδικίαν
ταύτην ἐσομένην.

XXVIII. Τριάκοντα δ᾽ ἡμερῶν διαγενομένων
ὁ Ἀλκιβιάδης ἵππου ποθὲν εὐπορήσας καὶ
ἀποδρὰς τοὺς φύλακας εἰς Κλαζομενὰς διέφυγε.
καὶ τὸν μὲν Τισαφέρνην προσδιέβαλλεν ὡς ὑπ᾽
ἐκείνου μεθειμένος, αὐτὸς δὲ πλεύσας εἰς τὸ
στρατόπεδον τῶν Ἀθηναίων καὶ πυθόμενος
Μίνδαρον ὁμοῦ καὶ Φαρνάβαζον ἐν Κυζίκῳ γε-
2 γονέναι, τοὺς μὲν στρατιώτας παρώρμησεν, ὡς
ἀνάγκην οὖσαν αὐτοῖς καὶ ναυμαχεῖν καὶ πεζο-
μαχεῖν καὶ νὴ Δία τειχομαχεῖν πρὸς τοὺς πολε-
μίους· χρήματα γὰρ οὐκ εἶναι μὴ πάντῃ κρατοῦσι·
πληρώσας δὲ τὰς ναῦς καὶ κατάρας εἰς Προικόν-

207

Their crews swam ashore, and here Pharnabazus
came to their aid with his infantry and fought along
the beach in defence of their ships. But finally the
Athenians captured thirty of them, rescued their
own, and erected a trophy of victory.

Taking advantage of a success so brilliant as this,
and ambitious to display himself at once before
Tissaphernes, Alcibiades supplied himself with gifts
of hospitality and friendship and proceeded, at the
head of an imperial retinue, to visit the satrap.
His reception, however, was not what he expected.
Tissaphernes had for a long time been accused by
the Lacedaemonians to the King, and being in fear
of the King's condemnation, it seemed to him that
Alcibiades had come in the nick of time. So he
arrested him and shut him up in Sardis, hoping that
such an outrage upon him as this would dispel the
calumnies of the Spartans.

XXVIII. After the lapse of thirty days Alcibiades
ran away from his guards, got a horse from some one
or other, and made his escape to Clazomenae. To
repay Tissaphernes, he alleged that he had escaped
with that satrap's connivance, and so brought additional calumny upon him. He himself sailed to
the camp of the Athenians,[1] where he learned that
Mindarus, along with Pharnabazus, was in Cyzicus.
Thereupon he roused the spirits of the soldiers,
declaring that they must now do sea-fighting and
land-fighting and even siege-fighting, too, against
their enemies, for poverty stared them in the face
unless they were victorious in every way. He then
manned his ships and made his way to Proconnesus,

---

[1] Early in the spring of 410 B.C. The Athenians were at
Cardia, a city of the Thracian Chersonese.

νησον ἐκέλευσεν ἐντὸς περιβάλλειν τὰ λεπτὰ
πλοῖα καὶ παραφυλάσσειν, ὅπως μηδεμία τοῖς
πολεμίοις ἐπιπλέοντος αὐτοῦ γένοιτο μηδαμόθεν
προαίσθησις.

3   Ἔτυχε δὲ καὶ πολὺν ὄμβρον ἐξαίφνης ἐπι-
πεσόντα καὶ βροντὰς καὶ ζόφον συνεργῆσαι καὶ
συνεπικρύψαι τὴν παρασκευήν. οὐ γὰρ μόνον
τοὺς πολεμίους ἔλαθεν, ἀλλὰ καὶ τοὺς Ἀθηναίους
ἀπεγνωκότας ἤδη ἐμβῆναι κελεύσας ἀνήχθη.
καὶ μετὰ μικρὸν ὅ τε ζόφος διελύθη καὶ κατώ-
φθησαν αἱ τῶν Πελοποννησίων νῆες αἰωρούμεναι
4   πρὸ τοῦ λιμένος τῶν Κυζικηνῶν. δείσας οὖν ὁ
Ἀλκιβιάδης μὴ διὰ τὸ πλῆθος αὐτὸν προϊδόντες
εἰς τὴν γῆν καταφύγωσι, τοὺς μὲν στρατηγοὺς
ἐκέλευσεν ἡσυχῇ πλέοντας ὑπολείπεσθαι, αὐτὸς
δὲ τετταράκοντα ναῦς ἔχων ἐφαίνετο καὶ προὐκαλεῖτο τοὺς πολεμίους. ἐπεὶ δ' ἐξηπάτηντο
καὶ καταφρονήσαντες ὡς ἐπὶ τοσαύτας ἀντεξή-
λασαν, αὐτοὶ μὲν εὐθὺς ἐξήπτοντο καὶ συνεπλέ-
κοντο, τῶν δ' ἄλλων ἤδη μαχομένοις ἐπιφερο-
μένων ἐκπλαγέντες ἔφευγον.

5   Ὁ δ' Ἀλκιβιάδης εἴκοσι ταῖς ἀρίσταις διεκπλεύ-
σας καὶ προσβαλὼν τῇ γῇ καὶ ἀποβάς, ἐνέκειτο
τοῖς φεύγουσιν ἐκ τῶν νεῶν καὶ πολλοὺς ἔφθειρε·
Μινδάρου δὲ καὶ Φαρναβάζου προσβοηθούντων
κρατήσας, τὸν μὲν Μίνδαρον ἀνεῖλεν ἐρρωμένως
6   ἀγωνιζόμενον, ὁ δὲ Φαρνάβαζος ἔφυγε. πολλῶν
δὲ καὶ νεκρῶν καὶ ὅπλων κρατήσαντες τάς τε
ναῦς ἁπάσας ἔλαβον, χειρωσάμενοι δὲ καὶ Κύζικον,

82

giving orders at once to seize all small trading craft and keep them under guard, that the enemy might get no warning of his approach from any source soever.

Now it chanced that copious rain fell all of a sudden, and thunder-peals and darkness coöperated with him in concealing his design. Indeed, not only did he elude the enemy, but even the Athenians themselves had already given up all expectation of fighting, when he suddenly ordered them aboard ship and put out to sea. After a little the darkness cleared away, and the Peloponnesian ships were seen hovering off the harbour of Cyzicus. Fearing then lest they catch sight of the full extent of his array and take refuge ashore, he ordered his fellow-commanders to sail slowly and so remain in the rear, while he himself, with only forty ships, hove in sight and challenged the foe to battle. The Peloponnesians were utterly deceived, and scorning what they deemed the small numbers of their enemy, put out to meet them, and closed at once with them in a grappling fight. Presently, while the battle was raging, the Athenian reserves bore down upon their foe, who were panic stricken and took to flight.

Then Alcibiades with twenty of his best ships broke though their line, put to shore, and disembarking his crews, attacked his enemy as they fled from their ships, and slew many of them. Mindarus and Pharnabazus, who came to their aid, he overwhelmed ; Mindarus was slain fighting sturdily, but Pharnabazus made his escape. Many were the dead bodies and the arms of which the Athenians became masters, and they captured all their enemy's ships. Then they also stormed Cyzicus, which Pharnabazus

ἐκλιπόντος τοῦ Φαρναβάζου καὶ τῶν Πελοποννησίων διαφθαρέντων, οὐ μόνον τὸν Ἑλλήσποντον
εἶχον βεβαίως, ἀλλὰ καὶ τῆς ἄλλης θαλάττης
ἐξήλασαν κατὰ κράτος τοὺς Λακεδαιμονίους.
ἑάλω δὲ καὶ γράμματα λακωνικῶς φράζοντα τοῖς
Ἐφόροις τὴν γεγενημένην ἀτυχίαν· "Ἔρρει τὰ
κᾶλα· Μίνδαρος ἀπεσσούα· πεινῶντι τὤνδρες·
ἀπορίομες τί χρὴ δρᾶν."

XXIX. Οὕτω δ' ἐπήρθησαν οἱ μετὰ τοῦ Ἀλκιβιάδου στρατευσάμενοι καὶ τοσοῦτον ἐφρόνησαν
ὥστ' ἀπαξιοῦν ἔτι τοῖς ἄλλοις καταμιγνύναι
στρατιώταις ἑαυτοὺς πολλάκις ἡττημένοις ἀητ-
τήτους ὄντας. καὶ γὰρ οὐ πολλῷ πρότερον συνε-
βεβήκει πταίσαντος περὶ Ἔφεσον τοῦ Θρασύλλου
τὸ χαλκοῦν ἀνεστάναι τρόπαιον ὑπὸ τῶν Ἐφεσίων
2 ἐπ' αἰσχύνῃ τῶν Ἀθηναίων. ταῦτ' οὖν ὠνείδιζον
οἱ μετὰ τοῦ Ἀλκιβιάδου τοῖς μετὰ τοῦ Θρασύλλου,
μεγαλύνοντες αὑτοὺς καὶ τὸν στρατηγόν, ἐκείνοις
δὲ μήτε γυμνασίων μήτε χώρας ἐν στρατοπέδῳ
κοινωνεῖν ἐθέλοντες. ἐπεὶ δὲ Φαρνάβαζος ἱππέας
τε πολλοὺς ἔχων καὶ πεζοὺς ἐπῆλθεν αὐτοῖς
ἐμβεβληκόσιν εἰς τὴν Ἀβυδηνῶν, ὁ δ' Ἀλκιβιάδης
ἐκβοηθήσας ἐπ' αὐτὸν ἐτρέψατο καὶ κατεδίωξεν
ἄχρι σκότους μετὰ τοῦ Θρασύλλου, καὶ ἀνεμίγ-
νυντο καὶ κοινῇ φιλοφρονούμενοι καὶ χαίροντες
ἐπανῇεσαν εἰς τὸ στρατόπεδον.
3 Τῇ δ' ὑστεραίᾳ στήσας τρόπαιον ἐλεηλάτει τὴν
Φαρναβάζου χώραν οὐδενὸς ἀμύνεσθαι τολμῶντος.
ἱερεῖς μέντοι καὶ ἱερείας ἔλαβε μέν, ἀλλ' ἀφῆκεν
ἄνευ λύτρων. Χαλκηδονίοις δ' ἀφεστῶσι καὶ

abandoned to its fate, and the Peloponnesians in it were annihilated. Thus the Athenians not only had the Hellespont under their sure control, but even drove the Lacedaemonians at a stroke from the rest of the sea. A dispatch was captured announcing the disaster to the ephors in true laconic style: "Our ships are lost; Mindarus is gone; our men are starving; we know not what to do."

XXIX. But the soldiers of Alcibiades were now so elated and filled with pride that they disdained longer to mingle with the rest of the army, since it had often been conquered, while they were unconquered. For not long before this,[1] Thrasyllus had suffered a reverse at Ephesus, and the Ephesians had erected their bronze trophy of victory, to the disgrace of the Athenians. This was what the soldiers of Alcibiades cast in the teeth of Thrasyllus' men, vaunting themselves and their general, and refusing to share either training or quarters in camp with them. But when Pharnabazus with much cavalry and infantry attacked the forces of Thrasyllus, who had made a raid into the territory of Abydos, Alcibiades sallied out to their aid, routed Pharnabazus, and pursued him till nightfall, along with Thrasyllus. Thus the two factions were blended, and returned to their camp with mutual friendliness and delight.

On the following day Alcibiades set up a trophy of victory and plundered the territory of Pharnabazus, no one venturing to defend it. He even captured some priests and priestesses, but let them go without ransom. On setting out to attack Chalcedon, which

---

[1] During the summer of 410 B.C., after the victory of Cyzicus.

δεδεγμένοις φρουρὰν καὶ ἁρμοστὴν Λακεδαιμονίων
ὡρμημένος πολεμεῖν, ἀκούσας δ᾿ ὅτι τὴν λείαν
πᾶσαν ἐκ τῆς χώρας συναγαγόντες εἰς Βιθυνοὺς
ὑπεκτίθενται [1] φίλους ὄντας, ἧκεν ἐπὶ τοὺς ὅρους
ἄγων τὸ στράτευμα, καὶ κήρυκα προπέμψας
ἐνεκάλει τοῖς Βιθυνοῖς. οἱ δὲ δείσαντες τήν τε
λείαν ἀπέδοσαν αὐτῷ καὶ φιλίαν ὡμολόγησαν.

XXX. Ἀποτειχιζομένης δὲ τῆς Χαλκηδόνος
ἐκ θαλάττης εἰς θάλατταν, ὁ Φαρνάβαζος ἧκεν
ὡς λύσων τὴν πολιορκίαν, καὶ Ἱπποκράτης ὁ
ἁρμοστὴς ἐκ τῆς πόλεως ἐξαγαγὼν τὴν σὺν 208
αὐτῷ δύναμιν ἐπεχείρει τοῖς Ἀθηναίοις. ὁ δ᾿
Ἀλκιβιάδης ἅμα πρὸς ἀμφοτέρους ἀντιτάξας τὸ
στράτευμα, τὸν μὲν Φαρνάβαζον αἰσχρῶς φεύγειν
ἠνάγκασε, τὸν δ᾿ Ἱπποκράτη διέφθειρε καὶ συχνοὺς
τῶν περὶ αὐτὸν ἡττηθέντας.

2 Εἶτ᾿ αὐτὸς μὲν ἐκπλεύσας εἰς τὸν Ἑλλήσποντον
ἠργυρολόγει καὶ Σηλυβρίαν εἷλεν, ἀφειδήσας
ἑαυτοῦ παρὰ τὸν καιρόν. οἱ γὰρ ἐνδιδόντες τὴν
πόλιν συνέθεντο μὲν ἀνασχήσειν πυρσὸν αὐτῷ
μεσούσης νυκτός, ἠναγκάσθησαν δὲ τοῦτο ποιῆσαι
πρὸ τοῦ καιροῦ, τῶν συνωμοτῶν τινα φοβηθέντες
ἐξαίφνης μεταβαλόμενον. ἀρθέντος οὖν τοῦ πυρ-
σοῦ μηδέπω τῆς στρατιᾶς οὔσης ἑτοίμης, ἀναλαβὼν ὅσον τριάκοντα περὶ αὐτὸν ἐπείγετο δρόμῳ
πρὸς τὰ τείχη, τοὺς ἄλλους ἕπεσθαι κατὰ τάχος
3 κελεύσας. ἀνοιχθείσης δὲ τῆς πύλης αὐτῷ καὶ
προσγενομένων τοῖς τριάκοντα πελταστῶν εἴκοσι
παρεισπεσὼν εὐθὺς ᾔσθετο τοὺς Σηλυβριανοὺς
ἐξ ἐναντίας μετὰ τῶν ὅπλων ἐπιφερομένους. ἐπεὶ

[1] ὑπεκτίθενται with Mᵃ and Cobet: ἐκτίθενται.

had revolted from Athens and received a Lacedaemonian garrison and governor, he heard that its
citizens had collected all their goods and chattels out
of the country and committed them for safe keeping
to the Bithynians, who were their friends. So he
marched to the confines of Bithynia with his army,
and sent on a herald with accusations and demands.
The Bithynians, in terror, gave up the booty to him,
and made a treaty of friendship.

XXX. While Chalcedon was being walled in from
sea to sea,[1] Pharnabazus came to raise the siege, and
at the same time Hippocrates, the Spartan governor,
led his forces out of the city and attacked the
Athenians. But Alcibiades arrayed his army so as
to face both enemies at once, put Pharnabazus to
shameful flight, and slew Hippocrates together with
many of his vanquished men.

Then he sailed in person into the Hellespont and
levied moneys there. He also captured Selymbria,
where he exposed himself beyond all bounds. For
there was a party in the city which offered to surrender it to him, and they had agreed with him upon
the signal of a lighted torch displayed at midnight.
But they were forced to give this signal before the
appointed time, through fear of one of the conspirators, who suddenly changed his mind. So the
torch was displayed before his army was ready ; but
Alcibiades took about thirty men and ran to the walls,
bidding the rest of his force follow with all speed.
The gate was thrown open for him and he rushed
into the city, his thirty men-at-arms reinforced by
twenty targeteers, but he saw at once that the
Selymbrians were advancing in battle array to attack

[1] In the spring of 409 B.C.

δ' ὑποστάντι μὲν οὐκ ἐφαίνετο σωτηρία, πρὸς δὲ
τὸ φυγεῖν, ἀήττητος ἄχρι τῆς ἡμέρας ἐκείνης ἐν
ταῖς στρατηγίαις γεγονώς, φιλονεικότερον εἶχε,
τῇ σάλπιγγι σημήνας σιωπὴν ἐκέλευσεν ἕνα τῶν
παρόντων ἀνειπεῖν Σηλυβριανοῖς Ἀθηναίους ἐναν-
4 τία ὅπλα μὴ τίθεσθαι. τοῦτο τὸ κήρυγμα τοὺς
μὲν ἀμβλυτέρους ἐποίησε πρὸς τὴν μάχην, ὡς
τῶν πολεμίων ἔνδον ὄντων ἁπάντων, οἱ δὲ ταῖς
ἐλπίσιν ἡδίους ἐγένοντο πρὸς τὰς διαλύσεις. ἐν
ᾧ δὲ συστάντες ἀλλήλοις ἐδίδοσαν λόγον, ἐπῆλθεν
ἡ στρατιὰ τῷ Ἀλκιβιάδῃ, καὶ τεκμαιρόμενος, ὅπερ
ἦν, εἰρηνικὰ φρονεῖν τοὺς Σηλυβριανούς, ἔδεισε
5 μὴ τὴν πόλιν οἱ Θρᾷκες διαρπάσωσιν. ἦσαν δὲ
πολλοί, χάριτι τοῦ Ἀλκιβιάδου καὶ δι' εὔνοιαν
στρατευόμενοι προθύμως. ἀπέπεμψεν οὖν τούτους ἅπαντας ἐκ τῆς πόλεως, τοὺς δὲ Σηλυβριανοὺς δεηθέντας οὐδὲν ἠδίκησεν, ἀλλὰ χρήματα
λαβὼν καὶ φρουρὰν ἐγκαταστήσας ἀπῆλθεν.

XXXI. Οἱ δὲ πολιορκοῦντες τὴν Χαλκηδόνα
στρατηγοὶ σπονδὰς ἐποιήσαντο πρὸς Φαρνάβαζον
ἐπὶ τῷ χρήματα λαβεῖν καὶ Χαλκηδονίους ὑπη-
κόους πάλιν Ἀθηναίοις εἶναι, τὴν δὲ Φαρναβάζου
χώραν μὴ ἀδικεῖν, Φαρνάβαζον δὲ πρέσβεσιν
Ἀθηναίων πρὸς βασιλέα πομπὴν μετ' ἀσφαλείας
2 παρασχεῖν. ὡς οὖν ἐπανελθόντα τὸν Ἀλκιβιάδην ὁ Φαρνάβαζος ἠξίου καὶ αὐτὸν ὀμόσαι περὶ
τῶν ὡμολογημένων, οὐκ ἔφη πρότερον ἢ ἐκεῖνον
αὐτοῖς ὀμόσαι.

Γενομένων δὲ τῶν ὅρκων ἐπὶ Βυζαντίους ἀφε-

him. In resistance he saw no safety, and for flight, undefeated as he was in all his campaigns down to that day, he had too much spirit. He therefore bade the trumpet signal silence, and then ordered formal proclamation to be made that Selymbria must not bear arms against Athens. This proclamation made some of the Selymbrians less eager for battle, if, as they supposed, their enemies were all inside the walls; and others were mollified by hopes of a peaceful settlement. While they were thus parleying with one another, up came the army of Alcibiades. Judging now, as was really the case, that the Selymbrians were disposed for peace, he was afraid that his Thracian soldiers might plunder the city. There were many of these, and they were zealous in their service, through the favour and good will they bore Alcibiades. Accordingly, he sent them all out of the city, and then, at the plea of the Selymbrians, did their city no injury whatever, but merely took a sum of money from it, set a garrison in it, and went his way.

XXXI. Meanwhile the Athenian generals who were besieging Chalcedon made peace with Pharnabazus on condition that they receive a sum of money, that Chalcedon be subject again to Athens, that the territories of Pharnabazus be not ravaged, and that the said Pharnabazus furnish safe escort for an Athenian embassy to the King. Accordingly, when Alcibiades came back from Selymbria, Pharnabazus demanded that he too take oath to the treaty; but Alcibiades refused to do so until Pharnabazus had taken his oath to it.

After the oaths had been taken, he went up against Byzantium, which was in revolt against

στῶτας ἦλθε καὶ περιετείχιζε τὴν πόλιν. Ἀνα-
ξιλάου δὲ καὶ Λυκούργου καί τινων ἄλλων συν-
θεμένων ἐπὶ σωτηρίᾳ παραδώσειν τὴν πόλιν,
διαδοὺς λόγον ὡς ἀνίστησιν αὐτοὺς πράγματα
νεώτερα συνιστάμενα περὶ τὴν Ἰωνίαν, ἡμέρας
3 ἀπέπλει ταῖς ναυσὶ πάσαις, νυκτὸς δ᾽ ὑποστρέψας
αὐτὸς μὲν ἀπέβη μετὰ τῶν ὁπλιτῶν καὶ προσελθὼν τοῖς τείχεσιν ἡσυχίαν ἦγεν, αἱ δὲ νῆες ἐπὶ
τὸν λιμένα πλεύσασαι καὶ βιαζόμεναι κραυγῇ τε
πολλῇ καὶ θορύβοις καὶ ψόφοις ἅμα μὲν ἐξέ-
πληττον τῷ ἀπροσδοκήτῳ τοὺς Βυζαντίους, ἅμα
δὲ τοῖς ἀττικίζουσι παρεῖχον ἐπ᾽ ἀδείας τὸν
Ἀλκιβιάδην δέχεσθαι, πάντων ἐπὶ τὸν λιμένα καὶ
4 τὰς ναῦς βοηθούντων. οὐ μὴν ἀμαχεὶ προσ-
εχώρησαν· οἱ γὰρ παρόντες ἐν τῷ Βυζαντίῳ Πελοποννήσιοι καὶ Βοιωτοὶ καὶ Μεγαρεῖς τοὺς μὲν ἀπὸ
τῶν νεῶν ἐτρέψαντο καὶ καθεῖρξαν εἰς τὰς ναῦς
πάλιν, τοὺς δ᾽ Ἀθηναίους ἔνδον ὄντας αἰσθόμενοι
καὶ συντάξαντες ἑαυτοὺς ἐχώρουν ὁμόσε. καρ-
τερᾶς δὲ μάχης γενομένης ἐνίκησεν Ἀλκιβιάδης
τὸ δεξιὸν κέρας ἔχων, Θηραμένης δὲ τὸ εὐώνυμον,
καὶ τῶν πολεμίων τοὺς περιγενομένους ὅσον
τριακοσίους ζῶντας ἔλαβε.
5 Βυζαντίων δὲ μετὰ τὴν μάχην οὐδεὶς ἀπέθανεν οὐδ᾽ ἔφυγεν· ἐπὶ τούτοις γὰρ οἱ ἄνδρες 209
παρέδοσαν τὴν πόλιν καὶ ταῦτα συνέθεντο,
μηδὲν αὐτοῖς ἴδιον ὑπεξελόμενοι. διὸ καὶ δίκην
προδοσίας ἐν Λακεδαίμονι φεύγων ὁ Ἀναξίλαος

Athens, and compassed the city with a wall.[1] But after Anaxilaüs, Lycurgus, and certain men besides had agreed to surrender the city to him on condition that it be not plundered, he spread abroad the story that threatening complications in Ionia called him away. Then he sailed off in broad daylight with all his ships; but in the night time stealthily returned. He disembarked with the men-at-arms under his own command, and stationed himself quietly within reach of the city's walls. His fleet, meanwhile, sailed to the harbour, and forcing its way in with much shouting and tumult and din, terrified the Byzantians by the unexpectedness of its attack, while it gave the party of Athens in the city a chance to admit Alcibiades in all security, since everybody had hurried off to the harbour and the fleet. However, the day was not won without a battle. The Peloponnesians, Boeotians and Megarians who were in garrison at Byzantium routed the ships' crews and drove them back on board again. Then, perceiving that the Athenians were inside the city, they formed in battle array and advanced to attack them. . A fierce battle followed, but Alcibiades was victorious with the right wing, as well as Theramenes with the left, and they took prisoners no less than three hundred of the enemy who survived.

Not a man of the Byzantians was put to death or sent into exile after the battle, for it was on these conditions that the men who surrendered the city had acted, and this was the agreement with them; they exacted no special grace for themselves. Therefore it was that when Anaxilaüs was prosecuted at Sparta for treachery, his words showed clearly

[1] During the winter of 409-408 B.C.

ἐφάνη τῷ λόγῳ τὸ ἔργον οὐκ αἰσχύνων. ἔφη γὰρ
οὐκ ὢν Λακεδαιμόνιος, ἀλλὰ Βυζάντιος, οὐδὲ τὴν
Σπάρτην κινδυνεύουσαν, ἀλλὰ τὸ Βυζάντιον
ὁρῶν, τῆς μὲν πόλεως ἀποτετειχισμένης, μηδενὸς
6 δ' εἰσαγομένου, τὸν δ' ὄντα σῖτον ἐν τῇ πόλει
Πελοποννησίων καὶ Βοιωτῶν ἐσθιόντων, Βυζαντίων δὲ πεινώντων σὺν τέκνοις καὶ γυναιξίν, οὐ
προδοῦναι τοῖς πολεμίοις, ἀλλὰ πολέμων καὶ
κακῶν ἀπαλλάξαι τὴν πόλιν, μιμούμενος τοὺς
ἀρίστους Λακεδαιμονίων, οἷς ἐν καλὸν ἁπλῶς καὶ
δίκαιόν ἐστι τὸ τῆς πατρίδος συμφέρον. οἱ μὲν
οὖν Λακεδαιμόνιοι ταῦτ' ἀκούσαντες ᾐδέσθησαν
καὶ ἀπέλυσαν τοὺς ἄνδρας.

XXXII. Ὁ δ' Ἀλκιβιάδης ἰδεῖν τε ποθῶν ἤδη
τὰ οἴκοι, καὶ ἔτι μᾶλλον ὀφθῆναι βουλόμενος
τοῖς πολίταις νενικηκὼς τοὺς πολεμίους τοσαυ-
τάκις, ἀνήχθη, πολλαῖς μὲν ἀσπίσι καὶ λαφύροις
κύκλῳ κεκοσμημένων τῶν Ἀττικῶν τριήρων,
πολλὰς δ' ἐφελκόμενος αἰχμαλώτους, ἔτι δὲ πλείω
κομίζων ἀκροστόλια τῶν διεφθαρμένων ὑπ' αὐτοῦ
καὶ κεκρατημένων. ἦσαν γὰρ οὐκ ἐλάττους συν-
αμφότεραι διακοσίων.

2 Ἃ δὲ Δοῦρις ὁ Σάμιος Ἀλκιβιάδου φάσκων
ἀπόγονος εἶναι προστίθησι τούτοις, αὐλεῖν μὲν
εἰρεσίαν τοῖς ἐλαύνουσι Χρυσόγονον τὸν πυθιο-
νίκην, κελεύειν δὲ Καλλιππίδην τὸν τῶν τραγῳ-
διῶν ὑποκριτήν, στατοὺς καὶ ξυστίδας καὶ τὸν

that his deeds had not been disgraceful. He said
that he was not a Lacedaemonian, but a Byzantian,
and it was not Sparta that was in peril. Considering
therefore the case of Byzantium, he saw that the
city was walled up, that no help could make its way
in, and that the provisions already in the city were
being consumed by Peloponnesians and Boeotians,
while the Byzantians were starving, together with
their wives and children. He had, therefore, not
betrayed the city to its enemies, but set it free from
war and its horrors, therein imitating the noblest
Lacedaemonians, in whose eyes the one unqualifiedly
honourable and righteous thing is their country's
good. The Lacedaemonians, on hearing this, were
moved with sincere respect, and acquitted the men.

XXXII. But Alcibiades, yearning at last to see
his home, and still more desirous of being seen by
his fellow citizens, now that he had conquered their
enemies so many times, set sail.[1] His Attic triremes
were adorned all round with many shields and spoils
of war ; many that he had captured in battle were
towed along in his wake ; and still more numerous
were the figure-heads he carried of triremes which
had been overwhelmed and destroyed by him.
There were not less than two hundred of these all
together.

Duris the Samian, who claims that he was a
descendant of Alcibiades, gives some additional
details. He says that the oarsmen of Alcibiades
rowed to the music of a flute blown by Chrysogonus
the Pythian victor ; that they kept time to a
rhythmic call from the lips of Callipides the tragic
actor ; that both these artists were arrayed in the

[1] From Samos, in the spring of 408 B.C.

ἄλλον ἐναγώνιον ἀμπεχομένους κόσμον, ἱστίῳ δ'
ἀλουργῷ τὴν ναυαρχίδα προσφέρεσθαι τοῖς λιμέ-
3 σιν, ὥσπερ ἐκ μέθης ἐπικωμάζοντος, οὔτε Θεόπομπος οὔτ' Ἔφορος οὔτε Ξενοφῶν γέγραφεν,
οὔτ' εἰκὸς ἦν οὕτως ἐντρυφῆσαι τοῖς Ἀθηναίοις
μετὰ φυγὴν καὶ συμφορὰς τοσαύτας κατερχόμε-
νον, ἀλλ' ἐκεῖνος καὶ δεδιὼς κατήγετο, καὶ καταχθεὶς οὐ πρότερον ἀπέβη τῆς τριήρους, πρὶν στὰς
ἐπὶ τοῦ καταστρώματος ἰδεῖν Εὐρυπτόλεμόν τε
τὸν ἀνεψιὸν παρόντα καὶ τῶν ἄλλων φίλων καὶ
οἰκείων συχνοὺς ἐκδεχομένους καὶ παρακαλοῦν-
τας.

4 Ἐπεὶ δ' ἀπέβη, τοὺς μὲν ἄλλους στρατηγοὺς
οὐδ' ὁρᾶν ἐδόκουν ἀπαντῶντες οἱ ἄνθρωποι, πρὸς
δ' ἐκεῖνον συντρέχοντες ἐβόων, ἠσπάζοντο, παρέ-
πεμπον, ἐστεφάνουν προσιόντες, οἱ δὲ μὴ δυνάμενοι προσελθεῖν ἄπωθεν ἐθεῶντο, καὶ τοῖς νέοις
ἐδείκνυσαν οἱ πρεσβύτεροι. πολὺ δὲ καὶ δά-
κρυον τῷ χαίροντι τῆς πόλεως ἀνεκέκρατο, καὶ
μνήμῃ πρὸς τὴν παροῦσαν εὐτυχίαν τῶν πρόσθεν
ἀτυχημάτων, λογιζομένοις ὡς οὔτ' ἂν Σικελίας
5 διήμαρτον οὔτ' ἄλλο τι τῶν προσδοκηθέντων
ἐξέφυγεν αὐτοὺς ἐάσαντας Ἀλκιβιάδην ἐπὶ τῶν
τότε πραγμάτων καὶ τῆς δυνάμεως ἐκείνης, εἰ νῦν
τὴν πόλιν παραλαβὼν ὀλίγου δέουσαν ἐκπεπτωκέναι τῆς θαλάττης, κατὰ γῆν δὲ μόλις τῶν
προαστείων κρατοῦσαν, αὐτὴν δὲ πρὸς ἑαυτὴν
στασιάζουσαν, ἐκ λυπρῶν ἔτι λειψάνων καὶ ταπεινῶν ἀναστήσας οὐ μόνον[1] τῆς θαλάττης τὸ κράτος

---

[1] μόνον with Mᵃ and Cobet : μόνον γε.

long tunics, flowing robes, and other adornment of
their profession ; and that the commander's ship
put into harbours with a sail of purple hue, as though,
after a drinking bout, he were off on a revel. But
neither Theopompus, nor Ephorus, nor Xenophon
mentions these things, nor is it likely that Alcibiades
put on such airs for the Athenians, to whom he was
returning after he had suffered exile and many great
adversities. Nay, he was in actual fear as he put
into the harbour, and once in, he did not leave his
trireme until, as he stood on deck, he caught sight
of his cousin Euryptolemus on shore, with many
other friends and kinsmen, and heard their cries of
welcome.

When he landed, however, people did not deign so
much as to look at the other generals whom they met,
but ran in throngs to Alcibiades with shouts of
welcome, escorting him on his way, and putting
wreaths on his head as they could get to him, while
those who could not come to him for the throng,
gazed at him from afar, the elderly men pointing him
out to the young. Much sorrow, too, was mingled
with the city's joy, as men called to mind their
former misfortunes and compared them with their
present good fortune, counting it certain that they
had neither lost Sicily, nor had any other great
expectation of theirs miscarried if they had only
left Alcibiades at the head of that enterprise and the
armament therefor. For now he had taken the
city when she was almost banished from the sea,
when on land she was hardly mistress of her own
suburbs, and when factions raged within her walls,
and had raised her up from this wretched and lowly
plight, not only restoring her dominion over the sea,

ἀποδέδωκεν, ἀλλὰ καὶ πεζῇ νικῶσαν ἀποδείκνυσι
πανταχοῦ τοὺς πολεμίους.

XXXIII. Τὸ μὲν οὖν ψήφισμα τῆς καθόδου
πρότερον ἐκεκύρωτο, Κριτίου τοῦ Καλλαίσχρου
γράψαντος, ὡς αὐτὸς ἐν ταῖς ἐλεγείαις πεποίηκεν, ὑπομιμνήσκων τὸν Ἀλκιβιάδην τῆς χάριτος
ἐν τούτοις·

Γνώμη δ' ἥ σε κατήγαγ', ἐγὼ ταύτην ἐν ἅπασιν
εἶπον, καὶ γράψας τοὔργον ἔδρασα τόδε.
σφραγὶς δ' ἡμετέρης γλώττης ἐπὶ τοῖσδεσι
κεῖται·

2 τότε δὲ τοῦ δήμου συνελθόντος εἰς τὴν ἐκκλησίαν
παρελθὼν ὁ Ἀλκιβιάδης, καὶ τὰ μὲν αὑτοῦ πάθη 21
κλαύσας καὶ ὀλοφυράμενος, ἐγκαλέσας δὲ μικρὰ
καὶ μέτρια τῷ δήμῳ, τὸ δὲ σύμπαν ἀναθεὶς αὑτοῦ
τινι τύχῃ πονηρᾷ καὶ φθονερῷ δαίμονι, πλεῖστα
δ' εἰς ἐλπίδας τῶν πολεμίων καὶ πρὸς τὸ θαρρεῖν
διαλεχθεὶς καὶ παρορμήσας, στεφάνοις μὲν ἐστε-
φανώθη χρυσοῖς, ᾑρέθη δ' ἅμα καὶ κατὰ γῆν καὶ
3 κατὰ θάλασσαν αὐτοκράτωρ στρατηγός. ἐψηφίσαντο δὲ τὴν οὐσίαν ἀποδοῦναι αὐτῷ, καὶ τὰς
ἀρὰς ἀφοσιώσασθαι πάλιν Εὐμολπίδας καὶ Κήρυ-
κας, ἃς ἐποιήσαντο τοῦ δήμου προστάξαντος.
ἀφοσιουμένων δὲ τῶν ἄλλων, Θεόδωρος ὁ ἱεροφάντης "Ἀλλ' ἐγώ," εἶπεν, "οὐδὲ κατηρασά-
μην αὐτῷ κακὸν οὐδέν, εἰ μηδὲν ἀδικεῖ τὴν
πόλιν."

but actually rendering her victorious over her enemies everywhere on land.

XXXIII. Now the decree for his recall had been passed before this,[1] on motion of Critias, the son of Callaeschrus, as Critias himself has written in his elegies, where he reminds Alcibiades of the favour in these words :—

"Mine was the motion that brought thee back ; I
    made it in public ;
    Words and writing were mine ; this the task I
        performed ;
Signet and seal of words that were mine give
    warrant as follows." [2]

At this time,[3] therefore, the people had only to meet in assembly, and Alcibiades addressed them. He lamented and bewailed his own lot, but had only little and moderate blame to lay upon the people. The entire mischief he ascribed to a certain evil fortune and envious genius of his own. Then he descanted at great length upon the vain hopes which their enemies were cherishing, and wrought his hearers up to courage. At last they crowned him with crowns of gold, and elected him general with sole powers by land and sea. They voted also that his property be restored to him, and that the Eumolpidae and Heralds revoke the curses wherewith they had cursed him at the command of the people. The others revoked their curses, but Theodorus the High Priest said : " Nay, I invoked no evil upon him if he does no wrong to the city."

---

[1] Nearly three years before, in the late autumn of 411 B.C., after the overthrow of the Four Hundred.

[2] Bergk, *Poet. Lyr. Graeci*, ii.[4] pp. 279 ff.

[3] In the early summer of 408 B.C.

XXXIV. Οὕτω δὲ τοῦ Ἀλκιβιάδου λαμπρῶς
εὐημεροῦντος ὑπέθραττεν ἐνίους ὅμως ὁ τῆς καθόδου καιρός. ᾗ γὰρ ἡμέρᾳ κατέπλευσεν, ἐδρᾶτο
τὰ Πλυντήρια τῇ θεῷ. δρῶσι δὲ τὰ ὄργια
Πραξιεργίδαι Θαργηλιῶνος ἕκτῃ φθίνοντος ἀπόρ-
ρητα, τόν τε κόσμον καθελόντες καὶ τὸ ἕδος
κατακαλύψαντες. ὅθεν ἐν ταῖς μάλιστα τῶν
ἀποφράδων τὴν ἡμέραν ταύτην ἄπρακτον Ἀθη-
2 ναῖοι νομίζουσιν. οὐ φιλοφρόνως οὖν οὐδ᾽ εὐ-
μενῶς ἐδόκει προσδεχομένη τὸν Ἀλκιβιάδην ἡ
θεὸς παρακαλύπτεσθαι καὶ ἀπελαύνειν ἑαυτῆς.
οὐ μὴν ἀλλὰ πάντων γεγονότων τῷ Ἀλκιβιάδῃ
κατὰ γνώμην, καὶ πληρουμένων ἑκατὸν τριήρων
αἷς αὖθις ἐκπλεῖν ἔμελλε, φιλοτιμία τις οὐκ
ἀγεννὴς προσπεσοῦσα κατέσχεν αὐτὸν ἄχρι
μυστηρίων.

3 Ἀφ᾽ οὗ γὰρ ἐπετειχίσθη Δεκέλεια καὶ τῶν
εἰς Ἐλευσῖνα παρόδων ἐκράτουν οἱ πολέμιοι
παρόντες, οὐδένα κόσμον εἶχεν ἡ τελετὴ πεμπο-
μένη κατὰ θάλατταν, ἀλλὰ καὶ θυσίαι καὶ
χορεῖαι καὶ πολλὰ τῶν δρωμένων καθ᾽ ὁδὸν
ἱερῶν, ὅταν ἐξελαύνωσι τὸν Ἴακχον, ὑπ᾽ ἀνάγκης
4 ἐξελείπετο. καλὸν οὖν ἐφαίνετο τῷ Ἀλκιβιάδῃ
καὶ πρὸς θεῶν ὁσιότητα καὶ πρὸς ἀνθρώπων
δόξαν ἀποδοῦναι τὸ πάτριον σχῆμα τοῖς ἱεροῖς,
παραπέμψαντα πεζῇ τὴν τελετὴν καὶ δορυφορή-
σαντα παρὰ τοὺς πολεμίους· ἢ γὰρ ἀτρεμήσαντα
κομιδῇ κολούσειν καὶ ταπεινώσειν τὸν Ἄγιν, ἢ
μάχην ἱερὰν καὶ θεοφιλῆ περὶ τῶν ἁγιωτάτων

XXXIV. But while Alcibiades was thus prospering brilliantly, some were nevertheless disturbed at the particular season of his return. For he had put into harbour on the very day when the Plynteria of the goddess Athene were being celebrated. The Praxiergidae celebrate these rites on the twenty-fifth day of Thargelion, in strict secrecy, removing the robes of the goddess and covering up her image. Wherefore the Athenians regard this day as the unluckiest of all days for business of any sort. The goddess, therefore, did not appear to welcome Alcibiades with kindly favour and good will, but rather to veil herself from him and repel him. However, all things fell out as he wished, and one hundred triremes were manned for service, with which he was minded to sail off again; but a great and laudable ambition took possession of him and detained him there until the Eleusinian mysteries.

Ever since Deceleia had been fortified, and the enemy, by their presence there, commanded the approaches to Eleusis, the festal rite had been celebrated with no splendour at all, being conducted by sea. Sacrifices, choral dances, and many of the sacred ceremonies usually held on the road, when Iacchus is conducted forth from Athens to Eleusis, had of necessity been omitted. Accordingly, it seemed to Alcibiades that it would be a fine thing, enhancing his holiness in the eyes of the gods and his good repute in the minds of men, to restore its traditional fashion to the sacred festival by escorting the rite with his infantry along past the enemy by land. He would thus either thwart and humble Agis, if the king kept entirely quiet, or would fight a fight that was sacred and approved by the

καὶ μεγίστων ἐν ὄψει τῆς πατρίδος μαχεῖσθαι,
καὶ πάντας ἕξειν μάρτυρας τοὺς πολίτας τῆς
ἀνδραγαθίας.

5 Ὡς δὲ ταῦτ' ἔγνω καὶ προεῖπεν Εὐμολπίδαις
καὶ Κήρυξι, σκοποὺς μὲν ἐπὶ τῶν ἄκρων ἐκάθισε
καὶ προδρόμους τινὰς ἅμ' ἡμέρᾳ προεξέπεμψεν,
ἱερεῖς δὲ καὶ μύστας καὶ μυσταγωγοὺς ἀναλαβὼν καὶ τοῖς ὅπλοις περικαλύψας ἦγεν ἐν κόσμῳ
καὶ μετὰ σιωπῆς, θέαμα σεμνὸν καὶ θεοπρεπὲς
τὴν στρατηγίαν ἐκείνην ἐπιδεικνύμενος, ὑπὸ τῶν
μὴ φθονούντων ἱεροφαντίαν καὶ μυσταγωγίαν
6 προσαγορευομένην. μηδενὸς δὲ τῶν πολεμίων
ἐπιθέσθαι τολμήσαντος ἀσφαλῶς ἐπαναγαγὼν
εἰς τὴν πόλιν, ἤρθη μὲν αὐτὸς τῷ φρονήματι
καὶ τὴν στρατιὰν ἐπῆρεν ὡς ἄμαχον καὶ
ἀήττητον οὖσαν ἐκείνου στρατηγοῦντος, τοὺς δὲ
φορτικοὺς καὶ πένητας οὕτως ἐδημαγώγησεν ὥστ'
ἐρᾶν ἔρωτα θαυμαστὸν ὑπ' ἐκείνου τυραννεῖσθαι,
καὶ λέγειν ἐνίους καὶ προσιέναι παρακελευομένους
ὅπως τοῦ φθόνου κρείττων γενόμενος καὶ καταβαλὼν ψηφίσματα καὶ νόμους καὶ φλυάρους
ἀπολλύντας τὴν πόλιν ὡς ἂν πράξῃ καὶ χρή-
σηται τοῖς πράγμασι, μὴ δεδιὼς τοὺς συκοφάντας.

XXXV. Αὐτὸς μὲν οὖν ἐκεῖνος ἣν εἶχε διάνοιαν
περὶ τῆς τυραννίδος ἄδηλόν ἐστιν· οἱ δὲ δυνατώτατοι τῶν πολιτῶν φοβηθέντες ἐσπούδασαν αὐτὸν
ἐκπλεῦσαι τὴν ταχίστην, τά τ' ἄλλα ψηφισά-
μενοι καὶ συνάρχοντας οὓς ἐκεῖνος ἠθέλησεν.

gods, in behalf of the greatest and holiest interests, in full sight of his native city, and with all his fellow citizens eye-witnesses of his valour.

When he had determined upon this course and made known his design to the Eumolpidae and Heralds, he stationed sentries on the heights, sent out an advance-guard at break of day, and then took the priests, mystae, and mystagogues, encompassed them with his men-at-arms, and led them over the road to Eleusis in decorous and silent array. So august and devout was the spectacle which, as general, he thus displayed, that he was hailed by those who were not unfriendly to him as High Priest, rather, and Mystagogue. No enemy dared to attack him, and he conducted the procession safely back to the city. At this he was exalted in spirit himself, and exalted his army with the feeling that it was irresistible and invincible under his command. People of the humbler and poorer sort he so captivated by his leadership that they were filled with an amazing passion to have him for their tyrant, and some proposed it, and actually came to him in solicitation of it. He was to rise superior to envy, abolish decrees and laws, and stop the mouths of the babblers who were so fatal to the life of the city, that he might bear an absolute sway and act without fear of the public informer.

XXXV. What thoughts he himself had about a tyranny, is uncertain. But the most influential citizens were afraid of it, and therefore anxious that he should sail away as soon as he could. They even voted him, besides everything else, the colleagues of his own choosing. Setting sail,[1] there-

---

[1] Towards the end of October, 408 B.C.

ἐκπλεύσας δὲ ταῖς ἑκατὸν ναυσὶ καὶ προσβαλὼν
Ἄνδρῳ, μάχῃ μὲν ἐκράτησεν αὐτῶν καὶ Λακεδαιμονίων ὅσοι παρῆσαν, οὐχ εἷλε δὲ τὴν πόλιν, 211
ἀλλὰ τοῦτο τῶν καινῶν[1] ἐγκλημάτων πρῶτον
ὑπῆρξε κατ᾽ αὐτοῦ τοῖς ἐχθροῖς.

2   Ἔοικε δ᾽, εἴ τις ἄλλος, ὑπὸ τῆς αὑτοῦ δόξης
καταλυθῆναι καὶ Ἀλκιβιάδης. μεγάλη γὰρ
οὖσα καὶ τόλμης καὶ συνέσεως γέμουσα ἀφ᾽ ὧν
κατώρθωσεν, ὕποπτον αὐτοῦ τὸ ἐλλεῖπον, ὡς οὐ
σπουδάσαντος, ἀπιστίᾳ τοῦ μὴ δυνηθῆναι παρεῖχε·
σπουδάσαντα γὰρ οὐδὲν ἂν διαφυγεῖν. ἤλπιζον
δὲ καὶ Χίους ἑαλωκότας ἀκούσεσθαι καὶ τὴν
3   ἄλλην Ἰωνίαν. ὅθεν ἠγανάκτουν μὴ ταχὺ πάντα
μηδ᾽ εὐθέως, ὡς ἐβούλοντο, πυνθανόμενοι δια-
πεπραγμένον, οὐχ ὑπολογιζόμενοι τὴν ἀχρη-
ματίαν, ἀφ᾽ ἧς πολεμῶν πρὸς ἀνθρώπους βασιλέα
μέγαν χορηγὸν ἔχοντας ἠναγκάζετο πολλάκις
ἐκπλέων καὶ ἀπολείπων τὸ στρατόπεδον μισθοὺς
καὶ τροφὰς πορίζειν. καὶ γὰρ τὸ τελευταῖον
ἔγκλημα διὰ ταύτην ἔλαβε τὴν αἰτίαν.

4   Λυσάνδρου γὰρ ἐπὶ τὴν ναυαρχίαν ἀποστα-
λέντος ὑπὸ Λακεδαιμονίων, καὶ τετρώβολον ἀντὶ
τριωβόλου τῷ ναύτῃ διδόντος ἐξ ὧν ἔλαβε παρὰ
Κύρου χρημάτων, αὐτὸς ἤδη γλίσχρως χορηγῶν
καὶ τὸ τριώβολον ἀπῆρεν ἀργυρολογήσων ἐπὶ
Καρίας. ὁ δ᾽ ἀπολειφθεὶς ἐπὶ τῶν νεῶν ἐπι-
μελητὴς Ἀντίοχος ἀγαθὸς μὲν ἦν κυβερνήτης,
5   ἀνόητος δὲ τἆλλα καὶ φορτικός· ἔχων δὲ πρόσ-

---

[1] καινῶν with Bekker, Mᵃ and Cobet : κοινῶν (public).

fore, with his one hundred ships, and assaulting
Andros, he conquered the islanders in battle, as
well as the Lacedaemonians who were there, but
he did not capture the city. This was the first
of the fresh charges brought against him by his
enemies.

And it would seem that if ever a man was
ruined by his own exalted reputation, that man
was Alcibiades. His continuous successes gave
him such repute for unbounded daring and sagacity,
that when he failed in anything, men suspected
his inclination; they would not believe in his
inability. Were he only inclined to do a thing,
they thought, naught could escape him. So they
expected to hear that the Chians also had been
taken, along with the rest of Ionia. They were
therefore incensed to hear that he had not accomplished everything at once and speedily, to
meet their wishes. They did not stop to consider
his lack of money. This compelled him, since he
was fighting men who had an almoner of bounty
in the Great King, to leave his camp frequently
and sail off in quest of money for rations and wages.
The final and prevailing charge against him was due
to this necessity.

Lysander, who had been sent out as admiral by
the Lacedaemonians, paid his sailors four obols a
day instead of three, out of the moneys he received
from Cyrus; while Alcibiades, already hard put to
it to pay even his three obols, was forced to sail
for Caria to levy money. The man whom he left
in charge of his fleet, Antiochus,[1] was a brave
captain, but otherwise a foolish and low-lived fellow.

[1] Cf. chapter x. 1.

τάγμα παρὰ τοῦ Ἀλκιβιάδου μηδ' ἂν ἐπιπλέω-
σιν οἱ πολέμιοι διαναυμαχεῖν, οὕτως ἐξύβρισε
καὶ κατεφρόνησεν ὥστε τὴν αὐτοῦ πληρωσάμενος
τριήρη καὶ τῶν ἄλλων μίαν ἐπιπλεῦσαι τῇ
Ἐφέσῳ καὶ παρὰ τὰς πρώρας τῶν πολεμίων
νεῶν πολλὰ καὶ πράττων καὶ φθεγγόμενος
6 ἀκόλαστα καὶ βωμολόχα παρεξελαύνειν. τὸ μὲν
οὖν πρῶτον Λύσανδρος ὀλίγαις ναυσὶν ἐπαναχθεὶς
ἐδίωκεν αὐτόν, τῶν δ' Ἀθηναίων ἐπιβοηθούντων
πάσαις ἀναχθεὶς καὶ κρατήσας αὐτόν τε διέφθειρε
τὸν Ἀντίοχον καὶ ναῦς ἔλαβε πολλὰς καὶ ἀνθρώπους καὶ τρόπαιον ἔστησεν. ὡς δὲ ταῦτ' ἤκουσεν
ὁ Ἀλκιβιάδης ἐπανελθὼν εἰς Σάμον, ἀνήχθη
παντὶ τῷ στόλῳ καὶ προὐκαλεῖτο τὸν Λύσανδρον.
ὁ δ' ἠγάπα νενικηκὼς καὶ οὐκ ἀντανήγετο.

XXXVI. Τῶν δὲ μισούντων τὸν Ἀλκιβιάδην
ἐν τῷ στρατοπέδῳ Θρασύβουλος ὁ Θράσωνος
ἐχθρὸς ὢν ἀπῆρεν εἰς Ἀθήνας κατηγορήσων. καὶ
τοὺς ἐκεῖ παροξύνας ἔλεγε πρὸς τὸν δῆμον ὡς
Ἀλκιβιάδης διέφθαρκε τὰ πράγματα καὶ τὰς
ναῦς ἀπολώλεκεν, ἐντρυφῶν τῇ ἀρχῇ καὶ παραδιδοὺς τὴν στρατηγίαν ἀνθρώποις ἐκ πότων καὶ
ναυτικῆς σπερμολογίας δυναμένοις παρ' αὐτῷ
2 μέγιστον, ὅπως αὐτὸς ἐπ' ἀδείας χρηματίζηται
περιπλέων καὶ ἀκολασταίνῃ μεθυσκόμενος καὶ
συνὼν ἑταίραις Ἀβυδηναῖς καὶ Ἰωνίσιν, ἐφορμούντων δι' ὀλίγου τῶν πολεμίων. ἐνεκάλουν

Although he had received explicit commands from
Alcibiades not to hazard a general engagement even
though the enemy sailed out to meet him, he showed
such wanton contempt of them as to man his own
trireme and one other and stand for Ephesus,
indulging in many shamelessly insulting gestures
and cries as he cruised past the prows of the
enemy's ships. At first Lysander put out with a
few ships only, and gave him chase. Then, when
the Athenians came to the aid of Antiochus,
Lysander put out with his whole fleet, won the day,
slew Antiochus himself, captured many ships and
men, and set up a trophy of victory. As soon as
Alcibiades heard of this, he came back to Samos, put
out to sea with his whole armament, and challenged
Lysander to battle. But Lysander was satisfied
with his victory, and would not put out to meet
him.

XXXVI. There were those who hated Alcibiades
in the camp, and of these Thrasybulus,[1] the son of
Thraso, his particular enemy, set sail for Athens to
denounce him. He stirred up the city against him
by declaring to the people that it was Alcibiades
who had ruined their cause and lost their ships by
his wanton conduct in office. He had handed over—so
Thrasybulus said—the duties of commander to men
who won his confidence merely by drinking deep
and reeling off sailors' yarns, in order that he himself
might be free to cruise about collecting moneys and
committing excesses of drunkenness and revelry
with courtezans of Abydos and Ionia, and this while
the enemy's fleet lay close to him. His enemies

---

[1] Not the illustrious commander (chapter xxvi. 6), who was
the son of Lycus.

δ' αὐτῷ καὶ τὴν τῶν τειχῶν κατασκευήν, ἃ κατε-
σκεύασεν ἐν Θράκῃ περὶ Βισάνθην αὐτῷ κατα-
φυγὴν ὡς ἐν τῇ πατρίδι μὴ δυνάμενος βιοῦν ἢ
3 μὴ βουλόμενος. οἱ δ' Ἀθηναῖοι πεισθέντες
ἑτέρους εἵλοντο στρατηγούς, ἐνδεικνύμενοι τὴν
πρὸς ἐκεῖνον ὀργὴν καὶ κακόνοιαν. ἃ δὴ πυνθανόμενος ὁ Ἀλκιβιάδης καὶ δεδοικὼς ἀπῆλθεν ἐκ τοῦ
στρατοπέδου παντάπασι, καὶ συναγαγὼν ξένους
ἐπολέμει τοῖς ἀβασιλεύτοις Θραξὶν ἰδίᾳ, καὶ
πολλὰ χρήματα συνήγαγεν ἀπὸ τῶν ἁλισκομένων,
καὶ τοῖς Ἕλλησιν ἅμα τοῖς προσοικοῦσιν ἄδειαν
ἀπὸ τῶν βαρβάρων παρεῖχεν.

4 Ἐπεὶ δ' οἱ περὶ Τυδέα καὶ Μένανδρον καὶ
Ἀδείμαντον στρατηγοί, πάσας ὁμοῦ τὰς ὑπαρ-
χούσας τότε ναῦς τοῖς Ἀθηναίοις ἔχοντες ἐν
Αἰγὸς ποταμοῖς, εἰώθεσαν ἐπιπλεῖν τῷ Λυσάνδρῳ
ναυλοχοῦντι περὶ Λάμψακον ἅμ' ἡμέρᾳ προκα-
λούμενοι καὶ πάλιν ἀναστρέφειν ὀπίσω καὶ
διημερεύειν ἀτάκτως καὶ ἀμελῶς, ἅτε δὴ κατα-
5 φρονοῦντες, ἐγγὺς ὢν ὁ Ἀλκιβιάδης οὐ περιεῖδεν   212
οὐδ' ἠμέλησεν, ἀλλ' ἵππῳ προσελάσας ἐδίδασκε
τοὺς στρατηγοὺς ὅτι κακῶς ὁρμοῦσιν ἐν χωρίοις
ἀλιμένοις καὶ πόλιν οὐκ ἔχουσιν, ἀλλὰ πόρρωθεν
ἐκ Σηστοῦ τὰ ἐπιτήδεια λαμβάνοντες, καὶ περι-
ορῶντες τὸ ναυτικόν, ὅταν ἐπὶ τῆς γῆς γένηται,
πλανώμενον ὅποι τις θέλοι καὶ διασπειρόμενον,
ἀντεφορμοῦντος αὐτοῖς στόλου πρὸς ἐπίταγμα
μοναρχικὸν εἰθισμένου σιωπῇ πάντα ποιεῖν.

---

[1] With these words Plutarch's story leaps over the events
of two and a half years, from the spring of 407 to the autumn
of 405 B.C.

also found ground for accusation against him in the
fortress which he had constructed in Thrace, near
Bisanthe. It was to serve, they said, as a refuge for
him in case he either could not or would not live at
home. The Athenians were persuaded, and chose
other generals in his place, thus displaying their
anger and ill-will towards him. On learning this,
Alcibiades was afraid, and departed from the camp
altogether, and assembling mercenary troops made
war on his own account against the Thracians who
acknowledge no king. He got together much money
from his captives, and at the same time afforded
security from barbarian inroads to the Hellenes on
the neighbouring frontier.

Tydeus, Menander, and Adeimantus, the generals,
who had all the ships which the Athenians could
finally muster in station at Aegospotami,[1] were wont
to sail out at daybreak against Lysander, who lay
with his fleet at Lampsacus, and challenge him to
battle. Then they would sail back again, to spend
the rest of the day in disorder and unconcern, since,
forsooth, they despised their enemy. Alcibiades,
who was near at hand,[2] could not see such conduct
with calmness or indifference, but rode up on
horseback and read the generals a lesson. He said
their anchorage was a bad one; the place had no
harbour and no city, but they had to get their
supplies from Sestos, a long way off; and they
permitted their crews, whenever they were on land,
to wander and scatter about at their own sweet wills,
while there lay at anchor over against them an
armament which was trained to do everything silently
at a word of absolute command.

[2] In his stronghold near Pactye (Xen. *Hell.* ii. 1, 25).

XXXVII. Ταῦτα δὲ λέγοντος τοῦ Ἀλκιβιάδου,
καὶ παραινοῦντος εἰς Σηστὸν μεθορμίσαι τὸν
στόλον, οὐ προσεῖχον οἱ στρατηγοί· Τυδεὺς δὲ
καὶ πρὸς ὕβριν ἐκέλευσεν ἀποχωρεῖν, οὐ γὰρ
ἐκεῖνον, ἀλλ᾽ ἑτέρους στρατηγεῖν. ὁ δ᾽ Ἀλκιβιάδης ὑπονοήσας τι καὶ προδοσίας ἐν αὐτοῖς
ἀπῄει, καὶ τοῖς προπέμπουσι τῶν ἀπὸ τοῦ στρατοπέδου γνωρίμων ἔλεγεν ὅτι μὴ προπηλακισθεὶς
οὕτως ὑπὸ τῶν στρατηγῶν ὀλίγαις ἂν ἡμέραις
ἠνάγκασε Λακεδαιμονίους διαναυμαχεῖν αὐτοῖς
2 ἄκοντας ἢ τὰς ναῦς ἀπολιπεῖν. ἐδόκει δὲ τοῖς
μὲν ἀλαζονεύεσθαι, τοῖς δ᾽ εἰκότα λέγειν, εἰ
Θρᾷκας ἐκ γῆς ἐπαγαγὼν πολλοὺς ἀκοντιστὰς
καὶ ἱππεῖς προσμάχοιτο καὶ διαταράττοι τὸ
στρατόπεδον αὐτῶν.

Ὅτι μέντοι τὰς ἁμαρτίας τῶν Ἀθηναίων ὀρθῶς
συνεῖδε, ταχὺ τὸ ἔργον ἐμαρτύρησεν. ἄφνω γὰρ
αὐτοῖς καὶ ἀπροσδοκήτως τοῦ Λυσάνδρου προσ-
πεσόντος, ὀκτὼ μόναι τριήρεις ἐξέφυγον μετὰ
Κόνωνος, αἱ δ᾽ ἄλλαι μικρὸν ἀπολείπουσαι
3 διακοσίων ἀπήχθησαν αἰχμάλωτοι. τῶν δ᾽ ἀνθρώπων τρισχιλίους ἑλὼν ζῶντας ἀπέσφαξεν ὁ
Λύσανδρος. ἔλαβε δὲ καὶ τὰς Ἀθήνας ὀλίγῳ
χρόνῳ καὶ τὰς ναῦς ἐνέπρησε καὶ τὰ μακρὰ
τείχη καθεῖλεν.

Ἐκ δὲ τούτου φοβηθεὶς ὁ Ἀλκιβιάδης ἄρχοντας ἤδη καὶ γῆς καὶ θαλάττης τοὺς Λακεδαιμονίους
εἰς Βιθυνίαν μετέστη, πολλὰ μὲν ἄγων χρήματα,
πολλὰ δὲ κομίζων, ἔτι δὲ πλείω καταλιπὼν ἐν
4 οἷς ᾤκει τείχεσιν. ἐν δὲ Βιθυνίᾳ πάλιν οὐκ
ὀλίγα τῶν ἰδίων ἀπολέσας καὶ περικοπεὶς ὑπὸ
τῶν ἐκεῖ Θρᾳκῶν, ἔγνω μὲν ἀναβαίνειν πρὸς

XXXVII. In spite of what Alcibiades said, and in spite of his advice to change their station to Sestos, the generals paid no heed. Tydeus actually insulted him by bidding him begone : he was not general now, but others. So Alcibiades departed, suspecting that some treachery was on foot among them. He told his acquaintances who were escorting him out of the camp that, had he not been so grievously insulted by the generals, within a few days he would have forced the Lacedaemonians to engage them whether they wished to do so or not, or else lose their ships. Some thought that what he said was arrant boasting ; but others that it was likely, since he had merely to bring up his numerous Thracian javelineers and horsemen to assault by land and confound the enemy's camp.

However, that he saw only too well the errors of the Athenians the event soon testified. Lysander suddenly and unexpectedly fell upon them, and only eight of their triremes escaped with Conon ; the rest, something less than two hundred, were captured and taken away. Three thousand of their crews were taken alive and executed by Lysander. In a short time [1] he also captured Athens, burned her ships, and tore down her long walls.

Alcibiades now feared the Lacedaemonians, who were supreme on land and sea, and betook himself into Bithynia, taking booty of every sort with him, but leaving even more behind him in the fortress where he had been living. In Bithynia he again lost much of his substance, being plundered by the Thracians there, and so he determined to go up to the court of

---

[1] In the spring of 404 B.C., some eight months later.

Ἀρταξέρξην, ἑαυτόν τε μὴ χείρονα Θεμιστο-
κλέους πειρωμένῳ βασιλεῖ φανεῖσθαι νομίζων,
καὶ κρείττονα τὴν πρόφασιν· οὐ γὰρ ἐπὶ τοὺς
πολίτας, ὡς ἐκεῖνος, ἀλλ᾽ ὑπὲρ τῆς πατρίδος
ἐπὶ τοὺς πολεμίους ὑπουργήσειν καὶ δεήσεσθαι
τῆς βασιλέως δυνάμεως· εὐπορίαν δὲ τῆς ἀνόδου
μετὰ ἀσφαλείας μάλιστα Φαρνάβαζον οἰόμενος
παρέξειν, ᾤχετο πρὸς αὐτὸν εἰς Φρυγίαν, καὶ
συνδιῆγε θεραπεύων ἅμα καὶ τιμώμενος.

XXXVIII. Ἀθηναῖοι δὲ χαλεπῶς μὲν ἔφερον
καὶ τῆς ἡγεμονίας ἀποστερηθέντες· ἐπεὶ δὲ καὶ
τὴν ἐλευθερίαν ἀφελόμενος αὐτῶν ὁ Λύσανδρος
ἀνδράσι τριάκοντα παρέδωκε τὴν πόλιν, οἷς οὐκ
ἐχρήσαντο σώζεσθαι δυνάμενοι λογισμοῖς, ἀπο-
λωλότων ἤδη τῶν πραγμάτων, συνίεσαν, ὀλοφυρό-
μενοι καὶ διεξιόντες τὰς ἁμαρτίας αὐτῶν καὶ
ἀγνοίας, ὧν μεγίστην ἐποιοῦντο τὴν δευτέραν
2 πρὸς Ἀλκιβιάδην ὀργήν. ἀπερρίφη γὰρ οὐδὲν
ἀδικῶν αὐτός, ἀλλ᾽ ὑπηρέτῃ χαλεπήναντες ὀλίγας ἀποβαλόντι ναῦς αἰσχρῶς, αἴσχιον αὐτοὶ
τὸν κράτιστον καὶ πολεμικώτατον ἀφείλοντο τῆς
πόλεως στρατηγόν. ἔτι δ᾽ οὖν ὅμως ἐκ τῶν
παρόντων ἀνέφερέ τις ἐλπὶς ἀμυδρὰ μὴ παντάπασιν ἔρρειν τὰ πράγματα τῶν Ἀθηναίων Ἀλκιβιάδου περιόντος· οὔτε γὰρ πρότερον ἠγάπησε
φεύγων ἀπραγμόνως ζῆν καὶ μεθ᾽ ἡσυχίας, οὔτε
νῦν, εἰ τὰ καθ᾽ ἑαυτὸν ἱκανῶς ἔχει, περιόψεται
Λακεδαιμονίους ὑβρίζοντας καὶ τοὺς τριάκοντα
παροινοῦντας.
3 Ταῦτα δ᾽ οὐκ ἦν ἄλογον οὕτως ὀνειροπολεῖν

Artaxerxes. He thought to show himself not inferior to Themistocles if the King made trial of his services, and superior in his pretext for offering them. For it was not to be against his fellow countrymen, as in the case of that great man, but in behalf of his country that he would assist the King and beg him to furnish forces against a common enemy. Thinking that Pharnabazus could best give him facilities for safely making this journey up to the King, he went to him in Phrygia, and continued there with him, paying him court and receiving marks of honour from him.

XXXVIII. The Athenians were greatly depressed at the loss of their supremacy. But when Lysander robbed them of their freedom too, and handed the city over to thirty men, then, their cause being lost, their eyes were opened to the course they would not take when salvation was yet in their power. They sorrowfully rehearsed all their mistakes and follies, the greatest of which they considered to be their second outburst of wrath against Alcibiades. He had been cast aside for no fault of his own ; but they got angry beeause a subordinate of his lost a few ships disgracefully, and then they themselves, more disgracefully still, robbed the city of its ablest and most experienced general. And yet, in spite of their present plight, a vague hope still prevailed that the cause of Athens was not wholly lost so long as Alcibiades was alive. He had not, in times past, been satisfied to live his exile's life in idleness and quiet ; nor now, if his means allowed, would he tolerate the insolence of the Lacedaemonians and the madness of the Thirty.

It was not strange that the multitude indulged in

τοὺς πολλούς, ὁπότε καὶ τοῖς τριάκοντα φροντί-
ζειν ἐπῄει καὶ διαπυνθάνεσθαι καὶ λόγον ἔχειν
πλεῖστον ὧν ἐκεῖνος ἔπραττε καὶ διενοεῖτο.
τέλος δὲ Κριτίας ἐδίδασκε Λύσανδρον ὡς Ἀθη-   21
ναίων οὐκ ἔστι δημοκρατουμένων ἀσφαλῶς ἄρχειν
4 Λακεδαιμονίοις τῆς Ἑλλάδος· Ἀθηναίους δέ,
κἂν πρᾴως πάνυ καὶ καλῶς πρὸς ὀλιγαρχίαν
ἔχωσιν, οὐκ ἐάσει ζῶν Ἀλκιβιάδης ἀτρεμεῖν
ἐπὶ τῶν καθεστώτων. οὐ μὴν ἐπείσθη γε πρότερον τούτοις ὁ Λύσανδρος ἢ παρὰ τῶν οἴκοι
τελῶν σκυτάλην ἐλθεῖν κελεύουσαν ἐκ ποδῶν
ποιήσασθαι τὸν Ἀλκιβιάδην, εἴτε κἀκείνων
φοβηθέντων τὴν ὀξύτητα καὶ μεγαλοπραγμοσύνην τοῦ ἀνδρός, εἴτε τῷ Ἄγιδι χαριζομένων.

XXXIX. Ὡς οὖν ὁ Λύσανδρος ἔπεμψε πρὸς
τὸν Φαρνάβαζον ταῦτα πράττειν κελεύων, ὁ δὲ
Μαγαίῳ τε τῷ ἀδελφῷ καὶ Σουσαμίθρῃ τῷ θείῳ
προσέταξε τὸ ἔργον, ἔτυχε μὲν ἐν κώμῃ τινὶ
τῆς Φρυγίας ὁ Ἀλκιβιάδης τότε διαιτώμενος,
ἔχων Τιμάνδραν μεθ' αὑτοῦ τὴν ἑταίραν, ὄψιν
2 δὲ κατὰ τοὺς ὕπνους εἶδε τοιαύτην· ἐδόκει περι-
κεῖσθαι μὲν αὐτὸς τὴν ἐσθῆτα τῆς ἑταίρας,
ἐκείνην δὲ τὴν κεφαλὴν ἐν ταῖς ἀγκάλαις ἔχουσαν αὐτοῦ κοσμεῖν τὸ πρόσωπον ὥσπερ γυναικὸς
ὑπογράφουσαν καὶ ψιμυθιοῦσαν. ἕτεροι δέ φασιν
ἰδεῖν τὴν κεφαλὴν ἀποτέμνοντας αὐτοῦ τοὺς περὶ
τὸν Μαγαῖον ἐν τοῖς ὕπνοις καὶ τὸ σῶμα καιό-
μενον. ἀλλὰ τὴν μὲν ὄψιν οὐ πολὺ γενέσθαι
λέγουσι πρὸ τῆς τελευτῆς.

Οἱ δὲ πεμφθέντες πρὸς αὐτὸν οὐκ ἐτόλμησαν
εἰσελθεῖν, ἀλλὰ κύκλῳ τὴν οἰκίαν περιστάντες
3 ἐνεπίμπρασαν. αἰσθόμενος δ' ὁ Ἀλκιβιάδης τῶν

such dreams, when even the Thirty were moved to anxious thought and inquiry, and made the greatest account of what Alcibiades was planning and doing. Finally, Critias tried to make it clear to Lysander that as long as Athens was a democracy the Lacedaemonians could not have safe rule over Hellas; and that Athens, even though she were very peacefully and well disposed towards oligarchy, would not be suffered, while Alcibiades was alive, to remain undisturbed in her present condition. However, Lysander was not persuaded by these arguments until a dispatch-roll came from the authorities at home bidding him put Alcibiades out of the way; either because they too were alarmed at the vigour and enterprise of the man, or because they were trying to gratify Agis.

XXXIX. Accordingly, Lysander sent to Pharnabazus and bade him do this thing, and Pharnabazus commissioned Magaeus, his brother, and Sousamithras, his uncle, to perform the deed. At that time Alcibiades was living in a certain village of Phrygia, where he had Timandra the courtezan with him, and in his sleep he had the following vision. He thought he had the courtezan's garments upon him, and that she was holding his head in her arms while she adorned his face like a woman's with paints and pigments. Others say that in his sleep he saw Magaeus' followers cutting off his head and his body burning. All agree in saying that he had the vision not long before his death.

The party sent to kill him did not dare to enter his house, but surrounded it and set it on fire. When Alcibiades was aware of this, he gathered together

μὲν ἱματίων τὰ πλεῖστα καὶ τῶν στρωμάτων
συναγαγὼν ἐπέρριψε τῷ πυρί, τῇ δ' ἀριστερᾷ
χειρὶ τὴν ἑαυτοῦ χλαμύδα περιελίξας, τῇ δεξιᾷ
σπασάμενος τὸ ἐγχειρίδιον ἐξέπεσεν ἀπαθὴς ὑπὸ
τοῦ πυρὸς πρὶν ἢ διαφλέγεσθαι τὰ ἱμάτια, καὶ
τοὺς βαρβάρους ὀφθεὶς διεσκέδασεν. οὐδεὶς γὰρ
ὑπέμεινεν αὐτὸν οὐδ' εἰς χεῖρας συνῆλθεν, ἀλλ'
ἀποστάντες ἔβαλλον ἀκοντίοις καὶ τοξεύμασιν.
4 οὕτω δ' αὐτοῦ πεσόντος καὶ τῶν βαρβάρων
ἀπελθόντων, ἡ Τιμάνδρα τὸν νεκρὸν ἀνείλετο, καὶ
τοῖς αὑτῆς περιβαλοῦσα καὶ περικαλύψασα χιτω-
νίσκοις, ἐκ τῶν παρόντων ἐκήδευσε λαμπρῶς καὶ
φιλοτίμως.

Ταύτης λέγουσι θυγατέρα γενέσθαι Λαΐδα τὴν
Κορινθίαν μὲν προσαγορευθεῖσαν, ἐκ δὲ Ὑκκάρων,
Σικελικοῦ πολίσματος, αἰχμάλωτον γενομένην.
5 ἔνιοι δὲ τὰ μὲν ἄλλα περὶ τῆς Ἀλκιβιάδου
τελευτῆς ὁμολογοῦσι τούτοις, αἰτίαν δέ φασιν οὐ
Φαρνάβαζον οὐδὲ Λύσανδρον οὐδὲ Λακεδαιμονίους
παρασχεῖν, αὐτὸν δὲ τὸν Ἀλκιβιάδην γνωρίμων
τινῶν διεφθαρκότα γύναιον ἔχειν σὺν αὑτῷ, τοὺς
δ' ἀδελφοὺς τοῦ γυναίου τὴν ὕβριν οὐ μετρίως
φέροντας ἐμπρῆσαί τε τὴν οἰκίαν νύκτωρ, ἐν ᾗ
διαιτώμενος ἐτύγχανεν ὁ Ἀλκιβιάδης, καὶ καταβαλεῖν αὐτόν, ὥσπερ εἴρηται, διὰ τοῦ πυρὸς
ἐξαλλόμενον.

most of the garments and bedding in the house and cast them on the fire. Then, wrapping his cloak about his left arm, and drawing his sword with his right, he dashed out, unscathed by the fire, before the garments were in flames, and scattered the Barbarians, who ran at the mere sight of him. Not a man stood ground against him, or came to close quarters with him, but all held aloof and shot him with javelins and arrows. Thus he fell, and when the Barbarians were gone, Timandra took up his dead body, covered and wrapped it in her own garments, and gave it such brilliant and honourable burial as she could provide.

This Timandra, they say, was the mother of that Lais who was called the Corinthian, although she was a prisoner of war from Hyccara, a small city of Sicily.[1] But some, while agreeing in all other details of the death of Alcibiades with what I have written, say that it was not Pharnabazus who was the cause of it, nor Lysander, nor the Lacedaemonians, but Alcibiades himself. He had corrupted a girl belonging to a certain well known family, and had her with him; and it was the brothers of this girl who, taking his wanton insolence much to heart, set fire by night to the house where he was living, and shot him down, as has been described, when he dashed out through the fire.

[1] See the *Nicias*, xv. 4.

CAIUS MARCIUS
CORIOLANUS

ΓΑΙΟΣ ΜΑΡΚΙΟΣ

I. Ὁ Μαρκίων οἶκος ἐν Ῥώμῃ τῶν πατρικίων
πολλοὺς παρέσχεν ἐνδόξους ἄνδρας, ὧν καὶ
Μάρκιος ἦν Ἄγκος, ὁ Νομᾶ θυγατριδοῦς καὶ
μετὰ Τύλλον Ὀστίλιον βασιλεὺς γενόμενος.
Μάρκιοι δ' ἦσαν καὶ Πόπλιος καὶ Κόϊντος οἱ
πλεῖστον ὕδωρ καὶ κάλλιστον ἐν Ῥώμῃ καταγαγ-
όντες, καὶ Κηνσωρῖνος, ὃν δὶς ἀπέδειξε τιμητὴν 2
ὁ Ῥωμαίων δῆμος, εἶτα ὑπ' αὐτοῦ πεισθεὶς
ἐκείνου νόμον ἔθετο καὶ ἐψηφίσατο μηδενὶ τὴν
2 ἀρχὴν δὶς ἐξεῖναι μετελθεῖν. Γάϊος δὲ Μάρκιος,
ὑπὲρ οὗ τάδε γέγραπται, τραφεὶς ὑπὸ μητρὶ χήρᾳ
πατρὸς ὀρφανός, ἀπέδειξε τὴν ὀρφανίαν ἄλλα μὲν
ἔχουσαν κακά, πρὸς δὲ τὸ γενέσθαι σπουδαῖον
ἄνδρα καὶ διαφέροντα τῶν πολλῶν οὐδὲν ἐμποδὼν
οὖσαν, ἄλλως δὲ τοῖς φαύλοις αἰτιᾶσθαι καὶ ψέγειν
παρέχουσαν αὐτὴν ὡς ἀμελείᾳ διαφθείρουσαν.
ὁ δ' αὐτὸς ἀνὴρ ἐμαρτύρησε καὶ τοῖς τὴν φύσιν
ἡγουμένοις, ἐὰν οὖσα γενναία καὶ ἀγαθὴ παιδείας
ἐνδεὴς γένηται, πολλὰ τοῖς χρηστοῖς ὁμοῦ φαῦλα
συναποτίκτειν, ὥσπερ εὐγενῆ χώραν ἐν γεωργίᾳ
3 θεραπείας μὴ τυχοῦσαν. τὸ γὰρ ἰσχυρὸν αὐτοῦ
πρὸς ἅπαντα τῆς γνώμης καὶ καρτερὸν ὁρμάς τε
μεγάλας καὶ τελεσιουργοὺς τῶν καλῶν ἐξέφερε,

118

CAIUS MARCIUS CORIOLANUS

I. THE patrician house of the Marcii at Rome furnished many men of distinction. One of them was Ancus Marcius, the grandson of Numa by his daughter, and the successor of Tullus Hostilius in the kingship. To this family belonged also Publius and Quintus Marcius, the men who brought into Rome its best and most abundant supply of water. So likewise did Censorinus, whom the Roman people twice appointed censor, and then, at his own instance, made a law by which it was decreed that no one should hold that office twice. Caius Marcius, whose life I now write, lost his father at an early age, and was reared by his widowed mother. He showed, however, that such loss of a father, although otherwise bad for a boy, need not prevent him from becoming a worthy and excellent man, and that it is wrong for worthless men to lay upon it the blame for their perverted natures, which are due, as they say, to early neglect. On the other hand, the same Marcius bore witness for those who hold that a generous and noble nature, if it lack discipline, is apt to produce much that is worthless along with its better fruits, like a rich soil deprived of the husbandman's culture. For while the force and vigour of his intelligence, which knew no limitations, led him into great undertakings, and such as were productive of the highest results, still, on the other hand, since he

θυμοῖς τε αὖ πάλιν χρώμενον ἀκράτοις καὶ φιλο-
νεικίαις ἀτρέπτοις οὐ ῥᾴδιον οὐδ' εὐάρμοστον
ἀνθρώποις συνεῖναι παρεῖχεν, ἀλλὰ τὴν ἐν ἡδοναῖς
καὶ πόνοις καὶ ὑπὸ χρημάτων ἀπάθειαν αὐτοῦ
θαυμάζοντες καὶ ὀνομάζοντες ἐγκράτειαν καὶ
δικαιοσύνην καὶ ἀνδρείαν, ἐν ταῖς πολιτικαῖς αὖ
πάλιν ὁμιλίαις ὡς ἐπαχθῆ καὶ ἄχαριν καὶ
4 ὀλιγαρχικὴν ἐδυσχέραινον. οὐδὲν γὰρ ἄλλο
Μουσῶν εὐμενείας ἀπολαύουσιν ἄνθρωποι τοσοῦτον ὅσον ἐξημερῶσαι τὴν φύσιν ὑπὸ λόγου καὶ
παιδείας, τῷ λόγῳ δεξαμένην τὸ μέτριον καὶ τὸ
ἄγαν ἀποβαλοῦσαν. ὅλως μὲν οὖν ἐν τοῖς τότε
χρόνοις ἡ Ῥώμη μάλιστα τῆς ἀρετῆς τὸ περὶ
τὰς πολεμικὰς καὶ στρατιωτικὰς ἐκύδαινε πράξεις,
καὶ μαρτυρεῖ τὸ τὴν ἀρετὴν ὑπ' αὐτῶν ἑνὶ τῷ τῆς
ἀνδρείας ὀνόματι προσαγορεύεσθαι, καὶ τοῦτο τοῦ
γένους ὄνομα κοινὸν ὑπάρχειν ᾧ τὴν ἀνδρείαν
ἰδίᾳ καλοῦσιν.

II. Ὁ δὲ Μάρκιος ἑτέρων μᾶλλον ἐμπαθὴς
γεγονὼς πρὸς τοὺς πολεμικοὺς ἀγῶνας, εὐθὺς ἐκ
παιδὸς τὰ ὅπλα διὰ χειρὸς εἶχε, καὶ τῶν ἐπι-
κτήτων οὐδὲν ἔργον οἰόμενος εἶναι τοῖς μὴ τὸ
σύμφυτον ὅπλον καὶ συγγενὲς ἐξηρτυμένον ἔχουσι
καὶ παρεσκευασμένον, οὕτως ἤσκησε τὸ σῶμα
πρὸς ἅπασαν ἰδέαν μάχης ὥστε καὶ θεῖν ἐλα-
φρὸν εἶναι καὶ βάρος ἔχειν ἐν λαβαῖς καὶ ἐν
διαπάλαις πολέμου δυσεκβίαστον. οἱ γοῦν ἔριν
ἔχοντες εὐψυχίας ἀεὶ καὶ ἀρετῆς πρὸς αὐτόν, ἐν
οἷς ἐλείποντο, τὴν τοῦ σώματος ᾐτιῶντο ῥώμην
ἄτρεπτον οὖσαν καὶ πρὸς μηδένα πόνον ἀπαγ-
ορεύουσαν.

indulged a vehement temper and displayed an unswerving pertinacity, it made him a difficult and unsuitable associate for others. They did indeed look with admiration upon his insensibility to pleasures, toils, and mercenary gains, to which they gave the names of self-control, fortitude, and justice ; but in their intercourse with him as a fellow-citizen they were offended by it as ungracious, burdensome, and arrogant. Verily, among all the benefits which men derive from the favour of the Muses, none other is so great as that softening of the nature which is produced by culture and discipline, the nature being induced by culture to take on moderation and cast off excess. It is perfectly true, however, that in those days Rome held in highest honour that phase of virtue which concerns itself with warlike and military achievements, and evidence of this may be found in the only Latin word for virtue, which signifies really *manly valour* ; they made valour, a specific form oɪ virtue, stand for virtue in general.

II. And so Marcius, who was by nature exceedingly fond of warlike feats, began at once, from his very boyhood, to handle arms. And since he thought that adventitious weapons were of little avail to such as did not have their natural and native armour developed and prepared for service, he so practised himself in every sort of combat that he was not only nimble of foot, but had also such a weight in grapplings and wrestlings that an enemy found it hard to extricate himself. At any rate, those who from time to time contended with him in feats of courage and valour, laid the blame for their inferiority upon his strength of body, which was inflexible and shrank from no hardship.

III. Ἐστρατεύσατο δὲ πρώτην στρατείαν ἔτι μειράκιον, ὅτε Ταρκυνίῳ τῷ βασιλεύσαντι τῆς Ῥώμης, εἶτα ἐκπεσόντι, μετὰ πολλὰς μάχας καὶ ἥττας ὥσπερ ἔσχατον κύβον ἀφιέντι πλεῖστοι μὲν Λατίνων, πολλοὶ δὲ καὶ τῶν ἄλλων Ἰταλιωτῶν συνελάμβανον καὶ συγκατῆγον ἐπὶ τὴν Ῥώμην, οὐκ ἐκείνῳ χαριζόμενοι μᾶλλον ἢ φόβῳ τὰ Ῥωμαίων αὐξόμενα καὶ φθόνῳ καταβάλλοντες.

2 ἐν ταύτῃ τῇ μάχῃ πολλὰς τροπὰς ἐπ᾽ ἀμφότερα λαμβανούσῃ Μάρκιος ἀγωνιζόμενος εὐρώστως ἐν ὄψει τοῦ δικτάτορος, ἄνδρα Ῥωμαῖον πεσόντα πλησίον ἰδὼν οὐκ ἠμέλησεν, ἀλλ᾽ ἔστη πρὸ αὐτοῦ καὶ τὸν ἐπιφερόμενον τῶν πολεμίων ἀμυνόμενος ἀπέκτεινεν. ὡς οὖν ἐκράτησεν ὁ στρατηγός, ἐν πρώτοις ἐκεῖνον ἐστεφάνωσε δρυὸς στεφάνῳ.

3 Τοῦτον γὰρ ὁ νόμος τῷ πολίτην ὑπερασπίσαντι τὸν στέφανον ἀποδέδωκεν, εἴτε δὴ μάλιστα τιμήσας δι᾽ Ἀρκάδας τὴν δρῦν βαλανηφάγους ὑπὸ τοῦ θεοῦ χρησμῷ προσαγορευθέντας, εἴτε ὡς ταχὺ καὶ πανταχοῦ δρυὸς οὖσαν εὐπορίαν στρατευομένοις, εἴτε Διὸς πολιέως ἱερὸν ὄντα τὸν τῆς δρυὸς στέφανον οἰόμενος ἐπὶ σωτηρίᾳ πολίτου δίδοσθαι πρεπόντως. ἔστι δὲ ἡ δρῦς τῶν μὲν ἀγρίων καλλικαρπότατον, τῶν δὲ τιθασῶν ἰσχυ-
4 ρότατον. ἦν δὲ καὶ σιτίον ἀπ᾽ αὐτῆς ἡ βάλανος καὶ ποτὸν τὸ μελίτειον, ὄψον δὲ παρεῖχε τὰ

---

[1] By Lake Regillus, 498 (?) B.C.
[2] Early colonists of Rome, under Evander.

III. He made his first campaign while yet a stripling, when Tarquin, who had been king of Rome, and then had been expelled, after many unsuccessful battles, staked his all, as it were, upon a final throw. Most of the people of Latium and many also of the other peoples of Italy were assisting him and marching with him upon Rome, to reinstate him there, not so much from a desire to gratify him, as because fear and envy led them to try to overthrow the growing power of the Romans. In the ensuing battle,[1] which long favoured now this side and now that, Marcius, who was fighting sturdily under the eyes of the dictator, saw a Roman soldier struck down near by. He ran to him at once, stood in front of him, defended him, and slew his assailant. Accordingly, after the Roman general had won the day, he crowned Marcius, among the first, with a garland of oak leaves.

This is the civic crown which the law bestows upon one who has saved the life of a fellow-citizen in battle, either because the oak was held in special honour for the sake of the Arcadians,[2] who were called acorn-eaters in an oracle of Apollo[3]; or because they could speedily find an abundance of oak wherever they fought; or because it was thought that the garland of oak leaves, being sacred to Jupiter, the city's guardian, was fittingly bestowed upon one who saved the life of a citizen. The oak, moreover, has the most beautiful fruit of all wild trees, and is the sturdiest of all trees under cultivation. Its acorn used to be food, and the honey found in it used to be drink[4] for men, and it furnished them with the flesh of most grazing

---

[3] Cf. Herodotus, i. 66.   [4] In the shape of mead.

πλεῖστα τῶν νεμομένων τε καὶ πτηνῶν, θήρας ὄργανον φέρουσα τὸν ἰξόν.

Ἐν ἐκείνῃ δὲ τῇ μάχῃ καὶ τοὺς Διοσκούρους ἐπιφανῆναι λέγουσι, καὶ μετὰ τὴν μάχην εὐθὺς 2 ὀφθῆναι ῥεομένοις ἱδρῶτι τοῖς ἵπποις ἐν ἀγορᾷ τὴν νίκην ἀπαγγέλλοντας, οὗ νῦν παρὰ τὴν κρήνην νεώς ἐστιν αὐτοῖς ἱδρυμένος. ὅθεν καὶ τὴν ἡμέραν ἐπινίκιον οὖσαν, ἐν τῷ Ἰουλίῳ μηνὶ τὰς εἰδούς, Διοσκούροις ἀνιερώκασι.

IV. Νέων δέ, ὡς ἔοικεν, ἀνδρῶν ἐπιφάνεια καὶ τιμὴ τὰς μὲν ἐλαφρῶς φιλοτίμους φύσεις πρωϊαίτερον παραγενομένη σβέννυσι, καὶ ἀποπίμπλησι ταχὺ τὸ διψῶδες αὐτῶν καὶ ἀψίκορον· τὰ δ' ἐμβριθῆ καὶ βέβαια φρονήματα αὔξουσιν αἱ τιμαὶ καὶ λαμπρύνουσιν ὥσπερ ὑπὸ πνεύματος ἐγειρόμενα πρὸς τὸ φαινόμενον καλόν. οὐ γὰρ ὡς μισθὸν ἀπολαμβάνοντες, ἀλλ' ὡς ἐνέχυρον διδόντες αἰσχύνονται τὴν δόξαν καταλιπεῖν καὶ μὴ τοῖς αὐτοῖς ἔργοις ὑπερβαλέσθαι. 2 τοῦτο παθὼν καὶ ὁ Μάρκιος αὐτὸς αὑτῷ ζῆλον ἀνδραγαθίας προὔθηκε, καινός τε ἀεὶ βουλόμενος εἶναι ταῖς πράξεσιν ἀριστείαις ἀριστείας συνῆπτε καὶ λάφυρα λαφύροις ἐπέφερε, καὶ τοῖς προτέροις ἀεὶ τοὺς ὑστέρους ἡγεμόνας εἶχε περὶ τῆς ἐκείνου τιμῆς ἐρίζοντας, καὶ μαρτυρίας ὑπερβαλέσθαι.[1] πολλῶν γέ τοι τότε Ῥωμαίοις ἀγώνων καὶ πολέμων γενομένων, ἐξ οὐδενὸς ἀστεφάνωτος ἦλθεν οὐδ' ἀγέραστος.

3 Ἦν δὲ τοῖς μὲν ἄλλοις ἡ δόξα τῆς ἀρετῆς τέλος, ἐκείνῳ δὲ τῆς δόξης ἡ τῆς μητρὸς εὐφροσύνη. τὸ

---

[1] καὶ μαρτυρίας ὑπερβαλέσθαι bracketed by Bekker.

creatures and birds, since it bore the mistletoe, from which they made bird-lime for snares.

In the battle of which I was speaking, it is said that Castor and Pollux appeared, and that immediately after the battle they were seen, their horses all a-drip with sweat, in the forum, announcing the victory, by the fountain where their temple now stands. Therefore the day on which this victory was won, the Ides of July, was consecrated to the Dioscuri.

IV. It would seem that when a young man's ambition is no integral part of his nature, it is apt to be quenched by an honourable distinction which is attained too early in life ; his thirst and fastidious appetite are speedily satisfied. But serious and firm spirits are stimulated by the honours they receive, and glow brightly, as if roused by a mighty wind to achieve the manifest good. They do not feel that they are receiving a reward for what they have done, but rather that they are giving pledges of what they will do, and they are ashamed to fall behind their reputation instead of surpassing it by their actual exploits. It was in this spirit that Marcius vied with himself in manly valour, and being ever desirous ot fresh achievement, he followed one exploit with another, and heaped spoils upon spoils, so that his later commanders were always striving with their predecessors in their efforts to do him honour, and to surpass in their testimonials to his prowess. Many indeed were the wars and conflicts which the Romans waged in those days, and from none did he return without laurels and rewards of valour.

But whereas other men found in glory the chief end of valour, he found the chief end of glory in his mother's gladness. That she should hear him praised

γὰρ ἐκείνην ἐπαινούμενον ἀκοῦσαι καὶ στεφανού-
μενον ἰδεῖν καὶ περιβαλεῖν δακρύουσαν ὑφ' ἡδονῆς
ἐντιμότατον αὐτὸν ἐνόμιζε ποιεῖν καὶ μακαριώ-
τατον. τοῦτο δ' ἀμέλει καὶ τὸν Ἐπαμεινώνδαν
φασὶν ἐξομολογήσασθαι τὸ πάθος, εὐτυχίαν
ποιούμενον αὐτοῦ μεγίστην ὅτι τὴν ἐν Λεύκτροις
στρατηγίαν αὐτοῦ καὶ νίκην ὁ πατὴρ καὶ ἡ μήτηρ
4 ἔτι ζῶντες ἐπεῖδον. ἀλλ' ἐκεῖνος μὲν ἀμφοτέρων
ἀπέλαυσε τῶν γονέων συνηδομένων καὶ συνευη-
μερούντων, Μάρκιος δὲ τῇ μητρὶ καὶ τὰς τοῦ
πατρὸς ὀφείλειν χάριτας οἰόμενος οὐκ ἐνεπίμ-
πλατο τὴν Οὐολουμνίαν εὐφραίνων καὶ τιμῶν,
ἀλλὰ καὶ γυναῖκα βουλομένης καὶ δεομένης
ἐκείνης,[1] ἔγημε καὶ τὴν οἰκίαν ᾤκει γενομένων
παίδων ὁμοῦ μετὰ τῆς μητρός.

V. Ἤδη δὲ καὶ δόξαν αὐτοῦ καὶ δύναμιν ἀπὸ
τῆς ἀρετῆς ἐν τῇ πόλει μεγάλην ἔχοντος, ἡ βουλὴ
τοῖς πλουσίοις ἀμύνουσα πρὸς τὸν δῆμον ἐστα-
σίασε πολλὰ καὶ δεινὰ πάσχειν ὑπὸ τῶν δανειστῶν δοκοῦντα. τοὺς μὲν γὰρ κεκτημένους μέτρια
πάντων ἀφῃροῦντο τῶν ὄντων ἐνεχυρασμοῖς καὶ
πράσεσι, τοὺς δὲ παντελῶς ἀπόρους αὐτοὺς
ἀπῆγον καὶ τὰ σώματα καθείργνυσαν αὐτῶν,
ὠτειλὰς ἔχοντα τετρωμένων πολλὰς καὶ πεπονη-
2 κότων ἐν ταῖς ὑπὲρ τῆς πατρίδος στρατείαις, ὧν
τὴν τελευταίαν ἐδέξαντο πρὸς Σαβίνους, τῶν τε
πλουσιωτάτων ἐπαγγειλαμένων μετριάσειν καὶ
τῆς βουλῆς τὸν ἄρχοντα Μάρκον Οὐαλλέριον
ἐγγυήσασθαι ψηφισαμένης. ἐπεὶ δὲ κἀκείνην
ἀγωνισαμένοις τὴν μάχην προθύμως καὶ κρατή-

---

[1] δεομένης ἐκείνης with Mᵃ : δεομένης.

and see him crowned and embrace him with tears of joy, this was what gave him, as he thought, the highest honour and felicity. And it was doubtless this feeling which Epaminondas also is said to have confessed, in considering it his greatest good fortune that his father and mother lived to know of his generalship and victory at Leuctra. But he was so blessed as to have both his parents share in his pleasure and success, whereas Marcius, who thought he owed his mother the filial gratitude also which would have been due to his father, could not get his fill of gladdening and honouring Volumnia, nay, he even married according to her wish and request, and continued to live in the same house with his mother after children were born to him.

V. The reputation and influence procured by his valour were already great in the city, when the senate, taking the part of the wealthy citizens, began to be at variance with the common people, who thought they suffered many grievous ills at the hands of the money-lenders. For those of them that were possessed of moderate means were stripped of all they had by means of pledges and sales, while those who were altogether without resources were led away in person and put in prison, although their bodies bore many marks of wounds received and hardships undergone in campaigns for the defence of their country. The last of these had been against the Sabines, and they had undertaken it upon a promise of their wealthiest creditors to deal moderately with them, and after a vote of the senate that Marcus Valerius, the consul, should guarantee the promise. But after they had fought zealously in that battle also, and had conquered the enemy, no

σασι τῶν πολεμίων οὐδὲν ἐγίνετο παρὰ τῶν
3 δανειστῶν ἐπιεικές, οὐδ' ἡ βουλὴ προσεποιεῖτο
μεμνῆσθαι τῶν ὡμολογημένων, ἀλλ' ἀγομένους
πάλιν περιεώρα καὶ ῥυσιαζομένους, θόρυβοι δὲ
καὶ συστάσεις ἦσαν ἐν τῇ πόλει πονηραί, καὶ
τοὺς πολεμίους οὐκ ἔλαθε ταραχωδῶς ἔχων ὁ
δῆμος, ἀλλ' ἐμβαλόντες ἐπυρπόλουν τὴν χώραν,
τῶν δ' ἀρχόντων εἰς τὰ ὅπλα τοὺς ἐν ἡλικίᾳ
καλούντων οὐδεὶς ὑπήκουεν, οὕτω διέστησαν αἱ
4 γνῶμαι πάλιν τῶν ἐν τέλει. καί τινες μὲν ᾤοντο
δεῖν ὑφίεσθαι τοῖς πένησι καὶ χαλάσαι τὸ σύν-
τονον ἄγαν καὶ νόμιμον, ἔνιοι δ' ἀντέτεινον, ὧν ἦν
καὶ Μάρκιος, οὐ τὸ τῶν χρημάτων μέγιστον
ἡγούμενος, ἀρχὴν δὲ καὶ πεῖραν ὕβρεως ὄχλου
καὶ θρασύτητος ἐπανισταμένου τοῖς νόμοις, εἰ
σωφρονοῦσι, παύειν καὶ σβεννύειν παρακελευό- 2
μενος.

VI. Συνιούσης δὲ περὶ τούτων πολλάκις ἐν
ὀλίγῳ χρόνῳ τῆς βουλῆς καὶ μηδὲν τέλος ἐκ-
φερούσης, συστάντες οἱ πένητες ἄφνω καὶ παρα-
καλέσαντες ἀλλήλους ἀπέλιπον τὴν πόλιν, καὶ
καταλαβόντες ὄρος ὃ νῦν ἱερὸν καλεῖται, παρὰ
τὸν Ἀνίωνα ποταμὸν ἐκαθέζοντο, πράττοντες μὲν
οὐδὲν βίαιον οὐδὲ στασιαστικόν, ἐκπεπτωκέναι δὲ
τῆς πόλεως ὑπὸ τῶν πλουσίων πάλαι βοῶντες,
ἀέρα δὲ καὶ ὕδωρ καὶ τόπον ἐνταφῆναι πανταχοῦ
2 τὴν Ἰταλίαν αὐτοῖς παρέξειν, ὧν πλέον οὐδὲν
οἰκοῦσι τὴν Ῥώμην ὑπάρχειν αὐτοῖς, ἀλλ' ἢ
τιτρώσκεσθαι καὶ ἀποθνήσκειν ὑπὲρ τῶν πλουσίων
στρατευομένοις.

Ταῦτ' ἔδεισεν ἡ βουλή, καὶ τοὺς ἐπιεικεῖς

consideration was shown them by their creditors, and the senate did not even pretend to remember its agreements, but again suffered them to be seized in pledge of payments and haled away to prison. Then there were tumults and disorderly gatherings in the city, and the enemy, not unaware of the popular confusion, burst in and ravaged the country, and when the consuls summoned those of military age to arms, no one responded. In this crisis, the opinions of those in authority were again at variance. Some thought that concessions should be made to the plebeians, and the excessive rigor of the law relaxed; but others opposed this, and among them was Marcius. He did not regard the financial difficulties as the main point at issue, and exhorted the magistrates to be wise enough to check and quell this incipient attempt at bold outrage on the part of a populace in revolt against the laws.

VI. The senate met to debate this question many times within the space of a few days, but came to no definite conclusion. The plebeians therefore banded together on a sudden, and after mutual exhortations forsook the city, and taking possession of what is now called the Sacred Mount, established themselves beside the river Anio.[1] They committed no acts of violence or sedition, but only cried aloud that they had for a long time been banished from the city by the rich, and that Italy would everywhere afford them air, water, and a place of burial, which was all they had if they dwelt in Rome, except for the privilege of wounds and death in campaigns for the defence of the rich.

These proceedings alarmed the senate, and it sent

---

[1] Three miles from the city (Livy, ii. 32, 2).

μάλιστα καὶ δημοτικοὺς τῶν πρεσβυτέρων ἐξαπ-
έστειλε. προηγόρει δὲ Μενήνιος Ἀγρίππας·
καὶ πολλὰ μὲν τοῦ δήμου δεόμενος, πολλὰ δ᾽ ὑπὲρ
τῆς βουλῆς παρρησιαζόμενος τελευτῶντι τῷ λόγῳ
περιῆλθεν εἰς σχῆμα μύθου διαμνημονευόμενον.
3 ἔφη γὰρ τοῦ ἀνθρώπου τὰ μέλη πάντα πρὸς τὴν
γαστέρα στασιάσαι, καὶ κατηγορεῖν αὐτῆς ὡς
μόνης ἀργοῦ καὶ ἀσυμβόλου καθεζομένης ἐν τῷ
σώματι, τῶν δ᾽ ἄλλων εἰς τὰς ἐκείνης ὀρέξεις
πόνους τε μεγάλους καὶ λειτουργίας ὑπομενόντων·
τὴν δὲ γαστέρα τῆς εὐηθείας αὐτῶν καταγελᾶν,
ἀγνοούντων ὅτι τὴν τροφὴν ὑπολαμβάνει μὲν εἰς
ἑαυτὴν ἅπασαν, ἀναπέμπει δ᾽ αὖθις ἐξ αὐτῆς καὶ
4 διανέμει τοῖς ἄλλοις. “Οὕτως οὖν,” ἔφη, “καὶ
τῆς συγκλήτου λόγος ἐστίν, ὦ πολῖται, πρὸς
ὑμᾶς· τὰ γὰρ ἐκεῖ τυγχάνοντα τῆς προσηκούσης
ἐπιμελείας καὶ οἰκονομίας βουλεύματα καὶ πράγματα πᾶσιν ὑμῖν ἐπιφέρει καὶ διανέμει τὸ χρήσιμον καὶ ὠφέλιμον.”

VII. Ἐκ τούτου διηλλάγησαν, αἰτησάμενοι
παρὰ τῆς βουλῆς καὶ τυχόντες ἄνδρας αἱρεῖσθαι
πέντε προστάτας τῶν δεομένων βοηθείας, τοὺς
νῦν δημάρχους καλουμένους. εἵλοντο δὲ πρώτους,
οἷς ἐχρήσαντο καὶ τῆς ἀποστάσεως ἡγεμόσι, τοὺς
περὶ Βροῦτον Ἰούνιον καὶ Σικίννιον Βέλλουτον.
ἐπεὶ δ᾽ ἡ πόλις εἰς ἓν ἦλθεν, εὐθὺς ἐν τοῖς ὅπλοις
ἦσαν οἱ πολλοί, καὶ παρεῖχον αὑτοὺς τοῖς ἄρχουσι
χρῆσθαι προθύμως ἐπὶ τὸν πόλεμον.

2 Ὁ δὲ Μάρκιος οὔτ᾽ αὐτὸς ἡδόμενος οἷς ὁ δῆμος

out those of its older members who were most
reasonably disposed towards the people to treat with
them. The chief spokesman was Menenius Agrippa,
and after much entreaty of the people and much
plain speaking in behalf of the senate, he concluded
his discourse with a celebrated fable. He said,
namely, that all the other members of man's body
once revolted against the belly, and accused it of
being the only member to sit idly down in its place
and make no contribution to the common welfare,
while the rest underwent great hardships and performed great public services only to minister to its
appetites; but that the belly laughed at their
simplicity in not knowing that it received into itself
all the body's nourishment only to send it back
again and duly distribute it among the other members.
"Such, then," said Agrippa, "is the relation of the
senate, my fellow-citizens, to you; the matters for
deliberation which there receive the necessary
attention and disposition bring to you all and severally
what is useful and helpful."[1]

VII. A reconciliation followed, after the people
had asked and obtained from the senate the privilege
of electing five men as protectors of those who
needed succour, the officers now called tribunes of
the people. And the first whom they chose to this
office were Junius Brutus and Sicinius Vellutus, who
had been their leaders in the secession.[2] When the
city was thus united, the common people at once
offered themselves as soldiers, and the consuls
found them ready and eager for service in the war.

As for Marcius, though he was displeased himself

[1] Cf. Livy, ii. 32, 9-11; Dionysius Hal., *Antiq. Rom.* vi. 86.
[2] Cf. Livy, ii. 33, 1-3.

ἴσχυεν ἐνδούσης τῆς ἀριστοκρατίας, καὶ τῶν
ἄλλων πατρικίων πολλοὺς ὁρῶν τὸ αὐτὸ πεπον-
θότας, ὅμως παρεκάλει μὴ ἀπολείπεσθαι τῶν
δημοτικῶν ἐν τοῖς περὶ τῆς πατρίδος ἀγῶσιν,
ἀλλὰ τῇ ἀρετῇ μᾶλλον ἢ τῇ δυνάμει φαίνεσθαι
διαφέροντας αὐτῶν.

VIII. Ἐν δὲ τῷ Οὐολούσκων ἔθνει, πρὸς οὓς
ἐπολέμουν, ἡ Κοριολανῶν πόλις ἀξίωμα μέγιστον
εἶχε. ταύτην οὖν τοῦ ὑπάτου Κομινίου περι-
στρατοπεδεύσαντος, οἱ λοιποὶ Οὐολοῦσκοι δείσαντες ἐπὶ τοὺς Ῥωμαίους συνεβοήθουν πανταχόθεν, ὡς πρὸς τῇ πόλει ποιησόμενοι μάχην καὶ
2 διχόθεν ἐπιχειρήσοντες αὐτοῖς. ἐπεὶ δ' ὁ Κομίνιος διελὼν τὴν δύναμιν αὐτὸς μὲν ἀπήντα τοῖς
ἔξωθεν ἐπιοῦσι τῶν Οὐολούσκων, Λάρκιον δὲ
Τίτον, ἄνδρα Ῥωμαίων ἐν τοῖς ἀρίστοις, ἐπὶ τῆς
πολιορκίας ἀπέλιπε, καταφρονήσαντες οἱ Κοριο-
λανοὶ τῶν παρόντων ἐπεξῆλθον, καὶ προσμαχό-
μενοι τὸ πρῶτον ἐκράτουν καὶ κατεδίωκον εἰς
3 τὸν χάρακα τοὺς Ῥωμαίους. ἔνθα δὴ Μάρκιος
ἐκδραμὼν σὺν ὀλίγοις καὶ καταβαλὼν τοὺς
προσμίξαντας αὐτῷ μάλιστα, τοὺς δ' ἄλλους
στήσας ἐπιφερομένους, ἀνεκαλεῖτο μεγάλῃ βοῇ
τοὺς Ῥωμαίους. καὶ γὰρ ἦν, ὥσπερ ἠξίου τὸν
στρατιώτην ὁ Κάτων, οὐ χειρὶ καὶ πληγῇ μόνον,
ἀλλὰ καὶ τόνῳ φωνῆς καὶ ὄψει προσώπου
φοβερὸς ἐντυχεῖν πολεμίῳ καὶ δυσυπόστατος.
ἀθροιζομένων δὲ πολλῶν καὶ συνισταμένων περὶ
4 αὐτὸν ἀπεχώρουν οἱ πολέμιοι δείσαντες. ὁ δ'
οὐκ ἠγάπησεν, ἀλλ' ἐπηκολούθει καὶ συνήλαυνεν

to have the people increase in power at the expense
of the aristocracy, and though he saw that many of the
other patricians were of the same mind, he nevertheless exhorted them not to fall behind the common
people in contending for their country's welfare, but
to show that they were superior to them in valour
rather than in political power.

VIII. Among the Volscians, with whom the
Romans were at war, the city of Corioli took highest
rank. When, therefore, Cominius the consul had
invested this place,[1] the rest of the Volscians, fearing
for its safety, came to its aid against the Romans
from all parts, designing to give them battle in front
of the city and to attack them on both sides.
Thereupon Cominius divided his forces, going forth
himself to meet the Volscians who were coming up
outside, and leaving Titus Lartius, one of the bravest
Romans of his day, in charge of the siege. Then the
men of Corioli, despising the forces that were left,
sallied out against them, overcame them in battle at
first, and pursued the Romans to their camp. At
this point Marcius darted out with a small band, and
after slaying those who came to close quarters and
bringing the rest of the assailants to a halt, called
the Romans back to the fight with loud cries. For
he had, as Cato thought a soldier should have,[2] not
only a vigour of stroke, but a voice and look which
made him a fearful man for a foe to encounter, and
hard to withstand. Many of his men rallied to
support him, and the enemy withdrew in terror.
With this, however, he was not satisfied, but followed

---

[1] It is in connection with the attack on Corioli that Livy
first mentions Marcius (ii. 33, 5–9) ; also Dionysius Hal.
(vi. 92). [2] Cf. *Cato the Elder*, i. 6.

ἤδη προτροπάδην φεύγοντας ἄχρι τῶν πυλῶν.
ἐκεῖ δ᾽ ὁρῶν ἀποτρεπομένους τοῦ διώκειν τοὺς 21
Ῥωμαίους, πολλῶν μὲν ἀπὸ τοῦ τείχους βελῶν
προσφερομένων, τὸ δὲ συνεισπεσεῖν τοῖς φεύγουσιν εἰς πόλιν ἀνδρῶν πολεμικῶν γέμουσαν ἐν
τοῖς ὅπλοις ὄντων οὐδενὸς εἰς νοῦν ἐμβαλέσθαι
τολμῶντος, ὅμως ἐπιστὰς παρεκάλει καὶ παρε-
θάρρυνεν, ἀνεῷχθαι βοῶν ὑπὸ τῆς τύχης τοῖς
διώκουσι μᾶλλον ἢ τοῖς φεύγουσι τὴν πόλιν.
5 οὐ πολλῶν δὲ βουλομένων ἐπακολουθεῖν, ὠσά-
μενος διὰ τῶν πολεμίων ἐνήλατο ταῖς πύλαις καὶ
συνεισέπεσε, μηδενὸς τὸ πρῶτον ἀντισχεῖν μηδ᾽
ὑποστῆναι τολμήσαντος, ἔπειτα δέ, ὡς κατεῖδον
ὀλίγους παντάπασιν ἔνδον ὄντας, συμβοηθούντων
6 καὶ προσμαχομένων, ἀναμεμιγμένος ὁμοῦ φίλοις
καὶ πολεμίοις ἄπιστον ἀγῶνα λέγεται καὶ χειρὸς
ἔργοις καὶ ποδῶν τάχει καὶ τολμήμασι ψυχῆς
ἀγωνιζόμενος ἐν τῇ πόλει, καὶ κρατῶν ἁπάντων
πρὸς οὓς ὁρούσειε, τοὺς μὲν ἐξῶσαι πρὸς τὰ
ἔσχατα μέρη, τῶν δ᾽ ἀπειπαμένων καὶ κατα-
βαλόντων τὰ ὅπλα πολλὴν ἄδειαν τῷ Λαρκίῳ
παρασχεῖν ἔξωθεν ἐπάγοντι τοὺς Ῥωμαίους.

IX. Οὕτω δὲ τῆς πόλεως ἁλούσης καὶ τῶν
πλείστων ἐν ἁρπαγαῖς ὄντων καὶ διαφορήσεσι
χρημάτων, ὁ Μάρκιος ἠγανάκτει καὶ ἐβόα, δεινὸν
ἡγούμενος, τοῦ ὑπάτου καὶ τῶν σὺν ἐκείνῳ πολιτῶν τάχα που συμπεπτωκότων τοῖς πολεμίοις
καὶ διαμαχομένων, αὐτοὺς χρηματίζεσθαι περι-
ιόντας ἢ προφάσει χρηματισμοῦ τὸν κίνδυνον
ἀποδιδράσκειν. ἐπεὶ δ᾽ οὐ πολλοὶ προσεῖχον

hard upon them, and drove them at last in headlong flight, up to the gate of their city. There, although he saw the Romans turning back from the pursuit, now that many missiles from the walls were reaching them, and although not a man of them dared to think of bursting into the city along with the fugitives, full as it was of enemies in arms, he nevertheless took his stand, and exhorted and encouraged them to the exploit, crying out that fortune had opened the city for the pursuers rather than for the pursued. Only a few were willing to follow him, but he pushed his way through the enemy, leaped against the gate, and burst in along with them, no man daring to oppose him at first or resist him. Then, however, when the citizens saw that few of the enemy all told were inside, they rallied and attacked them. Enveloped thus by friends and foes alike, Marcius is said to have waged a combat in the city which, for prowess of arm, speed of foot, and daring of soul, passes all belief; he overwhelmed all whom he assailed, driving some to the remotest parts of the city, while others gave up the struggle and threw down their arms. Thus he made it abundantly safe for Lartius to lead up the Romans who were outside.

IX. The city having been captured in this manner, most of the soldiers fell to plundering and pillaging it. At this Marcius was indignant, and cried out that he thought it a shame, when their consul and their fellow citizens who were with him had perhaps fallen in with the enemy and were fighting a battle with them, that they on their part should be going about after booty, or, under pretext of getting booty, should run away from the danger. Only a few paid

αὐτῷ, τοὺς βουλομένους ἀναλαβὼν ἐβάδιζε τὴν
ὁδὸν ᾗ τὸ στράτευμα προκεχωρηκὸς ᾖσθετο,
πολλάκις μὲν ἐποτρύνων τοὺς σὺν αὐτῷ καὶ
παρακαλῶν μὴ ἐνδιδόναι, πολλάκις δὲ τοῖς θεοῖς
εὐχόμενος μὴ ἀπολειφθῆναι τῆς μάχης, ἀλλ᾽ εἰς
καιρὸν ἐλθεῖν ἐν ᾧ συναγωνιεῖται καὶ συγκιν-
δυνεύσει τοῖς πολίταις.

Ἦν δὲ τότε τοῖς Ῥωμαίοις ἔθος εἰς τάξιν
καθισταμένοις καὶ μέλλουσι τοὺς θυρεοὺς ἀναλαμβάνειν καὶ περιζώννυσθαι τὴν τήβεννον ἅμα
καὶ διαθήκας ἀγράφους γίνεσθαι, τριῶν ἢ τεττά-
ρων ἐπακουόντων ὀνομάζοντας τὸν κληρονόμον.
3 ταῦτα δὴ πράττοντας ἤδη τοὺς στρατιώτας
Μάρκιος ἐν ὄψει τῶν πολεμίων ὄντων κατε-
λάμβανε. καὶ τὸ μὲν πρῶτον ἐνίους διετάραξεν
ὀφθεὶς μετ᾽ ὀλίγων, αἵματος περίπλεως καὶ
ἱδρῶτος· ἐπεὶ δὲ προσδραμὼν τῷ ὑπάτῳ περι-
χαρὴς τὴν δεξιὰν ἐνέβαλε καὶ τῆς πόλεως
ἀπήγγειλε τὴν ἅλωσιν, ὁ δὲ Κομίνιος περιεπτύ-
ξατο αὐτὸν καὶ κατησπάσατο, τοῖς μὲν πυθο-
μένοις τὸ γεγενημένον κατόρθωμα, τοῖς δ᾽ εἰκάσασι
θάρσος παρέστη, καὶ βοῇ παρεκάλουν ἄγειν
4 καὶ συνάπτειν. ὁ δὲ Μάρκιος ἠρώτησε τὸν
Κομίνιον πῶς διακεκόσμηται τὰ τῶν πολεμίων
ὅπλα καὶ ποῦ τέτακται τὸ μαχιμώτατον. ἐκείνου
δὲ φήσαντος οἴεσθαι τὰς κατὰ μέσον σπείρας
Ἀντιατῶν εἶναι, πολεμικωτάτων καὶ μηδενὶ
φρονήματος ὑφιεμένων, "Ἀξιῶ σε τοίνυν," ὁ
Μάρκιος ἔφη, "καὶ αἰτοῦμαι, κατὰ τούτους τάξον
ἡμᾶς τοὺς ἄνδρας." ἔδωκεν οὖν ὁ ὕπατος, θαυ-
μάσας αὐτοῦ τὸ πρόθυμον.
5 Ὡς δ᾽ ἦσαν ἐμβολαὶ δοράτων, καὶ τοῦ Μαρκίου

any heed to his words, whereupon he took those who were willing to follow, and set out on the road by which, as he learned, the consul's army had marched before him, often urging his companions on and beseeching them not to slacken their efforts, and often praying the gods that he might not be too late for the battle, but might come up in season to share in the struggles and perils of his fellow-citizens.

It was a custom with the Romans of that time, when they were going into action, and were about to gird up their cloaks and take up their bucklers, to make at the same time an unwritten will, naming their heirs in the hearing of three or four witnesses. This was just what the soldiers were doing when Marcius overtook them, the enemy being now in sight. At first some of them were confounded when they saw that he had a small following and was covered with blood and sweat; but when he ran to the consul with a glad countenance, gave him his hand, and announced the capture of the city, and when Cominius embraced and kissed him, then they were encouraged, some hearing of the success which had been gained, and some but guessing at it, and all called loudly upon the consul to lead them into battle. But Marcius asked Cominius how the enemy were arrayed, and where their best fighting men were placed. And when the consul told him he thought the troops in the centre were those of the Antiates, who were the most warlike of all and yielded to none in bravery, "I ask and demand of you, then," said Marcius, "post us opposite these men." The consul, accordingly, granted his request, astonished at his ardour.

As soon as spears began to fly, Marcius darted out

προεκδραμόντος οὐκ ἀντέσχον οἱ κατὰ στόμα τῶν
Οὐολούσκων, ἀλλ' ᾧ προσέμιξε μέρει τῆς
φάλαγγος εὐθὺς διεκέκοπτο, τῶν δ' ἑκατέρωθεν
ἐπιστρεφόντων καὶ περιλαμβανόντων τοῖς ὅπλοις
τὸν ἄνδρα, δείσας ὁ ὕπατος τοὺς κρατίστους τῶν
6 περὶ αὐτὸν ἐξέπεμπεν. ἰσχυρᾶς δὲ περὶ τὸν
Μάρκιον μάχης γενομένης καὶ πολλῶν ἐν ὀλίγῳ
νεκρῶν πεσόντων, ἐγκείμενοι καὶ καταβιαζόμενοι
τοὺς πολεμίους ἐώσαντο, καὶ τρεπόμενοι πρὸς
δίωξιν αὐτῶν τὸν Μάρκιον ἠξίουν ὑπό τε καμάτου
βαρὺν ὄντα καὶ τραυμάτων ἀναχωρεῖν ἐπὶ τὸ 2
στρατόπεδον. εἰπὼν δ' ἐκεῖνος ὅτι νικώντων οὐκ
ἔστι τὸ κάμνειν, ἐφείπετο τοῖς φεύγουσιν. ἡττήθη
δὲ καὶ τὸ λοιπὸν στράτευμα, πολλῶν μὲν διαφθαρέντων, πολλῶν δὲ ἁλόντων.

X. Τῇ δ' ὑστεραίᾳ τοῦ Λαρκίου παραγενομένου
καὶ τῶν ἄλλων ἀθροιζομένων πρὸς τὸν ὕπατον,
ἀναβὰς ἐπὶ τὸ βῆμα, καὶ τοῖς θεοῖς τὴν πρέπου-
σαν ἀποδοὺς ἐπὶ τηλικούτοις κατορθώμασιν
εὐφημίαν, πρὸς τὸν Μάρκιον τρέπεται. καὶ
πρῶτον μὲν αὐτοῦ θαυμαστὸν ἔπαινον εἶπε, τῶν
μὲν αὐτὸς ἐν τῇ μάχῃ γεγονὼς θεατής, τὰ δὲ τοῦ
2 Λαρκίου μαρτυροῦντος. ἔπειτα, πολλῶν χρημάτων καὶ ἵππων γεγονότων αἰχμαλώτων καὶ
ἀνθρώπων, ἐκέλευσεν αὐτὸν ἐξελέσθαι δέκα
πάντα πρὸ τοῦ νέμειν τοῖς ἄλλοις. ἄνευ δὲ
ἐκείνων ἀριστεῖον αὐτῷ κεκοσμημένον ἵππον
ἐδωρήσατο. τῶν δὲ Ῥωμαίων ἐπαινεσάντων ὁ
Μάρκιος προελθὼν τὸν μὲν ἵππον ἔφη δέχεσθαι

before the line, and the Volscians who faced him could not withstand his charge, but where he fell upon their ranks they were speedily cut asunder. Those on either side, however, wheeled about and encompassed him with their weapons, so that the consul, fearing for his safety, sent to his aid the choicest men he had about his person. Then a fierce battle raged around Marcius, and many were slain in short space of time; but the Romans pressed hard upon their enemies and put them to rout, and as they set out in pursuit of them, they insisted that Marcius, who was weighed down with fatigue and wounds, should retire to the camp. He answered, however, that weariness was not for victors, and took after the flying foe. The rest of their army also was defeated, many were slain, and many taken captive.[1]

X. On the following day, when Lartius had come up, and the rest of the army was assembled before the consul, Cominius mounted the rostra, and after rendering to the gods the praise that was their due for such great successes, addressed himself to Marcius. In the first place, he rehearsed with praise his astonishing exploits, some of which he had himself beheld in the battle, while to others Lartius bore witness. Then, out of the abundant treasures and the many horses and prisoners that had been taken, he ordered him to choose out a tenth, before any distribution to the rest of the army; and besides all this, he presented him with a horse, duly caparisoned, as a prize of valour. After the Romans had applauded this speech, Marcius came forward and said that he accepted the horse, and was de-

---

[1] Cf. Dionysius Hal. vi. 94.

καὶ χαίρειν τοῖς ἐπαίνοις τοῦ ἄρχοντος, τὰ δὲ
ἄλλα μισθόν, οὐ τιμὴν ἡγούμενος ἐᾶν, καὶ ἀγα-
3 πήσειν ὡς εἷς ἕκαστος τὴν νέμησιν. "'Εξαί-
ρετον δὲ μίαν αἰτοῦμαι χάριν," ἔφη, "καὶ δέομαι
λαβεῖν. ἦν μοι ξένος ἐν Οὐολούσκοις καὶ φίλος,
ἀνὴρ ἐπιεικὴς καὶ μέτριος· οὗτος ἑάλωκε νῦν
καὶ γέγονεν ἐκ πλουσίου καὶ μακαρίου δοῦλος.
πολλῶν οὖν αὐτῷ κακῶν παρόντων ἓν ἀφελεῖν
ἀρκεῖ, τὴν πρᾶσιν."

Ἐπὶ τούτοις λεχθεῖσι βοή τε μείζων ἀπήντησε
τῷ Μαρκίῳ, καὶ πλείονες οἱ θαυμάζοντες ἐγένοντο
τὸ μὴ κρατούμενον ὑπὸ χρημάτων τἀνδρὸς ἢ τὴν
4 ἐν τοῖς πολέμοις ἀνδραγαθίαν. καὶ γὰρ οἷς
φθόνου τι καὶ ζήλου πρὸς αὐτὸν ὑπέκειτο τιμώμενον ἐκπρεπῶς, κἀκείνοις τότε τοῦ λαβεῖν
μεγάλα τῷ μὴ λαβεῖν ἄξιος ἔδοξε, καὶ μᾶλλον
αὐτοῦ τὴν ἀρετὴν ἠγάπησαν, ἀφ' ἧς κατεφρόνει
τηλικούτων, ἢ δι' ὧν ἠξιοῦτο. τὸ μὲν γὰρ εὖ
χρῆσθαι χρήμασι κάλλιόν ἐστιν ἢ ὅπλοις, τοῦ δὲ
χρῆσθαι τὸ μὴ δεῖσθαι χρημάτων σεμνότερον.

XI. Ἐπεὶ δὲ ἐπαύσατο βοῆς καὶ θορύβου τὸ
πλῆθος, ὑπολαβὼν ὁ Κομίνιος, "Ἀλλ' ἐκείνας
μέν," εἶπεν, "ὦ συστρατιῶται, τὰς δωρεὰς οὐ
δύνασθε βιάζεσθαι μὴ δεχόμενον τὸν ἄνδρα μηδὲ
βουλόμενον λαβεῖν· ἣν δὲ οὐκ ἔστιν ἐπὶ τούτῳ διδο-
μένην ἀπώσασθαι, δῶμεν αὐτῷ καὶ ψηφισώμεθα
καλεῖσθαι Κοριολανόν, εἰ μὴ καὶ πρὸ ἡμῶν ἡ
πρᾶξις αὐτὴ τοῦτο δέδωκεν." ἐκ τούτου τρίτον
ἔσχεν ὄνομα τὸν Κοριολανόν.

lighted with the praises of the consul, but that he declined the rest, holding it to be pay, not honour, and would be content with his single share of the booty. "But I do ask one special favour," he said, "and beg that I may receive it. I had a guest-friend among the Volscians, a man of kindliness and probity. This man is now a prisoner, and from wealth and happiness is reduced to subjection. Since, then, many evils have befallen him, let me at least free him from one, that of being sold into bondage."

At such words as these still louder shouts greeted Marcius, and he found more admirers of his superiority to gain than of the bravery he had shown in war. For the very ones who secretly felt a certain jealous envy of him for his conspicuous honours, now thought him worthy of great rewards because he would not take them; and they were more delighted with the virtue which led him to despise such great rewards, than with the exploits which made him worthy of them. For the right use of wealth is a fairer trait than excellence in arms; but not to need wealth is loftier than to use it.

XI. When the multitude had ceased shouting their applause, Cominius took up the word again and said: "Ye cannot, indeed, my fellow-soldiers, force these gifts of yours upon the man, when he does not accept them and is unwilling to take them; but there is a gift which he cannot refuse when it is offered. Let us give him this gift, and pass a vote that he be surnamed Coriolanus, unless, indeed, before such act of ours, his exploit has itself given him this name." Thence came his third name of Coriolanus.[1]

---

[1] Cf. Dionysius Hal. vi. 94.

2 Ὧι καὶ μάλιστα δῆλόν ἐστιν ὅτι τῶν ὀνομάτων
ἴδιον ἦν ὁ Γάϊος, τὸ δὲ δεύτερον οἰκίας ἢ γένους
κοινὸν ὁ Μάρκιος, τῷ δὲ τρίτῳ ὕστερον ἐχρήσαντο
πράξεώς τινος ἢ τύχης ἢ ἰδέας ἢ ἀρετῆς ἐπιθέτῳ,
καθάπερ Ἕλληνες ἐτίθεντο πράξεως μὲν ἐπώνυ-
μον τὸν Σωτῆρα καὶ τὸν Καλλίνικον, ἰδέας δὲ τὸν
Φύσκωνα καὶ τὸν Γρυπόν, ἀρετῆς δὲ τὸν Εὐεργέτην καὶ τὸν Φιλάδελφον, εὐτυχίας δὲ τὸν
3 Εὐδαίμονα τῷ δευτέρῳ τῶν Βάττων. ἐνίοις δὲ
τῶν βασιλέων καὶ σκώμματα παρέσχεν ἐπι-
κλήσεις, ὡς Ἀντιγόνῳ τὸν Δώσωνα καὶ Πτολε-
μαίῳ τὸν Λάθυρον. ἐπὶ πλέον δὲ τῷ γένει τούτῳ
καὶ Ῥωμαῖοι κέχρηνται, Διαδήματόν τινα τῶν
Μετέλλων καλέσαντες, ὅτι πολὺν χρόνον ἕλκος
ἔχων περιενόστει διαδεδεμένος[1] τὸ μέτωπον,
ἕτερον δὲ Κέλερα σπεύσαντα μεθ᾽ ἡμέρας ὀλίγας
τῆς τοῦ πατρὸς τελευτῆς ἐπιταφίους μονομάχων
ἀγῶνας παρασχεῖν, τὸ τάχος καὶ τὴν ὀξύτητα τῆς
4 παρασκευῆς θαυμάσαντες. ἐνίους δὲ συντυχίᾳ
γενέσεως μέχρι νῦν καλοῦσι, Πρόκλον μέν, ἐὰν
ἀποδημοῦντος πατρὸς γένηται, καὶ Πόστουμον,
ἂν τεθνηκότος· ᾧ δ᾽ ἂν διδύμῳ γενομένῳ συμβῇ
περιβιῶναι, θατέρου τελευτήσαντος, Οὐοπίσκον.
τῶν δὲ σωματικῶν οὐ μόνον Σύλλας οὐδὲ Νίγρους

---

[1] διαδεδεμένος with Mᵃ : περιδεδεμένος.

---

[1] Soter, *Saviour* ; Callinicus, *Of noble victory* ; Physcon,
Fat-paunch ; Grypus, *Hook-nosed* ; Euergetes, *Benefactor* ;
Philadelphus, *Sister-* or *Brother-lover* ; Eudaemon, *Prosperous* ;

CAIUS MARCIUS CORIOLANUS

From this it is perfectly clear that Caius was the proper name; that the second name, in this case Marcius, was the common name of family or clan; and that the third name was adopted subsequently, and bestowed because of some exploit, or fortune, or bodily feature, or special excellence in a man. So the Greeks used to give surnames from an exploit, as for instance, Soter[1] and Callinicus; or from a bodily feature, as Physcon and Grypus; or from a special excellence, as Euergetes and Philadephus; or from some good fortune. as Eudaemon, the surname of the second Battus. And some of their kings have actually had surnames given them in mockery, as Antigonus Doson and Ptolemy Lathyrus. Surnames of this sort were even more common among the Romans. For instance, one of the Metelli was called Diadematus, because for a long time he suffered from a running sore and went about with a bandage on his forehead; another member of this family was called Celer, because he exerted himself to give the people funeral games of gladiators within a few days of his father's death, and the speed and swiftness of his preparations excited astonishment.[2] And at the present day some of them are named from casual incidents at their birth, Proculus, for instance, if a child is born when his father is away from home; or Postumus, if after his death; and when one of twin children survives, while the other dies, he is called Vopiscus. Moreover, from bodily features they not only bestow such surnames as Sulla, Niger, and Rufus, but also

Doson, *Always-promising*; Lathyrus, *Vetchling*; Sulla, *Blotches* (?); Niger, *Black*; Rufus, *Red*; Caecus, *Blind*; Claudius, *Lame*.   [2] Cf. *Romulus*, x. 2.

οὐδὲ Ῥούφους, ἀλλὰ καὶ Καίκους καὶ Κλωδίους
ἐπωνυμίας τίθενται, καλῶς ἐθίζοντες μήτε τυφλότητα μήτ' ἄλλην τινὰ σωματικὴν ἀτυχίαν ὄνει- 2
δος ἡγεῖσθαι μηδὲ λοιδορίαν, ἀλλ' ὡς οἰκείοις
ὑπακούειν ὀνόμασιν. ἀλλὰ ταῦτα μὲν ἑτέρῳ
γένει γραφῆς προσήκει.

XII. Παυσαμένῳ δὲ τῷ πολέμῳ τὴν στάσιν
ἐπήγειρον αὖθις οἱ δημαγωγοί, καινὴν μὲν οὐδεμίαν
αἰτίαν ἔχοντες οὐδ' ἔγκλημα δίκαιον, ἃ δὲ ταῖς
προτέραις αὐτῶν διαφοραῖς καὶ ταραχαῖς ἀναγ-
καίως ἐπηκολούθησε κακά, ταῦτα ποιούμενοι
πρόφασιν ἐπὶ τοὺς πατρικίους. ἄσπορος γὰρ ἡ
πλείστη καὶ ἀγεώργητος ἀπελείφθη τῆς χώρας,
ἀγορᾶς δ' ἐπεισάκτου παρασκευὴν διὰ τὸν πόλε-
2 μον ὁ καιρὸς οὐκ ἔδωκεν. ἰσχυρᾶς οὖν ἀπορίας
γενομένης, ὁρῶντες οἱ δημαγωγοὶ μήτ' ἀγορὰν
ἔχοντα μήτ', εἰ παρῆν ἀγορά, χρημάτων εὐ-
ποροῦντα τὸν δῆμον, ἐνέβαλλον λόγους καὶ
διαβολὰς κατὰ τῶν πλουσίων, ὡς ἐκεῖνοι τὸν
λιμὸν ἐπάγοιεν αὐτοῖς ὑπὸ μνησικακίας.

Ἐκ δὲ τῶν Οὐελιτρανῶν ἧκε πρεσβεία τὴν
πόλιν παραδιδόντων καὶ δεομένων ἀποίκους ἀπο-
στέλλειν. νόσος γὰρ ἐμπεσοῦσα λοιμώδης αὐτοῖς
τοσοῦτον ὄλεθρον καὶ φθορὰν ἀπειργάσατο τῶν
ἀνθρώπων ὥστε μόλις τὸ δέκατον τοῦ παντὸς
3 ἀπολειφθῆναι μέρος. ἔδοξεν οὖν τοῖς νοῦν
ἔχουσιν εἰς δέον γεγονέναι καὶ κατὰ καιρὸν ἡ
χρεία τῶν Οὐελιτρανῶν διά τε τὴν ἀπορίαν
κουφισμοῦ δεομένοις, καὶ τὴν στάσιν ἅμα σκε-
δάσειν ἤλπιζον, εἰ τὸ θορυβοῦν μάλιστα καὶ

such as Caecus and Claudius. And they do well thus to accustom men to regard neither blindness nor any other bodily misfortune as a reproach or a disgrace, but to answer to such names as though their own. This topic, however, would be more fittingly discussed elsewhere.

XII. The war was no sooner over than the popular leaders revived the internal dissensions, without any new cause of complaint, or just accusations, but making the very evils which had necessarily followed in the wake of their previous quarrels and disturbances a pretext for opposing the patricians. For the greater part of the land had been left unsown and untilled, and the war left no opportunity to arrange an importation of market supplies. There was, therefore, a great scarcity of food, and when the popular leaders saw that there were no market supplies, and that if there were, the people had no money to buy them, they assailed the rich with slanderous accusations of purposely arraying the famine against them, in a spirit of revenge.

Moreover, there came an embassy from the people of Velitrae, who offered to hand their city over to the Romans, and begged them to send out colonists for it. For a pestilential disease had assailed them, and wrought such death and destruction among their citizens that hardly the tenth part of the whole number was left. Accordingly, such of the Romans as were sensible thought that this request of the people of Velitrae had come at an advantageous and opportune time, since the scarcity of food made it needful to ease the city of its burdensome numbers; at the same time they also hoped to dissipate its sedition, if the most turbulent elements

145

συνεπηρμένον τοῖς δημαγωγοῖς ὥσπερ περίττωμα
τῆς πόλεως νοσερὸν καὶ ταραχῶδες ἀποκαθαρθείη.
4 τούτους τε δὴ καταλέγοντες εἰς τὴν ἀποικίαν ἐξέ-
πεμπον οἱ ὕπατοι, καὶ στρατείαν ἐπήγγελλον
ἑτέροις ἐπὶ τοὺς Οὐολούσκους, ἀσχολίαν τε τῶν
ἐμφυλίων μηχανώμενοι θορύβων, καὶ νομίζοντες
ἐν ὅπλοις καὶ στρατοπέδῳ καὶ κοινοῖς ἀγῶσιν
αὖθις γενομένους πλουσίους ὁμοῦ καὶ πένητας
καὶ δημοτικοὺς καὶ πατρικίους, ἡμερώτερον ἂν
διατεθῆναι πρὸς ἀλλήλους καὶ ἥδιον.

XIII. Ἐνίσταντο δὲ λοιπὸν οἱ περὶ Σικίννιον
καὶ Βροῦτον δημαγωγοί, βοῶντες ἔργον ὠμότατον
αὐτοὺς τῷ πραοτάτῳ τῶν ὀνομάτων ἀποικίαν
προσαγορεύσαντας ἀνθρώπους πένητας ὥσπερ
εἰς βάραθρον ὠθεῖν, ἐκπέμποντας εἰς πόλιν ἀέρος
τε νοσεροῦ καὶ νεκρῶν ἀτάφων γέμουσαν, ἀλ-
λοτρίῳ δαίμονι καὶ παλαμναίῳ συνοικιζομένους·
2 εἶτα ὥσπερ οὐκ ἀρκουμένους τοὺς μὲν ὑπὸ λιμοῦ
διολλύναι τῶν πολιτῶν, τοὺς δὲ λοιμῷ προσβάλλειν, ἔτι καὶ πόλεμον αὐθαίρετον ἐπάγειν, ὅπως
μηδὲν κακὸν ἀπῇ τῆς πόλεως, ὅτι δουλεύουσα
τοῖς πλουσίοις ἀπεῖπε. τοιούτων ἀναπιμπλά-
μενος λόγων ὁ δῆμος οὔτε τῷ καταλόγῳ προσῄει
τῶν ὑπάτων πρός τε τὴν ἀποικίαν διεβέβλητο.

3 Τῆς δὲ βουλῆς διαπορουμένης ὁ Μάρκιος, ἤδη
μεστὸς ὢν ὄγκου καὶ μέγας γεγονὼς τῷ φρονήματι καὶ θαυμαζόμενος ὑπὸ τῶν κρατίστων, φανε-

in it, and those which made most response to the
exciting appeals of the popular leaders, should be
purged away, like unhealthy and disturbing refuse
from the body. Such citizens, therefore, the consuls
selected as colonists and ordered them forth to
Velitrae. They also enlisted others in a campaign
against the Volscians, contriving thus that there
should be no leisure for intestine tumults, and
believing that when rich and poor alike, plebeians as
well as patricians, were once more united in military
service and in common struggles for the public good,
they would be more gently and pleasantly disposed
towards one another.

XIII. But the popular leaders, Sicinius and
Brutus, with their following, at once rose up in
opposition, crying out that the consuls were dis-
guising a most cruel deed under that most inoffensive
name, a colony, and were really pushing poor men
into a pit of death, as it were, by sending them forth
into a city which was full of deadly air and unburied
corpses, to be associated with a strange and
abominable deity ; and then, as if not satisfied with
destroying some of their fellow-citizens by famine,
and exposing others to pestilence, they proceeded
further to bring on a war of their own choosing, that
no evil might spare the city, which had but refused
to continue in servitude to the rich. With their
ears full of such speeches as these, the people would
neither answer the consular summons for enlistment,
nor look with any favour on the colony.[1]

The senate was in perplexity. But Marcius, who
was now full of importance, and had grown lofty in
spirit, and was looked upon with admiration by the

[1] Cf. Dionysius Hal. vii. 13.

ρὸς ἦν μάλιστα τοῖς δημαγωγοῖς ἀνθιστάμενος.
καὶ τὴν μὲν ἀποικίαν ἀπέστειλαν, ἐπιτιμίοις
μεγάλοις τοὺς λαχόντας ἐξελθεῖν ἀναγκάσαντες·
πρὸς δὲ τὴν στρατείαν παντάπασιν ἀπαγορευόν-
των, αὐτὸς ὁ Μάρκιος τούς τε πελάτας ἀναλαβὼν
καὶ τῶν ἄλλων ὅσους ἔπεισε, κατέδραμε τὴν
4 Ἀντιατῶν χώραν. καὶ πολὺν μὲν σῖτον εὑρών,
πολλῇ δὲ λείᾳ θρεμμάτων καὶ ἀνδραπόδων
περιτυχών, αὑτῷ μὲν οὐδὲν ἐξείλετο, τοὺς δὲ
στρατευσαμένους πολλὰ μὲν ἄγοντας ἔχων,
πολλὰ δὲ φέροντας, ἐπανῆλθεν εἰς τὴν Ῥώμην,
ὥστε τοὺς ἄλλους μεταμελομένους καὶ φθονήσαν-
τας τοῖς εὐπορήσασιν ἄχθεσθαι τῷ Μαρκίῳ καὶ
βαρύνεσθαι τὴν δόξαν αὐτοῦ καὶ τὴν δύναμιν, ὡς
ἐπὶ τὸν δῆμον αὐξομένην.

XIV. Ὀλίγου δὲ χρόνου μετῄει μὲν ὑπατείαν
ὁ Μάρκιος, ἐκάμπτοντο δὲ οἱ πολλοί, καὶ τὸν
δῆμον αἰδώς τις εἶχεν ἄνδρα καὶ γένει καὶ ἀρετῇ
πρῶτον ἀτιμάσαι καὶ καταβαλεῖν ἐπὶ τοσούτοις
καὶ τηλικούτοις εὐεργετήμασι. καὶ γὰρ ἔθος ἦν
τοῖς μετιοῦσι τὴν ἀρχὴν παρακαλεῖν καὶ δεξιοῦ-
σθαι τοὺς πολίτας ἐν ἱματίῳ κατιόντας εἰς τὴν
ἀγορὰν ἄνευ χιτῶνος, εἴτε μᾶλλον ἐκταπεινοῦντας 2
ἑαυτοὺς τῷ σχήματι πρὸς τὴν δέησιν, εἴτε δεικ-
νύντας οἷς ἦσαν ὠτειλαὶ προφανῆ τὰ σύμβολα
2 τῆς ἀνδρείας. οὐ γὰρ ὑποψίᾳ δήπου διανομῆς
ἀργυρίου καὶ δεκασμῶν ἄζωστον ἐβούλοντο προσιέναι καὶ ἀχίτωνα τοῖς πολίταις τὸν δεόμενον

---

[1] Cf. Dionysius Hal. vii. 19.

[2] There is nothing of this candidacy for the consulship in
Livy (ii. 34, 7-35). Marcius urges the senate to take advantage of the famine and exact from the plebeians a surrender

most powerful men of the city, openly took the lead
in resisting the popular leaders. The colony was
sent out, those that were chosen for it by lot being
compelled to go forth under severe penalties; and
when the people utterly refused military service,
Marcius himself mustered his clients and as many
others as he could persuade, and made an incursion
into the territory of Antium. There he found much
corn, and secured large booty in cattle and captives,
no part of which did he take out for himself, but
brought his followers back to Rome laden with
large spoils of every sort. The rest of the citizens
therefore repented themselves, envied their more
fortunate fellows, and were filled with hostility to
Marcius, not being able to endure the reputation and
power of the man, which was growing, as they
thought, to be detrimental to the people.[1]

XIV. But not long after, when Marcius stood for
the consulship,[2] the multitude relented, and the
people felt somewhat ashamed to slight and humble
a man who was foremost in birth and valour and had
performed so many and such great services. Now it
was the custom with those who stood for the office to
greet their fellow-citizens and solicit their votes,
descending into the forum in their toga, without a
tunic under it. This was either because they wished
the greater humility of their garb to favour their solicitations, or because they wished to display the tokens
of their bravery, in case they bore wounds. It was
certainly not owing to a suspicion of the dispensing
of money in bribery that the candidate for the votes

of their tribunate. This so exasperates the people that they
try Marcius *in absentia* and banish him, whereupon he goes
over to the Volsci. Plutarch's story (xiv.–xx.) agrees closely
with Dionysius Hal. vii. 21–64.

αὐτῶν· ὀψὲ γὰρ μετὰ πολὺν χρόνον ὠνὴ καὶ
πρᾶσις ἐπεισῆλθε, καὶ συνεμίγη ταῖς ἐκκλησιασ-
3 τικαῖς ψήφοις ἀργύριον. ἐκ δὲ τούτου καὶ δικασ-
τῶν θιγοῦσα καὶ στρατοπέδων ἡ δωροδοκία
περιέστησεν εἰς μοναρχίαν τὴν πόλιν, ἐξανδρα-
ποδισαμένη τὰ ὅπλα τοῖς χρήμασιν. οὐ γὰρ
κακῶς ἔοικεν εἰπεῖν ὁ εἰπὼν ὅτι πρῶτος κατέλυσε
τὸν δῆμον ὁ πρῶτος ἑστιάσας καὶ δεκάσας.
φαίνεται δὲ κρύφα καὶ κατὰ μικρὸν ὑπορρέον οὐκ
4 εὐθὺς ἔκδηλον ἐν Ῥώμῃ γενέσθαι τὸ κακόν. οὐ
γὰρ ἴσμεν ὅστις ἦν ὁ δεκάσας πρῶτος ἐν Ῥώμῃ
δῆμον ἢ δικαστήριον· Ἀθήνησι δὲ λέγεται πρῶτος ἀργύριον δοῦναι δικασταῖς Ἄνυτος ὁ Ἀνθεμίωνος, προδοσίας περὶ Πύλου κρινόμενος, ἐν τοῖς
Πελοποννησιακοῖς ἤδη τελευτῶσιν, ὁπηνίκα τὸ
χρυσοῦν ἔτι γένος καὶ ἀκήρατον ἐν Ῥώμῃ τὴν
ἀγορὰν κατεῖχεν.

XV. Ἀλλὰ τοῦ γε Μαρκίου πολλὰς ὑπο-
φαίνοντος ὠτειλὰς ἀπὸ πολλῶν ἀγώνων, ἐν οἷς
ἐπρώτευσεν ἑπτακαίδεκα ἔτη συνεχῶς στρατευό-
μενος, ἐδυσωποῦντο τὴν ἀρετήν, καὶ λόγον ἀλλήλοις ἐδίδοσαν ὡς ἐκεῖνον ἀποδείξοντες. ἐπεὶ δέ,
τῆς ἡμέρας ἐν ᾗ τὴν ψῆφον ἔδει φέρειν ἐνστάσης,
ὁ Μάρκιος εἰς ἀγορὰν ἐνέβαλε σοβαρῶς ὑπὸ τῆς
βουλῆς προπεμπόμενος, καὶ πάντες οἱ πατρίκιοι
περὶ αὐτὸν ἐγένοντο φανεροὶ πρὸς μηδὲν οὕτω
2 μηδέποτε σπουδάσαντες, ἐξέπεσον αὖθις οἱ πολλοὶ τῆς πρὸς αὐτὸν εὐνοίας, εἰς τὸ νεμεσᾶν καὶ

of the citizens was required to present himself before
them without a tunic and ungirt. For it was long
after this time that the buying and selling of votes
crept in and money became a feature of the elections.
But afterwards, bribery affected even courts and camps,
and converted the city into a monarchy, by making
armies the utter slaves of money. For it has been
well said that he first breaks down the power of the
people who first feasts and bribes them. But at
Rome the mischief seems to have crept in stealthily
and gradually, and not to have been noticed at once.
For we do not know who was the first man to bribe
her people or her courts of law; whereas at Athens,
Anytus, the son of Anthemion, is said to have been
the first man to give money to jurors, when he was
on trial for the treacherous failure to relieve Pylos,[1]
toward the close of the Peloponnesian war; a time
when the pure race of the golden age still possessed
the Roman forum.

XV. So when Marcius disclosed his many scars
from many contests, wherein he had been a foremost
soldier for seventeen years together, the people were
put out of countenance by his valour, and agreed
with one another to elect him. But when the day
for casting their votes came, and Marcius made a
pompous entry into the forum escorted by the senate,
and all the patricians about him were clearly more
bent on success than ever before, the multitude fell
away again from their good will towards him, and

---

[1] A stronghold on the western coast of Messenia, in
Peloponnesus. It was occupied and successfully defended by
the Athenians in 425 B.C. (Thuc. iv. 2–41). In 410, the
Lacedaemonians laid siege to its Messenian garrison, which
surrendered after an Athenian fleet had failed to relieve it
(Diodorus, xiii. 64, 5 f.).

PLUTARCH'S LIVES

φθονεῖν ὑποφερόμενοι. προσῆν δὲ τῷ πάθει
τούτῳ καὶ δέος, εἰ γένοιτο τῆς ἀρχῆς κύριος ἀνὴρ
ἀριστοκρατικὸς καὶ τοσοῦτον ἔχων ἐν τοῖς πατρι-
κίοις ἀξίωμα, μὴ παντάπασιν ἀφέλοιτο τοῦ δήμου
τὴν ἐλευθερίαν.

3   Οὕτω δὴ φρονήσαντες ἀπεψηφίσαντο τὸν
Μάρκιον. ὡς δ' ἀνηγορεύθησαν ἕτεροι, βαρέως
μὲν ἤνεγκεν ἡ βουλὴ δοκοῦσα προπεπηλακίσθαι
μᾶλλον ἑαυτὴν ἢ τὸν Μάρκιον, αὐτὸς δ' ἐκεῖνος
οὐ μετρίως ἔσχεν οὐδ' ἐπιεικῶς πρὸς τὸ συμβεβηκός, ἅτε δὴ πλεῖστα τῷ θυμοειδεῖ καὶ φιλο-
νείκῳ μέρει τῆς ψυχῆς, ὡς ἔχοντι μέγεθος καὶ
φρόνημα, κεχρημένος, τὸ δ' ἐμβριθὲς καὶ τὸ
πρᾷον, οὗ τὸ πλεῖστον ἀρετῇ πολιτικῇ μέτεστιν,
ἐγκεκραμένον οὐκ ἔχων ὑπὸ λόγου καὶ παιδείας,
4   οὐδὲ τὴν ἐρημίᾳ ξύνοικον, ὡς Πλάτων ἔλεγεν,
αὐθάδειαν εἰδὼς ὅτι δεῖ μάλιστα διαφεύγειν
ἐπιχειροῦντα πράγμασι κοινοῖς καὶ ἀνθρώποις
ὁμιλεῖν, καὶ γενέσθαι τῆς πολλὰ γελωμένης ὑπ'
ἐνίων ἀνεξικακίας ἐραστήν. ἀλλ' ἁπλοῦς τις ὢν
ἀεὶ καὶ ἀτενής, καὶ τὸ νικᾶν καὶ κρατεῖν ἁπάντων
πάντως ἀνδρείας ἔργον ἡγούμενος, οὐκ ἀσθενείας
καὶ μαλακίας, ἐκ τοῦ πονοῦντος καὶ πεπονθότος
μάλιστα τῆς ψυχῆς, ὥσπερ οἴδημα, τὸν θυμὸν
ἀναδιδούσης, ἀπῄει ταραχῆς μεστὸς ὢν καὶ
5   πικρίας πρὸς τὸν δῆμον. οἱ δ' ἐν ἡλικίᾳ τῶν
πατρικίων, ὅ τι περ ἦν ἐν τῇ πόλει μάλιστα
γαυρούμενον εὐγενείᾳ καὶ ἀνθοῦν, ἀεί τε θαυμαστῶς ἐσπουδάκεσαν περὶ τὸν ἄνδρα, καὶ τότε
προσκείμενοι καὶ παρόντες οὐκ ἐπ' ἀγαθῷ τὸν
θυμὸν ἐξερρίπιζον αὐτοῦ τῷ συναγανακτεῖν καὶ

drifted into feelings of resentment and envy. These feelings were reinforced by their fear that if an aristocrat, who had such weight with the patricians, should become supreme in the government, he might altogether deprive the people of their liberties.

So, being in such a state of mind, they rejected Marcius and others were proclaimed elected. The senators were indignant, thinking the insult directed rather at them than at Marcius, and he himself could not treat the occurrence with restraint or forbearance. He had indulged the passionate and contentious side of his nature, with the idea that there was something great and exalted in this, and had not been imbued, under the influence of reason and discipline, with that gravity and mildness which are the chief virtues of a statesman. Nor did he know that one who undertakes public business must avoid above all things that self-will which, as Plato says,[1] is the "companion of solitude"; must mingle with men, and be a lover of that submissiveness to injury which some people ridicule so much. But since he was ever a straightforward man and obstinate, and since he thought that conquest and mastery in all things and at all times was the prerogative of bravery, rather than of effeminate weakness (which breaks out in anger, like a swelling sore, from the troubled and wounded spirit), he went away full of indignation and bitterness towards the people. The younger patricians, too, that element in the city which made most vaunt of noble birth and was most showy, had always been amazingly devoted to the man, and, adhering to him now, when their presence did him no good, fanned his anger by their sympa-

[1] In a letter to Dio (*Epist.* iv. *ad fin.*).

συναλγεῖν. ἦν γὰρ ἡγεμὼν αὐτοῖς καὶ διδάσκαλος
εὐμενὴς τῶν πολεμικῶν ἐν ταῖς στρατείαις, καὶ
ζῆλον ἀρετῆς ἄνευ φθόνου πρὸς ἀλλήλους γαυ-
ρῶσαι τοὺς κατορθοῦντας.

XVI. Ἐν τούτῳ δὲ σῖτος ἧκεν εἰς Ῥώμην,
πολὺς μὲν ὠνητὸς ἐξ Ἰταλίας, οὐκ ἐλάττων δὲ
δωρητὸς ἐκ Συρακουσῶν, Γέλωνος τοῦ τυράννου
πέμψαντος· ὥστε τοὺς πλείστους ἐν ἐλπίσι
γενέσθαι χρησταῖς, ἅμα τῆς ἀπορίας καὶ τῆς
διαφορᾶς τὴν πόλιν ἀπαλλαγήσεσθαι προσδο-
κῶντας. εὐθὺς οὖν βουλῆς ἀθροισθείσης περι-
χυθεὶς ὁ δῆμος ἔξωθεν ἐκαραδόκει τὸ τέλος,
ἐλπίζων ἀγορᾷ τε χρήσεσθαι φιλανθρώπῳ καὶ
προῖκα τὰς δωρεὰς νεμήσεσθαι. καὶ γὰρ ἔνδον
2 ἦσαν οἱ ταῦτα τὴν βουλὴν πείθοντες. ὁ μέντοι
Μάρκιος ἀναστὰς σφόδρα καθήψατο τῶν χαριζομένων τοῖς πολλοῖς, δημαγωγοὺς καὶ προδότας
ἀποκαλῶν τῆς ἀριστοκρατίας καὶ σπέρματα
πονηρὰ θρασύτητος καὶ ὕβρεως εἰς ὄχλον
ἀφειμένα τρέφοντας καθ᾽ αὑτῶν, ἃ καλῶς μὲν
εἶχε μὴ περιϊδεῖν ἐν ἀρχῇ φυόμενα μηδ᾽ ἰσχυρὸν
ἀρχῇ τηλικαύτῃ ποιῆσαι τὸν δῆμον, ἤδη δὲ καὶ
φοβερὸν εἶναι τῷ πάντα βουλομένοις αὐτοῖς
ὑπάρχειν καὶ μηδὲν ἄκοντας βιάζεσθαι, μηδὲ
πείθεσθαι τοῖς ὑπάτοις, ἀλλ᾽ ἀναρχίας ἔχοντας
3 ἡγεμόνας ἰδίους ἄρχοντας προσαγορεύειν. ἐπιδόσεις μὲν οὖν καὶ διανομάς, ὥσπερ Ἑλλήνων οἱ
κράτιστα δημοκρατούμενοι, καθέξεσθαι ψηφιζο-
μένους ἔφη παντελῶς εἰς κοινὸν ὄλεθρον τὴν

thetic vexation and sorrow. For he was their leader and willing teacher of the art of war in their campaigns, and inspired them in their victories with a zeal for valour, which had no tinge of mutual jealousy.

XVI. In the meantime grain came to Rome, a great part of it bought in Italy, but an equal amount sent as a present from Syracuse, where Gelo was tyrant. Most of the people were consequently in great hope, expecting that the city would be delivered both from its scarcity and its discord. The senate, accordingly, was convened at once, and the people, flocking about the senate-house, awaited the result of its deliberations. They expected that the market-price for grain would now be moderate, and that what had been sent as a present would be distributed gratis. For there were some in the senate who so advised that body. But Marcius rose in his place and vehemently attacked those who favoured the multitude, calling them demagogues and betrayers of the aristocracy, and declaring that they were nourishing, to their own harm, the evil seeds of boldness and insolence which had been sown among the rabble; these they should have choked when they first sprang up, and not have strengthened the people by such a powerful magistracy as the tribunate. But now their body was formidable, because it got everything that it desired, allowed no constraint upon its will, and refused to obey the consuls, but had their own leaders in anarchy, whom they styled their rulers. To sit there, moreover, voting such a people largesses and supplies, like those Greeks where democracy is most extreme, he said was nothing more nor less than maintaining them in their disobedience, to the common destruc-

ἀπείθειαν αὐτῶν ἐφοδιάζειν. "Οὐ γὰρ χάριν γε
δήπου φήσουσιν ἀπολαμβάνειν τῶν στρατειῶν ἃς
ἐγκατέλιπον, καὶ τῶν ἀποστάσεων αἷς προήκαντο
τὴν πατρίδα, καὶ τῶν διαβολῶν ἃς ἐδέξαντο κατὰ
τῆς βουλῆς· ἀλλ᾿ ὑφιεμένους διὰ φόβον καὶ
κολακεύοντας ὑμᾶς ταῦτα διδόναι καὶ συγχωρεῖν
ἐλπίσαντες, οὐδὲν ἕξουσι πέρας ἀπειθείας, οὐδὲ
4 παύσονται διαφερόμενοι καὶ στασιάζοντες. ὥστε
τοῦτο μέν ἐστι κομιδῇ μανικόν· εἰ δὲ σωφρονοῦ-
μεν, ἀφαιρησόμεθα τὴν δημαρχίαν αὐτῶν, ἀναίρεσιν οὖσαν ὑπατείας καὶ διάστασιν τῆς πόλεως,
οὐκέτι μιᾶς, ὡς πρότερον, οὔσης, ἀλλὰ δεδεγμένης
τομὴν μηδέποτε συμφῦναι μηδ᾿ ὁμοφρονῆσαι μηδὲ
παύσασθαι νοσοῦντας ἡμᾶς καὶ ταραττομένους ὑπ᾿
ἀλλήλων ἐάσουσαν."

XVII. Πολλὰ τοιαῦτα λέγων ὁ Μάρκιος ὑπερ-
φυῶς εἶχε τοὺς νέους συνενθουσιῶντας αὐτῷ καὶ
τοὺς πλουσίους ὀλίγου δεῖν ἅπαντας, μόνον
ἐκεῖνον ἄνδρα τὴν πόλιν ἔχειν ἀήττητον καὶ
ἀκολάκευτον βοῶντας. ἔνιοι δὲ τῶν πρεσβυτέρων ἠναντιοῦντο, ὑφορώμενοι τὸ ἀποβησόμενον.
ἀπέβη δὲ χρηστὸν οὐδέν. οἱ γὰρ δήμαρχοι
παρόντες, ὡς ᾔσθοντο τῇ γνώμῃ κρατοῦντα τὸν
Μάρκιον, ἐξέδραμον εἰς τὸν ὄχλον μετὰ βοῆς
παρακελευόμενοι συνίστασθαι καὶ βοηθεῖν αὐτοῖς
2 τοὺς πολλούς. ἐκκλησίας δὲ θορυβώδους γενομένης, καὶ τῶν λόγων οὓς ὁ Μάρκιος εἶπεν ἀναγο-
ρευθέντων, ὀλίγον ἐδέησεν ἐμπεσεῖν ὑπ᾿ ὀργῆς
φερόμενος εἰς τὴν βουλὴν ὁ δῆμος· οἱ δὲ δήμαρχοι
τοῦ Μαρκίου τὴν αἰτίαν ἐποιοῦντο, καὶ πέμπον-

tion of all. "For they surely will not say that they are getting these as a grateful return for the military services which they omitted, and the secessions by which they renounced their country, and the calumnies against the senate which they have countenanced. They will rather be confident that your fears drive you to subserviency and flattery when you make them these gifts and concessions, and will set no limit to their disobedience, nor cease from their quarrels and seditions. Such action on our part would therefore be sheer madness; but if we are wise, we shall take their tribunate away from them, for it makes the consulship null and void, and divides the city. This is no longer one, as before, but has been cut in two, so that we can never grow together again, or be of one mind, or cease afflicting and confounding one another."

XVII. With many such words as these Marcius was beyond measure successful in filling the younger senators, and almost all the wealthy ones, with his own fierce enthusiasm, and they cried out that he was the only man in the city who disdained submission and flattery. But some of the older senators opposed him, suspecting the outcome. And the outcome was wholly bad. For the tribunes were present, and when they saw that the proposal of Marcius was likely to prevail, they ran out among the crowd with loud cries, calling upon the plebeians to rally to their help. Then there was a stormy session of the assembly, and when the speech of Marcius was reported to it, the people were carried away with fury and almost burst in upon the senate. But the tribunes made their formal denunciation of Marcius, and summoned him by messenger to come before them and

τες ἐκάλουν αὐτὸν ἀπολογησόμενον. ὡς δὲ
πρὸς ὕβριν τοὺς πεμφθέντας ἐξήλασεν ὑπηρέτας,
αὐτοὶ μετὰ τῶν ἀγορανόμων ἧκον ἄξοντες βίᾳ
τὸν ἄνδρα, καὶ τοῦ σώματος ἐπελαμβάνοντο.
συστάντες δ' οἱ πατρίκιοι τοὺς μὲν δημάρχους
ἀπετρίψαντο, τοῖς δ' ἀγορανόμοις καὶ πληγὰς
ἐνέβαλον.

3 Τότε μὲν οὖν ἑσπέρα καταλαβοῦσα τὴν ταρα-
χὴν διέλυσεν· ἅμα δ' ἡμέρᾳ τὸν δῆμον ἐξηγριω-
μένον ὁρῶντες οἱ ὕπατοι καὶ συντρέχοντα πανταχόθεν εἰς τὴν ἀγορὰν ἔδεισαν ὑπὲρ τῆς πόλεως,
καὶ τὴν βουλὴν ἀθροίσαντες ἐκέλευον σκοπεῖν
ὅπως ἐπιεικέσι λόγοις καὶ δόγμασι χρηστοῖς
πραΰνωσι καὶ καταστήσωσι τοὺς πολλούς, ὡς οὐ
φιλοτιμίας οὖσαν ὥραν, οὐδ' ὑπὲρ δόξης ἅμιλλαν,
εἰ σωφρονοῦσιν, ἀλλὰ καιρὸν ἐπισφαλῆ καὶ ὀξύν,
εὐγνώμονος πολιτείας καὶ φιλανθρώπου δεόμενον.
4 εἰξάντων δὲ τῶν πλείστων προελθόντες ὡς ἐνῆν
μάλιστα τῷ δήμῳ διελέγοντο καὶ κατεπράυνον,
ἀπολυόμενοί τε τὰς διαβολὰς ἐπιεικῶς καὶ τῷ
νουθετοῦντι καὶ δάκνοντι μετρίως χρώμενοι, περὶ
δὲ τιμῆς ὠνίων καὶ ἀγορᾶς οὐδὲν διοίσεσθαι πρὸς
αὐτοὺς φάσκοντες.

XVIII. Ὡς οὖν ἐνεδίδου τὸ πολὺ τοῦ δήμου 22
καὶ φανερὸν ἦν τῷ κοσμίως καὶ σωφρόνως
ἀκούειν ἀγόμενον καὶ κηλούμενον, ἀνέστησαν οἱ
δήμαρχοι, τῇ μὲν βουλῇ σωφρονούσῃ τὸν δῆμον
ἀνθυπείξειν ὅσα καλῶς ἔχει φάσκοντες, τὸν δὲ
Μάρκιον ἀπολογεῖσθαι κελεύοντες, εἰ μή φησιν

make his defence. And when he insolently drove away the officers who brought their message, they went themselves, attended by the aediles, to bring him by force, and tried to lay hands upon his person. But the patricians, banding together, drove the tribunes away, and actually beat the aediles.

By this time, then, evening had fallen, which put an end to the tumult; but as soon as it was day, the exasperated people came running together from all quarters into the forum. When the consuls saw this, they were alarmed for the city, and convening the senate, urged them to consider how, by reasonable proposals and suitable resolutions, they might soothe and pacify the multitude, since it was not a time for ambitious rivalry, nor would they be wise in contending for their dignity, but the crisis was severe and critical, and demanded measures that were considerate and humane. The majority of the senate acceding to these views, the consuls went out and reasoned with the people as well as they could, and tried to mollify them, answering their accusations in a reasonable manner, and making only a moderate use of admonition and rebuke; as regarded the price of provisions and market supplies, they declared there should be no difference between them.

XVIII. Accordingly, the greater part of the people showed signs of relenting, and it was evident, from their decorous and sober attention, that they were on the way to be controlled and won over. Then the tribunes rose and declared that since the senate was now acting soberly, the people in their turn would make such concessions as were fair and honourable. They insisted, however, that Marcius should make answer to the following charges: Could he deny that

ἐπὶ συγχύσει τῆς πολιτείας καὶ καταλύσει τοῦ
δήμου τήν τε βουλὴν παροξύνειν καὶ καλούμενος
2 ὑπ' αὐτῶν ἀπειθῆσαι, τέλος δὲ τοὺς ἀγορανόμους
τύπτων ἐν ἀγορᾷ καὶ προπηλακίζων ἐμφύλιον,
ὅσον ἐπ' αὐτῷ, πόλεμον ἐξεργάσασθαι καὶ προαγαγεῖν εἰς ὅπλα τοὺς πολίτας. ἔλεγον δὲ ταῦτα
βουλόμενοι τὸν Μάρκιον ἢ ταπεινὸν ἀποδεῖξαι,
παρὰ φύσιν ὑφέντα τὸ φρόνημα καὶ θεραπεύοντα
τὸν δῆμον, ἢ τῇ φύσει χρώμενον ἀνήκεστον
ἀπεργάσασθαι τὴν πρὸς αὐτὸν ὀργήν· ὃ μᾶλλον
ἤλπιζον, ὀρθῶς στοχαζόμενοι τοῦ ἀνδρός.

3 Ἔστη μὲν γὰρ ὡς ἀπολογησόμενος, καὶ παρέσχεν αὐτῷ σιωπὴν καὶ ἡσυχίαν ὁ δῆμος· ὡς δ'
ἤρξατο πρὸς τοὺς ἀνθρώπους δεητικόν τινα λόγον
προσδεχομένους οὐ μόνον ἐπαχθεῖ παρρησίᾳ χρῆσθαι καὶ πλείονι κατηγορίᾳ τῆς παρρησίας, ἀλλὰ
καὶ τόνῳ φωνῆς καὶ διαθέσει προσώπου τὴν ἐγγὺς
ὑπεροψίας καὶ ὀλιγωρίας ἀφοβίαν ἐπιδεικνύμενος,
4 ὁ μὲν δῆμος ἐξετραχύνθη καὶ φανερὸς ἦν δυσανασχετῶν καὶ βαρυνόμενος τοῖς λεγομένοις, τῶν δὲ
δημάρχων ὁ θρασύτατος Σικίννιος μικρὰ τοῖς
συνάρχουσι διαλεχθείς, εἶτ' εἰς μέσον ἀναγορεύσας
ὡς θάνατος ὑπὸ τῶν δημάρχων τοῦ Μαρκίου
κατέγνωσται, προσέταξε τοῖς ἀγορανόμοις ἀναγα-
γόντας αὐτὸν ἐπὶ τὴν ἄκραν εὐθὺς ὦσαι κατὰ
5 τῆς ὑποκειμένης φάραγγος. ἁπτομένων δὲ τῶν
ἀγορανόμων τοῦ σώματος ἔδοξε μὲν καὶ τῶν
δημοτῶν πολλοῖς φρικτὸν εἶναι τὸ γιγνόμενον καὶ
ὑπερήφανον, οἱ δὲ πατρίκιοι παντάπασιν ἐκστάντες

he had instigated the senate to violate the constitution and abrogate the powers of the people? When summoned to appear before them, had he not refused? And finally, by insulting and beating the aediles in the forum, had he not done all in his power to incite the citizens to arms and bring about a civil war? They made this demand with a desire either that Marcius should be publicly humiliated, if, contrary to his nature, he curbed his haughty spirit and sued for the favour of the people; or, if he yielded to his natural promptings, that he should do something which would justify their wrath against him and make it implacable. The latter was what they the rather expected, and they rightly estimated the man's character.

For he came and stood before them as one who would defend himself, and the people were quiet and silent in his presence. But when, instead of the more or less deprecatory language expected by his audience, he began not only to employ an offensive boldness of speech, which at last became actual denunciation, but also to show, by the tone of his voice and the cast of his countenance, that his fearlessness was not far removed from disdain and contempt, then the people was exasperated, and gave evident signs that his words roused their impatience and indignation. Upon this, Sicinius, the boldest of the tribunes, after a brief conference with his colleagues, made formal proclamation that Marcius was condemned to death by the tribunes of the people, and ordered the aediles to take him up to the Tarpeian rock at once, and cast him down the cliff below. But when the aediles laid hold of his person, it seemed, even to many of the plebeians, a horrible and monstrous act; the patricians,

161

καὶ περιπαθήσαντες ὥρμησαν ἀπὸ κραυγῆς βοηθεῖν, οἱ δὲ καὶ χερσὶ τοὺς ἐπιλαμβανομένους
ἀνείργοντες καὶ καταμιγνύντες ἑαυτοῖς τὸν Μάρ-
6 κιον· ἔνιοι δὲ καὶ τὰς χεῖρας ὀρέγοντες ἐδέοντο
τῶν πολλῶν, ἐπειδὴ λόγου τε καὶ φωνῆς οὐδὲν
ἔργον ἦν ἐν ἀκοσμίᾳ τοσαύτῃ καὶ θορύβοις, ἄχρι
οὗ συμφρονήσαντες οἱ φίλοι καὶ οἰκεῖοι τῶν
δημάρχων ὡς ἄνευ φόνου πολλοῦ τῶν πατρικίων
οὐκ ἔστιν ἐξαγαγεῖν οὐδὲ κολάσαι τὸν Μάρκιον,
ἔπεισαν αὐτοὺς ἀφελεῖν τῆς τιμωρίας τὸ ἀλλόκοτον
καὶ βαρύ, μὴ βίᾳ μηδ᾽ ἄκριτον ἀποκτιννύντας,
ἀλλὰ τῷ δήμῳ ψῆφον ἐπενεγκεῖν ἀποδόντας.
7 ἐκ τούτου καταστὰς ὁ Σικίννιος ἠρώτα τοὺς
πατρικίους τί βουλόμενοι τὸν Μάρκιον ἀφαιροῦν-
ται τοῦ δήμου βουλομένου κολάζειν. ἐκείνων δὲ
πάλιν ἀντερωτώντων· "Τί μὲν οὖν διανοεῖσθε
καὶ τί βούλεσθε ὑμεῖς, ἄνδρα Ῥωμαίων ἐν τοῖς
ἀρίστοις ἄνευ κρίσεως ἐπὶ τιμωρίαν ὠμὴν καὶ
8 παράνομον οὕτως ἄγοντες;" "'Ἀλλὰ ταύτην μέν,"
εἶπεν ὁ Σικίννιος, "ὑμεῖς μὴ ποιεῖσθε πρόφασιν
διαφορᾶς καὶ στάσεως πρὸς τὸν δῆμον· ὃ γὰρ
ἀξιοῦτε, δίδωσιν ὑμῖν, κριθῆναι τὸν ἄνδρα. σοὶ
δέ, Μάρκιε, προαγορεύομεν εἰς τρίτην ἀγορὰν
παρεῖναι καὶ πείθειν τοὺς πολίτας, εἰ μηδὲν ἀδικεῖς,
ὡς ψήφῳ κρινοῦντας."

XIX. Τότε μὲν οὖν ἠγάπησαν οἱ πατρίκιοι
τὴν διάλυσιν, καὶ τὸν Μάρκιον ἀσμένως ἔχοντες
ἀπῆλθον. ἐν δὲ τῷ μεταξὺ χρόνῳ τῆς τρίτης
ἀγορᾶς (ἀγορὰς δὲ ποιοῦσι Ῥωμαῖοι δι᾽ ἡμέρας
ἐνάτης, νουνδίνας καλοῦντες) ἐλπίδα μὲν αὐτοῖς
παρέσχε διακρούσεως στρατεία γενομένη πρὸς

moreover, utterly beside themselves, distressed and horror stricken, rushed with loud cries to his aid. Some of them actually pushed away the officers making the arrest, and got Marcius among themselves; some stretched out their hands in supplication of the multitude, since words and cries were of no avail amid such disorder and confusion. At last the friends and kindred of the tribunes, perceiving that it was impossible, without slaying many patricians, to lead Marcius away and punish him, persuaded them to remit what was unusual and oppressive in his sentence, not to use violence and put him to death without a trial, but to surrender him and refer his case to the people. Then Sicinius, becoming calm, asked the patricians what they meant by taking Marcius away from the people when it wished to punish him. But the patricians asked in their turn: "What then is your purpose, and what do ye mean, by thus dragging one of the foremost men of Rome, without a trial, to a savage and illegal punishment?" "Well then," said Sicinius, "ye shall not have any such excuse for factious quarrel with the people; for they grant your demand that the man have a trial. And we cite thee, Marcius, to appear before the citizens on the third market-day ensuing, and convince them, if you can, of your innocence, assured that they will decide your case by vote."

XIX. For the time being, then, the patricians were satisfied with this truce, and went away in glad possession of Marcius. But in the time which intervened before the third market-day (for the Romans hold their markets every ninth day, calling them, therefore, "nundinae"), a campaign was undertaken against the city of Antium, which led them to hope

Ἀντιάτας, ὡς μῆκος ἔξουσα καὶ χρόνον ἐν ᾧ
χειροήθης ὁ δῆμος ἔσται, τῆς ὀργῆς ἀπομαραν-
θείσης ἢ παντελῶς ἐκπεσούσης δι' ἀσχολίαν καὶ
2 πόλεμον· ἔπειτα δέ, ὡς ταχὺ διαλυσάμενοι πρὸς
τοὺς Ἀντιάτας ἐπανῆλθον, ἐγίνοντο σύνοδοι τῶν
πατρικίων πολλάκις, δεδιότων καὶ σκοπούντων
ὅπως τόν τε Μάρκιον οὐ προήσονται τόν τε δῆμον
αὖθις οὐ παρέξουσιν ἐκταράττειν τοῖς δημαγωγοῖς. Ἄππιος μὲν οὖν Κλαύδιος αἰτίαν ἔχων   2⋮
ἐν τοῖς μάλιστα μισόδημος εἶναι διεμαρτύρετο,
λέγων τήν τε βουλὴν αὐτοὺς ἀναιρήσειν καὶ
προήσεσθαι παντάπασι τὴν πολιτείαν, εἰ κύριον
τῆς ψήφου κατὰ τῶν πατρικίων δέξονται γενό-
3 μενον τὸν δῆμον· οἱ δὲ πρεσβύτατοι καὶ δημοτι-
κώτατοι τοὐναντίον ἠξίουν οὐ χαλεπὸν οὐδὲ
βαρύν, ἀλλὰ πρᾷον καὶ φιλάνθρωπον ὑπὸ τῆς
ἐξουσίας ἔσεσθαι τὸν δῆμον· οὐ γὰρ καταφρο-
νοῦντι τῆς βουλῆς, ἀλλ' οἰομένῳ καταφρονεῖσθαι
τιμὴν καὶ παραμυθίαν γενήσεσθαι τὴν κρίσιν,
ὥσθ' ἅμα τὴν ψῆφον λαβόντας ἀποθήσεσθαι τὴν
ὀργήν.

XX. Ὁρῶν οὖν ὁ Μάρκιος εὐνοίᾳ μὲν αὑτοῦ,
φόβῳ δὲ τοῦ δήμου τὴν σύγκλητον ἀπορουμένην,
ἠρώτησε τοὺς δημάρχους τί κατηγοροῦσιν αὐτοῦ
καὶ περὶ τίνος κριθησόμενον ἐπὶ τὸν δῆμον ἐξ-
άγουσιν. εἰπόντων δ' ἐκείνων ὅτι τυραννίς ἐστι τὸ
ἔγκλημα καὶ τυραννεῖν διανοούμενον ἀποδεί-
ξουσιν αὐτόν, οὕτως ἐξαναστὰς αὐτὸς ἔφη πρὸς

that the issue might be avoided altogether. The campaign would last long enough, they thought, for the people to become tractable, after their rage had languished or altogether disappeared by reason of their occupation with the war. But presently, when the citizens returned home after a speedy settlement of their dispute with Antium, the patricians were in frequent conclave, being full of fear, and deliberating how they might not surrender Marcius, and yet prevent the popular leaders from throwing the people again into tumult and disorder. Appius Claudius, indeed, who was counted among those most hostile to the claims of the people, said with all solemnity that the senate would destroy itself and utterly betray the government of the city, if it should suffer the people to wield their vote in judgement on the patricians. But the oldest senators, and those most inclined to favour the people, maintained on the contrary that it would not be rendered harsh or severe by its exercise of this power, but mild and humane ; for since it did not despise the senate, but rather thought itself despised by that body, the prerogative of trying a senator would be a solace to its feelings and a mark of honour, so that as soon as it proceeded to vote it would lay aside its wrath.

XX. Marcius, therefore, seeing that the senate was in suspense between its kindly feelings towards him and its fear of the people, asked the tribunes what the accusations against him were, and on what charge he would be tried if they led him before the people. They replied that the charge against him was usurpation, and that they would prove him guilty of planning a usurpation of the government. Thereupon he rose of his own accord and said he was going

τὸν δῆμον ἤδη βαδίζειν ἀπολογησόμενος καὶ
μηδένα τρόπον κρίσεως μηδέ, ἂν ἁλῷ, κολάσεως παραιτεῖσθαι· " Μόνον ὅπως," ἔφη,
"τοῦτο κατηγορήσητε καὶ μὴ ψεύσησθε τὴν
βουλήν." ὡς δ᾽ ὡμολόγησαν, ἐπὶ τούτοις ἡ
κρίσις ἐγίνετο.

2 Συνελθόντος δὲ τοῦ δήμου πρῶτον μὲν οὐ κατὰ
λόχους, ἀλλὰ κατὰ φυλὰς ἐβιάζοντο γίνεσθαι
τὴν ψηφοφορίαν, τῶν εὐπόρων καὶ γνωρίμων
καὶ στρατευομένων τὸν ἄπορον καὶ πολυπράγμονα
καὶ τοῦ καλοῦ φροντίζοντα μηδὲν ὄχλον ἐπί-
3 προσθεν ταῖς ψήφοις ποιοῦντες. ἔπειτα τὴν
τυραννίδος ἀφέντες αἰτίαν ἀναπόδεικτον οὖσαν,
ἐκείνων πάλιν ἐμέμνηντο τῶν λόγων οὓς ὁ Μάρκιος
πρότερον εἶπεν ἐν τῇ βουλῇ, κωλύων μὲν ἐπευω-
νίσαι τὴν ἀγοράν, ἀφελέσθαι δὲ τὴν δημαρχίαν
τοῦ δήμου κελεύων. καινὸν δὲ κατηγόρησαν
αὐτοῦ κατηγόρημα τὴν διανομὴν τῶν λαφύρων, ἃ
λαβὼν ἐκ τῆς Ἀντιατῶν χώρας οὐκ ἀνήνεγκεν εἰς
τὸ δημόσιον, ἀλλὰ διένειμε τοῖς μεθ᾽ αὑτοῦ στρα-
4 τευομένοις· ὑφ᾽ οὗ δὴ καὶ μάλιστα λέγεται
διαταραχθῆναι τὸν Μάρκιον. οὐ γὰρ προσεδόκησεν οὐδ᾽ εὐπόρησε πρὸς τὸν ὄχλον ἐκ τοῦ
παραυτίκα λόγων πιθανῶν, ἀλλ᾽ ἐπαινοῦντι τοὺς
στρατευσαμένους ἐθορύβησαν αὐτῷ πλείονες ὄντες
οἱ μὴ στρατευσάμενοι. τέλος δ᾽ οὖν ταῖς φυλαῖς

at once before the people to make his defence, and would deprecate no manner of trial, nor, should he be found guilty, any form of punishment; " Only," said he, " see that ye confine yourselves to the charge mentioned, and do not play false with the senate." The tribunes agreed to this, and on these terms the trial was held.

But when the people were come together, in the first place, the tribunes insisted that the votes be cast not by centuries,[1] but by tribes, thus making the indigent and officious rabble, which had no thought of honour, superior in voting power to the wealthy and well known citizens of the military class. In the second place, abandoning the charge of usurpation, which could not be proven, they dwelt again upon the speech which Marcius had previously made in the senate, when he protested against the lowering of the market-price of grain, and urged them to take the tribunate away from the people. They also added a fresh charge against him, namely, his distribution of the spoils which he had taken from the country of Antium; these, they said, he had not turned into the public treasury, but had distributed them among those who made the campaign with him. By this accusation Marcius is said to have been more disturbed than by all the rest. For he had not expected it, and was not ready at once with an answer which would satisfy the people, but began to praise those who had made the campaign, whereupon he was clamorously interrupted by those who had not made it, and they were the more numerous. In the end, therefore, the vote was taken

---

[1] Out of the 193 centuries, the richest class alone had 98, against 95 of all the other five classes put together.

τῆς ψήφου δοθείσης αἱ καθαιροῦσαι τρεῖς ἐγένοντο. ἦν δὲ τίμημα τῆς καταδίκης ἀΐδιος φυγή.
5 μετὰ δὲ τὴν ἀναγόρευσιν ὁ μὲν δῆμος οὐδέποτε
νικήσας μάχῃ πολεμίους τοσοῦτον ἐφρόνησεν
ὅσον τότε φρονῶν καὶ γεγηθὼς ἀπῄει, τὴν δὲ
βουλὴν ἄχος ἔσχε καὶ κατήφεια δεινή, μεταμελο-
μένην καὶ δυσφοροῦσαν ἐπὶ τῷ μὴ πάντα ποιῆσαι
καὶ παθεῖν πρότερον ἢ περιιδεῖν ὑβρίσαντα καὶ
χρησάμενον ἐξουσίᾳ τοσαύτῃ τὸν δῆμον. οὐδὲν δ'
ἔδει τότε πρὸς διάγνωσιν ἐσθῆτος ἢ παρασήμων
ἑτέρων, ἀλλ' εὐθὺς ἦν δῆλος ὅτι δημότης ὁ χαί-
ρων καὶ ὁ δυσφορῶν ὅτι πατρίκιος.

XXI. Πλὴν αὐτὸς ὁ Μάρκιος, ἀνέκπληκτος καὶ
ἀταπείνωτος, καὶ σχήματι καὶ βαδίσματι καὶ
προσώπῳ καθεστηκώς, ἐν πᾶσι τοῖς ἄλλοις ἐφαίνετο πεπονθόσιν ἀσυμπαθὴς ἑαυτῷ μόνος, οὐχ
ὑπὸ λογισμοῦ καὶ πρᾳότητος, οὐδὲ τῷ φέρειν
μετρίως τὸ συμβεβηκός, ἀλλ' ἐμπαθὴς ὢν ὑπ'
ὀργῆς καὶ βαρυφροσύνης, ὅπερ ἀγνοοῦσιν οἱ
2 πολλοὶ λύπην οὖσαν. ὅταν γὰρ εἰς θυμὸν μετα-
βάλῃ, καθάπερ ἐκπυρωθεῖσα τὸ ταπεινὸν ἀπο-
βάλλει καὶ ἀργόν· ᾗ καὶ δοκεῖ δραστικὸς ὁ
θυμούμενος ὡς θερμὸς ὁ πυρέττων, οἷον ἐν
σφυγμῷ καὶ διατάσει καὶ ὄγκῳ γενομένης τῆς
ψυχῆς. ἐδήλωσε δὲ τοῖς ἔργοις αὐτίκα μάλα τὴν
διάθεσιν ταύτην ὁ Μάρκιος.

3 Εἰσελθὼν γὰρ οἴκαδε, καὶ τὴν μητέρα καὶ τὴν
γυναῖκα μετὰ κλαυθμοῦ καὶ βοῆς ὀλοφυρομένας
ἀσπασάμενος καὶ κελεύσας μετρίως φέρειν τὸ

by tribes, and a majority of three condemned him.[1]
The penalty assigned was perpetual banishment.
After the result was announced, the people went off
in greater elation and delight than they had ever
shown for any victory in battle over their enemies;
but the senate was in distress and dire dejection,
repenting now and vexed to the soul that they had
not done and suffered all things rather than allow
the people to insult them in the exercise of such
great powers. And there was no need now of dress
or other marks of distinction in telling one class from
another, but it was clear at once that he who rejoiced
was a plebeian, and he who was vexed, a patrician.

XXI. Albeit Marcius himself, who was neither
daunted nor humbled, but in mien, port, and countenance fully composed, seemed the only man among
all the distressed patricians who was not touched by
his evil plight. And this was not due to calculation,
or gentleness, or to a calm endurance of his fate, but
he was stirred by rage and deep resentment, and
this, although the many know it not, is pain. For
when pain is transmuted into anger, it is consumed,
as it were, by its flames, and casts off its own humility
and sloth. Wherefore the angry man makes a show
of activity, as he who has a fever is hot, his spirit
being, so to speak, afflicted with throbbing, disten-
tion, and inflation. And that such was his condition,
Marcius showed right quickly by his conduct.

He went home, where his mother and his wife met
him with wailings and loud lamentations, and after
embracing them and bidding them to bear with
equanimity the fate that had come upon them, he

---

[1] Dionysius Hal. (vii. 64) says that nine of the twenty-one
tribes voted to acquit Marcius.

συμβεβηκός, εὐθὺς ἀπιὼν ἐβάδιζεν ἐπὶ τὰς πύλας.
ἐκεῖ δὲ τῶν πατρικίων ὁμοῦ πάντων προπεμ-
πόντων αὐτὸν οὔτε τι λαβὼν οὔτε τινὸς δεηθεὶς
ἀπηλλάττετο, τρεῖς ἢ τέτταρας πελάτας ἔχων
4 περὶ αὐτόν. ἡμέρας δ᾽ ὀλίγας ἔν τισιν ἀγροῖς
αὐτὸς καθ᾽ ἑαυτὸν ὑπὸ πολλῶν διενεχθεὶς διαλο-
γισμῶν, οἵους ὁ θυμὸς ὑπέβαλλεν, ὥστ᾽ οὔτ᾽ εἰς
καλὸν οὔτε συμφέρον οὐδέν, ἀλλ᾽ ἢ τὸ Ῥωμαίους
μετελθεῖν, ἐγίνωσκε πόλεμόν τινα βαρὺν καὶ
ὅμορον ἀναστῆσαι ἐπ᾽ αὐτούς. ὥρμησεν οὖν δια-
πειρᾶσθαι πρῶτον Οὐολούσκων, ἀκμάζοντας μὲν
εἰδὼς ἔτι καὶ σώμασι καὶ χρήμασι, ταῖς δὲ γεγενημέναις ἔναγχος ἥτταις οὐ τοσοῦτον ἀπολωλέναι τῆς δυνάμεως ὅσον ἐγγεγονέναι φιλονεικίας αὐτοῖς καὶ ὀργῆς οἰόμενος.

XXII. Ἦν δέ τις ἀνὴρ ἐξ Ἀντίου πόλεως διά
τε πλούτου καὶ ἀνδρείαν καὶ γένους ἐπιφάνειαν
ἀξίωμα βασιλικὸν ἔχων ἐν πᾶσιν Οὐολούσκοις,
ὄνομα Τύλλος Ἀμφίδιος. ὑπὸ τούτου μισούμενον
ὁ Μάρκιος ἑαυτὸν ὡς οὐδένα Ῥωμαίων ἐγίνωσκε·
πολλάκις γὰρ ἐν ἀπειλαῖς καὶ προκλήσεσι κατὰ
τὰς μάχας γενόμενοι, καὶ κομπάσαντες διὰ τὸ
ἐνάμιλλον οἷα νεανιῶν πολεμικῶν φιλοτιμίαι καὶ
ζῆλοι φέρουσιν, ἴδιον προσεκτήσαντο τῷ κοινῷ τὸ
2 κατ᾽ ἀλλήλων ἔχθος. οὐ μὴν ἀλλὰ μέγεθός τι
φρονήματος ἔχοντα τὸν Τύλλον ὁρῶν, καὶ μάλιστα
δὴ Οὐολούσκων ἐπιθυμοῦντα Ῥωμαίους λαβὴν
παρασχόντας ἐν μέρει κολοῦσαι, μαρτυρίαν ἀπέλιπε τῷ εἰπόντι· "Θυμῷ μάχεσθαι χαλεπόν· ὃ

straightway departed and went to the city gate.
Thither all the patricians in a body escorted him,
but without taking anything or asking for anything
he departed, having only three or four of his clients
with him. For a few days he remained by himself
at some country place, torn by many conflicting counsels, such as his anger suggested to him, purposing
no good or helpful thing at all, but only how he
might take vengeance on the Romans. At last he
determined to incite some neighbouring nation to a
formidable war against them. Accordingly, he set
out to make trial of the Volscians first, knowing that
they were still abundantly supplied with men and
money, and thinking that they had been not so
much crippled in power by their recent defeats as
filled with contentious wrath against the Romans.

XXII. Now there was a certain man of Antium,
Tullus Aufidius by name, who, by reason of his wealth
and bravery and conspicuous lineage, had the standing
of a king among all the Volscians. By this man
Marcius knew himself to be hated as no other Roman
was; for they had often exchanged threats and chal-
lenges in the battles which they had fought, and
such emulous boastings as the ambitious ardour of
youthful warriors prompts had given rise to a mutual
hatred of their own, in addition to that of their
peoples. However, since he saw that Tullus had a
certain grandeur of spirit, and that he, more than
all other Volscians, was eager to retaliate upon the
Romans, if they gave him any opportunity, Marcius
bore witness to the truth of him who said[1]: "With
anger it is hard to fight; for whatsoe'er it wishes,

---

[1] Heracleitus, Fragment 105 (Bywater, *Heracliti Ephesii
reliquiae*, p. 41).

γὰρ ἂν θέλῃ, ψυχῆς ὠνεῖται." λαβὼν γὰρ ἐσθῆτα
καὶ σκευὴν ἐν ᾗ μάλιστα μὴ δόξειν ὃς ἦν ἔμελλεν
ὁρώμενος, ὥσπερ Ὀδυσσεύς,

Ἀνδρῶν δυσμενέων κατέδυ πόλιν.

XXIII. Ἦν δ᾽ ἑσπέρα, καὶ πολλοὶ μὲν αὐτῷ
προσετύγχανον, ἐγνώριζε δ᾽ οὐδείς. ἐβάδιζεν οὖν
ἐπὶ τὴν οἰκίαν τοῦ Τύλλου, καὶ παρεισελθὼν
ἄφνω πρὸς τὴν ἑστίαν ἐκάθισε σιωπῇ, καὶ τὴν
κεφαλὴν ἐγκαλυψάμενος ἡσυχίαν ἦγεν. οἱ δὲ
κατὰ τὴν οἰκίαν θαυμάσαντες ἀναστῆσαι μὲν οὐκ
ἐτόλμησαν (ἦν γάρ τι καὶ περὶ αὐτὸν ἀξίωμα καὶ
τοῦ σχήματος καὶ τῆς σιωπῆς), ἔφρασαν δὲ τῷ
Τύλλῳ περὶ δεῖπνον ὄντι τὴν ἀτοπίαν τοῦ πράγ-
2 ματος. ὁ δ᾽ ἐξαναστὰς ἧκε πρὸς αὐτόν, καὶ
ἀνέκρινε τίς ὢν ἀφῖκται καὶ τίνων δεόμενος.
οὕτως οὖν ὁ Μάρκιος ἀποκαλυψάμενος καὶ μικρὸν ἀνασχών, "Εἰ μήπω με γινώσκεις, ὦ
Τύλλε," εἶπεν, "ἀλλ᾽ ὁρῶν ἀπιστεῖς, ἀνάγκη με
κατήγορον ἐμαυτοῦ γενέσθαι. Γάϊός εἰμι Μάρκιος, ὁ πλεῖστα σὲ καὶ Οὐολούσκους ἐργασάμενος
κακά, καὶ τὴν οὐκ ἐῶσαν ἀρνεῖσθαι ταῦτα περι-
3 φέρων προσηγορίαν τὸν Κοριολανόν. οὐδὲν γὰρ
ἄλλο τῶν πολλῶν πόνων καὶ κινδύνων ἐκείνων
ἐκτησάμην ἔπαθον ἢ τὸ παράσημον ὄνομα τῆς
πρὸς ὑμᾶς ἔχθρας. καὶ τοῦτό μοι περίεστιν
ἀναφαίρετον· τὰ δ᾽ ἄλλα ὁμοῦ πάντα φθόνῳ
δήμου καὶ ὕβρει, μαλακίᾳ δὲ καὶ προδοσίᾳ τῶν
ἐν τέλει καὶ ἰσοτίμων ἀπεστέρημαι, καὶ φυγὰς
ἐλήλαμαι, καὶ γέγονα τῆς ἑστίας τῆς σῆς ἱκέτης,
οὐχ ὑπὲρ ἀδείας καὶ σωτηρίας (τί γὰρ ἔδει με

that it buys, even at the cost of life." For, putting
on such clothing and attire as would make him seem,
to any one who saw him, least like the man he was,
like Odysseus,

"He went into the city of his deadly foes." [1]

XXIII. It was evening, and many met him, but
no man knew him. He proceeded, therefore, to the
house of Tullus, and slipping in unawares, took his
seat at the hearth [2] in silence, covered his head, and
remained there motionless. The people of the house
were amazed, and did not venture to raise him up,
for his mien and his silence gave him a certain dignity; but they told Tullus, who was at supper, what
a strange thing had happened. Tullus rose from table
and came to him, and asked him who he was, and
why he was come. At this, then, Marcius uncovered
his head, and after a slight pause, said: "If thou
dost not yet recognize me, Tullus, but disbelievest
thine eyes, I must be my own accuser. I am
Caius Marcius, he who has wrought thee and the
Volscians most harm, and the surname of Coriolanus
which I bear permits no denial of this. I have won
no other prize for all the toils and perils which I
have undergone than the name which is a badge of
my enmity to your people. This, indeed, cannot be
taken away from me; but of everything else I have
been stripped, through the envy and insolence of the
Roman people, and the cowardly treachery of the
magistrates and those of my own order. I have been
driven into exile, too, and am become a suppliant at
thy hearth, not for the sake of security and safety,—

[1] *Odyssey*, iv. 246.
[2] A sacred place of refuge for the suppliant. Cf. *Odyssey*,
vii. 153.

δεῦρο ἥκειν φοβούμενον ἀποθανεῖν;) ἀλλὰ δίκας
λαβεῖν χρήζων, καὶ λαμβάνων ἤδη παρὰ τῶν
4 ἐκβαλλόντων τῷ σὲ ποιεῖν ἐμαυτοῦ κύριον. εἰ
μὲν οὖν ἐστί σοι θυμὸς ἐπιχειρεῖν τοῖς πολεμίοις,
ἴθι, ταῖς ἐμαῖς συμφοραῖς, ὦ γενναῖε, χρῆσαι, καὶ
κοινὸν εὐτύχημα ποίησον Οὐολούσκων τὴν ἐμὴν
ἀτυχίαν, τοσούτῳ βέλτιον ὑπὲρ ὑμῶν πολεμή-
σοντος ἢ πρὸς ὑμᾶς, ὅσῳ πολεμοῦσι βέλτιον οἱ
γινώσκοντες τὰ παρὰ τοῖς πολεμίοις τῶν ἀγνοούντων. εἰ δ᾽ ἀπείρηκας, οὔτ᾽ ἐγὼ βούλομαι ζῆν 2
οὔτε σοὶ καλῶς ἔχει σώζειν πάλαι μὲν ἐχθρὸν
ἄνδρα καὶ πολέμιον, νῦν δ᾽ ἀνωφελῆ καὶ ἄχρηστον."

5   Ὡς οὖν ταῦτα ὁ Τύλλος ἤκουσεν, ἥσθη τε
θαυμαστῶς καὶ τὴν δεξιὰν ἐμβαλών, "Ἀνί-
στασο," εἶπεν, "ὦ Μάρκιε, καὶ θάρρει. μέγα γὰρ
ἡμῖν ἀγαθὸν ἥκεις διδοὺς σεαυτόν, ἔλπιζε δὲ
μείζονα παρὰ Οὐολούσκων." καὶ τότε μὲν εἱστία
φιλοφρονούμενος τὸν Μάρκιον, ἐν δὲ ταῖς ἐπιού-
σαις ἡμέραις ἐβουλεύοντο περὶ τοῦ πολέμου καθ᾽
ἑαυτούς.

XXIV. Τὴν δὲ Ῥώμην ἥ τε τῶν πατρικίων
δυσμένεια πρὸς τὸν δῆμον, οὐχ ἥκιστα τὴν τοῦ
Μαρκίου καταδίκην αἰτίαν ἐχόντων, ἐτάραττε,
καὶ πολλὰ δαιμόνια μάντεις καὶ ἱερεῖς καὶ ἰδιῶται
προσήγγελλον ἄξια φροντίδος. ἐν δὲ λέγεται
τοιοῦτό τι γενέσθαι. Τίτος ἦν Λατῖνος, ἀνὴρ οὐκ
ἄγαν ἐπιφανής, ἀπράγμων δὲ καὶ μέτριος ἄλλως

---

[1] Livy simply says that Marcius was kindly received by
the Volscians, and that he lodged with Tullus (ii. 35, 6).
Chapters xxi.–xxiii. agree closely with Dionysius Hal. vii. 67
and viii. 1.

for why should I come hither if I were afraid of death?—but with a desire to take vengeance on those who have driven me forth, which I take at once when I put myself in thy power. If, then, thou art eager to assail thine enemies, come, good Sir, take advantage of my calamities, and make my individual misfortune the good fortune of all the Volscians; I shall fight better for you than I have against you, in just so far as those who know the secrets of their enemies fight better than those who do not. But if thou hast given up hope, neither do I wish to live, nor is it for thine advantage to spare one who has long been an enemy and a foe, and now is unprofitable and useless."

When Tullus heard this, he was wonderfully pleased, and giving him his right hand, said : " Rise up, Marcius, and be of good courage. In giving thyself to us, thou bringest us a great good, and thou mayest expect a greater one still from the Volscians." Then he entertained Marcius at table with every mark of kindness, and during the ensuing days they took counsel together concerning the war.[1]

XXIV. But at Rome, owing to the hatred of the people by the patricians, who were especially embittered by the condemnation of Marcius, there were great commotions, and many signs from heaven were reported by seers, priests, and private persons, which could not be ignored. One of these is said to have been as follows. There was one Titus Latinus,[2] a man of no great prominence, but of quiet and modest life in general, and free from superstitious fears, as

[2] The story is found in Livy, ii. 36, and in Valerius Maximus, i. 7, 4.

καὶ καθαρὸς δεισιδαιμονίας, ἔτι δὲ μᾶλλον ἀλα-
2 ζονείας. οὗτος ὄναρ εἶδεν ὡς τοῦ Διὸς εἰς ὄψιν
ἥκοντος αὐτῷ καὶ κελεύοντος εἰπεῖν πρὸς τὴν
σύγκλητον ὅτι κακὸν τὸν ὀρχηστὴν ἔστειλαν
αὐτῷ πρὸ τῆς πομπῆς καὶ ἀτερπέστατον. ἰδὼν
δὲ τὴν ὄψιν ἔλεγε μὴ πάνυ φροντίσαι τὸ πρῶτον·
ὡς δὲ καὶ δεύτερον ἰδὼν καὶ τρίτον ἠμέλησε,
παιδός τε χρηστοῦ θάνατον ἐπιδεῖν καὶ τοῦ
σώματος ἄφνω παρεθέντος ἀκρατὴς γενέσθαι.
3 ταῦτα δ' ἐν κλινιδίῳ φοράδην κομισθεὶς εἰς τὴν
σύγκλητον ἀπήγγειλεν. ἀπαγγείλας δ', ὥς φασιν,
εὐθὺς ᾔσθετο ῥωννύμενον αὐτοῦ τὸ σῶμα, καὶ
ἀναστὰς ἀπῄει δι' αὐτοῦ βαδίζων. θαυμάσαντες
οὖν οἱ βουλευταὶ πολλὴν ἐποιήσαντο τοῦ πράγματος ζήτησιν.

Ἦν δὲ τοιοῦτον· οἰκέτην τις αὐτοῦ παραδοὺς
οἰκέταις ἑτέροις ἐκέλευσεν ἐξάγειν δι' ἀγορᾶς
4 μαστιγοῦντας, εἶτ' ἀποκτεῖναι. ταῦτα πράτ-
τουσιν αὐτοῖς καὶ τὸν ἄνθρωπον αἰκιζομένοις,
στροφάς τε παντοδαπὰς ὑπ' ὀδύνης στρεφόμενον
καὶ κινήσεις ἄλλας ἀτερπεῖς τῷ περιπαθεῖν
κινούμενον, ἡ πομπὴ κατὰ τύχην ἠκολουθήκει.
καὶ πολλοὶ μὲν ἐδυσχέραινον τῶν παρόντων, οὔτ'
ὄψιν ἱλαρὰν ὁρῶντες οὔτε κινήσεις πρεπούσας,
οὐδεὶς δ' ἐπεξῆλθεν, ἀλλὰ λοιδορίαι μόνον
ἐγένοντο καὶ κατάραι τῷ πικρῶς οὕτως κολάζοντι.
καὶ γὰρ ἐχρῶντο πολλῇ πρὸς τοὺς οἰκέτας
ἐπιεικείᾳ τότε, διὰ αὐτουργίαν καὶ τὸ κοινωνεῖν
διαίτης ἡμερώτερον ἔχοντες πρὸς αὐτοὺς καὶ
5 συνηθέστερον. ἦν δὲ μεγάλη κόλασις οἰκέτου
πλημμελήσαντος, εἰ ξύλον ἁμάξης, ᾧ τὸν ῥυμὸν

he was also, and yet more, from vain pretensions. This man dreamed that Jupiter appeared to him, and bade him tell the senate that the dancer, whom they had appointed to head his procession, was a bad one, and gave him the greatest displeasure. After having this vision, Titus said, he gave it no thought at all at first, but after he had seen it a second and a third time, and still neglected it, he had suffered the loss of an excellent son by death, and had himself become suddenly palsied. This story he told after having been brought into the senate on a litter, and no sooner had he told it, they say, than he at at once felt the strength return to his body, and rose up, and went away, walking without aid. In amazement, then, the senators made a careful investigation of the matter.

Now, what had happened was this. A certain man had handed over one of his slaves to other slaves, with orders to scourge him through the forum, and then put him to death. While they were executing this commission and tormenting the poor wretch, whose pain and suffering made him writhe and twist himself horribly, the sacred procession in honour of Jupiter chanced to come up behind. Many of those who took part in it were, indeed, scandalized at the joyless sight and the unseemly contortions of the victim, but no one made any protest; they merely heaped abuse and curses on the head of the master who was inflicting such a cruel punishment. For in those days the Romans treated their slaves with great kindness, because they worked and even ate with them themselves, and were therefore more familiar and gentle with them. And it was a severe punishment for a slave who had committed a fault, if he

ὑπερείδουσιν, ἀράμενος διεξέλθοι παρὰ τὴν γειτ-
νίασιν. ὁ γὰρ τοῦτο παθὼν καὶ ὀφθεὶς παρὰ τῶν
συνοίκων · καὶ γειτόνων οὐκέτι πίστιν εἶχεν.
ἐκαλεῖτο δὲ φούρκιφερ· ὃ γὰρ οἱ Ἕλληνες ὑπο-
στάτην καὶ στήριγμα, τοῦτο Ῥωμαῖοι φοῦρκαν
ὀνομάζουσιν.

XXV. Ὡς οὖν ὁ Λατῖνος ἀπήγγειλε τὴν ὄψιν
αὐτοῖς καὶ διηπόρουν ὅστις ἦν ὁ τῆς πομπῆς τότε
προηγούμενος ἀτερπὴς καὶ κακὸς ὀρχηστής,
ἀνεμνήσθησαν ἔνιοι διὰ τὴν ἀτοπίαν τῆς τιμωρίας ἐκείνου τοῦ θεράποντος, ὃν μαστιγοῦντες
ἐξήγαγον δι' ἀγορᾶς, εἶτ' ἐθανάτωσαν. συμφωνη-
σάντων οὖν τῶν ἱερέων ὅ τε δεσπότης δίκην ἔδωκε,
καὶ τῷ θεῷ τὴν πομπὴν καὶ τὰς θέας αὖθις ἐξ
ἀρχῆς ἐπετέλουν.

2 Ἔοικεν οὖν ὁ Νομᾶς τά τ' ἄλλα τῶν ἱερῶν
σοφώτατος ἐξηγητὴς γεγονέναι, καὶ τοῦτο παγκά-
λως γε νομοθετῆσαι πρὸς εὐλάβειαν αὐτοῖς. ὅταν
γὰρ ἄρχοντες ἢ ἱερεῖς πράττωσί τι τῶν θείων, ὁ
κῆρυξ πρόεισι μεγάλῃ φωνῇ βοῶν, "Ὂκ ἄγε."
σημαίνει δ' ἡ φωνή, τοῦτο πρᾶττε, προσέχειν
κελεύουσα τοῖς ἱεροῖς καὶ μηδὲν ἔργον ἐμβαλεῖν
μεταξὺ μηδὲ χρείαν ἀσχολίας, ὡς τὰ πλεῖστα τῶν
ἀνθρωπίνων ἀναγκαίῳ τινὶ τρόπῳ καὶ διὰ βίας
3 περαινόμενα. θυσίας δὲ καὶ πομπὰς καὶ θέας

---

[1] According to Livy (ii. 36 and 37), it was at the repetition
of the great games, which was made necessary by the

was obliged to take the piece of wood with which they prop up the pole of a waggon, and carry it around through the neighbourhood. For he who had been seen undergoing this punishment no longer had any credit in his own or neighbouring households. And he was called "furcifer"; for what the Greeks call a *prop*, or *support*, is called "furca" by the Romans.

XXV. When, therefore, Latinus had reported his vision to the senators, and they were at a loss to know who the unpleasant and bad dancer was who had headed the procession referred to, some of them were led, owing to the extraordinary nature of his punishment, to think of the slave who had been scourged through the forum and then put to death. Accordingly, with the concurrence of the priests, the master of the slave was punished, and the procession and spectacles in honour of the god were exhibited anew.[1]

Now it would seem that Numa, who in other respects also was a very wise director of sacred rites, had very properly sought to secure the people's reverent attention by means of the following ordinance. When, namely, magistrates or priests perform any religious function, a herald goes before, crying with a loud voice, "Hoc age." The meaning of the cry is, *Mind this!* and it warns the people to give heed to the sacred rites, and suffer no task or demand of business to intervene,[2] implying that men perform most of their duties under some sort of compulsion and by constraint. And it is customary for

profanation made known by the dream of Latinus, that the Volscians were out of the city, as described by Plutarch in chapter xxvi. 1.   Cf. *Numa*, xiv. 2.

οὐ μόνον ἐξ αἰτίας τηλικαύτης, ἀλλὰ καὶ διὰ
μικρὰς Ῥωμαίοις ἔθος ἐστὶν ἀναλαμβάνειν. ἵππου τε γὰρ ἑνὸς τῶν ἀγόντων τὰς καλουμένας
θήσσας ἀτονήσαντος, καὶ πάλιν τοῦ ἡνιόχου τῇ   226
ἀριστερᾷ χειρὶ τὰς ἡνίας συλλαβόντος, αὖθις
ἐψηφίσαντο τὴν πομπὴν ἐπιτελεῖν. ἐν δὲ τοῖς
κάτω χρόνοις μίαν θυσίαν τριακοντάκις ἐποίησαν,
ἀεί τινος ἐλλείμματος ἢ προσκρούσματος γίνεσθαι
δοκοῦντος. τοιαύτη μὲν εὐλάβεια πρὸς τὸ θεῖον
Ῥωμαίων.

XXVI. Ὁ δὲ Μάρκιος καὶ Τύλλος ἐν Ἀντίῳ
τοῖς δυνατωτάτοις κρύφα διελέγοντο, καὶ παρεκάλουν, ἕως στασιάζουσιν οἱ Ῥωμαῖοι πρὸς
ἀλλήλους, τὸν πόλεμον ἐξενεγκεῖν. τῶν δὲ
δυσωπουμένων, ὅτι σπονδαὶ διέτεις ἦσαν αὐτοῖς
καὶ ἀνοχαὶ γεγενημέναι, πρόφασιν αὐτοὶ Ῥωμαῖοι
παρέσχον, ἔκ τινος ὑποψίας ἢ διαβολῆς ἐν θέαις
καὶ ἀγῶσι κηρύξαντες ἀπιέναι Οὐολούσκους πρὸ
2 ἡλίου δύνοντος ἐκ τῆς πόλεως. ἔνιοι δέ φασιν
ἀπάτῃ τοῦ Μαρκίου καὶ δόλῳ γενέσθαι τοῦτο,
πέμψαντος εἰς Ῥώμην πρὸς τοὺς ἄρχοντας οὐκ
ἀληθῆ κατήγορον τῶν Οὐολούσκων, ὡς ἐν ταῖς
θέαις διανοουμένων ἐπιθέσθαι τοῖς Ῥωμαίοις καὶ
τὴν πόλιν ἐμπιπρᾶν. πάντας μὲν γὰρ αὐτοὺς τὸ
κήρυγμα τοῦτο δυσμενεστέρους ἐποίησε τοῖς
Ῥωμαίοις· ὁ δὲ Τύλλος ἐπὶ μεῖζον αἴρων τὸ
πρᾶγμα καὶ παροξύνων τέλος ἔπεισε πέμψαντας
εἰς Ῥώμην τήν τε χώραν ἀπαιτεῖν καὶ τὰς
πόλεις, ὅσας ἀφῄρηνται πολέμῳ τῶν Οὐολού-

---

[1] See the following *Comparison*, ii. 2.
[2] According to Livy (ii. 37, 1–7), it was Tullus himself

the Romans to renew sacrifices and processions and spectacles, not only for such a reason as the above, but also for trivial reasons. For instance, if one of the horses drawing the sacred chariots called Tensae gives out; or again, if the charioteer takes hold of the reins with his left hand, they decree that the procession be renewed. And in later ages, a single sacrifice has been performed thirty times, because again and again some failure or offence was thought to occur. Such is the reverent care of the Romans in religious matters.

XXVI. But Marcius and Tullus were secretly conferring at Antium with the chief men, and were urging them to begin the war while the Romans were torn by internal dissensions. And when shame restrained them from this course, because they had agreed to a truce and cessation of hostilities for two years, the Romans themselves furnished them with a pretext, by making proclamation at the spectacles and games, because of some suspicion or slanderous report, that the visiting Volscians must leave the city before sunset. Some say[1] that this was due to a deceitful stratagem of Marcius, who sent a man to the consuls in Rome, bearing the false charge that the Volscians purposed to fall upon the Romans at the spectacles, and set the city on fire.[2] This proclamation made all the Volscians more embittered against the Romans; and Tullus, magnifying the incident, and goading them on, at last persuaded them to send ambassadors to Rome[3] and demand back the territory and the cities which had been

who came to the consuls, as had been planned with Marcius. Plutarch agrees rather with Dionysius Hal. viii. 3.

[3] Livy speaks only of a revolt (ii. 38, *fin.*). Plutarch agrees with Dionysius Hal. viii. 4–10.

3 σκων. οἱ δὲ Ῥωμαῖοι τῶν πρέσβεων ἀκούσαντες
ἠγανάκτησαν, καὶ ἀπεκρίναντο προτέρους μὲν
ἀναλήψεσθαι τὰ ὅπλα τοὺς Οὐολούσκους, ὑστέρους δὲ καταθήσεσθαι Ῥωμαίους. ἐκ τούτου
συναγαγὼν ἐκκλησίαν πάνδημον ὁ Τύλλος, ἐπεὶ
τὸν πόλεμον ἐψηφίσαντο, συνεβούλευε τὸν Μάρκιον καλέσαι, μηδὲν αὐτῷ μνησικακοῦντας, ἀλλὰ
πιστεύσαντας ὅτι συμμαχῶν ὠφελήσει ὅσα πολεμῶν οὐκ ἔβλαψεν.

XXVII. Ἐπεὶ δὲ κληθεὶς ὁ Μάρκιος καὶ διαλεχθεὶς πρὸς τὸ πλῆθος οὐχ ἧττον ἀπὸ τῶν
λόγων ἢ τῶν ὅπλων ἀνὴρ δεινὸς ἐφάνη καὶ
πολεμικὸς καὶ τὸ φρονεῖν καὶ τολμᾶν περιττός,
ἀποδείκνυται μετὰ Τύλλου στρατηγὸς αὐτο-
2 κράτωρ τοῦ πολέμου. δεδιὼς δὲ τὸν χρόνον
ἐν ᾧ παρασκευάσασθαι τοὺς Οὐολούσκους ἔδει,
μὴ πολὺς γενόμενος τὸν καιρὸν ἀφέληται τῆς
πράξεως, τὰ μὲν ἄλλα τοὺς κατὰ πόλιν δυνατοὺς
καὶ ἄρχοντας ἐκέλευε συνάγειν καὶ πορίζειν,
αὐτὸς δὲ τοὺς προθυμοτάτους ἄνευ καταλόγου
πείσας ἑκόντας αὐτῷ συνεξελθεῖν, ἐνέβαλεν εἰς
τὴν τῶν Ῥωμαίων ἄφνω καὶ μηδενὸς προσδοκῶν-
3 τος. ὅθεν ηὐπόρησε λείας τοσαύτης ὅσην ἄγοντας
καὶ φέροντας καὶ χρωμένους ἐν τῷ στρατοπέδῳ
τοὺς Οὐολούσκους ἀπειπεῖν. ἦν δὲ μικρότατον
ἔργον αὐτῷ τῆς στρατείας ἐκείνης ἡ εὐπορία καὶ
τὸ πολλὰ βλάψαι καὶ κακῶσαι τὴν χώραν· οὗ
δ' ἕνεκα ταῦτ' ἔπραττε, μέγα, τὸ τοὺς πατρικίους

taken from the Volscians in war. But the Romans, after hearing the ambassadors, were full of indignation, and replied that the Volscians might be first to take up arms, but the Romans would be last to lay them down. Upon receiving this answer, Tullus called a general assembly of his people, and after they had voted for the war, advised them to call in Marcius, cherishing no resentment against him, but firmly convinced that he would be more helpful as an ally than he had been injurious as a foe.

XXVII. Marcius was therefore called in, and held a conference with the assembly; they saw from his speech that he was as eloquent as his exploits in arms had taught them that he was warlike, and were convinced of his surpassing intelligence and daring; so they appointed him general with Tullus, and gave him full powers to conduct the war. Fearing, then, that the time needed to equip and marshal the Volscians would be so long as to rob him of his best opportunity for action, he left orders with the magistrates and chief men of the city to assemble and provide the remaining forces and supplies that were requisite, while he himself, after persuading the most ardent spirits to march forth as volunteers with him and not stop for formal enrolment, burst into the Roman territory of a sudden, when no one expected it. Consequently he secured such abundance of booty that the Volscians had more than they could possibly do to use it in their camp or carry it off home. But the abundant supplies secured, and the great injury and damage done to the enemy's country, were, in his eyes, the most insignificant result of that expedition; its chief result, and his main object in making it, was to furnish the people of Rome with

προσδιαβαλεῖν τῷ δήμῳ. τὰ γὰρ ἄλλα πάντα λυ-
μαινόμενος καὶ διαφθείρων, τοὺς ἐκείνων ἀγροὺς
ἰσχυρῶς ἐφύλαττε, καὶ οὐκ εἴα κακουργεῖν οὐδὲ
4 λαμβάνειν ἐξ ἐκείνων οὐδέν. ὅθεν ἐν διαβολαῖς
ἔτι μᾶλλον ἐγένοντο καὶ ταραχαῖς πρὸς ἀλλήλους,
οἱ μὲν πατρίκιοι τοῖς πολλοῖς ἐγκαλοῦντες ὡς
ἄνδρα δυνατὸν ἀδίκως ἐκβαλοῦσιν, ὁ δὲ δῆμος
ἐκείνους ᾐτιᾶτο διὰ μνησικακίαν ἐπάγειν τὸν
Μάρκιον, εἶτα πολεμουμένων ἑτέρων θεατὰς
καθῆσθαι, φύλακα τοῦ πλούτου καὶ τῶν χρημάτων ἔξω τὸν πόλεμον αὐτὸν ἔχοντας. ταῦτα
διαπραξάμενος ὁ Μάρκιος, καὶ μεγάλα πρὸς τὸ
θαρρεῖν καὶ καταφρονεῖν τῶν πολεμίων τοὺς
Οὐολούσκους ὠφελήσας, ἀπήγαγεν ἀσφαλῶς.

XXVIII. Ἐπεὶ δὲ πᾶσα ταχὺ καὶ προθύμως
ἡ τῶν Οὐολούσκων δύναμις ἠθροίσθη πολλὴ
φανεῖσα, μέρος μὲν ἔγνωσαν ὑπολιπεῖν ταῖς
πόλεσιν ὑπὲρ ἀσφαλείας, μέρει δὲ στρατεύειν ἐπὶ
τοὺς Ῥωμαίους· ἑλέσθαι δὲ τῶν ἡγεμονιῶν ὁ
Μάρκιος ἔδωκε τῷ Τύλλῳ τὴν ἑτέραν. ὁ δὲ
Τύλλος, εἰπὼν ὡς οὐδὲν ἀρετῇ λειπόμενον αὐτοῦ
τὸν Μάρκιον ὁρᾷ, τύχῃ δὲ βελτίονι κεχρημένον ἐν
ταῖς μάχαις ἁπάσαις, ἐκέλευσεν ἡγεῖσθαι τῶν   227
ἐξιόντων, αὐτὸς δὲ τάς τε πόλεις ὑπομένων
φυλάξειν καὶ τοῖς στρατευομένοις ὑπουργήσειν
2 τὰ πρόσφορα. μᾶλλον οὖν ἐπιρρωσθεὶς ὁ Μάρκιος ἐχώρει πρῶτον ἐπὶ Κίρκαιον, πόλιν ἀποικίδα

---

[1] There is nothing of this preliminary foray in Livy. It is
on the main expedition (chap. xxviii.) that the patrician lands

fresh charges against the patricians. For while he maltreated and destroyed everything else, he kept a vigorous watch over the lands of the patricians, and would not suffer anyone to hurt them or take anything from them. This led to still further accusations and broils between the parties in the city; the patricians accused the people of unjustly driving out an influential man, and the people charged the patricians with bringing Marcius up against them in a spirit of revenge, and then enjoying the spectacle of what others suffered by the war, while the war itself protected their own wealth and property outside the city. After Marcius had accomplished his purposes, and greatly helped the Volscians towards courage and scorn of their enemies, he led his forces back in safety.[1]

XXVIII. The entire force of the Volscians was assembled with speed and alacrity, and was then seen to be so large that they determined to leave a part of it behind for the security of their cities, and with the other part to march against the Romans. Moreover, Marcius left it to the choice of Tullus which of the two divisions he would command. Then Tullus, remarking that Marcius was clearly in no wise inferior to himself in valour, and had enjoyed a better fortune in all his battles, bade him lead the division that was to take the field, and he himself would remain behind to guard the cities and provide what was requisite for the army abroad.[2] With a stronger force than before, then, Marcius set out first against Circeii, a city which was a colony of Rome;

are spared (ii. 39). According to Dionysius (viii. 12), Tullus led one division into the territory of the Latins, Marcius the other into that of Rome, and both brought back enormous booty. [2] Cf. Dionysius, viii. 13.

Ῥωμαίων, καὶ ταύτην ἐνδοῦσαν ἑκουσίως οὐδὲν
ἠδίκησε. μετὰ δὲ ταύτην ἐπόρθει τὴν Λατίνων
χώραν, ἐνταῦθα προσμαχεῖσθαι προσδεχόμενος
αὐτῷ τοὺς Ῥωμαίους ὑπὲρ τῶν Λατίνων συμμάχων ὄντων καὶ πολλάκις αὐτοὺς ἐπικαλου-
3 μένων. ἐπεὶ δὲ καὶ τὸ πλῆθος ἀπρόθυμον ἐγένετο
καὶ τοῖς ὑπάτοις ὀλίγος ἔτι περιῆν τῆς ἀρχῆς
χρόνος, ἐν ᾧ κινδυνεύειν οὐκ ἐβούλοντο, καὶ διὰ
ταῦτα τοὺς Λατίνους ἀπέπεμψαν, οὕτως ὁ Μάρκιος ἐπ' αὐτὰς τὰς πόλεις ἦγε, καὶ Τολερίνους καὶ
Λαουικανοὺς καὶ Πεδανοὺς, ἔτι δὲ Βωλανοὺς
ἀντιστάντας αὐτῷ κατὰ κράτος ἑλών, τά τε
σώματα λείαν ἐποιήσατο καὶ τὰ χρήματα δι-
ήρπασε. τῶν δὲ προστιθεμένων ἐπιμέλειαν
ἐποιεῖτο πολλήν, ὅπως μηδ' ἄκοντος αὐτοῦ
βλάπτοιντο, πορρωτάτω στρατοπεδεύων καὶ τῆς
χώρας ἀπεχόμενος.

XXIX. Ἐπεὶ δὲ καὶ Βόλλας πόλιν οὐ πλείους
σταδίους ἑκατὸν ἀπέχουσαν τῆς Ῥώμης ἑλὼν
χρημάτων πολλῶν ἐκράτησε καὶ πάντας ὀλίγου
δεῖν τοὺς ἐν ἡλικίᾳ διέφθειρε, τῶν δὲ Οὐολούσκων
οὐδ' οἱ μένειν ἐν ταῖς πόλεσι ταχθέντες ἐκαρ-
τέρουν, ἀλλ' ἐφέροντο σὺν τοῖς ὅπλοις πρὸς τὸν
Μάρκιον, ἕνα στρατηγὸν καὶ μόνον ἄρχοντα ἑαυτῶν γινώσκειν ἐκεῖνον εἶναι λέγοντες, ἦν ὄνομα
κατὰ πᾶσαν αὐτοῦ τὴν Ἰταλίαν μέγα καὶ δόξα
θαυμαστή, τῆς ἀρετῆς ἑνὸς σώματος μεταθέσει
τοσοῦτον ἀπεργασαμένης τὸ παράλογον ἐν τοῖς
πράγμασι.

2 Τὰ δὲ τῶν Ῥωμαίων οὐδένα κόσμον εἶχε,
μάχεσθαι μὲν ἀπεγνωκότων, ἐν δὲ συστάσεσι καὶ
λόγοις στασιαστικοῖς ὁσημέραι πρὸς ἀλλήλους

this surrendered to him of its own accord, and he
did it no harm. Next, he laid waste the country of
the Latins, where he expected that the Romans
would engage him in defence of the Latins, who
were their allies and by frequent messengers were
calling upon them for help. But the commons were
indifferent to the appeal, the consuls were unwilling
to risk a campaign during the short time left of their
term of office, and therefore the Latin envoys were
dismissed. Under these circumstances Marcius led
his forces against their cities, and taking by assault
those which offered resistance to him, namely, To-
lerium, Lavicum, Pedum, and later Bola, he made
slaves of the inhabitants and plundered their property.
But for those who came over to him of their own
accord he showed much concern, and that they might
suffer no harm, even against his wishes, he encamped
as far as he could from them, and held aloof from
their territory.

XXIX. But after he had taken Bola, a city not
more than twelve miles away from Rome, where he
got much treasure and put almost all the adults to
the sword; and after the Volscians even who had
been ordered to remain in their cities grew impatient,
and came trooping in arms to Marcius, declaring that
he was the sole and only general whom they would
recognize as their leader, then his name was great
throughout all Italy, and men thought with amazement how the valour of a single man, upon his
changing sides, had effected such a marvellous turn
in affairs.

At Rome, however, all was disorder; its citizens
refused to fight, and spent their whole time in cabals
and factious disputes with one another, until tidings

ὄντων, ἄχρι οὗ Λαουΐνιον ἀπηγγέλθη περιτειχι-
ζόμενον ὑπὸ τῶν πολεμίων, ὅπου καὶ θεῶν ἱερὰ
Ῥωμαίοις πατρῷων ἀπέκειτο, καὶ τοῦ γένους
ἦσαν αὐτοῖς ἀρχαί, διὰ τὸ πρώτην πόλιν ἐκείνην
3 κτίσαι τὸν Αἰνείαν. ἐκ δὲ τούτου θαυμαστὴ μὲν
ἔσχε καὶ ἀθρόα μεταβολὴ γνώμης τὸν δῆμον,
ἄτοπος δὲ κομιδῇ καὶ παράλογος τοὺς πατρικίους.
ὁ μὲν γὰρ δῆμος ὥρμησε λύειν τὴν τοῦ Μαρκίου
καταδίκην καὶ καλεῖν αὐτὸν εἰς τὴν πόλιν, ἡ δὲ
βουλὴ συναχθεῖσα καὶ σκοποῦσα περὶ τοῦ
βουλεύματος ἀπέγνω καὶ διεκώλυσεν, εἴτε πάντως ἐνίστασθαι φιλονεικοῦσα πᾶσιν οἷς ὁ δῆμος
4 ἐσπούδαζεν, εἴτ᾽ ἄλλως χάριτι τοῦ δήμου τὸν
ἄνδρα μὴ βουλομένη κατελθεῖν, εἴτε κἀκεῖνον
αὐτὸν ἤδη πεποιημένη δι᾽ ὀργῆς, ὅτι πάντας ἐποίει
κακῶς οὐχ ὑπὸ πάντων ἀγνωμονηθείς, καὶ τῆς
πατρίδος αὐτὸν ἔδειξεν ἐχθρόν, ἐν ᾗ τὸ κυριώτατον
καὶ κράτιστον μέρος ἐγίνωσκε συμπαθοῦν αὐτῷ
καὶ συναδικούμενον. ἐξενεχθείσης δὲ τῆς γνώμης
εἰς τοὺς πολλούς, ὁ μὲν δῆμος ἄκυρος ἦν τοῦ
ψήφῳ καὶ νόμῳ τι ποιεῖν ἄνευ προβουλεύματος.

XXX. Ὁ δὲ Μάρκιος ἀκούσας ἔτι μᾶλλον
ἐξετραχύνθη, καὶ τὴν πολιορκίαν ἀπολιπὼν ἐπὶ
τὴν πόλιν ὑπ᾽ ὀργῆς ἐχώρει, καὶ περὶ τὰς λεγομένας Κλοιλίας τάφρους κατεστρατοπέδευσε
τεσσαράκοντα τῆς πόλεως σταδίους ἀφεστώς.
ὀφθεὶς δὲ φοβερὸς καὶ πολὺν θόρυβον παρασχών,
ὅμως ἐν τῷ παρόντι τὴν στάσιν ἔπαυσεν· οὐδεὶς
γὰρ ἔτι τοῖς πολλοῖς ἐτόλμησεν ἀντειπεῖν οὔτ᾽
ἄρχων οὔτε βουλευτὴς περὶ τοῦ τὸν Μάρκιον
2 κατάγειν, ἀλλ᾽ ὁρῶντες ἐν τῇ πόλει διαδρομὰς

came that the enemy had laid close siege to Lavinium, where the sacred symbols of the ancestral gods of the Romans were stored up, and from which their nation took its origin, since that was the first city which Aeneas founded. This produced an astonishing and universal change of opinion in the commons, as well as one which was altogether strange and unexpected in the patricians. For the commons were eager to repeal the sentence against Marcius and invite him back to the city; whereas the senate, on assembling and considering the proposition, rejected and vetoed it; either because they were angrily bent on opposing all the people's desires; or else because they were unwilling that Marcius should owe his restoration to the kindness of the people; or because they were now angry at Marcius himself, seeing that he was injuring all alike, although he had not been ill-treated by all, and showed himself an enemy of his whole country, although he knew that the most influential and powerful men in it sympathised with him and shared in his wrongs. When this decision of the senate was made public, the people was powerless; it could not by its vote enact a law, without a previous decree of the senate.

XXX. But Marcius, when he heard of it, was yet more exasperated, and raising the siege of Lavinium, marched against Rome in wrath, and encamped at the so-called Fossae Cluiliae, only five miles distant from the city. Although the sight of him produced terror and great confusion there, still, it put a stop for the present to their dissensions; for no one longer, whether consul or senator, dared to oppose the people in the matter of restoring Marcius. On the contrary, when they saw the women running frantic in the

γυναικῶν καὶ πρὸς ἱεροῖς ἱκεσίας καὶ δάκρυα
πρεσβυτῶν καὶ δεήσεις, πάντα δ᾽ ἐνδεᾶ τόλμης
καὶ σωτηρίων λογισμῶν, συνέγνωσαν ὀρθῶς τὸν
δῆμον ἐπὶ τὰς διαλλαγὰς τοῦ Μαρκίου τραπέσθαι, τὴν δὲ βουλὴν τοῦ παντὸς ἁμαρτάνειν, ὅτε
παύσασθαι καλῶς εἶχεν ὀργῆς καὶ μνησικακίας,
ἀρχομένην. ἔδοξεν οὖν πᾶσι πρέσβεις ἀποστεῖλαι πρὸς τὸν Μάρκιον ἐκείνῳ τε κάθοδον
διδόντας εἰς τὴν πατρίδα καὶ τὸν πόλεμον αὐτοῖς
3 λῦσαι δεομένους. οἱ δὲ πεμφθέντες ἀπὸ βουλῆς
ἦσαν μὲν ἐπιτήδειοι τῷ Μαρκίῳ, προσεδέχοντο
δὲ πολλὴν περί γε τὰς πρώτας ἀπαντήσεις
φιλοφροσύνην παρ᾽ ἀνδρὸς οἰκείου καὶ συνήθους.
ἐγίνετο δὲ τοιοῦτον οὐδέν, ἀλλὰ διὰ τοῦ στρατοπέδου τῶν πολεμίων ἀχθέντες ἐνετύγχανον αὐτῷ
μετ᾽ ὄγκου καθεζομένῳ καὶ βαρύτητος οὐκ ἀνεκ-
4 τῆς. ἔχων δὲ τοὺς πρώτους τῶν Οὐολούσκων
περὶ αὑτόν, ἐκέλευε λέγειν ὧν δεόμενοι τυγχάνουσιν. εἰπόντων δὲ λόγους ἐπιεικεῖς καὶ φιλαν-
θρώπους ἐν ἤθει τῷ πρέποντι καὶ παυσαμένων,
ἀπεκρίνατο τὰ μὲν πικρῶς ὑπὲρ αὑτοῦ καὶ πρὸς
ὀργὴν ὧν ἔπαθε, τὰ δ᾽ ὑπὲρ τῶν Οὐολούσκων ὡς
στρατηγός, ἀποδοῦναι τὰς πόλεις καὶ τὴν χώραν,
ὅσην ἀπετέμοντο πολέμῳ, κελεύων, καὶ ψηφίσασθαι Οὐολούσκοις ἰσοπολιτείαν ἥνπερ Λατί-
5 νοις· ἄλλην γὰρ οὐκ εἶναι βέβαιον ἢ τὴν ἐπὶ τοῖς
ἴσοις καὶ δικαίοις ἀπαλλαγὴν τοῦ πολέμου.
χρόνον δὲ βουλῆς ἔδωκεν αὐτοῖς ἡμέρας τριά-

city, and the aged men resorting to the sacred shrines with suppliant tears and prayers, and everywhere an utter lack of courage and saving counsels, then all agreed that the people had done well to seek a reconciliation with Marcius, but that the senate had made a total mistake in beginning then to indulge its wrath and revengeful spirit, when it had been well to lay such feelings aside. It was, therefore, unanimously decided to send ambassadors to Marcius, offering him the privilege of returning to his country, and begging him to stop his war upon them. Moreover, the messengers from the senate were kinsmen and friends of Marcius, and expected to be treated with great friendliness in their first interview with a man who was a relative and associate of theirs. But matters turned out quite otherwise; for after being led through the camp of the enemy, they found him seated in great state, and looking insufferably stern. Surrounded by the chief men of the Volscians, he bade the Romans declare their wishes. They did so, in reasonable and considerate language, and with a manner suitable to their position, and when they had ceased, he made an answer which, so far as it concerned himself, was full of bitterness and anger at their treatment of him, and in behalf of the Volscians, as their general, he ordered the restitution of the cities and territory which had been torn from them in war, and the passage of a decree granting the Volscians, as allies, equal civic rights, as had been done for the Latins. For no respite from the war would be secure and lasting, he said, except it be based on just and equal rights. Moreover, he gave them thirty days for deliberation, and when the ambassadors were

κοντα· καὶ τῶν πρέσβεων ἀπελθόντων εὐθὺς
ἀνέζευξεν ἐκ τῆς χώρας.

XXXI. Τοῦτο δὴ πρῶτον αἰτίαμα τῶν Οὐολούσκων οἱ πάλαι βαρυνόμενοι τὴν δύναμιν αὐτοῦ
καὶ φθονοῦντες ἐλάμβανον· ὧν ἦν καὶ ὁ Τύλλος,
ἰδίᾳ μὲν ὑπὸ τοῦ Μαρκίου μηδὲν ἀδικούμενος, ἐν
δ' ἀνθρωπίνῳ πάθει γεγονώς. ἤχθετο γὰρ ἠμαυ-
ρωμένος παντάπασι τῇ δόξῃ καὶ παρορώμενος
ὑπὸ τῶν Οὐολούσκων, πάντα μόνον ἡγουμένων
αὐτοῖς εἶναι τὸν Μάρκιον, τοὺς δὲ ἄλλους ἀξιούντων, ὅσον ἐκεῖνος αὐτοῖς μεταδώσει δυνάμεως καὶ
2 ἀρχῆς, ἀγαπᾶν ἔχοντας. ὅθεν αἱ πρῶται κατη-
γορίαι κρύφα διεσπείροντο, καὶ συνιστάμενοι πρὸς
ἀλλήλους ἠγανάκτουν, καὶ προδοσίαν ἐκάλουν
τὴν ἀνάζευξιν, οὐ τειχῶν οὐδ' ὅπλων, ἀλλὰ
καιρῶν, οἷς καὶ τἆλλα πάντα σώζεσθαι καὶ πάλιν
ἀπόλλυσθαι πέφυκεν, ἡμερῶν τριάκοντα τῷ
πολέμῳ δεδομένων, οὗ μείζονας οὐδὲν ἐν ἐλάττονι
χρόνῳ λαμβάνειν μεταβολάς.

3   Καίτοι τὸν χρόνον τοῦτον ὁ Μάρκιος οὐκ ἀργὸν
διῆγεν, ἀλλὰ τοὺς συμμάχους τῶν πολεμίων
ἔφθειρεν ἐπιὼν καὶ περιέκοπτε καὶ πόλεις ἑπτὰ
μεγάλας καὶ πολυανθρώπους ἔλαβεν. οἱ δὲ
Ῥωμαῖοι βοηθεῖν μὲν οὐκ ἐτόλμων, ἀλλ' ὄκνου
πλήρεις ἦσαν αὐτῶν αἱ ψυχαί, καὶ τοῖς ἐκνεναρ-
κηκόσι κομιδῇ καὶ παραλελυμένοις σώμασιν
4 ὁμοίως διέκειντο πρὸς τὸν πόλεμον. ἐπεὶ δ' ὁ

---

[1] There is nothing of this withdrawal of forces in Livy
(ii. 39).

gone, he immediately withdrew his forces from the country.[1]

XXXI. This was the first ground of complaint against him which was laid hold of by those of the Volscians who had long been jealous of him, and uneasy at the influence which he had acquired. Among these was Tullus also, not because he had been personally wronged at all by Marcius, but because he was only too human. For he was vexed to find his reputation wholly obscured and himself neglected by the Volscians, who thought that Marcius alone was everything to them, and that their other leaders should be content with whatever share of influence and authority he might bestow upon them. This was the reason why the first seeds of denunciation were sown in secret, and now, banding together, the malcontents shared their resentment with one another, and called the withdrawal of Marcius a betrayal, not so much of cities and armies, as of golden opportunities, which prove the salvation or the loss of these as well as of everything else; for he had granted a respite of thirty days from war, although in war the greatest changes might occur in much less time than this.

And yet Marcius did not spend this time in idleness, but fell upon the enemy's allies, harassed and ravaged their territories, and captured seven of their large and populous cities.[2] And the Romans did not venture to come to their aid, but their spirits were full of hesitation, and their attitude toward the war was that of men who are completely benumbed and paralyzed. And when the time had passed, and

---

[2] Cf. Dionysius, viii. 36. Chapters xxviii.–xxx. in Plutarch agree closely with Dionysius viii. 14–35.

χρόνος διῆλθε καὶ παρῆν αὖθις ὁ Μάρκιος μετὰ
τῆς δυνάμεως ἀπάσης, ἐκπέμπουσι πρεσβείαν
πάλιν τοῦ Μαρκίου δεησομένην ὑφέσθαι τῆς
ὀργῆς καὶ τοὺς Οὐολούσκους ἐκ τῆς χώρας ἀπαγα-
γόντα πράττειν καὶ λέγειν ὅ τι ἂν ἀμφοτέροις
οἴηται βέλτιον εἶναι· φόβῳ μὲν γὰρ οὐδὲν ἐνδώσειν
Ῥωμαίους, ἐὰν δέ τινος τῶν φιλανθρώπων οἴηται
δεῖν τυχεῖν τοὺς Οὐολούσκους, ἅπαν αὐτοῖς
5 γενήσεσθαι τὰ ὅπλα καταθεμένοις. πρὸς ταῦθ᾽
ὁ Μάρκιος ἔφη μηδὲν ὡς Οὐολούσκων ἀποκρίνεσθαι
στρατηγός, ὡς δὲ Ῥωμαίων ἔτι πολίτης παραινεῖν
καὶ παρακαλεῖν μετριώτερα φρονήσαντας ἐπὶ
τοῖς δικαίοις ἥκειν πρὸς αὐτὸν ἐν ἡμέραις τρισίν,
ἃ προκαλεῖται ψηφισαμένους· εἰ δ᾽ ἕτερα δόξειε,
γιγνώσκειν οὐκ οὖσαν αὐτοῖς ἄδειαν αὖθις μετὰ
λόγων κενῶν βαδίζουσιν εἰς τὸ στρατόπεδον.

XXXII. Ἐπανελθόντων δὲ τῶν πρέσβεων ἀκού-
σασα ἡ βουλή, καθάπερ ἐν χειμῶνι πολλῷ καὶ
κλύδωνι τῆς πόλεως, ἄρασα τὴν ἀφ᾽ ἱερᾶς ἀφῆκεν.
ὅσοι γὰρ ἦσαν ἱερεῖς θεῶν ἢ μυστηρίων ὀργιασταὶ
ἢ φύλακες ἢ τὴν ἀπ᾽ οἰωνῶν πάτριον οὖσαν ἐκ
παλαιῶν μαντικὴν ἔχοντες, τούτους πάντας ἀπιέναι πρὸς τὸν Μάρκιον ἐψηφίσαντο, κεκοσμημένους
ὡς ἦν ἑκάστῳ νόμος ἐν ταῖς ἱερουργίαις· λέγειν δὲ
ταὐτά, καὶ παρακαλεῖν ὅπως ἀπαλλάξας τὸν
πόλεμον οὕτω διαλέγηται περὶ τῶν Οὐολούσκων
2 τοῖς πολίταις. ἐδέξατο μὲν οὖν εἰς τὸ στρατόπεδον
τοὺς ἄνδρας, ἄλλο δ᾽ οὐδὲν ἔδωκεν οὐδ᾽ ἔπραξεν
οὐδ᾽ εἶπε μαλακώτερον, ἀλλ᾽ ἐφ᾽ οἷς πρότερον

Marcius was at hand again with his entire force, they sent out another embassy to entreat him to moderate his wrath, withdraw the Volscian army from the country, and then make such proposals and settlements as he thought best for both nations; for the Romans would make no concessions through fear, but if he thought that the Volscians ought to obtain certain favours, all such would be granted them if they laid down their arms. Marcius replied that, as general of the Volscians, he would make no answer to this, but as one who was still a citizen of Rome, he advised and exhorted them to adopt more moderate views of what justice required, and come to him in three days with a ratification of his previous demands; but if they should decide otherwise, they must know well that it was not safe for them to come walking into his camp again with empty phrases.

XXXII. When the embassy had returned and the senate had heard its report, it was felt that the city was tossing on the billows of a great tempest, and therefore the last and sacred anchor was let down. A decree was passed that all the priests of the gods, and the celebrants or custodians of the mysteries, and those who practised the ancient and ancestral art of divination from the flight of birds,—that all these should go to Marcius, arrayed as was the custom of each in the performance of their sacred rites, and should urge him in the same manner as before to put a stop to the war, and then to confer with his fellow-citizens regarding the Volscians. He did, indeed, admit this embassy into his camp, but made no other concession, nor did he act or speak more mildly, but told them to make a settlement on his former

ἐκέλευε ποιεῖσθαι τὰς διαλύσεις ἢ δέχεσθαι τὸν
πόλεμον. ἐπανελθόντων οὖν τῶν ἱερέων ἔδοξεν
ἀτρεμοῦντας ἐν τῇ πόλει τὰ τείχη φυλάττειν καὶ
προσβάλλοντας ἀποκρούεσθαι τοὺς πολεμίους,
3 ἐν τῷ χρόνῳ μάλιστα καὶ τοῖς ἀπὸ τῆς τύχης
παραλόγοις τιθεμένοις τὰς ἐλπίδας, ἐπεὶ δι᾿ αὐτῶν
γε σωτήριον οὐδὲν ἠπίσταντο πράττοντες, ἀλλὰ
ταραχὴ καὶ πτοία καὶ φήμη πονηρὰ τὴν πόλιν
κατεῖχεν, ἄχρι οὗ συνέβη τι πρᾶγμα τῷ πολλάκις ὑφ᾿ Ὁμήρου λεγομένῳ,[1] μὴ πάνυ δὲ πείθοντι[2]
4 τοὺς πολλούς, ὅμοιον. λέγοντος γὰρ αὐτοῦ καὶ
ἀναφωνοῦντος ἐπὶ ταῖς μεγάλαις πράξεσι καὶ
παραλόγοις·

   Τῷ δ᾿ ἄρ᾿ ἐπὶ φρεσὶ θῆκε θεὰ γλαυκῶπις
     Ἀθήνη·

καὶ τὸ

   Ἀλλά τις ἀθανάτων τρέψεν φρένας, ὅς γ᾿ ἐνὶ
     θυμῷ
   δήμου θῆκε φάτιν·

καὶ τὸ

   Ἤ τι ὀϊσσάμενος ἢ καὶ θεὸς ὣς ἐκέλευε·

καταφρονοῦσιν ὡς ἀδυνάτοις πράγμασι καὶ μυθεύ-
μασιν ἀπίστοις τὸν ἑκάστου λογισμὸν τῆς προ-
5 αιρέσεως ἄπιστον[3] καθιστάντος. οὐ ποιεῖ δὲ
τοῦτο Ὅμηρος, ἀλλὰ τὰ μὲν εἰκότα καὶ συνήθη

---

[1] τῷ . . . λεγομένῳ Coraës and Bekker, after Reiske
(Amyot): τῶν . . . λεγομένων.

[2] πείθοντι Bekker, after Reiske : πεῖθον.

[3] ἄπιστον Bekker has ἀκρατῆ (*powerless to determine*).

terms, or else accept the war.[1] Accordingly, when the priests had returned, it was decided to remain quietly in the city, guarding its walls, and repulsing the enemy, should he make an attack. They put their hopes in time especially, and in the vicissitudes of fortune, since they knew not how to save themselves by their own efforts, but turmoil, terror, and rumours of evil possessed the city. At last something happened that was like what Homer often mentions, although people generally do not wholly believe it. For when some great and unusual deed is to be done, that poet declares in his stately manner :—

" He then was inspired by the goddess, flashing-eyed
    Athene " ; [2]

and again :—

" But some immortal turned his mind by lodging in
    his heart
  A fear of what the folk would say " ; [3]

and again :—

" Either through some suspicion, or else a god so
    bade him do " ; [4]

but people despise Homer and say that with his impossible exploits and incredible tales he makes it impossible to believe in every man's power to determine his own choice of action. This, however, is not what Homer does, but those acts which are natural, customary, and the result of reasoning, he

---

[1] Cf. Livy, ii. 39, 12 ; Dionysius, viii. 38.
[2] *Odyssey*, xviii. 158 = xxi. i. ($\tau\hat{\eta}$ δ' $\ddot{a}\rho a$).
[3] Not to be found now in Homer.   [4] *Odyssey*, ix. 339.

καὶ κατὰ λόγον περαινόμενα τῷ ἐφ' ἡμῖν ἀποδί-
δωσι, καὶ λέγει δήπου πολλάκις·

Αὐτὰρ ἐγὼ βούλευσα κατὰ μεγαλήτορα θυμόν·
καί,

  Ὡς φάτο, Πηλείωνι δ' ἄχος γένετ', ἐν δέ οἱ
    ἦτορ
  στήθεσσιν λασίοισι διάνδιχα μερμήριζεν·

καὶ πάλιν,

              ἀλλὰ τὸν οὔ τι
  πεῖθ' ἀγαθὰ φρονέοντα, δαΐφρονα Βελλεροφόν-
    την·

6 ἐν δὲ ταῖς ἀτόποις καὶ παραβόλοις πράξεσι καὶ
φορᾶς τινος ἐνθουσιώδους καὶ παραστάσεως δεο-
μέναις οὐκ ἀναιροῦντα ποιεῖ τὸν θεόν, ἀλλὰ
κινοῦντα τὴν προαίρεσιν, οὐδ' ὁρμὰς ἐνεργαζόμενον,
ἀλλὰ φαντασίας ὁρμῶν ἀγωγούς, αἷς οὐδὲ ποιεῖ
τὴν πρᾶξιν ἀκούσιον, ἀλλὰ τῷ ἑκουσίῳ δίδωσιν
ἀρχήν, καὶ τὸ θαρρεῖν καὶ τὸ ἐλπίζειν προστίθησιν.
7 ἢ γὰρ ἀπαλλακτέον ὅλως τὰ θεῖα πάσης αἰτίας
καὶ ἀρχῆς τῶν καθ' ἡμᾶς, ἢ τίς ἂν ἄλλος εἴη τρόπος
ᾧ βοηθοῦσιν ἀνθρώποις καὶ συνεργοῦσιν; οὐ τὸ
σῶμα δήπου πλάττοντες ἡμῶν, οὐδὲ τὰς χεῖρας,
ὡς δεῖ, μετατιθέντες αὐτοὶ καὶ τοὺς πόδας, ἀλλὰ
τῆς ψυχῆς τὸ πρακτικὸν καὶ προαιρετικὸν ἀρχαῖς
τισι καὶ φαντασίαις καὶ ἐπινοίαις ἐγείροντες ἢ
τοὐναντίον ἀποστρέφοντες καὶ ἱστάντες.

attributes to our own volition, and he certainly says frequently :—

" But I formed a plan within my lordly heart " ; [1]

and also :—

" So he spake, and Peleus' son was sore distressed,
  and his heart
  Within his shaggy breast between two courses was
      divided " ; [2]

and again :—

                    " But him no whit
  Could she persuade from his integrity, the fiery-
      hearted Bellerophon " ; [3]

while in exploits of a strange and extraordinary nature, requiring some rush of inspiration, and desperate courage, he does not represent the god as taking away, but as prompting, a man's choice of action ; nor yet as creating impulses in a man, but rather conceptions which lead to impulses, and by these his action is not made involuntary, but his will is set in motion, while courage and hope are added to sustain him. For either the influence of the gods must be wholly excluded from all initiating power over our actions, or in what other way can they assist and co-operate with men ? They certainly do not mould our bodies by their direct agency, nor give the requisite change to the action of our hands and feet, but rather, by certain motives, conceptions, and purposes, they rouse the active and elective powers of our spirits, or, on the other hand, divert and check them.

[1] *Odyssey*, ix. 299.   [2] *Iliad*, i. 188 f.   [3] *Iliad*, vi. 161 f.

XXXIII. Ἐν δὲ τῇ Ῥώμῃ τότε τῶν γυναικῶν
ἄλλαι μὲν πρὸς ἄλλοις ἱεροῖς, αἱ δὲ πλεῖσται καὶ
δοκιμώταται περὶ τὸν τοῦ Καπιτωλίου Διὸς βωμὸν
ἱκέτευον. ἐν δὲ ταύταις ἦν ἡ Ποπλικόλα τοῦ
μεγάλα καὶ πολλὰ Ῥωμαίους ἔν τε πολέμοις καὶ
πολιτείαις ὠφελήσαντος ἀδελφὴ Οὐαλερία. Ποπ-
λικόλας μὲν οὖν ἐτεθνήκει πρότερον, ὡς ἐν τοῖς
περὶ ἐκείνου γεγραμμένοις ἱστορήκαμεν, ἡ δὲ
Οὐαλερία δόξαν εἶχεν ἐν τῇ πόλει καὶ τιμήν,
2 δοκοῦσα τῷ βίῳ μὴ καταισχύνειν τὸ γένος. ὅπερ
οὖν λέγω πάθος ἐξαπίνης παθοῦσα, καὶ κατ᾿
ἐπίνοιαν οὐκ ἀθείαστον ἁψαμένη τοῦ συμφέροντος,
αὐτή τε ἀνέστη καὶ τὰς ἄλλας ἀναστήσασα πάσας
ἧκεν ἐπὶ τὴν οἰκίαν τῆς τοῦ Μαρκίου μητρὸς
Οὐολουμνίας. ὡς δ᾿ εἰσῆλθε καὶ κατέλαβε μετὰ
τῆς νυοῦ καθεζομένην καὶ τὰ παιδία τοῦ Μαρκίου
πρὸς τοῖς κόλποις ἔχουσαν, ἐν κύκλῳ περιστήσασα
3 τὰς γυναῖκας αὐτῆς· "Αὗται γε ἡμεῖς," εἶπεν, "ὦ 2
Οὐολουμνία, καὶ σύ, Οὐεργιλία, γυναῖκες ἥκομεν
πρὸς γυναῖκας, οὔτε βουλῆς ψηφισαμένης οὔτ᾿
ἄρχοντος κελεύσαντος, ἀλλ᾿ ὁ θεὸς ἡμῶν, ὡς
ἔοικεν, οἰκτείρας τὴν ἱκετείαν, ὁρμὴν παρέστησε
δευρὶ τραπέσθαι πρὸς ὑμᾶς καὶ δεηθῆναι σωτηρίαν μὲν αὐταῖς καὶ τοῖς ἄλλοις πολίταις, ὑμῖν
δὲ πεισθείσαις ἐπιφανεστέραν φέροντα δόξαν ἧς
αἱ Σαβίνων θυγατέρες ἔσχον, εἰς φιλίαν καὶ
εἰρήνην ἐκ πολέμων συναγαγοῦσαι πατέρας καὶ

---

[1] Chapter xxiii.

[2] "Then the matrons came in a body to Veturia, the
mother of Coriolanus, and Volumnia, his wife. Whether
this was the result of public counsel, or of the women's fear,

XXXIII. Now in Rome, at the time of which I speak, various groups of women visited the various temples, but the greater part of them, and those of highest station, carried their supplications to the altar of Jupiter Capitolinus. Among these was Valeria, a sister of that Publicola who had done the Romans so many eminent services both as warrior and statesman. Publicola, indeed, had died some time before, as I have related in his Life;[1] but Valeria was still enjoying her repute and honour in the city, where her life was thought to adorn her lineage. This woman, then, suddenly seized with one of those feelings which I have been describing, and laying hold of the right expedient with a purpose not uninspired of heaven, rose up herself, bade the other women all rise, and came with them to the house of Volumnia,[2] the mother of Marcius. After entering and finding her seated with her daughter-in-law, and holding the children of Marcius on her lap, Valeria called about her the women who had followed, and said: "We whom thou seest here, Volumnia, and thou, Vergilia, are come as women to women, obeying neither senatorial edict nor consular command; but our god, as it would seem, taking pity on our supplication, put into our hearts an impulse to come hither to you and beseech you to do that which will not only be the salvation of us ourselves and of the citizens besides, but also lift you who consent to do it to a more conspicuous fame than that which the daughters of the Sabines won, when they brought their fathers and husbands out

I cannot ascertain."—Livy, ii. **40**, 1. In Dionysius also (viii. 39, 40), whom Plutarch seems otherwise to be following, Veturia is the mother, and Volumnia the wife, of Marcius.

4 ἄνδρας. δεῦτε πρὸς Μάρκιον ἰοῦσαι μεθ' ἡμῶν
συνάψασθε τῆς ἱκετηρίας, καὶ μαρτυρήσατε τῇ
πατρίδι μαρτυρίαν ἀληθῆ καὶ δικαίαν, ὅτι πολλὰ
πάσχουσα κακῶς οὐδὲν οὔτ' ἔπραξε δεινὸν οὔτ'
ἐβούλευσε περὶ ὑμῶν δι' ὀργήν, ἀλλ' ἀποδίδωσιν
ὑμᾶς ἐκείνῳ κἂν μηδενὸς τυγχάνειν μέλλῃ τῶν
ἐπιεικῶν."

5 Ταῦτα τῆς Οὐαλερίας εἰπούσης ἀνεβόησαν αἱ
λοιπαὶ γυναῖκες, ἠμείψατο δὲ ἡ Οὐολουμνία·
"Καὶ τῶν κοινῶν ἡμῖν συμφορῶν, ὦ γυναῖκες,
ἴσον μέτεστι, καὶ ἰδίᾳ πράττομεν κακῶς ἀπολέ-
σασαι τὴν Μαρκίου δόξαν καὶ ἀρετήν, τὸ σῶμα δ'
αὐτοῦ τοῖς τῶν πολεμίων ὅπλοις φρουρούμενον
μᾶλλον ἢ σωζόμενον ἐφορῶσαι. μέγιστον δ' ἡμῖν
τῶν ἀτυχημάτων ἐστίν, εἰ τὰ τῆς πατρίδος οὕτως
6 ἐξησθένηκεν ὥστ' ἐν ἡμῖν ἔχειν τὰς ἐλπίδας. οὐκ
οἶδα γὰρ εἴ τινα ποιήσεται λόγον ἡμῶν ἐκεῖνος, εἴ
γε μηδένα ποιεῖται τῆς πατρίδος, ἣν καὶ μητρὸς
καὶ γυναικὸς καὶ τέκνων προετίμησεν. οὐ μὴν
ἀλλὰ χρῆσθε ἡμῖν λαβοῦσαι καὶ κομίζετε πρὸς
ἐκεῖνον, εἰ μηδὲν ἄλλο, ταῖς ὑπὲρ τῆς πατρίδος
ἱκεσίαις ἐναποπνεῦσαι δυναμένας."

XXXIV. Ἐκ τούτου τά τε παιδία καὶ τὴν
Οὐεργιλίαν ἀναστήσασα μετὰ τῶν ἄλλων γυναικῶν ἐβάδιζεν εἰς τὸ στρατόπεδον τῶν Οὐολούσκων. ἡ δ' ὄψις αὐτῶν τό τ' οἰκτρὸν καὶ τοῖς
πολεμίοις ἐνεποίησεν αἰδῶ καὶ σιωπήν. ἔτυχε δ'
ὁ Μάρκιος ἐπὶ βήματος καθεζόμενος μετὰ τῶν
2 ἡγεμονικῶν. ὡς οὖν εἶδε προσιούσας τὰς γυναῖκας, ἐθαύμασεν· ἐπιγνοὺς δὲ τὴν μητέρα πρώτην
βαδίζουσαν ἐβούλετο μὲν ἐμμένειν τοῖς ἀτρέπτοις

of war into friendship and peace. Arise, come with us to Marcius, and join with us in supplicating him, bearing this just and true testimony in behalf of your country, that, although she has suffered much wrong at his hands, she has neither done nor thought of doing harm to you, in her anger, but restores you to him, even though she is destined to obtain no equitable treatment at his hands."

These words of Valeria were seconded by the cries of the other women with her, and Volumnia gave them this answer:—"O women, not only have we an equal share with you in the common calamities, but we have an additional misery of our own, in that we have lost the fame and virtue of Marcius, and see his person protected in command, rather than preserved from death, by the arms of our enemies. And yet it is the greatest of our misfortunes that our native city is become so utterly weak as to place her hopes in us. For I know not whether the man will have any regard for us, since he has none for his country, which he once set before mother and wife and children. However, take us and use us and bring us to him; if we can do nothing else, we can at least breathe out our lives in supplications for our country."

XXXIV. After this, she took the children and Vergilia and went with the other women to the camp of the Volscians. The sight of them, and the pitifulness of it, produced even in their enemies reverence and silence. Now it chanced that Marcius was seated on a tribunal with his chief officers. When, accordingly, he saw the women approaching, he was amazed; and when he recognized his mother, who walked at their head, he would fain have persisted

ἐκείνοις καὶ ἀπαραιτήτοις λογισμοῖς, γενόμενος δὲ
τοῦ πάθους ἐλάττων καὶ συνταραχθεὶς πρὸς τὴν
ὄψιν οὐκ ἔτλη καθεζομένῳ προσελθεῖν, ἀλλὰ
καταβὰς θᾶττον ἢ βάδην καὶ ἀπαντήσας πρώτην
μὲν ἠσπάσατο τὴν μητέρα καὶ πλεῖστον χρόνον,
εἶτα δὲ τὴν γυναῖκα καὶ τὰ τέκνα, μήτε δακρύων
ἔτι μήτε τοῦ φιλοφρονεῖσθαι φειδόμενος, ἀλλ'
ὥσπερ ὑπὸ ῥεύματος φέρεσθαι τοῦ πάθους ἑαυτὸν
ἐνδεδωκώς.

XXXV. Ἐπεὶ δὲ τούτων ἅδην εἶχε καὶ τὴν
μητέρα βουλομένην ἤδη λόγων ἄρχειν ᾔσθετο,
τοὺς τῶν Οὐολούσκων προβούλους παραστησά-
μενος ἤκουσε τῆς Οὐολουμνίας τοιαῦτα λεγούσης·
" Ὁρᾷς μέν, ὦ παῖ, κἂν αὐταὶ μὴ λέγωμεν,
ἐσθῆτι καὶ μορφῇ τῶν ἀθλίων σωμάτων τεκμαιρόμενος, οἵαν οἰκουρίαν ἡμῖν ἡ σὴ φυγὴ περιεποιή-
2 σατο· λόγισαι δὲ νῦν ὡς ἀτυχέσταται πασῶν
ἀφίγμεθα γυναικῶν, αἷς τὸ ἥδιστον θέαμα φο-
βερώτατον ἡ τύχη πεποίηκεν, ἐμοὶ μὲν υἱόν,
ταύτῃ δ' ἄνδρα τοῖς τῆς πατρίδος τείχεσιν ἰδεῖν
ἀντικαθήμενον. ὃ δ' ἔστι τοῖς ἄλλοις ἀτυχίας
πάσης καὶ κακοπραγίας παραμύθιον, εὔχεσθαι
θεοῖς, ἡμῖν ἀπορώτατον γέγονεν. οὐ γὰρ οἷόν τε
καὶ τῇ πατρίδι νίκην ἅμα καὶ σοὶ σωτηρίαν
αἰτεῖσθαι παρὰ τῶν θεῶν, ἀλλ' ἅ τις ἂν ἡμῖν
καταράσαιτο τῶν ἐχθρῶν, ταῦτα ταῖς ἡμετέραις
3 ἔνεστιν εὐχαῖς. ἀνάγκη γὰρ ἢ τῆς πατρίδος ἢ
σοῦ στέρεσθαι γυναικὶ σῇ καὶ τέκνοις. ἐγὼ δ' οὐ
περιμενῶ ταύτην μοι διαιτῆσαι τὴν τύχην ζώσῃ
τὸν πόλεμον, ἀλλ' εἰ μή σε πείσαιμι φιλίαν καὶ
ὁμόνοιαν ἀντὶ διαφορᾶς καὶ κακῶν θέμενον ἀμφο-

in his previous inflexible and implacable course, but, mastered by his feelings, and confounded at what he saw, he could not endure to remain seated while they approached him, but descended quickly from the tribunal and ran to meet them. He saluted his mother first, and held her a long time in his embrace, and then his wife and children, sparing now neither tears nor caresses, but suffering himself as it were to be borne away by a torrent of emotion.

XXXV. But when he was sated with this, and perceived that his mother now wished to say something, he brought to his side the councillors of the Volscians, and heard Volumnia speak as follows: "Thou seest, my son, even if we do not speak ourselves, and canst judge from the wretchedness of our garb and aspect, to what a pitiful state thy banishment has reduced us. And now be sure that we who come to thee are of all women most unhappy, since fortune has made the sight which should have been most sweet, most dreadful for us, as I behold my son, and this wife of thine her husband, encamped against the walls of our native city. And that which for the rest is an assuagement of all misfortune and misery, namely prayer to the gods, has become for us most impracticable; for we cannot ask from the gods both victory for our country and at the same time safety for thee, but that which any one of our foes might imprecate upon us as a curse, this must be the burden of our prayers. For thy wife and children must needs be deprived either of their country or of thee. As for me, I will not wait to have the war decide this issue for me while I live, but unless I can persuade thee to substitute friendship and concord for dissension and hostility, and so

τερων εὐεργέτην γενέσθαι μᾶλλον ἢ λυμεῶνα τῶν
ἑτέρων, οὕτω διανοοῦ καὶ παρασκεύαζε σεαυτὸν
ὡς τῇ πατρίδι μὴ προσμῖξαι δυνάμενος πρὶν ἢ 2:
νεκρὰν ὑπερβῆναι τὴν τεκοῦσαν. οὐ γὰρ ἐκείνην
με δεῖ τὴν ἡμέραν ἀναμένειν ἐν ᾗ τὸν υἱὸν ἐπ-
όψομαι θριαμβευόμενον ὑπὸ τῶν πολιτῶν ἢ θριαμ-
4 βεύοντα κατὰ τῆς πατρίδος. εἰ μὲν οὖν ἀξιῶ σε
τὴν πατρίδα σῶσαι Οὐολούσκους ἀπολέσαντα,
χαλεπή σοι καὶ δυσδιαίτητος, ὦ παῖ, πρόκειται
σκέψις· οὔτε γὰρ διαφθεῖραι τοὺς πολίτας καλόν,
οὔτε τοὺς πεπιστευκότας προδοῦναι δίκαιον· νῦν
δ' ἀπαλλαγὴν κακῶν αἰτούμεθα, σωτήριον μὲν
ἀμφοτέροις ὁμοίως, ἔνδοξον δὲ καὶ καλὴν μᾶλλον
Οὐολούσκοις, ὅτι τῷ κρατεῖν δόξουσι διδόναι τὰ
μέγιστα τῶν ἀγαθῶν, οὐχ ἧττον λαμβάνοντες,
εἰρήνην καὶ φιλίαν, ὧν μάλιστα μὲν αἴτιος ἔσῃ
γινομένων, μὴ γινομένων δὲ μόνος αἰτίαν ἕξεις
5 παρ' ἀμφοτέροις. ἄδηλος δ' ὢν ὁ πόλεμος τοῦτ'
ἔχει πρόδηλον, ὅτι σοι νικῶντι μὲν ἀλάστορι τῆς
πατρίδος εἶναι περίεστιν, ἡττώμενος δὲ δόξεις ὑπ'
ὀργῆς εὐεργέταις ἀνδράσι καὶ φίλοις τῶν μεγίστων
συμφορῶν αἴτιος γεγονέναι."

XXXVI. Ταῦτα τῆς Οὐολουμνίας λεγούσης ὁ
Μάρκιος ἠκροᾶτο μηδὲν ἀποκρινόμενος. ἐπεὶ δὲ
καὶ παυσαμένης εἱστήκει σιωπῶν πολὺν χρόνον,
αὖθις ἡ Οὐολουμνία· "Τί σιγᾷς," εἶπεν, "ὦ παῖ;
πότερον ὀργῇ καὶ μνησικακίᾳ πάντα συγχωρεῖν
καλόν, οὐ καλὸν δὲ μητρὶ χαρίσασθαι δεομένῃ

to become a benefactor of both parties rather than a destroyer of one of them, then consider and be well assured that thou canst not assail thy country without first treading underfoot the corpse of her who bore thee. For it does not behoove me to await that day on which I shall behold my son either led in triumph by his fellow-citizens or triumphing over his country. If, then, I asked you to save your country by ruining the Volscians, the question before thee would be a grievous one, my son, and hard to decide, since it is neither honourable for a man to destroy his fellow-citizens, nor just for him to betray those who have put their trust in him; but as it is, we ask only a relief from evils, something which would be salutary for both parties alike, but more conducive to fame and honour for the Volscians, because their superiority in arms will give them the appearance of bestowing the greatest of blessings, namely peace and friendship, although they get these no less themselves. If these blessings are realized, it will be chiefly due to thee; if they are not, then thou alone wilt bear the blame from both nations. And though the issues of war are obscure, this is manifest, that if victorious, thou wilt only be thy country's destroying demon, and if defeated, the world will think that, to satisfy thy wrath, thou didst bring down the greatest calamities upon men who were thy benefactors and friends."

XXXVI. While Volumnia was saying this, Marcius listened without making any answer, and after she had ceased also, he stood a long time in silence. Volumnia therefore began once more: "Why art thou silent, my son? Is it right to yield everything to wrath and resentment, but wrong to gratify a

2 περὶ τηλικούτων; ἢ τὸ μεμνῆσθαι πεπονθότα
κακῶς ἀνδρὶ μεγάλῳ προσήκει, τὸ δ᾽ εὐεργεσίας,
αἷς εὐεργετοῦνται παῖδες ὑπὸ τῶν τεκόντων,
σέβεσθαι καὶ τιμᾶν οὐκ ἀνδρὸς ἔργον ἐστὶ
μεγάλου καὶ ἀγαθοῦ; καὶ μὴν οὐδενὶ μᾶλλον
ἔπρεπε τηρεῖν χάριν ὡς σοί, πικρῶς οὕτως ἀχαρι-
3 στίαν ἐπεξιόντι. καίτοι παρὰ τῆς πατρίδος ἤδη
μεγάλας δίκας ἀπείληφας, τῇ μητρὶ δ᾽ οὐδεμίαν
χάριν ἀποδέδωκας. ἦν μὲν οὖν ὁσιώτατον ἄνευ
τινὸς ἀνάγκης τυχεῖν με παρὰ σοῦ δεομένην
οὕτω καλῶν καὶ δικαίων· μὴ πείθουσα δὲ τί
φείδομαι τῆς ἐσχάτης ἐλπίδος ; " καὶ ταῦτ᾽
εἰποῦσα προσπίπτει τοῖς ποσὶν αὐτοῦ μετὰ τῆς
4 γυναικὸς ἅμα καὶ τῶν τέκνων. ὁ δὲ Μάρκιος
ἀναβοήσας· "Οἷα εἴργασαί με, ὦ μῆτερ," ἐξανί-
στησιν αὐτήν, καὶ τὴν δεξιὰν πιέσας σφόδρα·
"Νενίκηκας," εἶπεν, "εὐτυχῆ μὲν τῇ πατρίδι
νίκην, ἐμοὶ δ᾽ ὀλέθριον· ἄπειμι γὰρ ὑπὸ σοῦ
μόνης ἡττώμενος." τοῦτο δ᾽ εἰπών, καὶ βραχέα
τῇ μητρὶ καὶ τῇ γυναικὶ διαλεχθεὶς ἰδίᾳ, τὰς
μὲν ἀπέπεμψεν εἰς Ῥώμην πάλιν αὐτὰς δεομένας,
τῆς δὲ νυκτὸς παρελθούσης ἀπήγαγεν Οὐολούσκους, οὐ τὸν αὐτὸν τρόπον οὐδ᾽ ὁμοίως διακει-
5 μένους ἅπαντας. οἱ μὲν γὰρ ἐμέμφοντο καὶ τὸν
ἄνδρα καὶ τὴν πρᾶξιν, οἱ δὲ οὐδέτερα, πρὸς
διάλυσιν καὶ εἰρήνην οἰκείως ἔχοντες, ἔνιοι δὲ
δυσχεραίνοντες τὰ πραττόμενα τὸν Μάρκιον
ὅμως οὐ πονηρὸν ἐνόμιζον, ἀλλὰ συγγνωστὸν
ἐπικλασθέντα τηλικαύταις ἀνάγκαις. ἀντεῖπε

mother in such a prayer as this? Or is the remembrance of his wrongs becoming to a great man, while the remembrance, with reverence and honour, of the benefits which children have received from their parents is not the duty of a great and good man? Surely for no man were it more seemly to cherish gratitude than for thee, who dost so bitterly proceed against ingratitude. And yet, although thou hast already punished thy country severely, thou hast not shown thy mother any gratitude. It were, therefore, a most pious thing in thee to grant me, without any compulsion, so worthy and just a request as mine; but since I cannot persuade thee, why should I spare my last resource?" And with these words she threw herself at his feet, together with his wife and children. Then Marcius, crying out "What hast thou done to me, my mother!" lifted her up, and pressing her right hand warmly, said: "Thou art victorious, and thy victory means good fortune to my country, but death to me; for I shall withdraw vanquished, though by thee alone." When he had said this, and had held a little private conference with his mother and his wife, he sent them back again to Rome, as they desired, and on the next morning led away his Volscians, who were not all affected in the same way nor equally pleased by what had happened. For some found fault both with him and with what he had done; but others, who were favourably disposed towards a peaceful settlement of the dispute, with neither; while some, though displeased with his proceedings, nevertheless could not look upon Marcius as a bad man, but thought it pardonable in him to be broken down by such strong compulsions. No one, however, opposed him, but all followed

δ' οὐδείς, ἀλλὰ πάντες εἵποντο, τὴν ἀρετὴν μᾶλλον
αὐτοῦ θαυμάζοντες ἢ τὴν ἐξουσίαν.

XXXVII. Ὁ δὲ Ῥωμαίων δῆμος ἐν ὅσῳ φόβῳ
καὶ κινδύνῳ καθειστήκει τοῦ πολέμου παρόντος,
αἴσθησιν παρέσχε μᾶλλον λυθέντος. ἅμα γὰρ
ἀφεώρων τοὺς Οὐολούσκους ἀναζευγνύντας οἱ
περὶ τὰ τείχη, καὶ πᾶν εὐθὺς ἱερὸν ἀνεῴγει
στεφανηφορούντων ὥσπερ ἐπὶ νίκῃ καὶ θυόντων.
μάλιστα δὲ τῇ περὶ τὰς γυναῖκας ἀγαπήσει καὶ
τιμῇ τῆς τε βουλῆς τοῦ τε πλήθους ἅπαντος
ἔνδηλος ἦν ἡ χαρὰ τῆς πόλεως, καὶ λεγόντων
καὶ νομιζόντων γεγονέναι τῆς σωτηρίας περι-
2 φανῶς ἐκείνας αἰτίας. ψηφισαμένης δὲ τῆς
βουλῆς, ὅ τι ἂν αὐταῖς ἀξιώσωσι γενέσθαι πρὸς
δόξαν ἢ χάριν, τοῦτο ποιῆσαι καὶ παρασχεῖν
τοὺς ἄρχοντας, οὐδὲν ἠξίωσαν ἄλλο ἢ Τύχης
γυναικείας ἱερὸν ἱδρύσασθαι, τὸ μὲν ἀνάλωμα
συμβαλόμεναι παρ' αὑτῶν, ἱερουργίας δὲ καὶ
τιμάς, ὅσαι θεοῖς πρέπουσι, δημοσίᾳ τῆς πόλεως
3 ἀναλαβούσης. ἐπεὶ δὲ ἡ βουλὴ τὴν μὲν φιλοτιμίαν ἐπήνεσε, δημοσίαις δὲ δαπάναις ἐποιήσατο
τὸν νεὼν καὶ τὸ ἕδος, οὐδὲν ἧττον αὐταὶ χρήματα
συνεισενεγκοῦσαι δεύτερον ἄγαλμα κατεσκεύασαν,
ὃ δὴ καί φασι Ῥωμαῖοι καθιστάμενον ἐν τῷ ἱερῷ
φθέγξασθαί τι τοιοῦτον· "Θεοφιλεῖ με θεσμῷ
γυναῖκες δεδώκατε."

XXXVIII. Ταύτην καὶ δὶς γενέσθαι τὴν φωνὴν
μυθολογοῦσιν, ἀγενήτοις ὅμοια καὶ χαλεπὰ πει-

him obediently, though rather out of admiration for his virtue than regard for his authority.[1]

XXXVII. But the Roman people showed more plainly, when they were set free from the war, the greatness of their fear and peril while it lasted. For as soon as those who manned the walls descried the Volscians drawing their forces off, every temple was thrown open, and the people crowned themselves with garlands and offered sacrifices as if for victory. But the joy of the city was most apparent in the honour and loving favour which both the senate and the whole people bestowed upon the women, declaring their belief that the city's salvation was manifestly due to them. When, however, the senate passed a decree that whatsoever they asked for themselves in the way of honour or favour, should be furnished and done for them by the magistrates, they asked for nothing else besides the erection of a temple of Women's Fortune, the expense of which they offered to contribute of themselves, if the city would undertake to perform, at the public charge, all the sacrifices and honours, such as are due to the gods. The senate commended their public spirit, and erected the temple and its image at the public charge,[2] but they none the less contributed money themselves and set up a second image of the goddess, and this, the Romans say, as it was placed in the temple, uttered some such words as these : " Dear to the gods, O women, is your pious gift of me." [3]

XXXVIII. These words were actually uttered twice, as the story runs, which would have us be-

[1] Compare Livy's story of this interview and its results (ii. 40, 3–9). Plutarch agrees rather with Dionysius, viii. 39–54.

[2] Cf. Livy, ii. 40, 11.   [3] Cf. Dionysius, viii. 56.

σθῆναι πείθοντες ἡμᾶς. ἰδίοντα μὲν γὰρ ἀγάλματα φανῆναι καὶ δακρυρροοῦντα καί τινας
μεθιέντα νοτίδας αἱματώδεις οὐκ ἀδύνατόν ἐστι·
καὶ γὰρ ξύλα καὶ λίθοι πολλάκις μὲν εὐρῶτα
συνάγουσι γόνιμον ὑγρότητος, πολλὰς δὲ χροιὰς
ἀνιᾶσιν ἐξ ἑαυτῶν, καὶ δέχονται βαφὰς ἐκ τοῦ
περιέχοντος, οἷς ἔνια σημαίνειν τὸ δαιμόνιον οὐδὲν
2 ἂν δόξειε κωλύειν. δυνατὸν δὲ καὶ μυγμῷ καὶ
στεναγμῷ ψόφον ὅμοιον ἐκβάλλειν ἀγάλματα
κατὰ ῥῆξιν ἢ διάστασιν μορίων βιαιοτέραν ἐν
βάθει γενομένην· ἔναρθρον δὲ φωνὴν καὶ διά-
λεκτον οὕτω σαφῆ καὶ περιττὴν καὶ ἀρτίστομον
ἐν ἀψύχῳ γενέσθαι παντάπασιν ἀμήχανον, εἰ
μηδὲ τὴν ψυχὴν καὶ τὸν θεὸν ἄνευ σώματος
ὀργανικοῦ καὶ διηρμοσμένου μέρεσι λογικοῖς
3 γέγονεν ἠχεῖν καὶ διαλέγεσθαι. ὅπου δ' ἡμᾶς ἡ
ἱστορία πολλοῖς ἀποβιάζεται καὶ πιθανοῖς μάρ-
τυσιν, ἀνόμοιον αἰσθήσει πάθος ἐγγινόμενον τῷ
φανταστικῷ τῆς ψυχῆς συναναπείθει τὸ δόξαν,
ὥσπερ ἐν ὕπνοις ἀκούειν οὐκ ἀκούοντες καὶ
βλέπειν οὐ βλέποντες δοκοῦμεν. οὐ μὴν ἀλλὰ
τοῖς ὑπ' εὐνοίας καὶ φιλίας πρὸς τὸν θεὸν ἄγαν
ἐμπαθῶς ἔχουσι, καὶ μηδὲν ἀθετεῖν μηδ' ἀναίνε-
σθαι τῶν τοιούτων δυναμένοις, μέγα πρὸς πίστιν
ἐστὶ τὸ θαυμάσιον καὶ μὴ καθ' ἡμᾶς τῆς τοῦ
4 θεοῦ δυνάμεως. οὐδὲν γὰρ οὐδαμῶς ἀνθρωπίνῳ
προσέοικεν οὔτε φύσιν οὔτε κίνησιν οὔτε τέχνην
οὔτ' ἰσχύν, οὐδ' εἴ τι ποιεῖ τῶν ἡμῖν ἀποιήτων
καὶ μηχανᾶται τῶν ἀμηχάνων, παράλογόν ἐστιν,

lieve what is difficult of belief and probably never happened. For that statues have appeared to sweat, and shed tears, and exude something like drops of blood, is not impossible; since wood and stone often contract a mould which is productive of moisture, and cover themselves with many colours, and receive tints from the atmosphere; and there is nothing in the way of believing that the Deity uses these phenomena sometimes as signs and portents. It is possible also that statues may emit a noise like a moan or a groan, by reason of a fracture or a rupture, which is more violent if it takes place in the interior. But that articulate speech, and language so clear and abundant and precise, should proceed from a lifeless thing, is altogether impossible; since not even the soul of man, or the Deity, without a body duly organized and fitted with vocal parts, has ever spoken and conversed. But where history forces our assent with numerous and credible witnesses, we must conclude that an experience different from that of sensation arises in the imaginative part of the soul, and persuades men to think it sensation; as, for instance, in sleep, when we think we see and hear, although we neither see nor hear. However, those who cherish strong feelings of good-will and affection for the Deity, and are therefore unable to reject or deny anything of this kind, have a strong argument for their faith in the wonderful and transcendent character of the divine power. For the Deity has no resemblance whatever to man, either in nature, activity, skill, or strength; nor, if He does something that we cannot do, or contrives something that we cannot contrive, is this contrary to reason; but rather, since He differs from us in all

213

ἀλλὰ μᾶλλον ἐν πᾶσι διαφέρων πολὺ μάλιστα
τοῖς ἔργοις ἀνόμοιός ἐστι καὶ παρηλλαγμένος.
ἀλλὰ τῶν μὲν θείων τὰ πολλά, καθ᾽ Ἡράκλειτον,
ἀπιστίῃ διαφυγγάνει μὴ γινώσκεσθαι.

XXXIX. Τὸν δὲ Μάρκιον, ὡς ἐπανῆλθεν εἰς
τὸ Ἄντιον ἀπὸ τῆς στρατείας, μισῶν πάλαι
καὶ βαρυνόμενος διὰ φθόνον ὁ Τύλλος ἐπεβού-
λευεν ἀνελεῖν εὐθύς, ὡς εἰ νῦν διαφύγοι, λαβὴν
ἑτέραν οὐ παρέξοντα. πολλοὺς δὲ συστήσας καὶ
παρασκευάσας ἐπ᾽ αὐτὸν ἐκέλευσεν εὐθύνας ὑποσχεῖν τοῖς Οὐολούσκοις, ἀποδόντα τὴν ἀρχήν.
2 ὁ δὲ φοβούμενος ἰδιώτης γενέσθαι τοῦ Τύλλου
στρατηγοῦντος καὶ δυναμένου μέγιστον ἐν τοῖς
ἑαυτοῦ πολίταις, ἔλεγε τὴν ἀρχὴν ἀποδώσειν
Οὐολούσκοις, ἐὰν κελεύωσι, καὶ γὰρ λαβεῖν
πάντων κελευόντων, εὐθύνας δὲ διδόναι καὶ λόγον
οὐδὲ νῦν παραιτεῖσθαι τοῖς βουλομένοις Ἀντιατῶν. γενομένης οὖν ἐκκλησίας, οἱ παρεσκευασ-
μένοι τῶν δημαγωγῶν ἀνιστάμενοι παρώξυνον τὸ
3 πλῆθος. ἐπεὶ δ᾽ ἀναστάντι τῷ Μαρκίῳ τὸ μὲν
ἄγαν θορυβοῦν ὑπ᾽ αἰδοῦς ἐνεδίδου καὶ παρεῖχεν
ἀδεῶς λέγειν, οἱ δὲ βέλτιστοι καὶ μάλιστα
χαίροντες εἰρήνῃ τῶν Ἀντιατῶν ἐγένοντο φανεροὶ
μετ᾽ εὐνοίας ἀκουσόμενοι καὶ δικαίως κρινοῦντες,
ἔδεισεν ὁ Τύλλος τὴν ἀπολογίαν τοῦ ἀνδρός.
ἦν γὰρ ἐν τοῖς μάλιστα δεινὸς εἰπεῖν, καὶ τὰ

points, in His works most of all is He unlike us and far removed from us. But most of the Deity's powers, as Heracleitus says,[1] "escape our knowledge through incredulity."

XXXIX. But as for Marcius, when he came back to Antium from his expedition, Tullus, who had long hated him and been oppressed with jealousy of him, plotted to take him off at once, believing that if his enemy escaped him now, he would never give him another chance to seize him. Having, therefore, arrayed a large party against him, he bade him lay down his command and give the Volscians an account of his administration. But Marcius, afraid of being reduced to private station when Tullus was in command and exercising the greatest influence among his own countrymen, said he would resign his command to the Volscians, if they bade him do so, since it was at their general bidding that he had assumed it; and that he was ready, and would not refuse even before that, to give a full account of his administration to all the people of Antium who desired it. An assembly was therefore held, at which the popular leaders who had been set to the work rose and tried to embitter the multitude against him. But when Marcius rose to speak, the more disorderly part of his audience grew quiet, out of reverence for him, and gave him opportunity to speak fearlessly, while the best of the men of Antium, and those that were especially pleased with peace, made it clear that they would listen to him with favour and give a just decision. Tullus, therefore, began to fear the effect of the man's plea in self-defence; for he was one of the most powerful speakers, and his earlier achievements

[1] Fragment 116 (Bywater, p. 45).

πρόσθεν ἔργα μείζονα τὴν χάριν εἶχε τῆς ὕστερον αἰτίας, μᾶλλον δ' ὅλως τὸ ἔγκλημα τοῦ
4 μεγέθους τῆς χάριτος ἦν μαρτύριον. οὐ γὰρ ἂν
ἔδοξαν ἀδικεῖσθαι τὴν Ῥώμην ὑποχείριον μὴ
λαβόντες, εἰ μὴ τοῦ λαβεῖν ἐγγὺς ἐγένοντο διὰ
Μάρκιον.

Οὐκέτ' οὖν ἔδοξε διαμέλλειν οὐδὲ πειρᾶσθαι 23
τῶν πολλῶν, ἀλλ' ἐγκραγόντες οἱ θρασύτατοι
τῶν συνεστώτων ὡς οὐκ ἔστιν ἀκουστέον οὐδὲ
περιοπτέον Οὐολούσκοις τὸν προδότην τυραν-
νοῦντα καὶ μὴ κατατιθέμενον τὴν ἀρχήν, προσπεσόντες ἀθρόοι διέφθειραν αὐτόν, καὶ προσήμυνεν
5 οὐδεὶς τῶν παρόντων. ὅτι δὲ τοῖς πλείστοις οὐκ
ἐπράχθη κατὰ γνώμην, ἐδήλωσαν αὐτίκα συνδρα-
μόντες ἐκ τῶν πόλεων ἐπὶ τὸ σῶμα καὶ θάψαντες
ἐντίμως καὶ τὸν τάφον ὅπλοις καὶ λαφύροις
κοσμήσαντες ὡς ἀριστέως καὶ στρατηγοῦ. Ῥωμαῖοι δὲ τὴν τελευτὴν πυθόμενοι, ἄλλο μὲν οὐδὲν
ἀπεδείξαντο σημεῖον οὔτε τιμῆς οὔτ' ὀργῆς πρὸς
αὐτόν, αἰτησαμέναις δὲ ταῖς γυναιξὶν ἐπέτρεψαν
ἀποπενθῆσαι δέκα μῆνας, ὥσπερ ἔθος ἦν ἑκάστῃ
πατέρα καὶ παῖδα καὶ ἀδελφόν. οὗτος γὰρ ἦν
ὅρος τοῦ μακροτάτου πένθους, ὃν ὥρισε Νομᾶς
Πομπίλιος, ὡς ἐν τοῖς περὶ ἐκείνου γεγραμμένοις
δεδήλωται.

6 Τὸν δὲ Μάρκιον εὐθὺς ἐπόθει τὰ Οὐολούσκων
πράγματα. πρῶτον μὲν γὰρ στασιάσαντες πρὸς
Αἰκανοὺς συμμάχους καὶ φίλους ὄντας ὑπὲρ

---

[1] "Then, after he had withdrawn his troops from the
Roman territory, they say that he was overwhelmed with
hatred in consequence, and lost his life, different writers
giving different details of his death. In Fabius, who is by

secured him a gratitude which outweighed his later
fault; nay more, the very charge against him was
but so much proof of the great gratitude which was
his due. For they would not have thought themselves
wronged in not getting Rome into their power, had
not the efforts of Marcius brought them near to
taking it.

Accordingly, the conspirators decided to make no
more delay, and not to test the feelings of the multitude; but the boldest of them, crying out that the
Volscians must not listen to the traitor, nor suffer him
to retain his command and play the tyrant among
them, fell upon him in a body and slew him, and no
man present offered to defend him.[1] However, that
the deed was not wrought with the approval of the
majority of the Volscians, was seen at once from their
coming out of their cities in concourse to his body,
to which they gave honourable burial, adorning his
tomb with arms and spoils, as that of a chieftain and
general. But when the Romans learned of his death,
they paid him no other mark either of honour or
resentment, but simply granted the request of the
women that they might mourn for him ten months,
as was customary when any one of them lost a father,
or a son, or a brother. For this was the period fixed
for the longest mourning, and it was fixed by Numa
Pompilius, as is written in his Life.[2]

The loss of Marcius was keenly felt at once by the
Volscian state. For, in the first place, they quarrelled
with the Aequians, who were their allies and friends,
over the supreme command, and carried their quarrel

far the most ancient authority, I find that he lived even to
old age" (Livy, ii. 40, 10). Chapter xxxix. in Plutarch
agrees closely with Dionysius viii. 57-59, who says that
Marcius was stoned to death.   [2] Chapter xii. 2.

ἡγεμονίας, ἄχρι τραυμάτων καὶ φόνων προῆλθον·
ἔπειτα μάχῃ κρατηθέντες ὑπὸ Ῥωμαίων, ἐν ᾗ
Τύλλος ἀπέθανε καὶ τὸ ἀνθοῦν μάλιστα τῆς δυνάμεως διεφθάρη, διαλύσεις αἰσχίστας ἠγάπησαν
ὑπήκοοι γενόμενοι, καὶ τὸ προσταττόμενον αὐτοῖς
ποιήσειν ὁμολογήσαντες.

ΑΛΚΙΒΙΑΔΟΥ ΚΑΙ ΚΟΡΙΟΛΑΝΟΥ ΣΥΓΚΡΙΣΙΣ

I. Ἐκκειμένων δὲ τῶν πράξεων, ὅσας ἡγού-
μεθα λόγου καὶ μνήμης ἀξίας εἶναι, τὰς μὲν πολεμικὰς ἐπ' οὐδέτερον ποιούσας ῥοπὴν μεγάλην ὁρᾶν
ἔστιν. ὁμαλῶς γὰρ ἀμφότεροι πολλὰ μὲν στρα-
τιωτικῆς ἔργα τόλμης καὶ ἀνδρείας, πολλὰ δὲ καὶ
τέχνης καὶ προνοίας στρατηγοῦντες ἐπεδείξαντο,
2 πλὴν εἰ μή τις θέλοι τὸν Ἀλκιβιάδην, ὅτι καὶ
κατὰ γῆν καὶ κατὰ θάλατταν ἐν πολλοῖς ἀγῶσι
νικῶν καὶ κατορθῶν διετέλεσεν, ἀποφαίνειν τελειό-
τερον στρατηγόν· ἐπεὶ τό γε παρόντας καὶ ἄρχοντας ὀρθοῦν ἀεὶ προδήλως τὰ οἰκεῖα καὶ προ-
δηλότερον αὖ πάλιν βλάπτειν μεθισταμένους
3 ἀμφοτέροις ὑπῆρξε. πολιτείαν δὲ τὴν μὲν Ἀλκιβιάδου τὴν ἄγαν λαμυρὰν καὶ τὸ μὴ καθαρεῦον
ἀναγωγίας καὶ βωμολοχίας ἐν τῷ πρὸς χάριν
ὁμιλεῖν τοῖς πολλοῖς οἱ σώφρονες ἐβδελύττοντο,
τὴν δὲ Μαρκίου παντάπασιν ἄχαριν καὶ ὑπερη-

to the length of bloodshed and slaughter; in the
second place, they were defeated in battle by the
Romans, wherein Tullus was slain and the very flower
of their forces was cut to pieces, so that they were
glad to accept most disgraceful terms, becoming subjects of Rome, and pledging themselves to obey her
commands.[1]

COMPARISON OF ALCIBIADES AND CORIOLANUS

I. Now that all the deeds of these men are set
forth, so far as we consider them worthy of recol-
lection and record, it is plain that their military
careers do not incline the balance either way very
decidedly. For both alike gave many signal proofs
of daring and valour as soldiers, as well as of skill
and foresight as commanders; except that some may
give the preference to Alcibiades, because he was
continually successful and victorious in many struggles
by sea, as well as by land, and declare him therefore
the more consummate general. It is certainly true
of each that, when he was at home and in command,
he always conducted his country's cause with manifest
success, and, contrariwise, inflicted even more manifest injury upon it when he went over to the enemy.
As statesmen, if the exceeding wantonness of Alcibiades, and the stain of dissoluteness and vulgarity
upon all his efforts to win the favour of the multitude, won the loathing of sober-minded citizens, it
was equally true that the utter ungraciousness of

[1] Cf. Livy, ii. 40, 12 f.

φανον καὶ ὀλιγαρχικὴν γενομένην ἐμίσησεν ὁ
4 Ῥωμαίων δῆμος. οὐδετέραν μὲν οὖν ἐπαινετέον·
ὁ δὲ δημαγωγῶν καὶ χαριζόμενος τῶν ὅπως οὐ
δόξουσι δημαγωγεῖν προπηλακιζόντων τοὺς πολλοὺς ἀμεμπτότερος· αἰσχρὸν μὲν γὰρ τὸ κολακεύειν δῆμον ἐπὶ τῷ δύνασθαι, τὸ δ᾽ ἰσχύειν ἐκ τοῦ
φοβεροῦ εἶναι καὶ κακοῦν καὶ πιέζειν πρὸς τῷ
αἰσχρῷ καὶ ἄδικόν ἐστιν.

II. Ὅτι τοίνυν ἁπλοῦς τις ὁ Μάρκιος ὑπεί-
ληπται τῷ τρόπῳ γεγονέναι καὶ αὐθέκαστος, ὁ δὲ
Ἀλκιβιάδης πανοῦργος ἐν τῇ πολιτείᾳ καὶ ἀνα-
λήθης, οὐκ ἄδηλόν ἐστι. μάλιστα δὲ κατηγοροῦσιν αὐτοῦ κακοήθειαν καὶ ἀπάτην, ᾗ τοὺς Λακεδαιμονίων πρέσβεις παρακρουσάμενος, ὡς Θουκυ-
2 δίδης ἱστόρηκε, τὴν εἰρήνην ἔλυσεν. ἀλλ᾽ αὕτη
μὲν ἡ πολιτεία, καίπερ εἰς πόλεμον αὖθις ἐμ-
βαλοῦσα τὴν πόλιν, ἰσχυρὰν ἐποίησε καὶ φο-
βεράν, τῆς Μαντινέων καὶ Ἀργείων συμμαχίας δι᾽
Ἀλκιβιάδου προσγενομένης· Μάρκιος δ᾽ ὅτι μὲν
ἀπάτῃ καὶ αὐτὸς ἐξεπολέμωσε Ῥωμαίους καὶ
Οὐολούσκους διαβαλὼν ψευδῶς τοὺς ἥκοντας ἐπὶ
τὴν θέαν, Διονύσιος ἱστόρηκεν· ἡ δ᾽ αἰτία φαυλό-
3 τερον ποιεῖ τὸ ἔργον. οὐ γὰρ ἐκ φιλονεικίας οὐδὲ
πολιτικῆς μάχης ἢ ἁμίλλης, ὡς ἐκεῖνος, ἀλλ᾽
ὀργῇ χαριζόμενος, παρ᾽ ἧς οὐδένα φησὶν ὁ Δίων[1]
ἀπολαβεῖν χάριν, πολλὰ τῆς Ἰταλίας μέρη συνε-
τάραξε καὶ πολλὰς πόλεις οὐδὲν ἀδικούσας τῷ
πρὸς τὴν πατρίδα θυμῷ παρανάλωσε. καίτοι

---

[1] Δίων Bekker corrects to Ἴων, after Bryan. The verse
. . . οὐδεὶς γὰρ ὀργῆς χάριν ἀπείληφεν, πάτερ . . . is attributed
to Menander in Stobaeus, *Floril.* xx. 6 (Kock, *Com. Att.
Frag.* iii. p. 188).

Marcius, together with his pride and oligarchical demeanour, won the hatred of the Roman people. Neither course, then, is to be approved; although the man who seeks to win the people by his favours is less blameworthy than those who heap insults on the multitude, in order to avoid the appearance of trying to win them. For it is a disgrace to flatter the people for the sake of power; but to get power by acts of terror, violence, and oppression, is not only a disgrace, it is also an injustice.

II. Now, that Marcius is usually thought to have been rather simple in his nature, and straightforward, while Alcibiades was unscrupulous in his public acts, and false, is very clear. And Alcibiades is particularly denounced for the malicious deceit by which he cheated the Lacedaemonian ambassadors, as Thucydides relates,[1] and put an end to the peace. But this policy of his, although it did plunge the city again into war, made it nevertheless strong and formidable, by reason of the alliance with Mantinea and Argos which Alcibiades secured for it. And yet Marcius himself also used deceit to stir up war between the Romans and Volscians, when he brought a false charge against the visitors to the games, as Dionysius relates;[2] and the motive for his action makes it the worse of the two. For he was not influenced by ambition, or by rivalry in a political struggle, as Alcibiades was, but simply gave way to his anger, from which passion, as Dion says, "no one ever gets a grateful return," and threw many districts of Italy into confusion, and needlessly sacrificed many innocent cities to his rage against his country.

[1] V. 45; cf. Plutarch's *Nicias*, x. ; *Alcibiades*, xiv.
[2] See *Coriolanus*, xxvi. 2 ; Dionysius Hal., *Antiq. Rom.* viii. 2.

καὶ Ἀλκιβιάδης δι' ὀργὴν μεγάλων αἴτιος συμ-
4 φορῶν κατέστη τοῖς πολίταις. ἀλλ' ὅτε πρῶτον
ἔγνω μεταμελομένους, εὐγνωμόνησε, καὶ πάλιν
ἀπορριφεὶς οὐκ ἐφήσθη τοῖς στρατηγοῖς ἁμαρτά-
νουσιν οὐδὲ παρεῖδε κακῶς βουλευομένους καὶ
κινδυνεύοντας, ἀλλ', ὅπερ Ἀριστείδης ἐπαινεῖται
μάλιστα πράξας πρὸς Θεμιστοκλέα, τοῦτ' ἐποίησε,
πρὸς τοὺς τότ' ἄρχοντας οὐ φίλους ὄντας ἐλθὼν καὶ
5 φράσας τὸ δέον καὶ διδάξας. Μάρκιος δὲ πρῶτον
μὲν ὅλην κακῶς ἐποίει τὴν πόλιν οὐχ ὑφ' ὅλης
παθών, ἀλλὰ τοῦ βελτίστου καὶ κρατίστου μέρους
συναδικηθέντος αὐτῷ καὶ συναλγήσαντος· ἔπειτα
πολλαῖς πρεσβείαις καὶ δεήσεσι μίαν ἰωμένων
ὀργὴν καὶ ἄγνοιαν οὐ τεγχθεὶς οὐδ' εἴξας ἐδήλωσεν
ἐπὶ τῷ διαφθεῖραι τὴν πατρίδα καὶ καταβαλεῖν,
οὐχ ὅπως ἀπολάβῃ καὶ κατέλθῃ, βαρὺν πόλεμον
6 καὶ ἄσπονδον ἐπανῃρημένος. τούτῳ δὲ[1] φήσει
τις διαφέρειν· Ἀλκιβιάδην μὲν γὰρ ἐπιβουλευό-
μενον ὑπὸ Σπαρτιατῶν διὰ δέος ἅμα καὶ μῖσος
αὐτῶν μεταστῆναι πρὸς Ἀθηναίους, Μαρκίῳ δὲ
πάντα δίκαια ποιοῦντας Οὐολούσκους οὐ καλῶς
εἶχεν ἐγκαταλιπεῖν. καὶ γὰρ ἡγεμὼν ἀποδέδεικτο
7 καὶ μεγίστην πίστιν εἶχε μετὰ δυνάμεως, οὐχ ὡς
ἐκεῖνος, ἀποχρωμένων μᾶλλον ἢ χρωμένων αὐτῷ
Λακεδαιμονίων, ἐν τῇ πόλει περιϊὼν καὶ κυλιν-
δούμενος αὖθις ἐν τῷ στρατοπέδῳ τέλος εἰς τὰς

---

[1] τούτῳ δὲ Coraës and Bekker read τούτῳ γε with C, and
Bekker assumes a lacuna before the words.

It is true, indeed, that Alcibiades also, through his anger, was the cause of great calamities to his countrymen. But just as soon as he saw that they were repentant, he showed them his goodwill, and after he had been driven away a second time, he did not exult over the mistakes of their generals, nor look with indifference upon their bad and perilous plans, but did precisely what Aristides is so highly praised for doing to Themistocles: he came to the men who were then in command, although they were not his friends, and told them plainly what they ought to do. Marcius, however, in the first place, did injury to his whole city, although he had not been injured by the whole of it, but the best and strongest part of it shared his wrongs and his distress; in the second place, by resisting and not yielding to the many embassies and supplications with which his countrymen tried to heal his single wrath and folly, he made it clear that he had undertaken a fierce and implacable war for the overthrow and destruction of his country, not that he might recover and regain it. Further, in this point it may be said there was a difference between them, namely, that Alcibiades, when he went over to the side of the Athenians, was moved by fear and hatred of the Spartans, who were plotting to take his life; whereas it was dishonourable for Marcius to leave the Volscians in the lurch when they were treating him with perfect fairness. For he was appointed their leader, and had the greatest credit and influence among them, unlike Alcibiades, whom the Lacedaemonians misused rather than used, who wandered about aimlessly in their city, and again was tossed to and fro in their camp, and at last threw himself

Τισαφέρνου χεῖρας ἀφῆκεν αὐτόν· εἰ μὴ νὴ Δία
μὴ φθαρῆναι τὰς Ἀθήνας παντάπασι ποθῶν
κατελθεῖν ἐθεράπευε.

III. Χρήματα τοίνυν ὁ μὲν Ἀλκιβιάδης καὶ
λαβεῖν οὐκ εὖ πολλάκις ἐκ δωροδοκιῶν καὶ διαθέσθαι κακῶς εἰς τρυφὴν καὶ ἀκολασίαν ἱστόρηται·
Μάρκιον δὲ σὺν τιμῇ διδόντες οἱ στρατηγοὶ
λαβεῖν οὐκ ἔπεισαν. διὸ καὶ μάλιστα τοῖς πολλοῖς ἐπαχθὴς ἦν ἐν ταῖς περὶ χρεῶν διαφοραῖς
πρὸς τὸν δῆμον, ὡς οὐκ ἐπὶ κέρδεσιν, ἀλλὰ δι᾽
ὕβριν καὶ περιφροσύνην τοῖς πένησιν ἐπηρεάζων.

2   Ἀντίπατρος μὲν οὖν ἐν ἐπιστολῇ τινι γράφων
περὶ τῆς Ἀριστοτέλους τοῦ φιλοσόφου τελευτῆς,
"Πρὸς τοῖς ἄλλοις," φησίν, "ὁ ἀνὴρ καὶ τὸ
πείθειν εἶχε·" τὰς δὲ Μαρκίου πράξεις καὶ
ἀρετὰς τοῦτο μὴ προσὸν ἐπαχθεῖς ἐποίησεν
αὐτοῖς τοῖς εὖ παθοῦσι, τὸν ὄγκον αὐτοῦ καὶ τὴν
ἐρημίᾳ σύνοικον, ὡς Πλάτων εἶπεν, αὐθάδειαν
μὴ ὑπομείναντας. τοῦ δ᾽ Ἀλκιβιάδου τοὐναντίον
ἐπισταμένου χρῆσθαι τοῖς προστυγχάνουσιν οἰκείως, οὐδὲν θαυμαστὸν ἐν οἷς κατώρθου τὴν δόξαν
ἀνθεῖν μετ᾽ εὐνοίας καὶ τιμῆς εὐημεροῦσαν, ὅπου
καὶ τῶν ἁμαρτημάτων ἔνια πολλάκις [1] χάριν εἶχε
3   καὶ ὥραν. ὅθεν οὗτος μὲν οὐ μικρὰ βλάψας οὐδ᾽
ὀλίγα τὴν πόλιν ὅμως ἀπεδείκνυτο πολλάκις
ἡγεμὼν καὶ στρατηγός, ἐκεῖνος δὲ μετιὼν ἐπὶ

---

[1] πολλάκις bracketed by Bekker.

into the hands of Tissaphernes; unless, indeed, he
was all the while paying him court in order that the
Athens to which he longed to return might not be
utterly destroyed.

III. Furthermore, in the matter of money, we are
told that Alcibiades often got it ill by taking bribes,
and spent it ill in luxury and dissipation; whereas
Marcius could not be persuaded to take it even when
it was offered to him as an honour by his commanders.
And for this reason he was especially odious to the
multitude in the disputes with the people concerning
debts, because they saw that it was not for gain, but
out of insolence and scorn, that he acted despitefully
towards the poor.

Antipater, writing in one of his letters about the
death of Aristotle the philosopher,[1] says: "In addition to all his other gifts, the man had also that of
persuasion"; and the absence of this gift in Marcius
made his great deeds and virtues obnoxious to the
very men whom they benefited, since they could not
endure the arrogant pride of the man, and that self-
will which is, as Plato says,[2] "the companion of
solitude." Alcibiades, on the contrary, understood
how to treat in a friendly manner those who met
him, and we cannot wonder that when he was successful his fame was attended with goodwill and
honour, and flowered luxuriantly, since some of his
errors even had often charm and felicity. This was
the reason why, in spite of the great and frequent
harm done by him to the city, he was nevertheless
many times appointed leader and general; while
Marcius, when he stood for an office which was his

---

[1] See *Comparison of Aristides and Cato*, ii. 4.
[2] See *Coriolanus*, xv. 4.

πολλαῖς ἀριστείαις καὶ ἀνδραγαθίαις ἀρχὴν
προσήκουσαν ἐξέπεσεν. οὕτω τὸν μὲν οὐδὲ
πάσχοντες κακῶς ἐδύναντο μισεῖν οἱ πολῖται, τῷ
δὲ περιῆν θαυμαζομένῳ μὴ φιλεῖσθαι.

IV. Καὶ γάρ τοι Μάρκιος μὲν οὐδὲν ἀπεδείξατο
τῇ πόλει στρατηγῶν, ἀλλὰ τοῖς πολεμίοις κατὰ
τῆς πατρίδος· Ἀλκιβιάδου δὲ καὶ στρατευομένου
πολλάκις καὶ στρατηγοῦντος ἀπέλαυσαν οἱ Ἀθη-
ναῖοι· καὶ παρὼν ἐκράτει τῶν ἐχθρῶν ὅσον ἐβούλετο, καὶ μὴ παρόντος ἴσχυσαν αἱ διαβολαί·
2 Μάρκιος δὲ παρὼν ὑπὸ Ῥωμαίων κατεδικάσθη,
παρόντα δὲ Οὐολοῦσκοι διέφθειραν, οὐ δικαίως
μὲν οὐδ' ὁσίως, αἰτίαν δὲ τοῦ εὐλόγου παρέσχεν
αὐτός, ὅτι δημοσίᾳ τὰς διαλύσεις μὴ προσδεξά-
μενος, ἰδίᾳ δὲ πεισθεὶς ὑπὸ τῶν γυναικῶν οὐκ 235
ἔλυσε τὴν ἔχθραν, ἀλλὰ τοῦ πολέμου μένοντος
3 ἀπώλεσε τὸν καιρὸν καὶ διέφθειρε. πείσαντα
γὰρ ἔδει τοὺς πεπιστευκότας ἀπελθεῖν, εἰ τοῦ
πρὸς ἐκείνους δικαίου πλεῖστον ἐποιεῖτο λόγον.
εἰ δὲ μηδὲν ἐφρόντιζεν Οὐολούσκων, ἀλλὰ τὴν
ὀργὴν ἐμπλῆσαι τὴν ἑαυτοῦ βουλόμενος ἐνῆγε τὸν
πόλεμον, εἶτ' ἔληξεν, οὐ διὰ τὴν μητέρα καλῶς
εἶχε φείσασθαι τῆς πατρίδος, ἀλλὰ σὺν τῇ πατρίδι
τῆς μητρός· μέρος γὰρ ἦν καὶ ἡ μήτηρ καὶ ἡ γυνὴ
4 τῆς πατρίδος ἣν ἐπολιόρκει. τὸ δὲ δημοσίαις
ἱκεσίαις καὶ δεήσει πρέσβεων καὶ λιταῖς ἱερέων

due in view of his valorous achievements, was defeated. And so it was that the one could not make himself hated by his countrymen, even when he was doing them harm; while the other was after all not beloved, even while he was admired.

IV. For Marcius did not, as a commander, obtain any great successes for his city, but only for his enemies against his country; whereas Alcibiades was often of service to the Athenians, both as a private soldier and as a commander. When he was at home, he mastered his adversaries to his heart's content; it was when he was absent that their calumnies prevailed. Marcius, on the contrary, was with the Romans when they condemned him, and with the Volscians when they slew him. The deed was not in accordance with justice or right, it is true, and yet his own acts supplied an excuse for it, because, after rejecting the terms of peace publicly offered, and suffering himself to be persuaded by the private solicitations of the women, he did not put an end to hostilities, but allowed the war to continue, while he threw away for ever its golden opportunity. For he should have won the consent of those who had put their trust in him, before retiring from his position, if he had the highest regard for their just claims upon him. If, on the other hand, he cared nothing for the Volscians, but was prosecuting the war merely to satisfy his own anger, and then stopped it abruptly, the honourable course had been, not to spare his country for his mother's sake, but his mother together with his country; since his mother and his wife were part and parcel of the native city which he was besieging. But after giving harsh treatment to public supplications, entreaties of embassies, and prayers of

ἀπηνῶς χρησάμενον εἶτα χαρίσασθαι τῇ μητρὶ
τὴν ἀναχώρησιν, οὐ τῆς μητρὸς ἦν τιμή, ἀλλ'
ἀτιμία τῆς πατρίδος, οἴκτῳ καὶ παραιτήσει διὰ
μίαν γυναῖκα σωζομένης, ὡς οὐκ ἀξίας σώζεσθαι
δι' αὐτήν. ἐπίφθονος γὰρ ἡ χάρις καὶ ὠμὴ καὶ
ἀχάριστος ἀληθῶς καὶ πρὸς οὐδετέρους ἔχουσα
τὸ εὐγνῶμον· ἀνεχώρησε γὰρ μήτε πεισθεὶς ὑπὸ
τῶν πολεμουμένων μήτε πείσας τοὺς συμπολε-
μοῦντας.

5 Ὧν αἴτιον ἀπάντων τὸ ἀνομίλητον τοῦ τρόπου
καὶ λίαν ὑπερήφανον καὶ αὔθαδες, ὃ καθ' αὑτὸ
μὲν ἐπαχθές ἐστι τοῖς πολλοῖς, τῷ δὲ φιλοτίμῳ
προσὸν γίνεται παντάπασιν ἄγριον καὶ ἀπα-
ραίτητον. οὐ γὰρ θεραπεύουσι τοὺς πολλοὺς ὡς
μὴ δεόμενοι τιμῆς, εἶτα χαλεπαίνουσι μὴ τυγχά-
νοντες. ἐπεὶ τό γε μὴ λιπαρῇ μηδὲ θεραπευτικὸν
ὄχλων εἶναι καὶ Μέτελλος εἶχε καὶ Ἀριστείδης
6 καὶ Ἐπαμεινώνδας· ἀλλὰ τῷ καταφρονεῖν ἀληθῶς
ὧν δῆμός ἐστι καὶ δοῦναι καὶ ἀφελέσθαι κύριος,
ἐξοστρακιζόμενοι καὶ ἀποχειροτονούμενοι καὶ
καταδικαζόμενοι πολλάκις οὐκ ὠργίζοντο τοῖς
πολίταις ἀγνωμονοῦσιν, ἀλλ' ἠγάπων αὖθις μεταμελομένους καὶ διηλλάττοντο παρακαλούντων.
τὸν γὰρ ἥκιστα θεραπευτικὸν ἥκιστα πρέπει
τιμωρητικὸν εἶναι τῶν πολλῶν, ὡς τὸ χαλεπαίνειν
μάλιστα μὴ τυγχάνοντα τῆς τιμῆς ἐκ τοῦ σφόδρα
γλίχεσθαι φυόμενον.

V. Ἀλκιβιάδης μὲν οὖν οὐκ ἠρνεῖτο τιμώμενος
χαίρειν καὶ δυσφορεῖν παρορώμενος, ὅθεν ἐπειρᾶτο

priests, then to concede his withdrawal as a favour
to his mother, was not so much an honour to that
mother, as it was a dishonour to his country, which
was thus saved by the pitiful intercession of a single
woman, and held unworthy of salvation for its own
sake. Surely the favour was invidious, and harsh,
and really no favour at all, and unacceptable to both
parties; for he retired without listening to the per-
suasions of his antagonists, and without gaining the
consent of his comrades-in-arms.

The cause of all this lay in his unsociable, very
overweening, and self-willed disposition, which of
itself is offensive to most people, and when combined
with an ambitious spirit, becomes altogether savage
and implacable. Such men pay no court to the
multitude, professing not to want their honours, and
then are vexed if they do not get them. Certainly
there was no tendency to importune or court the
favour of the multitude in men like Metellus, Aristides, and Epaminondas; but owing to their genuine
contempt for what a people has the power to give
and take away, though they were repeatedly ostra-
cised, defeated at elections, and condemned in courts
of justice, they cherished no anger against their
countrymen for their ingratitude, but showed them
kindness again when they repented, and were reconciled with them when they asked it. Surely he who
least courts the people's favour, ought least to resent
their neglect, since vexation over failure to receive
their honours is most apt to spring from an excessive
longing after them.

V. Well, then, Alcibiades would not deny that he
rejoiced to be honoured, and was displeased to be
overlooked, and he therefore tried to be agreeable

προσφιλὴς εἶναι τοῖς παροῦσι καὶ κεχαρισμένος·
Μάρκιον δὲ θεραπεύειν μὲν οὐκ εἴα τοὺς τιμᾶν
δυναμένους καὶ αὔξειν τὸ ὑπερήφανον, ὀργὴν δὲ
καὶ λύπην ἀμελουμένῳ τὸ φιλότιμον παρεῖχε.
2 καὶ ταῦτ' ἔστιν ἅ τις ἂν αἰτιάσαιτο τοῦ ἀν-
δρός· τὰ δ' ἄλλα πάντα λαμπρά. σωφροσύνης
δὲ καὶ χρημάτων ἐγκρατείας ἕνεκα τοῖς ἀρίστοις
καὶ καθαρωτάτοις τῶν Ἑλλήνων ἄξιον αὐτὸν
παραβάλλειν, οὐκ Ἀλκιβιάδῃ μὰ Δία τῷ θρασυ-
τάτῳ περὶ ταῦτα καὶ ὀλιγωροτάτῳ τοῦ καλοῦ
γενομένῳ.

and pleasant to his associates; but the overweening pride of Marcius would not suffer him to pay court to those who had the power to honour and advance him, while his ambition made him feel angry and hurt when he was neglected. These are the blame-worthy traits in the man, but all the rest are brilliant. And for his temperance and superiority to wealth, he deserves to be compared with the best and purest of the Greeks, not with Alcibiades, who, in these regards, was the most unscrupulous of men, and the most careless of the claims of honour.

LYSANDER

ΛΥΣΑΝΔΡΟΣ

I. Ὁ Ἀκανθίων θησαυρὸς ἐν Δελφοῖς ἐπιγραφὴν ἔχει τοιαύτην· "Βρασίδας καὶ Ἀκάνθιοι ἀπ' Ἀθηναίων·" διὸ καὶ πολλοὶ τὸν ἐντὸς ἑστῶτα τοῦ οἴκου παρὰ ταῖς θύραις λίθινον ἀνδριάντα Βρασίδου νομίζουσιν εἶναι. Λυσάνδρου δέ ἐστιν εἰκονικός, εὖ μάλα κομῶντος ἔθει τῷ παλαιῷ καὶ 2 πώγωνα καθειμένου γενναῖον. οὐ γάρ, ὡς ἔνιοί φασιν, Ἀργείων μετὰ τὴν μεγάλην ἧτταν ἐπὶ πένθει καρέντων οἱ Σπαρτιᾶται πρὸς τὸ ἀντίπαλον αὐτοῖς τὰς κόμας ἀγαλλόμενοι τοῖς πεπραγμένοις ἀνῆκαν, οὐδὲ Βακχιαδῶν τῶν ἐκ Κορίνθου φυγόντων εἰς Λακεδαίμονα ταπεινῶν καὶ ἀμόρφων διὰ τὸ κείρασθαι τὰς κεφαλὰς φανέντων εἰς ζῆλον αὐτοὶ τοῦ κομᾶν ἦλθον, ἀλλὰ καὶ τοῦτο Λυκούργειόν ἐστι. καί φασιν αὐτὸν εἰπεῖν ὡς ἡ κόμη τοὺς μὲν καλοὺς εὐπρεπεστέρους ὁρᾶσθαι ποιεῖ, τοὺς δὲ αἰσχροὺς φοβερωτέρους.

II. Λέγεται δὲ ὁ Λυσάνδρου πατὴρ Ἀριστόκλειτος οἰκίας μὲν οὐ γενέσθαι βασιλικῆς, ἄλλως δὲ γένους εἶναι τοῦ τῶν Ἡρακλειδῶν. ἐτράφη δὲ ὁ Λύσανδρος ἐν πενίᾳ, καὶ παρέσχεν ἑαυτὸν εὔτακτον, ὡς εἴ τις ἄλλος, πρὸς τοὺς ἐθισμοὺς καὶ

---

[1] In B.C. 424, Brasidas won Acanthus, a town on the Chalcidic peninsula, away from its alliance with Athens (Thuc. iv. 84–88).　　[2] Herodotus, i. 82.

LYSANDER

I. THE treasury of the Acanthians at Delphi bears
this inscription: "Brasidas and the Acanthians, with
spoil from the Athenians." [1] For this reason many
think that the marble figure standing within the
edifice, by the door, is a statue of Brasidas. But it
really represents Lysander, with his hair very long,
after the ancient custom, and growing a generous
beard. For it is not true, as some state, that because
the Argives, after their great defeat, shaved their
heads for sorrow, the Spartans, in contrary fashion,
let their hair grow long in exultation over their
victory; [2] nor was it because the Bacchiadae, [3] when
they fled from Corinth to Lacedaemon, looked mean
and unsightly from having shaved their heads, that
the Spartans, on their part, became eager to wear
their hair long; but this custom also goes back to
Lycurgus. And he is reported to have said that a
fine head of hair makes the handsome more comely
to look upon, and the ugly more terrible. [4]

II. The father of Lysander, Aristocleitus, is said
to have been of the lineage of the Heracleidae,
though not of the royal family. But Lysander was
reared in poverty, and showed himself as much as
any man conformable to the customs of his people;

---

[3] An oligarchical family, deposed from rule in Corinth by
Cypselus, about 650 B.C. (Herod. v. 92).

[4] Cf. *Lycurgus*, xxii. 1.

ἀνδρώδη καὶ κρείττονα πάσης ἡδονῆς, πλὴν εἴ
τινα τιμωμένοις καὶ κατορθοῦσιν αἱ καλαὶ πράξεις
ἐπιφέρουσι. ταύτης δὲ οὐκ αἰσχρόν ἐστιν ἡττᾶ-
2 σθαι τοὺς νέους ἐν Σπάρτῃ. βούλονται γὰρ εὐθὺς ἐξ
ἀρχῆς πάσχειν τι τοὺς παῖδας αὐτῶν πρὸς δόξαν,
ἀλγυνομένους τε τοῖς ψόγοις καὶ μεγαλυνομένους
ὑπὸ τῶν ἐπαίνων· ὁ δὲ ἀπαθὴς καὶ ἀκίνητος ἐν
τούτοις ὡς ἀφιλότιμος πρὸς ἀρετὴν καὶ ἀργὸς
καταφρονεῖται. τὸ μὲν οὖν φιλότιμον αὐτῷ καὶ
φιλόνεικον ἐκ τῆς Λακωνικῆς παρέμεινε παιδείας
ἐγγενόμενον, καὶ οὐδέν τι μέγα χρὴ τὴν φύσιν ἐν
3 τούτοις αἰτιᾶσθαι· θεραπευτικὸς δὲ τῶν δυνατῶν
μᾶλλον ἢ κατὰ Σπαρτιάτην φύσει δοκεῖ γενέσθαι,
καὶ βάρος ἐξουσίας διὰ χρείαν ἐνεγκεῖν εὔκολος·
ὃ πολιτικῆς δεινότητος οὐ μικρὸν ἔνιοι ποιοῦνται
μέρος. Ἀριστοτέλης δὲ τὰς μεγάλας φύσεις ἀπο-
φαίνων μελαγχολικάς, ὡς τὴν Σωκράτους καὶ
Πλάτωνος καὶ Ἡρακλέους, ἱστορεῖ καὶ Λύσανδρον
οὐκ εὐθύς, ἀλλὰ πρεσβύτερον ὄντα τῇ μελαγχολίᾳ
περιπεσεῖν.
4 Ἴδιον δὲ αὐτοῦ μάλιστα τὸ καλῶς πενίαν
φέροντα, καὶ μηδαμοῦ κρατηθέντα μηδὲ διαφθα-
ρέντα χρήμασιν αὐτόν, ἐμπλῆσαι τὴν πατρίδα
πλούτου καὶ φιλοπλουτίας καὶ παῦσαι θαυμαζο-
μένην ἐπὶ τῷ μὴ θαυμάζειν πλοῦτον, εἰσάγοντα
χρυσίου καὶ ἀργυρίου πλῆθος μετὰ τὸν Ἀττικὸν
πόλεμον, ἑαυτῷ δὲ μηδεμίαν δραχμὴν ὑπολειπό-
5 μενον. Διονυσίου δὲ τοῦ τυράννου πέμψαντος
αὐτοῦ ταῖς θυγατράσι πολυτελῆ χιτώνια τῶν

of a manly spirit, too, and superior to every pleasure, excepting only that which their good deeds bring to those who are successful and honoured. To this pleasure it is no disgrace for the youth in Sparta to succumb. Indeed, from the very first they wish their boys to be sensitive towards public opinion, distressed by censure, and exalted by praise; and he who is insensible and stolid in these matters, is looked down upon as without ambition for excellence, and a cumberer of the ground. Ambition, then, and the spirit of emulation, were firmly implanted in him by his Laconian training, and no great fault should be found with his natural disposition on this account. But he seems to have been naturally subservient to men of power and influence, beyond what was usual in a Spartan, and content to endure an arrogant authority for the sake of gaining his ends, a trait which some hold to be no small part of political ability. And Aristotle, when he sets forth that great natures, like those of Socrates and Plato and Heracles, have a tendency to melancholy, writes also [1] that Lysander, not immediately, but when well on in years, was a prey to melancholy.

But what is most peculiar in him is that, though he bore poverty well, and though he was never mastered nor even corrupted by money, yet he filled his country full of wealth and the love of wealth, and made her cease to be admired for not admiring wealth, importing as he did an abundance of gold and silver after the war with Athens, although he kept not a single drachma for himself. And when Dionysius the tyrant sent his daughters some costly tunics of Sicilian make, he would not receive them,

---

[1] *Problems*, xxx. 1.

Σικελῶν, οὐκ ἔλαβεν, εἰπὼν φοβεῖσθαι μὴ διὰ
ταῦτα μᾶλλον αἰσχραὶ φανῶσιν. ἀλλ᾽ ὀλίγον
ὕστερον πρὸς τὸν αὐτὸν τύραννον ἐκ τῆς αὐτῆς
πόλεως ἀποσταλεὶς πρεσβευτής, προσπέμψαντος
αὐτῷ δύο στολὰς ἐκείνου καὶ κελεύσαντος ἣν
βούλεται τούτων ἑλόμενον τῇ θυγατρὶ κομίζειν,
αὐτὴν ἐκείνην ἔφη βέλτιον αἱρήσεσθαι, καὶ λαβὼν
ἀμφοτέρας ἀπῆλθεν.

III. Ἐπεὶ δὲ τοῦ Πελοποννησιακοῦ πολέμου
μῆκος λαμβάνοντος, καὶ μετὰ τὴν ἐν Σικελίᾳ τῶν
Ἀθηναίων κακοπραγίαν αὐτίκα μὲν ἐπιδόξων
ὄντων ἐκπεσεῖσθαι τῆς θαλάττης, οὐ πολλῷ δὲ
ὕστερον ἀπαγορεύσειν παντάπασιν, Ἀλκιβιάδης
ἀπὸ τῆς φυγῆς ἐπιστὰς τοῖς πράγμασι μεγάλην
μεταβολὴν ἐποίησε καὶ κατέστησε τοὺς ναυτικοὺς
2 ἀγῶνας εἰς ἀντίπαλον αὐτοῖς, δείσαντες οὖν οἱ
Λακεδαιμόνιοι πάλιν καὶ γενόμενοι ταῖς προ-
θυμίαις καινοὶ πρὸς τὸν πόλεμον, ὡς ἡγεμόνος τε
δεινοῦ καὶ παρασκευῆς ἐρρωμενεστέρας δεόμενοι,
ἐκπέμπουσιν ἐπὶ τὴν τῆς θαλάττης ἡγεμονίαν
Λύσανδρον. γενόμενος δ᾽ ἐν Ἐφέσῳ, καὶ τὴν
πόλιν εὑρὼν εὔνουν μὲν αὐτῷ καὶ λακωνίζουσαν
προθυμότατα, πράττουσαν δὲ τότε λυπρῶς καὶ κινδυνεύουσαν ἐκβαρβαρωθῆναι τοῖς Περσικοῖς ἔθεσι
διὰ τὰς ἐπιμιξίας, ἅτε δὴ τῆς Λυδίας περικεχυμέ-
νης καὶ τῶν βασιλικῶν στρατηγῶν αὐτόθι τὰ
3 πολλὰ διατριβόντων, στρατόπεδον βαλόμενος καὶ
τὰ πλοῖα πανταχόθεν ἕλκεσθαι κελεύσας ἐκεῖ τὰ
φορτηγά, καὶ ναυπηγίαν τριήρων ἐκεῖ κατα-
σκευασάμενος, ταῖς μὲν ἐμπορίαις τοὺς λιμένας
αὐτῶν ἀνέλαβεν, ἐργασίαις δὲ τὴν ἀγοράν, χρη-
ματισμῶν δὲ τοὺς οἴκους καὶ τὰς τέχνας ἐνέ-

saying he was afraid they would make his daughters look more ugly. But a little later, when he was sent as ambassador to the same tyrant from the same city, and was presented by him with two robes, and ordered to choose which of them he would, and carry it to his daughter, he said that she could choose better herself, and went off with both of them.

III. The Peloponnesian war had now been carried on for a long time, and after their disaster in Sicily[1] it was expected that the Athenians would straightway lose their control of the sea, and presently give up the struggle altogether. But Alcibiades, returning from exile and taking the command, wrought a great change, and made his countrymen again a match for their enemies by sea.[2] The Lacedaemonians, accordingly, were frightened again, and summoning up fresh zeal for the war, which required, as they thought, an able leader and a more powerful armament, sent out Lysander to take command upon the sea.[3] When he came to Ephesus, he found the city well disposed to him and very zealous in the Spartan cause, although it was then in a low state of prosperity and in danger of becoming utterly barbarized by the admixture of Persian customs, since it was enveloped by Lydia, and the King's generals made it their headquarters. He therefore pitched his camp there, and ordered the merchant vessels from every quarter to land their cargoes there, and made preparations for the building of triremes. Thus he revived the traffic of their harbours, and the business of their market, and filled their houses and workshops with

---

[1] 413 B.C. Cf. Thuc. viii. 2.   [2] Cf. *Alcibiades*, xxxii. 4.
[3] In the autumn of 408 B.C.

πλησεν, ὥστε πρῶτον ἀπ' ἐκείνου τοῦ χρόνου
τὴν πόλιν ἐν ἐλπίδι τοῦ περὶ αὐτὴν νῦν ὄντος
ὄγκου καὶ μεγέθους διὰ Λύσανδρον γενέσθαι.

IV. Πυθόμενος δὲ Κῦρον εἰς Σάρδεις ἀφῖχθαι
τὸν βασιλέως υἱόν, ἀνέβη διαλεξόμενος αὐτῷ καὶ   43
Τισαφέρνου κατηγορήσων, ὃς ἔχων πρόσταγμα
Λακεδαιμονίοις βοηθεῖν καὶ τῆς θαλάσσης ἐξ-
ελάσαι τοὺς Ἀθηναίους, ἐδόκει δι' Ἀλκιβιάδην
ὑφιέμενος ἀπρόθυμος εἶναι καὶ γλίσχρως χορη-
2 γῶν τὸ ναυτικὸν φθείρειν. ἦν δὲ καὶ Κύρῳ βουλομένῳ τὸν Τισαφέρνην ἐν αἰτίαις εἶναι καὶ κακῶς
ἀκούειν, πονηρὸν ὄντα καὶ πρὸς αὐτὸν ἰδίᾳ
διαφερόμενον. ἔκ τε δὴ τούτων καὶ τῆς ἄλλης
συνδιαιτήσεως ὁ Λύσανδρος ἀγαπηθεὶς καὶ τῷ
θεραπευτικῷ μάλιστα τῆς ὁμιλίας ἑλὼν τὸ μειρά-
3 κιον ἐπέρρωσε πρὸς τὸν πόλεμον. ἐπεὶ δὲ ἀπαλ-
λάττεσθαι βουλόμενον αὐτὸν ἑστιῶν ὁ Κῦρος
ἠξίου μὴ διωθεῖσθαι τὰς παρ' αὐτοῦ φιλοφρο-
σύνας, ἀλλ' αἰτεῖν ὃ βούλοιτο καὶ φράζειν ὡς
οὐδενὸς ἁπλῶς ἀποτευξόμενον, ὑπολαβὼν ὁ Λύσανδρος, "Ἐπεὶ τοίνυν," εἶπεν, "οὕτως ἔχεις, ὦ
Κῦρε, προθυμίας, αἰτοῦμαί σε καὶ παρακαλῶ
προσθεῖναι τῷ μισθῷ τῶν ναυτῶν ὀβολόν, ὅπως
4 τετρώβολον ἀντὶ τριωβόλου λαμβάνωσιν." ἡσθεὶς οὖν ὁ Κῦρος ἐπὶ τῇ φιλοτιμίᾳ τοῦ ἀνδρὸς
μυρίους αὐτῷ δαρεικοὺς ἔδωκεν, ἐξ ὧν ἐπιμετρήσας
τὸν ὀβολὸν τοῖς ναύταις καὶ λαμπρυνάμενος ὀλίγῳ
χρόνῳ τὰς ναῦς τῶν πολεμίων κενὰς ἐποίησεν.
ἀπεφοίτων γὰρ οἱ πολλοὶ πρὸς τοὺς πλέον δι-

profits, so that from that time on, and through his efforts, the city had hopes of achieving the stateliness and grandeur which it now enjoys.

IV. When he learned that Cyrus, the King's son, was come to Sardis,[1] he went up to confer with him and to accuse Tissaphernes, who, though he was commissioned to aid the Lacedaemonians and drive the Athenians from the sea, was thought to be remiss in his duty, through the efforts of Alcibiades,[2] showing lack of zeal, and destroying the efficiency of the fleet by the meagre subsidies which he gave. Now Cyrus was well pleased that Tissaphernes, who was a base man and privately at feud with him, should be accused and maligned. By this means, then, as well as by his behaviour in general, Lysander made himself agreeable, and by the submissive deference of his conversation, above all else, he won the heart of the young prince, and roused him to prosecute the war with vigour. At a banquet which Cyrus gave him as he was about to depart, the prince begged him not to reject the tokens of his friendliness, but to ask plainly for whatever he desired, since nothing whatsoever would be refused him. "Since, then," said Lysander in reply, "thou art so very kind, I beg and entreat thee, Cyrus, to add an obol to the pay of my sailors, that they may get four obols instead of three."[3] Cyrus, accordingly, delighted with his public spirit, gave him ten thousand darics, out of which he added the obol to the pay of his seamen, and, by the renown thus won, soon emptied the ships of his enemies. For most of their seamen

---

[1] He succeeded Tissaphernes as satrap of Lydia.
[2] Cf. *Alcibiades*, xxv. 1-2.
[3] Cf. Xen. *Hell.* i. 5, 6 f.

δόντας, οἱ δὲ μένοντες ἀπρόθυμοι καὶ στασιώδεις
ἐγίνοντο καὶ κακὰ παρεῖχον ὁσημέραι τοῖς στρατη-
5 γοῖς. οὐ μὴν ἀλλὰ καίπερ οὕτως περισπάσας
καὶ κακώσας τοὺς πολεμίους ὁ Λύσανδρος ὠρρώδει
ναυμαχεῖν, δραστήριον ὄντα τὸν Ἀλκιβιάδην καὶ
νεῶν πλήθει περιόντα καὶ μάχας καὶ κατὰ γῆν
καὶ κατὰ θάλατταν εἰς ἐκεῖνο χρόνου πάσας ἀητ-
τητον ἠγωνισμένον δεδοικώς.

V. Ἐπεὶ δὲ ὁ μὲν Ἀλκιβιάδης εἰς Φώκαιαν ἐκ
Σάμου διέπλευσεν ἐπὶ τοῦ στόλου καταλιπὼν
Ἀντίοχον τὸν κυβερνήτην, ὁ δὲ Ἀντίοχος οἷον
ἐφυβρίζων τῷ Λυσάνδρῳ καὶ θρασυνόμενος ἐπέ-
πλευσε δυσὶ τριήρεσιν εἰς τὸν λιμένα τῶν
Ἐφεσίων καὶ παρὰ τὸν ναύσταθμον γέλωτι καὶ
πατάγῳ χρώμενος σοβαρῶς παρήλαυνεν, ἀγανακ-
τήσας ὁ Λύσανδρος καὶ κατασπάσας τὸ πρῶτον
οὐ πολλὰς τῶν τριήρων ἐδίωκεν αὐτόν, ἰδὼν δὲ
αὖ τοὺς Ἀθηναίους βοηθοῦντας ἄλλας ἐπλήρου,
2 καὶ τέλος ἐναυμάχουν συμπεσόντες. ἐνίκα δὲ
Λύσανδρος, καὶ πεντεκαίδεκα τριήρεις λαβὼν
ἔστησε τρόπαιον. ἐπὶ τούτῳ τὸν Ἀλκιβιάδην ὁ
μὲν ἐν ἄστει δῆμος ὀργισθεὶς ἀπεχειροτόνησεν,
ὑπὸ δὲ τῶν ἐν Σάμῳ στρατιωτῶν ἀτιμαζόμενος
καὶ κακῶς ἀκούων ἀπέπλευσεν εἰς Χερρόνησον ἐκ
τοῦ στρατοπέδου. ταύτην μὲν οὖν τὴν μάχην,
καίπερ οὐ μεγάλην τῇ πράξει γενομένην, ἡ τύχη
δι' Ἀλκιβιάδην ὀνομαστὴν ἐποίησεν.

3 Ὁ δὲ Λύσανδρος ἀπὸ τῶν πόλεων εἰς Ἔφεσον
μεταπεμπόμενος οὓς ἑώρα μάλιστα ταῖς τε τόλ-
μαις καὶ τοῖς φρονήμασιν ὑπὲρ τοὺς πολλοὺς
ὄντας, ἀρχὰς ὑπέσπειρε τῶν ὕστερον ἐπ' αὐτοῦ
γενομένων δεκαδαρχιῶν καὶ νεωτερισμῶν, προ-

came over to those who offered higher pay, and those who remained were listless and mutinous, and gave daily trouble to their officers. However, although he had thus injured and weakened his enemies, Lysander shrank from a naval battle, through fear of Alcibiades, who was energetic, had a greater number of ships, and in all his battles by land and sea up to that time had come off victorious.

V. But after this, Alcibiades sailed away from Samos to Phocaea, leaving Antiochus, his pilot, in command of the fleet; and Antiochus, as if in bold mockery of Lysander, put in to the harbour of Ephesus with two triremes, and rowed ostentatiously past his ships, as they lay drawn up on shore, with noise and laughter. Lysander was incensed, and launching at first only a few of his triremes, pursued him; then seeing that the Athenians were coming to the rescue, he manned others, and at last the action became general. Lysander was victorious, too, captured fifteen triremes, and set up a trophy. Thereupon the people of Athens, flying into a passion, deposed Alcibiades from his command, and finding himself slighted and abused by the soldiers at Samos, he left the camp and sailed off to the Chersonese. This battle, then, although actually not a great one, was made memorable by its bearing on the fortunes of Alcibiades.[1]

Lysander now summoned from their various cities to Ephesus men whom he saw to be most eminent for confidence and daring, and sowed in their minds the seeds of the revolutionary decadarchies[2] afterwards instituted by him, urging and inciting them to

---

[1] Cf. *Alcibiades*, xxxv.-xxxvi.
[2] Governing bodies of ten men.

τρέπων καὶ παροξύνων ἑταιρικὰ συνίστασθαι καὶ
προσέχειν τὸν νοῦν τοῖς πράγμασιν, ὡς ἅμα τῷ
καταλυθῆναι τοὺς Ἀθηναίους τῶν τε δήμων
ἀπαλλαξομένους καὶ δυναστεύσοντας ἐν ταῖς
4 πατρίσι. τούτων δὲ τὴν πίστιν ἑκάστῳ δι᾽
ἔργων παρεῖχε, τοὺς ἤδη γεγονότας φίλους αὐτῷ
καὶ ξένους εἰς μεγάλα πράγματα καὶ τιμὰς καὶ
στρατηγίας ἀνάγων, καὶ συναδικῶν καὶ συνεξ-
αμαρτάνων αὐτὸς ὑπὲρ τῆς ἐκείνων πλεονεξίας,
ὥστε προσέχειν ἅπαντας αὐτῷ καὶ χαρίζεσθαι
καὶ ποθεῖν, ἐλπίζοντας οὐδενὸς ἀτυχήσειν τῶν
5 μεγίστων ἐκείνου κρατοῦντος. διὸ καὶ Καλλικρατίδαν οὔτ᾽ εὐθὺς ἡδέως εἶδον ἐλθόντα τῷ
Λυσάνδρῳ διάδοχον τῆς ναυαρχίας, οὔτε, ὡς
ὕστερον διδοὺς πεῖραν ἀνὴρ ἐφαίνετο πάντων
ἄριστος καὶ δικαιότατος, ἠρέσκοντο τῷ τρόπῳ 436
τῆς ἡγεμονίας ἁπλοῦν τι καὶ Δώριον ἐχούσης καὶ
ἀληθινόν. ἀλλὰ τούτου μὲν τὴν ἀρετὴν ὥσπερ
ἀγάλματος ἡρωϊκοῦ κάλλος ἐθαύμαζον, ἐπόθουν
δὲ τὴν ἐκείνου σπουδὴν καὶ τὸ φιλέταιρον καὶ
χρειώδες ἐζήτουν, ὥστε ἀθυμεῖν ἐκπλέοντος αὐτοῦ
καὶ δακρύειν.

VI. Ὁ δὲ τούτους τε τῷ Καλλικρατίδᾳ δυσμενεστέρους ἐποίει ἔτι μᾶλλον, καὶ τῶν ὑπὸ
Κύρου χρημάτων αὐτῷ δεδομένων εἰς τὸ ναυτικὸν
τὰ περιόντα πάλιν εἰς Σάρδεις ἀνέπεμψεν, αὐτὸν
αἰτεῖν, εἰ βούλοιτο, τὸν Καλλικρατίδαν καὶ σκοπεῖν ὅπως θρέψοι τοὺς στρατιώτας κελεύσας.
2 τέλος δὲ ἀποπλέων ἐμαρτύρατο πρὸς αὐτὸν ὅτι

form political clubs in their several cities, and apply themselves to public affairs, assuring them that as soon as the Athenian empire was destroyed, they could rid themselves of their democracies and become themselves supreme in power. Moreover, by actual benefits he gave them all a confidence in this future, promoting those who were already his friends and allies to large enterprises and honours and commands, and taking a share himself in their injustice and wickedness in order to gratify their rapacity. Therefore all attached themselves to him, courted his favour, and fixed their hearts upon him, expecting to attain all their highest ambitions if only he remained in power. Therefore, too, they neither looked kindly upon Callicratidas at the first, when he came to succeed Lysander in the admiralty,[1] nor afterwards, when he had shown by manifest proofs that he was the justest and noblest of men, were they pleased with the manner of his leadership, which had a certain Doric simplicity and sincerity. They did, indeed, admire his virtue, as they would the beauty of a hero's statue; but they yearned for the zealous support of Lysander, and missed the interest which he took in the welfare of his partisans, so that when he sailed away they were dejected and shed tears.

VI. Lysander made these men yet more disaffected towards Callicratidas. He also sent back to Sardis what remained of the money which Cyrus had given him for the navy, bidding Callicratidas ask for it himself, if he wished, and see to the maintenance of his soldiers. And finally, as he sailed away, he called Callicratidas to witness that

---

[1] Late in the year 407 B.C. It was Spartan policy to change their admiral yearly.

θαλασσοκρατοῦν τὸ ναυτικὸν παραδίδωσιν. ὁ δὲ
βουλόμενος ἐλέγξαι τὴν φιλοτιμίαν ἀλαζονικὴν
καὶ κενὴν οὖσαν, "Οὐκοῦν," ἔφη, "λαβὼν ἐν
ἀριστερᾷ Σάμον καὶ περιπλεύσας εἰς Μίλητον
ἐκεῖ μοι παράδος τὰς τριήρεις· δεδιέναι γὰρ οὐ
χρὴ παραπλέοντας ἡμᾶς τοὺς ἐν Σάμῳ πολεμίους,
3 εἰ θαλασσοκρατοῦμεν." πρὸς ταῦτα εἰπὼν ὁ
Λύσανδρος ὅτι οὐκ αὐτός, ἀλλ' ἐκεῖνος ἄρχοι τῶν
νεῶν, ἀπέπλευσεν εἰς Πελοπόννησον, ἐν πολλῇ
τὸν Καλλικρατίδαν ἀπορίᾳ καταλιπών. οὔτε
γὰρ οἴκοθεν ἀφῖκτο χρήματα κομίζων, οὔτε τὰς
πόλεις ἀργυρολογεῖν καὶ βιάζεσθαι μοχθηρὰ
4 πραττούσας ὑπέμεινε. λοιπὸν οὖν ἦν ἐπὶ θύρας
ἰόντα τῶν βασιλέως στρατηγῶν, ὥσπερ Λύσανδρος, αἰτεῖν· πρὸς ὃ πάντων ἀφυέστατος ἐτύγχανεν, ἀνὴρ ἐλευθέριος καὶ μεγαλόφρων, καὶ πᾶσαν
ὑφ' Ἑλλήνων ἧτταν Ἕλλησιν ἡγούμενος εὐπρε-
πεστέραν εἶναι τοῦ κολακεύειν καὶ φοιτᾶν ἐπὶ
θύρας ἀνθρώπων βαρβάρων, πολὺ χρυσίον, ἄλλο
δ' οὐδὲν καλὸν ἐχόντων.
5 Ἐκβιαζόμενος δὲ ὑπὸ τῆς ἀπορίας, ἀναβὰς εἰς
Λυδίαν εὐθὺς ἐπορεύετο εἰς τὴν οἰκίαν τοῦ Κύρου,
καὶ φράζειν προσέταξεν ὅτι Καλλικρατίδας ὁ
ναύαρχος ἥκει διαλεχθῆναι βουλόμενος αὐτῷ.
τῶν δ' ἐπὶ θύραις τινὸς εἰπόντος, "Ἀλλ' οὐ
σχολὴ νῦν, ὦ ξένε, Κύρῳ· πίνει γάρ," ἀφε-
λέστατά πως ὁ Καλλικρατίδας, "Οὐδέν," ἔφη,
"δεινόν· αὐτοῦ γὰρ ἑστὼς ἀναμενῶ, μέχρι πίῃ."
6 τότε μὲν οὖν δόξας ἀγροῖκός τις εἶναι καὶ κατα-
γελασθεὶς ὑπὸ τῶν βαρβάρων ἀπῆλθεν· ἐπεὶ δὲ
καὶ δεύτερον ἐλθὼν ἐπὶ θύρας οὐ παρείθη, βαρέως

the fleet which he handed over to him was in command of the sea. But he, wishing to prove the emptiness and vanity of this ambitious boast, said : "In that case, keep Samos on the left, sail to Miletus, and there hand the triremes over to me ; surely we need not fear to sail past the enemy at Samos if we are masters of the sea." To this Lysander answered that Callicratidas, and not he, was in command of the ships, and sailed off to Peloponnesus, leaving Callicratidas in great perplexity.[1] For neither had he brought money from home with him, nor could he bear to lay the cities under forced contribution when they were already in an evil plight. The only course left, therefore, was to go to the doors of the King's generals, as Lysander had done, and ask for money. For this he was of all men least fitted by nature, being of a free and lofty spirit, and one who thought any and every defeat of Greeks at the hands of Greeks more becoming to them than visits of flattery to the houses of Barbarians, who had much gold, but nothing else worth while.

Constrained, however, by his necessities, he went up into Lydia, proceeded at once to the house of Cyrus, and ordered word to be sent in that Callicratidas the admiral was come and wished to confer with him. And when one of the door-keepers said to him : "But Cyrus is not at leisure now, Stranger, for he is at his wine"; Callicratidas replied with the utmost simplicity : "No matter, I will stand here and wait till he has had his wine." This time, then, he merely withdrew, after being taken for a rustic fellow and laughed at by the Barbarians. But when he was come a second time to the door and

[1] Cf. Xen. *Hell.* i. 6, 2 f.

ἐνεγκὼν εἰς Ἔφεσον ᾤχετο, πολλὰ μὲν ἐπα-
ρώμενος κακὰ τοῖς πρώτοις ἐντρυφηθεῖσιν ὑπὸ
βαρβάρων καὶ διδάξασιν αὐτοὺς ὑβρίζειν διὰ
7 πλοῦτον, ὀμνύων δὲ πρὸς τοὺς παρόντας ἦ μήν,
ὅταν πρῶτον εἰς Σπάρτην παραγένηται, πάντα
ποιήσειν ὑπὲρ τοῦ διαλυθῆναι τοὺς Ἕλληνας, ὡς
φοβεροὶ τοῖς βαρβάροις εἶεν αὐτοὶ καὶ παύσαιντο
τῆς ἐκείνων ἐπ' ἀλλήλους δεόμενοι δυνάμεως.

VII. Ἀλλὰ Καλλικρατίδας μὲν ἄξια τῆς
Λακεδαίμονος διανοηθείς, καὶ γενόμενος τοῖς ἄκ-
ροις ἐνάμιλλος τῶν Ἑλλήνων διὰ δικαιοσύνην καὶ
μεγαλοψυχίαν καὶ ἀνδρείαν, μετ' οὐ πολὺν χρόνον
ἐν Ἀργινούσαις καταναυμαχηθεὶς ἠφανίσθη. τῶν
δὲ πραγμάτων ὑποφερομένων οἱ σύμμαχοι πρεσβείαν πέμποντες εἰς Σπάρτην ᾐτοῦντο Λύσανδρον
ἐπὶ τὴν ναυαρχίαν, ὡς πολὺ προθυμότερον ἀν-
τιληψόμενοι τῶν πραγμάτων ἐκείνου στρατηγοῦν-
2 τος. τὰ δὲ αὐτὰ καὶ Κῦρος ἀξιῶν ἐπέστελλεν.
ἐπεὶ δὲ νόμος ἦν οὐκ ἐῶν δὶς τὸν αὐτὸν ναυαρχεῖν,
ἐβούλοντό τε χαρίζεσθαι τοῖς συμμάχοις οἱ Λακεδαιμόνιοι, τὸ μὲν ὄνομα τῆς ναυαρχίας Ἀράκῳ
τινὶ περιέθεσαν, τὸν δὲ Λύσανδρον ἐπιστολέα τῷ
λόγῳ, τῷ δ' ἔργῳ κύριον ἁπάντων ἐξέπεμψαν.
τοῖς μὲν οὖν πλείστοις τῶν πολιτευομένων καὶ
δυναμένων ἐν ταῖς πόλεσι πάλαι ποθούμενος
ἦκεν· ἤλπιζον γὰρ ἔτι μᾶλλον ἰσχύσειν δι' αὐτοῦ
3 παντάπασι τῶν δήμων καταλυθέντων· τοῖς δὲ
τὸν ἁπλοῦν καὶ γενναῖον ἀγαπῶσι τῶν ἡγεμόνων 437

was refused admittance, he was indignant, and set off for Ephesus, invoking many evils upon those who first submitted to the mockery of the Barbarians and taught them to be insolent because of their wealth, and swearing roundly to the bystanders that as soon as he got back to Sparta, he would do all he could to reconcile the Greeks with one another, in order that they might themselves strike fear into the Barbarians, and cease soliciting their power against each other.

VII. But Callicratidas, after cherishing purposes worthy of Lacedaemon, and showing himself worthy to compete with the most eminent of the Greeks by reason of his righteousness, magnanimity, and valour, not long afterwards lost the sea-fight at Arginusae and vanished from among men.[1]   Then, their cause declining, the allies sent an embassy to Sparta and asked that Lysander be made admiral, declaring that they would grapple much more vigorously with the situation if he were their commander.   Cyrus also sent to make the same request.   Now the Lacedaemonians had a law forbidding that the same man should be admiral twice, and yet they wished to gratify their allies; they therefore invested a certain Aracus with the title of admiral, and sent out Lysander as vice-admiral,[2] nominally, but really with supreme power.   So he came out, as most of those who had political power and influence in the cities had long desired, for they expected to become still stronger by his aid when the popular governments had been utterly overthrown; but to those who loved simplicity and nobility in the character of their leaders,

---

[1] In the late summer of 406 B.C. (Xen. *Hell.* i. 6, 33).

[2] In the spring of 405 B.C. (Xen. *Hell.* ii. 1, 7).

τρόπον, ὁ Λύσανδρος τῷ Καλλικρατίδᾳ παρα-
βαλλόμενος ἐδόκει πανοῦργος εἶναι καὶ σοφιστής,
ἀπάταις τὰ πολλὰ διαποικίλλων τοῦ πολέμου
καὶ τὸ δίκαιον ἐπὶ τῷ λυσιτελοῦντι μεγαλύνων,
εἰ δὲ μή, τῷ συμφέροντι χρώμενος ὡς καλῷ, καὶ
τὸ ἀληθὲς οὐ φύσει τοῦ ψεύδους κρεῖττον ἡγούμενος, ἀλλ' ἑκατέρου τῇ χρείᾳ τὴν τιμὴν ὁρίζων.
4 τῶν δ' ἀξιούντων μὴ πολεμεῖν μετὰ δόλου τοὺς
ἀφ' Ἡρακλέους γεγονότας καταγελᾶν ἐκέλευεν·
"'Ὅπου γὰρ ἡ λεοντῆ μὴ ἐφικνεῖται, προσραπτέον
ἐκεῖ τὴν ἀλωπεκῆν."

VIII. Τοιαῦτα δὲ αὐτοῦ καὶ τὰ περὶ Μίλητον
ἱστόρηται. τῶν γὰρ φίλων καὶ ξένων, οἷς ὑπέσχετο συγκαταλύσειν τε τὸν δῆμον καὶ συνεκ-
βαλεῖν τοὺς διαφόρους, μεταβαλομένων καὶ διαλ-
λαγέντων τοῖς ἐχθροῖς, φανερῶς μὲν ἥδεσθαι
προσεποιεῖτο καὶ συνδιαλλάττειν, κρύφα δὲ
λοιδορῶν αὐτοὺς καὶ κακίζων παρώξυνεν ἐπι-
2 θέσθαι τοῖς πολλοῖς. ὡς δὲ ᾔσθετο γινομένην
τὴν ἐπανάστασιν, ὀξέως βοηθήσας καὶ παρεισελθὼν εἰς τὴν πόλιν οἷς πρώτοις ἐπιτύχοι τῶν
νεωτεριζόντων ἐχαλέπαινε τῇ φωνῇ καὶ προσῆγε
τραχυνόμενος ὡς ἐπιθήσων δίκην αὐτοῖς, τοὺς
δὲ ἄλλους ἐκέλευε θαρρεῖν καὶ μηδὲν ἔτι προσ-
3 δοκᾶν δεινὸν αὐτοῦ παρόντος. ὑπεκρίνετο δὲ
ταῦτα καὶ διεποίκιλλε, τοὺς δημοτικωτάτους καὶ
κρατίστους βουλόμενος μὴ φεύγειν, ἀλλ' ἀποθανεῖν ἐν τῇ πόλει μείναντας. ὃ καὶ συνέβη·
πάντες γὰρ ἀπεσφάγησαν οἱ καταπιστεύσαντες.

Ἀπομνημονεύεται δὲ ὑπὸ Ἀνδροκλείδου λόγος
πολλήν τινα κατηγορῶν τοῦ Λυσάνδρου περὶ τοὺς

Lysander, compared with Callicratidas, seemed to be unscrupulous and subtle, a man who tricked out most of what he did in war with the varied hues of deceit, extolling justice if it was at the same time profitable, but if not, adopting the advantageous as the honourable course, and not considering truth as inherently better than falsehood, but bounding his estimate of either by the needs of the hour. Those who demanded that the descendants of Heracles should not wage war by deceit he held up to ridicule, saying that "where the lion's skin will not reach, it must be patched out with the fox's."

VIII. Of such a sort were his dealings with Miletus, according to the record. For when his friends and allies, whom he had promised to aid in overthrowing the democracy and expelling their opponents, changed their minds and became reconciled to their foes, openly he pretended to be pleased and to join in the reconciliation; but in secret he reviled and abused them, and incited them to fresh attacks upon the multitude. And when he perceived that the uprising was begun, he quickly came up and entered the city, where he angrily rebuked the first conspirators whom he met, and set upon them roughly, as though he were going to punish them, but ordered the rest of the people to be of good cheer and to fear no further evil now that he was with them. But in this he was playing a shifty part, wishing the leading men of the popular party not to fly, but to remain in the city and be slain. And this was what actually happened; for all who put their trust in him were slaughtered.

Furthermore, there is a saying of Lysander's, recorded by Androcleides, which makes him guilty of

4 ὅρκους εὐχέρειαν. ἐκέλευε γάρ, ὥς φησι, τοὺς
μὲν παῖδας ἀστραγάλοις, τοὺς δὲ ἄνδρας ὅρκοις
ἐξαπατᾶν, ἀπομιμούμενος Πολυκράτη τὸν Σάμιον,
οὐκ ὀρθῶς τύραννον στρατηγός, οὐδὲ Λακωνικὸν
τὸ χρῆσθαι τοῖς θεοῖς ὥσπερ τοῖς πολεμίοις,
μᾶλλον δὲ ὑβριστικώτερον. ὁ γὰρ ὅρκῳ παρα-
κρουόμενος τὸν μὲν ἐχθρὸν ὁμολογεῖ δεδιέναι, τοῦ
δὲ θεοῦ καταφρονεῖν.

IX. Ὁ δ᾽ οὖν Κῦρος εἰς Σάρδεις μεταπεμψά-
μενος τὸν Λύσανδρον, τὰ μὲν ἔδωκε, τὰ δὲ ὑπέσχετο,
νεανιευσάμενος εἰς τὴν ἐκείνου χάριν καὶ εἰ μηδὲν
ὁ πατὴρ διδῴη καταχορηγήσειν τὰ οἰκεῖα· κἂν
ἐπιλίπῃ πάντα, κατακόψειν ἔφη τὸν θρόνον ἐφ᾽
ᾧ καθήμενος ἐχρημάτιζε, χρυσοῦν καὶ ἀργυροῦν
2 ὄντα. τέλος δὲ εἰς Μηδίαν ἀναβαίνων πρὸς τὸν
πατέρα, τούς τε φόρους ἀπέδειξε τῶν πόλεων
λαμβάνειν ἐκεῖνον, καὶ τὴν αὐτοῦ διεπίστευσεν
ἀρχήν· ἀσπασάμενος δὲ καὶ δεηθεὶς μὴ ναυμαχεῖν
Ἀθηναίοις, πρὶν αὐτὸν ἀφικέσθαι πάλιν, ἀφίξ-
εσθαι δὲ ναῦς ἔχοντα πολλὰς ἔκ τε Φοινίκης καὶ
Κιλικίας, ἀνέβαινεν ὡς βασιλέα.

Λύσανδρος δὲ μήτε ναυμαχεῖν ἀγχωμάλῳ πλήθει δυνάμενος μήτε ἀργὸς καθέζεσθαι μετὰ νεῶν
τοσούτων, ἀναχθεὶς ἐνίας προσηγάγετο τῶν νήσων,
Αἴγινάν τε καὶ Σαλαμῖνα προσμίξας κατέδραμεν.
3 εἰς δὲ τὴν Ἀττικὴν ἀποβὰς καὶ τὸν Ἆγιν ἀσπασάμενος, κατέβη γὰρ αὐτὸς ἐκ Δεκελείας πρὸς αὐτόν,
ἐπέδειξε τῷ πεζῷ παρόντι τὴν τοῦ ναυτικοῦ

---

[1] Cf. Xen. *Hell.* ii. 1, 13 f.
[2] In the spring of 413 B.C. the Spartans had fortified
Deceleia, a few miles N.W. of Athens, and stationed there a

the greatest recklessness in the matter of oaths. It
was his policy, according to this authority, "to cheat
boys with knuckle-bones, but men with oaths," thus
imitating Polycrates of Samos; not a proper attitude
in a general towards a tyrant, nor yet a Laconian
trait to treat the gods as one's enemies are treated,
nay, more outrageously still; since he who over-
reaches his enemy by means of an oath, confesses
that he fears that enemy, but despises God.

IX. Well, then, Cyrus summoned Lysander to
Sardis, and gave him this, and promised him that,
ardently protesting, to gratify him, that he would
actually squander his own fortune, if his father gave
him nothing for the Spartans; and if all else failed,
he said he would cut up the throne on which he sat
when giving audience, a throne covered with gold
and silver. And finally, as he was going up into
Media to wait upon his father, he assigned to Lysander
the tribute of the cities, and entrusted his own
government to him; and embracing him in farewell,
and begging him not to fight the Athenians at sea
until he was come back, and promising to come back
with many ships from Phoenicia and Cilicia, he set
out to go up to the King.[1]

Then Lysander, who could neither fight a naval
battle on equal terms, nor remain idle with the large
fleet at his disposal, put out to sea and reduced some
of the islands, and touching at Aegina and Salamis,
overran them. Then he landed in Attica and saluted
Agis, who came down in person from Deceleia[2] to
meet him, and displayed to the land forces there the

permanent garrison under Agis the king. Lysander's ravaging
of Aegina and Salamis was just before his siege of Athens,
according to Xenophon (*Hell.* ii. 2, 9).

ῥώμην, ὡς πλέων ᾗ βούλοιτο, κρατῶν τῆς θαλάττης. οὐ μὴν ἀλλὰ τοὺς Ἀθηναίους αἰσθόμενος
διώκοντας αὐτὸν ἄλλῳ δρόμῳ διὰ νήσων ἔφευγεν
εἰς τὴν Ἀσίαν.

4 Καὶ τὸν Ἑλλήσποντον ἔρημον καταλαβὼν
ἐπεχείρει Λαμψακηνοῖς αὐτὸς ἐκ θαλάττης ταῖς
ναυσί, Θώραξ δὲ τῷ πεζῷ στρατῷ συνανύσας εἰς
τὸ αὐτὸ προσέβαλε τοῖς τείχεσιν. ἑλὼν δὲ τὴν
πόλιν κατὰ κράτος διαρπάσαι τοῖς στρατιώταις
ἔδωκεν. ὁ δὲ τῶν Ἀθηναίων στόλος ὀγδοήκοντα
καὶ ἑκατὸν τριήρων ἐτύγχανε μὲν ἄρτι καθωρμισ-
μένος εἰς Ἐλαιοῦντα τῆς Χερρονήσου, πυνθανόμενοι δὲ ἀπολωλέναι τὴν Λάμψακον εὐθὺς εἰς 438
5 Σηστὸν καταίρουσι. κἀκεῖθεν ἐπισιτισάμενοι
παρέπλευσαν εἰς Αἰγὸς ποταμούς, ἀντιπέρας
τῶν πολεμίων ἔτι ναυλοχούντων περὶ τὴν Λάμψακον. ἐστρατήγουν δὲ τῶν Ἀθηναίων ἄλλοι τε
πλείους καὶ Φιλοκλῆς ὁ πείσας ποτὲ ψηφίσασθαι
τὸν δῆμον ἀποκόπτειν τὸν δεξιὸν ἀντίχειρα τῶν
ἁλισκομένων κατὰ πόλεμον, ὅπως δόρυ μὲν φέρειν
μὴ δύνωνται, κώπην δὲ ἐλαύνωσι.

X. Τότε μὲν οὖν ἀνεπαύοντο πάντες, ἐλπίζοντες
εἰς τὴν ὑστεραίαν ναυμαχήσειν. ὁ δὲ Λύσανδρος
ἄλλα μὲν διενοεῖτο, προσέταττε δὲ ναύταις καὶ
κυβερνήταις, ὡς ἀγῶνος ἅμα ἡμέρᾳ γενησομένου,
περὶ ὄρθρον ἐμβαίνειν εἰς τὰς τριήρεις καὶ καθέζεσθαι κόσμῳ καὶ σιωπῇ, δεχομένους τὸ παραγ-
γελλόμενον, ὡς δ' αὕτως καὶ τὸ πεζὸν ἐν τάξει
2 παρὰ τὴν θάλατταν ἡσυχάζειν. ἀνίσχοντος δὲ
τοῦ ἡλίου καὶ τῶν Ἀθηναίων μετωπηδὸν ἁπάσαις
ἐπιπλεόντων καὶ προκαλουμένων, ἀντιπρώρους

strength of his fleet, with the mien of one who
sailed where he pleased and was master of the sea.
But on learning that the Athenians were pursuing
him, he fled by another route through the islands
to Asia.

Finding the Hellespont unguarded, he himself
attacked Lampsacus from the sea with his ships,
while Thorax, co-operating with the land forces,
assaulted the walls. He took the city by storm,
and gave it up to his soldiers to plunder.[1] Meanwhile the Athenian fleet of a hundred and eighty
triremes had just arrived at Elaeus in the Chersonese,
and learning that Lampsacus had fallen, they straightway put in at Sestos. There they took in provisions,
and then sailed along to Aegospotami, over against
their enemies, who were still in station at Lampsacus.
The Athenians were under the command of several
generals, among whom was Philocles, the man who
had recently persuaded the people to pass a decree
that their prisoners of war should have the right
thumb cut off, that they might not be able to wield
a spear, though they might ply an oar.[2]

X. For the time being, then, all rested, expecting
that on the morrow the fleets would engage. But
Lysander was planning otherwise, and ordered his
seamen and pilots, as though there would be a
struggle at daybreak, to go on board their triremes
in the early morning, and take their seats in order
and in silence, awaiting the word of command, and
that the land forces also, in the same manner, remain
quietly in their ranks by the sea. When the sun
rose, however, and the Athenians sailed up with all
their ships in line and challenged to battle, although

[1] Cf. Xen. *Hell.* ii. 1, 18 f.   [2] See the note on xiii. 1.

ἔχων τὰς ναῦς καὶ πεπληρωμένας ἔτι νυκτὸς οὐκ
ἀνήγετο, πέμπων δὲ ὑπηρετικὰ παρὰ τὰς πρώτας
τῶν νεῶν ἀτρεμεῖν ἐκέλευε καὶ μένειν ἐν τάξει μὴ
3 θορυβουμένους μηδ᾽ ἀντεκπλέοντας. οὕτω δὲ περὶ
δείλην ἀποπλεόντων ὀπίσω τῶν Ἀθηναίων οὐ
πρότερον ἐκ τῶν νεῶν τοὺς στρατιώτας ἀφῆκεν,
εἰ μὴ δύο καὶ τρεῖς τριήρεις, ἃς ἔπεμψε κατασκόπους, ἐλθεῖν ἰδόντας ἀποβεβηκότας τοὺς πολεμίους. τῇ δ᾽ ὑστεραίᾳ πάλιν ἐγίνοντο ταῦτα καὶ
τῇ τρίτῃ μέχρι τετάρτης, ὥστε πολὺ τοῖς Ἀθηναίοις θράσος ἐγγενέσθαι καὶ καταφρόνησιν ὡς
δεδιότων καὶ συνεσταλμένων τῶν πολεμίων.

4   Ἐν τούτῳ δὲ Ἀλκιβιάδης (ἐτύγχανε γὰρ περὶ
Χερρόνησον ἐν τοῖς ἑαυτοῦ τείχεσι διαιτώμενος)
ἵππῳ προσελάσας πρὸς τὸ στράτευμα τῶν Ἀθηναίων ᾐτιᾶτο τοὺς στρατηγοὺς πρῶτον μὲν οὐ
καλῶς οὐδ᾽ ἀσφαλῶς στρατοπεδεύειν ἐν αἰγιαλοῖς
δυσόρμοις καὶ ἀναπεπταμένοις· ἔπειτα πόρρωθεν
ἐκ Σηστοῦ τὰ ἐπιτήδεια λαμβάνοντας ἁμαρτάνειν,
5 δέον εἰς λιμένα καὶ πόλιν Σηστὸν δι᾽ ὀλίγου
περιπλεύσαντας, ἀπωτέρω γενέσθαι τῶν πολεμίων
ἐφορμούντων στρατεύματι μοναρχουμένῳ καὶ
πάντα πρὸς φόβον ὀξέως ἀπὸ συνθήματος ὑπηρε-
τοῦντι. ταῦτα δὲ αὐτοῦ διδάσκοντος οὐκ ἐπείθοντο, Τυδεὺς δὲ καὶ πρὸς ὕβριν ἀπεκρίνατο, φήσας
οὐκ ἐκεῖνον, ἀλλ᾽ ἑτέρους στρατηγεῖν.

XI. Ὁ μὲν οὖν Ἀλκιβιάδης ὑποπτεύσας τι
καὶ προδοσίας ἐν αὐτοῖς ἀπηλλάττετο. πέμπτῃ

256

he had his ships drawn up in line to meet them and fully manned before it was light, he did not put out from his position, but sending despatch-boats to the foremost of his ships, ordered them to keep quiet and remain in line, not getting into confusion nor sailing out to meet the enemy. And so towards evening, when the Athenians sailed back, he did not allow his men to leave their ships until two or three triremes, which he sent to reconnoitre, came back, after seeing that the enemy had disembarked. On the following day this was done again, and on the third, and at last on the fourth, so that the Athenians became very bold and contemptuous, believing that their enemies were huddling together in fear.

At this juncture, Alcibiades, who was living in his own fortress on the Chersonese, rode up to the Athenian army and censured the generals, first, for having pitched their camp in a bad and even danger-ous place on an open beach where there was no road-stead ; and second, for the mistake of getting their provisions from distant Sestos, when they ought to sail round the coast a little way to the harbour and city of Sestos, where they would be at a longer remove from their enemies, who lay watching them with an army commanded by a single man, the fear of whom led it to obey his every order promptly. These were the lessons he gave them, but they would not receive them, and Tydeus actually gave him an insolent answer, saying that he was not general now, but others.[1]

XI. Alcibiades, accordingly, suspecting that some treachery was afoot among them, went away. But

[1] Cf. Xen. *Hell*. ii. 1, 20–26 ; Plutarch, *Alcibiades*, xxxvi. 4–xxxvii. 1.

δὲ ἡμέρᾳ τῶν Ἀθηναίων ποιησαμένων τὸν ἐπί-
πλουν καὶ πάλιν ἀπερχομένων, ὥσπερ εἰώθεσαν,
ὀλιγώρως πάνυ καὶ καταφρονητικῶς, ὁ Λύσανδρος
ἐκπέμπων τὰς κατασκόπους ναῦς ἐκέλευσε τοὺς
τριηράρχους, ὅταν ἴδωσι τοὺς Ἀθηναίους ἐκβε-
βηκότας, ἐλαύνειν ἀποστρέψαντας ὀπίσω τάχει
παντί, καὶ γενομένους κατὰ μέσον τὸν πόρον
ἀσπίδα χαλκῆν ἐπάρασθαι πρώραθεν ἐπίπλου
2 σύμβολον. αὐτὸς δὲ τοὺς κυβερνήτας καὶ τριηράρχους ἐπιπλέων ἀνεκαλεῖτο καὶ παρώρμα συν-
έχειν ἕκαστον ἐν τάξει τὸ πλήρωμα καὶ τοὺς
ναύτας καὶ τοὺς ἐπιβάτας, ὅταν δὲ σημανθῇ, μετὰ
προθυμίας καὶ ῥώμης ἐλαύνειν ἐπὶ τοὺς πολεμίους. ὡς δὲ ἥ τε ἀσπὶς ἀπὸ τῶν νεῶν ἤρθη καὶ
τῇ σάλπιγγι τὴν ἀναγωγὴν ἐσήμαινεν ἀπὸ τῆς
ναυαρχίδος, ἐπέπλεον μὲν αἱ νῆες, ἡμιλλῶντο δὲ
3 οἱ πεζοὶ παρὰ τὸν αἰγιαλὸν ἐπὶ τὴν ἄκραν. τὸ δὲ
μεταξὺ τῶν ἠπείρων διάστημα ταύτῃ πεντεκαίδεκα σταδίων ἐστί, καὶ ταχέως ὑπὸ σπουδῆς καὶ
προθυμίας τῶν ἐλαυνόντων συνῄρητο. Κόνων δὲ
πρῶτος ὁ τῶν Ἀθηναίων στρατηγὸς ἀπὸ τῆς γῆς
ἰδὼν ἐπιπλέοντα τὸν στόλον ἐξαίφνης ἀνεβόησεν
ἐμβαίνειν, καὶ περιπαθῶν τῷ κακῷ τοὺς μὲν
ἐκάλει, τῶν δὲ ἐδεῖτο, τοὺς δὲ ἠνάγκαζε πληροῦν
4 τὰς τριήρεις. ἦν δὲ οὐδὲν ἔργον αὐτοῦ τῆς σπουδῆς 43
ἐσκεδασμένων τῶν ἀνθρώπων. ὡς γὰρ ἐξέβησαν,
εὐθύς, ἅτε μηδὲν προσδοκῶντες, ἠγόραζον, ἐπλα-
νῶντο περὶ τὴν χώραν, ἐκάθευδον ὑπὸ ταῖς
σκηναῖς, ἠριστοποιοῦντο, πορρωτάτω τοῦ μέλλον-
5 τος ἀπειρίᾳ τῶν ἡγουμένων ὄντες. ἤδη δὲ κραυγῇ
καὶ ῥοθίῳ προσφερομένων τῶν πολεμίων ὁ μὲν

on the fifth day, when the Athenians had sailed over
to the enemy and back again, as was now their wont,
very carelessly and contemptuously, Lysander, as he
sent out his reconnoitring ships, ordered their commanders, as soon as they saw that the Athenians
had disembarked, to put about and row back with
all speed, and when they were half way across, to
hoist a brazen shield at the prow, as a signal for the
onset. And he himself sailed round and earnestly
exhorted the pilots and trierarchs to keep all their
crews at their post, sailors and soldiers alike, and as
soon as the signal was given, to row with ardour and
vigour against the enemy. When, therefore, the
shield was hoisted on the lookout ships, and the
trumpet on the admiral's ship signalled the attack,
the ships sailed forth, and the land forces ran their
fastest along the shore to seize the promontory. The
distance between the two continents at this point is
fifteen furlongs, and such was the zealous ardour of
the rowers that it was quickly consumed. Conon,
the Athenian general, who was the first to see from
the land the onset of the fleet, suddenly shouted
orders to embark, and deeply stirred by the threatening disaster, called upon some, besought others,
and forced others still to man the triremes. But his
eager efforts were of no avail, since the men were
scattered. For just as soon as they had disembarked,
since they expected no trouble, some went to market,
some walked about the country, some lay down to
sleep in their tents, and some began to get their
suppers ready, being as far as possible removed from
any thought of what was to happen, through the
inexperience of their commanders. The shouts and
splashing oars of the oncoming enemy were already

259

s 2

Κόνων ὀκτὼ ναυσὶν ὑπεξέπλευσε καὶ διαφυγὼν
ἀπεπέρασεν εἰς Κύπρον πρὸς Εὐαγόραν, ταῖς δὲ
ἄλλαις ἐπιπεσόντες οἱ Πελοποννήσιοι τὰς μὲν
κενὰς παντάπασιν ἤρουν, τὰς δ' ἔτι πληρουμένας
ἔκοπτον. οἱ δὲ ἄνθρωποι πρός τε ταῖς ναυσὶν
ἀπέθνησκον ἄνοπλοι καὶ σποράδες ἐπιβοηθοῦντες,
ἔν τε τῇ γῇ φεύγοντες ἀποβάντων τῶν πολεμίων
6 ἐκτείνοντο. λαμβάνει δὲ ὁ Λύσανδρος τρισχιλίους
ἄνδρας αἰχμαλώτους μετὰ τῶν στρατηγῶν, ἅπαν
δὲ τὸ ναύσταθμον ἄνευ τῆς Παράλου καὶ τῶν
μετὰ Κόνωνος ἐκφυγουσῶν. ἀναδησάμενος δὲ
τὰς ναῦς καὶ διαπορθήσας τὸ στρατόπεδον μετὰ
αὐλοῦ καὶ παιάνων ἀνέπλευσεν εἰς Λάμψακον,
ἔργον ἐλαχίστῳ πόνῳ μέγιστον ἐξειργασμένος,
καὶ συνῃρηκὼς ὥρᾳ μιᾷ χρόνου μήκιστον καὶ
ποικιλώτατον πάθεσί τε καὶ τύχαις ἀπιστότατον
7 τῶν πρὸ αὐτοῦ πολέμων, ὃς μυρίας μορφὰς ἀγώνων καὶ πραγμάτων μεταβολὰς ἀμείψας, καὶ
στρατηγοὺς ὅσους οὐδὲ οἱ σύμπαντες οἱ πρὸ αὐτοῦ
τῆς Ἑλλάδος ἀναλώσας, ἑνὸς ἀνδρὸς εὐβουλίᾳ
καὶ δεινότητι συνῄρητο· διὸ καὶ θεῖόν τινες ἡγή-
σαντο τοῦτο τὸ ἔργον.

XII. Ἦσαν δέ τινες οἱ τοὺς Διοσκούρους ἐπὶ
τῆς Λυσάνδρου νεὼς ἑκατέρωθεν, ὅτε τοῦ λιμένος
ἐξέπλει πρῶτον ἐπὶ τοὺς πολεμίους, ἄστρα τοῖς
οἴαξιν ἐπιλάμψαι λέγοντες. οἱ δὲ καὶ τὴν τοῦ
λίθου πτῶσιν ἐπὶ τῷ πάθει τούτῳ σημεῖόν φασι

heard, when Conon, with eight ships, sailed stealthily away, and making his escape, proceeded to Cyprus, to Evagoras; but the Peloponnesians fell upon the rest of the ships, some of which they took entirely empty, and others they disabled while their crews were still getting aboard. And the men, coming up unarmed and in straggling fashion, perished at their ships, or if they fled by land, their enemies, who had disembarked, slew them. Lysander took three thousand men prisoners, together with their generals, and captured the whole fleet, excepting the Paralus[1] and the ships that had made their escape with Conon. So after plundering his enemy's camp and taking their ships in tow, he sailed back to Lampsacus, to the sound of pipes and hymns of victory. He had wrought a work of the greatest magnitude with the least toil and effort, and had brought to a close in a single hour a war which, in length, and the incredible variety of its incidents and fortunes, surpassed all its predecessors. Its struggles and issues had assumed ten thousand changing shapes, and it had cost Hellas more generals than all her previous wars together, and yet it was brought to a close by the prudence and ability of one man. Therefore some actually thought the result due to divine intervention.

XII. There were some who declared that the Dioscuri[2] appeared as twin stars on either side of Lysander's ship just as he was sailing out of the harbour against the enemy, and shone out over the rudder-sweeps. And some say also that the falling of the stone was a portent of this disaster; for ac-

---

[1] One of the sacred state-galleys. It now carried the news of the disaster to Athens (Xen. *Hell.* ii. 1, 28).

[2] Castor and Pollux.

γενέσθαι· κατηνέχθη γάρ, ὡς ἡ δόξα τῶν πολλῶν,
ἐξ οὐρανοῦ παμμεγέθης λίθος εἰς Αἰγὸς ποταμούς.
2 καὶ δείκνυται μὲν ἔτι νῦν, σεβομένων αὐτὸν τῶν
Χερρονησιτῶν· λέγεται δὲ Ἀναξαγόραν προειπεῖν
ὡς τῶν κατὰ τὸν οὐρανὸν ἐνδεδεμένων σωμάτων,
γενομένου τινὸς ὀλισθήματος ἢ σάλου, ῥῖψις
ἔσται καὶ πτῶσις ἑνὸς ἀπορραγέντος· εἶναι δὲ καὶ
τῶν ἄστρων ἕκαστον οὐκ ἐν ᾗ πέφυκε χώρᾳ·
λιθώδη γὰρ ὄντα καὶ βαρέα λάμπειν μὲν ἀντερείσει
καὶ περικλάσει τοῦ αἰθέρος, ἕλκεσθαι δὲ ὑπὸ βίας
σφιγγόμενα δίνῃ καὶ τόνῳ τῆς περιφορᾶς, ὥς που
καὶ τὸ πρῶτον ἐκρατήθη μὴ πεσεῖν δεῦρο, τῶν
ψυχρῶν καὶ βαρέων ἀποκρινομένων τοῦ παντός.
3 Ἔστι δέ τις πιθανωτέρα δόξα ταύτης, εἰρηκότων
ἐνίων ὡς οἱ διάττοντες ἀστέρες οὐ ῥύσις εἰσὶν οὐδ᾽
ἐπινέμησις αἰθερίου πυρὸς ἐν ἀέρι κατασβεννυμένου
περὶ τὴν ἔξαψιν αὐτήν, οὐδὲ ἀέρος εἰς τὴν ἄνω
χώραν πλήθει λυθέντος ἔκπρησις καὶ ἀνάφλεξις,
ῥῖψις δὲ καὶ πτῶσις οὐρανίων σωμάτων οἷον
ἐνδόσει τινὶ τόνου καὶ περιτρόπου [1] κινήσεως
ἐκπαλῶν φερομένων οὐ πρὸς τὸν οἰκούμενον τόπον
τῆς γῆς, ἀλλὰ τῶν πλείστων ἐκτὸς εἰς τὴν
μεγάλην ἐκπιπτόντων θάλατταν· διὸ καὶ λανθά-
νουσι.
4 Τῷ δ᾽ Ἀναξαγόρᾳ μαρτυρεῖ καὶ Δαΐμαχος ἐν
τοῖς Περὶ εὐσεβείας, ἱστορῶν ὅτι πρὸ τοῦ πεσεῖν
τὸν λίθον ἐφ᾽ ἡμέρας ἑβδομήκοντα καὶ πέντε
συνεχῶς κατὰ τὸν οὐρανὸν ἑωρᾶτο πύρινον σῶμα

---

[1] περιτρόπου the correction of Coraës: παρατρόπου (unusual).

cording to the common belief, a stone of vast size had fallen from heaven at Aegospotami,[1] and it is shown to this day by the dwellers in the Chersonese, who hold it in reverence. Anaxagoras is said to have predicted that if the heavenly bodies should be loosened by some slip or shake, one of them might be torn away, and might plunge and fall down to earth; and he said that none of the stars was in its original position; for being of stone, and heavy, their shining light is caused by friction with the revolving aether, and they are forced along in fixed orbits by the whirling impulse which gave them their circular motion, and this was what prevented them from falling to our earth in the first place, when cold and heavy bodies were separated from universal matter.

But there is a more plausible opinion than this, and its advocates hold that shooting stars are not a flow or emanation of aetherial fire, which the lower air quenches at the very moment of its kindling, nor are they an ignition and blazing up of a quantity of lower air which has made its escape into the upper regions; but they are plunging and falling heavenly bodies, carried out of their course by some relaxation in the tension of their circular motion, and falling, not upon the inhabited region of the earth, but for the most part outside of it and into the great sea; and this is the reason why they are not noticed.

But Daïmachus, in his treatise "On Religion," supports the view of Anaxagoras. He says that before the stone fell, for seventy-five days continually, there was seen in the heavens a fiery body of

---

[1] In 468-7 B.C., according to the Parian marble (*ep.* 57) and Pliny, *N.H.* ii. 149 f.

παμμέγεθες, ὥσπερ νέφος φλογοειδές, οὐ σχολάζον,
ἀλλὰ πολυπλόκους καὶ κεκλασμένας φορὰς φερό-
μενον, ὥστε ὑπὸ σάλου καὶ πλάνης ἀπορρηγνύ-
μενα πυροειδῆ σπάσματα φέρεσθαι πολλαχοῦ
καὶ ἀστράπτειν, ὥσπερ οἱ διᾴττοντες ἀστέρες.
5 ἐπεὶ δὲ ἐνταῦθα τῆς γῆς ἔβρισε καὶ παυσάμενοι
φόβου καὶ θάμβους οἱ ἐπιχώριοι συνῆλθον, ὤφθη
πυρὸς μὲν οὐδὲν ἔργον οὐδ' ἴχνος τοσοῦτο,[1] λίθος
δὲ κείμενος, ἄλλως μὲν μέγας, οὐθὲν δὲ μέρος, ὡς
εἰπεῖν, ἐκείνης τῆς πυροειδοῦς περιοχῆς ἔχων.   440
ὅτι μὲν οὖν εὐγνωμόνων ὁ Δαΐμαχος ἀκροατῶν
6 δεῖται δῆλός ἐστιν· εἰ δὲ ἀληθὴς ὁ λόγος, ἐξελέγχει
κατὰ κράτος τοὺς φάσκοντας ἔκ τινος ἀκρωρείας
ἀποκοπεῖσαν πνεύμασι καὶ ζάλαις πέτραν, ὑπο-
ληφθεῖσαν δ' ὥσπερ οἱ στρόβιλοι, καὶ φερομένην,
ᾗ πρῶτον ἐνέδωκε καὶ διελύθη τὸ περιδινῆσαν,
7 ἐκριφῆναι καὶ πεσεῖν. εἰ μὴ νὴ Δία πῦρ μὲν ἦν
ὄντως τὸ φαινόμενον ἐπὶ πολλὰς ἡμέρας, σβέσις
δὲ καὶ φθορὰ μεταβολὴν ἀέρι παρέσχεν εἰς πνεύ-
ματα βιαιότερα καὶ κινήσεις, ὑφ' ὧν συνέτυχε καὶ
τὸν λίθον ἐκριφῆναι. ταῦτα μὲν οὖν ἑτέρῳ γένει
γραφῆς διακριβωτέον.

XIII. Ὁ δὲ Λύσανδρος, ἐπεὶ τῶν τρισχιλίων
Ἀθηναίων, οὓς ἔλαβεν αἰχμαλώτους, ὑπὸ τῶν
συνέδρων θάνατος κατέγνωστο, καλέσας Φιλοκλέα
τὸν στρατηγὸν αὐτῶν ἠρώτησεν τίνα τιμᾶται
δίκην ἑαυτῷ τοιαῦτα περὶ Ἑλλήνων συμβεβου-

---

[1] τοσοῦτο Coraës and Bekker adopt Reiske's correction to
τοσούτου.

[1] See chapter ix. 5. According to Xenophon (*Hell.* ii. 1, 31 f.),
however, the Athenians had passed a decree that, if
victorious in the sea-fight, they would cut off the right hand

vast size, as if it had been a flaming cloud, not resting in one place, but moving along with intricate and irregular motions, so that fiery fragments, broken from it by its plunging and erratic course, were carried in all directions and flashed fire, just as shooting stars do. But when it had fallen in that part of the earth, and the inhabitants, after recovering from their fear and amazement, were assembled about it, no action of fire was seen, nor even so much as a trace thereof, but a stone lying there, of large size, it is true, but one which bore almost no proportion at all to the fiery mass seen in the heavens. Well, then, that Daïmachus must needs have indulgent readers, is clear; but if his story is true, he refutes utterly those who affirm that a rock, which winds and tempests had torn from some mountain top, was caught up and borne along like a spinning top, and that at the point where the whirling impetus given to it first relaxed and ceased, there it plunged and fell. Unless, indeed, what was seen in the heavens for many days was really fire, the quenching and extinction of which produced a change in the air resulting in unusually violent winds and agitations, and these brought about the plunge of the stone. However, the minute discussion of this subject belongs to another kind of writing.

XIII. Lysander, after the three thousand Athenians whom he had taken prisoners had been condemned to death by the special council of allies, calling Philocles, their general, asked him what punishment he thought should be visited upon him for having given his fellow-citizens such counsel regarding Greeks.[1]

of every prisoner; and the crime of Philocles was that he had ordered the crews of two captured triremes to be thrown over a precipice.

2 λευκὼς τοῖς πολίταις. ὁ δὲ οὐδέν τι πρὸς τὴν
συμφορὰν ἐνδοὺς ἐκέλευσε μὴ κατηγορεῖν ὧν
οὐδείς ἐστι δικαστής, ἀλλὰ νικῶντα πράττειν
ἅπερ ἂν νικηθεὶς ἔπασχεν· εἶτα λουσάμενος καὶ
λαβὼν χλανίδα λαμπρὰν πρῶτος ἐπὶ τὴν σφαγὴν
ἡγεῖτο τοῖς πολίταις, ὡς ἱστορεῖ Θεόφραστος. ἐκ
δὲ τούτου πλέων ὁ Λύσανδρος ἐπὶ τὰς πόλεις
Ἀθηναίων μὲν οἷς ἐπιτύχοι ἐκέλευε πάντας εἰς
Ἀθήνας ἀπιέναι· φείσεσθαι γὰρ οὐδενός, ἀλλ'
3 ἀποσφάξειν ὃν ἂν ἔξω λάβῃ τῆς πόλεως. ταῦτα
δ' ἔπραττε καὶ συνήλαυνεν ἅπαντας εἰς τὸ ἄστυ
βουλόμενος ἐν τῇ πόλει ταχὺ λιμὸν ἰσχυρὸν
γενέσθαι καὶ σπάνιν, ὅπως μὴ πράγματα παρά-
σχοιεν αὐτῷ τὴν πολιορκίαν εὐπόρως ὑπομένοντες.
καταλύων δὲ τοὺς δήμους καὶ τὰς ἄλλας πολιτείας,
ἕνα μὲν ἁρμοστὴν ἑκάστῃ Λακεδαιμόνιον κατέλιπε,
δέκα δὲ ἄρχοντας ἐκ τῶν ὑπ' αὐτοῦ συγκεκροτη-
4 μένων κατὰ πόλιν ἑταιρειῶν. καὶ ταῦτα πράττων ὁμοίως ἔν τε ταῖς πολεμίαις καὶ ταῖς συμμάχοις γεγενημέναις πόλεσι, παρέπλει σχολαίως,
τρόπον τινὰ κατασκευαζόμενος ἑαυτῷ τὴν τῆς
Ἑλλάδος ἡγεμονίαν. οὔτε γὰρ ἀριστίνδην οὔτε
πλουτίνδην ἀπεδείκνυε τοὺς ἄρχοντας, ἀλλ' ἑταιρείαις καὶ ξενίαις χαριζόμενος τὰ πράγματα καὶ
κυρίους ποιῶν τιμῆς τε καὶ κολάσεως, πολλαῖς
δὲ παραγινόμενος αὐτὸς σφαγαῖς καὶ συνεκβάλ-
λων τοὺς τῶν φίλων ἐχθρούς, οὐκ ἐπιεικὲς ἐδίδου
τοῖς Ἕλλησι δεῖγμα τῆς Λακεδαιμονίων ἀρχῆς,

LYSANDER

But he, not one whit softened by his misfortunes, bade him not play the prosecutor in a case where there was no judge, but to inflict, as victor, the punishment he would have suffered if vanquished. Then, after bathing and putting on a rich robe, he went first to the slaughter and showed his countrymen the way, as Theophrastus writes. After this, Lysander sailed to the various cities, and ordered all the Athenians whom he met to go back to Athens, for he would spare none, he said, but would slaughter any whom he caught outside the city. He took this course, and drove them all into the city together, because he wished that scarcity of food and a mighty famine should speedily afflict the city, in order that they might not hinder him by holding out against his siege with plenty of provisions. He also suppressed the democratic, and the other forms of government, and left one Lacedaemonian harmost [1] in each city, and ten rulers chosen from the political clubs which he had organized throughout the cities. This he did alike in the cities which had been hostile, and in those which had become his allies, and sailed along in leisurely fashion, in a manner establishing for himself the supremacy over Hellas. For in his appointments of the rulers he had regard neither to birth nor wealth, but put control of affairs into the hands of his comrades and partisans, and made them masters of rewards and punishments. He also took part himself in many massacres, and assisted in driving out the enemies of his friends. Thus he gave the Greeks no worthy specimen of Lacedaemonian rule, nay,

---

[1] The specific name for the governor whom the Lacedaemonians sent out to the islands and cities of Greece during their supremacy.

5 ἀλλὰ καὶ ὁ κωμικὸς Θεόπομπος ἔοικε ληρεῖν
ἀπεικάζων τοὺς Λακεδαιμονίους ταῖς καπηλίσιν,
ὅτι τοὺς Ἕλληνας ἥδιστον ποτὸν τῆς ἐλευθερίας
γεύσαντες ὄξος ἐνέχεαν· εὐθὺς γὰρ ἦν τὸ γεῦμα
δυσχερὲς καὶ πικρόν, οὔτε τοὺς δήμους κυρίους
τῶν πραγμάτων ἐῶντος εἶναι τοῦ Λυσάνδρου, καὶ
τῶν ὀλίγων τοῖς θρασυτάτοις καὶ φιλονεικοτάτοις
τὰς πόλεις ἐγχειρίζοντος.

XIV. Διατρίψας δὲ περὶ ταῦτα χρόνον οὐ
πολύν, καὶ προπέμψας εἰς Λακεδαίμονα τοὺς
ἀπαγγελοῦντας ὅτι προσπλεῖ μετὰ νεῶν διακοσίων,
συνέμιξε περὶ Ἀττικὴν Ἄγιδι καὶ Παυσανίᾳ τοῖς
βασιλεῦσιν ὡς ταχὺ συναιρήσων τὴν πόλιν. ἐπεὶ
δὲ ἀντεῖχον οἱ Ἀθηναῖοι, λαβὼν τὰς ναῦς πάλιν
εἰς Ἀσίαν διεπέρασε· καὶ τῶν μὲν ἄλλων πόλεων
ὁμαλῶς ἁπασῶν κατέλυε τὰς πολιτείας καὶ καθίστη δεκαδαρχίας, πολλῶν μὲν ἐν ἑκάστῃ σφαττομένων, πολλῶν δὲ φευγόντων, Σαμίους δὲ πάντας
ἐκβαλὼν παρέδωκε τοῖς φυγάσι τὰς πόλεις.
2 Σηστὸν δ' Ἀθηναίων ἐχόντων ἀφελόμενος οὐκ
εἴασεν οἰκεῖν Σηστίους, ἀλλὰ τοῖς γενομένοις ὑπ'
αὐτῷ κυβερνήταις καὶ κελευσταῖς ἔδωκε τὴν
πόλιν καὶ τὴν χώραν νέμεσθαι. πρὸς ὃ καὶ πρῶτον
ἀντέκρουσαν οἱ Λακεδαιμόνιοι καὶ τοὺς Σηστίους
3 αὖθις ἐπὶ τὴν χώραν κατήγαγον. ἀλλ' ἐκεῖνά γε
τοῦ Λυσάνδρου πάντες ἡδέως ἑώρων οἱ Ἕλληνες, 441
Αἰγινήτας τε διὰ πολλοῦ χρόνου τὴν αὐτῶν πόλιν

268

even the comic poet Theopompus was thought absurd in likening the Lacedaemonians to tavernwomen, because they gave the Greeks a very pleasant sip of freedom, and then dashed the wine with vinegar; for from the very first the taste was harsh and bitter, since Lysander not only would not suffer the people to be masters of their affairs, but actually put the cities into the hands of the boldest and most contentious of the oligarchs.

XIV. After he had spent some little time in this business, and had sent messengers to Lacedaemon to report that he was sailing up with two hundred ships, he made a junction in Attica with the forces of Agis and Pausanias, the kings, believing that he would speedily capture the city.[1] But since the Athenians held out against them, he took his ships and crossed again to Asia. Here he suppressed the governments of all the remaining cities in like manner, and set up decadarchies, many citizens being slain in each city, and many banished; he also drove out all the Samians, and handed their cities over to the men whom they had banished.[2] Moreover, when he had taken Sestos out of the hands of the Athenians, he would not permit the Sestians to dwell there, but gave the city and its territory to be divided among men who had been pilots and boatswains under him. And this was the first step of his which was resisted by the Lacedaemonians, who restored the Sestians again to their country. But there were other measures of Lysander upon which all the Greeks looked with pleasure, when, for instance, the Aeginetans, after a long time,[3] re-

---

[1] Cf. Xen. *Hell.* ii. 2, 5-9.
[2] This was after the fall of Athens (Xen. *Hell.* ii. 3, 6 f.).
[3] They had been expelled by the Athenians in 431 B.C.

ἀπολαμβάνοντας καὶ Μηλίους καὶ Σκιωναίους ὑπ᾽
αὐτοῦ συνοικιζομένους, ἐξελαυνομένων Ἀθηναίων
καὶ τὰς πόλεις ἀποδιδόντων.

Ἤδη δὲ καὶ τοὺς ἐν ἄστει κακῶς ἔχειν ὑπὸ
λιμοῦ πυνθανόμενος κατέπλευσεν εἰς τὸν Πειραιᾶ
καὶ παρεστήσατο τὴν πόλιν, ἀναγκασθεῖσαν ἐφ᾽
οἷς ἐκεῖνος ἐκέλευε ποιήσασθαι τὰς διαλύσεις.

4 καίτοι Λακεδαιμονίων ἐστὶν ἀκοῦσαι λεγόντων ὡς
Λύσανδρος μὲν ἔγραψε τοῖς ἐφόροις τάδε· "Ἁλώ-
καντι ταὶ Ἀθᾶναι," Λυσάνδρῳ δ᾽ ἀντέγραψαν
οἱ ἔφοροι· "Ἀρκεῖ τό γε ἑαλώκειν." ἀλλ᾽
εὐπρεπείας χάριν οὗτος ὁ λόγος πέπλασται.
τὸ δ᾽ ἀληθινὸν δόγμα τῶν ἐφόρων οὕτως εἶχε·
"Τάδε τὰ τέλη τῶν Λακεδαιμονίων ἔγνω· καβ-
βαλόντες τὸν Πειραιᾶ καὶ τὰ μακρὰ σκέλη,
καὶ ἐκβάντες ἐκ πασῶν τῶν πόλεων τὰν αὐτῶν
γᾶν ἔχοντες, ταῦτά κα δρῶντες τὰν εἰράναν
ἔχοιτε, αἰ χρήδοιτε, καὶ τοὺς φυγάδας ἀνέντες.
5 περὶ τᾶν ναῶν τῶ πλήθεος, ὁκοῖόν τί κα τηνεὶ
δοκέῃ, ταῦτα ποιέετε." ταύτην δὲ προσεδέξαντο
τὴν σκυτάλην οἱ Ἀθηναῖοι Θηραμένους τοῦ
Ἅγνωνος συμβουλεύσαντος· ὅτε καί φασιν ὑπὸ
τῶν νέων τινὸς δημαγωγῶν Κλεομένους ἐρωτώ-
μενον εἰ τολμᾷ τἀναντία Θεμιστοκλεῖ πράττειν
καὶ λέγειν, παραδιδοὺς τὰ τείχη τοῖς Λακεδαιμονίοις, ἃ Λακεδαιμονίων ἀκόντων ἐκεῖνος ἀν-
6 έστησεν, εἰπεῖν· "Ἀλλ᾽ οὐδέν, ὦ μειράκιον, ὑπε-
ναντίον ἐγὼ πράττω Θεμιστοκλεῖ· τὰ γὰρ αὐτὰ
τείχη κἀκεῖνος ἐπὶ σωτηρίᾳ τῶν πολιτῶν ἀν-

ceived back their own city, and when the Melians[1]
and Scionaeans[2] were restored to their homes by
him, after the Athenians had been driven out and
had delivered back the cities.

And now, when he learned that the people of
Athens were in a wretched plight from famine, he
sailed into the Piraeus, and reduced the city, which
was compelled to make terms on the basis of his
commands. It is true one hears it said by Lacedaemonians that Lysander wrote to the ephors thus:
" Athens is taken "; and that the ephors wrote back
to Lysander: " 'Taken' were enough "; but this
story was invented for its neatness' sake.[3] The actual
decree of the ephors ran thus: " This is what the
Lacedaemonian authorities have decided: tear down
the Piraeus and the long walls; quit all the cities
and keep to your own land; if you do these things,
and restore your exiles, you shall have peace, if you
want it. As regards the number of your ships, whatsoever shall be decided there, this do."[4] This edict
was accepted by the Athenians, on the advice of
Theramenes the son of Hagnon, who, they say, being
asked at this time by Cleomenes, one of the young
orators, if he dared to act and speak the contrary to
Themistocles, by surrendering those walls to the
Lacedaemonians which that statesman had erected
in defiance of the Lacedaemonians, replied: " But
I am doing nothing, young man, that is contrary to
Themistocles; for the same walls which he erected

---

[1] The island and city of Melos were captured and depopulated by the Athenians in the winter of 416–415 B.C.

[2] The city of Scionè, on the Chalcidic peninsula, was
captured and depopulated by the Athenians in 421 B.C.

[3] To illustrate the Spartan passion for brevity of speech.

[4] Cf. Xen. *Hell.* ii. 2, 20.

ἔστησε καὶ ἡμεῖς ἐπὶ σωτηρίᾳ καταβαλοῦμεν.
εἰ δὲ τὰ τείχη τὰς πόλεις εὐδαίμονας ἐποίει,
πασῶν ἔδει πράττειν κάκιστα τὴν Σπάρτην
ἀτείχιστον οὖσαν."

XV. Ὁ δ᾽ οὖν Λύσανδρος, ὡς παρέλαβε τάς
τε ναῦς ἁπάσας πλὴν δώδεκα καὶ τὰ τείχη τῶν
Ἀθηναίων, ἕκτῃ ἐπὶ δεκάτῃ Μουνυχιῶνος μηνός,
ἐν ᾗ καὶ τὴν ἐν Σαλαμῖνι ναυμαχίαν ἐνίκων τὸν
βάρβαρον, ἐβούλευσεν εὐθὺς καὶ τὴν πολιτείαν
2 μεταστῆσαι. δυσπειθῶς δὲ καὶ τραχέως φερόν-
των, ἀποστείλας πρὸς τὸν δῆμον ἔφη τὴν πόλιν
εἰληφέναι παρασπονδοῦσαν· ἑστάναι γὰρ τὰ
τείχη τῶν ἡμερῶν ἐν αἷς ἔδει καθῃρῆσθαι παρῳ-
χημένων. ἑτέραν οὖν ἐξ ἀρχῆς προθήσειν γνώμην περὶ αὐτῶν ὡς τὰς ὁμολογίας λελυκότων.
ἔνιοι δὲ καὶ προτεθῆναί φασιν ὡς ἀληθῶς ὑπὲρ
ἀνδραποδισμοῦ γνώμην ἐν τοῖς συμμάχοις, ὅτε
καὶ τὸν Θηβαῖον Ἐρίανθον εἰσηγήσασθαι τὸ
μὲν ἄστυ κατασκάψαι, τὴν δὲ χώραν ἀνεῖναι
3 μηλόβοτον. εἶτα μέντοι συνουσίας γενομένης
τῶν ἡγεμόνων παρὰ πότον, καί[1] τινος Φωκέως
ᾄσαντος ἐκ τῆς Εὐριπίδου Ἠλέκτρας τὴν πάροδον
ἧς ἡ ἀρχή

Ἀγαμέμνονος ὦ κόρα,
    ἤλυθον, Ἠλέκτρα, ποτὶ σὰν ἀγρότειραν αὐλάν,

πάντας ἐπικλασθῆναι, καὶ φανῆναι σχέτλιον
ἔργον τὴν οὕτως εὐκλεᾶ καὶ τοιούτους ἄνδρας
φέρουσαν ἀνελεῖν καὶ διεργάσασθαι πόλιν.
4   Ὁ δ᾽ οὖν Λύσανδρος ἐνδόντων τῶν Ἀθηναίων

---

[1] παρὰ πότον καί Bekker follows Coraës in transposing to
καὶ παρὰ πότον.

for the safety of the citizens, we shall tear down for their safety. And if walls made cities prosperous, then Sparta must be in the worst plight of all, since she has none."

XV. Lysander, accordingly, when he had taken possession of all the ships of the Athenians except twelve, and of their walls, on the sixteenth day of the month Munychion, the same on which they conquered the Barbarian in the sea-fight at Salamis, took measures at once to change their form of government. And when the Athenians opposed him bitterly in this, he sent word to the people that he had caught the city violating the terms of its surrender; for its walls were still standing, although the days were past within which they should have been pulled down; he should therefore present their case anew for the decision of the authorities, since they had broken their agreements. And some say that in very truth a proposition to sell the Athenians into slavery was actually made in the assembly of the allies, and that at this time Erianthus the Theban also made a motion that the city be razed to the ground, and the country about it left for sheep to graze. Afterwards, however, when the leaders were gathered at a banquet, and a certain Phocian sang the first chorus in the "Electra" of Euripides,[1] which begins with

"O thou daughter of Agamemnon,
    I am come, Electra, to thy rustic court,"

all were moved to compassion, and felt it to be a cruel deed to abolish and destroy a city which was so famous, and produced such poets.

So then, after the Athenians had yielded in all

----

[1] Verses 167 f. (Kirchhoff).

πρὸς ἅπαντα, πολλὰς μὲν ἐξ ἄστεος μεταπεμψά-
μενος αὐλητρίδας, πάσας δὲ τὰς ἐν τῷ στρατοπέδῳ συναγαγών, τὰ τείχη κατέσκαπτε καὶ τὰς
τριήρεις κατέφλεγε πρὸς τὸν αὐλόν, ἐστεφανω-
μένων καὶ παιζόντων ἅμα τῶν συμμάχων, ὡς
ἐκείνην τὴν ἡμέραν ἄρχουσαν τῆς ἐλευθερίας.
5 εὐθὺς δὲ καὶ τὰ περὶ τὴν πολιτείαν ἐκίνησε,
τριάκοντα μὲν ἐν ἄστει, δέκα δὲ ἐν Πειραιεῖ
καταστήσας ἄρχοντας, ἐμβαλὼν δὲ φρουρὰν εἰς
τὴν ἀκρόπολιν, καὶ Καλλίβιον ἁρμοστήν, ἄνδρα
Σπαρτιάτην, ἐπιστήσας. ἐπεὶ δὲ οὗτος Αὐτόλυκον τὸν ἀθλητήν, ἐφ' ᾧ τὸ συμπόσιον ὁ Ξενοφῶν πεποίηκε, τὴν βακτηρίαν διαράμενος παίσειν
ἔμελλεν, ὁ δὲ τῶν σκελῶν συναράμενος ἀνέτρεψεν
αὐτόν, οὐ συνηγανάκτησεν ὁ Λύσανδρος, ἀλλὰ
καὶ συνεπετίμησε,[1] φήσας αὐτὸν οὐκ ἐπίστασθαι   442
ἐλευθέρων ἄρχειν. ἀλλὰ τὸν μὲν Αὐτόλυκον
οἱ τριάκοντα τῷ Καλλιβίῳ χαριζόμενοι μικρὸν
ὕστερον ἀνεῖλον.

XVI. Ὁ δὲ Λύσανδρος ἀπὸ τούτων γενόμενος,
αὐτὸς μὲν ἐπὶ Θρᾴκης ἐξέπλευσε, τῶν δὲ χρημάτων τὰ περιόντα καὶ ὅσας δωρεὰς αὐτός ἢ
στεφάνους ἐδέξατο, πολλῶν, ὡς εἰκός, διδόντων
ἀνδρὶ δυνατωτάτῳ καὶ τρόπον τινὰ κυρίῳ τῆς
Ἑλλάδος, ἀπέστειλεν εἰς Λακεδαίμονα διὰ Γυλίππου τοῦ στρατηγήσαντος περὶ Σικελίαν. ὁ
δέ, ὡς λέγεται, τὰς ῥαφὰς τῶν ἀγγείων κάτωθεν

---

[1] συνεπετίμησε Bekker adopts Reiske's correction to ἐπετί-
μησε.

---

[1] Cf. Xen. *Hell.* ii. 2, 23.
[2] The scene of the "Symposium" is laid at the house of

points, Lysander sent for many flute-girls from the
city, and assembled all those who were already
in the camp, and then tore down the walls, and
burned up the triremes, to the sound of the flute,
while the allies crowned themselves with garlands
and made merry together, counting that day as the
beginning of their freedom.[1] Then, without delay,
he also made changes in the form of government,
establishing thirty rulers in the city and ten in
Piraeus. Further, he put a garrison into the acropolis, and made Callibius, a Spartan, its harmost.
He it was who once lifted his staff to smite Autolycus, the athlete, whom Xenophon makes the chief
character in his "Symposium";[2] and when Autolycus seized him by the legs and threw him down,
Lysander did not side with Callibius in his vexation,
but actually joined in censuring him, saying that he
did not understand how to govern freemen. But
the Thirty, to gratify Callibius, soon afterwards put
Autolycus to death.

XVI. Lysander, after settling these matters, sailed
for Thrace himself, but what remained of the public
moneys, together with all the gifts and crowns which
he had himself received, — many people, as was
natural, offering presents to a man who had the
greatest power, and who was, in a manner, master
of Hellas,—he sent off to Lacedaemon by Gylippus,
who had held command in Sicily.[3] But Gylippus,
as it is said, ripped open the sacks at the bottom,

Callias, to which Autolycus and his father have been invited,
together with Socrates and some of his friends.
[3] As Spartan general sent out to aid the Syracusans, he
had turned the success of the besieging Athenians into
disaster. See the *Nicias*, chapters xviii. ff.

ἀναλύσας καὶ ἀφελὼν συχνὸν ἀργύριον ἐξ ἑκάστου πάλιν συνέρραψεν, ἀγνοήσας ὅτι γραμ-
ματίδιον ἐνῆν ἑκάστῳ τὸν ἀριθμὸν σημαῖνον.
2 ἐλθὼν δὲ εἰς Σπάρτην ἃ μὲν ὑφῄρητο κατέκρυψεν
ὑπὸ τὸν κέραμον τῆς οἰκίας, τὰ δὲ ἀγγεῖα παρέδωκε τοῖς ἐφόροις καὶ τὰς σφραγῖδας ἐπέδειξεν.
ἐπεὶ δὲ ἀνοιξάντων καὶ ἀριθμούντων διεφώνει
πρὸς τὰ γράμματα τὸ πλῆθος τοῦ ἀργυρίου
καὶ παρεῖχε τοῖς ἐφόροις ἀπορίαν τὸ πρᾶγμα,
φράζει θεράπων τοῦ Γυλίππου πρὸς αὐτοὺς αἰνι-
ξάμενος ὑπὸ τῷ κεραμικῷ κοιτάζεσθαι πολλὰς
γλαῦκας. ἦν γάρ, ὡς ἔοικε, τὸ χάραγμα τοῦ
πλείστου τότε νομίσματος διὰ τοὺς Ἀθηναίους
γλαῦκες.

XVII. Ὁ μὲν οὖν Γύλιππος αἰσχρὸν οὕτω
καὶ ἀγεννὲς ἔργον ἐπὶ λαμπροῖς τοῖς ἔμπροσθεν
καὶ μεγάλοις ἐργασάμενος μετέστησεν ἑαυτὸν
ἐκ Λακεδαίμονος. οἱ δὲ φρονιμώτατοι τῶν Σπαρτιατῶν οὐχ ἥκιστα καὶ διὰ τοῦτο τὴν τοῦ νομίσματος ἰσχὺν φοβηθέντες, ὡς οὐχὶ τῶν τυχόντων
ἁπτομένην πολιτῶν, τόν τε Λύσανδρον ἐλοιδόρουν
καὶ διεμαρτύραντο τοῖς ἐφόροις ἀποδιοπομπεῖ-
σθαι πᾶν τὸ ἀργύριον καὶ τὸ χρυσίον ὥσπερ
κῆρας ἐπαγωγίμους. οἱ δὲ προὔθεσαν γνώμην.
2 καὶ Θεόπομπος μέν φησι Σκιραφίδαν, Ἔφορος
δὲ Φλογίδαν εἶναι τὸν ἀποφηνάμενον ὡς οὐ
χρὴ προσδέχεσθαι νόμισμα χρυσοῦν καὶ ἀργυροῦν εἰς τὴν πόλιν, ἀλλὰ χρῆσθαι τῷ πατρίῳ.
τοῦτο δὲ ἦν σιδηροῦν, πρῶτον μὲν ὄξει κατα-
βαπτόμενον ἐκ πυρός, ὅπως μὴ καταχαλκεύοιτο,
ἀλλὰ διὰ τὴν βαφὴν ἄστομον καὶ ἀδρανὲς γίνοιτο,
ἔπειτα βαρύσταθμον καὶ δυσπαρακόμιστον καὶ

276

and after taking a large amount of silver from each, sewed them up again, not knowing that there was a writing in each indicating the sum it held. And when he came to Sparta, he hid what he had stolen under the tiles of his house, but delivered the sacks to the ephors, and showed the seals upon them. When, however, the ephors opened the sacks and counted the money, its amount did not agree with the written lists, and the thing perplexed them, until a servant of Gylippus made the truth known to them by his riddle of many owls sleeping under the tiling. For most of the coinage of the time, as it seems, bore the effigy of an owl, owing to the supremacy of Athens.

XVII. Gylippus, then, after adding a deed so disgraceful and ignoble as this to his previous great and brilliant achievements, removed himself from Lacedaemon. And the wisest of the Spartans, being led by this instance in particular to fear the power of money, which they said was corrupting influential as well as ordinary citizens, reproached Lysander, and fervently besought the ephors to purify the city of all the silver and the gold, as imported curses. The ephors deliberated on the matter. And it was Sciraphidas, according to Theopompus, or Phlogidas, according to Ephorus, who declared that they ought not to receive gold and silver coinage into the city, but to use that of the country. Now this was of iron, and was dipped in vinegar as soon as it came from the fire, that it might not be worked over, but be made brittle and intractable by the dipping.[1] Besides, it was very heavy and troublesome

---

[1] Cf. *Lycurgus*, ix. 2.

ἀπὸ πολλοῦ τινος πλήθους καὶ ὄγκου μικράν
3 τινα ἀξίαν δυνάμενον. κινδυνεύει δὲ καὶ τὸ
πάμπαν ἀρχαῖον οὕτως ἔχειν, ὀβελίσκοις χρωμένων νομίσμασι[1] σιδηροῖς, ἐνίων δὲ χαλκοῖς· ἀφ'
ὧν παραμένει πλῆθος ἔτι καὶ νῦν τῶν κερμάτων
ὀβολοὺς καλεῖσθαι, δραχμὴν δὲ τοὺς ἓξ ὀβολούς·
τοσούτων γὰρ ἡ χεὶρ περιεδράττετο.

4 Τῶν δὲ Λυσάνδρου φίλων ὑπεναντιουμένων
καὶ σπουδασάντων ἐν τῇ πόλει καταμεῖναι τὰ
χρήματα, δημοσίᾳ μὲν ἔδοξεν εἰσάγεσθαι νόμισμα
τοιοῦτον, ἂν δέ τις ἁλῷ κεκτημένος ἰδίᾳ, ζημίαν
ὥρισαν θάνατον, ὥσπερ τοῦ Λυκούργου τὸ
νόμισμα φοβηθέντος, οὐ τὴν ἐπὶ τῷ νομίσματι
φιλαργυρίαν, ἣν οὐκ ἀφῄρει τὸ μὴ κεκτῆσθαι
τὸν ἰδιώτην, ὡς τὸ κεκτῆσθαι τὴν πόλιν εἰσεποιεῖτο,[2] τῆς χρείας ἀξίαν προσλαμβανούσης καὶ
5 ζῆλον. οὐ γὰρ ἦν δημοσίᾳ τιμώμενον ὁρῶντας
ἰδίᾳ καταφρονεῖν ὡς ἀχρήστου, καὶ πρὸς τὰ
οἰκεῖα νομίζειν ἑκάστῳ μηδενὸς ἄξιον πρᾶγμα τὸ
κοινῇ οὕτως εὐδοκιμοῦν καὶ ἀγαπώμενον, ἀλλὰ
καὶ πολλῷ τάχιον ἀπὸ τῶν κοινῶν ἐπιτηδευμάτων
ἐπιρρέουσιν οἱ ἐθισμοὶ τοῖς ἰδιωτικοῖς βίοις ἢ τὰ
καθ' ἕκαστον ὀλισθήματα καὶ πάθη τὰς πόλεις
6 ἀναπίμπλησι πραγμάτων πονηρῶν. τῷ γὰρ ὅλῳ
συνδιαστρέφεσθαι τὰ μέρη μᾶλλον, ὅταν ἐνδῷ
πρὸς τὸ χεῖρον, εἰκός, αἱ δὲ ἀπὸ μέρους εἰς ὅλον
ἁμαρτίαι πολλὰς ἐνστάσεις καὶ βοηθείας ἀπὸ
τῶν ὑγιαινόντων ἔχουσιν. οἱ δὲ ταῖς μὲν οἰκίαις
τῶν πολιτῶν, ὅπως οὐ πάρεισιν εἰς αὐτὰς νόμισ- 443
μα, τὸν φόβον ἐπέστησαν φύλακα καὶ τὸν νόμον,

---

[1] νομίσμασι Bekker corrects to νομίσματι.
[2] εἰσεποιεῖτο Bekker adopts Coraës' correction to εἰσεποίει.

to carry, and a great quantity and weight of it had but little value. Probably, too, all the ancient money was of this sort, some peoples using iron spits for coins, and some bronze; whence it comes that even to this day many small pieces of money retain the name of "oboli," or *spits*, and six "oboli" make a "drachma," or *handful*, since that was as many as the hand could grasp.

But since Lysander's friends opposed this measure, and insisted that the money remain in the city, it was resolved that money of this sort could be introduced for public use, but that if any private person should be found in possession of it, he should be punished with death; just as though Lycurgus had feared the coin, and not the covetousness which the coin produced. And this vice was not removed by allowing no private person to possess money, so much as it was encouraged by allowing the city to possess money, its use thereby acquiring dignity and honour. Surely it was not possible for those who saw money publicly honoured, to despise it privately as of no service; or to consider as worthless for the individual's private use that which was publicly held in such repute and esteem. Moreover, it takes far less time for public practices to affect the customs of private life, than it does for individual lapses and failings to corrupt entire cities. For it is natural that the parts should rather be perverted along with the whole, when that deteriorates; but the diseases which flow from a part into the whole find many correctives and aids in the parts which remain sound. And so these magistrates merely set the fear of the law to guard the houses of the citizens, that money might have no entrance there, but did not keep their

αὐτὰς δὲ τὰς ψυχὰς ἀνεκπλήκτους καὶ ἀπαθεῖς
πρὸς ἀργύριον οὐ διετήρησαν, ἐμβαλόντες εἰς
ζῆλον ὡς σεμνοῦ δή τινος καὶ μεγάλου τοῦ πλου-
τεῖν ἅπαντας. περὶ μὲν οὖν τούτων καὶ δι᾽ ἑτέρας
που γραφῆς ἡψάμεθα Λακεδαιμονίων.

XVIII. Ὁ δὲ Λύσανδρος ἔστησεν ἀπὸ τῶν
λαφύρων ἐν Δελφοῖς αὑτοῦ χαλκῆν εἰκόνα καὶ
τῶν ναυάρχων ἑκάστου καὶ χρυσοῦς ἀστέρας
τῶν Διοσκούρων, οἳ πρὸ τῶν Λευκτρικῶν ἠφανί-
σθησαν. ἐν δὲ τῷ Βρασίδου καὶ Ἀκανθίων
θησαυρῷ τριήρης ἔκειτο διὰ χρυσοῦ πεποιημένη
καὶ ἐλέφαντος δυεῖν πηχῶν, ἣν Κῦρος αὐτῷ νικη-
2 τήριον ἔπεμψεν. Ἀναξανδρίδης δὲ ὁ Δελφὸς
ἱστορεῖ καὶ παρακαταθήκην ἐνταῦθα Λυσάνδρου
κεῖσθαι τάλαντον ἀργυρίου καὶ μνᾶς πεντήκοντα
δύο καὶ πρὸς τούτοις ἕνδεκα στατῆρας, οὐχ ὁμο-
λογούμενα γράφων τοῖς περὶ τῆς πενίας τοῦ
ἀνδρὸς ὁμολογουμένοις. τότε δ᾽ οὖν ὁ Λύσανδρος
ὅσον οὐδεὶς τῶν πρόσθεν Ἑλλήνων δυνηθεὶς
ἐδόκει φρονήματι καὶ ὄγκῳ μείζονι κεχρῆσθαι τῆς
3 δυνάμεως. πρώτῳ μὲν γάρ, ὡς ἱστορεῖ Δοῦρις,
Ἑλλήνων ἐκείνῳ βωμοὺς αἱ πόλεις ἀνέστησαν ὡς
θεῷ καὶ θυσίας ἔθυσαν, εἰς πρῶτον δὲ παιᾶνες
ᾔσθησαν, ὧν ἑνὸς ἀρχὴν ἀπομνημονεύουσι
τοιάνδε·

> Τὸν Ἑλλάδος ἀγαθέας
> στραταγὸν ἀπ᾽ εὐρυχόρου
> Σπάρτας ὑμνήσομεν, ὦ,
> ἰὴ Παιάν.

4 Σάμιοι δὲ τὰ παρ᾽ αὑτοῖς Ἡραῖα Λυσάνδρεια
καλεῖν ἐψηφίσαντο. τῶν δὲ ποιητῶν Χοιρίλον

spirits undaunted by the power of money and in
sensible to it; they rather inspired them all with an
emulous desire for wealth as a great and noble object
of pursuit. On this point, however, we have censured
the Lacedaemonians in another treatise.[1]

XVIII. Out of the spoils, Lysander set up at
Delphi bronze statues of himself and each of his
admirals, as well as golden stars of the Dioscuri,
which disappeared before the battle of Leuctra.[2]
And in the treasury of Brasidas and the Acanthians[3]
there was stored a trireme two cubits long, made of
gold and ivory, which Cyrus sent Lysander as a prize
for his victory. Moreover, Anaxandrides the Delphian
writes that a deposit of Lysander's was also stored
there, consisting of a talent of silver, and fifty-two
minas, and eleven staters besides; a statement that
is inconsistent with the generally accepted accounts
of his poverty. At any rate, Lysander was at this
time more powerful than any Greek before him had
been, and was thought to cherish a pretentious pride
that was greater even than his power. For he was
the first Greek, as Duris writes, to whom the cities
erected altars and made sacrifices as to a god, the
first also to whom songs of triumph were sung. One
of these is handed down, and begins as follows :—

> "The general of sacred Hellas
>   who came from wide-spaced Sparta
> will we sing, O! io! Paean."

The Samians, too, voted that their festival of Hera
should be called Lysandreia. And the poet Choe-

---

[1] *Inst. Lacon.* 42 (*Morals*, p. 239 f.).
[2] An omen of the defeat of the Spartans in that battle
(371 B.C.).   [3] Cf. chapter i. 1.

μὲν ἀεὶ περὶ αὐτὸν εἶχεν ὡς κοσμήσοντα τὰς
πράξεις διὰ ποιητικῆς, Ἀντιλόχῳ δὲ ποιήσαντι
μετρίους τινὰς εἰς αὐτὸν στίχους ἡσθεὶς ἔδωκε
πλήσας ἀργυρίου τὸν πῖλον. Ἀντιμάχου δὲ τοῦ
Κολοφωνίου καὶ Νικηράτου τινὸς Ἡρακλεώτου
ποιήμασι Λυσάνδρεια διαγωνισαμένων ἐπ' αὐτοῦ
τὸν Νικήρατον ἐστεφάνωσεν, ὁ δὲ Ἀντίμαχος
5 ἀχθεσθεὶς ἠφάνισε τὸ ποίημα. Πλάτων δὲ νέος
ὢν τότε, καὶ θαυμάζων τὸν Ἀντίμαχον ἐπὶ τῇ
ποιητικῇ, βαρέως φέροντα τὴν ἧτταν ἀνελάμβανε
καὶ παρεμυθεῖτο, τοῖς ἀγνοοῦσι κακὸν εἶναι φάμενος τὴν ἄγνοιαν, ὥσπερ τὴν τυφλότητα τοῖς μὴ
βλέπουσιν. ἐπεὶ μέντοι ὁ κιθαρῳδὸς Ἀριστόνους
ἑξάκις Πύθια νενικηκὼς ἐπηγγέλλετο τῷ Λυσάνδρῳ φιλοφρονούμενος, ἂν νικήσῃ πάλιν,
Λυσάνδρου κηρύξειν ἑαυτόν, "Ἦ δοῦλον;" εἶπεν.

XIX. Ἀλλ' ἡ μὲν φιλοτιμία τοῦ Λυσάνδρου
τοῖς πρώτοις καὶ ἰσοτίμοις ἦν ἐπαχθὴς μόνον.
ὑπεροψίας δὲ πολλῆς ἅμα τῇ φιλοτιμίᾳ διὰ τοὺς
θεραπεύοντας ἐγγενομένης τῷ ἤθει καὶ βαρύτητος,
οὔτε τιμῆς οὔτε τιμωρίας μέτρον ἦν παρ' αὐτῷ
δημοτικόν, ἀλλὰ φιλίας μὲν ἆθλα καὶ ξενίας
ἀνυπεύθυνοι δυναστεῖαι πόλεων καὶ τυραννίδες
ἀνεξέταστοι, θυμοῦ δὲ μία πλήρωσις ἀπολέσθαι
2 τὸν ἀπεχθόμενον· οὐδὲ γὰρ φυγεῖν ἐξῆν. ἀλλὰ
καὶ Μιλησίων ὕστερον τοὺς τοῦ δήμου προΐστα-
μένους δεδιὼς μὴ φύγωσι, καὶ προαγαγεῖν τοὺς
κεκρυμμένους βουλόμενος, ὤμοσε μὴ ἀδικήσειν·

rilus was always kept in his retinue, to adorn his
achievements with verse; while with Antilochus,
who composed some verses in his honour, he was so
pleased that he filled his cap with silver and gave it
to him. And when Antimachus of Colophon and a
certain Niceratus of Heracleia competed with one
another at the Lysandreia in poems celebrating his
achievements, he awarded the crown to Niceratus,
and Antimachus, in vexation, suppressed his poem.
But Plato, who was then a young man, and admired
Antimachus for his poetry, tried to cheer and console
him in his chagrin at this defeat, telling him that it
is the ignorant who suffer from their ignorance, just
as the blind do from their blindness. However, when
Aristonoüs the harper, who had been six times victor
at the Pythian games, told Lysander in a patronizing
way that if he should be victorious again, he would
have himself proclaimed under Lysander's name,
"That is," Lysander replied, "as my slave?"

XIX. Now to the leading men, and to his equals,
the ambition of Lysander was annoying merely. But
since, owing to the court that was paid to him, great
haughtiness and severity crept into his character
along with his ambition, there was no such moderation as would become a popular leader either in his
rewards or punishments, but the prizes he awarded
to his friends and allies were irresponsible lordships
over cities, and absolute sovereignties, while the sole
punishment that could satisfy his wrath was the
death of his enemy; not even exile was allowed.
Nay, at a later time, fearing lest the active popular
leaders of Miletus should go into exile, and desiring
to bring from their retreats those also who were in
hiding, he made oath that he would do them no

πιστεύσαντας δὲ καὶ προελθόντας ἀποσφάξαι
τοῖς ὀλιγαρχικοῖς παρέδωκεν, οὐκ ἐλάττονας
3 ὀκτακοσίων συναμφοτέρους ὄντας. ἦν δὲ καὶ
τῶν ἄλλων ἐν ταῖς πόλεσι δημοτικῶν φόνος οὐκ
ἀριθμητός, ἅτε δὴ μὴ κατ᾽ ἰδίας μόνον αἰτίας
αὐτοῦ κτείνοντος, ἀλλὰ πολλαῖς μὲν ἔχθραις,
πολλαῖς δὲ πλεονεξίαις τῶν ἑκασταχόθι φίλων
χαριζομένου τὰ τοιαῦτα καὶ συνεργοῦντος. ὅθεν
εὐδοκίμησεν Ἐτεοκλῆς ὁ Λακεδαιμόνιος εἰπὼν ὡς
οὐκ ἂν ἡ Ἑλλὰς δύο Λυσάνδρους ἤνεγκε. τὸ δὲ
αὐτὸ τοῦτο καὶ περὶ Ἀλκιβιάδου φησὶ Θεό- 444
4 φραστος εἰπεῖν Ἀρχέστρατον. ἀλλ᾽ ἐκεῖ μὲν
ὕβρις ἦν καὶ τρυφὴ σὺν αὐθαδείᾳ τὸ μάλιστα
δυσχεραινόμενον· τὴν δὲ Λυσάνδρου δύναμιν ἡ
τοῦ τρόπου χαλεπότης φοβερὰν ἐποίει καὶ
βαρεῖαν.

Οἱ δὲ Λακεδαιμόνιοι τοῖς μὲν ἄλλοις οὐ πάνυ
προσεῖχον ἐγκαλοῦσιν· ἐπεὶ δὲ Φαρνάβαζος ἀδικούμενος ὑπ᾽ αὐτοῦ τὴν χώραν ἄγοντος καὶ
φέροντος ἀπέστειλεν εἰς τὴν Σπάρτην κατηγόρους,
ἀγανακτήσαντες οἱ ἔφοροι τῶν μὲν φίλων αὐτοῦ
καὶ συστρατήγων ἕνα Θώρακα λαβόντες ἀργύριον
ἰδίᾳ κεκτημένον ἀπέκτειναν, ἐκείνῳ δὲ σκυτάλην
ἔπεμψαν ἥκειν κελεύοντες.

5 Ἔστι δὲ ἡ σκυτάλη τοιοῦτον. ἐπὰν ἐκπέμ-
πωσι ναύαρχον ἢ στρατηγὸν οἱ ἔφοροι, ξύλα δύο
στρογγύλα μῆκος καὶ πάχος ἀκριβῶς ἀπισώ-
σαντες, ὥστε ταῖς τομαῖς ἐφαρμόζειν πρὸς ἄλληλα,
τὸ μὲν αὐτοὶ φυλάττουσι, θάτερον δὲ τῷ πεμπο-
μένῳ διδόασι. ταῦτα δὲ τὰ ξύλα σκυτάλας
6 καλοῦσιν. ὅταν οὖν ἀπόρρητόν τι καὶ μέγα

harm; but when the first put faith in him and the
second came forth, he delivered them all over to the
oligarchs for slaughter, being no less than eight
hundred of both classes. In the other cities also
untold numbers of the popular party were slain,
since he killed not only for his own private reasons,
but also gratified by his murders the hatred and
cupidity of his many friends everywhere, and shared
the bloody work with them. Wherefore Eteocles the
Lacedaemonian won great approval when he said
that Hellas could not have borne two Lysanders.
Now this same utterance was made by Archestratus
concerning Alcibiades also,[1] as Theophrastus tells us.
But in his case it was insolence, and wanton self-will,
that gave most offence; whereas Lysander's power
was made dreadful and oppressive by the cruelty
of his disposition.

The Lacedaemonians paid little heed to the rest of
his accusers, but when Pharnabazus, who was outraged by Lysander's pillaging and wasting his territory, sent men to Sparta to denounce him, the ephors
were incensed, and when they found Thorax, one of
Lysander's friends and fellow-generals, with money
in his private possession, they put him to death, and
sent a dispatch-scroll to Lysander, ordering him
home.

The dispatch-scroll is of the following character.
When the ephors send out an admiral or a general,
they make two round pieces of wood exactly alike
in length and thickness, so that each corresponds to
the other in its dimensions, and keep one themselves,
while they give the other to their envoy. These pieces
of wood they call "scytalae." Whenever, then, they

---

[1] Cf. *Alcibiades*, xvi. 5.

φράσαι βουληθῶσι, βιβλίον ὥσπερ ἱμάντα
μακρὸν καὶ στενὸν ποιοῦντες περιελίττουσι τὴν
παρ' αὑτοῖς σκυτάλην, οὐδὲν διάλειμμα ποιοῦντες,
ἀλλὰ πανταχόθεν κύκλῳ τὴν ἐπιφάνειαν αὐτῆς
τῷ βιβλίῳ καταλαμβάνοντες. τοῦτο δὲ ποιήσαντες ἃ βούλονται καταγράφουσιν εἰς τὸ
βιβλίον, ὥσπερ ἐστὶ τῇ σκυτάλῃ περικείμενον·
ὅταν δὲ γράψωσιν, ἀφελόντες τὸ βιβλίον ἄνευ
τοῦ ξύλου πρὸς τὸν στρατηγὸν ἀποστέλλουσι.
7 δεξάμενος δὲ ἐκεῖνος ἄλλως μὲν οὐδὲν ἀναλέξα-
σθαι δύναται τῶν γραμμάτων συναφὴν οὐκ ἐχόντων, ἀλλὰ διεσπασμένων, τὴν δὲ παρ' αὑτῷ
σκυτάλην λαβὼν τὸ τμῆμα τοῦ βιβλίου περὶ
αὐτὴν περιέτεινεν, ὥστε, τῆς ἕλικος εἰς τάξιν
ὁμοίως ἀποκαθισταμένης, ἐπιβάλλοντα τοῖς πρώτοις τὰ δεύτερα, κύκλῳ τὴν ὄψιν ἐπάγειν τὸ
συνεχὲς ἀνευρίσκουσαν. καλεῖται δὲ ὁμωνύμως
τῷ ξύλῳ σκυτάλη τὸ βιβλίον, ὡς τῷ μετροῦντι
τὸ μετρούμενον.

XX. Ὁ δὲ Λύσανδρος, ἐλθούσης τῆς σκυτάλης
πρὸς αὐτὸν εἰς τὸν Ἑλλήσποντον, διεταράχθη,
καὶ μάλιστα τὰς τοῦ Φαρναβάζου δεδιὼς κατηγορίας, ἐσπούδασεν εἰς λόγους αὐτῷ συνελθεῖν,
ὡς λύσων τὴν διαφοράν. καὶ συνελθὼν ἐδεῖτο
γράψαι περὶ αὐτοῦ πρὸς τοὺς ἄρχοντας ἑτέραν
ἐπιστολὴν ὡς οὐδὲν ἠδικημένον οὐδ' ἐγκαλοῦντα.
2 πρὸς Κρῆτα δὲ ἄρα, τὸ τοῦ λόγου, κρητίζων
ἠγνόει τὸν Φαρνάβαζον. ὑποσχόμενος γὰρ
ἅπαντα ποιήσειν, φανερῶς μὲν ἔγραψεν οἵαν ὁ
Λύσανδρος ἠξίωσεν ἐπιστολήν, κρύφα δὲ εἶχεν
ἑτέραν αὐτόθι γεγραμμένην. ἐν δὲ τῷ τὰς σφρα-

wish to send some secret and important message, they make a scroll of parchment long and narrow, like a leathern strap, and wind it round their "scytale," leaving no vacant space thereon, but covering its surface all round with the parchment. After doing this, they write what they wish on the parchment, just as it lies wrapped about the "scytale"; and when they have written their message, they take the parchment off, and send it, without the piece of wood, to the commander. He, when he has received it, cannot otherwise get any meaning out of it,—since the letters have no connection, but are disarranged,—unless he takes his own "scytale" and winds the strip of parchment about it, so that, when its spiral course is restored perfectly, and that which follows is joined to that which precedes, he reads around the staff, and so discovers the continuity of the message. And the parchment, like the staff, is called "scytale," as the thing measured bears the name of the measure.

XX. But Lysander, when the dispatch-scroll reached him at the Hellespont, was much disturbed, and since he feared the denunciations of Pharnabazus above all others, he hastened to hold a conference with him, hoping to compose their quarrel. At this conference he begged Pharnabazus to write another letter about him to the magistrates, stating that he had not been wronged at all, and had no complaints to make. But in thus " playing the Cretan against a Cretan," as the saying is, he misjudged his opponent. For Pharnabazus, after promising to do all that he desired, openly wrote such a letter as Lysander demanded, but secretly kept another by him ready written. And when it came to putting on the seals,

γῖδας ἐπιβάλλειν ἐναλλάξας τὰ βιβλία μηδὲν
διαφέροντα τῇ ὄψει, δίδωσιν ἐκείνην αὐτῷ τὴν
3 κρύφα γεγραμμένην. ἀφικόμενος οὖν ὁ Λύσανδρος
εἰς Λακεδαίμονα καὶ πορευθείς, ὥσπερ ἔθος ἐστίν,
εἰς τὸ ἀρχεῖον, ἀπέδωκε τοῖς ἐφόροις τὰ γράμματα
τοῦ Φαρναβάζου, πεπεισμένος ἀνῃρῆσθαι τὸ
μέγιστον αὐτοῦ τῶν ἐγκλημάτων· ἠγαπᾶτο γὰρ ὁ
Φαρνάβαζος ὑπὸ τῶν Λακεδαιμονίων, προθυμό-
τατος ἐν τῷ πολέμῳ τῶν βασιλέως στρατηγῶν
4 γεγενημένος. ἐπεὶ δὲ ἀναγνόντες οἱ ἔφοροι τὴν
ἐπιστολὴν ἔδειξαν αὐτῷ, καὶ συνῆκεν ὡς

Οὐκ ἄρ' Ὀδυσσεύς ἐστιν αἰμύλος μόνος,

τότε μὲν ἰσχυρῶς τεθορυβημένος ἀπῆλθεν· ἡμέραις
δὲ ὀλίγαις ὕστερον ἐντυχὼν τοῖς ἄρχουσιν ἔφη
δεῖν αὐτὸν εἰς Ἄμμωνος ἀναβῆναι καὶ τῷ θεῷ
5 θῦσαι θυσίας ἃς εὔξατο πρὸ τῶν ἀγώνων. ἔνιοι
μὲν οὖν ἀληθῶς φασιν αὐτῷ πολιορκοῦντι τὴν τῶν
Ἀφυταίων πόλιν ἐν Θρᾴκῃ κατὰ τοὺς ὕπνους
παραστῆναι τὸν Ἄμμωνα· διὸ καὶ τὴν πολιορκίαν ἀφείς, ὡς τοῦ θεοῦ προστάξαντος, ἐκέλευσε
τοὺς Ἀφυταίους Ἄμμωνι θύειν καὶ τὸν θεὸν
ἐσπούδασεν εἰς τὴν Λιβύην πορευθεὶς ἐξιλάσα-
6 σθαι. τοῖς δὲ πλείστοις ἐδόκει πρόσχημα ποιεῖσθαι τὸν θεόν, ἄλλως δὲ τοὺς ἐφόρους δεδοικὼς 445
καὶ τὸν οἴκοι ζυγὸν οὐ φέρων οὐδ' ὑπομένων ἄρ-
χεσθαι πλάνης ὀρέγεσθαι καὶ περιφοιτήσεως
τινός, ὥσπερ ἵππος ἐκ νομῆς ἀφέτου καὶ λειμῶνος
αὖθις ἥκων ἐπὶ φάτνην καὶ πρὸς τὸ σύνηθες ἔργον

he exchanged the documents, which looked exactly alike, and gave him the letter which had been secretly written. Accordingly, when Lysander arrived at Sparta and went, as the custom is, into the senate-house, he gave the ephors the letter of Pharnabazus, convinced that the greatest of the complaints against him was thus removed; for Pharnabazus was in high favour with the Lacedaemonians, because he had been, of all the King's generals, most ready to help them in the war. But when the ephors, after reading the letter, showed it to him, and he understood that

"Odysseus, then, is not the only man of guile," [1]

for the time being he was mightily confounded and went away. But a few days afterwards, on meeting the magistrates, he said that he was obliged to go up to the temple of Ammon [2] and sacrifice to the god the sacrifices which he had vowed before his battles. Now some say that when he was besieging the city of Aphytae in Thrace, Ammon really stood by him in his sleep; wherefore he raised the siege, declaring that the god had commanded it, and ordered the Aphytaeans to sacrifice to Ammon, and was eager to make a journey into Libya and propitiate the god. But the majority believed that he made the god a pretext, and really feared the ephors, and was impatient of the yoke at home, and unable to endure being under authority, and therefore longed to wander and travel about somewhat, like a horse which comes back from unrestricted pasturage in the meadows to his stall, and is put once more to his accustomed work.

[1] An iambic trimeter of some unknown poet.
[2] In an oasis of the great desert of Libya. Cf. *Cimon*, xviii. 6 f.

αὖθις ἀγόμενος. ἦν μὲν γὰρ Ἔφορος τῆς ἀποδη-
μίας ταύτης αἰτίαν ἀναγράφει, μετὰ μικρὸν
ἀφηγήσομαι.

XXI. Μόλις δὲ καὶ χαλεπῶς ἀφεθῆναι διαπραξάμενος ὑπὸ τῶν ἐφόρων ἐξέπλευσεν. οἱ δὲ
βασιλεῖς ἀποδημήσαντος αὐτοῦ συμφρονήσαντες
ὅτι ταῖς ἑταιρείαις τὰς πόλεις κατέχων διὰ παντὸς
ἄρχει καὶ κύριός ἐστι τῆς Ἑλλάδος, ἔπρασσον
ὅπως ἀποδώσουσι τοῖς δημόταις τὰ πράγματα
2 τοὺς ἐκείνου φίλους ἐκβαλόντες. οὐ μὴν ἀλλὰ
πάλιν πρὸς ταῦτα κινήματος γενομένου, καὶ πρώτων τῶν ἀπὸ Φυλῆς Ἀθηναίων ἐπιθεμένων τοῖς
τριάκοντα καὶ κρατούντων, ἐπανελθὼν διὰ ταχέων
ὁ Λύσανδρος ἔπεισε τοὺς Λακεδαιμονίους ταῖς
ὀλιγαρχίαις βοηθεῖν καὶ τοὺς δήμους κολάζειν.
καὶ πρώτοις τοῖς τριάκοντα πέμπουσιν ἑκατὸν
τάλαντα πρὸς τὸν πόλεμον καὶ στρατηγὸν αὐτὸν
3 Λύσανδρον. οἱ δὲ βασιλεῖς φθονοῦντες καὶ δεδιό-
τες μὴ πάλιν ἕλῃ τὰς Ἀθήνας, ἔγνωσαν ἐξιέναι
τὸν ἕτερον αὐτῶν. ἐξῆλθε δὲ ὁ Παυσανίας, λόγῳ
μὲν ὑπὲρ τῶν τυράννων ἐπὶ τὸν δῆμον, ἔργῳ δὲ
καταλύσων τὸν πόλεμον, ὡς μὴ πάλιν ὁ Λύσανδρος διὰ τῶν φίλων κύριος γένοιτο τῶν Ἀθηνῶν. τοῦτο μὲν οὖν διεπράξατο ῥᾳδίως· καὶ τοὺς
Ἀθηναίους διαλλάξας καὶ καταπαύσας τὴν στάσιν
4 ἀφείλετο τοῦ Λυσάνδρου τὴν φιλοτιμίαν. ὀλίγῳ
δὲ ὕστερον ἀποστάντων πάλιν τῶν Ἀθηναίων
αὐτὸς μὲν αἰτίαν ἔλαβεν, ὡς ἐγκεχαλινωμένον τῇ
ὀλιγαρχίᾳ τὸν δῆμον ἀνεὶς αὖθις ἐξυβρίσαι καὶ

Ephorus, it is true, assigns another reason for this absence abroad, which I shall mention by and by.[1]

XXI. After he had with great difficulty procured his release by the ephors, he set sail. But the kings, when he had gone abroad, became aware that by means of the societies which he had formed, he had the cities entirely in his power and was master of Hellas; they therefore took measures for deposing his friends everywhere and restoring the management of affairs to the people. However, fresh disturbances broke out in connection with these changes, and first of all the Athenians from Phyle attacked the Thirty and overpowered them. Lysander therefore came home in haste, and persuaded the Lacedaemonians to aid the oligarchies and chastise the democracies. Accordingly, they sent to the Thirty, first of all, a hundred talents for the war, and Lysander himself as general. But the kings were jealous of him, and feared to let him capture Athens a second time; they therefore determined that one of them should go out with the army. And Pausanias did go out, ostensibly in behalf of the tyrants[2] against the people, but really to put a stop to the war, in order that Lysander might not again become master of Athens through the efforts of his friends. This object, then, he easily accomplished, and by reconciling the Athenians and putting a stop to their discord, he robbed Lysander of his ambitious hopes. A short time afterwards, however, when the Athenians revolted again, he himself was censured for taking the curb of the oligarchy out of the mouth of the people, and letting them grow bold and insolent again; while

[1] Chapter xxv. 3.　　　[2] That is, the Thirty in Athens.

θρασύνασθαι, τῷ δὲ Λυσάνδρῳ προσεθήκατο δόξαν ἀνδρὸς οὐ πρὸς ἑτέρων χάριν οὐδὲ θεατρικῶς, ἀλλὰ πρὸς τὸ τῇ Σπάρτῃ συμφέρον αὐθεκάστως στρατηγοῦντος.

XXII. Ἦν δὲ καὶ τῷ λόγῳ θρασὺς καὶ καταπληκτικὸς πρὸς τοὺς ἀντιτείνοντας. Ἀργείοις μὲν γὰρ ἀμφιλογουμένοις περὶ γῆς ὅρων καὶ δικαιότερα τῶν Λακεδαιμονίων οἰομένοις λέγειν δείξας τὴν μάχαιραν, "Ὁ ταύτης," ἔφη, "κρατῶν βέλτιστα περὶ γῆς ὅρων διαλέγεται." Μεγαρέως δὲ ἀνδρὸς ἔν τινι συλλόγῳ παρρησίᾳ χρησαμένου πρὸς αὐτόν, "Οἱ λόγοι σου," εἶπεν, "ὦ ξένε, 2 πόλεως δέονται." τοὺς δὲ Βοιωτοὺς ἐπαμφοτερίζοντας ἠρώτα πότερον ὀρθοῖς τοῖς δόρασιν ἢ κεκλιμένοις διαπορεύηται τὴν χώραν αὐτῶν. ἐπεὶ δὲ τῶν Κορινθίων ἀφεστώτων παρερχόμενος πρὸς τὰ τείχη τοὺς Λακεδαιμονίους ἑώρα προσβάλλειν ὀκνοῦντας, καὶ λαγώς τις ὤφθη διαπηδῶν τὴν τάφρον, "Οὐκ αἰσχύνεσθε," ἔφη, "τοιούτους φοβούμενοι πολεμίους, ὧν οἱ λαγωὶ δι' ἀργίαν τοῖς τείχεσιν ἐγκαθεύδουσιν;"

3 Ἐπεὶ δὲ Ἆγις ὁ βασιλεὺς ἐτελεύτησεν ἀδελφὸν μὲν Ἀγησίλαον καταλιπών, υἱὸν δὲ νομιζόμενον Λεωτυχίδαν, ἐραστὴς τοῦ Ἀγησιλάου γεγονὼς ὁ Λύσανδρος ἔπεισεν αὐτὸν ἀντιλαμβάνεσθαι τῆς βασιλείας ὡς Ἡρακλείδην ὄντα γνήσιον. ὁ γὰρ Λεωτυχίδας διαβολὴν εἶχεν ἐξ Ἀλκιβιάδου γεγονέναι, συνόντος κρύφα τῇ Ἄγιδος γυναικὶ Τιμαίᾳ καθ' ὃν χρόνον φεύγων ἐν Σπάρτῃ διέ4 τριβεν. ὁ δὲ Ἆγις, ὥς φασι, χρόνου λογισμῷ τὸ πρᾶγμα συνελών, ὡς οὐ κυήσειεν ἐξ αὐτοῦ, παρη-

Lysander won fresh repute as a man who exercised his command in downright fashion, not for the gratification of others, nor yet to win applause, but for the good of Sparta.

XXII. He was harsh of speech also, and terrifying to his opponents. For instance, when the Argives were disputing about boundaries, and thought they made a juster plea than the Lacedaemonians, he pointed to his sword, and said to them: "He who is master of this discourses best about boundaries." And when a Megarian, in some conference with him, grew bold in speech, he said: "Thy words, Stranger, lack a city." And when the Boeotians tried to play a double game with him, he asked them whether he should march through their territory with spears upright, or levelled. And once when the Corinthians had revolted, and, on coming to their walls, he saw that the Lacedaemonians hesitated to make an assault, a hare was seen leaping across the moat; whereupon he said: "Are ye not ashamed to fear enemies who are so lazy that hares sleep on their walls?"

When Agis the king died,[1] leaving a brother, Agesilaüs, and a reputed son, Leotychides, Lysander, who had been a lover of Agesilaüs, persuaded him to lay claim to the kingdom, on the ground that he was a genuine descendant of Heracles. For Leotychides was accused of being a son of Alcibiades, who had secret commerce with Timaea, the wife of Agis, while he was living in exile at Sparta. Now Agis, as they tell us, being convinced by a computation of time that his wife had not conceived by him, ignored

[1] In 398 B.C., after returning home from a victorious campaign (Xen. *Hell.* iii. 3, 1).

μέλει τοῦ Λεωτυχίδου καὶ φανερὸς ἦν ἀναινόμενος
αὐτὸν παρά γε τὸν λοιπὸν χρόνον. ἐπεὶ δὲ νοσῶν
εἰς Ἡραίαν ἐκομίσθη καὶ τελευτᾶν ἔμελλε, τὰ
μὲν ὑπ' αὐτοῦ τοῦ νεανίσκου, τὰ δὲ ὑπὸ τῶν
φίλων ἐκλιπαρηθεὶς ἐναντίον πολλῶν ἀπέφηνεν
υἱὸν αὑτοῦ τὸν Λεωτυχίδαν, καὶ δεηθεὶς τῶν
παρόντων ἐπιμαρτυρῆσαι ταῦτα πρὸς τοὺς Λα-
5 κεδαιμονίους ἀπέθανεν. οὗτοι μὲν οὖν ἐμαρ-   44
τύρουν ταῦτα τῷ Λεωτυχίδᾳ· τὸν δ' Ἀγησίλαον
λαμπρὸν ὄντα τἆλλα καὶ συναγωνιστῇ τῷ Λυσάνδρῳ χρώμενον ἔβλαπτε Διοπείθης, ἀνὴρ εὐδό-
κιμος ἐπὶ χρησμολογίᾳ, τοιόνδε μάντευμα προφέ-
ρων εἰς τὴν χωλότητα τοῦ Ἀγησιλάου·

Φράζεο δή, Σπάρτη, καίπερ μεγάλαυχος ἐοῦσα,
μὴ σέθεν ἀρτίποδος βλάστῃ χωλὴ βασιλεία.
δηρὸν γὰρ μόχθοι σε κατασχήσουσιν ἄελπτοι
φθισιβρότου τ' ἐπὶ κῦμα κυλινδόμενον πολέ-
μοιο.

6 πολλῶν οὖν ὑποκατακλινομένων πρὸς τὸ λόγιον
καὶ τρεπομένων πρὸς τὸν Λεωτυχίδαν, ὁ Λύσανδρος οὐκ ὀρθῶς ἔφη τὸν Διοπείθη τὴν μαντείαν
ὑπολαμβάνειν· οὐ γὰρ ἂν προσπταίσας τις ἄρχῃ
Λακεδαιμονίων, δυσχεραίνειν τὸν θεόν, ἀλλὰ
χωλὴν εἶναι τὴν βασιλείαν εἰ νόθοι καὶ κακῶς
γεγονότες βασιλεύσουσι σὺν[1] Ἡρακλείδαις. τοιαῦτα λέγων καὶ δυνάμενος πλεῖστον ἔπεισε, καὶ
γίνεται βασιλεὺς Ἀγησίλαος.

---

[1] σὺν supplied by Sintenis alone.

Leotychides, and manifestly repudiated him up to the last. But when he was carried sick to Heraea and was about to die, he yielded to the entreaties of the young man himself and of his friends, and declared in the hearing of many that Leotychides was his own son, and after begging those who were present to bear witness of this to the Lacedaemonians, died. Accordingly, they did so bear witness in favour of Leotychides. Moreover, Agesilaüs, who was otherwise illustrious, and had Lysander as a champion, was injured in his claim by Diopeithes, a man in high repute for his interpretation of oracles, who published the following prophecy with reference to the lameness of Agesilaüs [1] :—

'Bethink thee now, O Sparta, although thou art
    very proud,
Lest from thee, sound of foot, there spring a maimed
    royalty;
For long will unexpected toils oppress thee,
And onward rolling billows of man-destroying
    war."

Many, therefore, out of deference to the oracle, inclined to Leotychides, but Lysander declared that Diopeithes did not interpret the prophecy correctly; for it did not mean that the god would be displeased if one who was lame should rule the Lacedaemonians, but the kingdom would be maimed if bastards and ill-born men should be kings in a line with the posterity of Heracles. By such arguments, and because he had very great influence, he prevailed, and Agesilaüs became king.[2]

[1] Cf. Plutarch's *Agesilaüs*, ii. 2.
[2] Cf. Plutarch's *Agesilaüs*, iii. 3–5 ; Xen. *Hell*. iii. 3, 2 f.

XXIII. Εὐθὺς οὖν αὐτὸν ἐξώρμα καὶ πρού-
τρεπεν ὁ Λύσανδρος εἰς τὴν Ἀσίαν στρατεύειν,
ὑποτιθεὶς ἐλπίδας ὡς καταλύσοντι Πέρσας καὶ
μεγίστῳ γενησομένῳ, πρός τε τοὺς ἐν Ἀσίᾳ
φίλους ἔγραψεν αἰτεῖσθαι κελεύων παρὰ Λακεδαιμονίων στρατηγὸν Ἀγησίλαον ἐπὶ τὸν πρὸς
2 τοὺς βαρβάρους πόλεμον. οἱ δὲ ἐπείθοντο καὶ
πρέσβεις ἔπεμπον εἰς Λακεδαίμονα δεομένους· ὃ
δοκεῖ τῆς βασιλείας οὐκ ἔλαττον Ἀγησιλάῳ καλὸν
ὑπάρξαι διὰ Λύσανδρον. ἀλλ᾽ αἱ φιλότιμοι
φύσεις ἄλλως μὲν οὐ κακαὶ πρὸς τὰς ἡγεμονίας
εἰσί, τὸ δὲ φθονεῖν τοῖς ὁμοίοις διὰ δόξαν οὐ
μικρὸν ἐμπόδιον τῶν καλῶν πράξεων ἔχουσι·
ποιοῦνται γὰρ ἀνταγωνιστὰς τῆς ἀρετῆς οἷς πάρ-
3 εστι χρῆσθαι συνεργοῖς. Ἀγησίλαος μὲν οὖν
ἐπηγάγετο Λύσανδρον ἐν τοῖς τριάκοντα συμ-
βούλοις ὡς μάλιστα καὶ πρώτῳ τῶν φίλων
χρησόμενος· ἐπεὶ δὲ εἰς τὴν Ἀσίαν παραγενομένων πρὸς ἐκεῖνον μὲν οὐκ ἔχοντες οἱ ἄνθρωποι
συνήθως βραχέα καὶ σπανίως διελέγοντο, τὸν δὲ
Λύσανδρον ἐκ πολλῆς τῆς πρόσθεν ὁμιλίας οἵ τε
φίλοι θεραπεύοντες οἵ τε ὕποπτοι δεδοικότες
4 ἐφοίτων ἐπὶ θύρας καὶ παρηκολούθουν, οἷον ἐν
τραγῳδίαις ἐπιεικῶς συμβαίνει περὶ τοὺς ὑπο-
κριτάς, τὸν μὲν ἀγγέλου τινὸς ἢ θεράποντος
ἐπικείμενον[1] πρόσωπον εὐδοκιμεῖν καὶ πρωταγων-
ιστεῖν, τὸν δὲ διάδημα καὶ σκῆπτρον φοροῦντα
μηδὲ ἀκούεσθαι φθεγγόμενον, οὕτω περὶ τὸν
σύμβουλον ἦν τὸ πᾶν ἀξίωμα τῆς ἀρχῆς, τῷ δὲ
βασιλεῖ τοὔνομα τῆς δυνάμεως ἔρημον ἀπελείπετο.

---

[1] ἐπικείμενον Bekker adopts Coraës' correction to περικεί-
μενον.

XXIII. At once, then, Lysander tried to rouse
and incite him to make an expedition into Asia,
suggesting hopes that he would put down the
Persians and become a very great man. He also
wrote letters to his friends in Asia, bidding them
ask Agesilaüs of the Lacedaemonians as general for
their war against the Barbarians.[1] They obeyed,
and sent ambassadors to Lacedaemon with the
request, and thus an honour not inferior to that of
being made king was obtained for Agesilaüs through
the efforts of Lysander. But with ambitious natures,
which are otherwise not ill qualified for command,
jealousy of their equals in reputation is no slight
obstacle to the performance of noble deeds; for they
make those their rivals in the path of virtue, whom
they might have as helpers. Agesilaüs did indeed
take Lysander with him among his thirty counsellors,
intending to treat him with special favour as his
chief friend; but when they were come into Asia,
the people there, who were not acquainted with him,
conferred with him but rarely and briefly, whereas
Lysander, in consequence of their large intercourse
with him in former times, had them always at his
door and in his train, those who were his friends
coming out of deference, and those whom he
suspected, out of fear. And just as in tragedies it
naturally happens that an actor who takes the part
of some messenger or servant is in high repute and
plays leading rôles, while the one who bears the
crown and sceptre is not even listened to when he
speaks, so in this case the whole honour of the government was associated with the counsellor, and there
was left for the king only the empty name of power.

---

[1] Cf. Plutarch's *Agesilaüs*, vi. 1 f.

5 γενέσθαι μὲν οὖν ἴσως ἔδει τινὰ τῆς ἐκμελοῦς
ταύτης φιλοτιμίας ἐπαφὴν καὶ συσταλῆναι τὸν
Λύσανδρον ἄχρι τῶν δευτερείων· τὸ δὲ παντελῶς
ἀπορρῖψαι καὶ προπηλακίσαι διὰ δόξαν εὐεργέτην
ἄνδρα καὶ φίλον οὐκ ἦν ἄξιον Ἀγησιλάῳ προσ-
εῖναι.

Πρῶτον μὲν οὖν οὐ παρεῖχεν αὐτῷ πράξεων
ἀφορμάς, οὐδὲ ἔταττεν ἐφ᾽ ἡγεμονίας· ἔπειτα
ὑπὲρ ὧν αἴσθοιτό τι πράττοντα καὶ σπουδάζοντα
τὸν Λύσανδρον, ἀεὶ τούτους πάντων ἀπράκτους
καὶ τῶν ἐπιτυχόντων ἔλαττον ἔχοντας ἀπέπεμπε,
παραλύων ἡσυχῇ καὶ διαψύχων τὴν ἐκείνου
6 δύναμιν. ἐπεὶ δὲ τῶν πάντων διαμαρτάνων ὁ
Λύσανδρος ἔγνω τοῖς φίλοις τὴν παρ᾽ αὐτοῦ
σπουδὴν ἐναντίωμα γινομένην, αὐτός τε τὸ βοηθεῖν
ἐξέλιπε κἀκείνων ἐδεῖτο μὴ προσιέναι μηδὲ θεραπεύειν αὐτόν, ἀλλὰ τῷ βασιλεῖ διαλέγεσθαι καὶ
τοῖς δυναμένοις ὠφελεῖν τοὺς τιμῶντας αὐτοὺς
7 μᾶλλον ἐν τῷ παρόντι. ταῦτα ἀκούοντες οἱ
πολλοὶ τοῦ μὲν ἐνοχλεῖν αὐτὸν περὶ πραγμάτων
ἀπείχοντο, τὰς δὲ θεραπείας οὐ κατέλιπον, ἀλλὰ
προσφοιτῶντες ἐν τοῖς περιπάτοις καὶ γυμνασίοις   447
ἔτι μᾶλλον ἢ πρότερον ἠνίων τὸν Ἀγησίλαον ὑπὸ
φθόνου τῆς τιμῆς, ὥστε τοῖς πολλοῖς Σπαρτιάταις[1]
ἡγεμονίας πραγμάτων καὶ διοικήσεις πόλεων ἀπο-
διδοὺς τὸν Λύσανδρον ἀπέδειξε κρεοδαίτην. εἶτα
οἷον ἐφυβρίζων πρὸς τοὺς Ἴωνας, "Ἀπιόντες,"
ἔφη, "νῦν τὸν ἐμὸν κρεοδαίτην θεραπευέτωσαν."
8 ἔδοξεν οὖν τῷ Λυσάνδρῳ διὰ λόγων πρὸς αὐτὸν

---

[1] Σπαρτιάταις the correction of Emperius : στρατιώταις
(soldiers).

It is true, perhaps, that there should have been some gentle handling of this excessive ambition, and that Lysander should have been reduced to the second place; but entirely to cast off and insult, for fame's sake, a benefactor and a friend, was not worthy of the character of Agesilaüs.

In the first place, then, he did not give him opportunities for achievement, nor even assign him to a command; and secondly, those in whose behalf he perceived that Lysander was earnestly exerting himself, these he always sent away with less reward than an ordinary suitor, or wholly unsuccessful, thus quietly undoing and chilling his influence. So when Lysander missed all his aims, and saw that his interested efforts for his friends were an obstacle to their success, he not only ceased to give them his own aid, but begged them not to wait upon him nor pay him their court, but to confer with the king, and with such as had more power to benefit those who showed them honour than was his at present. Most of those who heard this refrained from troubling him about their affairs, but did not cease paying him their court, nay rather, by waiting upon him in the public walks and places of exercise, they gave Agesilaüs even more annoyance than before, because he envied him the honour. Therefore, though he offered most of the Spartans [1] commands in the field and governments of cities, he appointed Lysander his carver of meats. And presently, as if by way of insult to the Ionians, he said: "Let them be off, and pay their court now to my carver of meats." Accordingly, Lysander determined to have a con-

[1] Agis took thirty Spartans with him as counsellors and captains (Plutarch's *Agesilaüs*, vi. 3; Xenophon's *Agesilaüs*, i. 7).

ἐλθεῖν· καὶ γίνεται βραχὺς καὶ Λακωνικὸς αὐτῶν
διάλογος. "Ἦ καλῶς ᾔδεις, ὦ Ἀγησίλαε, φίλους
ἐλαττοῦν." καὶ ὅς· "Ἄν γε ἐμοῦ βούλωνται
μείζονες εἶναι· τοὺς δὲ αὔξοντας τὴν ἐμὴν δύναμιν
9 καὶ μετέχειν αὐτῆς δίκαιον." "Ἀλλ' ἴσως μέν,
ὦ Ἀγησίλαε, σοὶ λέλεκται κάλλιον ἢ ἐμοὶ πέ-
πρακται· δέομαι δέ σου καὶ διὰ τοὺς ἐκτὸς
ἀνθρώπους, οἳ πρὸς ἡμᾶς ἀποβλέπουσιν, ἐνταῦθά
με τῆς σεαυτοῦ στρατηγίας τάξον, ὅπου τεταγμένον ἥκιστα μὲν ἐπαχθῆ, μᾶλλον δὲ χρήσιμον
ἔσεσθαι σεαυτῷ νομίζεις."

XXIV. Ἐκ τούτου πρεσβευτὴς εἰς Ἑλλήσποντον ἐπέμπετο· καὶ τὸν μὲν Ἀγησίλαον δι' ὀργῆς
εἶχεν, οὐκ ἠμέλει δὲ τοῦ τὰ δέοντα πράττειν,
Σπιθριδάτην δὲ τὸν Πέρσην προσκεκρουκότα
Φαρναβάζῳ, γενναῖον ἄνδρα καὶ στρατιὰν ἔχοντα
περὶ αὑτόν, ἀποστήσας ἤγαγε πρὸς τὸν Ἀγη-
2 σίλαον. ἄλλο δὲ οὐδὲν ἐχρήσατο αὐτῷ πρὸς τὸν
πόλεμον, ἀλλὰ τοῦ χρόνου διελθόντος ἀπέπλευσεν
εἰς τὴν Σπάρτην ἀτίμως, ὀργιζόμενος μὲν τῷ
Ἀγησιλάῳ, μισῶν δὲ καὶ τὴν ὅλην πολιτείαν ἔτι
μᾶλλον ἢ πρότερον, καὶ τὰ πάλαι δοκοῦντα
συγκεῖσθαι καὶ μεμηχανῆσθαι πρὸς μεταβολὴν
καὶ νεωτερισμὸν ἐγνωκὼς ἐγχειρεῖν τότε καὶ μὴ
διαμέλλειν.

3 Ἦν δὲ τοιάδε. τῶν ἀναμιχθέντων Δωριεῦσιν
Ἡρακλειδῶν καὶ κατελθόντων εἰς Πελοπόννησον
πολὺ μὲν ἐν Σπάρτῃ καὶ λαμπρὸν ἤνθησε γένος,
οὐ παντὶ δὲ αὐτῶν τῆς βασιλικῆς μετῆν διαδοχῆς,

ference with him, at which a brief and laconic
dialogue passed between them. "Verily, thou
knowest well, Agesilaüs, how to abase friends." To
which Agesilaüs: "Yes, if they would be greater
than I; but those who increase my power should
also share in it." "Well, perhaps thy words,
Agesilaüs, are fairer than my deeds; but I beg thee,
even because of the strangers who have their eyes
upon us, to give me a post under thy command
where thou believest that I shall be least annoying
to thyself, and more serviceable than now." [1]

XXIV. Upon this, he was sent as ambassador to
the Hellespont; and though he was angry with
Agesilaüs, he did not neglect to do his duty, but
induced Spithridates the Persian, a high-minded
man with forces at his command, to revolt from
Pharnabazus, with whom he was at odds, and
brought him to Agesilaüs.[2] The king made no
further use of Lysander, however, in the war, and
when his time had expired, he sailed back to Sparta
without honour, not only enraged at Agesilaüs, but
hating the whole form of government more than ever,
and resolved to put into execution at once, and
without delay, the plans for a revolutionary change
which he is thought to have devised and concocted
some time before.

They were as follows. Of the Heracleidae who
united with the Dorians and came down into Peloponnesus, there was a numerous and glorious stock
flourishing in Sparta; however, not every family
belonging to it participated in the royal succession,

---

[1] Cf. Plutarch's *Agesilaüs*, vii.–viii. 1–2; Xen. *Hell.* iii. 4,
7–9.
[2] Cf. Plutarch's *Agesilaüs*, viii. 3; Xen. *Hell.* iii. 4, 10.

ἀλλ' ἐβασίλευον ἐκ δυεῖν οἴκων μόνον Εὐρυπων-
τίδαι καὶ Ἀγιάδαι προσαγορευόμενοι, τοῖς δὲ
ἄλλοις οὐδὲν ἑτέρου πλέον ἔχειν ἐν τῇ πολιτείᾳ
διὰ τὴν εὐγένειαν ὑπῆρχεν, αἱ δὲ ἀπ' ἀρετῆς
4 τιμαὶ πᾶσι προύκειντο τοῖς δυναμένοις. τούτων
οὖν γεγονὼς ὁ Λύσανδρος, ὡς εἰς δόξαν τῶν πράξεων ἤρθη μεγάλην καὶ φίλους ἐκέκτητο πολλοὺς
καὶ δύναμιν, ἤχθετο τὴν πόλιν ὁρῶν ὑπ' αὐτοῦ
μὲν αὐξανομένην, ὑφ' ἑτέρων δὲ βασιλευομένην
οὐδὲν βέλτιον αὐτοῦ γεγονότων, καὶ διενοεῖτο τὴν
ἀρχὴν ἐκ τῶν δυεῖν οἴκων μεταστήσας εἰς κοινὸν
5 ἀποδοῦναι πᾶσιν Ἡρακλείδαις, ὡς δὲ ἔνιοί φασιν,
οὐχ Ἡρακλείδαις, ἀλλὰ Σπαρτιάταις, ἵνα μὴ ᾖ
τῶν ἀφ' Ἡρακλέους, ἀλλὰ τῶν οἷος Ἡρακλῆς τὸ
γέρας, ἀρετῇ κρινομένων, ἣ κἀκεῖνον εἰς θεῶν
τιμὰς ἀνήγαγεν. ἤλπιζε δὲ τῆς βασιλείας οὕτω
δικαζομένης οὐδένα πρὸ αὐτοῦ Σπαρτιάτην ἂν
αἱρεθήσεσθαι.

XXV. Πρῶτον μὲν οὖν ἐπεχείρησε καὶ παρε-
σκευάσατο πείθειν δι' ἑαυτοῦ τοὺς πολίτας, καὶ
λόγον ἐξεμελέτα πρὸς τὴν ὑπόθεσιν γεγραμμένον
ὑπὸ Κλέωνος τοῦ Ἁλικαρνασσέως. ἔπειτα τὴν
ἀτοπίαν καὶ τὸ μέγεθος τοῦ καινοτομουμένου
πράγματος ὁρῶν ἰταμωτέρας δεόμενον βοηθείας,
ὥσπερ ἐν τραγῳδίᾳ μηχανὴν αἴρων ἐπὶ τοὺς
2 πολίτας, λόγια πυθόχρηστα καὶ χρησμοὺς συν-
ετίθει καὶ κατεσκεύαζεν, ὡς οὐδὲν ὠφελησό-

---

[1] Cf. Plutarch's *Agesilaüs*, viii. 3.

but the kings were chosen from two houses only, and were called Eurypontidae and Agiadae. The rest had no special privileges in the government because of their high birth, but the honours which result from superior excellence lay open to all who had power and ability. Now Lysander belonged to one of these families, and when he had risen to great fame for his deeds, and had acquired many friends and great power, he was vexed to see the city increased in power by his efforts, but ruled by others who were of no better birth than himself. He therefore planned to take the government away from the two houses, and restore it to all the Heracleidae in common, or, as some say, not to the Heracleidae, but to the Spartans in general,[1] in order that its high prerogatives might not belong to those only who were descended from Heracles, but to those who, like Heracles, were selected for superior excellence, since it was this which raised him to divine honours. And he hoped that when the kingdom was awarded on this principle, no Spartan would be chosen before himself.

XXV. In the first place, then, he undertook and made preparations to persuade the citizens by his own efforts, and committed to memory a speech written by Cleon, the Halicarnassian, for the purpose. In the second place, seeing that the novelty and magnitude of his innovation demanded a more audacious support, he brought stage machinery to bear upon the citizens,[2] as it were, by collecting and arranging responses and oracles of Apollo ; convinced

---

[2] In the Greek theatre, gods were swung into view, above the plane of the action, by means of a huge crane. Cf. *Themistocles*, x. 1.

μενος ὑπὸ τῆς Κλέωνος δεινότητος, εἰ μὴ φόβῳ
θεοῦ τινι καὶ δεισιδαιμονίᾳ προεκπλήξας καὶ
χειρωσάμενος ὑπαγάγοι πρὸς τὸν λόγον τοὺς πολί-
3 τας. Ἔφορος μὲν οὖν φησιν αὐτόν, ὡς τήν τε
Πυθίαν ἐπιχειρήσας διαφθεῖραι καὶ τὰς Δωδω-
νίδας αὖθις ἀναπείθων διὰ Φερεκλέους ἀπέ-
τυχεν, εἰς Ἄμμωνος ἀναβῆναι καὶ διαλέγεσθαι
τοῖς προφήταις πολὺ χρυσίον διδόντα, τοὺς δὲ
δυσχεραίνοντας εἰς Σπάρτην τινὰς ἀποστεῖλαι
τοῦ Λυσάνδρου κατηγορήσοντας, ἐπεὶ δὲ ἀπε-
λύθη, τοὺς Λίβυας ἀπιόντας εἰπεῖν· "Ἀλλ'
ἡμεῖς γε βέλτιον, ὦ Σπαρτιᾶται, κρινοῦμεν, ὅταν   448
ἥκητε πρὸς ἡμᾶς εἰς Λιβύην οἰκήσοντες," ὡς
δὴ χρησμοῦ τινος ὄντος παλαιοῦ Λακεδαιμονίους
4 ἐν Λιβύῃ κατοικῆσαι. τὴν δὲ ὅλην ἐπιβουλὴν
καὶ σκευωρίαν τοῦ πλάσματος οὐ φαύλην οὖσαν
οὐδὲ ἀφ' ὧν ἔτυχεν ἀρξαμένην, ἀλλὰ πολλὰς
καὶ μεγάλας ὑποθέσεις, ὥσπερ ἐν διαγράμματι
μαθηματικῷ, προσλαβοῦσαν καὶ διὰ λημμάτων
χαλεπῶν καὶ δυσπορίστων ἐπὶ τὸ συμπέρασμα
προϊοῦσαν, ἡμεῖς ἀναγράψομεν ἀνδρὸς ἱστορικοῦ
καὶ φιλοσόφου λόγῳ κατακολουθήσαντες.

XXVI. Ἦν γύναιον ἐν Πόντῳ κύειν ἐξ Ἀπόλλωνος φάμενον, ᾧ πολλοὶ μέν, ὡς εἰκὸς ἦν,
ἠπίστουν, πολλοὶ δὲ καὶ προσεῖχον, ὥστε καὶ
τεκούσης παιδάριον ἄρρεν ὑπὸ πολλῶν καὶ γνωρίμων σπουδάζεσθαι τὴν ἐκτροφὴν αὐτοῦ καὶ
τὴν ἐπιμέλειαν. ὄνομα δὲ τῷ παιδὶ Σειληνὸς
ἐκ δή τινος αἰτίας ἐτέθη. ταύτην λαβὼν ὁ

that Cleon's clever rhetoric would not help him at all unless he should first terrify and subdue his countrymen by vague religious fear and superstitious terror, and then bring them under the influence of his argument. Well, then, Ephorus tells us that after an attempt to corrupt the Pythian priestess, and after a second failure to persuade the priestesses of Dodona by means of Pherecles, he went up to the temple of Ammon and had a conference with that god's interpreters there, at which he offered them much money, but that they took this ill, and sent certain messengers to Sparta to denounce him; and further, that when Lysander was acquitted of their charges, the Libyans said, as they went away, "But we will pass better judgments than yours, O Spartans, when ye come to dwell with us in Libya"; for they knew that there was a certain ancient oracle bidding the Lacedaemonians to settle in Libya. But since the whole plot and concoction was no insignificant one, nor yet carelessly undertaken, but made many important assumptions, like a mathematical demonstration, and proceeded to its conclusion through premises which were difficult and hard to obtain, we shall follow, in our description of it, the account of one who was both a historian and a philosopher.[1]

XXVI. There was a woman in Pontus who declared that she was with child by Apollo. Many disbelieved her, as was natural, but many also lent an ear to her, so that when she gave birth to a male child, many notable persons took an interest in its care and rearing. For some reason or other, the name given to the boy was Silenus. Lysander

----

[1] Probably Ephorus.

Λύσανδρος ἀρχήν, τὰ λοιπὰ παρ' ἑαυτοῦ προσε-
τεκταίνετο καὶ συνύφαινεν, οὐκ ὀλίγοις χρώμενος οὐδὲ φαύλοις τοῦ μύθου συναγωνισταῖς,
2 οἳ τήν τε φήμην τῆς γενέσεως τοῦ παιδὸς εἰς
πίστιν ἀνυπόπτως προῆγον, ἄλλον τε λόγον ἐκ
Δελφῶν ἀντικομίσαντες εἰς τὴν Σπάρτην κατέβαλον καὶ διέσπειραν, ὡς ἐν γράμμασιν ἀπορ-
ρήτοις ὑπὸ τῶν ἱερέων φυλάττοιντο παμπάλαιοι
δή τινες χρησμοί, καὶ λαβεῖν οὐκ ἔξεστι τούτους
οὐδ' ἐντυχεῖν θεμιτόν, εἰ μή τις ἄρα γεγονὼς
ἐξ Ἀπόλλωνος ἀφίκοιτο τῷ πολλῷ χρόνῳ καὶ
σύνθημα τοῖς φυλάττουσι τῆς γενέσεως γνώρι-
μον παρασχὼν κομίσαιτο τὰς δέλτους ἐν αἷς ἦσαν
3 οἱ χρησμοί. τούτων δὲ προκατεσκευασμένων ἔδει
τὸν Σειληνὸν ἐλθόντα τοὺς χρησμοὺς ἀπαιτεῖν
ὡς Ἀπόλλωνος παῖδα, τοὺς δὲ συμπράττοντας
τῶν ἱερέων ἐξακριβοῦν ἕκαστα καὶ διαπυνθάνεσθαι περὶ τῆς γενέσεως, τέλος δὲ πεπεισμένους
δῆθεν ὡς Ἀπόλλωνος υἱῷ δεῖξαι τὰ γράμματα,
τὸν δὲ ἀναγνῶναι πολλῶν παρόντων ἄλλας τε
μαντείας καὶ ἧς ἕνεκα τἄλλα πέπλασται [1] τὴν
περὶ τῆς βασιλείας, ὡς ἄμεινον εἴη καὶ λῷον
Σπαρτιάταις ἐκ τῶν ἀρίστων πολιτῶν αἱρουμένοις
τοὺς βασιλέας.
4 Ἤδη δὲ τοῦ Σειληνοῦ μειρακίου γεγονότος καὶ
πρὸς τὴν πρᾶξιν ἥκοντος, ἐξέπεσε τοῦ δράματος ὁ
Λύσανδρος ἀτολμίᾳ τῶν ὑποκριτῶν καὶ συνεργῶν
ἑνός, ὡς ἐπ' αὐτὸ τὸ ἔργον ἦλθεν, ἀποδειλιάσαντος
καὶ ἀναδύντος. οὐ μὴν ἐφωράθη γε τοῦ Λυσάνδρου ζῶντος οὐθέν, ἀλλὰ μετὰ τὴν τελευτήν.

---

[1] τἄλλα πέπλασται the correction of Coraës; πᾶσαι Bekker·
πλάσαι, with the MSS.

took these circumstances for his foundation, and supplied the rest of his cunning fabric himself, making use of not a few, nor yet insignificant, champions of the tale, who brought the story of the boy's birth into credit without exciting suspicion. They also brought back another response from Delphi, and caused it to be circulated in Sparta, which declared that sundry very ancient oracles were kept in secret writings by the priests there, and that it was not possible to get these, nor even lawful to read them, unless someone born of Apollo should come after a long lapse of time, give the keepers an intelligible token of his birth, and obtain the tablets containing the oracles. The way being thus prepared, Silenus was to come and demand the oracles as Apollo's son, and the priests who were in the secret were to insist on precise answers to all their questions about his birth, and finally, persuaded, forsooth, that he was the son of Apollo, were to show him the writing. Then Silenus, in the presence of many witnesses, was to read aloud the prophecies, especially the one relating to the kingdom, for the sake of which the whole scheme had been invented, and which declared that it was more for the honour and interest of the Spartans to choose their kings from the best citizens.

But when at last Silenus was grown to be a youth, and was ready for the business, Lysander's play was ruined for him by the cowardice of one of his actors, or co-workers, who, just as he came to the point, lost his courage and drew back. However, all this was actually found out, not while Lysander was alive, but after his death.

XXVII. Ἐτελεύτησε δὲ πρὶν ἐξ Ἀσίας ἐπαν-
ελθεῖν τὸν Ἀγησίλαον, ἐμπεσὼν εἰς τὸν Βοιω-
τικὸν πόλεμον, ἢ μᾶλλον ἐμβαλὼν τὴν Ἑλλάδα.
λέγεται γὰρ ἀμφοτέρως· καὶ τὴν αἰτίαν οἱ μέν
τινες ἐκείνου ποιοῦσιν, οἱ δὲ Θηβαίων, οἱ δὲ
κοινήν, Θηβαίοις μὲν ἐγκαλοῦντες τὴν ἐν Αὐλίδι
τῶν ἱερῶν διάρριψιν καὶ ὅτι τῶν περὶ Ἀνδρο-
κλείδην καὶ Ἀμφίθεον χρήμασι βασιλικοῖς διαφθαρέντων ἐπὶ τῷ Λακεδαιμονίοις Ἑλληνικὸν
περιστῆσαι πόλεμον ἐπέθεντο Φωκεῦσι καὶ τὴν
2 χώραν αὐτῶν ἐπόρθησαν, Λύσανδρον δέ φασιν
ὀργῇ φέρειν ὅτι τῆς δεκάτης ἀντεποιήσαντο τοῦ
πολέμου Θηβαῖοι μόνοι, τῶν ἄλλων συμμάχων
ἡσυχαζόντων, καὶ περὶ χρημάτων ἠγανάκτησαν
ἃ Λύσανδρος εἰς Σπάρτην ἀπέστειλε, μάλιστα
δὲ ἐπὶ τῷ παρασχεῖν ἀρχὴν Ἀθηναίοις ἐλευθε-
ρώσεως ἀπὸ τῶν τριάκοντα τυράννων, οὓς Λύσανδρος μὲν κατέστησε, Λακεδαιμόνιοι δὲ δύναμιν
καὶ φόβον αὐτοῖς προστιθέντες ἐψηφίσαντο τοὺς
φεύγοντας ἐξ Ἀθηνῶν ἀγωγίμους εἶναι πανταχόθεν, ἐκσπόνδους δὲ τοὺς ἐνισταμένους τοῖς
3 ἄγουσι. πρὸς ταῦτα γὰρ ἀντεψηφίσαντο Θηβαῖοι ψηφίσματα πρέποντα καὶ ἀδελφὰ ταῖς
Ἡρακλέους καὶ Διονύσου πράξεσιν, οἰκίαν μὲν
ἀνεῷχθαι πᾶσαν καὶ πόλιν ἐν Βοιωτίᾳ τοῖς
δεομένοις Ἀθηναίων, τὸν δὲ τῷ ἀγομένῳ φυγάδι
μὴ βοηθήσαντα ζημίαν ὀφείλειν τάλαντον, ἂν   449
δέ τις Ἀθήναζε διὰ τῆς Βοιωτίας ἐπὶ τοὺς τυράν-

---

[1] In 395 B.C., the aggressions of Sparta led to an alliance
between Thebes and Athens against her. In the following
year Corinth and Argos joined the alliance, and the whole

XXVII. And he died before Agesilaüs returned
from Asia, after he had plunged, or rather had plunged
Hellas, into the Boeotian war.[1] For it is stated in both
ways; and some hold him responsible for the war,
others the Thebans, and others both together. It is
charged against the Thebans that they cast away the
sacrifices at Aulis,[2] and that, because Androcleides and
Amphitheus[3] had been bribed with the King's
money to stir up a war in Greece against the Lacedaemonians, they set upon the Phocians and ravaged
their country. It is said, on the other hand, that
Lysander was angry with the Thebans because they
alone laid claim to a tenth part of the spoils of the
war, while the rest of the allies held their peace;
and because they were indignant about the money
which he sent to Sparta; but above all, because they
first put the Athenians in the way of freeing themselves from the thirty tyrants whom he had set up,
whose terrorizing power the Lacedaemonians had
increased by decreeing that fugitives from Athens
might be brought back from every place of refuge, and
that all who impeded their return should be declared
enemies of Sparta. In reply to this the Thebans issued
counter decrees, akin in spirit to the beneficent deeds
of Heracles and Dionysus, to the effect that every
house and city in Boeotia should be open to such
Athenians as needed succour; and that whosoever
did not help a fugitive under arrest, should be fined
a talent; and that if any one should carry arms

war, which dragged along until 387 B.C., is usually known as
the "Corinthian war."

[2] In the spring of 396, when Agesilaüs vainly tried to
sacrifice there, in imitation of Agamemnon (Plutarch's
Agesilaüs, vi. 4–6 ; Xen. *Hell.* iii. 4, 3 f., and 5, 5).

[3] Cf. Xen. *Hell.* iii. 5, 1 and 4.

νους ὅπλα κομίζῃ, μήτε ὁρᾶν τινα Θηβαῖον μήτε
4 ἀκούειν. καὶ οὐκ ἐψηφίσαντο μὲν οὕτως Ἑλ-
ληνικὰ καὶ φιλάνθρωπα, τὰς δὲ πράξεις τοῖς
γράμμασιν ὁμοίας οὐ παρέσχον, ἀλλὰ Θρασύβουλος καὶ οἱ σὺν αὐτῷ Φυλὴν καταλαβόντες
ἐκ Θηβῶν ὡρμήθησαν, ὅπλα καὶ χρήματα καὶ
τὸ λαθεῖν καὶ τὸ ἄρξασθαι Θηβαίων αὐτοῖς
συμπαρασκευασάντων. αἰτίας μὲν οὖν ταύτας
ἔλαβε κατὰ τῶν Θηβαίων ὁ Λύσανδρος.

XXVIII. Ἤδη δὲ παντάπασι χαλεπὸς ὢν
ὀργὴν διὰ τὴν μελαγχολίαν ἐπιτείνουσαν εἰς
γῆρας, παρώξυνε τοὺς ἐφόρους καὶ συνέπεισε
φῆναι φρουρὰν ἐπ' αὐτούς, καὶ λαβὼν τὴν ἡγεμονίαν ἐξεστράτευσεν. ὕστερον δὲ καὶ Παυ-
σανίαν τὸν βασιλέα μετὰ στρατιᾶς ἀπέστειλαν.
2 ἀλλὰ Παυσανίας μὲν κύκλῳ περιελθὼν διὰ τοῦ
Κιθαιρῶνος ἐμβάλλειν ἔμελλεν εἰς τὴν Βοιωτίαν,
Λύσανδρος δὲ διὰ Φωκέων ἀπήντα στρατιώτας
ἔχων πολλούς· καὶ τὴν μὲν Ὀρχομενίων πόλιν
ἑκουσίως προσχωρήσασαν ἔλαβε, τὴν δὲ Λεβά-
δειαν ἐπελθὼν διεπόρθησεν. ἔπεμψε δὲ τῷ Παυσανίᾳ γράμματα κελεύων εἰς Ἁλίαρτον ἐκ Πλαταιῶν συνάπτειν, ὡς αὐτὸς ἅμ' ἡμέρᾳ πρὸς τοῖς
τείχεσι τῶν Ἁλιαρτίων γενησόμενος. ταῦτα τὰ
γράμματα πρὸς τοὺς Θηβαίους ἀπηνέχθη, τοῦ
κομίζοντος εἰς κατασκόπους τινὰς ἐμπεσόντος.
3 οἱ δὲ προσβεβοηθηκότων αὐτοῖς Ἀθηναίων τὴν
μὲν πόλιν ἐκείνοις διεπίστευσαν, αὐτοὶ δὲ περὶ

―――――――――
[1] Cf. Xen. *Hell.* ii. 4, 1 f.
[2] Lysander was commissioned to raise a force of allies in
Phocis and the neighbouring country, with which Pausanias

through Boeotia against the tyrants in Athens, no
Theban would either see him or hear about it. And
they did not merely vote such Hellenic and humane
decrees, without at the same time making their deeds
correspond to their edicts; but Thrasybulus and
those who with him occupied Phyle, set out from
Thebes to do so,[1] and the Thebans not only provided
them with arms and money, but also with secrecy
and a base of operations. Such, then, were the
grounds of complaint which Lysander had against
the Thebans.

XXVIII. And since he was now of an altogether
harsh disposition, owing to the melancholy which
persisted into his old age, he stirred up the ephors,
and persuaded them to fit out an expedition against
the Thebans; and assuming the command, he set
out on the campaign.[2] Afterwards the ephors sent
out Pausanias the king also with an army. Now it
was the plan that Pausanias should make a circuit
by the way of Mount Cithaeron, and then invade
Boeotia, while Lysander marched through Phocis to
meet him, with a large force. He took the city of
Orchomenus, which came over to him of its own
accord, and assaulted and plundered Lebadeia.
Then he sent a letter to Pausanias, bidding him move
from Plataea and join forces with him at Haliartus,
and promising that he himself would be before the
walls of Haliartus at break of day. This letter was
brought to Thebes by some scouts, into whose hands
its bearer fell. The Thebans therefore entrusted
their city to a force of Athenians which had come to
their aid, while they themselves set out early in the

was to unite his troops (Xen. *Hell.* iii. 5, 6). Plutarch's
language is obscure.

πρῶτον ὕπνον ἐξορμήσαντες ἔφθασαν ὀλίγῳ τὸν
Λύσανδρον ἐν Ἁλιάρτῳ γενόμενοι, καὶ μέρει τινὶ
παρῆλθον εἰς τὴν πόλιν. ἐκεῖνος δὲ τὸ μὲν
πρῶτον ἔγνω τὴν στρατιὰν ἱδρύσας ἐπὶ λόφου
περιμένειν τὸν Παυσανίαν· ἔπειτα προϊούσης τῆς
ἡμέρας ἀτρεμεῖν οὐ δυνάμενος, λαβὼν τὰ ὅπλα καὶ
τοὺς συμμάχους παρορμήσας ὀρθίῳ τῇ φάλαγγι
4 παρὰ τὴν ὁδὸν ἦγε πρὸς τὸ τεῖχος. τῶν δὲ
Θηβαίων οἱ μὲν ἔξω μεμενηκότες ἐν ἀριστερᾷ
τὴν πόλιν λαβόντες ἐβάδιζον ἐπὶ τοὺς ἐσχάτους
τῶν πολεμίων ὑπὸ τὴν κρήνην τὴν Κισσοῦσαν
προσαγορευομένην, ἔνθα μυθολογοῦσι τὰς τιθήνας
νήπιον ἐκ τῆς λοχείας ἀπολοῦσαι τὸν Διόνυσον·
καὶ γὰρ οἰνωπὸν ἐπιστίλβει τὸ χρῶμα καὶ διαυγὲς
καὶ πιεῖν ἥδιστον. οἱ δὲ Κρήσιοι στύρακες οὐ
πρόσω περιπεφύκασιν, ἃ τεκμήρια τῆς Ῥαδα-
μάνθυος αὐτόθι κατοικήσεως Ἁλιάρτιοι ποιοῦνται, καὶ τάφον αὐτοῦ δεικνύουσιν Ἀλεᾶ καλοῦν-
5 τες. ἔστι δὲ καὶ τὸ τῆς Ἀλκμήνης μνημεῖον
ἐγγύς· ἐνταῦθα γάρ, ὥς φασιν, ἐκηδεύθη συνοικ-
ήσασα Ῥαδαμάνθυϊ μετὰ τὴν Ἀμφιτρύωνος
τελευτήν.

Οἱ δὲ ἐν τῇ πόλει Θηβαῖοι μετὰ τῶν Ἁλιαρτίων συντεταγμένοι τέως μὲν ἡσύχαζον, ἐπεὶ δὲ
τὸν Λύσανδρον ἅμα τοῖς πρώτοις προσπελάζοντα
τῷ τείχει κατεῖδον, ἐξαπίνης ἀνοίξαντες τὰς
πύλας καὶ προσπεσόντες αὐτόν τε μετὰ τοῦ
μάντεως κατέβαλον καὶ τῶν ἄλλων ὀλίγους
τινάς· οἱ γὰρ πλεῖστοι ταχέως ἀνέφυγον πρὸς
6 τὴν φάλαγγα. τῶν δὲ Θηβαίων οὐκ ἀνιέντων,
ἀλλὰ προσκειμένων αὐτοῖς, ἐτράποντο πάντες
ἀνὰ τοὺς λόφους φεύγειν, καὶ χίλιοι πίπτουσιν

night, and succeeded in reaching Haliartus a little before Lysander, and a considerable part of them entered the city. Lysander at first decided to post his army on a hill and wait for Pausanias; then, as the day advanced, being unable to remain inactive, he took his arms, encouraged his allies, and led them along the road in column towards the wall of the city. But those of the Thebans who had remained outside, taking the city on their left, advanced upon the rear of their enemy, at the spring called Cissusa. Here, as the story goes, his nurses bathed the infant Dionysus after his birth; for the water has the colour and sparkle of wine, is clear, and very pleasant to the taste. And not far away the Cretan storax-shrub grows in profusion, which the Haliartians regard as a proof that Rhadamanthus once dwelt there; and they show his tomb, which they call Alea. And near by is also the memorial of Alcmene; for she was buried there, as they say, having lived with Rhadamanthus after the death of Amphitryon.

But the Thebans inside the city, drawn up in battle array with the Haliartians, kept quiet for some time; when, however, they saw Lysander with his foremost troops approaching the wall, they suddenly threw open the gate and fell upon them, and killed Lysander himself with his soothsayer, and a few of the rest; for the greater part of them fled swiftly back to the main body. And when the Thebans made no halt, but pressed hard upon them, the whole force turned to the hills in flight, and a thousand of them were slain. Three hundred of

αὐτῶν. ἀπέθανον δὲ καὶ Θηβαίων τριακόσιοι
πρὸς τὰ τραχέα καὶ καρτερὰ τοῖς πολεμίοις
συνεκπεσόντες. οὗτοι δὲ ἦσαν ἐν αἰτίᾳ τοῦ
λακωνίζειν, ἣν σπουδάζοντες ἀπολύσασθαι τοῖς
πολίταις καὶ σφῶν αὐτῶν ἀφειδοῦντες ἐν τῇ
διώξει παραναλώθησαν.

XXIX. Τῷ δὲ Παυσανίᾳ τὸ πάθος ἀγγέλλεται
καθ᾽ ὁδὸν ἐκ Πλαταιῶν εἰς Θεσπιὰς πορευομένῳ·
καὶ συνταξάμενος ἧκε πρὸς τὸν Ἁλίαρτον. ἧκε
δὲ καὶ Θρασύβουλος ἐκ Θηβῶν ἄγων τοὺς Ἀθηναίους. βουλευομένου δὲ τοῦ Παυσανίου τοὺς
νεκροὺς ὑποσπόνδους ἀπαιτεῖν, δυσφοροῦντες οἱ
πρεσβύτεροι τῶν Σπαρτιατῶν αὐτοί τε καθ᾽
ἑαυτοὺς ἠγανάκτουν, καὶ τῷ βασιλεῖ προσιόντες
ἐμαρτύραντο μὴ διὰ σπονδῶν ἀναιρεῖσθαι Λύ-   450
σανδρον, ἀλλὰ δι᾽ ὅπλων περὶ τοῦ σώματος
ἀγωνισαμένους καὶ νικήσαντας οὕτω τὸν ἄνδρα
θάπτειν, ἡττωμένοις δὲ καλὸν ἐνταῦθα κεῖσθαι
2 μετὰ τοῦ στρατηγοῦ. ταῦτα τῶν πρεσβυτέρων
λεγόντων ὁρῶν ὁ Παυσανίας μέγα μὲν ἔργον
ὑπερβαλέσθαι μάχῃ τοὺς Θηβαίους ἄρτι κεκρατη-
κότας, ἐγγὺς δὲ τῶν τειχῶν τὸ σῶμα τοῦ Λυσάνδρου παραπεπτωκός, ὥστε χαλεπὴν ἄνευ
σπονδῶν καὶ νικῶσιν εἶναι τὴν ἀναίρεσιν, ἔπεμψε
κήρυκα καὶ σπεισάμενος ἀπήγαγε τὴν δύναμιν
3 ὀπίσω. τὸν δὲ Λύσανδρον ᾗ πρῶτον κομίζοντες
ὑπὲρ τοὺς ὅρους ἐγένοντο τῆς Βοιωτίας ἐν φίλῃ
καὶ συμμαχίδι χώρᾳ τῇ Πανοπέων κατέθεσαν, οὗ
νῦν τὸ μνημεῖόν ἐστι παρὰ τὴν ὁδὸν εἰς Χαιρώνειαν ἐκ Δελφῶν πορευομένοις.

Ἐνταῦθα δὴ τῆς στρατιᾶς καταυλισαμένης

the Thebans also lost their lives by pursuing their
enemies into rough and dangerous places. These
had been accused of favouring the Spartan cause, and
in their eagerness to clear themselves of this charge
in the eyes of their fellow-citizens, they exposed
themselves needlessly in the pursuit, and so threw
away their lives.[1]

XXIX. Tidings of the disaster were brought to
Pausanias while he was on the march from Plataea
to Thespiae, and putting his army in battle array, he
came to Haliartus. Thrasybulus also came from
Thebes, leading his Athenians. But when Pausanias
was minded to ask for the bodies of the dead under
a truce, the elders of the Spartans could not brook
it, and were angry among themselves, and coming
to the king, they protested that the body of Lysander
must not be taken up under cover of a truce, but by
force of arms, in open battle for it; and that if they
conquered, then they would give him burial, but if
they were vanquished, it would be a glorious thing
to lie dead with their general. Such were the words
of the elders; but Pausanias saw that it would be a
difficult matter to conquer the Thebans, flushed as
they were with victory, and that the body of
Lysander lay near the walls, so that its recovery
would be difficult without a truce, even if they were
victorious; he therefore sent a herald, and after
making a truce, led his forces back. And as soon as
they had come beyond the boundary of Boeotia with
Lysander's body, they buried it in the friendly soil
of their allies, the Panopeans, where his monument
now stands, by the road leading from Delphi to
Chaeroneia.

Here the army bivouacked; and it is said that a

[1] Cf. Xen. *Hell*. iii. 5, 17–20.

λέγεταί τινα τῶν Φωκέων ἑτέρῳ μὴ παρατυχόντι
τὸν ἀγῶνα διηγούμενον, εἰπεῖν ὡς οἱ πολέμιοι
προσπέσοιεν αὐτοῖς τοῦ Λυσάνδρου τὸν Ὁπλίτην
4 ἤδη διαβεβηκότος. θαυμάσαντα δὲ Σπαρτιάτην
ἄνδρα τοῦ Λυσάνδρου φίλον ἐρέσθαι τίνα λέγοι
τὸν Ὁπλίτην· οὐ γὰρ εἰδέναι τοὔνομα· "Καὶ μὴν
ἐκεῖ γε," φάναι, "τοὺς πρώτους ἡμῶν οἱ πολέμιοι
κατέβαλον. τὸ γὰρ παρὰ τὴν πόλιν ῥεῖθρον
Ὁπλίτην καλοῦσιν." ἀκούσαντα δὲ τὸν Σπαρτιάτην ἐκδακρῦσαι καὶ εἰπεῖν ὡς ἄφευκτόν ἐστιν
5 ἀνθρώπῳ τὸ πεπρωμένον. ἦν γάρ, ὡς ἔοικε, τῷ
Λυσάνδρῳ δεδομένος χρησμὸς οὕτως ἔχων·

Ὁπλίτην κελάδοντα φυλάξασθαί σε κελεύω
γῆς τε δράκονθ᾽ υἱὸν δόλιον κατόπισθεν ἰόντα.

τινὲς δὲ τὸν Ὁπλίτην οὐ πρὸς Ἁλιάρτῳ ῥεῖν
λέγουσιν, ἀλλὰ πρὸς Κορώνειαν χειμάρρουν εἶναι
τῷ Φιλάρῳ ποταμῷ συμφερόμενον παρὰ τὴν
πόλιν, ὃν πάλαι μὲν Ὁπλίαν, νῦν δὲ Ἰσόμαντον
6 προσαγορεύουσιν. ὁ δὲ ἀποκτείνας τὸν Λύσανδρον
Ἁλιάρτιος ἀνὴρ ὄνομα Νέοχωρος ἐπίσημον εἶχε
τῆς ἀσπίδος δράκοντα· καὶ τοῦτο σημαίνειν ὁ
χρησμὸς εἰκάζετο. λέγεται δὲ καὶ Θηβαίοις ὑπὸ
τὸν Πελοποννησιακὸν πόλεμον ἐν Ἰσμηνίῳ γενέσθαι χρησμὸν ἅμα τήν τε πρὸς Δηλίῳ μάχην καὶ
τὴν πρὸς Ἁλιάρτῳ ταύτην ἐκείνης ὕστερον ἔτει
7 τριακοστῷ γενομένην προμηνύοντα. ἦν δὲ τοιοῦ-
τος·

Ἐσχατιὰν πεφύλαξο λύκους καμάκεσσι δοκ-
εύων
καὶ λόφον Ὀρχαλίδην, ὃν ἀλώπηξ οὔποτε
λείπει.

certain Phocian, recounting the action to another who was not in it, said that the enemy fell upon them just after Lysander had crossed the Hoplites. Then a Spartan, who was a friend of Lysander, asked in amazement what he meant by Hoplites, for he did not know the name. "Indeed it was there," said the Phocian, "that the enemy slew the foremost of us ; for the stream that flows past the city is called Hoplites." On hearing this, the Spartan burst into tears, and said that man could not escape his destiny. For Lysander, as it appears, had received an oracle running thus :—

"Be on thy guard, I bid thee, against a sounding Hoplites,
  And an earth-born dragon craftily coming behind thee."

Some, however, say that the Hoplites does not flow before Haliartus, but is a winter torrent near Coroneia, which joins the Philarus and then flows past that city ; in former times it was called Hoplias, but now Isomantus. Moreover, the man of Haliartus who killed Lysander, Neochorus by name, had a dragon as emblem on his shield, and to this, it was supposed, the oracle referred. And it is said that the Thebans also, during the Peloponnesian war, received an oracle at the sanctuary of Ismenus which indicated beforehand not only the battle at Delium,[1] but also this battle at Haliartus, thirty years later. It ran as follows :—

"When thou huntest the wolf with the spear, watch closely the border,
  Orchalides, too, the hill which foxes never abandon."

[1] 424 B.C.

τὸν μὲν οὖν περὶ Δήλιον τόπον ἐσχατιὰν προσ-
εῖπε, καθ' ὃν ἡ Βοιωτία τῇ Ἀττικῇ σύνορός ἐστιν,
Ὀρχαλίδην δὲ λόφον, ὃν νῦν Ἀλώπεκον καλοῦσιν,
ἐν τοῖς πρὸς τὸν Ἑλικῶνα μέρεσι τοῦ Ἁλιάρτου
κείμενον.

XXX. Τοιαύτης δὲ τῷ Λυσάνδρῳ τῆς τελευτῆς γενομένης παραχρῆμα μὲν οὕτως ἤνεγκαν οἱ
Σπαρτιᾶται βαρέως, ὥστε τῷ βασιλεῖ κρίσιν
προγράψαι θανατικήν· ἣν οὐχ ὑποστὰς ἐκεῖνος
εἰς Τεγέαν ἔφυγε, κἀκεῖ κατεβίωσεν ἱκέτης ἐν τῷ
2 τεμένει τῆς Ἀθηνᾶς. καὶ γὰρ ἡ πενία τοῦ Λυσάνδρου τελευτήσαντος ἐκκαλυφθεῖσα φανερω-
τέραν ἐποίησε τὴν ἀρετήν, ἀπὸ χρημάτων πολλῶν
καὶ δυνάμεως θεραπείας τε πόλεων καὶ βασιλέως
τοσαύτης μηδὲ μικρὸν ἐπιλαμπρύναντος τὸν οἶκον
εἰς χρημάτων λόγον, ὡς ἱστορεῖ Θεόπομπος, ᾧ
μᾶλλον ἐπαινοῦντι πιστεύσειεν ἄν τις ἢ ψέγοντι,
3 ψέγει γὰρ ἥδιον ἢ ἐπαινεῖ. χρόνῳ δὲ ὕστερον
Ἔφορός φησιν ἀντιλογίας τινὸς συμμαχικῆς ἐν
Σπάρτῃ γενομένης, καὶ τὰ γράμματα δια-
σκέψασθαι δεῆσαν ἃ παρ' ἑαυτῷ κατέσχεν ὁ
Λύσανδρος, ἐλθεῖν ἐπὶ τὴν οἰκίαν τὸν Ἀγησίλαον.
εὑρόντα δὲ τὸ βιβλίον ἐν ᾧ γεγραμμένος ἦν ὁ
περὶ τῆς πολιτείας λόγος, ὡς χρὴ τῶν Εὐρυπων-
τιδῶν καὶ Ἀγιαδῶν τὴν βασιλείαν ἀφελομένους
εἰς μέσον θεῖναι καὶ ποιεῖσθαι τὴν αἵρεσιν ἐκ τῶν
4 ἀρίστων, ὁρμῆσαι μὲν εἰς τοὺς πολίτας τὸν λόγον
ἐξενεγκεῖν καὶ παραδεικνύναι τὸν Λύσανδρον,
οἷος ὢν πολίτης διαλάθοι, Λακρατίδαν δέ, ἄνδρα 45

318

Now by "border," the god meant the region about Delium, where Boeotia is conterminous with Attica; and by Orchalides, the hill which is now called Alopecus, or *Fox-hill,* in the parts of Haliartus which stretch towards Mount Helicon.

XXX. Now that Lysander had met with such an end, at the outset the Spartans were so indignant about it that they summoned the king to trial for his life; but he evaded it, and fled to Tegea, where he spent the rest of his days as a suppliant in the sanctuary of Athena. For the poverty of Lysander, which was discovered at his death, made his excellence more apparent to all, since from the vast wealth and power in his hands, and from the great homage paid him by cities and the Great King, he had not, even in the slightest degree, sought to amass money for the aggrandizement of his family. This is the testimony of Theopompus, who is more to be trusted when he praises than when he blames; for he takes more pleasure in blaming than in praising. But after some time had passed, according to Ephorus, some dispute arose at Sparta with her allies, and it became necessary to inspect the writings which Lysander had kept by him; for which purpose Agesilaüs went to his house. And when he found the book containing the speech on the constitution,[1] which argued that the kingship ought to be taken from the Eurypontidae and Agiadae and made accessible to all Spartans alike, and that the choice should be made from the best of these, he was eager to produce the speech before his countrymen, and show them what the real character of Lysander's citizenship had been. But Lacratidas, a prudent man, and

[1] Cf. chapter xxv. 1.

φρόνιμον καὶ τότε προεστῶτα τῶν ἐφόρων, ἐπι-
λαβέσθαι τοῦ Ἀγησιλάου, καὶ εἰπεῖν ὡς δεῖ μὴ
ἀνορύττειν τὸν Λύσανδρον, ἀλλὰ καὶ τὸν λόγον
αὐτῷ συγκατορύττειν οὕτω συντεταγμένον πιθα-
νῶς καὶ πανούργως.

5   Οὐ μὴν ἀλλὰ τάς τε ἄλλας τιμὰς ἀπέδοσαν
αὐτῷ τελευτήσαντι, καὶ τοὺς μνηστευσαμένους
τὰς θυγατέρας, εἶτα μετὰ τὴν τελευτὴν τοῦ
Λυσάνδρου πένητος εὑρεθέντος ἀπειπαμένους ἐζη-
μίωσαν, ὅτι πλούσιον μὲν νομίζοντες ἐθεράπευον,
δίκαιον δὲ καὶ χρηστὸν ἐκ τῆς πενίας ἐπιγνόντες
ἐγκατέλιπον. ἦν γάρ, ὡς ἔοικεν, ἐν Σπάρτῃ καὶ
ἀγαμίου δίκη καὶ ὀψιγαμίου καὶ κακογαμίου·
ταύτῃ δὲ ὑπῆγον μάλιστα τοὺς ἀντὶ τῶν ἀγαθῶν
καὶ οἰκείων τοῖς πλουσίοις κηδεύοντας. τὰ μὲν
οὖν περὶ Λύσανδρον οὕτως ἱστορήσαμεν ἔχοντα.

at that time the principal ephor, held Agesilaüs
back, saying that they ought not to dig Lysander
up again, but rather to bury the speech along with
him, since it was composed with such a subtle per-
suasiveness.

However, they paid him many honours at his
death. In particular, they imposed a fine upon the
men who had engaged to marry his daughters, and
then, after Lysander's death, when he was discovered
to be poor, had renounced the engagement. The
reason given for the fine was that the men had paid
court to Lysander while they thought him rich, but
when his poverty showed them that he was a just
and good man, they forsook him. For there was, as it
appears, a penalty at Sparta not only for not marrying
at all, and for a late marriage, but also for a bad
marriage ; and to this last they subjected those
especially who sought alliance with the rich, instead
of with the good and with their own associates.
Such, then, are the accounts we have found given of
Lysander.

SULLA

ΣΥΛΛΑΣ

I. Λεύκιος δὲ Κορνήλιος Σύλλας γένει μὲν ἦν
ἐκ πατρικίων, οὓς εὐπατρίδας ἄν τις εἴποι, τῶν δὲ
προγόνων αὐτοῦ λέγουσι Ῥουφῖνον ὑπατεῦσαι,
καὶ τούτῳ δὲ τῆς τιμῆς ἐπιφανεστέραν γενέσθαι
τὴν ἀτιμίαν. εὑρέθη γὰρ ἀργυρίου κοίλου κεκτημένος ὑπὲρ δέκα λίτρας, τοῦ νόμου μὴ διδόντος·
ἐπὶ τούτῳ δὲ τῆς βουλῆς ἐξέπεσεν. οἱ δὲ μετ᾽
ἐκεῖνον ἤδη ταπεινὰ πράττοντες διετέλεσαν, αὐτός
τε Σύλλας ἐν οὐκ ἀφθόνοις ἐτράφη τοῖς πατρῴοις.
2 γενόμενος δὲ μειράκιον ᾤκει παρ᾽ ἑτέροις ἐνοίκιον
οὐ πολὺ τελῶν, ὡς ὕστερον ὠνειδίζετο παρ᾽ ἀξίαν
εὐτυχεῖν δοκῶν. σεμνυνομένῳ μὲν γὰρ αὐτῷ καὶ
μεγαληγοροῦντι μετὰ τὴν ἐν Λιβύῃ στρατείαν
λέγεταί τις εἰπεῖν τῶν καλῶν τε κἀγαθῶν ἀνδρῶν,
" Καὶ πῶς ἂν εἴης σὺ χρηστός, ὃς τοῦ πατρός σοι
3 μηδὲν καταλιπόντος τοσαῦτα κέκτησαι;" καὶ γὰρ
οὐκ ἔτι τῶν βίων ἐν ἤθεσιν ὀρθίοις καὶ καθαροῖς
μενόντων, ἀλλ᾽ ἐγκεκλικότων καὶ παραδεδεγ-
μένων τρυφῆς καὶ πολυτελείας ζῆλον, εἰς ἴσον
ὅμως ὄνειδος ἐτίθεντο τοὺς ὑπάρχουσαν εὐπορίαν
ἀπολέσαντας καὶ τοὺς πενίαν πατρῴαν μὴ δια-
4 φυλάξαντας. ὕστερον δὲ ἤδη κρατοῦντος αὐτοῦ
καὶ πολλοὺς ἀποκτιννύντος, ἀπελευθερικὸς ἄνθρωπος, δοκῶν κρύπτειν ἕνα τῶν προγεγραμμένων
καὶ κατακρημνίζεσθαι διὰ τοῦτο μέλλων, ὠνείδισε

SULLA

I. LUCIUS CORNELIUS SULLA belonged to a patrician, or noble, family, and one of his ancestors, Rufinus, is said to have been consul, although he was not so conspicuous for this honour as for the dishonour which he incurred. For he was found to be possessed of more than ten pounds of silver plate, contrary to the law, and was for this reason expelled from the senate. His posterity became at once obscure, and continued so, nor did Sulla himself enjoy a wealthy parentage. When he was a youth, he lived in lodgings, at a low price, and this was afterwards cast in his teeth when men thought him unduly prosperous. For instance, we are told that when he was putting on boastful airs after his campaign in Libya, a certain nobleman said to him : " How canst thou be an honest man, when thy father left thee nothing, and yet thou art so rich?" For although the Romans of that time no longer retained their ancient purity and uprightness of life, but had degenerated, and yielded to the appetite for luxury and extravagance, they nevertheless held in equal opprobrium those who lost an inherited wealth and those who forsook an ancestral poverty. And afterwards, when he had at last become absolute in power, and was putting many to death, a freedman, who was thought to be concealing one of the proscribed, and was therefore to be thrown down the Tarpeian rock,

τὸν Σύλλαν ὅτι πολὺν χρόνον ἐν μιᾷ συνοικίᾳ
διῃτῶντο, φέροντες ἐνοίκιον αὐτὸς μὲν τῶν ἄνω
δισχιλίους νούμμους, ἐκεῖνος δὲ τῶν ὑποκάτω
τρισχιλίους, ὥστε τῆς τύχης αὐτῶν τὸ μεταξὺ
χιλίους εἶναι νούμμους, οἳ πεντήκοντα καὶ διακοσίας δραχμὰς Ἀττικὰς δύνανται. ταῦτα μὲν οὖν
ἱστοροῦσι περὶ τῆς παλαιᾶς τοῦ Σύλλα τύχης.

II. Τοῦ δὲ σώματος αὐτοῦ τὸ μὲν ἄλλο εἶδος
ἐπὶ τῶν ἀνδριάντων φαίνεται, τὴν δὲ τῶν ὀμμάτων
γλαυκότητα δεινῶς πικρὰν καὶ ἄκρατον οὖσαν ἡ
χρόα τοῦ προσώπου φοβερωτέραν ἐποίει προσιδεῖν. ἐξήνθει γὰρ τὸ ἐρύθημα τραχὺ καὶ σποράδην
καταμεμιγμένον τῇ λευκότητι· πρὸς ὃ καὶ τοὔνομα λέγουσιν αὐτῷ γενέσθαι τῆς χρόας ἐπίθετον,
καὶ τῶν Ἀθήνησι γεφυριστῶν ἐπέσκωψέ τις εἰς
τοῦτο ποιήσας·

συκάμινόν ἐσθ' ὁ Σύλλας ἀλφίτῳ πεπασμένον.

2 τοῖς δὲ τοιούτοις τῶν τεκμηρίων οὐκ ἄτοπόν ἐστι
χρῆσθαι περὶ ἀνδρός, ὃν οὕτω φιλοσκώμμονα
φύσει γεγονέναι λέγουσιν, ὥστε νέον μὲν ὄντα καὶ
ἄδοξον ἔτι μετὰ μίμων καὶ γελωτοποιῶν διαιτᾶσθαι καὶ συνακολασταίνειν, ἐπεὶ δὲ κύριος
ἁπάντων κατέστη, συναγαγόντα τῶν ἀπὸ σκηνῆς
καὶ θεάτρου τοὺς ἰταμωτάτους ὁσημέραι πίνειν
καὶ διαπληκτίζεσθαι τοῖς σκώμμασι, τοῦ τε
γήρως ἀωρότερα πράττειν δοκοῦντα καὶ πρὸς τῷ
καταισχύνειν τὸ ἀξίωμα τῆς ἀρχῆς πολλὰ τῶν
3 δεομένων ἐπιμελείας προϊέμενον. οὐ γὰρ ἦν τῷ
Σύλλᾳ περὶ δεῖπνον ὄντι χρήσασθαι σπουδαῖον

cast it in his teeth that they had long lived together in one lodging house, himself renting the upper rooms at two thousand sesterces,[1] and Sulla the lower rooms at three thousand. The difference in their fortunes, therefore, was only a thousand sesterces, which are equivalent to two hundred and fifty Attic drachmas. Such, then, is the account we find of Sulla's earlier fortune.

II. His personal appearance, in general, is given by his statues; but the gleam of his gray eyes, which was terribly sharp and powerful, was rendered even more fearful by the complexion of his face. This was covered with coarse blotches of red, interspersed with white. For this reason, they say, his surname was given him because of his complexion, and it was in allusion to this that a scurrilous jester at Athens made the verse :—

" Sulla is a mulberry sprinkled o'er with meal."

Nor is it out of place to mention such testimonies in the case of a man said to have been by nature so fond of raillery, that when he was still young and obscure he spent much time with actors and buffoons and shared their dissolute life ; and when he had made himself supreme master, he would daily assemble the most reckless stage and theatre folk to drink and bandy jests with them, although men thought that he disgraced his years, and although he not only dishonoured his high office, but neglected much that required attention. For when Sulla was once at table, he refused to be serious at all, but,

[1] In Sulla's time the *sestertius* was a silver coin worth between two and three pence, or about five cents. The Attic drachma was a silver coin worth about eight pence, or twenty cents.

οὐδέν, ἀλλ᾽ ἐνεργὸς ὢν καὶ σκυθρωπότερος παρὰ
τὸν ἄλλον χρόνον, ἀθρόαν ἐλάμβανε μεταβολὴν
ὁπότε πρῶτον ἑαυτὸν εἰς συνουσίαν καταβάλοι
καὶ πότον, ὥστε μιμῳδοῖς καὶ ὀρχησταῖς τιθασὸς
εἶναι καὶ πρὸς πᾶσαν ἔντευξιν ὑποχείριος καὶ
κατάντης. ταύτης δὲ τῆς ἀνέσεως ἔοικε γεγονέναι νόσημα καὶ ἡ πρὸς τοὺς ἔρωτας εὐχέρεια
καὶ ῥύσις αὐτοῦ τῆς φιληδονίας, ἧς οὐδὲ γηράσας
4 ἐπαύσατο, Μητροβίου δὲ τῶν ἀπὸ σκηνῆς τινος
ἐρῶν διετέλεσεν ἔτι νέος ὤν.[1] καὶ συνήντησεν
αὐτῷ τὸ τοιοῦτον· ἀρξάμενος γὰρ ἐρᾶν κοινῆς μέν,
εὐπόρου δὲ γυναικός, ὄνομα Νικοπόλεως, καὶ διὰ
συνήθειαν καὶ χάριν, ἣν ἀφ᾽ ὥρας εἶχεν, εἰς ἐρω-
μένου σχῆμα περιελθών, ἀπελείφθη κληρονόμος
ὑπὸ τῆς ἀνθρώπου τελευτώσης. ἐκληρονόμησε
δὲ καὶ τὴν μητρυιάν, ἀγαπηθεὶς ὥσπερ υἱὸς ὑπ᾽
αὐτῆς· καὶ μετρίως μὲν ἀπὸ τούτων εὐπόρησεν.

III. Ἀποδειχθεὶς δὲ ταμίας ὑπατεύοντι Μαρίῳ
τὴν πρώτην ὑπατείαν, συνεξέπλευσεν εἰς Λιβύην
πολεμήσων Ἰογόρθαν. γενόμενος δὲ ἐπὶ στρατοπέδου τά τε ἄλλα παρεῖχεν ἑαυτὸν εὐδόκιμον, καὶ
καιρῷ παραπεσόντι χρησάμενος εὖ φίλον ἐποιήσατο τὸν τῶν Νομάδων βασιλέα Βόκχον. πρεσ-
βευτὰς γὰρ αὐτοῦ λῃστήριον Νομαδικὸν ἐκφυγόν-
τας ὑποδεξάμενος καὶ φιλοφρονηθείς, δῶρα καὶ
2 πομπὴν ἀσφαλῆ παρασχὼν ἀπέστειλεν. ὁ δὲ
Βόκχος ἐτύγχανε μὲν ἔτι γε πάλαι γαμβρὸν ὄντα
μισῶν καὶ φοβούμενος τὸν Ἰογόρθαν, τότε δὲ
ἡττημένῳ καὶ πεφευγότι πρὸς αὐτὸν ἐπιβουλεύων
ἐκάλει τὸν Σύλλαν, δι᾽ ἐκείνου μάλιστα βουλό-

---

[1] ἔτι νέος ὢν before this phrase Bekker assumes a lacuna in
the text; Sintenis would transpose it to follow ἀρξάμενος γάρ.

although at other times he was a man of business and wore an austere look, he underwent a complete change as soon as he betook himself to good-fellowship and drinking, so that comic singers and dancers found him anything but ferocious, and ready to listen and yield to every request. It was this laxity, as it seems, which produced in him a diseased propensity to amorous indulgence and an unrestrained voluptuousness, from which he did not refrain even in his old age, but continued his youthful love for Metrobius, an actor.[1] He also had the following experience. He began by loving a common but wealthy woman, Nicopolis by name, and such was the charm of his intimacy and youthful grace that in the end he was beloved by her, and was left her heir when she died. He also inherited the property of his step-mother, who loved him as her own son. By these means he became moderately well off.

III. Having been appointed quaestor to Marius in his first consulship,[2] he sailed with him to Libya, to make war upon Jugurtha. He was put in charge of the camp, and won great credit for himself, especially by improving a favourable opportunity and making a friend of Bocchus, the king of Numidia. For he hospitably entertained ambassadors of the king, who had escaped from Numidian robbers, and sent them on their way with gifts and a safe escort. Now Bocchus had for a long time hated and feared his son-in-law, Jugurtha, who had been defeated and had fled to him for safety, and was then plotting against him. He therefore invited Sulla to come

---

[1] The sense of the obscure Greek is clear from chapter xxxvi. 1 *fin.* Capps suggests ὡς . . . . ὤν.   [2] 107 B.C.

μενος τὴν σύλληψιν καὶ παράδοσιν τοῦ Ἰογόρθα
γενέσθαι ἢ δι᾽ αὑτοῦ. κοινωσάμενος δὲ τῷ Μαρίῳ
καὶ λαβὼν στρατιώτας ὀλίγους ὁ Σύλλας τὸν
μέγιστον ὑπέδυ κίνδυνον, ὅτι βαρβάρῳ καὶ πρὸς
τοὺς οἰκειοτάτους ἀπίστῳ πιστεύσας, ὑπὲρ τοῦ
3 παραλαβεῖν ἕτερον ἑαυτὸν ἐνεχείρισεν. οὐ μὴν
ἀλλὰ ὁ Βόκχος ἀμφοτέρων κύριος γενόμενος, καὶ
καταστήσας ἑαυτὸν εἰς ἀνάγκην τοῦ παρασπον-
δῆσαι τὸν ἕτερον, καὶ πολλὰ διενεχθεὶς τῇ γνώμῃ,
τέλος ἐκύρωσε τὴν πρώτην προδοσίαν καὶ παρέδωκε τῷ Σύλλᾳ τὸν Ἰογόρθαν. ὁ μὲν οὖν θρι-
αμβεύων ἐπὶ τούτῳ Μάριος ἦν, ἡ δὲ δόξα τοῦ
κατορθώματος, ἣν ὁ Μαρίου φθόνος Σύλλᾳ
4 προσετίθει, παρελύπει τὸν Μάριον ἡσυχῇ. καὶ
γὰρ αὐτὸς ὁ Σύλλας φύσει τε μεγάλαυχος ὢν καὶ
τότε πρῶτον ἐκ βίου ταπεινοῦ καὶ ἀγνῶτος ἔν
τινι λόγῳ γεγονὼς παρὰ τοῖς πολίταις, καὶ τοῦ
τιμᾶσθαι γευόμενος, εἰς τοῦτο φιλοτιμίας προῆλ-
θεν ὥστε γλυψάμενος ἐν δακτυλίῳ φορεῖν εἰκόνα
τῆς πράξεως, καὶ ταύτῃ γε χρώμενος ἀεὶ διετέλεσεν. ἦν δὲ ἡ γραφὴ Βόκχος μὲν παραδιδούς,
Σύλλας δὲ παραλαμβάνων τὸν Ἰογόρθαν.

IV. Ἡνία μὲν οὖν ταῦτα τὸν Μάριον· ἔτι δὲ
ἡγούμενος ἐλάττονα τοῦ φθονεῖσθαι τὸν Σύλλαν,
ἐχρῆτο πρὸς τὰς στρατείας, τὸ μὲν δεύτερον
ὑπατεύων πρεσβευτῇ, τὸ δὲ τρίτον χιλιάρχῳ, καὶ
πολλὰ δι᾽ ἐκείνου τῶν χρησίμων κατωρθοῦτο.
πρεσβεύων τε γὰρ ἡγεμόνα Τεκτοσάγων Κόπιλ-
λον εἷλε, καὶ χιλιαρχῶν μέγα καὶ πολυάνθρωπον
ἔθνος Μαρσοὺς ἔπεισε φίλους γενέσθαι καὶ συμ-
2 μάχους Ῥωμαίων. ἐκ δὲ τούτων τὸν Μάριον   4

to him, wishing to have the seizure and surrender
of Jugurtha effected through Sulla rather than
through himself. Sulla imparted the matter to
Marius, and taking with him a few soldiers, underwent the greatest peril; he put faith in a Barbarian,
and one who was faithless towards his own relations,
and to secure his surrender of another, placed himself
in his hands. However, Bocchus, now that he had
both in his power, and had laid himself under the
necessity of proving false to one or the other, although
he vacillated long, finally decided upon his original
betrayal, and handed Jugurtha over to Sulla. It
is true that the one who celebrated a triumph for this
was Marius, but those who envied him attributed the
glory of the success to Sulla, and this secretly
annoyed Marius. And indeed Sulla himself was
naturally vainglorious, and now that he had for the
first time emerged from his lowly and obscure
condition and become of some account among his
countrymen, and was enjoying a taste of honour, he
was arrogant enough to have a representation of
his exploit engraved on a seal-ring which he wore,
and continued to use it ever after. The device was,
Bocchus delivering, and Sulla receiving, Jugurtha.

IV. Of course this distressed Marius; but since he
considered Sulla to be beneath his envy, he used him
in his campaigns, during his second consulship as
legate, or lieutenant, and during his third as military
tribune, and through his agency performed many
successful services. For instance, as legate, Sulla
captured Copillus, chieftain of the Tectosages; and
as tribune, he persuaded the great and populous
nation of the Marsi to become friends and allies of
Rome. But perceiving that Marius was vexed with

331

αἰσθόμενος ἀχθόμενον αὐτῷ καὶ μηκέτι προϊέμενον ἡδέως πράξεων ἀφορμάς, ἀλλὰ ἐνιστάμενον
τῇ αὐξήσει, Κάτλῳ, τῷ συνάρχοντι τοῦ Μαρίου,
προσένειμεν ἑαυτόν, ἀνδρὶ χρηστῷ μέν, ἀμβλυ-
τέρῳ δὲ πρὸς τοὺς ἀγῶνας. ὑφ' οὗ τὰ πρῶτα καὶ
μέγιστα πιστευόμενος εἰς δύναμιν ἅμα δόξῃ
3 προῄει. καὶ πολέμῳ μὲν αἱρεῖ πολὺ μέρος τῶν ἐν
ταῖς Ἄλπεσι βαρβάρων, ἐπιλιπούσης δὲ τῆς
ἀγορᾶς ἀναδεξάμενος τὴν ἐπιμέλειαν τοσαύτην
ἐποίησε περιουσίαν, ὥστε τῶν Κάτλου στρατιωτῶν ἐν ἀφθόνοις διαγόντων καὶ τοῖς Μαρίου
προσπαρασχεῖν. ἐφ' ᾧ φησιν αὐτὸς ἰσχυρῶς¹
4 ἀνιᾶσαι τὸν Μάριον. ἡ μὲν οὖν ἔχθρα βραχεῖαν
οὕτω καὶ μειρακιώδη λαβοῦσα τὴν πρώτην ὑπόθεσιν καὶ ἀρχήν, εἶτα χωροῦσα δι' αἵματος
ἐμφυλίου καὶ στάσεων ἀνηκέστων ἐπὶ τυραννίδα
καὶ σύγχυσιν ἁπάντων πραγμάτων, ἀπέδειξε τὸν
Εὐριπίδην σοφὸν ἄνδρα καὶ πολιτικῶν ἐπιστή-
μονα νοσημάτων, διακελευσάμενον φυλάττεσθαι
τὴν φιλοτιμίαν ὡς ὀλεθριωτάτην καὶ κακίστην
δαίμονα τοῖς χρωμένοις.²

V. Ὁ δὲ Σύλλας οἰόμενος αὐτῷ τὴν ἀπὸ τῶν
πολεμικῶν δόξαν ἐπὶ τὰς πολιτικὰς πράξεις διαρ-
κεῖν, καὶ δοὺς ἑαυτὸν ἀπὸ τῆς στρατείας εὐθὺς ἐπὶ
τὴν τοῦ δήμου πρᾶξιν, ἐπὶ στρατηγίαν πολιτικὴν
ἀπεγράψατο καὶ διεψεύσθη· τὴν δ' αἰτίαν τοῖς
ὄχλοις ἀνατίθησι. φησὶ γὰρ αὐτοὺς τὴν πρὸς
Βόκχον εἰδότας φιλίαν, καὶ προσδεχομένους, εἰ
πρὸ τῆς στρατηγίας ἀγορανομοίη, κυνηγέσια λαμ-

---

¹ In his *Memoirs*. Cf. chapter vi. 5.
² *Phoenissae*, 532 ff. (Kirchhoff).

him for these successes, and that he was no longer
glad to give him opportunities for action, but
opposed his advancement, he attached himself to
Catulus, the colleague of Marius in the consulship, a
worthy man, but too sluggish for arduous contests.
By him he was entrusted with the leading and most
important enterprises, and rose to power and fame.
He not only subdued in war a large part of the
Barbarians of the Alps, but when provisions ran low,
he undertook the task of furnishing them, and made
them so abundant that the soldiers of Catulus lived
in plenty, and had some to spare for those of Marius.
At this, as Sulla himself says,[1] Marius was greatly
distressed.   So slight and puerile were the first
foundations and occasions of that hatred between
them, which afterwards led them through civil
bloodshed and irreparable discords to tyranny and
the confusion of the whole state.   This proved that
Euripides was a wise man, and acquainted with the
distempers of civil government, when he exhorted
men to beware of ambition as a deity most injurious
and fatal to its votaries.[2]

V. Sulla now thought that the reputation which
he had won in war was sufficient to justify political
activities, and therefore at once exchanged military
service for public life,[3] offered himself as a candidate
for the city praetorship, and was defeated.   The
responsibility for his defeat, however, he lays upon
the populace.   They knew, he says, about his
friendship with Bocchus, and expected that if he
should be made aedile before his praetorship, he
would treat them to splendid hunting scenes and

[3] He returned to Rome in 101 B.C., and was elected praetor
in 93 B.C.

πρὰ καὶ Λιβυκῶν θηρίων ἀγῶνας, ἑτέρους ἀποδεῖξαι στρατηγοὺς ὡς αὐτὸν ἀγορανομεῖν ἀναγκά-
2 σοντας. ἔοικε δὲ τὴν ἀληθῆ τῆς ἀποτεύξεως
αἰτίαν οὐχ ὁμολογῶν ὁ Σύλλας ἐλέγχεσθαι τοῖς
πράγμασιν. ἐνιαυτῷ γὰρ κατόπιν ἔτυχε τῆς
στρατηγίας, τοῦ δήμου τὸ μέν τι θεραπείᾳ, τὸ δὲ
καὶ χρήμασι προσαγαγόμενος. διὸ δὴ καὶ στρατηγοῦντος αὐτοῦ, καὶ πρὸς Καίσαρα μετ' ὀργῆς
εἰπόντος ὡς χρήσεται τῇ ἰδίᾳ πρὸς αὐτὸν ἐξουσίᾳ,
γελάσας ὁ Καῖσαρ, "Ὀρθῶς," ἔφη, "τὴν ἀρχὴν
ἰδίαν νομίζεις· ἔχεις γὰρ αὐτὴν πριάμενος."

3 Μετὰ δὲ τὴν στρατηγίαν εἰς τὴν Καππαδοκίαν
ἀποστέλλεται, τὸν μὲν ἐμφανῆ λόγον ἔχων πρὸς
τὴν στρατείαν Ἀριοβαρζάνην καταγαγεῖν, αἰτίαν
δὲ ἀληθῆ Μιθριδάτην ἐπισχεῖν πολυπραγ-
μονοῦντα καὶ περιβαλλόμενον ἀρχὴν καὶ δύναμιν
οὐκ ἐλάττονα τῆς ὑπαρχούσης. ἰδίαν μὲν οὖν
δύναμιν οὐ πολλὴν ἐπήγετο, χρησάμενος δὲ τοῖς
συμμάχοις προθύμοις, καὶ πολλοὺς μὲν αὐτῶν
Καππαδοκῶν, πλείονας δ' αὖθις Ἀρμενίων προσ-
βοηθοῦντας ἀποκτείνας, Γόρδιον μὲν ἐξήλασεν,
Ἀριοβαρζάνην δὲ ἀπέδειξε βασιλέα.

4 Διατρίβοντι δὲ αὐτῷ παρὰ τὸν Εὐφράτην
ἐντυγχάνει Πάρθος Ὀρόβαζος, Ἀρσάκου βασιλέως πρεσβευτής, οὔπω πρότερον ἀλλήλοις ἐπι-
μεμιγμένων τῶν γενῶν· ἀλλὰ καὶ τοῦτο τῆς με-
γάλης δοκεῖ Σύλλα τύχης γενέσθαι, τὸ πρώτῳ
Ῥωμαίων ἐκείνῳ Πάρθους συμμαχίας καὶ φιλίας
δεομένους διὰ λόγων ἐλθεῖν. ὅτε καὶ λέγεται

334

combats of Libyan wild beasts, and therefore appointed others to the praetorship, in order to force him into the aedileship. But subsequent events would seem to show that Sulla does not confess the real reason for his failure. For in the following year he obtained the praetorship, partly because he was subservient to the people, and partly because he used money to win their support. And so it happened that, during his praetorship, when he angrily told Caesar[1] that he would use his own authority against him, Caesar laughed and said: "You do well to consider the office your own, for you bought it."

After his praetorship, he was sent out to Cappadocia, ostensibly to reinstate Ariobarzanes, but really to check the restless activities of Mithridates, who was adding to his dominion and power fully as much as he had inherited. Accordingly, he took out with him no large force of his own, but made use of the allies, whom he found eager to serve him, and after slaying many of the Cappadocians themselves, and yet more of the Armenians who came to their aid, he drove out Gordius, and made Ariobarzanes king again.

As he lingered on the banks of the Euphrates, he received a visit from Orobazus, a Parthian, who came as an ambassador from king Arsaces, although up to this time the two nations had held no intercourse with one another. This also is thought to have been part of Sulla's great good fortune, that he should be the first Roman with whom the Parthians held conference when they wanted alliance and friendship

[1] Not the dictator, who was only seven years old at this time.

τρεῖς δίφρους προθέμενος, τὸν μὲν Ἀριοβαρζάνῃ,
τὸν δὲ Ὀροβάζῳ, τὸν δὲ αὑτῷ, μέσος ἀμφοῖν
5 καθεζόμενος χρηματίζειν. ἐφ' ᾧ τὸν μὲν Ὀρο-
βάζον ὕστερον ὁ τῶν Πάρθων βασιλεὺς ἀπέ-
κτεινε, τὸν δὲ Σύλλαν οἱ μὲν ἐπῄνεσαν ἐντρυφή-
σαντα τοῖς βαρβάροις, οἱ δὲ ὡς φορτικὸν
ᾐτιάσαντο καὶ ἀκαίρως φιλότιμον. ἱστορεῖται δέ
τις ἀνὴρ τῶν μετὰ Ὀροβάζου καταβεβηκότων,
Χαλδαῖος, εἰς τὸ τοῦ Σύλλα πρόσωπον ἀπιδὼν
καὶ ταῖς κινήσεσι τῆς τε διανοίας καὶ τοῦ σώμα-
6 τος οὐ παρέργως ἐπιστήσας, ἀλλὰ πρὸς τὰς τῆς
τέχνης ὑποθέσεις τὴν φύσιν ἐπισκεψάμενος,
εἰπεῖν ὡς ἀναγκαῖον εἴη τοῦτον τὸν ἄνδρα μέγιστον γενέσθαι, θαυμάζειν δὲ καὶ νῦν πῶς ἀνέχεται
μὴ πρῶτος ὢν ἁπάντων. ἀναχωρήσαντι δὲ αὐτῷ
δίκην ἔλαχε δώρων Κηνσωρῖνος, ὡς πολλὰ χρήματα συνειλοχότι παρὰ τὸν νόμον ἐκ φίλης καὶ
συμμάχου βασιλείας. οὐ μὴν ἀπήντησεν ἐπὶ τὴν
κρίσιν, ἀλλ' ἀπέστη τῆς κατηγορίας.

VI. Ἡ μέντοι πρὸς Μάριον αὐτῷ στάσις ἀνερ-
ριπίζετο καινὴν ὑπόθεσιν λαβοῦσα τὴν Βόκχου
φιλοτιμίαν, ὃς τόν τε δῆμον ἅμα θεραπεύων ἐν
Ῥώμῃ καὶ τῷ Σύλλᾳ χαριζόμενος ἀνέθηκε εἰκόνας[1]
ἐν Καπιτωλίῳ τροπαιοφόρους καὶ παρ' αὐταῖς
χρυσοῦν Ἰογόρθαν ὑφ' ἑαυτοῦ Σύλλᾳ παραδιδό-
2 μενον. ἐφ' ᾧ τοῦ Μαρίου βαρυθυμουμένου καὶ
καθαιρεῖν ἐπιχειροῦντος, ἑτέρων δὲ ἀμύνειν τῷ
Σύλλᾳ, καὶ τῆς πόλεως ὅσον οὔπω διακεκαυμένης
ὑπ' ἀμφοῖν, ὁ συμμαχικὸς πόλεμος πάλαι τυφό-

---

[1] εἰκόνας Coraës, Sintenis[1], and Bekker, with the MSS.
Sintenis[2] adopts Cobet's correction to Νίκας (*Victories*), to
agree with *Marius*, xxxii. 2.

On this occasion, too, it is said that he ordered three chairs to be set, one for Ariobarzanes, one for Orobazus, and one for himself, and that he sat between them both and gave them audience. For this the king of Parthia afterwards put Orobazus to death ; and while some people commended Sulla for the airs which he assumed with the Barbarians, others accused him of vulgarity and ill-timed arrogance. It is also recorded that a certain man in the retinue of Orobazus, a Chaldaean, after looking Sulla intently in the face, and studying carefully the movements of his mind and body, and investigating his nature according to the principles of his peculiar art, declared that this man must of necessity become the greatest in the world, and that even now the wonder was that he consented not to be first of all men. When Sulla came back to Rome, however, Censorinus brought suit against him for bribery, alleging that he had collected large sums of money illegally from a friendly and allied kingdom. However, Censorinus did not put in an appearance at the trial, but dropped his impeachment.

VI. Moreover, Sulla's quarrel with Marius broke out afresh on being supplied with fresh material by the ambition of Bocchus, who, desiring to please the people at Rome, and at the same time to gratify Sulla, dedicated on the Capitol some images bearing trophies, and beside them gilded figures representing Jugurtha being surrendered by Bocchus to Sulla. Thereupon Marius was very angry, and tried to have the figures taken down, but others were minded to aid Sulla in opposing this, and the city was all but in flames with their dispute, when the Social war,[1]

---

[1] 90–89 B.C., following the revolt of Rome's Italian allies.

μενος ἐπὶ τὴν πόλιν ἀναλάμψας τότε τὴν στάσιν
ἐπέσχεν. ἐν τούτῳ, μεγίστῳ καὶ ποικιλωτάτῳ
γενομένῳ καὶ πλεῖστα κακὰ καὶ βαρυτάτους
παρασχόντι κινδύνους Ῥωμαίοις, Μάριος μὲν
οὐδὲν ἀποδεῖξαι μέγα δυνηθεὶς ἤλεγχε τὴν πολε-
μικὴν ἀρετὴν ἀκμῆς καὶ ῥώμης δεομένην, Σύλλας
δὲ πολλὰ δράσας ἄξια λόγου δόξαν ἔσχεν ἡγεμόνος μεγάλου μὲν παρὰ τοῖς πολίταις, μεγίστου
δὲ παρὰ τοῖς φίλοις, εὐτυχεστάτου δὲ καὶ παρὰ
3 τοῖς ἐχθροῖς. ἀλλ᾽ οὐκ ἔπαθε ταὐτὸ Τιμοθέῳ τῷ
τοῦ Κόνωνος, ὅς, εἰς τὴν τύχην αὐτοῦ τὰ κατορ-
θώματα τῶν ἐχθρῶν τιθεμένων καὶ γραφόντων ἐν
πίναξι κοιμώμενον ἐκεῖνον, τὴν δὲ Τύχην δικτύῳ
τὰς πόλεις περιβάλλουσαν, ἀγροικιζόμενος καὶ
χαλεπαίνων πρὸς τοὺς ταῦτα ποιοῦντας ὡς ἀπο-
στερούμενος ὑπ᾽ αὐτῶν τῆς ἐπὶ ταῖς πράξεσι δόξης,
ἔφη ποτὲ πρὸς τὸν δῆμον, ἐπανήκων ἐκ στρατείας
εὖ κεχωρηκέναι δοκούσης, "Ἀλλὰ ταύτης γε
τῆς στρατείας οὐδέν, ἄνδρες Ἀθηναῖοι, τῇ τύχῃ
4 μέτεστι." πρὸς Τιμόθεον μὲν οὖν φασιν οὕτω
φανέντα φιλότιμον ἀντιμειρακιεύεσθαι τὸ δαιμόνιον, ὥστε μηδὲν ἔτι πρᾶξαι λαμπρόν, ἀλλὰ ὅλως
ἀποτυγχάνοντα ταῖς πράξεσι καὶ προσκρούοντα
τῷ δήμῳ τέλος ἐκπεσεῖν τῆς πόλεως· Σύλλας δὲ
οὐ μόνον ἡδέως προσιέμενος τὸν τοιοῦτον εὐδαι-
μονισμὸν καὶ ζῆλον, ἀλλὰ καὶ συναύξων καὶ
συνεπιθειάζων τὰ πραττόμενα, τῆς τύχης ἐξῆ-
πτεν, εἴτε κόμπῳ χρώμενος εἴθ᾽ οὕτως ἔχων τῇ
5 δόξῃ πρὸς τὸ θεῖον. καὶ γὰρ ἐν τοῖς ὑπομνήμασι

which had long been smouldering, blazed up against the city and put a stop for the time being to the quarrel. In this war, which proved of the greatest moment and most varied fortunes, and brought innumerable mischiefs and the gravest perils upon the Romans, Marius was unable to render any great service, and proved that military excellence requires a man's highest strength and vigour. Sulla, on the other hand, did much that was memorable, and achieved the reputation of a great leader among his fellow-citizens, that of the greatest of leaders among his friends, and that of the most fortunate even among his enemies. But he did not feel about this as Timotheus the son of Conon did, who, when his adversaries ascribed his successes to Fortune, and had him represented in a painting as lying asleep, while Fortune cast her net about the cities, was rudely angry with those who had done this, because, as he thought, they were robbing him of the glory due to his exploits, and said to the people once, on returning from a campaign in which he was thought to have been successful: " In this campaign, at least, men of Athens, Fortune has no share." Upon Timotheus, then, who had shown himself so covetous of honour, the deity is said to have requited his youthful petulance, so that from that time on he did nothing brilliant, but miscarried in all his undertakings, gave offence to the people, and was finally banished the city ; whereas Sulla not only accepted with pleasure such felicitations and admiration, but actually joined in magnifying the aid of Heaven in what he did, and gave the credit of it to Fortune, either out of boastfulness, or because he had such a belief in the divine agency. For in his Memoirs he writes

γέγραφεν ὅτι τῶν καλῶς αὐτῷ βεβουλεῦσθαι
δοκούντων αἱ μὴ κατὰ γνώμην, ἀλλὰ πρὸς καιρὸν
ἀποτολμώμεναι πράξεις ἔπιπτον εἰς ἄμεινον. ἔτι
δὲ καὶ δι' ὧν φησι πρὸς τύχην εὖ πεφυκέναι μᾶλλον ἢ πρὸς πόλεμον, τῇ τύχῃ τῆς ἀρετῆς πλέον
ἔοικε νέμειν καὶ ὅλως ἑαυτὸν τοῦ δαίμονος ποιεῖν,
ὅς γε καὶ τῆς πρὸς Μέτελλον ὁμονοίας, ἰσότιμον
ἄνδρα καὶ κηδεστήν, εὐτυχίαν τινὰ θείαν αἰτιᾶται·
πολλὰ γὰρ αὐτῷ πράγματα παρέξειν ἐπίδοξον
ὄντα πρᾳότατον ἐν τῇ κοινωνίᾳ γενέσθαι τῆς
6 ἀρχῆς. ἔτι δὲ Λευκόλλῳ μὲν ἐν τοῖς ὑπομνήμασιν, ὧν ἐκείνῳ τὴν γραφὴν ἀνατέθεικε, παραινεῖ
μηδὲν οὕτως ἡγεῖσθαι βέβαιον ὡς ὅ τι ἂν αὐτῷ
προστάξῃ νύκτωρ τὸ δαιμόνιον. ἐκπεμπομένου
δὲ αὐτοῦ μετὰ δυνάμεως εἰς τὸν συμμαχικὸν
πόλεμον ἱστορεῖ χάσμα τῆς γῆς μέγα γενέσθαι
περὶ Λαβέρνην· ἐκ δὲ τούτου πῦρ ἀναβλῦσαι
πολὺ καὶ φλόγα λαμπρὰν στηρίσαι πρὸς τὸν
7 οὐρανόν. εἰπεῖν δὴ καὶ τοὺς μάντεις ὡς ἀνὴρ
ἀγαθὸς ὄψει διάφορος καὶ περιττὸς ἄρξας ἀπαλ-
λάξει τῇ πόλει ταραχὰς τὰς παρούσας. τοῦτον
δὲ αὐτὸν εἶναί φησιν ὁ Σύλλας· τῆς μὲν γὰρ
ὄψεως ἴδιον εἶναι τὸ περὶ τὴν κόμην χρυσωπόν,
ἀρετὴν δὲ οὐκ αἰσχύνεσθαι μαρτυρῶν ἑαυτῷ μετὰ
πράξεις καλὰς οὕτω καὶ μεγάλας. ταῦτα μὲν
οὖν περὶ τῆς θειότητος.

Τὸν δὲ ἄλλον τρόπον ἀνώμαλός τις ἔοικε
γεγονέναι καὶ διάφορος πρὸς ἑαυτόν, ἀφελέσθαι
πολλά, χαρίσασθαι πλείονα, τιμῆσαι παραλόγως, 45
παραλόγως ἐφυβρίσαι, θεραπεύειν ὧν δέοιτο,

that, of the undertakings which men thought well-advised, those upon which he had boldly ventured, not after deliberation, but on the spur of the moment, turned out for the better. And further, from what he says about his being well endowed by nature for Fortune rather than for war, he seems to attribute more to Fortune than to his own excellence, and to make himself entirely the creature of this deity, since he accounts even his concord with Metellus, a man his equal in rank, and a relative by marriage, a piece of divine felicity; for whereas he expected much annoyance from him as a colleague in office, he found him most obliging. And still further, in the dedication of his Memoirs to Lucullus, he advises him to deem nothing so secure as what the divine power enjoins upon him in his dreams. And he relates that when he was dispatched with an army to the Social war, a great chasm in the earth opened near Laverna, from which a great quantity of fire burst forth and a bright flame towered up towards the heavens; whereupon the soothsayers declared that a brave man, of rare courage and surpassing appearance, was to take the government in hand and free the city from its present troubles. And Sulla says that he himself was this man, for his golden head of hair gave him a singular appearance, and as for bravery, he was not ashamed to testify in his own behalf, after such great and noble deeds as he had performed. So much, then, regarding his attitude towards the divine powers.

In other respects he seems to have been of very uneven character, and at variance with himself; he robbed much, but gave more; bestowed his honours unexpectedly, as unexpectedly his insults; fawned on

θρύπτεσθαι πρὸς τοὺς δεομένους, ὥστε ἀγνοεῖσθαι
πότερον ὑπερόπτης φύσει μᾶλλον ἢ κόλαξ γέγονε.
8 τὴν μὲν γὰρ ἐν ταῖς τιμωρίαις ἀνωμαλίαν, ἐξ ὧν
ἔτυχεν αἰτιῶν ἀποτυμπανίζοντος αὐτοῦ καὶ πάλιν
τὰ μέγιστα τῶν ἀδικημάτων πράως φέροντος,
καὶ διαλλαττομένου μὲν ἐπὶ τοῖς ἀνηκέστοις μετὰ
εὐκολίας, τὰ δὲ μικρὰ καὶ φαῦλα προσκρούσματα
σφαγαῖς καὶ δημεύσεσιν οὐσιῶν μετιόντος, οὕτως
ἄν τις διαιτήσειεν ὡς φύσει μὲν ὀργὴν χαλεπὸν
ὄντα καὶ τιμωρητικόν, ὑφιέμενον δὲ τῆς πικρίας
9 λογισμῷ πρὸς τὸ συμφέρον. ἐν αὐτῷ γε τούτῳ
τῷ συμμαχικῷ πολέμῳ τῶν στρατιωτῶν αὐτοῦ
στρατηγικὸν ἄνδρα πρεσβευτήν, Ἀλβῖνον ὄνομα,
ξύλοις καὶ λίθοις διαχρησαμένων, παρῆλθε καὶ
οὐκ ἐπεξῆλθεν ἀδίκημα τοσοῦτον, ἀλλὰ καὶ
σεμνυνόμενος διεδίδου λόγον ὡς προθυμοτέροις
διὰ τοῦτο χρήσοιτο πρὸς τὸν πόλεμον αὐτοῖς
ἰωμένοις τὸ ἁμάρτημα δι' ἀνδραγαθίας. τῶν δ'
ἐγκαλούντων οὐδὲν ἐφρόντιζεν, ἀλλὰ ἤδη καταλῦ-
σαι Μάριον διανοούμενος καὶ τοῦ πρὸς τοὺς συμμάχους πολέμου τέλος ἔχειν δοκοῦντος ἀποδει-
χθῆναι στρατηγὸς ἐπὶ Μιθριδάτην, ἐθεράπευε τὴν
ὑφ' ἑαυτῷ στρατιάν.
10   Καὶ παρελθὼν εἰς τὴν πόλιν ὕπατος μὲν ἀποδείκνυται μετὰ Κοΐντου Πομπηΐου, πεντήκοντα
ἔτη γεγονώς, γαμεῖ δὲ γάμον ἐνδοξότατον Και-
κιλίαν τὴν Μετέλλου θυγατέρα τοῦ ἀρχιερέως.
ἐφ' ᾧ πολλὰ μὲν εἰς αὐτὸν ᾖδον οἱ δημοτικοί,
πολλοὶ δὲ τῶν πρώτων ἐνεμέσων, οὐκ ἄξιον
ἡγούμενοι τῆς γυναικὸς ὃν ἄξιον ὑπατείας ἔκριναν,

---

[1] In 88 B.C.
[2] In the seventy-seventh, one of the lost books.

those he needed, but gave himself airs towards those
who needed him; so that one cannot tell whether
he was more inclined by nature to disdain or flattery.
For as regards the irregularity of his punishments,
cudgelling to death as he did on any chance grounds,
and again gently submitting to the greatest wrongs;
readily open to reconciliation after the most irreparable injuries, but visiting small and insignificant
offences with death and confiscation of goods; here
one might decide that he was naturally of a stern
and revengeful temper, but relaxed his severity out
of calculating regard for his interests. In this very
Social war, for example, when his soldiers with clubs
and stones did to death a legate, a man of praetorian
dignity, Albinus by name, he passed over without
punishment this flagrant crime, and solemnly passed
the word about that he would find his men more ready
and willing for the war on account of this transgression,
since they would try to atone for it by their bravery.
To those who censured the crime he paid no heed,
but purposing already to put down the power of
Marius and, now that the Social war was thought
to be at an end, to get himself appointed general
against Mithridates, he treated the soldiers under
him with deference.

When he returned to the city, he was appointed
consul with Quintus Pompeius,[1] in the fiftieth year
of his age, and made a most illustrious marriage with
Caecilia, the daughter of Metellus, the Pontifex
Maximus. On the theme of this marriage many
verses were sung in ridicule of him by the common
people, and many of the leading men were indignant
at it, deeming him, as Livy says,[2] unworthy of the
woman although they had judged him worthy of the

11 ὥς φησιν ὁ Τίτος. οὐ μόνην δὲ ταύτην ἔγημεν,
ἀλλὰ πρώτην μὲν ἔτι μειράκιον ὢν Ἰλίαν ἔσχε
τὴν καὶ θυγάτριον αὐτῷ τεκοῦσαν, εἶτα μετ'
ἐκείνην Αἰλίαν· τρίτην δὲ Κλοιλίαν, ἣν ἀπεπέμ-
ψατο μὲν ὡς στεῖραν ἐντίμως καὶ μετ' εὐφημίας
καὶ δῶρα προσθείς, ὀλίγαις δὲ ὕστερον ἡμέραις
ἀγαγόμενος τὴν Μετέλλαν ἔδοξε διὰ τοῦτο τὴν
12 Κλοιλίαν οὐ καλῶς αἰτιάσασθαι. τὴν μέντοι
Μετέλλαν ἐν πᾶσι θεραπεύων διετέλεσεν, ὥστε
καὶ τὸν Ῥωμαίων δῆμον, ὅτε τοὺς περὶ Μάριον
φυγάδας ἐπεθύμει καταγαγεῖν, ἀρνουμένου τοῦ
Σύλλα, δεόμενον ἐπιβοήσασθαι τὴν Μετέλλαν.
ἐδόκει δὲ καὶ τοῖς Ἀθηναίοις ἑλὼν τὸ ἄστυ προσ-
ενεχθῆναι τραχύτερον, ὅτι τὴν Μετέλλαν ἀπὸ
τοῦ τείχους γεφυρίζοντες ἐλοιδόρησαν. ἀλλὰ
ταῦτα μὲν ὕστερον.

VII. Τότε δὲ τὴν ὑπατείαν πρὸς τὰ μέλλοντα
μικρὸν ἡγούμενος, ἐπτόητο τῇ γνώμῃ πρὸς τὸν
Μιθριδατικὸν πόλεμον. ἀντανίστατο δὲ αὐτῷ
Μάριος ὑπὸ δοξομανίας καὶ φιλοτιμίας, ἀγηράτων
παθῶν, ἀνὴρ τῷ τε σώματι βαρὺς καὶ ταῖς
ἔναγχος ἀπειρηκὼς στρατείαις διὰ γῆρας ἐκδήμων
2 καὶ διαποντίων πολέμων ἐφιέμενος. καὶ τοῦ
Σύλλα πρὸς τὰς ἐπιλιπεῖς πράξεις ὁρμήσαντος
εἰς τὸ στρατόπεδον, αὐτὸς οἰκουρῶν ἐτεκταίνετο
τὴν ὀλεθριωτάτην ἐκείνην καὶ ὅσα σύμπαντες οἱ
πόλεμοι τὴν Ῥώμην οὐκ ἔβλαψαν ἀπεργασα-
μένην στάσιν, ὡς καὶ τὸ δαιμόνιον αὐτοῖς προεσή-
μηνε. πῦρ μὲν γὰρ αὐτόματον ἐκ τῶν τὰ σημεῖα

consulship. And this was not the only woman whom he married, but first, when he was still a stripling, he took Ilia to wife, and she bore him a daughter; then Aelia, after her; and thirdly, Cloelia, whom he divorced for barrenness, honourably, and with words of praise, to which he added gifts. But since he married Metella only a few days afterwards, he was thought to have accused Cloelia unfairly. To Metella, however, he always showed great deference in all things, so that the Roman people, when it longed for the restoration of the exiled partisans of Marius, and Sulla refused it, in its need called upon Metella for aid. It was thought also that when he took the city of Athens, he treated its people more harshly because they had scurrilously abused Metella from the walls. But this was later.[1]

VII. At the time of which I speak, deeming the consulship a slight matter in comparison with things to come, his thoughts soared to the Mithridatic war. But here he found a rival in Marius, who was possessed by ambition and a mad desire for fame, those never ageing passions. He was now unwieldy in body, and in the recent campaigns had given up service on account of his age, and yet set his heart upon foreign wars beyond the seas. And when Sulla had set out for his camp on unfinished business,[2] he himself kept at home and contrived that most fatal sedition, which wrought Rome more harm than all her wars together had done, as indeed the heavenly powers foreshowed to them. For fire broke forth of its own accord from the staves which supported

---

[1] Cf. chapter xiii. 1.
[2] Sulla was occupied with the siege of Nola, in Campania.

δοράτων ὑποφερόντων ἀνέλαμψε καὶ κατεσβέσθη
μόλις, κόρακες δὲ τρεῖς τοὺς νεοσσοὺς εἰς τὴν
ὁδὸν προαγαγόντες κατέφαγον, τὰ δὲ λείψανα
3 πάλιν εἰς τὴν νεοσσιὰν ἀνήνεγκαν. καὶ μυῶν δὲ
ἐν ἱερῷ χρυσὸν ἀνακείμενον διαφαγόντων μίαν οἱ
ζάκοροι πάγῃ θήλειαν λαμβάνουσιν, ἡ δὲ ἐν αὐτῇ
τῇ πάγῃ τεκοῦσα πέντε καταναλωσε τὰ τρία. τὸ
δὲ πάντων μέγιστον, ἐξ ἀνεφέλου καὶ διαίθρου
τοῦ περιέχοντος ἤχησε φωνὴ σάλπιγγος ὀξὺν
ἀποτείνουσα καὶ θρηνώδη φθόγγον, ὥστε πάντας
ἔκφρονας γενέσθαι καὶ καταπτῆξαι διὰ τὸ μέγε-   456
θος. Τυρρηνῶν δὲ οἱ λόγιοι μεταβολὴν ἑτέρου
γένους ἀπεφαίνοντο καὶ μετακόσμησιν ἀποσημαί-
4 νειν τὸ τέρας. εἶναι μὲν γὰρ ὀκτὼ[1] τὰ σύμπαντα
γένη, διαφέροντα τοῖς βίοις καὶ τοῖς ἤθεσιν ἀλλήλων, ἑκάστῳ δὲ ἀφωρίσθαι χρόνων ἀριθμὸν ὑπὸ
τοῦ θεοῦ συμπεραινόμενον ἐνιαυτοῦ μεγάλου
περιόδῳ. καὶ ὅταν αὕτη σχῇ τέλος, ἑτέρας
ἐνισταμένης κινεῖσθαί τι σημεῖον ἐκ γῆς ἢ
οὐρανοῦ θαυμάσιον, ὡς δῆλον εἶναι τοῖς πεφρον-
τικόσι τὰ τοιαῦτα καὶ μεμαθηκόσιν εὐθὺς ὅτι καὶ
τρόποις ἄλλοις καὶ βίοις ἄνθρωποι χρώμενοι
γεγόνασι, καὶ θεοῖς ἧττον ἢ μᾶλλον τῶν προ-
5 τέρων μέλοντες. τά τε γὰρ ἄλλα φασὶν ἐν τῇ
τῶν γενῶν ἀμείψει λαμβάνειν μεγάλας καινοτομίας, καὶ τὴν μαντικὴν ποτὲ μὲν αὔξεσθαι τῇ
τιμῇ καὶ κατατυγχάνειν ταῖς προαγορεύσεσι,
καθαρὰ καὶ φανερὰ σημεῖα τοῦ δαιμονίου προπέμ-
ποντος, αὖθις δ' ἐν ἑτέρῳ γένει ταπεινὰ πράττειν,
αὐτοσχέδιον οὖσαν τὰ πολλὰ καὶ δι' ἀμυδρῶν

---

[1] ὀκτὼ before this word Sintenis[2] reads ἀνθρώπων, after
Suidas.

the ensigns, and was with difficulty extinguished;
and three ravens brought their young forth into the
street and devoured them, and then carried the
remains back again into their nest; and after mice
had gnawed consecrated gold in a temple, the
keepers caught one of them, a female, in a trap,
and in the very trap she brought forth five young
ones, and ate up three of them. But most important of all, out of a cloudless and clear air there
rang out the voice of a trumpet, prolonging a shrill
and dismal note, so that all were amazed and
terrified at its loudness. The Tuscan wise men
declared that the prodigy foretokened a change of
conditions and the advent of a new age. For
according to them there are eight ages in all,
differing from one another in the lives and customs
of men, and to each of these God has appointed a
definite number of times and seasons, which is
completed by the circuit of a great year. And
whenever this circuit has run out, and another
begins, some wonderful sign is sent from earth or
heaven, so that it is at once clear to those who
have studied such subjects and are versed in them,
that men of other habits and modes of life have
come into the world, who are either more or less
of concern to the gods than their predecessors
were. All things, they say, undergo great changes,
as one age succeeds another, and especially the art
of divination; at one period it rises in esteem and
is successful in its predictions, because manifest and
genuine signs are sent forth from the Deity; and
again, in another age, it is in small repute, being
off-hand, for the most part, and seeking to grasp

καὶ σκοτεινῶν ὀργάνων τοῦ μέλλοντος ἁπτομένην.
ταῦτα μὲν οὖν οἱ λογιώτατοι Τυρρηνῶν καὶ πλέον
6 τι τῶν ἄλλων εἰδέναι δοκοῦντες ἐμυθολόγουν. τῆς
δὲ συγκλήτου τοῖς μάντεσι περὶ τούτων σχολα-
ζούσης καὶ καθημένης ἐν τῷ ναῷ τῆς Ἐννοῦς,
στρουθὸς εἰσέπτη πάντων ὁρώντων τέττιγα φέρων
τῷ στόματι, καὶ τὸ μὲν ἐκβαλὼν μέρος αὐτοῦ
κατέλιπε, τὸ δὲ ἔχων ἀπῆλθεν. ὑφεωρῶντο δὴ
στάσιν οἱ τερατοσκόποι καὶ διαφορὰν τῶν κτη-
ματικῶν πρὸς τὸν ἀστικὸν ὄχλον καὶ ἀγοραῖον·
φωνάεντα γὰρ τοῦτον εἶναι καθάπερ τέττιγα,
τοὺς δὲ χωρίτας ἀρουραίους.

VIII. Μάριος δὴ προσλαμβάνει δημαρχοῦντα
Σουλπίκιον, ἄνθρωπον οὐδενὸς δεύτερον ἐν ταῖς
ἄκραις κακίαις, ὥστε μὴ ζητεῖν τίνος ἐστὶν ἑτέρου
μοχθηρότερος, ἀλλὰ πρὸς τί μοχθηρότατος ἑαυτοῦ. καὶ γὰρ ὠμότης καὶ τόλμα καὶ πλεονεξία
περὶ αὐτὸν ἦν ἀπερίσκεπτος αἰσχροῦ καὶ παντὸς
κακοῦ, ὅς γε τὴν Ῥωμαίων πολιτείαν ἐξελευ-
θερικοῖς καὶ μετοίκοις πωλῶν ἀναφανδὸν ἠρίθμει
2 τιμὴν διὰ τραπέζης ἐν ἀγορᾷ κειμένης. ἔτρεφε δὲ
τρισχιλίους μαχαιροφόρους, καὶ πλῆθος ἱππικῶν
νεανίσκων πρὸς ἅπαν ἑτοίμων περὶ αὐτὸν εἶχεν,
οὓς ἀντισύγκλητον ὠνόμαζε. νόμον δὲ κυρώσας
μηδένα συγκλητικὸν ὑπὲρ δισχιλίας δραχμὰς
ὀφείλειν, αὐτὸς ἀπέλιπε μετὰ τὴν τελευτὴν ὀφλή-
ματος μυριάδας τριακοσίας. οὗτος εἰς τὸν δῆμον
ἀφεθεὶς ὑπὸ τοῦ Μαρίου, καὶ συνταράξας πάντα

---

[1] The Greek of this sentence is acknowledged by all editors
to be corrupt.   The translation follows Coraës.

the future by means of faint and blind senses.
Such, at any rate, was the tale told by the wisest
of the Tuscans, who were thought to know much
more about it than the rest. Moreover, while
the senate was busied with the soothsayers about
these prodigies, and holding its session in the temple
of Bellona, a sparrow came flying in, before the eyes
of all, with a grasshopper in its mouth, a part of
which it threw down and left there, and then went
away with the other part. From this the diviners
apprehended a quarrelsome dissension between the
landed proprietors and the populace of the city and
forum; for the latter is vociferous like a grasshopper, while the former haunt the fields (like the
sparrow).[1]

VIII. Marius now made alliance with Sulpicius
who was a tribune of the people, a man second to
none in prime villainies, so that the question was
not whom else he surpassed in wickedness, but in
what he surpassed his own wickedness. For the
combination of cruelty, effrontery, and rapacity in
him was regardless of shame and of all evil, since
he sold the Roman citizenship to freedmen and
aliens at public sale, and counted out the price on
a money-table which stood in the forum. Moreover, he maintained three thousand swordsmen,
and had about him a body of young men of the
equestrian order who were ready for everything,
and whom he called his anti-senate. Further,
though he got a law passed that no senator should
incur a debt of more than two thousand drachmas,
he himself left behind him after death a debt of
three millions. This man was now let loose upon
the people by Marius, and after confounding all

τὰ πράγματα βίᾳ καὶ σιδήρῳ, νόμους ἔγραφεν
ἄλλους τε μοχθηροὺς καὶ τὸν διδόντα Μαρίῳ τοῦ
3 Μιθριδατικοῦ πολέμου τὴν ἡγεμονίαν. ἀπραξίας
δὲ διὰ ταῦτα τῶν ὑπάτων ψηφισαμένων, ἐπαγαγὼν αὐτοῖς ἐκκλησιάζουσι περὶ τὸν νεὼν τῶν
Διοσκούρων ὄχλον ἄλλους τε πολλοὺς καὶ τὸ
Πομπηΐου τοῦ ὑπάτου μειράκιον ἐπὶ τῆς ἀγορᾶς
ἀνεῖλεν· αὐτὸς δὲ Πομπήϊος λαθὼν ἐξέφυγε.
Σύλλας δὲ εἰς τὴν οἰκίαν τοῦ Μαρίου συνδιωχθεὶς
4 ἠναγκάσθη προελθὼν τὰς ἀπραξίας λῦσαι· καὶ διὰ
τοῦτο τὸν Πομπήϊον ἐπάρχοντα παύσας[1] ὁ Σουλπίκιος οὐκ ἀφείλετο τοῦ Σύλλα τὴν ὑπατείαν, ἀλλὰ
τὴν ἐπὶ Μιθριδάτην στρατείαν μόνον εἰς Μάριον
μετήνεγκε· καὶ πέμπει χιλιάρχους εὐθὺς εἰς
Νῶλαν παραληψομένους τὸ στράτευμα καὶ πρὸς
τὸν Μάριον ἄξοντας.

IX. Φθάσαντος δὲ τοῦ Σύλλα διαφυγεῖν εἰς τὸ
στρατόπεδον, καὶ τῶν στρατιωτῶν, ὡς ἐπύθοντο
ταῦτα, καταλευσάντων τοὺς χιλιάρχους, οἱ περὶ
τὸν Μάριον αὖθις ἐν τῇ πόλει τοὺς Σύλλα φίλους
ἀνῄρουν καὶ χρήματα διήρπαζον αὐτῶν. ἦσαν δὲ
μεταστάσεις καὶ φυγαί, τῶν μὲν εἰς πόλιν ἀπὸ
στρατοπέδου, τῶν δ᾽ ἐκεῖσε διαφοιτώντων ἐκ τῆς
2 πόλεως. ἡ δὲ σύγκλητος ἦν μὲν οὐχ αὑτῆς, ἀλλὰ
τοῖς Μαρίου καὶ Σουλπικίου διῳκεῖτο προστάγ-
μασι, πυθομένη δὲ τὸν Σύλλαν ἐπὶ τὴν πόλιν   457
ἐλαύνειν ἔπεμψε δύο τῶν στρατηγῶν, Βροῦτον
καὶ Σερουΐλιον, ἀπαγορεύσοντας αὐτῷ βαδίζειν.
τούτους θρασύτερον Σύλλᾳ διαλεχθέντας ὥρμησαν μὲν ἀνελεῖν οἱ στρατιῶται, τὰς δὲ ῥάβδους

---

[1] παύσας Coraës and Bekker, after Muretus : ποιήσας.

things by force and the sword, he proposed certain vicious laws, and particularly one offering to Marius the command in the Mithridatic war. To prevent voting on these, the consuls decreed suspension of public business, whereupon Sulpicius led a mob against them, as they were holding an assembly near the temple of Castor and Pollux, and, amongst many others, slew also the young son of Pompeius the consul in the forum; but Pompeius himself made his escape unnoticed. Sulla, however, after having been pursued into the house of Marius, was forced to come forth and rescind the decree for suspension of public business; and it was because he did this that Sulpicius, although he deposed Pompeius, did not take the consulship away from Sulla, but merely tansferred the expedition against Mithridates to the command of Marius. He also sent military tribunes at once to Nola, who were to take over the army there and conduct it to Marius.

IX. But Sulla succeeded in making his escape and reaching the camp first, and his soldiers, when they learned what had happened, stoned the tribunes to death; in return for which, Marius and his partisans in the city went to slaying the friends of Sulla and plundering their property. Then there were removals and flights, some passing continually from camp to city, and others from city to camp. The senate was not its own master, but was governed by the dictates of Marius and Sulpicius, and when it learned that Sulla was marching against the city, it sent two of the praetors, Brutus and Servilius, to forbid his advance. These men addressed Sulla with too much boldness, whereupon his soldiers

κατέκλασαν καὶ τὰς περιπορφύρους ἀφείλοντο
καὶ πολλὰ περιυβρισμένους ἀπέπεμψαν, αὐτόθεν τε δεινὴν κατήφειαν, ὁρωμένους τῶν στρατη-
γικῶν παρασήμων ἐρήμους, καὶ τὴν στάσιν οὐκέτι
καθεκτήν, ἀλλ' ἀνήκεστον ἀπαγγέλλοντας.

3   Οἱ μὲν οὖν περὶ τὸν Μάριον ἐν παρασκευαῖς
ἦσαν· ὁ δὲ Σύλλας ἄγων ἓξ τάγματα τέλεια μετὰ
τοῦ συνάρχοντος ἀπὸ Νώλης ἐκίνει, τὸν μὲν
στρατὸν ὁρῶν πρόθυμον ὄντα χωρεῖν εὐθὺς ἐπὶ
τὴν πόλιν, ἐνδοιάζων δὲ τῇ γνώμῃ παρ' ἑαυτῷ
καὶ δεδοικὼς τὸν κίνδυνον. ὁ δὲ μάντις Ποστού-
μιος θύσαντος αὐτοῦ καταμαθὼν τὰ σημεῖα, καὶ
τὰς χεῖρας ἀμφοτέρας τῷ Σύλλᾳ προτείνας, ἠξίου
δεθῆναι καὶ φυλάττεσθαι μέχρι τῆς μάχης, ὡς, εἰ
μὴ πάντα ταχὺ καὶ καλῶς αὐτῷ συντελεσθείη,
4   τὴν ἐσχάτην δίκην ὑποσχεῖν βουλόμενος. λέγεται δὲ καὶ κατὰ τοὺς ὕπνους αὐτῷ Σύλλᾳ φανῆναι θεὸν ἣν τιμῶσι Ῥωμαῖοι παρὰ Καππαδοκῶν
μαθόντες, εἴτε δὴ Σελήνην οὖσαν εἴτε Ἀθηνᾶν εἴτε
Ἐννώ. ταύτην ὁ Σύλλας ἔδοξεν ἐπιστᾶσαν ἐγχειρί-
σαι κεραυνὸν αὐτῷ, καὶ τῶν ἐχθρῶν ἕκαστον ὀνομά-
ζουσαν τῶν ἐκείνου βάλλειν κελεῦσαι, τοὺς δὲ
πίπτειν βαλλομένους καὶ ἀφανίζεσθαι. θαρσήσας
δὲ τῇ ὄψει καὶ φράσας τῷ συνάρχοντι μεθ' ἡμέραν
ἐπὶ τὴν Ῥώμην ἡγεῖτο.

5   Καὶ περὶ Πικτὰς αὐτῷ πρεσβείας ἐντυχούσης

---

[1] Plutarch must mean the "Great Mother," Cybele. Cf.
Themistocles, xxx. 1.

would have gladly torn them to pieces, but contented themselves with breaking their fasces, stripping them of their senatorial togas, insulting them in many ways, and then sending them back to the city. Here a terrible dejection was produced by the mere sight of them, stripped of their praetorial insignia, and by their announcement that the sedition could no longer be checked, but must run its course.

Marius and his partisans, then, busied themselves with preparations; while Sulla, at the head of six full legions, moved with his colleague from Nola, his army, as he saw, being eager to march at once against the city, although he himself wavered in his own mind, and feared the danger. But after he had offered a sacrifice, Postumius the soothsayer learned what the omens were, and stretching out both hands to Sulla, begged that he might be bound and kept a prisoner until the battle, assuring him that he was willing to undergo the extremest penalty if all things did not speedily come to a good issue for him. It is said, also, that to Sulla himself there appeared in his dreams a goddess whom the Romans learned to worship from the Cappadocians,[1] whether she is Luna, or Minerva, or Bellona. This goddess, as Sulla fancied, stood by his side and put into his hand a thunder-bolt, and naming his enemies one by one, bade him smite them with it; and they were all smitten, and fell, and vanished away. Encouraged by the vision, he told it to his colleague, and at break of day led on towards Rome.

When he had reached Pictae,[2] he was met by a

---

[2] A place of public entertainment a few miles south of Rome (Strabo, v. 3, 9). The name has been substituted for the Picinae of the best MS., about which nothing is known.

καὶ δεομένης μὴ βαδίζειν εὐθὺς ἐξ ἐφόδου, πάντα
γὰρ ἔσεσθαι τὰ δίκαια τῆς βουλῆς ψηφισαμένης,
ὡμολόγησε μὲν αὐτοῦ καταστρατοπεδεύσειν καὶ
διαμετρεῖν ἐκέλευε χώρας, ὥσπερ εἰώθει, τῷ
στρατοπέδῳ τοὺς ἡγεμόνας, ὥστε τοὺς πρέσβεις
ἀπελθεῖν πιστεύσαντας· ἐκείνων δὲ ἀπελθόντων
εὐθὺς ἐκπέμψας Λεύκιον Βάσιλλον καὶ Γάιον
Μόμμιον καταλαμβάνει τὴν πύλην δι' αὐτῶν καὶ
τὰ τείχη τὰ περὶ τὸν λόφον τὸν Αἰσκυλῖνον· εἶτ'
6 αὐτὸς ἁπάσῃ σπουδῇ συνῆπτε. τῶν δὲ περὶ τὸν
Βάσιλλον εἰς τὴν πόλιν ἐμπεσόντων καὶ κρατούντων, ὁ πολὺς καὶ ἄνοπλος δῆμος ἀπὸ τῶν τεγῶν
κεράμῳ καὶ λίθῳ βάλλοντες ἐπέσχον αὐτοὺς τοῦ
πρόσω χωρεῖν καὶ συνέστειλαν εἰς τὸ τεῖχος. ἐν
τούτῳ δὲ ὁ Σύλλας παρῆν ἤδη, καὶ συνιδὼν τὸ
γινόμενον ἐβόα τὰς οἰκίας ὑφάπτειν, καὶ λαβὼν
δᾷδα καιομένην ἐχώρει πρῶτος αὐτός, καὶ τοὺς
τοξότας ἐκέλευε χρῆσθαι τοῖς πυροβόλοις ἄνω τῶν
στεγασμάτων ἐφιεμένους, κατ' οὐδένα λογισμόν,
7 ἀλλ' ἐμπαθὴς ὢν καὶ τῷ θυμῷ παραδεδωκὼς τὴν
τῶν πρασσομένων ἡγεμονίαν, ὅς γε τοὺς ἐχθροὺς
μόνον ἑώρα, φίλους δὲ καὶ συγγενεῖς καὶ οἰκείους
εἰς οὐδένα λόγον θέμενος οὐδ' οἶκτον κατῄει διὰ
πυρός, ᾧ τῶν αἰτίων καὶ μὴ διάγνωσις οὐκ ἦν.
τούτων δὲ γινομένων Μάριος ἐξωσθεὶς πρὸς τὸ
τῆς Γῆς ἱερὸν ἐκάλει διὰ κηρύγματος ἐπ' ἐλευ-
θερίᾳ τὸ οἰκετικόν· ἐπελθόντων δὲ τῶν πολεμίων
κρατηθεὶς ἐξέπεσε τῆς πόλεως.

X. Σύλλας δὲ τὴν βουλὴν συναγαγὼν καταψη-
φίζεται θάνατον αὐτοῦ τε Μαρίου καὶ ὀλίγων

deputation from the city, which begged him not to advance to an immediate attack, since the senate had voted that he should have all his rights; he therefore agreed to encamp there, and ordered his officers to measure out the ground, as was usual, for the camp, so that the deputation returned to the city believing that he would do so. But no sooner were they gone than he sent forward Lucius Basillus and Caius Mummius, who seized for him the city-gate and the walls on the Esquiline hill; then he himself followed hard after them with all speed. Basillus and his men burst into the city and were forcing their way along, when the unarmed multitude pelted them with stones and tiles from the roofs of the houses, stopped their further progress, and crowded them back to the wall. But by this time Sulla was at hand, and seeing what was going on, shouted orders to set fire to the houses, and seizing a blazing torch, led the way himself, and ordered his archers to use their fire-bolts and shoot them up at the roofs. This he did not from any calm calculation, but in a passion, and having surrendered to his anger the command over his actions, since he thought only of his enemies, and without any regard or even pity for friends and kindred and relations, made his entry by the aid of fire, which made no distinction between the guilty and the innocent. Meanwhile Marius, who had been driven back to the temple of Tellus, made a proclamation calling the slaves to his support under promise of freedom; but the enemy coming on, he was overpowered and fled from the city.

X. Sulla now called together the senate, and had sentence of death passed on Marius himself and a

355

ἄλλων, ἐν οἷς Σουλπίκιος ἦν ὁ δήμαρχος. ἀλλὰ
Σουλπίκιος μὲν ἀπεσφάγη προδοθεὶς ὑπὸ θεράποντος, ὃν ὁ Σύλλας ἠλευθέρωσεν, εἶτα κατε-
κρήμνισε, Μαρίῳ δ' ἐπεκήρυξεν ἀργύριον, οὐκ
εὐγνωμόνως οὐδὲ πολιτικῶς, ᾧ γε μικρὸν ἔμπροσθεν ὑποχείριον εἰς τὴν οἰκίαν δοὺς ἑαυτὸν
2 ἀσφαλῶς ἀφείθη. καίτοι Μαρίῳ τότε μὴ διέντι
Σύλλαν, ἀλλ' ἀποθανεῖν ὑπὸ Σουλπικίου προε-
μένῳ, πάντων κρατεῖν ὑπῆρχεν, ἀλλ' ὅμως ἐφεί-
σατο· καὶ μεθ' ἡμέρας ὀλίγας τὴν αὐτὴν λαβὴν
παρασχὼν οὐκ ἔτυχε τῶν ὁμοίων. ἐφ' οἷς ὁ
Σύλλας τὴν μὲν σύγκλητον ἀδήλως ἠνίασεν· ἡ δὲ
παρὰ τοῦ δήμου δυσμένεια καὶ νέμεσις αὐτῷ
3 φανερὰ δι' ἔργων ἀπήντα. Νώνιον μέν γε τὸν   458
ἀδελφιδοῦν αὐτοῦ καὶ Σερουήϊον ἀρχὰς μετι-
όντας ἀποψηφισάμενοι καὶ καθυβρίσαντες ἑτέρους
κατέστησαν ἄρχοντας, οὓς μάλιστα τιμῶντες
ᾤοντο λυπεῖν ἐκεῖνον. ὁ δὲ τούτοις τε προσεποιεῖτο χαίρειν, ὡς τοῦ δήμου τῷ ποιεῖν ἃ βούλοιτο δι' αὐτὸν ἀπολαύοντος τῆς ἐλευθερίας, καὶ
θεραπεύων τὸ τῶν πολλῶν μῖσος ὕπατον κατέ-
στησεν ἀπὸ τῆς ἐναντίας στάσεως Λεύκιον
Κίνναν, ἀραῖς καὶ ὅρκοις καταλαβὼν εὐνοήσειν
4 τοῖς ἑαυτοῦ πράγμασιν. ὁ δὲ ἀναβὰς εἰς τὸ
Καπιτώλιον ἔχων ἐν τῇ χειρὶ λίθον ὤμνυεν, εἶτα
ἐπαρασάμενος ἑαυτῷ μὴ φυλάττοντι τὴν πρὸς
ἐκεῖνον εὔνοιαν ἐκπεσεῖν τῆς πόλεως, ὥσπερ ὁ
λίθος διὰ τῆς χειρός, κατέβαλε χαμᾶζε τὸν λίθον
οὐκ ὀλίγων παρόντων. παραλαβὼν δὲ τὴν ἀρ-

few others, among whom was Sulpicius the tribune of the people. But Sulpicius was killed, after he had been betrayed by a servant, to whom Sulla first gave his freedom, and then had him thrown down the Tarpeian rock; moreover, he set a price on the head of Marius, an act both ungrateful and impolitic, since it was in his house that he had found refuge and surrendered himself a little before this, and had been let off safe. And yet had Marius at that time not let Sulla go, but given him up to death at the hands of Sulpicius, he might have been absolute master in Rome; nevertheless he spared his life, and when after a few days he had given him the same opportunity, he did not obtain like mercy. By these proceedings Sulla won the secret dislike of the senate; but the people's hatred and indignation was made manifest to him by their acts. For instance, they ignominiously rejected Nonius his nephew, and Servius, who were his candidates for offices, and appointed others, whose preferment they thought would be most vexing to him. But he pretended to be pleased at this, saying that the people, in doing as it pleased, enjoyed a freedom which was due to him, and out of deference to the hatred of the multitude allowed Lucius Cinna, a man of the opposite faction, to be invested with the consulship, after binding him by solemn oaths to be favourable to his policies. And Cinna went up to the Capitol with a stone in his hand and took the oaths, and then, after praying that if he did not maintain his goodwill towards Sulla, he might be cast out of the city, as the stone from his hand, he threw the stone upon the ground in the sight of many people. But as soon as he had entered upon his office, he

χὴν εὐθὺς ἐπεχείρει τὰ καθεστῶτα κινεῖν, καὶ
δίκην ἐπὶ τὸν Σύλλαν παρεσκεύασε καὶ κατηγορεῖν ἐπέστησεν Οὐεργίνιον, ἕνα τῶν δημάρχων,
ὃν ἐκεῖνος ἅμα τῷ δικαστηρίῳ χαίρειν ἐάσας ἐπὶ
Μιθριδάτην ἀπῆρε.

XI. Λέγεται δὲ ὑπὸ τὰς ἡμέρας ἐκείνας ἐν αἷς
ὁ Σύλλας ἀπὸ τῆς Ἰταλίας ἐκίνει τὸν στόλον,
ἄλλα τε πολλὰ Μιθριδάτῃ διατρίβοντι περὶ τὸ
Πέργαμον ἐπισκῆψαι δαιμόνια, καὶ Νίκην στε-
φανηφόρον καθιεμένην ὑπὸ τῶν Περγαμηνῶν ἐπ᾽
αὐτὸν ἔκ τινων ὀργάνων ἄνωθεν ὅσον οὔπω τῆς
κεφαλῆς ψαύουσαν συντριβῆναι, καὶ τὸν στέφανον ἐκπεσόντα κατὰ τοῦ θεάτρου φέρεσθαι
χαμᾶζε διαθρυπτόμενον, ὥστε φρίκην μὲν τῷ
δήμῳ, ἀθυμίαν δὲ πολλὴν Μιθριδάτῃ παρασχεῖν,
καίπερ αὐτῷ τότε τῶν πραγμάτων ἐλπίδος πέρα
2 προχωρούντων. αὐτὸς μὲν γὰρ Ἀσίαν τε Ῥωμαίων καὶ Βιθυνίαν καὶ Καππαδοκίαν τῶν βασιλέων ἀφῃρημένος ἐν Περγάμῳ καθῆστο, πλούτους
καὶ δυναστείας καὶ τυραννίδας διανέμων τοῖς
φίλοις, τῶν δὲ παίδων ὁ μὲν ἐν Πόντῳ καὶ
Βοσπόρῳ τὴν παλαιὰν ἄχρι τῶν ὑπὲρ τὴν Μαιῶ-
τιν ἀοικήτων ἀρχὴν κατεῖχεν οὐδενὸς παρεν-
οχλοῦντος, Ἀριαράθης δὲ Θρᾴκην καὶ Μακεδονίαν
3 ἐπῄει στρατῷ μεγάλῳ προσαγόμενος, ἄλλους δὲ
οἱ στρατηγοὶ τόπους ἐχειροῦντο δυνάμεις ἔχοντες,
ὧν ὁ μέγιστος Ἀρχέλαος ταῖς μὲν ναυσὶν ὁμοῦ
τι συμπάσης ἐπικρατῶν τῆς θαλάττης τάς τε
Κυκλάδας νήσους ἐδουλοῦτο καὶ τῶν ἄλλων ὅσαι
Μαλέας ἐντὸς ἵδρυνται, καὶ τὴν Εὔβοιαν αὐτὴν
εἶχεν, ἐκ δὲ Ἀθηνῶν ὁρμώμενος τὰ μέχρι Θετ-

tried to subvert the existing order of things, and
had an impeachment prepared against Sulla, and
appointed Virginius, a tribune of the people, to be
his accuser. But Sulla, ignoring alike accuser and
court, set out against Mithridates.[1]

XI. And it is said that about the time when Sulla
was moving his armament from Italy, Mithridates,
who was staying at Pergamum, was visited with many
other portents from Heaven, and that a Victory with
a crown in her hand, which the Pergamenians were
lowering towards him by machinery of some sort,
was broken to pieces just as she was about to touch
his head, and the crown went tumbling from her
hand to the ground in the midst of the theatre, and
was shattered, whereat the people shuddered, and
Mithridates was greatly dejected, although at that
time his affairs were prospering beyond his hopes.
For he himself had wrested Asia from the Romans,
and Bithynia and Cappadocia from their kings, and
was now set down in Pergamum, dispensing riches,
principalities, and sovereignties to his friends ; and
of his sons, one was in Pontus and Bosporus, holding
without any opposition the ancient realm as far as the
deserts beyond Lake Maeotis, while Ariarathes was
overrunning Thrace and Macedonia with a large
army, and trying to win them over; his generals, too,
with forces under them, were subduing other regions,
and the greatest of them, Archelaüs, who with his
fleet controlled the entire sea, was subjugating the
Cyclades, and all the other islands which lie to the
east of Cape Malea, and was in possession of Euboea
itself, while from his head-quarters at Athens he was
bringing into revolt from Rome the peoples of Greece

[1] In 87 B.C.

ταλίας ἔθνη τῆς Ἑλλάδος ἀφίστη, μικρὰ προσ-
4 κρούσας περὶ Χαιρώνειαν. ἐνταῦθα γὰρ αὐτῷ
Βρέττιος Σούρρας ἀπήντησε, πρεσβευτὴς μὲν
ὢν Σεντίου, τοῦ στρατηγοῦ τῆς Μακεδονίας,
ἀνὴρ δὲ τόλμῃ καὶ φρονήσει διαφέρων. οὗτος
Ἀρχελάῳ δίκην ῥεύματος φερομένῳ διὰ τῆς
Βοιωτίας ἐπὶ πλεῖστον ἀντιστάς, καὶ τρισὶ
μάχαις διαγωνισάμενος περὶ Χαιρώνειαν, ἐξέωσε
5 καὶ συνέστειλε πάλιν ἐπὶ τὴν θάλατταν. Λευ-
κίου δὲ Λευκόλλου κελεύσαντος αὐτὸν ὑποχω-
ρεῖν ἐπιόντι Σύλλᾳ καὶ τὸν ἐψηφισμένον ἐκείνῳ
ἐᾶν πόλεμον, εὐθὺς ἐκλιπὼν τὴν Βοιωτίαν ὀπίσω
πρὸς Σέντιον ἀπήλαυνε, καίπερ αὐτῷ τῶν πραγμάτων ἐλπίδος πέρα προχωρούντων καὶ τῆς Ἑλλάδος οἰκείως ἐχούσης πρὸς μεταβολὴν διὰ τὴν
ἐκείνου καλοκἀγαθίαν. ἀλλὰ γὰρ Βρεττίῳ μὲν
ταῦτα λαμπρότατα τῶν πεπραγμένων.

XII. Σύλλας δὲ τὰς μὲν ἄλλας πόλεις εὐθὺς
εἶχεν ἐπιπρεσβευομένας καὶ καλούσας, ταῖς δὲ
Ἀθήναις διὰ τὸν τύραννον Ἀριστίωνα βασι-
λεύεσθαι ἠναγκασμέναις ἄθρους ἐπέστη καὶ τὸν
Πειραιᾶ περιλαβὼν ἐπολιόρκει, μηχανήν τε
πᾶσαν ἐφιστὰς καὶ μάχας παντοδαπὰς ποιού-
2 μενος. καίτοι χρόνον οὐ πολὺν ἀνασχομένῳ
παρῆν ἀκινδύνως ἑλεῖν τὴν ἄνω πόλιν, ὑπὸ
λιμοῦ συνηγμένην ἤδη τῇ χρείᾳ τῶν ἀναγκαίων
εἰς τὸν ἔσχατον καιρόν· ἀλλ' ἐπειγόμενος εἰς
Ῥώμην καὶ δεδιὼς τὸν ἐκεῖ νεωτερισμόν, πολλοῖς μὲν κινδύνοις, πολλαῖς δὲ μάχαις, μεγά- 459
λαις δὲ δαπάναις κατέσπευδε τὸν πόλεμον, ᾧ
γε δίχα τῆς ἄλλης παρασκευῆς ἡ περὶ τὰ
μηχανήματα πραγματεία ζεύγεσι μυρίοις ὀρικοῖς

as far as Thessaly, although he met with slight reverses at Chaeroneia. For here he was confronted by Bruttius Sura, who was a lieutenant of Sentius the praetor of Macedonia, and a man of superior courage and prudence. This man, as Archelaüs came rushing like a torrent through Boeotia, opposed him most fiercely, and after thrice giving him battle at Chaeroneia, repulsed him, and drove him back to the sea. But when Lucius Lucullus ordered him to give place to Sulla, who was coming, and to leave the conduct of the war to him, as the senate had voted, he at once abandoned Boeotia and marched back to Sentius, although his efforts were proving successful beyond hope, and although the nobility of his bearing was making Greece well-disposed towards a change of allegiance. However, these were the most brilliant achievements of Bruttius.

XII. As for Sulla, he at once received deputations and invitations from the other cities, but Athens was compelled by the tyrant Aristion to side with Mithridates. Against this city, therefore, Sulla led up all his forces, and investing the Piraeus, laid siege to it, bringing to bear upon it every sort of siege-engine, and making all sorts of assaults upon it. And yet if he had been patient a little while, he might have captured the upper city without hazard, since it lacked the necessities of life and was already reduced by famine to the last extremity. But since he was eager to get back to Rome, and feared the spirit of revolution there, he ran many risks, fought many battles, and made great outlays that he might hasten on the war, in which, not to speak of his other munitions, the operation of the siege-engines

ἐχορηγεῖτο, καθ' ἡμέραν ἐνεργοῖς οὖσι πρὸς τὴν
3 ὑπηρεσίαν. ἐπιλειπούσης δὲ τῆς ὕλης διὰ τὸ
κόπτεσθαι πολλὰ τῶν ἔργων περικλώμενα τοῖς
αὐτῶν βρίθεσι καὶ πυρπολεῖσθαι βαλλόμενα
συνεχῶς ὑπὸ τῶν πολεμίων, ἐπεχείρησε τοῖς
ἱεροῖς ἄλσεσι, καὶ τήν τε Ἀκαδήμειαν ἔκειρε
δενδροφορωτάτην προαστείων οὖσαν καὶ τὸ Λύ-
κειον. ἐπεὶ δὲ καὶ χρημάτων ἔδει πολλῶν
πρὸς τὸν πόλεμον, ἐκίνει τὰ τῆς Ἑλλάδος ἄσυλα,
τοῦτο μὲν ἐξ Ἐπιδαύρου, τοῦτο δὲ ἐξ Ὀλυμπίας,
τὰ κάλλιστα καὶ πολυτελέστατα τῶν ἀναθη-
4 μάτων μεταπεμπόμενος. ἔγραψε δὲ καὶ τοῖς
Ἀμφικτύοσιν εἰς Δελφοὺς ὅτι τὰ χρήματα τοῦ
θεοῦ βέλτιον εἴη κομισθῆναι πρὸς αὐτόν· ἢ γὰρ
φυλάξειν ἀσφαλέστερον ἢ καὶ ἀποχρησάμενος
ἀποδώσειν οὐκ ἐλάττω· καὶ τῶν φίλων ἀπέστειλε
Κάφιν τὸν Φωκέα κελεύσας σταθμῷ παραλαβεῖν
ἕκαστον. ὁ δὲ Κάφις ἧκε μὲν εἰς Δελφούς,
ὤκνει δὲ τῶν ἱερῶν θιγεῖν, καὶ πολλὰ τῶν Ἀμφι-
κτυόνων παρόντων ἀπεδάκρυσε τὴν ἀνάγκην.
5 ἐνίων δὲ φασκόντων ἀκοῦσαι φθεγγομένης τῆς
ἐν τοῖς ἀνακτόροις κιθάρας, εἴτε πιστεύσας εἴτε
τὸν Σύλλαν βουλόμενος ἐμβαλεῖν εἰς δεισιδαι-
μονίαν, ἐπέστειλε πρὸς αὐτόν. ὁ δὲ σκώπτων
ἀντέγραψε θαυμάζειν τὸν Κάφιν, εἰ μὴ συνίησιν
ὅτι χαίροντος, οὐ χαλεπαίνοντος, εἴη τὸ ᾄδειν·
ὥστε θαρροῦντα λαμβάνειν ἐκέλευσεν, ὡς ἡδο-
μένου τοῦ θεοῦ καὶ διδόντος.
6   Τὰ μὲν οὖν ἄλλα διέλαθε τούς γε πολλοὺς
Ἕλληνας ἐκπεμπόμενα, τὸν δὲ ἀργυροῦν πίθον,
ὃς ἦν ὑπόλοιπος ἔτι τῶν βασιλικῶν, διὰ βάρος

called for ten thousand pairs of mules, which were
employed daily for this service. And when timber
began to fail, owing to the destruction of many of
the works, which broke down of their own weight,
and to the burning of those which were continually
smitten by the enemy's fire-bolts, he laid hands upon
the sacred groves, and ravaged the Academy, which
was the most wooded of the city's suburbs, as well
as the Lyceum. And since he needed much money
also for the war, he diverted to his uses the sacred
treasures of Hellas, partly from Epidaurus, and
partly from Olympia, sending for the most beautiful
and most precious of the offerings there. He wrote
also to the Amphictyons at Delphi that it was
better to have the treasures of the god sent to him ;
for he would either keep them more safely, or, if he
spent them, would restore as much. And he sent
Caphis, the Phocian, one of his friends, with the
letter, bidding him receive each article by weight.
Caphis came to Delphi, but was loth to touch the
sacred objects, and shed many tears, in the presence
of the Amphictyons, over the necessity of it. And
when some of them declared they heard the sound
of the god's lyre in the inner sanctuary, Caphis,
either because he believed them, or because he
wished to strike Sulla with superstitious fear, sent
word to him about it. But Sulla wrote back jocosely,
expressing his amazement that Caphis did not
understand that singing was done in joy, not anger ;
his orders were therefore to take boldly, assured that
the god was willing and glad to give.

Accordingly, the rest of the treasures were sent
away without the knowledge of the most, certainly,
of the Greeks ; but the silver jar, the only one of

καὶ μέγεθος οὐ δυναμένων ἀναλαβεῖν τῶν ὑπο-
ζυγίων, ἀναγκαζόμενοι κατακόπτειν οἱ Ἀμφι-
κτύονες εἰς μνήμην ἐβάλοντο τοῦτο μὲν Τίτον
Φλαμινῖνον καὶ Μάνιον Ἀκύλιον, τοῦτο δὲ
Αἰμίλιον Παῦλον, ὧν ὁ μὲν Ἀντίοχον ἐξελάσας
τῆς Ἑλλάδος, οἱ δὲ τοὺς Μακεδόνων βασιλεῖς
καταπολεμήσαντες οὐ μόνον ἀπέσχοντο τῶν
ἱερῶν τῶν Ἑλληνικῶν, ἀλλὰ καὶ δῶρα καὶ
τιμὴν αὐτοῖς καὶ σεμνότητα πολλὴν προσέθε-
7 σαν. ἀλλ' ἐκεῖνοι μὲν ἀνδρῶν τε σωφρόνων καὶ
μεμαθηκότων σιωπῇ τοῖς ἄρχουσι παρέχειν τὰς
χεῖρας ἡγούμενοι κατὰ νόμον, αὐτοί τε ταῖς
ψυχαῖς βασιλικοὶ καὶ ταῖς δαπάναις εὐτελεῖς
ὄντες, μετρίοις ἐχρῶντο καὶ τεταγμένοις ἀναλώ-
μασι, τὸ κολακεύειν τοὺς στρατιώτας αἴσχιον
8 ἡγούμενοι τοῦ δεδιέναι τοὺς πολεμίους· οἱ δὲ
τότε στρατηγοὶ βίᾳ τὸ πρωτεῖον, οὐκ ἀρετῇ,
κτώμενοι, καὶ μᾶλλον ἐπ' ἀλλήλους δεόμενοι τῶν
ὅπλων ἢ τοὺς πολεμίους, ἠναγκάζοντο δημαγωγεῖν ἐν τῷ στρατηγεῖν, εἶθ' ὧν εἰς τὰς ἡδυπαθείας
τοῖς στρατευομένοις ἀνήλισκον ὠνούμενοι τοὺς
πόνους αὐτῶν, ἔλαθον ὤνιον ὅλην τὴν πατρίδα
ποιήσαντες ἑαυτούς τε δούλους τῶν κακίστων ἐπὶ
τῷ τῶν βελτιόνων ἄρχειν. ταῦτα ἐξήλαυνε
Μάριον, εἶτ' αὖθις ἐπὶ Σύλλαν κατῆγε, ταῦτα
Ὀκταουίου τοὺς περὶ Κίνναν, ταῦτα Φλάκκου
9 τοὺς περὶ Φιμβρίαν αὐτόχειρας ἐποίησεν. ὧν

---

[1] The gifts of Croesus, king of Lydia (Herodotus, i. 51).
[2] Manius Acilius Glabrio, consul in 191 B.C., defeated
Antiochus the Great at Thermopylae, and forced him to
return to Asia.

the royal gifts[1] which still remained, was too large
and heavy for any beast of burden to carry, and the
Amphictyons were compelled to cut it into pieces.
As they did so, they called to mind now Titus
Flamininus and Manius Acilius, and now Aemilius
Paulus, of whom one had driven Antiochus out of
Greece,[2] and the others had subdued in war the
kings of Macedonia[3]; these had not only spared
the sanctuaries of the Greeks, but had even made
additional gifts to them, and greatly increased their
honour and dignity. But these were lawful commanders of men who were self-restrained and had
learned to serve their leaders without a murmur,
and they were themselves kingly in spirit and
simple in their personal expenses, and indulged in
moderate and specified public expenditures, deeming it more disgraceful to flatter their soldiers than
to fear their enemies; the generals of this later
time, however, who won their primacy by force, not
merit, and who needed their armies for service
against one another, rather than against the public
enemy, were compelled to merge the general in the
demagogue, and then, by purchasing the services
of their soldiers with lavish sums to be spent on
luxurious living, they unwittingly made their whole
country a thing for sale, and themselves slaves
of the basest men for the sake of ruling over
the better. This was what drove out Marius, and
then brought him back again against Sulla; this
made Cinna the assassin of Octavius, and Fimbria of

---

[3] Flamininus defeated Philip V. of Macedon at Cynos-
cephalae in 197 B.C., and Aemilius Paulus crushed Perseus,
the last king of Macedonia, at Pydna, in 168 B.C. See
Plutarch's *Flamininus*, xv. ; *Aemilius Paulus*, xvi.–xxii.

οὐχ ἥκιστα Σύλλας ἐνέδωκεν ἀρχάς, ἐπὶ τῷ
διαφθείρειν καὶ μετακαλεῖν τοὺς ὑπ' ἄλλοις ταττομένους
καταχορηγῶν εἰς τοὺς ὑφ' αὑτῷ καὶ
δαπανώμενος, ὥστε ἅμα τοὺς ἄλλους μὲν εἰς
προδοσίαν, τοὺς δὲ ὑφ' αὑτῷ εἰς ἀσωτίαν διαφθείρων
χρημάτων δεῖσθαι πολλῶν, καὶ μάλιστα
πρὸς τὴν πολιορκίαν ἐκείνην.

XIII. Δεινὸς γάρ τις ἄρα καὶ ἀπαραίτητος
εἶχεν αὐτὸν ἔρως ἑλεῖν τὰς Ἀθήνας, εἴτε ζήλῳ
τινὶ πρὸς τὴν πάλαι σκιαμαχοῦντα τῆς πόλεως
δόξαν, εἴτε θυμῷ τὰ σκώμματα φέροντα καὶ τὰς 46(
βωμολοχίας, αἷς αὐτόν τε καὶ τὴν Μετέλλαν ἀπὸ
τῶν τειχῶν ἑκάστοτε γεφυρίζων καὶ κατορχούμενος
ἐξηρέθιζεν ὁ τύραννος Ἀριστίων, ἄνθρωπος
ἐξ ἀσελγείας ὁμοῦ καὶ ὠμότητος ἔχων συγκει-
2 μένην τὴν ψυχήν, καὶ τὰ χείριστα τῶν Μιθριδατικῶν συνερρυηκότα νοσημάτων καὶ παθῶν εἰς
ἑαυτὸν ἀνειληφώς, καὶ τῇ πόλει μυρίους μὲν
πολέμους, πολλὰς δὲ τυραννίδας καὶ στάσεις
διαπεφευγυίᾳ πρότερον ὥσπερ νόσημα θανατη-
φόρον εἰς τοὺς ἐσχάτους καιροὺς ἐπιτιθέμενος· ὅς,
χιλίων δραχμῶν ὠνίου τοῦ μεδίμνου τῶν πυρῶν
ὄντος ἐν ἄστει τότε, τῶν ἀνθρώπων σιτουμένων τὸ
3 περὶ τὴν ἀκρόπολιν φυόμενον παρθένιον, ὑποδή-
ματα δὲ καὶ ληκύθους ἐφθὰς ἐσθιόντων, αὐτὸς
ἐνδελεχῶς πότοις μεθημερινοῖς καὶ κώμοις χρώμενος καὶ πυρριχίζων καὶ γελωτοποιῶν πρὸς τοὺς
πολεμίους τὸν μὲν ἱερὸν τῆς θεοῦ λύχνον ἀπε-

---

[1] According to Appian, *Bell. Civ.* i. 71, Octavius, the
consul, a supporter of Sulla, was killed at Rome by Censorinus, acting under the orders of Marius and Cinna, in 86 B.C.
Valerius Flaccus, chosen consul to succeed Marius, in 86 B.C.,

Flaccus.[1] And it was Sulla who, more than any one else, paved the way for these horrors, by making lavish expenditures upon the soldiers under his own command that he might corrupt and win over those whom others commanded, so that in making traitors of the rest, and profligates of his own soldiers, he had need of much money, and especially for this siege.

XIII. For he was possessed by some dreadful and inexorable passion for the capture of Athens, either because he was fighting with a sort of ardour against the shadow of the city's former glory, or because he was provoked to anger by the scurrilous abuse which had been showered from the walls upon himself and Metella by the tyrant Aristion, who always danced in mockery as he scoffed. This man's spirit was compounded of licentiousness and cruelty; he had made himself a sink for the worst of the diseases and passions of Mithridates; and in these her last days he had fixed himself, like a fatal malady, upon a city which had previously passed safely through countless wars, and many usurpations and seditions. This man, although at the time a bushel of wheat sold in the city for a thousand drachmas, and although men made food for themselves of the fever-few which grew on the acropolis, and boiled down shoes and leather oil-flasks to eat, was himself continually indulging in drinking-bouts and revels by daylight, was dancing in armour and making jokes to deride the enemy, while he suffered the sacred

---

was sent into Asia to thwart Sulla and conduct the war against Mithridates, but was murdered there by his mutinous lieutenant, Fimbria, in the following year. See chapters xx. 1; xxiii. 6; *Lucullus*, xxxiv. 2.

σβηκότα διὰ σπάνιν ἐλαίου περιεῖδε, τῇ δὲ ἱερο-
φάντιδι πυρῶν ἡμίεκτον προσαιτούσῃ πεπέρεως
ἔπεμψε, τοὺς δὲ βουλευτὰς καὶ ἱερεῖς ἱκετεύοντας
οἰκτεῖραι τὴν πόλιν καὶ διαλύσασθαι πρὸς Σύλ-
4 λαν τοξεύμασι βάλλων διεσκέδασεν. ὀψὲ δὲ ἤδη
που μόλις ἐξέπεμψεν ὑπὲρ εἰρήνης δύο ἢ τρεῖς
τῶν συμποτῶν· πρὸς οὓς οὐδὲν ἀξιοῦντας σωτήριον, ἀλλὰ τὸν Θησέα καὶ τὸν Εὔμολπον καὶ τὰ
Μηδικὰ σεμνολογουμένους ὁ Σύλλας "᾽Ἄπιτε,"
εἶπεν, "ὦ μακάριοι, τοὺς λόγους τούτους ἀνα-
λαβόντες· ἐγὼ γὰρ οὐ φιλομαθήσων εἰς ᾽Αθήνας
ὑπὸ ῾Ρωμαίων ἐπέμφθην, ἀλλὰ τοὺς ἀφιστα-
μένους καταστρεψόμενος."

XIV. ᾽Εν δὲ τούτῳ λέγεταί τινας ἐν Κεραμεικῷ[1]
πρεσβυτῶν ἀκούσαντας διαλεγομένων πρὸς ἀλλήλους καὶ κακιζόντων τὸν τύραννον, ὡς μὴ φυλάτ-
τοντα τοῦ τείχους τὴν περὶ τὸ ῾Επτάχαλκον
ἔφοδον καὶ προσβολήν, ᾗ μόνῃ δυνατὸν εἶναι καὶ
ῥᾴδιον ὑπερβῆναι τοὺς πολεμίους, ἀπαγγεῖλαι
2 ταῦτα πρὸς τὸν Σύλλαν. ὁ δὲ οὐ κατεφρόνησεν,
ἀλλὰ ἐπελθὼν νυκτὸς καὶ θεασάμενος τὸν τόπον
ἁλώσιμον εἴχετο τοῦ ἔργου. λέγει δὲ αὐτὸς ὁ
Σύλλας ἐν τοῖς ὑπομνήμασι τὸν πρῶτον ἐπιβάντα
τοῦ τείχους Μάρκον ᾽Ατήιον ἀντιστάντος αὐτῷ
πολεμίου δόντα πληγὴν ἐκ καταφορᾶς τῷ κράνει
περικλάσαι τὸ ξίφος, οὐ μὴν ὑφέσθαι τῆς χώρας,
ἀλλὰ μεῖναι καὶ κατασχεῖν. κατελήφθη μὲν οὖν
ἡ πόλις ἐκεῖθεν, ὡς ᾽Αθηναίων οἱ πρεσβύτατοι

---

[1] The Outer Cerameicus, *i.e.* the suburb before the Dipylon,
or Sacred Gate, through which one left the city for
Eleusis.

lamp of the goddess to go out for lack of oil; and
when the chief priestess begged him for a twelfth of
a bushel of wheat, he sent her so much pepper; and
when the senators and priests came to him in suppliant array, and entreated him to take pity on the
city and come to terms with Sulla, he scattered them
with a volley of arrows. But after a long time, at
last, with much ado, he sent out two or three of his
fellow-revellers to treat for peace, to whom Sulla,
when they made no demands which could save the
city, but talked in lofty strains about Theseus and
Eumolpus and the Persian wars, said : " Be off, my
dear Sirs, and take these speeches with you; for I
was not sent to Athens by the Romans to learn its
history, but to subdue its rebels."

XIV. But at this juncture, as it is said, certain
soldiers in the Cerameicus [1] overheard some old men
talking with one another, and abusing the tyrant
because he did not guard the approaches to the wall
at the Heptachalcum,[2] at which point alone it was
possible and easy for the enemy to get over. When
this was reported to Sulla, he did not make light of
it, but went thither by night, and after seeing that
the place could be taken, set himself to the work.
And Sulla himself says, in his Memoirs, that Marcus
Ateius was the first man to mount the wall, and that
when an enemy confronted him, he gave him a
downward cut on the helmet with his sword, and
shattered the weapon; he did not, however, yield
ground, but remained and held his own. At any
rate, the city was taken at this point, as the oldest

[2] An unknown feature of the wall, somewhere between the
Piraïc, or western gate, and the Dipylon, or Sacred Gate,
opening to the N.W.

3 διεμνημόνευον. αὐτὸς δὲ Σύλλας τὸ μεταξὺ τῆς
Πειραϊκῆς πύλης καὶ τῆς ἱερᾶς κατασκάψας καὶ
συνομαλύνας, περὶ μέσας νύκτας εἰσήλαυνε,
φρικώδης ὑπό τε σάλπιγξι καὶ κέρασι πολλοῖς,
ἀλαλαγμῷ καὶ κραυγῇ τῆς δυνάμεως ἐφ' ἁρπαγὴν
καὶ φόνον ἀφειμένης ὑπ' αὐτοῦ, καὶ φερομένης
διὰ τῶν στενωπῶν[1] ἐσπασμένοις τοῖς ξίφεσιν,
ὥστε ἀριθμὸν μηδένα γενέσθαι τῶν ἀποσφαγέν-
των, ἀλλὰ τῷ τόπῳ τοῦ ῥυέντος αἵματος ἔτι νῦν
4 μετρεῖσθαι τὸ πλῆθος. ἄνευ γὰρ τῶν κατὰ τὴν
ἄλλην πόλιν ἀναιρεθέντων ὁ περὶ τὴν ἀγορὰν
φόνος ἐπέσχε πάντα τὸν ἐντὸς τοῦ Διπύλου
Κεραμεικόν· πολλοῖς δὲ λέγεται καὶ διὰ πυλῶν
κατακλύσαι τὸ προάστειον. ἀλλὰ τῶν οὕτως
ἀποθανόντων, τοσούτων γενομένων, οὐκ ἐλάσ-
σονες ἦσαν οἱ σφᾶς αὐτοὺς διαφθείροντες οἴκτῳ
καὶ πόθῳ τῆς πατρίδος ὡς ἀναιρεθησομένης.
τοῦτο γὰρ ἀπογνῶναι καὶ φοβηθῆναι τὴν σωτηρίαν ἐποίησε τοὺς βελτίστους, οὐδὲν ἐν τῷ
Σύλλα φιλάνθρωπον οὐδὲ μέτριον ἐλπίσαντας.
5 ἀλλὰ γὰρ τοῦτο μὲν Μειδίου καὶ Καλλιφῶντος
τῶν φυγάδων δεομένων καὶ προκυλινδουμένων
αὐτοῦ, τοῦτο δὲ τῶν συγκλητικῶν, ὅσοι συνε-
στράτευον, ἐξαιτουμένων τὴν πόλιν, αὐτός τε
μεστὸς ὢν ἤδη τῆς τιμωρίας, ἐγκώμιόν τι τῶν
παλαιῶν Ἀθηναίων ὑπειπὼν ἔφη χαρίζεσθαι
πολλοῖς μὲν ὀλίγους, ζῶντας δὲ τεθνηκόσιν.
6 Ἑλεῖν δὲ τὰς Ἀθήνας αὐτός φησιν ἐν τοῖς
ὑπομνήμασι Μαρτίαις καλάνδαις, ἥτις ἡμέρα

46

---

[1] τῶν στενωπῶν Bekker, after Coraës : στενωπῶν.

---

[1] In Plutarch's time.

Athenians used to testify.[1] And Sulla himself, after
he had thrown down and levelled with the ground
the wall between the Piraïc and the Sacred Gate, led
his army into the city at midnight. The sight of
him was made terrible by blasts of many trumpets
and bugles, and by the cries and yells of the soldiery
now let loose by him for plunder and slaughter, and
rushing through the narrow streets with drawn
swords.   There was therefore no counting of the
slain, but their numbers are to this day determined
only by the space that was covered with blood.
For without mention of those who were killed in the
rest of the city, the blood that was shed in the
market-place covered all the Cerameicus inside the
Dipylon gate; nay, many say that it flowed through
the gate and deluged the suburb. But although
those who were thus slain were so many, there were
yet more who slew themselves, out of yearning pity
for their native city, which they thought was going
to be destroyed.   For this conviction made the best
of them give up in despair and fear to survive, since
they expected no humanity or moderation in Sulla.
However, partly at the instance of the exiles Meidias
and Calliphon, who threw themselves at his feet in
supplication, and partly because all the Roman
senators who were in his following interceded for
the city, being himself also by this time sated
with vengeance, after some words in praise of the
ancient Athenians, he said that he forgave a few for
the sake of many, the living for the sake of the dead.

He took Athens, as he says himself in his Memoirs,
on the Calends of March,[2] a day which corresponds

[2] 86 B.C. Cf. the description of the capture of Athens
given by Appian, *Bell. Mith.* xxx.

μάλιστα συμπίπτει τῇ νουμηνίᾳ τοῦ Ἀνθε-
στηριῶνος μηνός, ἐν ᾧ κατὰ τύχην ὑπομνήματα
πολλὰ τοῦ διὰ τὴν ἐπομβρίαν ὀλέθρου καὶ τῆς
φθορᾶς ἐκείνης δρῶσιν, ὡς τότε καὶ περὶ τὸν
χρόνον ἐκεῖνον μάλιστα τοῦ κατακλυσμοῦ συμ-
7 πεσόντος. ἑαλωκότος δὲ τοῦ ἄστεος ὁ μὲν τύραννος εἰς τὴν ἀκρόπολιν καταφυγὼν ἐπολιορκεῖτο,
Κουρίωνος ἐπὶ τούτῳ τεταγμένου· καὶ χρόνον
ἐγκαρτερήσας συχνὸν αὐτὸς ἑαυτὸν ἐνεχείρισε
δίψει πιεσθείς. καὶ τὸ δαιμόνιον εὐθὺς ἐπεσή-
μηνε· τῆς γὰρ αὐτῆς ἡμέρας τε καὶ ὥρας ἐκεῖνόν
τε Κουρίων κατῆγε, καὶ νεφῶν ἐξ αἰθρίας συνδρα-
μόντων πλῆθος ὄμβρου καταρραγὲν ἐπλήρωσεν
ὕδατος τὴν ἀκρόπολιν. εἷλε[1] δὲ καὶ τὸν Πειραιᾶ
μετ' οὐ πολὺν χρόνον ὁ Σύλλας, καὶ τὰ πλεῖστα
κατέκαυσεν, ὧν ἦν καὶ ἡ Φίλωνος ὁπλοθήκη,
θαυμαζόμενον ἔργον.

XV. Ἐν δὲ τούτῳ Ταξίλης ὁ Μιθριδάτου
στρατηγὸς ἐκ Θρᾴκης καὶ Μακεδονίας καταβεβηκὼς
δέκα μυριάσι πεζῶν καὶ μυρίοις ἱππεῦσι καὶ
τεθρίπποις ἐνενήκοντα δρεπανηφόροις ἐκάλει τὸν
Ἀρχέλαον, ἔτι ναυλοχοῦντα περὶ τὴν Μουνυχίαν
καὶ μήτε τῆς θαλάττης βουλόμενον ἀποστῆναι
μήτε πρόθυμον ὄντα συμπλέκεσθαι τοῖς Ῥωμαίοις, ἀλλὰ χρονοτριβεῖν τὸν πόλεμον καὶ τὰς
2 εὐπορίας αὐτῶν ἀφαιρεῖν. ἃ δὴ πολὺ μᾶλλον
ἐκείνου συνορῶν ὁ Σύλλας ἀνέζευξεν εἰς Βοιωτίαν
ἐκ χωρίων γλίσχρων καὶ μηδὲ ἐν εἰρήνῃ τρέφειν
ἱκανῶν ὄντων. καὶ τοῖς πολλοῖς ἐδόκει σφάλ-

---

[1] εἷλε Bekker, after Emperius : εἶχε.

---

[1] In the time of Deucalion, the Noah of Greek tradition. (Cf. Pausanias, i. 18, 7.)

very nearly with the first of the month Anthesterion. In this month, as it happens, the Athenians perform many rites commemorating the destruction and devastation caused by the flood, believing that the ancient deluge [1] occurred at about this time. On the capture of the town, the tyrant took refuge in the acropolis, and was besieged there by Curio, who was appointed to this task. He held out for a considerable time, but was driven by the pangs of thirst to give himself up. And the Deity at once gave a manifest token in the matter; for at the very hour of the day when Curio brought his prisoner down, clouds gathered in an open sky, and a quantity of rain fell and filled the acropolis with water. Not long after, Sulla took the Piraeus also, and burnt most of it, including the arsenal of Philo,[2] a marvellous work.

XV. Meanwhile Taxiles, the general of Mithridates had come down from Thrace and Macedonia with a hundred thousand footmen, ten thousand horse, and ninety scythe-bearing four-horse chariots, and summoned Archelaüs to join him. Archelaüs still lay with his fleet at Munychia,[3] and was neither willing to quit the sea, nor eager to join battle with the Romans, but planned to protract the war and cut off their supplies. But Sulla understood the situation much better than Archelaüs did, and therefore transferred his forces into Boeotia, away from regions that were far from fertile, and unable to maintain a population even in time of peace. Most people thought that he had erred in his calculations,

[2] It must have been finished in 330–329 B.C. See Frazer on Pausanias, i. 1, 2.

[3] One of the three harbours of the Piraeus.

λεσθαι τὸν λογισμόν, ὅτι τὴν Ἀττικὴν τραχεῖαν
οὖσαν καὶ δύσιππον ἀπολιπὼν ἐνέβαλεν ἑαυτὸν
πεδιάσι καὶ ἀναπεπταμέναις ταῖς περὶ τὴν Βοιωτίαν χώραις, ὁρῶν ἐν ἅρμασι καὶ ἵπποις τὴν
3 βαρβαρικὴν οὖσαν ἀλκήν. ἀλλὰ φεύγων, ὥσπερ
εἴρηται, λιμὸν καὶ σπάνιν ἠναγκάζετο διώκειν τὸν
ἐκ τῆς μάχης κίνδυνον. ἔτι δὲ Ὀρτήσιος αὐτὸν
ἐφόβει, στρατηγικὸς ἀνὴρ καὶ φιλόνεικος, ὃν ἐκ
Θετταλίας ἄγοντα τῷ Σύλλᾳ δύναμιν ἐν τοῖς
στενοῖς οἱ βάρβαροι παρεφύλαττον. διὰ ταῦτα
μὲν εἰς τὴν Βοιωτίαν ἀνέζευξεν ὁ Σύλλας· Ὀρτή-
σιον δὲ Κάφις, ἡμέτερος ὤν, ἑτέραις ὁδοῖς ψευσά-
μενος τοὺς βαρβάρους διὰ τοῦ Παρνασσοῦ κατ-
ῆγεν ὑπ' αὐτὴν τὴν Τιθόραν, οὔπω τοσαύτην πόλι
4 οὖσαν ὅση νῦν ἐστιν, ἀλλὰ φρούριον ἀπορρῶγι
κρημνῷ περικοπτόμενον, εἰς ὃ καὶ πάλαι ποτὲ
Φωκέων οἱ Ξέρξην ἐπιόντα φεύγοντες ἀνεσκευά-
σαντο καὶ διεσώθησαν. ἐνταῦθα καταστρατο-
πεδεύσας Ὀρτήσιος ἡμέρας μὲν ἀπεκρούσατο
τοὺς πολεμίους, νύκτωρ δ' ἐπὶ Πατρωνίδα ταῖς
δυσχωρίαις καταβὰς ἀπαντήσαντι τῷ Σύλλᾳ
μετὰ τῆς δυνάμεως συνέμιξε.

XVI. Γενόμενοι δὲ κοινῇ καταλαμβάνονται
βουνὸν ἐκ μέσων ἑστῶτα τῶν Ἐλατικῶν πεδίων,
εὔγεων καὶ ἀμφιλαφῆ καὶ παρὰ τὴν ῥίζαν ὕδωρ
ἔχοντα· Φιλοβοιωτὸς καλεῖται, καὶ τὴν φύσιν
αὐτοῦ καὶ τὴν θέσιν ἐπαινεῖ θαυμασίως ὁ Σύλλας.
στρατοπεδεύσαντες δὲ παντάπασιν ὀλίγοι τοῖς
πολεμίοις κατεφάνησαν· ἱππεῖς μὲν γὰρ οὐ
πλείους πεντακοσίων καὶ χιλίων ἐγένοντο, πεζοὶ

because he had abandoned Attica, which was a rough country and ill-suited for cavalry movements, and thrown himself into the plains and open districts of Boeotia, although he saw that the strength of the Barbarians consisted in chariots and cavalry. But in flying from scarcity and famine, as has been said, he was compelled to pursue the danger arising from battle. And furthermore, he was anxious about Hortensius, a bold and capable general, who was leading a force from Thessaly to Sulla while the Barbarians were closely watching for him in the passes.[1] For these reasons Sulla transferred his army into Boeotia. But Hortensius was rescued by Caphis, a countryman of mine, and conducted by different routes, of which the Barbarians were ignorant, past Parnassus to a spot just below Tithora. This was not so large a city then as it is now, but a fortress surrounded on all sides by steep cliffs, into which those of the Phocians who in ancient times fled before the advance of Xerxes betook themselves and were saved.[2] Having encamped here, Hortensius repulsed the enemy by day, and at night descended to Patronis by difficult paths and made a junction with Sulla, who came to meet him with his army.

XVI. When they had thus united their forces, they occupied a hill which rose out of the midst of the plains of Elatea, a fertile hill, thickly grown with trees, and supplied with water at its base. Philoboeotus is its name, and its situation and natural advantages are most highly praised by Sulla. As they lay encamped here, they appeared to the enemy altogether few in numbers; for they were not more than fifteen hundred horse, and less than fifteen

---

[1] At Thermopylae.   [2] Cf. Herodotus, viii. 32.

2 δὲ πεντακισχιλίων καὶ μυρίων ἐλάττους. ὅθεν
ἐκβιασάμενοι τὸν Ἀρχέλαον οἱ λοιποὶ στρατηγοὶ
καὶ παρατάξαντες τὴν δύναμιν, ἐνέπλησαν ἵππων,
ἁρμάτων, ἀσπίδων, θυρεῶν τὸ πεδίον.

Τὴν δὲ κραυγὴν καὶ ἀλαλαγμὸν οὐκ ἔστεγεν ὁ
ἀὴρ ἐθνῶν τοσούτων ἅμα καθισταμένων εἰς τάξιν.
ἦν δὲ ἅμα καὶ τὸ κομπῶδες καὶ σοβαρὸν αὐτῶν
τῆς πολυτελείας οὐκ ἀργὸν οὐδὲ ἄχρηστον εἰς
ἔκπληξιν, ἀλλ' αἵ τε μαρμαρυγαὶ τῶν ὅπλων
3 ἠσκημένων χρυσῷ τε καὶ ἀργύρῳ διαπρεπῶς, αἵ
τε βαφαὶ τῶν Μηδικῶν καὶ Σκυθικῶν χιτώνων
ἀναμεμιγμέναι χαλκῷ καὶ σιδήρῳ λάμποντι 462
πυροειδῆ καὶ φοβερὰν ἐν τῷ σαλεύεσθαι καὶ
διαφέρεσθαι προσέβαλον ὄψιν, ὥστε τοὺς Ῥωμαίους ὑπὸ τὸν χάρακα συστέλλειν ἑαυτούς, καὶ
τὸν Σύλλαν μηδενὶ λόγῳ τὸ θάμβος αὐτῶν
ἀφελεῖν δυνάμενον, βιάζεσθαί τε ἀποδιδράσκον-
τας οὐ βουλόμενον, ἡσυχίαν ἄγειν καὶ φέρειν
βαρέως ἐφυβρίζοντας ὁρῶντα κομπασμῷ καὶ
γέλωτι τοὺς βαρβάρους. ὤνησε μέντοι τοῦτο
4 μάλιστα πάντων αὐτόν. οἱ γὰρ ἐναντίοι καταφρονήσαντες ἐτράποντο πρὸς ἀταξίαν πολλήν,
οὐδὲ ἄλλως ὑπήκοοι τῶν στρατηγῶν διὰ πολυ-
αρχίαν ὄντες· ὥστε[1] ὀλίγοι μὲν ἐν τῷ χάρακι
διεκαρτέρουν, ὁ δὲ πλεῖστος ὄχλος ἁρπαγαῖς καὶ
πορθήμασι δελεαζόμενος ὁδὸν ἡμερῶν πολλῶν
ἀπὸ τοῦ στρατοπέδου διεσπείρετο. καὶ τήν τε
τῶν Πανοπέων πόλιν ἐκκόψαι λέγονται καὶ τὴν
Λεβαδέων διαρπάσαι καὶ συλῆσαι τὸ μαντεῖον,
οὐδενὸς στρατηγοῦ πρόσταγμα δόντος.

---

[1] ὥστε supplied by Coraës and Bekker ; Sintenis prefers
καί, with Schaefer.

thousand foot. Wherefore the rest of his generals overpowered the objections of Archelaüs and drew up for battle, filling the plain with their horses, chariots, shields, and bucklers.

The air could not contain the shouts and clamour of so many nations forming in array. At the same time also the pomp and ostentation of their costly equipment was not without its effect and use in exciting terror; indeed, the flashing of their armour, which was magnificently embellished with gold and silver, and the rich colours of their Median and Scythian vests, intermingled with bronze and flashing steel, presented a flaming and fearful sight as they surged to and fro, so that the Romans huddled together behind their trenches, and Sulla, unable by any reasoning to remove their fear, and unwilling to force them into a fight from which they wanted to run away, had to sit still and endure as best he could the sight of the Barbarians insulting him with boasts and laughter. This, however, was of service to him above all else. For owing to their contempt of him, his opponents lapsed into great disorder, since even at their best they were not obedient to their generals, owing to the great number in command. Few of them therefore consented to remain within their entrenchments, but the largest part of the throng was lured away by plunder and pillage, and was scattered about the country many days march from their camp. They are said to have destroyed the city of Panope, and to have sacked Lebadeia and despoiled its oracle, although none of their generals ordered them to do so.

5 Ὁ δὲ Σύλλας, ἐν ὄμμασιν αὐτοῦ πόλεων ἀπολ-
λυμένων, δυσανασχετῶν καὶ λυπούμενος, οὐκ εἴα
τοὺς στρατιώτας σχολάζειν, ἀλλὰ προσάγων
αὐτοὺς ἠνάγκαζε τόν τε Κηφισὸν ἐκ τοῦ ῥείθρου
παρατρέπειν καὶ τάφρους ὀρύσσειν, ἀνάπαυλαν
οὐδενὶ διδοὺς καὶ τῶν ἐνδιδόντων ἀπαραίτητος
ἐφεστὼς κολαστής, ὅπως ἀπαγορεύσαντες πρὸς
τὰ ἔργα διὰ τὸν πόνον ἀσπάσωνται τὸν κίνδυνον.
6 ὃ καὶ συνέβη. τρίτην γὰρ ἡμέραν ἐργαζόμενοι
τοῦ Σύλλα παρεξιόντος ἐδέοντο μετὰ κραυγῆς
ἄγειν ἐπὶ τοὺς πολεμίους. ὁ δὲ οὐ μάχεσθαι
βουλομένων, ἀλλὰ μὴ βουλομένων πονεῖν ἔφησεν
εἶναι τὸν λόγον· εἰ δὲ ὄντως ἔχουσιν ἀγωνιστικῶς,
ἐκέλευσεν ἤδη μετὰ τῶν ὅπλων ἐλθεῖν ἐκεῖσε,
δείξας αὐτοῖς τὴν πρότερον μὲν γενομένην ἀκρό-
7 πολιν τῶν Παραποταμίων, τότε δὲ ἀνηρημένης
τῆς πόλεως λόφος ἐλείπετο πετρώδης καὶ περί-
κρημνος, τοῦ Ἡδυλίου διωρισμένος ὅρους ὅσον ὁ
Ἄσσος ἐπέχει ῥέων, εἶτα συμπίπτων ὑπὸ τὴν
ῥίζαν αὐτὴν τῷ Κηφισῷ καὶ συνεκτραχυνόμενος
ὀχυρὰν ἐνστρατοπεδεῦσαι τὴν ἄκραν ποιεῖ. διὸ
καὶ τοὺς χαλκάσπιδας ὁρῶν τῶν πολεμίων ὠθου-
μένους ἐπ᾽ αὐτὴν ὁ Σύλλας· ἐβούλετο φθῆναι
καταλαβὼν τὸν τόπον· καὶ κατέλαβε χρησάμενος
8 τοῖς στρατιώταις προθύμοις. ἐπεὶ δὲ ἀποκρουσ-
θεὶς ἐκεῖθεν ὁ Ἀρχέλαος ὥρμησεν ἐπὶ τὴν Χαιρώνειαν, οἱ δὲ συστρατευσάμενοι τῶν Χαιρωνέων
ἐδέοντο τοῦ Σύλλα μὴ προέσθαι τὴν πόλιν,
ἐκπέμπει τῶν χιλιάρχων ἕνα Γαβίνιον μετὰ τάγ-
ματος ἑνὸς καὶ τοὺς Χαιρωνεῖς ἀφίησι, βουλη-
θέντας μέν, οὐ μὴν δυνηθέντας φθῆναι τὸν

But Sulla, though chafing and fretting while cities were destroyed before his eyes, would not suffer his soldiers to be idle, but led them out and forced them to dig ditches and divert the Cephisus from its channel, giving no man a respite, and showing himself an inexorable chastiser of those who were remiss, in order that they might be worn out at their tasks and induced by their hardships to welcome danger. And so it fell out. For on the third day of their drudgery, as Sulla passed by, they begged and clamoured to be led against the enemy. But Sulla said their words showed not a willingness to fight, but an unwillingness to labour; if, however, they were really disposed to fight, then he bade them take their arms and go at once yonder, pointing them to what had formerly been the acropolis of Parapotamii. At this time, however, the city had been destroyed, and only a rocky and precipitous crest remained, separated from Mount Hedylium by the breadth of the river Assus, which then falls into the Cephisus at the very base of the mountain, becomes impetuous in its flow after the confluence, and makes the citadel a strong place for a camp. For this reason, and because he saw the Chalcaspides, or *Bronze-shields,* of the enemy pushing their way towards it, Sulla wished to occupy the place first; and he did occupy it, now that he found his soldiers eager for action. And when Archelaüs, repulsed from this site, set out against Chaeroneia, and the Chaeroneians in Sulla's army besought him not to abandon their city to its fate, he sent out Gabinius, one of his tribunes, with one legion, and let the Chaeroneians also go, who wished, but were unable, to get into the city before Gabinius. So

379

Γαβίνιον. οὕτως ἦν ἀγαθὸς καὶ προθυμότερος
εἰς τὸ σῶσαι τῶν σωθῆναι δεομένων. ὁ δὲ Ἰόβας
οὐ Γαβίνιόν φησι πεμφθῆναι, ἀλλὰ Ἐρίκιον.
ἡ μὲν οὖν πόλις ἡμῶν παρὰ τοσοῦτον ἐξέφυγε τὸν
κίνδυνον.

XVII. Ἐκ δὲ Λεβαδείας καὶ τοῦ Τροφωνίου
φῆμαί τε χρησταὶ καὶ νικηφόρα μαντεύματα τοῖς
Ῥωμαίοις ἐξεπέμποντο. περὶ ὧν οἱ μὲν ἐπιχώριοι
πλείονα λέγουσιν· ὡς δὲ Σύλλας αὐτὸς ἐν δεκάτῳ
τῶν ὑπομνημάτων γέγραφε, Κόϊντος Τίτιος, οὐκ
ἀφανὴς ἀνὴρ τῶν ἐν τῇ Ἑλλάδι πραγματευο-
μένων, ἧκε πρὸς αὐτὸν ἤδη τὴν ἐν Χαιρωνείᾳ
νενικηκότα μάχην, ἀπαγγέλλων ὅτι καὶ δευτέραν
ὁ Τροφώνιος αὐτόθι μάχην καὶ νίκην προσημαίνει
2 ἐντὸς ὀλίγου χρόνου. μετὰ δὲ τοῦτον ἀνὴρ τῶν
ἐν τάξει στρατευομένων ὄνομα Σαλουήνιος ἀνή-
νεγκε παρὰ τοῦ θεοῦ τέλος οἷον αἱ κατὰ τὴν
Ἰταλίαν πράξεις ἔμελλον ἕξειν. ἀμφότεροι δὲ
ταὐτὰ περὶ τῆς ὀμφῆς ἔφραζον· τῷ γὰρ Ὀλυμπίῳ
Διὶ καὶ τὸ κάλλος καὶ τὸ μέγεθος παραπλήσιον
ἰδεῖν ἔφασαν.

3 Ἐπειδὴ δὲ διέβη τὸν Ἄσσον ὁ Σύλλας, παρελθὼν ὑπὸ τὸ Ἡδύλιον τῷ Ἀρχελάῳ παρεστρατο-
πέδευσε, βεβλημένῳ χάρακα καρτερὸν ἐν μέσῳ
τοῦ Ἀκοντίου καὶ τοῦ Ἡδυλίου πρὸς τοῖς λεγομένοις Ἀσσίοις. ὁ μέντοι τόπος ἐν ᾧ κατεσκή- 463
νωσεν ἄχρι νῦν Ἀρχέλαος ἀπ' ἐκείνου καλεῖται.
διαλιπὼν δὲ μίαν ἡμέραν ὁ Σύλλας Μουρήναν
μὲν ἔχοντα τάγμα καὶ σπείρας δύο πρὸς τὸ τοῖς
πολεμίοις ἐνοχλῆσαι παραταττομένοις ἀπέλιπεν,

efficient was he, and more eager to bring succour than those who begged that succour should be given. Juba, however, says it was not Gabinius, but Ericius, who was thus sent. At any rate, so narrowly did my native city escape its peril.

XVII. From Lebadeia and the cave of Trophonius favourable utterances and oracles announcing victory were now sent out to the Romans. Of these the inhabitants of the country have more to say; but Sulla himself has written in the tenth book of his Memoirs, how Quintus Titius, a prominent man among the Romans doing business in Greece, came to him immediately after he had won his victory at Chaeroneia,[1] with tidings that Trophonius predicted for him a second battle and victory in that neighbourhood within a short time.[2] And after him, a legionary soldier, Salvenius by name, brought him from the god a statement of the issue which affairs in Italy were going to have. But both agreed about the source of their oracle; for they said they had beheld one who in beauty and majesty was like unto Olympian Jove.

Sulla now crossed the Assus, and after advancing to the foot of Mount Hedylium, encamped over against Archelaüs, who had thrown up strong entrenchments between Mounts Acontium and Hedylium, at the so-called Assian plain. The spot in which he encamped, moreover, is to this day called Archelaüs, after him. After one day's respite, Sulla left Murena behind with one legion and two cohorts, to obstruct the enemy if they attempted to draw up their forces, while he himself held sacrifices on the

---

[1] As described in chapter xix.
[2] Near Orchomenus, as described in chapter xxi.

4 αὐτὸς δὲ παρὰ τὸν Κηφισὸν ἐσφαγιάζετο, καὶ
τῶν ἱερῶν γενομένων ἐχώρει πρὸς τὴν Χαιρώνειαν,
ἀναληψόμενός τε τὴν αὐτόθι στρατιὰν καὶ κατοψ-
όμενος τὸ καλούμενον Θούριον ὑπὸ τῶν πολεμίων προκατειλημμένον. ἔστι δὲ κορυφὴ τραχεῖα
καὶ στροβιλῶδες ὄρος, ὃ καλοῦμεν Ὀρθόπαγον,
ὑπὸ δὲ αὐτὸ τὸ ῥεῦμα τοῦ Μόλου καὶ Θουρίου
νεὼς Ἀπόλλωνος. ὠνόμασται δὲ ὁ θεὸς ἀπὸ
Θουροῦς, τῆς Χαίρωνος μητρός, ὃν οἰκιστὴν γεγο-
5 νέναι τῆς Χαιρωνείας ἱστοροῦσιν. οἱ δέ φασι
τὴν Κάδμῳ δοθεῖσαν ὑπὸ τοῦ Πυθίου καθηγεμόνα
βοῦν ἐκεῖ φανῆναι, καὶ τὸν τόπον ἀπ᾽ αὐτῆς οὕτω
προσαγορευθῆναι· θὼρ γὰρ οἱ Φοίνικες τὴν βοῦν
καλοῦσι.

Προσιόντος δὲ τοῦ Σύλλα πρὸς τὴν Χαιρώνειαν
ὁ τεταγμένος ἐν τῇ πόλει χιλίαρχος, ἐξωπλισ-
μένους ἄγων τοὺς στρατιώτας, ἀπήντησε στέφα-
6 νον δάφνης κομίζων. ὡς δὲ δεξάμενος ἠσπάσατο
τοὺς στρατιώτας καὶ παρώρμησε πρὸς τὸν κίνδυνον, ἐντυγχάνουσιν αὐτῷ δύο τῶν Χαιρωνέων
ἄνδρες, Ὁμολόιχος καὶ Ἀναξίδαμος, ὑφιστάμενοι
τοὺς τὸ Θούριον κατασχόντας ἐκκόψειν, ὀλίγους
στρατιώτας παρ᾽ ἐκείνου λαβόντες· ἀτραπὸν γὰρ
εἶναι τοῖς βαρβάροις ἄδηλον, ἀπὸ τοῦ καλου-
μένου Πετράχου παρὰ τὸ Μουσεῖον ἐπὶ τὸ Θούριον ὑπὲρ κεφαλῆς ἄγουσαν, ᾗ πορευθέντες οὐ
χαλεπῶς ἐπιπεσεῖσθαι καὶ καταλεύσειν ἄνωθεν
7 αὐτοὺς ἢ συνώσειν εἰς τὸ πεδίον. τοῦ δὲ Γαβι-
νίου τοῖς ἀνδράσι μαρτυρήσαντος ἀνδρείαν καὶ
πίστιν, ἐκέλευσεν ἐπιχειρεῖν ὁ Σύλλας· αὐτὸς δὲ
συνέταττε τὴν φάλαγγα καὶ διένειμε τοὺς ἱππό-
τας ἐπὶ κέρως ἑκατέρου, τὸ δεξιὸν αὐτὸς ἔχων, τὸ

banks of the Cephisus, and, when the rites were
over, moved on towards Chaeroneia, to pick up the
forces stationed there, and to reconnoitre Thurium, as
it is called, which had been already occupied by the
enemy. This is a conical-shaped hill with a craggy
peak (we call it Orthopagus), and at its foot is the
river Molus and a temple of Apollo Thurius. The
god got this surname from Thuro, the mother of
Chaeron, who was founder of Chaeroneia, according to tradition. But some say that the cow which
was given by Apollo to Cadmus as his guide, appeared there, and that the place was named as it
is from her, "thor" being the Phoenician word
for *cow*.

As Sulla drew near to Chaeroneia, the tribune who
had been stationed in the city, with his men in full
armour, came to meet him, carrying a wreath of
laurel. After Sulla had accepted this, greeted the
soldiers, and animated them for the coming danger,
two men of Chaeroneia accosted him, Homoloïchus
and Anaxidamus, and engaged to cut off the troops
in possession of Thurium if he would give them a
few soldiers; for there was a path out of sight of
the Barbarians, leading from the so-called Petrachus
along past the Museum to that part of Thurium
which was over their heads, and by taking this path
it would not be difficult, they said, to fall upon them
and either stone them to death from above, or force
them into the plain. After Gabinius had borne
testimony to the men's courage and fidelity, Sulla
ordered them to make the attempt, while he himself
proceeded to form his line of battle, and to dispose
his cavalry on either wing, taking command of the

δ᾽ εὐώνυμον ἀποδοὺς Μουρήνᾳ. Γάλβας δὲ καὶ
Ὁρτήσιος οἱ πρεσβευταὶ σπείρας ἐπιτάκτους
ἔχοντες ἔσχατοι παρενέβαλον ἐπὶ τῶν ἄκρων
φύλακες πρὸς τὰς κυκλώσεις· ἑωρῶντο γὰρ οἱ
πολέμιοι κατασκευάζοντες ἱππεῦσι πολλοῖς καὶ
ψιλοῖς ποδώκεσιν εἰς ἐπιστροφὴν τὸ κέρας εὐ-
καμπὲς καὶ κοῦφον, ὡς μακρὰν ἀνάξοντες καὶ
κυκλωσόμενοι τοὺς Ῥωμαίους.

XVIII. Ἐν δὲ τούτῳ τῶν Χαιρωνέων Ἐρίκιον
ἄρχοντα παρὰ τοῦ Σύλλα λαβόντων καὶ περιελ-
θόντων ἀδήλως τὸ Θούριον, εἶτα ἐπιφανέντων,
θόρυβος ἦν πολὺς καὶ φυγὴ τῶν βαρβάρων καὶ
φόνος ὑπ᾽ ἀλλήλων ὁ πλεῖστος. οὐ γὰρ ὑπέ-
μειναν, ἀλλὰ κατὰ πρανοῦς φερόμενοι τοῖς τε
δόρασι περιέπιπτον αὐτοὶ τοῖς ἑαυτῶν καὶ κατε-
κρήμνιζον ὠθοῦντες ἀλλήλους, ἄνωθεν ἐπικειμένων τῶν πολεμίων καὶ τὰ γυμνὰ παιόντων,
2 ὥστε τρισχιλίους πεσεῖν περὶ τὸ Θούριον. τῶν
δὲ φευγόντων τοὺς μὲν εἰς τάξιν ἤδη καθεστὼς ὁ
Μουρήνας ἀπετέμνετο καὶ διέφθειρεν ὑπαντιάζων,
οἱ δὲ ὠσάμενοι πρὸς τὸ φίλιον στρατόπεδον καὶ
τῇ φάλαγγι φύρδην ἐμπεσόντες ἀνέπλησαν δέους
καὶ ταραχῆς τὸ πλεῖστον μέρος, καὶ διατριβὴν
τοῖς στρατηγοῖς ἐνεποίησαν οὐχ ἥκιστα βλάψα-
σαν αὐτούς. ὀξέως γὰρ ὁ Σύλλας ταρασσομένοις
ἐπαγαγὼν καὶ τὸ μέσον διάστημα τῷ τάχει συν-
ελὼν ἀφείλετο τὴν τῶν δρεπανηφόρων ἐνέργειαν.
3 ἔρρωται γὰρ μάλιστα μήκει δρόμου σφοδρότητα
καὶ ῥύμην τῇ διεξελάσει διδόντος, αἱ δὲ ἐκ

right himself, and assigning the left to Murena.[1]
His lieutenants, Galba and Hortensius, with cohorts
of reserves, stationed themselves on the heights in
the rear, to guard against attacks on the flanks. For
the enemy were observed to be making their wing
flexible and light for evolution with large bodies of
horse and light infantry, purposing to extend it and
envelop the Romans.

XVIII. Meanwhile the Chaeroneians, over whom
Ericius had been placed in command by Sulla, made
their way unnoticed around Thurium and then showed
themselves suddenly, producing great confusion and
rout among the Barbarians, and slaughter at one
another's hands for the most part. For they did not
hold their ground, but rushed down the steeps, falling
upon their own spears and crowding one another
down the precipices, while their enemies pressed
upon them from above and smote their exposed
bodies, so that three thousand of them fell on
Thurium. Of the fugitives, some were met by
Murena, who had already formed his array, and were
cut off and slain; others pushed their way towards
the camp of their friends, and falling pell-mell upon
their lines, filled the greater part of them with
terror and confusion, and inflicted a delay upon their
generals which was especially harmful to them. For
Sulla promptly charged upon them while they were
in confusion, and by abridging the space between
the armies with the speed of his approach, robbed
the scythe-bearing chariots of their efficiency. For
these are of most avail after a long course, which
gives them velocity and impetus for breaking through

---

[1] Cf. chapter xvii. 3. Archelaüs had followed Sulla towards
Chaeroneia, leaving Murena free to join his chief.

βραχέος ἀφεσεις ἄπρακτοι καὶ ἀμβλεῖαι, καθάπερ βελῶν τάσιν οὐ λαβόντων. ὃ δὴ καὶ τότε
τοῖς βαρβάροις ἀπήντα· καὶ τὰ πρῶτα τῶν ἁρμάτων ἀργῶς ἐξελαυνόμενα καὶ προσπίπτοντα
νωθρῶς ἐκκρούσαντες οἱ Ῥωμαῖοι μετὰ κρότου
καὶ γέλωτος ἄλλα ἤτουν, ὥσπερ εἰώθασιν ἐν ταῖς
4 θεατρικαῖς ἱπποδρομίαις. τοὐντεῦθεν αἱ πεζαὶ   464
δυνάμεις συνερράγησαν, τῶν μὲν βαρβάρων προ-
βαλλομένων τὰς σαρίσας μακρὰς καὶ πειρωμένων
τῷ συνασπισμῷ τὴν φάλαγγα διατηρεῖν ἐν τάξει,
τῶν δὲ Ῥωμαίων τοὺς μὲν ὑσσοὺς αὐτοῦ κατα-
βαλόντων, σπασαμένων δὲ τὰς μαχαίρας καὶ
παρακρουομένων τὰς σαρίσας, ὡς τάχιστα προσ-
5 μίξειαν αὐτοῖς δι' ὀργήν. προτεταγμένους γὰρ
ἑώρων τῶν πολεμίων μυρίους καὶ πεντακισχιλίους
θεράποντας, οὓς ἐκ τῶν πόλεων κηρύγμασιν ἐλευ-
θεροῦντες οἱ βασιλέως στρατηγοὶ κατελόχιζον
εἰς τοὺς ὁπλίτας. καί τις ἑκατοντάρχης λέγεται
Ῥωμαῖος εἰπεῖν ὡς ἐν Κρονίοις μόνον εἰδείη τῆς
6 παρρησίας δούλους μετέχοντας. τούτους μὲν οὖν
διὰ βάθος καὶ πυκνότητα βραδέως ἐξωθουμένους
ὑπὸ τῶν ὁπλιτῶν καὶ παρὰ φύσιν μένειν τολμῶν-
τας αἵ τε βελοσφενδόναι καὶ οἱ γρόσφοι, χρωμένων ἀφειδῶς τῶν κατόπιν Ῥωμαίων, ἀπέστρε-
φον καὶ συνετάραττον.

XIX. Ἀρχελάου δὲ τὸ δεξιὸν κέρας εἰς κύκλω-
σιν ἀνάγοντος, Ὁρτήσιος ἐφῆκε τὰς σπείρας
δρόμῳ προσφερομένας ὡς ἐμβαλῶν πλαγίοις.
ἐπιστρέψαντος δὲ ταχέως ἐκείνου τοὺς περὶ αὑτὸν

----

[1] The festival of Saturn, a time of general license and
mirth, when masters treated their slaves as equals.

an opposing line, but short starts are ineffectual and
feeble, as in the case of missiles which do not get
full propulsion. And this proved true now in the
case of the Barbarians. The first of their chariots
were driven along feebly and engaged sluggishly,
so that the Romans, after repulsing them, clapped
their hands and laughed and called for more, as they
are wont to do at the races in the circus. Thereupon
the infantry forces engaged, the Barbarians holding
their pikes before them at full length, and en-
deavouring, by locking their shields together, to
keep their line of battle intact; while the Romans
threw down their javelins, drew their swords, and
sought to dash the pikes aside, that they might get
at their enemies as soon as possible, in the fury that
possessed them. For they saw drawn up in front of
the enemy fifteen thousand slaves, whom the king's
generals had set free by proclamation in the cities
and enrolled among the men-at-arms. And a certain
Roman centurion is reported to have said that it was
only at the Saturnalia,[1] so far as he knew, that slaves
participated in the general license. These men,
however, owing to the depth and density of their
array, and the unnatural courage with which they
held their ground, were only slowly repulsed by the
Roman men-at-arms; but at last the fiery bolts and
the javelins which the Romans in the rear ranks plied
unsparingly, threw them into confusion and drove
them back.

XIX. Archelaüs now extended his right wing to
envelop Sulla's line, whereupon Hortensius[2] sent his
cohorts against him on a quick run, intending to
attack his flank. But Archelaüs wheeled swiftly

[2] See chapter xvii. 7.

ἱππεῖς δισχιλίους, ἐκθλιβόμενος ὑπὸ πλήθους
προσεστέλλετο τοῖς ὀρεινοῖς, κατὰ μικρὸν ἀπορ-
ρηγνύμενος τῆς φάλαγγος καὶ περιλαμβανόμενος
2 ὑπὸ τῶν πολεμίων. πυθόμενος δὲ ὁ Σύλλας ἀπὸ
τοῦ δεξιοῦ μήπω συμπεπτωκότος εἰς μάχην
ἐδίωκε βοηθῶν. Ἀρχέλαος δὲ τῷ κονιορτῷ τῆς
ἐλάσεως ὅπερ ἦν τεκμηράμενος, Ὁρτήσιον μὲν εἴα
χαίρειν, αὐτὸς δὲ ἐπιστρέψας ὥρμησεν ὅθεν ὁ
Σύλλας πρὸς τὸ δεξιόν, ὡς ἔρημον ἄρχοντος αἱρή-
σων. ἅμα δὲ καὶ Μουρήνᾳ Ταξίλης ἐπῆγε τοὺς
χαλκάσπιδας, ὥστε τῆς κραυγῆς διχόθεν φερομένης καὶ τῶν ὀρῶν ἀνταποδιδόντων τὴν περι-
ήχησιν, ἐπιστήσαντα τὸν Σύλλαν διαπορεῖν
3 ὁποτέρωσε χρὴ προσγενέσθαι. δόξαν δὲ τὴν
ἑαυτοῦ τάξιν ἀναλαμβάνειν, Μουρήνᾳ μὲν ἀρω-
γὸν ἔπεμψεν Ὁρτήσιον ἔχοντα τέσσαρας σπείρας, αὐτὸς δὲ τὴν πέμπτην ἕπεσθαι κελεύσας
ἐπὶ τὸ δεξιὸν ἠπείγετο καὶ καθ᾽ ἑαυτὸ μὲν ἀξιο-
μάχως ἤδη τῷ Ἀρχελάῳ συνεστηκός, ἐκείνου
δὲ ἐπιφανέντος παντάπασιν ἐξεβιάσαντο, καὶ
κρατήσαντες ἐδίωκον πρός τε τὸν ποταμὸν καὶ
4 τὸ Ἀκόντιον ὄρος προτροπάδην φεύγοντας. οὐ
μὴν ὅ γε Σύλλας ἠμέλησε Μουρήνα κινδυνεύον-
τος, ἀλλὰ ὥρμησε τοῖς ἐκεῖ βοηθεῖν· ἰδὼν δὲ
νικῶντας, τότε τῆς διώξεως μετεῖχε. πολλοὶ
μὲν οὖν ἐν τῷ πεδίῳ τῶν βαρβάρων ἀνηροῦντο,
πλεῖστοι δὲ τῷ χάρακι προσφερόμενοι κατεκόπησαν, ὥστε μυρίους διαπεσεῖν εἰς Χαλκίδα
μόνους ἀπὸ τοσούτων μυριάδων. ὁ δὲ Σύλλας
λέγει τέσσαρας καὶ δέκα ἐπιζητῆσαι τῶν αὐτοῦ
στρατιωτῶν, εἶτα καὶ τούτων δύο πρὸς τὴν
5 ἑσπέραν παραγενέσθαι. διὸ καὶ τοῖς τροπαίοις

against him his two thousand horsemen, and Hortensius, forced aside by superior numbers, was keeping close to the hills, separating himself little by little from the main line, and getting surrounded by the enemy. When Sulla learned of this, he came swiftly to his aid from the right wing, which was not yet engaged. But Archelaüs, guessing the truth from the dust raised by Sulla's troops, gave Hortensius the go-by, and wheeling, set off for the right wing whence Sulla had come, thinking to surprise it without a commander. At the same time Murena also was attacked by Taxiles with his Bronze-shields, so that when shouts were borne to his ears from both places, and reëchoed by the surrounding hills, Sulla halted, and was at a loss to know in which of the two directions he ought to betake himself. But having decided to resume his own post, he sent Hortensius with four cohorts to help Murena, while he himself, bidding the fifth cohort to follow, hastened to the right wing. This of itself had already engaged Archelaüs on equal terms, but when Sulla appeared, they drove the enemy back at all points, obtained the mastery, and pursued them to the river and Mount Acontium in a headlong flight. Sulla, however, did not neglect Murena in his peril, but set out to aid the forces in that quarter; he saw, however, that they were victorious, and then joined in the pursuit. Many of the Barbarians, then, were slain in the plain, but most were cut to pieces as they rushed for their entrenchments, so that only ten thousand out of so many myriads made their escape into Chalcis. But Sulla says he missed only fourteen of his soldiers, and that afterwards, towards evening, two of these came in. He therefore

ἐπέγραψεν Ἄρη καὶ Νίκην καὶ Ἀφροδίτην, ὡς
οὐχ ἧττον εὐτυχίᾳ κατορθώσας ἢ δεινότητι καὶ
δυνάμει τὸν πόλεμον. ἀλλὰ τοῦτο μὲν τὸ τρόπαιον ἕστηκε τῆς πεδιάδος μάχης ᾗ πρῶτον
ἐνέκλιναν οἱ περὶ Ἀρχέλαον παρὰ[1] τὸ Μόλου
ῥεῖθρον, ἕτερον δέ ἐστι τοῦ Θουρίου κατὰ κορυ-
φὴν βεβηκὸς ἐπὶ τῇ κυκλώσει τῶν βαρβάρων,
γράμμασιν Ἑλληνικοῖς ἐπισημαῖνον Ὁμολόϊχον
6 καὶ Ἀναξίδαμον ἀριστεῖς. ταύτης τὰ ἐπινίκια
τῆς μάχης ἦγεν ἐν Θήβαις, περὶ τὴν Οἰδιπό-
δειον κρήνην κατασκευάσας θυμέλην. οἱ δὲ
κρίνοντες ἦσαν Ἕλληνες ἐκ τῶν ἄλλων ἀνακε-
κλημένοι πόλεων, ἐπεὶ πρός γε Θηβαίους ἀδιαλ-
λάκτως εἶχε, καὶ τῆς χώρας αὐτῶν ἀποτεμόμενος
τὴν ἡμίσειαν τῷ Πυθίῳ καὶ τῷ Ὀλυμπίῳ καθιέ-
ρωσεν, ἐκ τῶν προσόδων κελεύσας ἀποδίδοσθαι
τὰ χρήματα τοῖς θεοῖς ἅπερ αὐτὸς εἰλήφει.

XX. Μετὰ ταῦτα πυνθανόμενος Φλάκκον ἀπὸ
τῆς ἐναντίας στάσεως ὕπατον ᾑρημένον διαπερᾶν
τὸν Ἰόνιον μετὰ δυνάμεως, λόγῳ μὲν ἐπὶ Μιθριδάτην, ἔργῳ δὲ ἐπ' ἐκεῖνον αὐτόν, ὥρμησεν ἐπὶ
Θετταλίας ὡς ἀπαντήσων. γενομένῳ δὲ αὐτῷ
περὶ πόλιν Μελίτειαν ἀφικνοῦντο πολλαχόθεν
ἀγγελίαι πορθεῖσθαι τὰ κατόπιν αὖθις οὐκ ἐλάτ-
2 τονι στρατιᾷ βασιλικῇ τῆς πρότερον. Δορύλαος
γὰρ εἰς Χαλκίδα καταχθεὶς παρασκευῇ νεῶν
πολλῇ, ἐν αἷς ἦγεν ὀκτὼ μυριάδας ἠσκημένας
καὶ συντεταγμένας ἄριστα δὴ τῆς Μιθριδατικῆς

---

[1] παρὰ with Bekker, after Emperius : μέχρι παρά.

---

[1] A deity of good fortune among the Romans.
[2] So named "because in it Oedipus washed off the blood
of his murdered father" (Pausanias, ix. 18, 4).

inscribed upon his trophies the names of Mars, Victory and Venus,[1] in the belief that his success in the war was due no less to good fortune than to military skill and strength. This trophy of the battle in the plain stands on the spot where the troops of Archelaüs first gave way, by the brook Molus, but there is another planted on the crest of Thurium, to commemorate the envelopment of the Barbarians there, and it indicates in Greek letters that Homoloïchus and Anaxidamus were the heroes of the exploit. The festival in honour of this victory was celebrated by Sulla in Thebes, where he prepared a stage near the fountain of Oedipus.[2] But the judges were Greeks invited from the other cities, since towards the Thebans he was irreconcileably hostile. He also took away half of their territory and consecrated it to Pythian Apollo and Olympian Zeus, giving orders that from its revenues the moneys should be paid back to the gods which he had taken from them.[3]

XX. After this, learning that Flaccus, a man of the opposite faction, had been chosen consul [4] and was crossing the Ionian sea with an army, ostensibly against Mithridates, but really against himself, he set out towards Thessaly in order to meet him. But when he was come to the city of Meliteia, tidings reached him from many quarters that the regions behind him were ravaged again by an army of the king which was no smaller than the former. For Dorylaüs, having put in at Chalcis with a large fleet, on which he brought eighty thousand of the best trained and disciplined men in the army of

[3] Cf. chapter xii. 3-6.
[4] With Cinna, to succeed Marius, who died in 86 B.C.

στρατιᾶς, εὐθὺς εἰς Βοιωτίαν ἐνέβαλε καὶ κατεῖχε
τὴν χώραν, προθυμούμενος εἰς μάχην ἐπισπά-
σασθαι τὸν Σύλλαν, οὐ προσέχων Ἀρχελάῳ
διακωλύοντι, καὶ λόγον περὶ τῆς προτέρας μάχης
διαδιδοὺς ὡς οὐκ ἄνευ προδοσίας μυριάδες τοσαῦ-
3 ται διαφθαρεῖεν. οὐ μὴν ἀλλὰ ὁ Σύλλας ταχέως
ὑποστρέψας ἀπέδειξε τῷ Δορυλάῳ τὸν Ἀρχέλαον ἄνδρα φρόνιμον καὶ τῆς Ῥωμαίων ἐμπει-
ρότατον ἀρετῆς, ὥστε μικρὰ αὐτὸν τῷ Σύλλᾳ
περὶ τὸ Τιλφώσσιον ἐμπεσόντα πρῶτον εἶναι
τῶν οὐκ ἀξιούντων κρίνεσθαι διὰ μάχης, ἀλλὰ
δαπάναις καὶ χρόνῳ τρίβειν τὸν πόλεμον. ὅμως
δὲ θάρσος τι τῷ Ἀρχελάῳ παρεῖχεν ὁ πρὸς
Ὀρχομενῷ τόπος, ἐν ᾧ κατεστρατοπέδευσαν,
εὐφυέστατος ὢν ἱπποκρατοῦσιν ἐναγωνίσασθαι.
4 τῶν γὰρ Βοιωτίων πεδίων ὅ τί πέρ ἐστι κάλλιστον καὶ μέγιστον, τοῦτο τῆς Ὀρχομενίων
ἐξηρτημένον πόλεως ὁμαλὸν ἀναπέπταται καὶ
ἄδενδρον ἄχρι τῶν ἑλῶν ἐν οἷς ὁ Μέλας κατ-
αναλίσκεται ποταμός, ἀνατέλλων μὲν ὑπὸ τὴν
πόλιν τῶν Ὀρχομενίων πολὺς καὶ πλώϊμος ἐν
πηγαῖς μόνος τῶν Ἑλληνικῶν ποταμῶν, αὐξόμενος δὲ ὑπὸ τροπὰς θερινάς, ὥσπερ ὁ Νεῖλος,
καὶ φέρων ὅμοια τοῖς ἐκεῖ τὰ φυόμενα, πλὴν
5 ἄκαρπα καὶ ἀναυξῆ. πόρρω δὲ οὐ πρόεισιν,
ἀλλὰ τὸ μὲν πλεῖστον εὐθὺς εἰς λίμνας τυφλὰς
καὶ ἑλώδεις ἀφανίζεται, μέρος δὲ οὐ πολὺ τῷ
Κηφισῷ συμμίγνυται, περὶ ὃν μάλιστα τόπον
ἡ λίμνη δοκεῖ τὸν αὐλητικὸν ἐκφέρειν κάλαμον.

XXI. Ἐπεὶ δὲ ἐγγὺς κατεστρατοπέδευσαν, ὁ
μὲν Ἀρχέλαος ἡσύχαζεν, ὁ δὲ Σύλλας ὤρυττε

Mithridates, at once burst into Boeotia and occupied the country. He was eager to entice Sulla to battle, disregarding the protests of Archelaüs, and giving it out that in the previous battle so many myriads had not perished without treachery. Sulla, however, turning swiftly back, showed Dorylaüs that Archelaüs was a man of prudence and best acquainted with the Roman valour, so that after a slight skirmish with Sulla near Tilphossium, he was first of those who thought it expedient not to decide the issue by a battle, but rather to wear out the war by dint of time and treasure. Nevertheless, Archelaüs was much encouraged by the nature of the country about Orchomenus, where they were encamped, since it was most favourable as a battle-field for an army superior in cavalry. For of all the plains of Boeotia this is the largest and fairest, and beginning from the city of Orchomenus, it spreads out smooth and treeless as far as the marshes in which the river Melas loses itself. This rises close under the city of Orchomenus, and is the only Greek river that is copious and navigable at its sources; moreover, it increases towards the time of the summer solstice, like the Nile, and produces plants like those which grow there, only stunted and without fruit. Its course is short, however, and the greater part of it disappears at once in blind and marshy lakes, while a small portion of it unites with the Cephisus, somewhere near the place in which the stagnant water is reputed to produce the famous reed for flutes.[1]

XXI. When the two armies had encamped near each other, Archelaüs lay still, but Sulla proceeded

[1] The Boeotians excelled with the flute. See *Alcibiades*, ii. 4-6.

τάφρους ἑκατέρωθεν, ὅπως, εἰ δύναιτο, τῶν στε-
ρεῶν καὶ ἱππασίμων ἀποτεμόμενος τοὺς πολεμίους ὤσειεν εἰς τὰ ἕλη. τῶν δὲ οὐκ ἀνασχο-
μένων, ἀλλ' ὡς ἀφείθησαν ὑπὸ τῶν στρατηγῶν,
ἐντόνως καὶ ῥύδην ἐλαυνόντων, οὐ μόνον οἱ περὶ
τὰ ἔργα τοῦ Σύλλα διεσκεδάσθησαν, ἀλλὰ καὶ
τοῦ παρατεταγμένου συνεχύθη τὸ πλεῖστον φυγ-
2 όντος. ἔνθα δὴ Σύλλας αὐτὸς ἀποπηδήσας τοῦ
ἵππου καὶ σημεῖον ἁρπάσας ὠθεῖτο διὰ τῶν
φευγόντων εἰς τοὺς πολεμίους, βοῶν "Ἐμοὶ μὲν
ἐνταῦθά που καλόν, ὦ Ῥωμαῖοι, τελευτᾶν, ὑμεῖς
δὲ τοῖς πυνθανομένοις ποῦ προδεδώκατε τὸν
αὐτοκράτορα, μεμνημένοι φράζειν ὡς ἐν Ὀρχομενῷ." τούτους τε δὴ τὸ ῥηθὲν ἐπέστρεψε,
καὶ τῶν ἐπὶ τοῦ δεξιοῦ κέρως σπειρῶν δύο
προσεβοήθησαν, ἃς ἐπαγαγὼν τρέπεται τοὺς
3 πολεμίους. ἀναγαγὼν δὲ μικρὸν ὀπίσω, καὶ
δοὺς ἄριστον αὐτοῖς, αὖθις ἀπετάφρευε τὸν χάρακα τῶν πολεμίων. οἱ δὲ αὖθις ἐν τάξει μᾶλλον ἢ πρότερον προσεφέροντο. καὶ Διογένης
μὲν ὁ τῆς Ἀρχελάου γυναικὸς υἱὸς ἀριστεύων
ἐπὶ τοῦ δεξιοῦ περιόπτως ἔπεσεν, οἱ δὲ τοξόται,
τῶν Ῥωμαίων ἐκβιαζομένων, οὐκ ἔχοντες ἀνα-
στροφὴν ἀθρόοις τοῖς ὀϊστοῖς ἐκ χειρὸς ὥσπερ
ξίφεσι παίοντες ἀνέκοπτον αὐτούς, τέλος δὲ
κατακλεισθέντες εἰς τὸν χάρακα μοχθηρῶς ὑπὸ
τραυμάτων καὶ φόνου[1] διενυκτέρευσαν. ἡμέρας
δὲ πάλιν τῷ χάρακι τοὺς στρατιώτας προσαγα-
4 γὼν ὁ Σύλλας ἀπετάφρευεν. ἐξελθόντας δὲ τοὺς
πολλοὺς ὡς ἐπὶ μάχην συμβαλὼν τρέπεται, καὶ

---

[1] φόνου Bekker adopts Reiske's correction to φόβου (terror).

to dig trenches on either side, in order that, if possible, he might cut the enemy off from the solid ground which was favourable for cavalry, and force them into the marshes. The enemy, however, would not suffer this, but when their generals sent them forth, charged impetuously and at full speed, so that not only Sulla's labourers were dispersed, but also the greater part of the corps drawn up to protect them was thrown into confusion and fled. Then Sulla threw himself from his horse, seized an ensign, and pushed his way through the fugitives against the enemy, crying : " For me, O Romans, an honourable death here ; but you, when men ask you where you betrayed your commander, remember to tell them, at Orchomenus." The fugitives rallied at these words, and two of the cohorts on his right wing came to his aid ; these he led against the enemy and routed them. Then he fell back a little distance, and after giving his men breakfast, again proceeded to fence the enemy's entrenchments off with his ditches. But they attacked him again in better order than before, Diogenes, the step-son of Archelaüs, fought gallantly on their right wing, and fell gloriously, and their archers, being hard pressed by the Romans, so that they had no room to draw their bows, took their arrows by handfuls, struck with them as with swords, at close quarters, and tried to beat back their foes, but were finally shut up in their entrenchments, and had a miserable night of it with their slain and wounded. Next day Sulla again led his soldiers up to the enemy's fortifications and continued trenching them off, and when the greater part of them came out to give him battle, he engaged with them and routed

πρὸς τὸν ἐκείνων φόβον οὐδενὸς μένοντος αἱρεῖ
κατὰ κράτος τὸ στρατόπεδον. καὶ κατέπλησαν   466
ἀποθνήσκοντες αἵματος τὰ ἕλη καὶ νεκρῶν τὴν
λίμνην, ὥστε μέχρι νῦν πολλὰ βαρβαρικὰ τόξα
καὶ κράνη καὶ θωράκων σπάσματα σιδηρῶν καὶ
μαχαίρας ἐμβεβαπτισμένας τοῖς τέλμασιν εὑρί-
σκεσθαι, σχεδὸν ἐτῶν διακοσίων ἀπὸ τῆς μάχης
ἐκείνης διαγεγονότων. τὰ μὲν οὖν περὶ Χαιρώνειαν καὶ πρὸς Ὀρχομενῷ τοιαῦτα λέγεται
γενέσθαι.

XXII. Κίννα δὲ καὶ Κάρβωνος ἐν Ῥώμῃ τοῖς
ἐπιφανεστάτοις ἀνδράσι χρωμένων παρανόμως καὶ
βιαίως, πολλοὶ τὴν τυραννίδα φεύγοντες ὥσπερ εἰς
λιμένα τοῦ Σύλλα τὸ στρατόπεδον κατεφέροντο,
καὶ περὶ αὐτὸν ὀλίγου χρόνου σχῆμα βουλῆς ἐγε-
γόνει. καὶ Μετέλλα μόλις διακλέψασα ἑαυτὴν
καὶ τοὺς παῖδας, ἧκεν ἀγγέλλουσα τὴν οἰκίαν
αὐτοῦ καὶ τὰς ἐπαύλεις ὑπὸ τῶν ἐχθρῶν ἐμπε-
2 πρῆσθαι καὶ δεομένη τοῖς οἴκοι βοηθεῖν. ἀπορου-
μένῳ δ᾽ αὐτῷ, καὶ μήτε τῆς πατρίδος ἀμελεῖν
ὑπομένοντι κακουμένης μήτε ὅπως ἄπεισιν ἀτελὲς
λιπὼν τοσοῦτον ἔργον, τὸν Μιθριδατικὸν πόλεμον,
ἐπινοοῦντι, παραγίνεται Δηλιακὸς ἔμπορος Ἀρχέλαος, ἐλπίδας τινὰς καὶ λόγους κρύφα παρὰ τοῦ
βασιλικοῦ κομίζων Ἀρχελάου. καὶ τὸ πρᾶγμα
Σύλλας οὕτως ἠγάπησεν ὥστε αὐτὸς εἰς λόγους
3 σπεῦσαι τῷ Ἀρχελάῳ συνελθεῖν· καὶ συνῆλθον
ἐπὶ θαλάττῃ περὶ Δήλιον, οὗ τὸ ἱερὸν τοῦ Ἀπόλ-
λωνός ἐστιν. ἀρξαμένου δὲ τοῦ Ἀρχελάου διαλέγεσθαι, καὶ τὸν Σύλλαν ἀξιοῦντος ἀφέντα τὴν

---

[1] Plutarch must, therefore, have written this *Life* shortly
before 115 A.D.

them, and such was their panic that no resistance was made, and he took their camp by storm. The marshes were filled with their blood, and the lake with their dead bodies, so that even to this day many bows, helmets, fragments of steel breastplates, and swords of barbarian make are found embedded in the mud, although almost two hundred years have passed since this battle.[1] Such, then, are the accounts given of the actions at Chaeroneia and Orchomenus.

XXII. Now since Cinna and Carbo [2] at Rome were treating the most eminent men with injustice and violence, many of these had fled from their tyranny and were repairing to Sulla's camp as to a harbour of refuge, and in a little time he had about him a semblance of a senate. Metella, also, who had with difficulty stolen herself and her children away, came with tidings that his house and his villas had been burned by his enemies, and with entreaties that he would come to the help of his partisans at home. But while he was in doubt what to do, and could neither consent to neglect his country when she was outraged, nor see his way clear to go away and leave unfinished so great a task as the war with Mithridates, there came to him a merchant of Delos, named Archelaüs, who secretly brought from Archelaüs the king's general certain vague hopes and propositions. The matter was so welcome to Sulla that he was eager to have a personal conference with Archelaüs; and they had a meeting on the sea-coast near Delium, where the temple of Apollo is. Archelaüs began the conference by urging Sulla to abandon Asia and Pontus and sail

[2] Elected consul with Cinna in 85 B.C.

Ἀσίαν καὶ τὸν Πόντον ἐπὶ τὸν ἐν Ῥώμῃ πόλεμον
πλεῖν, χρήματα λαβόντα καὶ τριήρεις καὶ δύναμιν ὅσην βούλοιτο παρὰ τοῦ βασιλέως, ὑπολαβὼν ὁ Σύλλας Μιθριδάτου μὲν ἀμελεῖν ἐκέλευεν,
αὐτὸν δὲ βασιλεύειν ἀντ' ἐκείνου σύμμαχον
Ῥωμαίων γενόμενον καὶ παραδόντα τὰς ναῦς.
4 ἀφοσιουμένου δὲ τοῦ Ἀρχελάου τὴν προδοσίαν, "Εἶτα," ἔφη, "σὺ μέν, ὦ Ἀρχέλαε, Καπ-
παδόκης ὢν καὶ βαρβάρου βασιλέως δοῦλος, εἰ
δὲ βούλει, φίλος, οὐχ ὑπομένεις ἐπὶ τηλικούτοις
ἀγαθοῖς τὸ αἰσχρόν, ἐμοὶ δὲ ἡγεμόνι Ῥωμαίων
ὄντι καὶ Σύλλᾳ τολμᾷς διαλέγεσθαι περὶ προδοσίας, ὥσπερ οὐκ ἐκεῖνος ὢν Ἀρχέλαος, ὁ φυγὼν
μὲν ἐκ Χαιρωνείας ὀλιγοστὸς ἀπὸ μυριάδων δυο-
καίδεκα, κρυφθεὶς δὲ δύο ἡμέρας ἐν τοῖς Ὀρχομενίων ἕλεσιν, ἄβατον δὲ τὴν Βοιωτίαν ὑπὸ
5 νεκρῶν πλήθους ἀπολελοιπώς;" ἐκ τούτου μετα-
βαλὼν ὁ Ἀρχέλαος καὶ προσκυνήσας ἐδεῖτο
παύσασθαι τοῦ πολέμου καὶ διαλλαγῆναι πρὸς
τὸν Μιθριδάτην. δεξαμένου δὲ τοῦ Σύλλα τὴν
πρόκλησιν ἐγένοντο συνθῆκαι, Μιθριδάτην μὲν
Ἀσίαν ἀφεῖναι καὶ Παφλαγονίαν, ἐκστῆναι δὲ
Βιθυνίας Νικομήδει καὶ Καππαδοκίας¹ Ἀριοβαρζάνῃ, καταβαλεῖν δὲ Ῥωμαίοις δισχίλια
τάλαντα καὶ δοῦναι ναῦς ἑβδομήκοντα χαλ-
κήρεις μετὰ τῆς οἰκείας παρασκευῆς, Σύλλαν
δὲ ἐκείνῳ τήν τε ἄλλην ἀρχὴν βεβαιοῦν καὶ σύμμαχον Ῥωμαίων ψηφίζεσθαι.

XXIII. Τούτων ὁμολογηθέντων ἀναστρέψας
ἐβάδιζε διὰ Θετταλίας καὶ Μακεδονίας ἐπὶ τὸν
Ἑλλήσποντον, ἔχων μεθ' αὑτοῦ τὸν Ἀρχέλαον ἐν

¹ καὶ Καππαδοκίας Bekker, after Coraës: Καππαδοκίας.

for the war in Rome, on condition of receiving
money, triremes, and as large a force as he wished,
from the king. Sulla rejoined by bidding him take
no further thought for Mithridates, but assume the
crown himself in his stead, becoming an ally of
the Romans, and surrendering to them his ships.
And when Archelaüs expressed his abhorrence of
such treason, Sulla said : " So then, thou, Archelaüs,
who art a Cappadocian, and a slave of a barbarian
king, or, if thou wilt, his friend, wilt not consent
to a disgraceful deed for such great rewards ; but
to me, who am a Roman commander, and Sulla,
thou darest to propose treachery ? as if thou wert
not that Archelaüs who fled from Chaeroneia with
a few survivors out of one hundred and twenty
thousand men, and who lay hid for two days in
the marshes of Orchomenus, and who left Boeotia
impassable for the multitude of dead bodies ! "
Upon this, Archelaüs changed his tone, and as a
humble suppliant besought him to desist from the
war and be reconciled with Mithridates. Sulla
granted the request, and terms of agreement were
made as follows : Mithridates was to renounce
Asia and Paphlagonia, restore Bithynia to Nicomedes
and Cappadocia to Ariobarzanes, pay down to the
Romans two thousand talents, and give them seventy
bronze-armoured ships with their proper equipment ;
Sulla, on his part, was to confirm Mithridates in the
rest of his dominions, and get him voted an ally of
the Romans.

XXIII. When these agreements had been made,
Sulla turned back and proceeded by way of Thessaly
and Macedonia towards the Hellespont, having

399

τιμῇ. καὶ νοσήσαντος ἐπισφαλῶς περὶ Λάρισσαν
ἐπιστήσας τὴν πορείαν, ὡς ἑνὸς τῶν ὑπ' αὐτὸν
2 ἡγεμόνων καὶ στρατηγῶν ἐπεμελήθη. ταῦτά τε
δὴ διέβαλλε τὸ περὶ Χαιρώνειαν ἔργον ὡς οὐχὶ
καθαρῶς ἀγωνισθέν, καὶ ὅτι τοὺς ἄλλους Μιθριδάτῃ φίλους, οὓς εἶχεν αἰχμαλώτους, ἀποδοὺς ὁ
Σύλλας Ἀριστίωνα μόνον τὸν τύραννον ἀνεῖλε
διὰ φαρμάκων Ἀρχελάῳ διάφορον ὄντα· μάλιστα
δ' ἡ δοθεῖσα γῆ τῷ Καππαδόκῃ μυρίων πλέθρων
ἐν Εὐβοίᾳ, καὶ τὸ Ῥωμαίων φίλον αὐτὸν καὶ
σύμμαχον ὑπὸ Σύλλα ἀναγραφῆναι. περὶ μὲν
οὖν τούτων αὐτὸς ὁ Σύλλας ἐν τοῖς ὑπομνήμασιν
ἀπολογεῖται.

3   Τότε δὲ πρεσβευτῶν παρὰ τοῦ Μιθριδάτου   467
παραγενομένων καὶ τὰ μὲν ἄλλα φασκόντων
δέχεσθαι, Παφλαγονίαν δὲ ἀξιούντων μὴ ἀφαι-
ρεθῆναι, τὰς δὲ ναῦς οὐδὲ ὅλως ὁμολογηθῆναι,
χαλεπήνας ὁ Σύλλας, "Τί φατε;" εἶπε, "Μιθριδάτης Παφλαγονίας ἀντιποιεῖται καὶ περὶ τῶν
νεῶν ἔξαρνός ἐστιν, ὃν ἐγὼ προσκυνήσειν ἐνόμιζον,
εἰ τὴν δεξιὰν αὐτῷ καταλείποιμι χεῖρα, δι' ἧς
4 τοσούτους Ῥωμαίων ἀνεῖλεν; ἑτέρας μέντοι τάχα
φωνὰς ἀφήσει διαβάντος εἰς Ἀσίαν ἐμοῦ· νῦν δὲ
ἐν Περγάμῳ καθήμενος ὃν οὐχ ἑώρακε διαστρα-
τηγεῖ πόλεμον." οἱ μὲν οὖν πρέσβεις φοβηθέντες
ἡσύχαζον, ὁ δὲ Ἀρχέλαος ἐδεῖτο τοῦ Σύλλα καὶ
κατεπράϋνε τὴν ὀργήν, ἁπτόμενος τῆς δεξιᾶς
αὐτοῦ καὶ δακρύων. τέλος δ' ἔπεισεν ἀποσταλῆναι αὐτὸς[1] πρὸς τὸν Μιθριδάτην· διαπράξ-

---

[1] ἀποσταλῆναι αὐτὸς Sintenis[1] and Bekker, after Emperius:
ἀποσταλῆναι. The best MS. (S^g) has αὐτούς.

Archelaüs with him, and in honour. And when Archelaüs fell dangerously ill at Larissa, Sulla stopped his
march, and cared for him as if he had been one
of his own commanding officers. This raised the
suspicion that the action at Chaeroneia had not
been fairly fought, as well as the fact that Sulla
released the other friends of Mithridates whom
he had taken captive, but put to death Aristion
the tyrant alone, by poison, who was at enmity
with Archelaüs; the strongest ground for the suspicion, however, was his gift to the Cappadocian
of ten thousand acres of land in Euboea, and his
bestowing upon him the title of friend and ally of
the Romans. At any rate, on these points Sulla
defends himself in his Memoirs.

At this time also ambassadors from Mithridates
arrived, and when they declared that he accepted
the other terms, but demanded that Paphlagonia
be not taken away from him, and that as to the
ships no agreement whatsoever should be made,
Sulla flew into a passion and said: "What say
ye? Mithridates maintains his claim to Paphlagonia,
and refuses to give the ships, when I thought he
would prostrate himself humbly before me if I
should leave him but that right hand of his, with
which he took the lives of so many Romans?
However, he will quickly talk in another strain after
I have crossed into Asia; now he sits in Pergamum
and directs a war which he has not seen." The ambassadors, accordingly, were frightened, and held
their peace; but Archelaüs entreated Sulla, and
tried to soften his anger, laying hold of his right
hand and weeping. And finally he obtained Sulla's
consent to send him in person to Mithridates; for

εσθαι γὰρ ἐφ᾽ οἷς βούλεται τὴν εἰρήνην, εἰ δὲ μὴ
5 πείθοι, κτενεῖν αὐτὸς αὑτόν. ἐπὶ τούτοις ἐκπέμψας ἐκεῖνον αὐτὸς εἰς τὴν Μαιδικὴν ἐνέβαλε,
καὶ τὰ πολλὰ διαπορθήσας πάλιν ἀνέστρεψεν εἰς
Μακεδονίαν, καὶ τὸν Ἀρχέλαον ἐδέξατο περὶ
Φιλίππους ἀγγέλλοντα καλῶς ἔχειν πάντα·
6 δεῖσθαι δὲ πάντως αὐτῷ τὸν Μιθριδάτην εἰς
λόγους ἐλθεῖν. αἴτιος δ᾽ ἦν μάλιστα Φιμβρίας,
ὃς τὸν ἀπὸ τῆς ἑτέρας στάσεως ἄρχοντα Φλάκκον
ἀνελὼν καὶ τῶν Μιθριδατικῶν στρατηγῶν κρατήσας ἐπ᾽ αὐτὸν ἐκεῖνον ἐβάδιζε. ταῦτα γὰρ
δείσας ὁ Μιθριδάτης μᾶλλον εἵλετο τῷ Σύλλᾳ
φίλος γενέσθαι.

XXIV. Συνῆλθον οὖν τῆς Τρῳάδος ἐν Δαρδάνῳ,
Μιθριδάτης μὲν ἔχων ναῦς αὐτόθι διακοσίας
ἐνήρεις καὶ τῆς πεζῆς δυνάμεως ὁπλίτας μὲν
δισμυρίους, ἱππεῖς δὲ ἑξακισχιλίους καὶ συχνὰ
τῶν δρεπανηφόρων, Σύλλας δὲ τέσσαρας σπείρας
καὶ διακοσίους ἱππεῖς. ἀπαντήσαντος δὲ τοῦ
Μιθριδάτου καὶ τὴν δεξιὰν προτείναντος, ἠρώτησεν αὐτὸν εἰ καταλύσεται τὸν πόλεμον ἐφ᾽ οἷς
ὡμολόγησεν Ἀρχέλαος· σιωπῶντος δὲ τοῦ βασιλέως, ὁ Σύλλας "Ἀλλὰ μήν," ἔφη, "τῶν δεομένων ἐστὶ τὸ προτέρους λέγειν, τοῖς δὲ νικῶσιν
2 ἐξαρκεῖ τὸ σιωπᾶν." ἐπεὶ δὲ ἀρξάμενος τῆς
ἀπολογίας ὁ Μιθριδάτης ἐπειρᾶτο τοῦ πολέμου
τὰ μὲν εἰς δαίμονας τρέπειν, τὰ δὲ αὐτοὺς αἰτιᾶσθαι τοὺς Ῥωμαίους, ὑπολαβὼν ὁ Σύλλας ἔφη
πάλαι μὲν ἑτέρων ἀκούειν, νῦν δ᾽ αὐτὸς ἐγνωκέναι
τὸν Μιθριδάτην δεινότατον ὄντα ῥητορεύειν, ὃς

he said that he would have the peace ratified on Sulla's terms, or, if he could not persuade the king, would kill himself. Upon these assurances Sulla sent him away, and then himself invaded the country of the Maedi, and after ravaging the most of it, turned back again into Macedonia, and received Archelaüs at Philippi. Archelaüs brought him word that all was well, but that Mithridates insisted on a conference with him. Fimbria was chiefly responsible for this, who, after killing Flaccus, the consul of the opposite faction,[1] and overpowering the generals of Mithridates, was marching against the king himself. For this terrified Mithridates, and he chose rather to seek the friendship of Sulla.

XXIV. They met, accordingly, at Dardanus, in the Troad, Mithridates having two hundred ships there, equipped with oars, twenty thousand men-at-arms from his infantry force, six thousand horse, and a throng of scythe-bearing chariots; Sulla, on the other hand, having four cohorts and two hundred horse. When Mithridates came towards him and put out his hand, Sulla asked him if he would put a stop to the war on the terms which Archelaüs had made, and as the king was silent, Sulla said: "But surely it is the part of suppliants to speak first, while victors need only to be silent." Then Mithridates began a defence of himself, and tried to shift the blame for the war partly upon the gods, and partly upon the Romans themselves. But Sulla cut him short, saying that he had long ago heard from others, but now knew of himself, that Mithridates was a very powerful orator, since he

---

[1] See chapter xii. 8 and note.

ἐπὶ πράξεσιν οὕτω πονηραῖς καὶ παρανόμοις
3 λόγων ἐχόντων εὐπρέπειαν οὐκ ἠπόρηκεν. ἐξ-
ελέγξας δὲ τὰ πεπραγμένα πικρῶς ὑπ' αὐτοῦ καὶ
κατηγορήσας, πάλιν ἠρώτησεν εἰ ποιεῖ τὰ συγ-
κείμενα δι' Ἀρχελάου. φήσαντος δὲ ποιεῖν,
οὕτως ἠσπάσατο καὶ περιλαβὼν ἐφίλησεν αὐτόν,
Ἀριοβαρζάνην δὲ αὖθις καὶ Νικομήδην τοὺς
βασιλεῖς προσαγαγὼν διήλλαξεν. ὁ μὲν οὖν
Μιθριδάτης ἑβδομήκοντα ναῦς παραδοὺς καὶ
τοξότας πεντακοσίους εἰς Πόντον ἀπέπλευσεν.
4 Ὁ δὲ Σύλλας, αἰσθόμενος ἀχθομένους τοὺς
στρατιώτας τῇ διαλύσει (τὸν γὰρ ἔχθιστον τῶν
βασιλέων καὶ δεκαπέντε μυριάδας ἡμέρᾳ μιᾷ τῶν
ἐν Ἀσίᾳ Ῥωμαίων κατασφαγῆναι παρασκευά-
σαντα δεινὸν ἡγοῦντο μετὰ πλούτου καὶ λαφύρων
ὁρᾶν ἐκπλέοντα τῆς Ἀσίας, ἣν ἔτη τέσσαρα
λεηλατῶν καὶ φορολογῶν διετέλεσεν), ἀπελογεῖτο
πρὸς αὐτοὺς ὡς οὐκ ἂν ἅμα Φιμβρίᾳ καὶ Μιθριδάτῃ πολεμεῖν, εἰ συνέστησαν ἀμφότεροι κατ'
αὐτοῦ, δυνηθείς.

XXV. Ὁρμήσας δὲ ἐκεῖθεν ἐπὶ Φιμβρίαν πρὸς
Θυατείροις στρατοπεδεύοντα καὶ πλησίον κατα-
ζεύξας, τάφρον τῷ στρατοπέδῳ περιέβαλεν. οἱ
δὲ τοῦ Φιμβρίου στρατιῶται μονοχίτωνες ἐκ τοῦ
στρατοπέδου προϊόντες ἠσπάζοντο τοὺς ἐκείνου
καὶ συνελάμβανον αὐτοῖς τῶν ἔργων προθύμως.
ὁρῶν δὲ ὁ Φιμβρίας τὴν μεταβολὴν καὶ τὸν
Σύλλαν ὡς ἀδιάλλακτον δεδοικὼς αὐτὸς ἑαυτὸν
ἐν τῷ στρατοπέδῳ διέφθειρε.

---

1 In the late autumn of 88 B.C. The cities of Asia Minor
were glad to obey the orders of Mithridates for a general

had not been at a loss for plausible arguments to defend such baseness and injustice as his. Then he reproached him bitterly and denounced him for what he had done, and asked him again if he would keep the agreements made through Archelaüs. And when he said that he would, then Sulla greeted him with an embrace and a kiss, and later, bringing to him Ariobarzanes and Nicomedes the kings, he reconciled him with them. Mithridates, accordingly, after handing over to Sulla seventy ships and five hundred archers, sailed away to Pontus.

But Sulla perceived that his soldiers were incensed at the peace which he had made; they thought it a terrible thing to see the most hostile of kings, who had caused one hundred and fifty thousand of the Romans in Asia to be massacred in a single day [1] go sailing off with wealth and spoils from Asia, which he had for four years continued to plunder and levy taxes on. He therefore defended himself to them by saying that he would not have been able to carry on war with Mithridates and Fimbria too, if they had both joined forces against him.

XXV. Then he set out from thence against Fimbria, who was encamped near Thyateira, and halting his army near by, began to fortify his camp. But the soldiers of Fimbria came forth from their camp without any armour on, and welcomed Sulla's soldiers, and joined them eagerly in their labours, and when Fimbria saw this change in their allegiance, fearing that Sulla was irreconcileable, he laid violent hands on himself in the camp.

massacre of the resident Romans. Cf. Appian, *Mithridates*, xxii. Valerius Maximus (ix. 2, 4, Ext. 3) gives the number of slain as 80,000.

2 Σύλλας δὲ κοινῇ μὲν ἐζημίωσε τὴν Ἀσίαν
δισμυρίοις ταλάντοις, ἰδίᾳ δὲ τοὺς οἴκους ἐξέ- 468
τριψεν ὕβρει καὶ πολιορκίᾳ[1] τῶν ἐπισταθμευόν-
των. ἐτέτακτο γὰρ ἑκάστης ἡμέρας τῷ καταλύτῃ
τὸν ξένον διδόναι τέσσαρα τετράδραχμα καὶ
παρέχειν δεῖπνον αὐτῷ καὶ φίλοις, ὅσους ἂν
ἐθέλῃ καλεῖν, ταξίαρχον δὲ πεντήκοντα δραχμὰς
λαμβάνειν τῆς ἡμέρας, ἐσθῆτα δὲ ἄλλην μὲν
οἰκουρῶν, ἄλλην δὲ εἰς ἀγορὰν προερχόμενος.

XXVI. Ἀναχθεὶς δὲ πάσαις ταῖς ναυσὶν ἐξ
Ἐφέσου τριταῖος ἐν Πειραιεῖ καθωρμίσθη· καὶ
μυηθεὶς ἐξεῖλεν ἑαυτῷ τὴν Ἀπελλικῶνος τοῦ
Τηΐου βιβλιοθήκην, ἐν ᾗ τὰ πλεῖστα τῶν Ἀριστοτέλους καὶ Θεοφράστου βιβλίων ἦν, οὔπω τότε
σαφῶς γνωριζόμενα τοῖς πολλοῖς. λέγεται δὲ
κομισθείσης αὐτῆς εἰς Ῥώμην Τυραννίωνα τὸν
γραμματικὸν ἐνσκευάσασθαι τὰ πολλά, καὶ παρ'
αὐτοῦ τὸν Ῥόδιον Ἀνδρόνικον εὐπορήσαντα τῶν
ἀντιγράφων εἰς μέσον θεῖναι καὶ ἀναγράψαι τοὺς
2 νῦν φερομένους πίνακας. οἱ δὲ πρεσβύτεροι
Περιπατητικοὶ φαίνονται μὲν καθ' ἑαυτοὺς γενόμενοι χαρίεντες καὶ φιλόλογοι, τῶν δὲ Ἀριστοτέλους καὶ Θεοφράστου γραμμάτων οὔτε πολλοῖς
οὔτε ἀκριβῶς ἐντετυχηκότες διὰ τὸ τὸν Νηλέως
τοῦ Σκηψίου κλῆρον, ᾧ τὰ βιβλία κατέλιπε
Θεόφραστος, εἰς ἀφιλοτίμους καὶ ἰδιώτας ἀνθρώπους περιγενέσθαι.

---

[1] πολιορκίᾳ MSS., Coraës, Sintenis[1], Bekker : πλεονεξίᾳ after
Solanus.

---

[1] Cf. *Lucullus*, iv. 1.
[2] Cf. Strabo, xiii. 1, 54. Scepsis was a city of the Troad,

Sulla now laid a public fine upon Asia of twenty thousand talents,[1] and utterly ruined individual families by the insolent outrages of the soldiers quartered on them. For orders were given that the host should give his guest four tetradrachms every day, and furnish him, and as many friends as he might wish to invite, with a supper; and that a military tribune should receive fifty drachmas a day, and two suits of clothing, one to wear when he was at home, and another when he went abroad.

XXVI. Having put to sea with all his ships from Ephesus, on the third day he came to anchor in Piraeus. He was now initiated into the mysteries, and seized for himself the library of Apellicon the Teian, in which were most of the treatises of Aristotle and Theophrastus, at that time not yet well known to the public. But it is said that after the library was carried to Rome, Tyrannio the grammarian arranged most of the works in it, and that Andronicus the Rhodian was furnished by him with copies of them, and published them, and drew up the lists now current. The older Peripatetics were evidently of themselves accomplished and learned men, but they seem to have had neither a large nor an exact acquaintance with the writings of Aristotle and Theophrastus, because the estate of Neleus of Scepsis, to whom Theophrastus bequeathed his books, came into the hands of careless and illiterate people.[2]

---

and a centre of learning under the Attalid dynasty of Pergamum. The writings of Aristotle and Theophrastus were hidden in an underground cellar by their owners, to keep them from being taken to Pergamum, and came in a damaged condition into the possession of Apellicon.

3 Σύλλᾳ δὲ διατρίβοντι περὶ τὰς Ἀθήνας ἄλγημα
ναρκῶδες μετὰ βάρους εἰς τοὺς πόδας ἐνέπεσεν, ὅ
φησιν ὁ Στράβων ποδάγρας ψελλισμὸν εἶναι.
διαπλεύσας οὖν εἰς Αἴδηψον ἐχρῆτο τοῖς θερμοῖς
ὕδασι, ῥᾳθυμῶν ἅμα καὶ συνδιημερεύων τοῖς περὶ
τὸν Διόνυσον τεχνίταις. περιπατοῦντος δὲ πρὸς
τὴν θάλατταν ἁλιεῖς τινες ἰχθῦς αὐτῷ παγκάλους
προσήνεγκαν. ἡσθεὶς δὲ τοῖς δώροις, καὶ πυθόμενος ὡς ἐξ Ἁλῶν[1] εἶεν, "Ἔτι γὰρ ζῇ τις
4 Ἁλαίων;" ἔφη· ἐτύγχανε γάρ, ὅτε τὴν πρὸς
Ὀρχομενῷ μάχην νενικηκὼς ἐδίωκε τοὺς πολεμίους, ἅμα τρεῖς πόλεις τῆς Βοιωτίας, Ἀνθηδόνα,
Λάρυμναν, Ἁλὰς[1] ἀνῃρηκώς. τῶν δ᾽ ἀνθρώπων
ὑπὸ δέους ἀφώνων γενομένων, διαμειδιάσας ἐκέλευσεν ἀπιέναι χαίροντας, ὡς οὐ μετὰ φαύλων
οὐδὲ ἀξίων ὀλιγωρίας ἥκοντας παραιτητῶν.
Ἁλαῖοι μὲν ἐκ τούτου λέγουσι θαρρήσαντες αὖθις
εἰς τὴν πόλιν συνελθεῖν.

XXVII. Σύλλας δὲ διὰ Θετταλίας καὶ Μακεδονίας καταβὰς ἐπὶ θάλατταν παρεσκευάζετο
χιλίαις ναυσὶ καὶ διακοσίαις ἀπὸ Δυρραχίου
διαβάλλειν εἰς Βρεντέσιον. ἡ δὲ Ἀπολλωνία
πλησίον ἐστί, καὶ πρὸς αὐτῇ τὸ Νύμφαιον, ἱερὸς
τόπος ἐκ χλοερᾶς νάπης καὶ λειμώνων ἀναδιδοὺς
2 πυρὸς πηγὰς σποράδας ἐνδελεχῶς ῥέοντος. ἐνταῦθά φασι κοιμώμενον ἁλῶναι σάτυρον, οἷον οἱ
πλάσται καὶ γραφεῖς εἰκάζουσιν, ἀχθέντα δὲ ὡς
Σύλλαν ἐρωτᾶσθαι δι᾽ ἑρμηνέων πολλῶν ὅστις
εἴη· φθεγξαμένου δὲ μόλις οὐδὲν συνετῶς, ἀλλὰ

---

[1] Ἁλῶν, Ἁλὰς with Coraës (in notes): Ἁλαιῶν, Ἁλαίας.

---

[1] In some passage not now extant.

While Sulla was tarrying at Athens, his feet were attacked by numbness and a feeling of heaviness, which Strabo says [1] is premonitory gout. He therefore crossed the straits to Aedepsus and used the hot waters there, taking a holiday at the same time, and passing his time pleasantly with the theatrical artists. Once, as he was walking along the sea-shore, certain fishermen brought him some very fine fish. Being delighted with their gift, and learning that they were from Halae, "What!" said he, "is any man of Halae still alive?" For when he was pursuing the enemy after his victory at Orchomenus, he had destroyed three cities of Boeotia together, Anthedon, Larymna, and Halae. The men were speechless with terror, but Sulla smiled and bade them depart in peace, since they had brought with them no mean or despicable intercessors. The men of Halae say that this gave them courage to go back again in a body to their city.

XXVII. And now Sulla, having passed through Thessaly and Macedonia down to the sea, was preparing to cross from Dyrrhachium to Brundisium with twelve hundred ships.[2] Near by is Apollonia, and in its vicinity is the Nymphaeum, a sacred precinct, which sends forth in various places from its green dell and meadows, streams of perpetually flowing fire. Here, they say, a satyr was caught asleep, such an one as sculptors and painters represent, and brought to Sulla, where he was asked through many interpreters who he was. And when at last he uttered nothing intelligible, but with difficulty

----

[2] His fleet had sailed round Peloponnesus from Piraeus. According to Appian (*Bell. Civ.* i. 79), Sulla crossed from Patras to Brundisium.

τραχεῖάν τινα καὶ μάλιστα μεμιγμένην ἵππου τε
χρεμετισμῷ καὶ τράγου μηκασμῷ φωνὴν ἀφέντος,
ἐκπλαγέντα τὸν Σύλλαν ἀποδιοπομπήσασθαι.

3 Μέλλοντος δὲ τοὺς στρατιώτας διαπεραιοῦν,
καὶ δεδιότος μὴ τῆς Ἰταλίας ἐπιλαβόμενοι κατὰ
πόλεις ἕκαστοι διαρρυῶσι, πρῶτον μὲν ὤμοσαν
ἀφ᾽ αὑτῶν παραμενεῖν καὶ μηδὲν ἑκουσίως κακ-
ουργήσειν τὴν Ἰταλίαν, ἔπειτα χρημάτων δεόμενον πολλῶν ὁρῶντες, ἀπήρχοντο καὶ συνεισέ-
φερον ὡς ἕκαστος εἶχεν εὐπορίας. οὐ μὴν ἐδέξατο
τὴν ἀπαρχὴν ὁ Σύλλας, ἀλλ᾽ ἐπαινέσας καὶ
παρορμήσας διέβαινεν, ὥς φησιν αὐτός, ἐπὶ
πεντεκαίδεκα στρατηγοὺς πολεμίους πεντήκοντα
καὶ τετρακοσίας σπείρας ἔχοντας, ἐκδηλότατα
τοῦ θεοῦ τὰς εὐτυχίας προσημαίνοντος αὐτῷ,

4 θύσαντος μὲν γὰρ εὐθέως ᾗ διέβη περὶ Τάραντα,
δάφνης στεφάνου τύπον ἔχων ὁ λοβὸς ὤφθη, καὶ
λημνίσκων δύο κατηρτημένων. μικρὸν δὲ πρὸ   469
τῆς διαβάσεως ἐν Καμπανίᾳ περὶ τὸ Τίφατον
ὄρος ἡμέρας ὤφθησαν δύο τράγοι μεγάλοι συμ-
φερόμενοι καὶ πάντα δρῶντες καὶ πάσχοντες
ἃ συμβαίνει μαχομένοις ἀνθρώποις. ἦν δὲ ἄρα
φάσμα, καὶ κατὰ μικρὸν αἰρόμενον ἀπὸ γῆς διεσπείρετο πολλαχοῦ τοῦ ἀέρος εἰδώλοις ἀμαυροῖς

5 ὅμοιον, εἶτα οὕτως ἠφανίσθη. καὶ μετ᾽ οὐ πολὺν
χρόνον ἐν τῷ τόπῳ τούτῳ Μαρίου τοῦ νέου καὶ
Νορβανοῦ τοῦ ὑπάτου μεγάλας δυνάμεις ἐπαγα-
γόντων, ὁ Σύλλας οὔτε τάξιν ἀποδοὺς οὔτε
λοχίσας τὸ οἰκεῖον στράτευμα, ῥώμῃ δὲ προθυμίας κοινῆς καὶ φορᾷ τόλμης ἀποχρησάμενος

---

[1] In the spring of 83 B.C. The main part of his forces, at
any rate, must have landed at Brundisium.

emitted a hoarse cry that was something between
the neighing of a horse and the bleating of a goat,
Sulla was horrified, and ordered him out of his sight.

When Sulla was about to transport his soldiers,
and was in fear lest, when they had reached Italy,
they should disperse to their several cities, in the
first place, they took an oath of their own accord to
stand by him, and to do no damage to Italy without
his orders ; and then, seeing that he needed much
money, they made a free-will offering and contribution, each man according to his abundance.
Sulla, however, would not accept their offering, but
after thanking them and rousing their courage,
crossed over to confront, as he himself says, fifteen
hostile commanders with four hundred and fifty
cohorts. But the Deity gave him most unmistake-
able foretokens of his successes. For after he had
sacrificed at once where he landed at Tarentum,[1]
the victim's liver was seen to have an impression of
a wreath of laurel, with two fillets hanging from it.[2]
And a little while before he crossed over from
Greece, there were seen on Mount Tifatum in
Campania, in the day time, two great he-goats
fighting together, and doing everything that men do
when they fight a battle. But it proved to be an
apparition, and gradually rising from earth it dispersed
itself generally in the air, like vague phantoms, and
then vanished from sight. And not long after,[3] in
this very place, when Marius the younger and
Norbanus the consul led large forces up against him,
Sulla, without either giving out an order of battle or
forming his own army in companies, but taking
advantage of a vigorous general alacrity and a

[2] The typical triumphal crown.   [3] In 83 B.C.

ἐτρέψατο τοὺς πολεμίους καὶ κατέκλεισεν εἰς
Καπύην πόλιν τὸν Νορβανόν, ἑπτακισχιλίους
6 ἀποκτείνας. τοῦτο αἴτιον αὐτῷ γενέσθαι φησὶ
τοῦ μὴ διαλυθῆναι τοὺς στρατιώτας κατὰ πόλεις,
ἀλλὰ συμμεῖναι καὶ καταφρονῆσαι τῶν ἐναντίων
πολλαπλασίων ὄντων. ἐν δὲ Σιλβίῳ φησὶν
οἰκέτην Ποντίου θεοφόρητον ἐντυχεῖν αὐτῷ λέ-
γοντα παρὰ τῆς Ἐννοῦς κράτος πολέμου καὶ
νίκην ἀπαγγέλλειν· εἰ δὲ μὴ σπεύσειεν, ἐμπεπρή-
σεσθαι τὸ Καπιτώλιον· ὃ καὶ συμβῆναι τῆς
ἡμέρας ἐκείνης ἧς ὁ ἄνθρωπος προηγόρευσεν· ἦν
δὲ αὕτη πρὸ μιᾶς νωνῶν Κυντιλίων, ἃς νῦν
7 Ἰουλίας καλοῦμεν. ἔτι δὲ Μάρκος Λεύκολλος, εἷς
τῶν ὑπὸ Σύλλᾳ στρατηγούντων, περὶ Φιδεντίαν
ἑκκαίδεκα σπείραις πρὸς πεντήκοντα τῶν πολεμίων ἀντιταχθεὶς τῇ μὲν προθυμίᾳ τῶν
στρατιωτῶν ἐπίστευεν, ἀνόπλους δὲ τοὺς πολλοὺς ἔχων ὤκνει. βουλευομένου δὲ αὐτοῦ καὶ
διαμέλλοντος, ἀπὸ τοῦ πλησίον πεδίου λειμῶνα
ἔχοντος αὔρα φέρουσα μαλακὴ πολλὰ τῶν ἀνθέων
ἐπέβαλε τῇ στρατιᾷ καὶ κατέσπειρεν, αὐτομάτως
ἐπιμένοντα καὶ περιπίπτοντα τοῖς θυρεοῖς καὶ
τοῖς κράνεσιν αὐτῶν, ὥστε φαίνεσθαι τοῖς πο-
8 λεμίοις ἐστεφανωμένους. γενόμενοι δὲ ὑπὸ τούτου προθυμότεροι συνέβαλον· καὶ νικήσαντες
ὀκτακισχιλίους ἐπὶ μυρίοις ἀπέκτειναν καὶ τὸ
στρατόπεδον εἷλον. οὗτος ὁ Λεύκολλος ἀδελφὸς
ἦν Λευκόλλου τοῦ Μιθριδάτην ὕστερον καὶ
Τιγράνην καταπολεμήσαντος.

XXVIII. Ὁ δὲ Σύλλας ἔτι πολλοῖς στρατο-
πέδοις καὶ μεγάλαις δυνάμεσι περικεχυμένους

transport of courage in them, routed the enemy and
shut up Norbanus in the city of Capua, after slaying
seven thousand of his men. It was on account of
this success, he says, that his soldiers did not disperse
into their several cities, but held together and
despised their opponents, though these were many
times more numerous. He says, moreover, that at
Silvium, a servant of Pontius met him, in an
inspired state, declaring that he brought him from
Bellona triumph in war and victory, but that if he
did not hasten, the Capitol would be burnt; and
this actually happened, he says, on the day which
the man foretold, namely, the sixth day of Quintilis,
which we now call July.[1] And still further, at Fidentia,
when Marcus Lucullus, one of Sulla's commanders,
with sixteen cohorts confronted fifty cohorts of the
enemy, although he had confidence in the readiness
of his soldiers, still, as most of them were without
arms, he hesitated to attack. But while he was
waiting and deliberating, from the neighbouring
plain, which was a meadow, a gentle breeze brought
a quantity of flowers and scattered them down
upon his army; they settled of their own accord
and enveloped the shields and helmets of the
soldiers, so that to the enemy these appeared to be
crowned with garlands. This circumstance made
them more eager for the fray, and they joined battle,
won the victory, killed eighteen thousand of the
enemy, and took their camp. This Lucullus was a
brother of the Lucullus who afterwards subdued
Mithridates and Tigranes.

XXVIII. But Sulla, seeing that his enemies still
surrounded him on all sides with many armies and

---

[1] Cf. *Publicola*, xv. 1.

αὐτῷ τοὺς πολεμίους ὁρῶν πανταχόθεν ἥπτετο
δυνάμει καὶ δι' ἀπάτης, προκαλούμενος εἰς δια-
2 λύσεις τὸν ἕτερον τῶν ὑπάτων Σκηπίωνα. δεξαμένου δ' ἐκείνου σύλλογοι μὲν ἐγίνοντο καὶ
κοινολογίαι πλείονες, ἀεὶ δέ τινα παραγωγὴν καὶ
πρόφασιν ἐμβάλλων ὁ Σύλλας διέφθειρε τοὺς
περὶ Σκηπίωνα τοῖς ἑαυτοῦ στρατιώταις, ἠσκη-
μένοις πρὸς ἀπάτην καὶ γοητείαν ἅπασαν ὥσπερ
αὐτὸς ὁ ἡγεμών. εἰσιόντες γὰρ εἰς τὸν χάρακα
τῶν πολεμίων καὶ ἀναμιγνυμένοι τοὺς μὲν εὐθὺς
ἀργυρίῳ, τοὺς δὲ ὑποσχέσεσι, τοὺς δὲ κολακεύ-
3 οντες καὶ ἀναπείθοντες προσήγοντο. τέλος δὲ
τοῦ Σύλλα μετὰ σπειρῶν εἴκοσι προσελθόντος
ἐγγὺς οἱ μὲν ἠσπάσαντο τοὺς τοῦ Σκηπίωνος, οἱ
δὲ ἀντασπασάμενοι προσεχώρησαν· ὁ δὲ Σκηπίων
ἔρημος ἐν τῇ σκηνῇ ληφθεὶς ἠφείθη, Σύλλας δὲ
ταῖς εἴκοσι σπείραις ὥσπερ ἤθασιν ὄρνισι τεσσαράκοντα τὰς τῶν πολεμίων παλεύσας ἀπήγαγεν εἰς τὸ στρατόπεδον ἅπαντας. ὅτε καὶ
Κάρβωνά φασιν εἰπεῖν ὡς ἀλώπεκι καὶ λέοντι
πολεμῶν ἐν τῇ Σύλλα ψυχῇ κατοικοῦσιν ὑπὸ
τῆς ἀλώπεκος ἀνιῷτο μᾶλλον.

4 Ἐκ τούτου περὶ Σίγνιον Μάριος ὀγδοήκοντα
καὶ πέντε σπείρας ἔχων προὐκαλεῖτο Σύλλαν. ὁ
δὲ καὶ πάνυ πρόθυμος ἦν διαγωνίσασθαι κατ'
ἐκείνην τὴν ἡμέραν· ἐτύγχανε γὰρ ὄψιν ἑωρακὼς
τοιάνδε κατὰ τοὺς ὕπνους. ἐδόκει τὸν γέροντα
Μάριον τεθνηκότα πάλαι τῷ παιδὶ Μαρίῳ παραινεῖν φυλάξασθαι τὴν ἐπιοῦσαν ἡμέραν ὡς μεγάλην αὐτῷ δυστυχίαν φέρουσαν. διὰ τοῦτο μὲν
δὴ πρόθυμος ὁ Σύλλας ἦν μάχεσθαι, καὶ μετε- 470
πέμπετο τὸν Δολοβέλλαν ἄπωθεν στρατοπε-

414

large forces, had recourse to craft as well as force, and invited Scipio, the other consul, to make terms of peace. He accepted the proposal, and several meetings and conferences were held; but Sulla continually interposed some pretext for gaining time, and gradually corrupted Scipio's soldiers by means of his own, who were practised in deceit and every kind of jugglery, like their general himself. For they entered the camp of their enemies, mingled freely with them, and gradually won them over to Sulla's cause, some at once with money, others with promises, and others still with persuasive flatteries. And finally, when Sulla drew near with twenty cohorts, his men greeted those of Scipio, who answered their greetings and went over to them. Scipio, who was left alone, was taken in his tent, but dismissed; while Sulla, who had used his twenty cohorts as decoy-birds to catch the forty cohorts of the enemy, led them all back to his camp. It was on this occasion, too, that Carbo is said to have remarked that in making war upon the fox and the lion in Sulla, he was more annoyed by the fox.

After this, at Signia, Marius, with eighty-five cohorts, challenged Sulla to battle. Now Sulla was very eager to have the issue settled on that day; for he had seen a vision in his dreams, as follows. He thought he saw the elder Marius, who was long since dead, advising his son Marius to beware of the ensuing day, since it would bring him a great calamity. For this reason, then, Sulla was eager to fight a battle, and was trying to get Dolabella, who was encamped at some distance, to join him. But

5 δεύοντα. τῶν δὲ πολεμίων ἐφισταμένων ταῖς
ὁδοῖς καὶ ἀποφραττόντων οἱ τοῦ Σύλλα προσ-
μαχόμενοι καὶ ὁδοποιοῦντες ἔκαμνον· καὶ πολὺς
ὄμβρος ἅμα τοῖς ἔργοις ἐπιγενόμενος μᾶλλον
ἐκάκωσεν αὐτούς. ὅθεν οἱ ταξίαρχοι προσιόντες
τῷ Σύλλᾳ ἐδέοντο τὴν μάχην ἀναβαλέσθαι,
δεικνύντες ἅμα τοὺς στρατιώτας ἐρριμμένους ὑπὸ
κόπου καὶ προσαναπαυομένους χαμᾶζε τοῖς θυ-
6 ρεοῖς κεκλιμένοις. ἐπεὶ δὲ συνεχώρησεν ἄκων καὶ
πρόσταγμα καταζεύξεως ἔδωκεν, ἀρχομένων αὐτῶν τὸν χάρακα βάλλειν καὶ τάφρον ὀρύσσειν
πρὸ τῆς στρατοπεδείας, ἐπήλαυνε σοβαρῶς ὁ
Μάριος προϊππεύων ὡς ἀτάκτους καὶ τεθορυβη-
μένους διασκεδάσων. ἐνταῦθα τῷ Σύλλᾳ τὴν
κατὰ τοὺς ὕπνους φωνὴν ὁ δαίμων συνετέλει.
ὀργὴ γὰρ αὐτοῦ τοῖς στρατιώταις παρέστη, καὶ
παυσάμενοι τῶν ἔργων τοὺς μὲν ὑσσοὺς κατέ-
πηξαν ἐπὶ τῇ τάφρῳ, σπασάμενοι δὲ τὰ ξίφη καὶ
συναλαλάξαντες ἐν χερσὶν ἦσαν τῶν πολεμίων.
7 οἱ δὲ οὐ πολὺν ὑπέστησαν χρόνον, ἀλλὰ γίνεται
πολὺς φόνος αὐτῶν τραπέντων. Μάριος δὲ φεύγων εἰς Πραινεστὸν ἤδη τὰς πύλας εὗρε κεκλει-
μένας· καλωδίου δὲ ἄνωθεν ἀφεθέντος ἐνζώσας
ἑαυτὸν ἀνελήφθη πρὸς τὸ τεῖχος. ἔνιοι δέ φασιν,
ὧν καὶ Φαινεστέλλας ἐστίν, οὐδὲ αἰσθέσθαι τῆς
μάχης τὸν Μάριον, ἀλλ᾿ ἐξ ἀγρυπνιῶν καὶ κόπων
ὑπὸ σκιᾷ τινι χαμαὶ κατακλινέντα τοῦ συνθήματος δοθέντος ἐνδοῦναι πρὸς ὕπνον, εἶτα μόλις
8 ἐξεγείρεσθαι τῆς φυγῆς γενομένης. ἐν ταύτῃ τῇ
μάχῃ Σύλλας φησὶν εἰκοσιτρεῖς μόνους ἀποβαλεῖν,
ἀποκτεῖναι δὲ τῶν πολεμίων δισμυρίους καὶ λαβεῖν ζῶντας ὀκτακισχιλίους. καὶ τἆλλα δὲ ὁμοίως

the enemy beset the roads and hemmed Sulla in,
and his soldiers were worn out with fighting to open
a passage. Much rain also came upon them while
they were at work and added to their distress. The
tribunes therefore came to Sulla and begged him to
defer the battle, showing him the soldiers prostrated
with weariness and resting on their shields, which
they had laid upon the ground. Sulla yielded
reluctantly, and gave orders to pitch a camp, but
just as his men were beginning to dig a trench and
throw up the rampart before it, Marius attacked them
confidently, riding ahead of his lines, and hoping to
scatter his enemies while they were in disorder and
confusion. There the Deity fulfilled the words
which Sulla had heard in his dreams. For Sulla's rage
imparted itself to his soldiers, and leaving off their
work, they planted their javelins in the trench, drew
their swords, and with a general shout came to close
quarters with their enemies. These did not hold
their ground long, but took to flight, and were slain
in great numbers. Marius fled to Præneste, but
found the gate already closed. A rope was thrown
down to him, however, and after fastening this
around his waist, he was hoisted to the top of the
wall. But there are some who say, and Fenestella
is one of these, that Marius knew nothing of the
battle, but was forced by loss of sleep and weariness
to cast himself upon the ground in a shady place
when the signal for battle was given, and there gave
way to sleep, and was then roused with difficulty
when the rout took place. In this battle Sulla says
he lost only twenty-three men, but killed twenty
thousand of the enemy, and took eight thousand
prisoners. His other plans were carried out with like

εὐτυχεῖτο διὰ τῶν στρατηγῶν, Πομπηΐου, Κρασ-
σου, Μετέλλου, Σερουϊλίου. οὐδὲν γὰρ ἢ μικρὰ
προσκρούσαντες οὗτοι μεγάλας συνέτριψαν δυνάμεις τῶν πολεμίων, ὥστε τὸν μάλιστα τὴν
ἐναντίαν στάσιν συνέχοντα Κάρβωνα νύκτωρ
ἀποδράντα τὴν ἑαυτοῦ στρατιὰν εἰς Λιβύην ἐκπλεῦσαι.

XXIX. Τὸν μέντοι τελευταῖον ἀγῶνα καθάπερ
ἔφεδρος ἀθλητῇ καταπόνῳ προσενεχθεὶς ὁ Σαυ-
νίτης Τελεσῖνος ἐγγὺς ἦλθε τοῦ σφῆλαι καὶ
καταβαλεῖν ἐπὶ θύραις τῆς Ῥώμης. ἔσπευδε μὲν
γὰρ ἅμα Λαμπωνίῳ τῷ Λευκανῷ χεῖρα πολλὴν
ἀθροίσας ἐπὶ Πραινεστὸν ὡς ἐξαρπασόμενος τῆς
2 πολιορκίας τὸν Μάριον· ἐπεὶ δὲ ᾔσθετο Σύλλαν
μὲν κατὰ στόμα, Πομπήϊον δὲ κατ' οὐρὰν βοη-
δρομοῦντας ἐπ' αὐτόν, εἰργόμενος τοῦ πρόσω καὶ
ὀπίσω πολεμιστὴς ἀνὴρ καὶ μεγάλων ἀγώνων
ἔμπειρος ἄρας νυκτὸς ἐπ' αὐτὴν ἐχώρει παντὶ τῷ
στρατοπέδῳ τὴν Ῥώμην. καὶ μικροῦ μὲν ἐδέησεν
ἐμπεσεῖν εἰς ἀφύλακτον· ἀποσχὼν δὲ τῆς Κολ-
λίνης πύλης δέκα σταδίους ἐπηυλίσατο τῇ πόλει,
μεγαλοφρονῶν καὶ ταῖς ἐλπίσιν ἐπηρμένος ὡς
τοσούτους ἡγεμόνας καὶ τηλικούτους κατεστρατη-
3 γηκώς. ἅμα δ' ἡμέρᾳ τῶν λαμπροτάτων νέων
ἐξιππασαμένων ἐπ' αὐτὸν ἄλλους τε πολλοὺς καὶ
Κλαύδιον Ἄππιον, εὐγενῆ καὶ ἀγαθὸν ἄνδρα,
κατέβαλε. θορύβου δ', οἷον εἰκός, ὄντος ἐν τῇ
πόλει καὶ βοῆς γυναικείας καὶ διαδρομῶν ὡς
ἁλισκομένων κατὰ κράτος, πρῶτος ὤφθη Βάλβος

---

[1] Cf. Plutarch's *Pompey*, vi.-viii.
[2] Cf. Plutarch's *Crassus*, vi.

success by his generals, Pompey,[1] Crassus,[2] Metellus, and Servilius. For with few or no reverses these annihilated large forces of the enemy, so that Carbo, the chief supporter of the opposite faction, ran away from his own army by night, and sailed off to Libya.

XXIX. In Sulla's last struggle, however, Telesinus the Samnite,[3] like a third wrestler who sits by to contend with a weary victor, came near tripping and throwing him at the gates of Rome. For he had collected a large force, and was hastening, together with Lamponius the Lucanian, to Praeneste, in order to relieve Marius from the siege. But when he learned that Sulla to his front, and Pompey to his rear, were hurrying up against him, since he was being hemmed in before and behind, valiant and highly experienced soldier that he was, he broke camp by night, and marched with all his army against Rome itself. And he came within a little of breaking into the city in its unguarded state; indeed, he was only ten furlongs from the Colline gate when he bivouacked against it, highly encouraged and elated with hopes at the thought of having outgeneralled so many great commanders. And when, at day-break, the noblest youth of the city rode out against him, he overwhelmed many of them, including Appius Claudius, a man of high birth and character. There was a tumult in the city, naturally, and shrieking of women, and running hither and thither, as though the city were taken by storm, when Balbus, sent forward by Sulla, was first

---

[3] At the close of the Social war, in 89 B.C., the Samnites and Lucanians alone persisted in their hostility to Rome. The Marian party had conciliated them, but they regarded Sulla as their bitterest foe.

ἀπὸ Σύλλα προσελαύνων ἀνὰ κράτος ἱππεῦσιν
ἑπτακοσίοις. διαλιπὼν δὲ ὅσον ἀναψῦξαι τὸν
ἱδρῶτα τῶν ἵππων, εἶτ' αὖθις ἐγχαλινώσας διὰ
ταχέων ἐξήπτετο τῶν πολεμίων.

4 Ἐν τούτῳ δὲ καὶ Σύλλας ἐφαίνετο· καὶ τοὺς
πρώτους εὐθὺς ἀριστᾶν κελεύων εἰς τάξιν καθίστη.
πολλὰ δὲ Δολοβέλλα καὶ Τουρκουάτου δεομένων
ἐπισχεῖν καὶ μὴ κατακόπους ἔχοντα τοὺς ἄνδρας
ἀποκινδυνεῦσαι περὶ τῶν ἐσχάτων (οὐ γὰρ Κάρβωνα καὶ Μάριον, ἀλλὰ Σαυνίτας καὶ Λευκανούς,   47
τὰ ἔχθιστα τῇ Ῥώμῃ καὶ τὰ πολεμικώτατα φῦλα,
συμφέρεσθαι), παρωσάμενος αὐτοὺς ἐκέλευσε σημαίνειν τὰς σάλπιγγας ἀρχὴν ἐφόδου, σχεδὸν εἰς
ὥραν δεκάτην ἤδη τῆς ἡμέρας καταστρεφούσης.

5 γενομένου δὲ ἀγῶνος, οἷος οὐχ ἕτερος, τὸ μὲν
δεξιόν, ἐν ᾧ Κράσσος ἐτέτακτο, λαμπρῶς ἐνίκα,
τῷ δὲ εὐωνύμῳ πονοῦντι καὶ κακῶς ἔχοντι Σύλλας
παρεβοήθει, λευκὸν ἵππον ἔχων θυμοειδῆ καὶ
ποδωκέστατον· ἀφ' οὗ γνωρίσαντες αὐτὸν δύο
τῶν πολεμίων διετείνοντο τὰς λόγχας ὡς ἀφή-
σοντες. αὐτὸς μὲν οὖν οὐ προενόησε, τοῦ δ'
ἱπποκόμου μαστίξαντος τὸν ἵππον ἔφθη παρε-
νεχθεὶς τοσοῦτον ὅσον περὶ τὴν οὐρὰν τοῦ ἵππου
τὰς αἰχμὰς συμπεσούσας εἰς τὴν γῆν παγῆναι.

6 λέγεται δὲ ἔχων τι χρυσοῦν Ἀπόλλωνος ἀγαλ-
μάτιον ἐκ Δελφῶν ἀεὶ μὲν αὐτὸ κατὰ τὰς μάχας
περιφέρειν ἐν τῷ κόλπῳ, ἀλλὰ καὶ τότε τοῦτο
καταφιλεῖν οὕτω δὴ λέγων· "Ὦ Πύθιε Ἄπολλον,
τὸν εὐτυχῆ Σύλλαν Κορνήλιον ἐν τοσούτοις ἀγῶσιν ἄρας λαμπρὸν καὶ μέγαν ἐνταῦθα ῥίψεις ἐπὶ

seen riding up at full speed with seven hundred horsemen. He paused just long enough to let the sweat of the horses dry off, and then quickly bridled them again and attacked the enemy.

At this juncture, Sulla also made his appearance, and ordering his vanguard to take food at once, proceeded to form them in order of battle. Dolabella and Torquatus earnestly besought him to wait a while, and not to hazard the supreme issue with his men fatigued and spent; for they were to contend not with Carbo and Marius, but with Samnites and Lucanians, the most inveterate enemies of Rome, and the most warlike of peoples. But he put them by, and commanded the trumpets to sound the charge, though it was now getting on towards four o'clock in the afternoon. In the struggle which followed, and no other was so fierce, the right wing, where Crassus was posted, was brilliantly successful; but the left was hard pressed and in a sorry plight, when Sulla came to its assistance, mounted on a white horse that was mettlesome and very swift. By this horse two of enemy recognised him, and poised their spears for the cast. Sulla himself, now, did not notice this, but his groom did, and with a cut of the lash succeeded in sending Sulla's horse along so that the spear-heads just grazed its tail and fixed themselves in the ground. There is also a story that Sulla had a little golden image of Apollo from Delphi which he always carried in his bosom when he was in battle, but that on this occasion he took it out and kissed it affectionately, saying: "O Pythian Apollo, now that thou hast in so many struggles raised the fortunate Cornelius Sulla to glory and greatness, can it be that thou hast brought

θύραις τῆς πατρίδος ἀγαγών, αἴσχιστα τοῖς
7 ἑαυτοῦ συναπολούμενον πολίταις;" τοιαῦτά
φασι τὸν Σύλλαν θεοκλυτοῦντα τοὺς μὲν ἀντιβολεῖν, τοῖς δὲ ἀπειλεῖν, τῶν δὲ ἐπιλαμβάνεσθαι·
τέλος δὲ τοῦ εὐωνύμου συντριβέντος ἀναμι-
χθέντα τοῖς φεύγουσιν εἰς τὸ στρατόπεδον κατα-
φυγεῖν, πολλοὺς ἀποβαλόντα τῶν ἑταίρων καὶ
γνωρίμων. οὐκ ὀλίγοι δὲ καὶ τῶν ἐκ τῆς πόλεως
ἐπὶ θέαν προελθόντες ἀπώλοντο καὶ κατεπατή-
8 θησαν, ὥστε τὴν μὲν πόλιν οἴεσθαι διαπεπρᾶχθαι,
παρ' ὀλίγον δὲ καὶ τὴν Μαρίου πολιορκίαν λυ-
θῆναι, πολλῶν ἐκ τῆς τροπῆς ὠσαμένων ἐκεῖ καὶ
τὸν ἐπὶ τῇ πολιορκίᾳ τεταγμένον Ὀφέλλαν
Λουκρήτιον ἀναζευγνύναι κατὰ τάχος κελευόντων,
ὡς ἀπολωλότος τοῦ Σύλλα καὶ τῆς Ῥώμης ἐχο-
μένης ὑπὸ τῶν πολεμίων.

XXX. Ἤδη δὲ νυκτὸς οὔσης βαθείας ἧκον εἰς τὸ
τοῦ Σύλλα στρατόπεδον παρὰ τοῦ Κράσσου
δεῖπνον αὐτῷ καὶ τοῖς στρατιώταις μετιόντες· ὡς
γὰρ ἐνίκησε τοὺς πολεμίους, εἰς Ἄντεμναν κατα-
διώξαντες ἐκεῖ κατεστρατοπέδευσαν. ταῦτ' οὖν
πυθόμενος ὁ Σύλλας, καὶ ὅτι τῶν πολεμίων οἱ
πλεῖστοι διολώλασιν, ἧκεν εἰς Ἄντεμναν ἅμ'
ἡμέρᾳ, καὶ τρισχιλίων ἐπικηρυκευσαμένων πρὸς
αὐτὸν ὑπέσχετο δώσειν τὴν ἀσφάλειαν, εἰ κακόν
τι τοὺς ἄλλους ἐργασάμενοι πολεμίους ἔλθοιεν πρὸς
2 αὐτόν. οἱ δὲ πιστεύσαντες ἐπέθεντο τοῖς λοιποῖς,
καὶ πολλοὶ κατεκόπησαν ὑπ' ἀλλήλων. οὐ μὴν
ἀλλὰ καὶ τούτους καὶ τῶν ἄλλων τοὺς περιγενομένους εἰς ἑξακισχιλίους ἀθροίσας παρὰ τὸν ἱπ-
πόδρομον, ἐκάλει τὴν σύγκλητον εἰς τὸ τῆς

him to the gates of his native city only to cast him down there, to perish most shamefully with his fellow-countrymen?" Thus invoking the god, they say, he entreated some of his men, threatened others, and laid hands on others still; but at last his left wing was completely shattered, and with the fugitives he sought refuge in his camp, after losing many friends and acquaintances. Not a few also of those who had come out of the city to see the battle were trodden under foot and killed, so that it was thought that all was over with the city, and that the siege of Marius in Praeneste was all but raised; indeed many of the fugitives made their way thither and urged Lucretius Ofella, who had been appointed to conduct the siege, to break camp with all speed, since Sulla had fallen, and Rome was in the hands of the enemy.

XXX. But when the night was now far advanced, messengers came to the camp of Sulla from Crassus, to fetch supper for him and his soldiers; for after conquering the enemy, he had pursued them into Antemnae, and was encamped before that city. When, therefore, Sulla learned this, and also that the greater part of the enemy had been destroyed, he came to Antemnae at break of day. There three thousand of the inhabitants sent a deputation to him to sue for mercy, and he promised them safety if they would do some mischief to the rest of his enemies before coming to him. So they, trusting to his promise, attacked the rest of the people in the city, and many were slain by one another's hands. However, the survivors of both parties alike, to the number of six thousand, were collected by Sulla in the circus at Rome, and then the senate was

Ἐννοῦς ἱερόν. ἅμα δ' αὐτός τε λέγειν ἐνήρχετο
καὶ κατέκοπτον οἱ τεταγμένοι τοὺς ἑξακισχιλίους.
3 κραυγῆς δέ, ὡς εἰκός, ἐν χωρίῳ μικρῷ τοσούτων
σφαττομένων φερομένης καὶ τῶν συγκλητικῶν
ἐκπλαγέντων, ὥσπερ ἐτύγχανε λέγων ἀτρέπτῳ καὶ
καθεστηκότι τῷ προσώπῳ προσέχειν ἐκέλευσεν
αὐτοὺς τῷ λόγῳ, τὰ δ' ἔξω γινόμενα μὴ πολυ-
πραγμονεῖν· νουθετεῖσθαι γὰρ αὐτοῦ κελεύσαντος
ἐνίους τῶν πονηρῶν.
4   Τοῦτο καὶ τῷ βραδυτάτῳ Ῥωμαίων νοῆσαι
παρέστησεν ὡς ἀλλαγὴ τὸ χρῆμα τυραννίδος,
οὐκ ἀπαλλαγὴ γέγονε. Μάριος μὲν οὖν ἀπ'
ἀρχῆς χαλεπὸς ὢν ἐπέτεινεν, οὐ μετέβαλε τῇ
ἐξουσίᾳ τὴν φύσιν· Σύλλας δὲ μετρίως τὰ
πρῶτα καὶ πολιτικῶς ὁμιλήσας τῇ τύχῃ καὶ
δόξαν ἀριστοκρατικοῦ καὶ δημωφελοῦς ἡγεμόνος
5 παρασχών, ἔτι δὲ καὶ φιλόγελως ἐκ νέου γενόμενος καὶ πρὸς οἶκτον ὑγρός, ὥστε ῥᾳδίως ἐπι-
δακρύειν, εἰκότως προσετρίψατο ταῖς μεγάλαις
ἐξουσίαις διαβολὴν ὡς τὰ ἤθη μένειν οὐκ ἐώσαις
ἐπὶ τῶν ἐξ ἀρχῆς τρόπων, ἀλλ' ἔμπληκτα καὶ
χαῦνα καὶ ἀπάνθρωπα ποιούσαις. τοῦτο μὲν οὖν
εἴτε κίνησίς ἐστι καὶ μεταβολὴ φύσεως ὑπὸ 472
τύχης, εἴτε μᾶλλον ὑποκειμένης ἀποκάλυψις ἐν
ἐξουσίᾳ κακίας, ἑτέρα τις ἂν διορίσειε πραγματεία.
XXXI. Τοῦ δὲ Σύλλα πρὸς τὸ σφάττειν τρα-

summoned by him to meet in the temple of Bellona,[1] and at one and the same moment he himself began to speak in the senate, and those assigned to the task began to cut to pieces the six thousand in the circus. The shrieks of such a multitude, who were being massacred in a narrow space, filled the air, of course, and the senators were dumbfounded; but Sulla, with the calm and unmoved countenance with which he had begun to speak, ordered them to listen to his words and not concern themselves with what was going on outside, for it was only that some criminals were being admonished, by his orders.

This gave even the dullest Roman to understand that, in the matter of tyranny, there had been an exchange, but not a deliverance. Marius the elder, at any rate, had been naturally harsh at the outset, and power had intensified, not altered, his disposition; but Sulla had used his good fortune moderately, at first, and like a statesman, and had led men to expect in him a leader who was attached to the aristocracy, and at the same time helpful to the common people. Furthermore, from his youth up he had been of a merry temper, and easily moved to tears of pity. Naturally, therefore, his conduct fixed a stigma upon offices of great power, which were thought to work a change in men's previous characters, and render them capricious, vain, and cruel. However, whether this is a change and reversal of nature, brought about by fortune, or rather a revelation, when a man is in authority, of underlying baseness, were matter for determination in some other treatise.

XXXI. Sulla now busied himself with slaughter,

---

[1] Both the circus (Flaminius) and the temple were in the Campus Martius.

πομένου καὶ φόνων οὔτε ἀριθμὸν οὔτε ὅρον ἐχόντων ἐμπιπλάντος τὴν πόλιν, ἀναιρουμένων πολλῶν καὶ κατ' ἰδίας ἔχθρας, οἷς οὐδὲν ἦν πρᾶγμα
πρὸς Σύλλαν, ἐφιέντος αὐτοῦ καὶ χαριζομένου
τοῖς περὶ αὐτόν, ἐτόλμησε τῶν νέων εἷς, Γάϊος
Μέτελλος, ἐν τῇ συγκλήτῳ τοῦ Σύλλα πυθέσθαι τί πέρας ἔσται τῶν κακῶν, καὶ ποῖ προ-
ελθόντος αὐτοῦ δεῖ πεπαῦσθαι τὰ γινόμενα
2 προσδοκᾶν. "Παραιτούμεθα γάρ," εἶπεν, "οὐχ
οὓς σὺ ἔγνωκας ἀναιρεῖν τῆς τιμωρίας, ἀλλὰ
τῆς ἀμφιβολίας οὓς ἔγνωκας σώζειν." ἀπο-
κριναμένου δὲ τοῦ Σύλλα μηδέπω γινώσκειν οὓς
ἀφίησιν, ὑπολαβὼν ὁ Μέτελλος, "Οὐκοῦν," ἔφη,
"δήλωσον οὓς μέλλεις κολάζειν." καὶ ὁ Σύλλας
3 ἔφη τοῦτο ποιήσειν. ἔνιοι δὲ οὐ τὸν Μέτελλον,
ἀλλὰ Φουφίδιόν τινα τῶν πρὸς χάριν ὁμιλούν-
των τῷ Σύλλᾳ τὸ τελευταῖον εἰπεῖν λέγουσιν.
ὁ δ' οὖν Σύλλας εὐθὺς ὀγδοήκοντα προέγραψεν,
οὐδενὶ τῶν ἐν τέλει κοινωσάμενος. ἀγανακτούντων δὲ πάντων, μίαν ἡμέραν διαλιπὼν ἄλλους
προέγραψεν εἴκοσι καὶ διακοσίους, εἶτα τρίτῃ
4 πάλιν οὐκ ἐλάττους. ἐπὶ δὲ τούτοις δημηγορῶν
εἶπεν ὅσους μεμνημένος τυγχάνοι προγράφειν,
τοὺς δὲ νῦν διαλανθάνοντας αὖθις προγράψειν.
προέγραψε δὲ τῷ μὲν ὑποδεξαμένῳ καὶ διασώ-
σαντι τὸν προγεγραμμένον, ζημίαν τῆς φιλανθρωπίας ὁρίζων θάνατον, οὐκ ἀδελφόν, οὐχ υἱόν,
οὐ γονεῖς ὑπεξελόμενος, τῷ δὲ ἀποκτείναντι γέρας

and murders without number or limit filled the city. Many, too, were killed to gratify private hatreds, although they had no relations with Sulla, but he gave his consent in order to gratify his adherents. At last one of the younger men, Caius Metellus, made bold to ask Sulla in the senate what end there was to be of these evils, and how far he would proceed before they might expect such doings to cease. " We do not ask thee," he said, "to free from punishment those whom thou hast determined to slay, but to free from suspense those whom thou hast determined to save." And when Sulla answered that he did not yet know whom he would spare, " Well, then," said Metellus in reply, " let us know whom thou intendest to punish." This Sulla said he would do. Some, however, say that it was not Metellus, but Fufidius, one of Sulla's fawning creatures, who made this last speech to him. Be that as it may, Sulla at once proscribed[1] eighty persons, without communicating with any magistrate; and in spite of the general indignation, after a single day's interval, he proscribed two hundred and twenty others, and then on the third day, as many more. Referring to these measures in a public harangue, he said that he was proscribing as many as he could remember, and those who now escaped his memory, he would proscribe at a future time. He also proscribed any one who harboured and saved a proscribed person, making death the punishment for such humanity, without exception of brother, son, or parents, but offering any one who slew a proscribed

---

[1] A list of the persons proscribed was posted in public, and those whose names were on the list might be killed by any one who chose to do it.

δύο τάλαντα τῆς ἀνδροφονίας, κἂν δοῦλος δεσπό-
την κἂν πατέρα υἱὸς ἀνέλῃ. ὃ δὲ πάντων ἀδι-
κώτατον ἔδοξε, τῶν γὰρ προγεγραμμένων ἠτί-
μωσε καὶ υἱοὺς καὶ υἱωνούς, καὶ τὰ χρήματα
5 πάντων ἐδήμευσε. προεγράφοντο δὲ οὐκ ἐν
Ῥώμῃ μόνον, ἀλλὰ καὶ ἐν πάσῃ πόλει τῆς
Ἰταλίας· καὶ φονευομένων οὔτε ναὸς ἦν καθαρὸς
θεοῦ οὔτε ἑστία ξένιος οὔτε οἶκος πατρῷος, ἀλλὰ
καὶ παρὰ γυναιξὶ γαμεταῖς ἄνδρες ἐσφάττοντο
καὶ παρὰ μητράσι παῖδες. ἦσαν δὲ οἱ δι'
ὀργὴν ἀπολλύμενοι καὶ δι' ἔχθραν οὐδὲν μέρος
τῶν διὰ χρήματα σφαττομένων, ἀλλὰ καὶ λέγειν
ἐπῄει τοῖς κολάζουσιν ὡς τόνδε μὲν ἀνῄρηκεν
οἰκία μεγάλη, τόνδε δὲ κῆπος, ἄλλον ὕδατα
6 θερμά. Κόϊντος δὲ Αὐρήλιος, ἀνὴρ ἀπράγμων
καὶ τοσοῦτον αὐτῷ μετεῖναι τῶν κακῶν νομίζων
ὅσον ἄλλοις συναλγεῖν ἀτυχοῦσιν, εἰς ἀγορὰν
ἐλθὼν ἀνεγίνωσκε τοὺς προγεγραμμένους· εὑρὼν
δὲ ἑαυτόν, "Οἴμοι τάλας," εἶπε, "διώκει με τὸ ἐν
Ἀλβανῷ χωρίον." καὶ βραχὺ προελθὼν ὑπό
τινος ἀπεσφάγη καταδιώξαντος.

XXXII. Ἐν τούτῳ δὲ Μάριος μὲν ἁλισκόμενος
ἑαυτὸν διέφθειρε, Σύλλας δὲ εἰς Πραινεστὸν
ἐλθὼν πρῶτα μὲν ἰδίᾳ κατ' ἄνδρα κρίνων ἐκό-
λαζεν, εἶτα ὡς οὐ σχολῆς οὔσης πάντας ἀθρόως
εἰς ταὐτὸ συναγαγών, μυρίους καὶ δισχιλίους
ὄντας, ἐκέλευσεν ἀποσφάττειν, μόνῳ τῷ ξένῳ

person two talents as a reward for his murderous
deed, even though a slave should slay his master, or
a son his father. And what seemed the greatest
injustice of all, he took away all civil rights from the
sons and grandsons of those who had been proscribed, and confiscated the property of all. Moreover,
proscriptions were made not only in Rome, but also
in every city of Italy, and neither temple of God,
nor hearth of hospitality, nor paternal home was free
from the stain of bloodshed, but husbands were
butchered in the embraces of their wedded wives,
and sons in the arms of their mothers. Those who
fell victims to political resentment and private hatred
were as nothing compared with those who were
butchered for the sake of their property, nay, even
the executioners were prompted to say that his great
house killed this man, his garden that man, his warm
baths another. Quintus Aurelius, a quiet and
inoffensive man, who thought his only share in the
general calamity was to condole with others in their
misfortunes, came into the forum and read the list of
the proscribed, and finding his own name there, said,
" Ah! woe is me! my Alban estate is prosecuting
me." And he had not gone far before he was
dispatched by some one who had hunted him down.

XXXII. Meanwhile Marius the younger, at the
point of being captured,[1] slew himself; and Sulla,
coming to Praeneste, at first gave each man there
a separate trial before he executed him, but afterwards, since time failed him, gathered them all together in one place—there were twelve thousand of
them—and gave orders to slaughter them, his host

[1] According to Appian (*Bell. Civ.* i. 94), as he was trying
to escape from Praeneste by an underground passage.

διδοὺς ἄδειαν. ὁ δὲ εὐγενῶς πάνυ φήσας πρὸς
αὐτὸν ὡς οὐδέποτε σωτηρίας χάριν εἴσεται τῷ
φονεῖ τῆς πατρίδος, ἀναμιχθεὶς ἑκὼν συγκατε-
2 κόπη τοῖς πολίταις. ἔδοξε δὲ καινότατον γενέσθαι τὸ περὶ Λεύκιον Κατιλίναν. οὗτος γὰρ
οὔπω τῶν πραγμάτων κεκριμένων ἀνῃρηκὼς
ἀδελφὸν ἐδεήθη τοῦ Σύλλα τότε προγράψαι
τὸν ἄνθρωπον ὡς ζῶντα· καὶ προεγράφη. τούτου δὲ τῷ Σύλλᾳ χάριν ἐκτίνων Μάρκον τινὰ
Μάριον τῶν ἐκ τῆς ἐναντίας στάσεως ἀποκτείνας τὴν μὲν κεφαλὴν ἐν ἀγορᾷ καθεζομένῳ
τῷ Σύλλᾳ προσήνεγκε, τῷ δὲ περιρραντηρίῳ τοῦ
Ἀπόλλωνος ἐγγὺς ὄντι προσελθὼν ἀπενίψατο
τὰς χεῖρας.

XXXIII. Ἔξω δὲ τῶν φονικῶν καὶ τὰ λοιπὰ   473
τοὺς ἀνθρώπους ἐλύπει. δικτάτορα μὲν γὰρ
ἑαυτὸν ἀνηγόρευσε, δι' ἐτῶν ἑκατὸν εἴκοσι τοῦτο
τὸ γένος τῆς ἀρχῆς ἀναλαβών. ἐψηφίσθη δὲ
αὐτῷ πάντων ἄδεια τῶν γεγονότων, πρὸς δὲ τὸ
μέλλον ἐξουσία θανάτου, δημεύσεως, κληρου-
χιῶν, κτίσεως, πορθήσεως, ἀφελέσθαι βασιλείαν,
2 καὶ ᾧ[1] βούλοιτο χαρίσασθαι. τὰς δὲ δια-
πράσεις τῶν δεδημευμένων οἴκων οὕτως ὑπερηφάνως ἐποιεῖτο καὶ δεσποτικῶς ἐπὶ βήματος
καθεζόμενος, ὥστε τῶν ἀφαιρέσεων ἐπαχθεστέρας
αὐτοῦ τὰς δωρεὰς εἶναι, καὶ γυναιξὶν εὐμόρφοις
καὶ λυρῳδοῖς καὶ μίμοις καὶ καθάρμασιν ἐξε-
λευθερικοῖς ἐθνῶν χώρας καὶ πόλεων χαριζομένου προσόδους, ἐνίοις δὲ γάμους ἀκουσίως
3 ζευγνυμένων γυναικῶν. Πομπήϊον γέ τοι βου-

---

[1] καὶ ᾧ with Bekker, after Reiske : ᾧ.

alone receiving immunity. But this man, with a noble spirit, told Sulla that he would never owe his safety to the slayer of his country, and joining his countrymen of his own accord, was cut down with them. But that which Lucius Catiline did was thought to be most monstrous of all. This man, namely, had killed his brother before the civil struggle was decided, and now asked Sulla to proscribe the man, as one still living; and he was proscribed. Then Catiline, returning this favour of Sulla's, killed a certain Marcus Marius, one of the opposite faction, and brought his head to Sulla as he was sitting in the forum, and then going to the lustral water of Apollo which was near, washed the blood off his hands.

XXXIII. But besides his massacres, the rest of Sulla's proceedings also gave offence. For he proclaimed himself dictator,[1] reviving this particular office after a lapse of a hundred and twenty years. Moreover, an act was passed granting him immunity for all his past acts, and for the future, power of life and death, of confiscation, of colonization, of founding or demolishing cities, and of taking away or bestowing kingdoms at his pleasure. He conducted the sales of confiscated estates in such arrogant and imperious fashion, from the tribunal where he sat, that his gifts excited more odium than his robberies. He bestowed on handsome women, musicians, comic actors, and the lowest of freedmen, the territories of nations and the revenues of cities, and women were married against their will to some of his favourites. In the case of Pompey the Great,[2] at least,

[1] In 81 B.C.
[2] The title of Great was first bestowed on him by Sulla himself (cf. *Pompey*, xiii. 4).

λόμενος οἰκειώσασθαι τὸν Μάγνον, ἣν μὲν εἶχε
γαμετὴν ἀφεῖναι προσέταξεν, Αἰμιλίαν δέ, Σκαύ-
ρου θυγατέρα καὶ Μετέλλης τῆς ἑαυτοῦ γυναικός,
ἀποσπάσας Μανίου Γλαβρίωνος ἐγκύμονα, συν-
ῴκισεν αὐτῷ· ἀπέθανε δὲ ἡ κόρη παρὰ τῷ
4 Πομπηΐῳ τίκτουσα. Λουκρητίου δὲ Ὀφέλλα
τοῦ Μάριον ἐκπολιορκήσαντος αἰτουμένου καὶ
μετιόντος ὑπατείαν πρῶτον μὲν ἐκώλυεν· ὡς δὲ
ἐκεῖνος ὑπὸ πολλῶν σπουδαζόμενος εἰς τὴν ἀγορὰν ἐνέβαλε, πέμψας τινὰ τῶν περὶ αὐτὸν
ἑκατονταρχῶν ἀπέσφαξε τὸν ἄνδρα, καθεζόμενος
αὐτὸς ἐπὶ βήματος ἐν τῷ Διοσκουρείῳ καὶ τὸν
φόνον ἐφορῶν ἄνωθεν. τῶν δὲ ἀνθρώπων τὸν
ἑκατοντάρχην συλλαβόντων καὶ προσαγαγόντων
τῷ βήματι, σιωπῆσαι κελεύσας τοὺς θορυβοῦντας
αὐτὸς ἔφη κελεῦσαι τοῦτο, καὶ τὸν ἑκατοντάρχην
ἀφεῖναι προσέταξεν.

XXXIV. Ὁ μέντοι θρίαμβος αὐτοῦ τῇ πολυτελείᾳ καὶ καινότητι τῶν βασιλικῶν λαφύρων
σοβαρὸς γενόμενος μείζονα κόσμον ἔσχε καὶ
καλὸν θέαμα τοὺς φυγάδας. οἱ γὰρ ἐνδοξότατοι
καὶ δυνατώτατοι τῶν πολιτῶν ἐστεφανωμένοι
παρείποντο, σωτῆρα καὶ πατέρα τὸν Σύλλαν
ἀποκαλοῦντες, ἅτε δὴ δι' ἐκεῖνον εἰς τὴν πατρίδα
κατιόντες καὶ κομιζόμενοι παῖδας καὶ γυναῖκας.
2 ἤδη δὲ συνηρημένων ἁπάντων, ἀπολογισμὸν ἐν
ἐκκλησίᾳ τῶν πράξεων ποιούμενος οὐκ ἐλάσσονι
σπουδῇ τὰς εὐτυχίας ἢ τὰς ἀνδραγαθίας κατη-
ριθμεῖτο, καὶ πέρας ἐκέλευσεν ἑαυτὸν ἐπὶ τούτοις Εὐτυχῆ προσαγορεύεσθαι· τοῦτο γὰρ ὁ

wishing to establish relationship with him, he ordered him to divorce the wife he had, and then gave him in marriage Aemilia, daughter of Scaurus and his own wife Metella, whom he tore away from Manius Glabrio when she was with child by him; and the young woman died in childbirth at the house of Pompey.[1] Lucretius Ofella, who had reduced Marius by siege, gave himself out as a candidate for the consulship, and Sulla at first tried to stop him; but when Ofella came down into the forum with a large and eager following, he sent one of the centurions in his retinue and slew him, himself sitting on a tribunal in the temple of Castor and beholding the murder from above. The people in the forum seized the centurion and brought him before the tribunal, but Sulla bade them cease their clamour, and said that he himself had ordered this deed, and commanded them to let the centurion go.

XXXIV. His triumph, however, which was imposing from the costliness and rarity of the royal spoils, had a greater ornament in the noble spectacle of the exiles. For the most distinguished and influential of the citizens, crowned with garlands, followed in the procession, calling Sulla their saviour and father, since indeed it was through him that they were returning to their native city and bringing with them their wives and children. And when at last the whole spectacle was over, he gave an account of his achievements in a speech to the people, enumerating the instances of his good fortune with no less emphasis than his deeds of valour, and finally, in view of these, he ordered that he receive the surname of *Fortunate* (for this is what the word

[1] Cf. Plutarch's *Pompey*, ix. 2.

Φῆλιξ μάλιστα βούλεται δηλοῦν· αὐτὸς δὲ τοῖς
"Ελλησι γράφων καὶ χρηματίζων ἑαυτὸν Ἐπα-
φρόδιτον ἀνηγόρευε, καὶ παρ' ἡμῖν ἐν τοῖς τροπαίοις οὕτως ἀναγέγραπται· ΛΕΥΚΙΟΣ ΚΟΡ-
3 ΝΗΛΙΟΣ ΣΥΛΛΑΣ ΕΠΑΦΡΟΔΙΤΟΣ. ἔτι δὲ
τῆς Μετέλλης παιδία τεκούσης δίδυμα τὸ μὲν
ἄρρεν Φαῦστον, τὸ δὲ θῆλυ Φαῦσταν ὠνόμασε·
τὸ γὰρ εὐτυχὲς καὶ ἱλαρὸν Ῥωμαῖοι φαῦστον
καλοῦσιν. οὕτω δὲ ἄρα οὐ ταῖς πράξεσιν ὡς
τοῖς εὐτυχήμασιν ἐπίστευεν, ὥστε, παμπόλλων
μὲν ἀνῃρημένων ὑπ' αὐτοῦ, καινοτομίας δὲ γενομένης καὶ μεταβολῆς ἐν τῇ πόλει τοσαύτης, ἀπο-
θέσθαι τὴν ἀρχὴν καὶ τὸν δῆμον ἀρχαιρεσιῶν
ὑπατικῶν ποιῆσαι κύριον, αὐτὸς δὲ μὴ προσελθεῖν, ἀλλ' ἐν ἀγορᾷ τὸ σῶμα παρέχων τοῖς βουλομένοις ὑπεύθυνον ὥσπερ ἰδιώτης ἀναστρέφε-
4 σθαι. καί τις παρὰ γνώμην αὐτοῦ θρασὺς ἀνὴρ
καὶ πολέμιος ἐπίδοξος ἦν ὕπατος αἱρεθήσεσθαι,
Μάρκος Λέπιδος, οὐ δι' ἑαυτόν, ἀλλὰ Πομπηΐῳ
σπουδάζοντι καὶ δεομένῳ τοῦ δήμου χαριζομένου.
5 διὸ καὶ χαίροντα τῇ νίκῃ τὸν Πομπήϊον ὁ Σύλλας
ἰδὼν ἀπιόντα καλέσας πρὸς ἑαυτόν, "Ὡς καλόν,"
ἔφη, "σοῦ τὸ πολίτευμα, ὦ νεανία, τὸ Κάτλου
πρότερον ἀναγορεῦσαι Λέπιδον, τοῦ πάντων ἀρί-
στου τὸν ἐμπληκτότατον. ὥρα μέντοι σοι μὴ
καθεύδειν ὡς ἰσχυρότερον πεποιηκότι κατὰ σαυτοῦ
τὸν ἀνταγωνιστήν." τοῦτο μὲν οὖν ὁ Σύλλας 47
ὥσπερ ἀπεθέσπισε· ταχὺ γὰρ ἐξυβρίσας ὁ Λέπι-

"Felix" most nearly means). But he himself, in writing to the Greeks on official business, styled himself Epaphroditus, or *Favourite of Venus*,[1] and on his trophies in our country his name is thus inscribed: Lucius Cornelius Sulla Epaphroditus. Besides this, when Metella bore him twin children, he named the male child Faustus, and the female Fausta; for the Romans call what is *auspicious* and *joyful*, "faustum." And to such an extent did he put more confidence in his good fortunes than in his achievements, that, although he had slain great numbers of the citizens, and introduced great innovations and changes in the government of the city,[2] he laid down his office of dictator, and put the consular elections in the hands of the people; and when they were held, he did not go near them himself, but walked up and down the forum like a private man, exposing his person freely to all who wished to call him to account. Contrary to his wishes, a certain bold enemy of his was likely to be chosen consul, Marcus Lepidus, not through his own efforts, but owing to the success which Pompey had in soliciting votes for him from the people. And so, when Sulla saw Pompey going away from the polls delighted with his victory, he called him to him, and said:[3] "What a fine policy this is of thine, young man, to elect Lepidus in preference to Catulus, the most unstable instead of the best of men! Now, surely, it is high time for thee to be watchful, after strengthening thine adversary against thyself." And in saying this, Sulla was something of a prophet; for

---

[1] Cf. chapter xix. 5 and note.
[2] Sulla restored the ancient powers of the senate, and reduced those of the tribunate. He resigned the dictatorship in 79 B.C.   [3] Cf. *Pompey*, xv. 1 f.

δος εἰς πόλεμον κατέστη τοῖς περὶ τὸν Πομπήϊον.

XXXV. Ἀποθύων δὲ τῆς οὐσίας ἁπάσης ὁ
Σύλλας τῷ Ἡρακλεῖ δεκάτην ἑστιάσεις ἐποιεῖτο
τῷ δήμῳ πολυτελεῖς· καὶ τοσοῦτον περιττὴ ἦν ἡ
παρασκευὴ τῆς χρείας ὥστε παμπληθῆ καθ'
ἑκάστην ἡμέραν εἰς τὸν ποταμὸν ὄψα ῥιπτεῖσθαι,
πίνεσθαι δὲ οἶνον ἐτῶν τεσσαράκοντα καὶ παλαιό-
2 τερον. διὰ μέσου δὲ τῆς θοίνης πολυημέρου
γενομένης ἀπέθνησκεν ἡ Μετέλλα νόσῳ· καὶ
τῶν ἱερέων τὸν Σύλλαν οὐκ ἐώντων αὐτῇ προσελθεῖν οὐδὲ τὴν οἰκίαν τῷ κήδει μιανθῆναι, γραψά-
μενος διάλυσιν τοῦ γάμου πρὸς αὐτὴν ὁ Σύλλας
ἔτι ζῶσαν ἐκέλευσεν εἰς ἑτέραν οἰκίαν μετακομι-
σθῆναι. καὶ τοῦτο μὲν ἀκριβῶς τὸ νόμιμον ὑπὸ
δεισιδαιμονίας ἐτήρησε· τὸν δὲ τῆς ταφῆς ὁρίζοντα
τὴν δαπάνην νόμον αὐτὸς εἰσενηνοχὼς παρέβη,
3 μηδενὸς ἀναλώματος φεισάμενος. παρέβαινε δὲ
καὶ τὰ περὶ τῆς εὐτελείας τῶν δείπνων ὑπ' αὐτοῦ
τεταγμένα, πότοις καὶ συνδείπνοις τρυφὰς καὶ
βωμολοχίας ἔχουσι παρηγορῶν τὸ πένθος.

Ὀλίγων δὲ μηνῶν διαγενομένων ἦν μὲν θέα μονομάχων, οὔπω δὲ τῶν τόπων διακεκριμένων, ἀλλ'
ἔτι τοῦ θεάτρου συμμιγοῦς ἀνδράσι καὶ γυναιξὶν
ὄντος, ἔτυχε πλησίον τοῦ Σύλλα καθεζομένη
γυνὴ τὴν ὄψιν εὐπρεπὴς καὶ γένους λαμπροῦ·
4 Μεσσάλα γὰρ ἦν θυγάτηρ, Ὁρτησίου δὲ τοῦ
ῥήτορος ἀδελφή, Οὐαλλερία δὲ τοὔνομα· συνεβε-
βήκει δὲ αὐτῇ νεωστὶ πρὸς ἄνδρα διάστασις.
αὕτη παρὰ τὸν Σύλλαν ἐξόπισθεν παραπορευο-
μένη τήν τε χεῖρα πρὸς αὐτὸν ἀπηρείσατο καὶ

Lepidus speedily waxed insolent and went to war with Pompey and his party.[1]

XXXV. On consecrating the tenth of all his substance to Hercules, Sulla feasted the people sumptuously, and his provision for them was so much beyond what was needed that great quantities of meats were daily cast into the river, and wine was drunk that was forty years old and upwards. In the midst of the feasting, which lasted many days, Metella lay sick and dying. And since the priests forbade Sulla to go near her, or to have his house polluted by her funeral, he sent her a bill of divorce, and ordered her to be carried to another house while she was still living. In doing this, he observed the strict letter of the law, out of superstition; but the law limiting the expense of the funeral, which law he had himself introduced, he transgressed, and spared no outlays. He transgressed also his own ordinances limiting the cost of banquets, when he tried to assuage his sorrow by drinking parties and convivial banquets, where extravagance and ribaldry prevailed.

A few months afterwards there was a gladiatorial spectacle, and since the places for men and women in the theatre were not yet separated,[2] but still promiscuous, it chanced that there was sitting near Sulla a woman of great beauty and splendid birth; she was a daughter of Messala, a sister of Hortensius the orator, and her name was Valeria, and it so happened that she had recently been divorced from her husband. As she passed along behind Sulla, she rested her hand upon him, plucked off a bit of nap

---

[1] On the death of Sulla, in 78 B.C., Lepidus headed an insurrection, and attempted to overthrow the constitution. Pompey adhered to the senatorial party (Cf. *Pompey*, xvi.).

[2] As they were in the time of Augustus.

κροκύδα τοῦ ἱματίου σπάσασα παρῆλθεν ἐπὶ τὴν
ἑαυτῆς χώραν. ἐμβλέψαντος δὲ τοῦ Σύλλα καὶ
θαυμάσαντος, "Οὐδέν," ἔφη, "δεινόν, αὐτό-
κρατορ, ἀλλὰ βούλομαι τῆς σῆς κἀγὼ μικρὸν
5 εὐτυχίας μεταλαβεῖν." τοῦτο ἤκουσεν οὐκ ἀηδῶς
ὁ Σύλλας, ἀλλὰ καὶ δῆλος εὐθὺς ἦν ὑποκεκνισ-
μένος· ἠρώτα γὰρ ὑποπέμπων αὐτῆς ὄνομα, καὶ
γένος καὶ βίον ἐμάνθανεν. ἐκ δὲ τούτων ῥίψεις
ὀμμάτων ἐπ᾽ ἀλλήλους ἐγίνοντο καὶ παρεπιστρο-
φαὶ συνεχεῖς προσώπων καὶ μειδιαμάτων δια-
δόσεις, τέλος δὲ ὁμολογίαι καὶ συνθέσεις περὶ
γάμων, ἐκείνῃ μὲν ἴσως ἄμεμπτοι, Σύλλας δέ, εἰ
καὶ τὰ μάλιστα σώφρονα καὶ γενναίαν, ἀλλ᾽ οὐκ
ἐκ σώφρονος καὶ καλῆς ἔγημεν ἀρχῆς, ὄψει καὶ
λαμπρίᾳ μειρακίου δίκην παραβληθείς, ὑφ᾽ ὧν
τὰ αἴσχιστα καὶ ἀναιδέστατα πάθη κινεῖσθαι
πέφυκεν.

XXXVI. Οὐ μὴν ἀλλὰ καὶ ταύτην ἔχων ἐπὶ
τῆς οἰκίας συνῆν μίμοις γυναιξὶ καὶ κιθαριστρίαις
καὶ θυμελικοῖς ἀνθρώποις, ἐπὶ στιβάδων ἀφ᾽
ἡμέρας συμπίνων. οὗτοι γὰρ οἱ τότε παρ᾽ αὐτῷ
δυνάμενοι μέγιστον ἦσαν, Ῥώσκιος ὁ κωμῳδὸς καὶ
Σῶριξ ὁ ἀρχιμῖμος καὶ Μητρόβιος ὁ λυσιῳδός,
οὗ καίπερ ἐξώρου γενομένου διετέλει μέχρι παν-
2 τὸς ἐρᾶν οὐκ ἀρνούμενος. ὅθεν καὶ τὴν νόσον ἀπ᾽
αἰτίας ἐλαφρᾶς ἀρξαμένην ἐξέθρεψε, καὶ πολὺν
χρόνον ἠγνόει περὶ τὰ σπλάγχνα γεγονὼς ἔμπυος,
ὑφ᾽ ἧς καὶ τὴν σάρκα διαφθαρεῖσαν εἰς φθεῖρας
μετέβαλε πᾶσαν, ὥστε πολλῶν δι᾽ ἡμέρας ἅμα
καὶ νυκτὸς ἀφαιρούντων μηδὲν εἶναι μέρος τοῦ
ἐπιγινομένου τὸ ἀποκρινόμενον, ἀλλὰ πᾶσαν
ἐσθῆτα καὶ λουτρὸν καὶ ἀπόνιμμα καὶ σιτίον
438

from his mantle, and then proceeded to her own place. When Sulla looked at her in astonishment, she said: "It's nothing of importance, Dictator, but I too wish to partake a little in thy felicity." Sulla was not displeased at hearing this, nay, it was at once clear that his fancy was tickled, for he secretly sent and asked her name, and inquired about her family and history. Then followed mutual glances, continual turnings of the face to gaze, interchanges of smiles, and at last a formal compact of marriage. All this was perhaps blameless on her part, but Sulla, even though she was ever so chaste and reputable, did not marry her from any chaste and worthy motive; he was led away, like a young man, by looks and languishing airs, through which the most disgraceful and shameless passions are naturally excited.

XXXVI. However, even though he had such a wife at home, he consorted with actresses, harpists, and theatrical people, drinking with them on couches all day long. For these were the men who had most influence with him now: Roscius the comedian, Sorex the archmime, and Metrobius the impersonator of women, for whom, though past his prime, he continued up to the last to be passionately fond, and made no denial of it.[1] By this mode of life he aggravated a disease which was insignificant in its beginnings, and for a long time he knew not that his bowels were ulcerated. This disease corrupted his whole flesh also, and converted it into worms, so that although many were employed day and night in removing them, what they took away was as nothing compared with the increase upon him, but all his clothing,

[1] Cf. chapter ii. 4.

ἀναπίμπλασθαι τοῦ ῥεύματος ἐκείνου καὶ τῆς
3 φθορᾶς· τοσοῦτον ἐξήνθει. διὸ πολλάκις τῆς
ἡμέρας εἰς ὕδωρ ἐνέβαινεν ἐκκλύζων τὸ σῶμα καὶ
ἀπορρυπτόμενος. ἦν δὲ οὐδὲν ὄφελος· ἐκράτει
γὰρ ἡ μεταβολὴ τῷ τάχει, καὶ περιεγίνετο παντὸς
καθαρμοῦ τὸ πλῆθος.

Λέγεται δὲ τῶν μὲν πάνυ παλαιῶν Ἄκαστον
φθειριάσαντα τὸν Πελίου τελευτῆσαι, τῶν δὲ
ὑστέρων Ἀλκμᾶνα τὸν μελοποιὸν καὶ Φερεκύδην
τὸν θεολόγον καὶ Καλλισθένη τὸν Ὀλύνθιον ἐν
εἱρκτῇ φρουρούμενον, ἔτι δὲ Μούκιον τὸν νομικόν. 47
4 εἰ δὲ δεῖ καὶ τῶν ἀπ' οὐδενὸς μὲν χρηστοῦ γνωρίμων δὲ ἄλλως ἐπιμνησθῆναι, λέγεται τὸν ἄρξαντα
τοῦ δουλικοῦ πολέμου περὶ Σικελίαν δραπέτην,
Εὔνουν ὄνομα, μετὰ τὴν ἅλωσιν εἰς Ῥώμην ἀγόμενον ὑπὸ φθειριάσεως ἀποθανεῖν.

XXXVII. Ὁ δὲ Σύλλας οὐ μόνον προέγνω
τὴν ἑαυτοῦ τελευτήν, ἀλλὰ τρόπον τινὰ καὶ
γέγραφε περὶ αὐτῆς. τὸ γὰρ εἰκοστὸν καὶ δεύτερον τῶν ὑπομνημάτων πρὸ δυεῖν ἡμερῶν ἢ
ἐτελεύτα γράφων ἐπαύσατο· καί φησι τοὺς
Χαλδαίους αὐτῷ προειπεῖν ὡς δέοι βεβιωκότα
καλῶς αὐτὸν ἐν ἀκμῇ τῶν εὐτυχημάτων κατα-
2 στρέψαι· λέγει δὲ καὶ τὸν υἱὸν αὐτοῦ, τεθνηκότα
μικρὸν ἔμπροσθεν τῆς Μετέλλης, φανῆναι κατὰ
τοὺς ὕπνους ἐν ἐσθῆτι φαύλῃ παρεστῶτα καὶ
δεόμενον τοῦ πατρὸς παύσασθαι τῶν φροντίδων,
ἰόντα δὲ σὺν αὐτῷ παρὰ τὴν μητέρα Μετέλλαν
ἐν ἡσυχίᾳ καὶ ἀπραγμόνως ζῆν μετ' αὐτῆς. οὐ
3 μὴν ἐπαύσατό γε τοῦ πράττειν τὰ δημόσια. δέκα
μὲν γὰρ ἡμέραις ἔμπροσθεν τῆς τελευτῆς τοὺς
ἐν Δικαιαρχείᾳ στασιάζοντας διαλλάξας νόμον

baths, hand-basins, and food, were infected with that
flux of corruption, so violent was its discharge. Therefore he immersed himself many times a-day in water
to cleanse and scour his person. But it was of no
use; for the change gained upon him rapidly, and
the swarm of vermin defied all purification.

We are told that in very ancient times, Acastus
the son of Pelias was thus eaten of worms and died,
and in later times, Alcman the lyric poet, Pherecydes
the theologian, Callisthenes of Olynthus, who was
kept closely imprisoned, as also Mucius the jurist;
and if mention is to be made of men who had no
excellence to commend them, but were notorious for
other reasons, it is said that the runaway slave who
headed the servile war in Sicily,[1] Eunus by name,
was taken to Rome after his capture, and died there
of this disease.

XXXVII. Sulla not only foresaw his own death,
but may be said to have written about it also. For
he stopped writing the twenty-second book of his
Memoirs two days before he died, and he there says
that the Chaldaeans foretold him that, after an honourable life, he was to end his days at the height of
his good fortunes. He says also that his son, who
had died a little while before Metella, appeared to
him in his dreams, clad in mean attire, and besought
his father to put an end to anxious thoughts, and
come with him to his mother Metella, there to live
in peace and quietness with her. However, he did not
cease to transact the public business. For instance,
ten days before he died, he reconciled the opposing
factions in Dicaearchia,[2] and prescribed a code of

---

[1] B.C. 134; cf. Diodorus, xxxiv. 2, 23.
[2] An earlier name for Puteoli.

ἔγραψεν αὐτοῖς καθ᾽ ὃν πολιτεύσονται· πρὸ μιᾶς
δὲ ἡμέρας πυθόμενος τὸν ἄρχοντα Γράνιον, ὡς
ὀφείλων δημόσιον χρέος οὐκ ἀποδίδωσιν, ἀλλ᾽
ἀναμένει τὴν αὐτοῦ τελευτήν, μετεπέμψατο τὸν
ἄνθρωπον εἰς τὸ δωμάτιον· καὶ περιστήσας τοὺς
ὑπηρέτας ἐκέλευσε πνίγειν, τῇ δὲ κραυγῇ καὶ τῷ
σπαραγμῷ τὸ ἀπόστημα ῥήξας πλῆθος αἵματος
4 ἐξέβαλεν. ἐκ δὲ τούτου τῆς δυνάμεως ἐπιλιπούσης διαγαγὼν τὴν νύκτα μοχθηρῶς ἀπέθανε, δύο
παῖδας ἐκ τῆς Μετέλλης νηπίους καταλιπών. ἡ
γὰρ Οὐαλλερία μετὰ τὴν τελευτὴν αὐτοῦ θυγάτριον ἀπεκύησεν, ὃ Πόστουμαν ἐκάλουν· τοὺς γὰρ
ὕστερον τῆς τῶν πατέρων τελευτῆς γενομένους
οὕτω Ῥωμαῖοι προσαγορεύουσιν.

XXXVIII. Ὥρμησαν μὲν οὖν πολλοὶ καὶ
συνέστησαν πρὸς Λέπιδον ὡς εἴρξοντες τὸ σῶμα
κηδείας τῆς νενομισμένης· Πομπήιος δέ, καίπερ
ἐγκαλῶν τῷ Σύλλᾳ (μόνον γὰρ αὐτὸν ἐν ταῖς
διαθήκαις τῶν φίλων παρέλιπε), τοὺς μὲν χάριτι
καὶ δεήσει, τοὺς δὲ ἀπειλῇ διακρουσάμενος εἰς
Ῥώμην παρέπεμψε τὸ σῶμα, καὶ ταῖς ταφαῖς
2 ἀσφάλειαν ἅμα καὶ τιμὴν παρέσχε. λέγεται δὲ
τοσοῦτο πλῆθος ἀρωμάτων ἐπενεγκεῖν τὰς γυναῖκας αὐτῷ ὥστε ἄνευ τῶν ἐν φορήμασι δέκα καὶ
διακοσίοις διακομιζομένων πλασθῆναι μὲν εἴδωλον εὐμέγεθες αὐτοῦ Σύλλα, πλασθῆναι δὲ καὶ
ῥαβδοῦχον ἔκ τε λιβανωτοῦ πολυτελοῦς καὶ
κινναμώμου. τῆς δὲ ἡμέρας συννεφοῦς ἕωθεν
οὔσης, ὕδωρ ἐξ οὐρανοῦ προσδοκῶντες ἐνάτης
3 ἦραν μόλις ὥρας τὸν νεκρόν. ἀνέμου δὲ λαμπροῦ

laws for their conduct of the city's government; and one day before he died, on learning that the magistrate there, Granius, refused to pay a debt he owed the public treasury, in expectation of his death, he summoned him to his room, stationed his servants about him, and ordered them to strangle him; but with the strain which he put upon his voice and body, he ruptured his abscess and lost a great quantity of blood. In consequence of this his strength failed, and after a night of wretchedness, he died, leaving two young children by Metella.[1] For it was after his death that Valeria gave birth to a daughter, who was called Postuma, this being the name which the Romans give to children who are born after their father's death.

XXXVIII. Many now joined themselves eagerly to Lepidus, purposing to deprive Sulla's body of the usual burial honours; but Pompey, although offended at Sulla (for he alone, of all his friends, was not mentioned in his will), diverted some from their purpose by his kindly influence and entreaties, and others by his threats, and then conveyed the body to Rome, and secured for it an honourable as well as a safe interment. And it is said that the women contributed such a vast quantity of spices for it, that, apart from what was carried on two hundred and ten litters, a large image of Sulla himself, and another image of a lictor, was moulded out of costly frankincense and cinnamon. The day was cloudy in the morning, and the expectation was that it would rain, but at last, at the ninth hour,[2] the corpse was placed upon the funeral pyre. Then a strong wind smote

---

[1] Cf. chapter xxxiv. 3.
[2] *I.e.* in the middle of the afternoon.

καταιγίσαντος εἰς τὴν πυρὰν καὶ φλόγα πολλὴν
ἐγείραντος ἔφθη τὸ σῶμα συγκομισθὲν ὅσον ἤδη
τῆς πυρᾶς μαραινομένης καὶ τοῦ πυρὸς ἀπιόντος
ἐκχυθῆναι πολὺν ὄμβρον καὶ κατασχεῖν ἄχρι
νυκτός, ὥστε τὴν τύχην αὐτοῦ δοκεῖν τὸ σῶμα
4 συνθάπτειν παραμένουσαν. τὸ μὲν οὖν μνημεῖον
ἐν τῷ πεδίῳ τοῦ Ἄρεώς ἐστι· τὸ δὲ ἐπίγραμμά
φασιν αὐτὸν ὑπογραψάμενον καταλιπεῖν, οὗ
κεφάλαιόν ἐστιν ὡς οὔτε τῶν φίλων τις αὐτὸν εὖ
ποιῶν οὔτε τῶν ἐχθρῶν κακῶς ὑπερεβάλετο.

ΛΥΣΑΝΔΡΟΥ ΚΑΙ ΣΥΛΛΑ ΣΥΓΚΡΙΣΙΣ

I. Ἐπεὶ δὲ καὶ τὸν τούτου διεληλύθαμεν βίον,
ἴωμεν ἤδη πρὸς τὴν σύγκρισιν. τὸ μὲν οὖν ἀφ'
ἑαυτῶν αὐξήσεως ἀρχὴν λαβοῦσι μεγάλοις γενέσθαι κοινὸν ἀμφοτέροις ὑπῆρξεν, ἴδιον δὲ
Λυσάνδρου τὸ βουλομένων τῶν πολιτῶν καὶ
ὑγιαινόντων ὅσας ἔσχεν ἀρχὰς λαβεῖν, βιά-
σασθαι δὲ μηδὲν ἀκόντων μηδ' ἰσχῦσαι παρὰ
τοὺς νόμους.

2 Ἐν δὲ διχοστασίῃ καὶ ὁ πάγκακος ἔλλαχε
τιμῆς,

ὥσπερ ἐν Ῥώμῃ τότε διεφθαρμένου τοῦ δήμου
καὶ νοσοῦντος αὐτοῖς τοῦ πολιτεύματος ἄλλος 4
ἀλλαχόθεν ἀνίστατο δυνάστης. καὶ οὐδὲν ἦν
θαυμαστὸν εἰ Σύλλας ἦρχεν, ὅτε Γλαυκίαι καὶ

the pyre, and roused a mighty flame, and there was just time to collect the bones for burial, while the pyre was smouldering and the fire was going out, when a heavy rain began to fall, which continued till night. Therefore his good fortune would seem to have lasted to the very end, and taken part in his funeral rites. At any rate, his monument stands in the Campus Martius, and the inscription on it, they say, is one which he wrote for it himself, and the substance of it is, that no friend ever surpassed him in kindness, and no enemy in mischief.

COMPARISON OF LYSANDER AND SULLA

I. AND now since we have completed this Life also, let us come at once to the Comparison. In this respect, then, they were alike, namely, that both were founders of their own greatness; but it was a peculiar virtue in Lysander that he obtained all his high offices with the consent of his fellow-citizens, and when affairs were in a sound condition; he did not force anything from them against their will, nor did he acquire any power which was contrary to the laws.

" But in a time of sedition, the base man too is in honour," [1]

and so in Rome at that time, since the people was corrupt and their government in a distempered state, men of various origin rose to power. And it was no wonder that Sulla held sway, when such men as

[1] A proverb in hexameter verse, attributed to Callimachus of Alexandria. Plutarch uses it also in the *Nicias*, xi. 3, and in *Morals*, p. 479 a.

Σατορνῖνοι Μετέλλους ἤλαυνον ἐκ τῆς πόλεως,
ὑπάτων δὲ ἀπεσφάττοντο παῖδες ἐν ἐκκλησίαις,
ἀργυρίῳ δὲ καὶ χρυσίῳ τὰ ὅπλα παρελάμβανον
ὠνούμενοι τοὺς στρατευομένους, πυρὶ δὲ καὶ
σιδήρῳ τοὺς νόμους ἐτίθεσαν βιαζόμενοι τοὺς
3 ἀντιλέγοντας. οὐκ αἰτιῶμαι δὲ τὸν ἐν τοιούτοις
πράγμασι μέγιστον ἰσχῦσαι διαπραξάμενον, ἀλλὰ
σημεῖον οὐ τίθεμαι τοῦ βέλτιστον εἶναι τὸ γενέσθαι πρῶτον οὕτω πονηρὰ πραττούσης τῆς
πόλεως. ὁ δὲ ἀπὸ τῆς Σπάρτης εὐνομουμένης
τότε μάλιστα καὶ σωφρονούσης ἐπὶ τὰς μεγίστας
ἐκπεμπόμενος ἡγεμονίας καὶ πράξεις σχεδὸν
ἀρίστων ἄριστος ἐκρίνετο καὶ πρώτων πρῶτος.
4 ὅθεν ὁ μὲν πολλάκις τὴν ἀρχὴν ἀποδοὺς τοῖς
πολίταις ἀνέλαβε πολλάκις· διέμενε γὰρ ἡ τιμὴ
τῆς ἀρετῆς ἔχουσα τὸ πρωτεῖον· ὁ δὲ ἅπαξ
αἱρεθεὶς στρατεύματος ἡγεμών, ἔτη συνεχῶς
δέκα, νῦν μὲν ὕπατον, νῦν δὲ δικτάτορα ποιῶν
ἑαυτόν, ἀεὶ δὲ ὢν τύραννος, ἐν τοῖς ὅπλοις
ἔμενεν.

II. Ἐπεχείρησε μὲν οὖν ὁ Λύσανδρος, ὡς
εἴρηται, μεταστῆσαι τὰ περὶ τὴν πολιτείαν πρᾳό-
τερον καὶ νομιμώτερον ἢ Σύλλας· πειθοῖ γάρ,
οὐ δι᾽ ὅπλων οὐδὲ πάντα συλλήβδην ἀναιρῶν,
ὥσπερ ἐκεῖνος, ἀλλ᾽ αὐτὴν ἐπανορθούμενος τὴν
κατάστασιν τῶν βασιλέων· ὃ καὶ φύσει που
δίκαιον ἐδόκει, τὸν ἐξ ἀρίστων ἄριστον ἄρχειν
ἐν πόλει τῆς Ἑλλάδος ἡγουμένῃ δι᾽ ἀρετήν, οὐ
2 δι᾽ εὐγένειαν. ὥσπερ γὰρ κυνηγὸς οὐ ζητεῖ τὸ
ἐκ κυνός, ἀλλὰ κύνα, καὶ ἱππικὸς ἵππον, οὐ τὸ
ἐξ ἵππου· τί γάρ, ἂν ἐξ ἵππου ἡμίονος γένηται;

Glaucia and Saturninus drove such men as Metellus from the city, when sons of consuls were butchered in assemblies, when silver and gold purchased arms and men to wield them, and laws were enacted with fire and sword in defiance of all opposition. Now I do not blame the man who, in such a state of affairs, forced his way to supreme power; but I cannot regard his becoming first man, when the city was in such an evil plight, as a proof that he was also the best man. Whereas Lysander, since Sparta was at the height of good government and sobriety when she sent him forth upon the greatest commands and undertakings, was virtually decided to be first of her first men, and best of her best. Lysander, therefore, though he often surrendered his power into the hands of his fellow-citizens, as often received it back again, since the honour accorded to virtue continued to rank highest in the state; but Sulla, when he had once been chosen leader of an army, remained in arms for ten years together, making himself now consul, and now dictator, but always being a usurper.

II. It is true, indeed, that Lysander attempted, as I have said, to change the form of government, but it was by milder and more legal methods than Sulla's; by persuasion, namely, not by force of arms, nor by subverting everything at once, as Sulla did, but by amending merely the appointment of the kings. And it seemed but natural justice, in a way, that the best of the best should rule in a city which had the leadership in Hellas by virtue of his excellence, and not of his noble birth. For just as a hunter looks for a dog, and not the whelp of a certain bitch, and a horseman for a horse, and not the foal of a certain mare (for what if the foal should prove to be a mule?),

447

οὕτως ὁ πολιτικὸς ἁμαρτήσεται τοῦ παντός,
ἐὰν μὴ ζητῇ τὸν ἄρχοντα τίς ἐστιν, ἀλλὰ ἐκ
τίνος. αὐτοί γέ τοι Σπαρτιᾶται βασιλεύοντας
ἐνίους ἀφείλοντο τὴν ἀρχήν, ὡς οὐ βασιλικούς,
ἀλλὰ φαύλους καὶ τὸ μηδὲν ὄντας. εἰ δὲ κακία
καὶ μετὰ γένους ἄτιμον, οὐδ᾽ ἀρετὴ δι᾽ εὐγένειαν,
ἀλλ᾽ ἀφ᾽ ἑαυτῆς ἔντιμον.

3   Αἱ τοίνυν ἀδικίαι τῷ μὲν ὑπὲρ φίλων, τῷ δ᾽
ἄχρι φίλων ἐπράχθησαν. Λύσανδρος μὲν γὰρ
ὁμολογεῖται τὰ πλεῖστα διὰ τοὺς ἑταίρους ἐξαμαρτεῖν καὶ τὰς πλείστας σφαγὰς ὑπὲρ τῆς
ἐκείνων ἀπεργάσασθαι δυναστείας καὶ τυραννίδος·
4   Σύλλας δὲ καὶ Πομπηΐου περιέκοψε τὸ στρατι-
ωτικὸν φθονήσας, καὶ Δολοβέλλα τὴν ναυαρχίαν
ἐπεχείρησε δοὺς ἀφελέσθαι, καὶ Λουκρήτιον
Ὀφέλλαν ἀντὶ πολλῶν καὶ μεγάλων ὑπατείαν
μνώμενον ἐν ὀφθαλμοῖς ἀποσφάξαι προσέταξε,
φρίκην καὶ δέος ἐμποιῶν πρὸς αὐτὸν ἀνθρώποις
ἅπασι διὰ τῆς τῶν φιλτάτων ἀναιρέσεως.

III. Ἔτι δὲ μᾶλλον ἡ περὶ τὰς ἡδονὰς καὶ τὰ
χρήματα σπουδὴ δείκνυσι τοῦ μὲν ἡγεμονικήν,
τοῦ δὲ τυραννικὴν τὴν προαίρεσιν οὖσαν. ὁ μὲν
γὰρ οὐδὲν ἀκόλαστον οὐδὲ μειρακιῶδες ἐν ἐξουσίᾳ
καὶ δυνάμει τηλικαύτῃ φαίνεται διαπεπραγμένος,
ἀλλ᾽, εἰ δή τις ἄλλος, ἐκπεφευγὼς τουτὶ τὸ
περίακτον· "Οἴκοι λέοντες, ἐν ὑπαίθρῳ δὲ ἀλώ-
πεκες·" οὕτω σώφρονα καὶ Λακωνικὴν καὶ
κεκολασμένην ἐπεδείκνυτο πανταχοῦ τὴν δίαιταν.
2   ὁ δὲ οὔτε νέος ὢν περὶ τὰς ἐπιθυμίας ἐμετρίαζε
διὰ τὴν πενίαν οὔτε γηράσας διὰ τὴν ἡλικίαν,

so the statesman makes an utter mistake if he enquires, not what sort of a man the ruler is, but from whom he is descended. And indeed the Spartans themselves deposed some of their kings, for the reason that they were not kingly men, but insignificant nobodies. And if vice, even in one of ancient family, is dishonourable, then it must be virtue itself, and not good birth, that makes virtue honourable.

Moreover, the acts of injustice which one wrought, were in behalf of his friends; while the other's extended to his friends. For it is generally agreed that Lysander committed the most of his transgressions for the sake of his comrades, and that most of his massacres were perpetrated to maintain their power and sovereignty; but Sulla cut down the number of Pompey's soldiers out of jealousy, and tried to take away from Dolabella the naval command which he had given him, and when Lucretius Ofella sued for the consulship as a reward for many great services, ordered him to be slain before his eyes, causing all men to regard him with fear and horror because of his murdering his dearest friends.

III. Still further, in their pursuit of riches and pleasures we discover that the purpose of one was more befitting a commander, that of the other more characteristic of a tyrant. For Lysander appears to have perpetrated no act of wantonness or youthful folly while he enjoyed such great authority and power, nay, if ever man did, he avoided the praise and reproach of the proverb: "Lions at home, but foxes abroad"; so sober, Spartan, and restrained was the way of life which he everywhere manifested. But Sulla allowed neither the poverty of his youth to set bounds to his desires, nor the years of his old age,

449

ἀλλὰ τοὺς περὶ γάμων καὶ σωφροσύνης εἰσηγεῖτο
νόμους τοῖς πολίταις αὐτὸς ἐρῶν καὶ μοιχεύων,
ὥς φησι Σαλούστιος. ὅθεν οὕτω τὴν πόλιν
πτωχὴν καὶ κενὴν ἐποίησε χρημάτων ὥστε ταῖς
συμμαχίσι καὶ φίλαις πόλεσιν ἀργυρίου πωλεῖν
τὴν ἐλευθερίαν καὶ τὴν αὐτονομίαν, καίτοι τοὺς
πολυαργυρωτάτους οἴκους καὶ μεγίστους ὁσημέραι
3 δημεύοντος αὐτοῦ καὶ ἀποκηρύττοντος. ἀλλὰ
μέτρον οὐδὲν ἦν τῶν ῥιπτουμένων καὶ καταχορη-
γουμένων εἰς τοὺς κόλακας. τίνα γὰρ εἰκὸς εἶναι
λογισμὸν ἢ φειδὼ πρὸς τὰς παρ' οἶνον συνουσίας 4
αὐτοῦ καὶ χάριτας, ὃς ἐν φανερῷ ποτε τοῦ δήμου
περιεστῶτος οὐσίαν μεγάλην διαπιπράσκων τιμῆς
τῆς τυχούσης εἰς ἕνα τῶν φίλων ἐκέλευε κατα-
κηρύσσειν, ἑτέρου δὲ τὴν τιμὴν ὑπερβαλομένου
καὶ τοῦ κήρυκος τὸ προστεθὲν ἀγορεύσαντος
διηγανάκτησε, "Δεινά γε, ὦ φίλοι πολῖται, καὶ
τυραννικὰ πάσχω," φάμενος, "εἰ τὰ ἐμά μοι
λάφυρα διαθέσθαι μὴ ἔξεστιν ὡς βούλομαι."
4 Λύσανδρος δὲ καὶ τὰς αὐτῷ δοθείσας δωρεὰς μετὰ
τῶν ἄλλων ἀπέπεμψε τοῖς πολίταις. καὶ οὐκ
ἐπαινῶ τὸ ἔργον· ἴσως γὰρ ἔβλαψε τῇ κτήσει
τῶν χρημάτων τὴν Σπάρτην οὗτος ὅσον οὐκ
ἔβλαψε τῇ ἀφαιρέσει τὴν Ῥώμην ἐκεῖνος· ἀλλὰ
τεκμήριον τοῦτο ποιοῦμαι τῆς ἀφιλοπλουτίας
5 τοῦ ἀνδρός. ἴδιον δέ τι πρὸς τὴν ἑαυτοῦ πόλιν
ἑκάτερος ἔπαθε. Σύλλας μὲν γὰρ ἀκόλαστος ὢν
καὶ πολυτελὴς ἐσωφρόνιζε τοὺς πολίτας, Λύσανδρος δ' ὢν αὐτὸς ἀπείχετο παθῶν ἐνέπλησε τὴν
πόλιν, ὥστε ἁμαρτάνειν τὸν μὲν αὐτὸν ὄντα
χείρονα τῶν ἰδίων νόμων, τὸν δὲ αὐτοῦ χείρονας
ἀπεργαζόμενον τοὺς πολίτας· δεῖσθαι γὰρ ἐδίδαξε

but continued to introduce marriage and sumptuary laws for the citizens, while he himself was living in lewdness and adultery, as Sallust says. In these courses he so beggared and emptied the city of her wealth that he sold to allied and friendly cities their freedom and independence for money, although he was daily confiscating and selling at public auction the wealthiest and greatest estates. Nay, there was no measuring what he lavishly squandered and threw away upon his flatterers. For what calculation or economy could be expected in his convivial associations and delights, when, on a public occasion, with the people standing about, at the sale of a large property, he ordered the crier to knock it down to one of his friends at a nominal price, and when another bidder raised the price and the crier announced the advance, he flew into a rage, saying: "It is a dreadful wrong, my dear citizens, and a piece of usurpation, that I cannot dispose of my own spoils as I wish." But Lysander sent home for public use even the presents which had been given to him along with the rest of his spoils. Not that I commend what he did; for he, perhaps, by his acquisition of money for Sparta, injured her more than Sulla injured Rome by robbing her of it; but I offer this as a proof of the man's indifference to riches. Moreover, each had a peculiar experience with his own city. Sulla, who knew no restraint in his extravagance, tried to bring the citizens into ways of sobriety; while Lysander filled his city with the passions to which he himself was a stranger. The former erred, therefore, in falling below the standard of his own laws; the latter, in causing the citizens to fall below his own standard, since he taught Sparta to want

451

τὴν Σπάρτην ὧν αὐτὸς ἔμαθε μὴ προσδεῖσθαι.
καὶ τὰ μὲν πολιτικὰ ταῦτα.

IV. Πολέμων δὲ ἀγῶσι καὶ στρατηγικαῖς
πράξεσι καὶ πλήθει τροπαίων καὶ μεγέθει κινδύνων ἀσύγκριτος ὁ Σύλλας. ὁ μέντοι γε δύο
νίκας ἐξηνέγκατο ναυμαχίαις δυσί· προσθήσω
δὲ αὐτῷ τὴν Ἀθηνῶν πολιορκίαν, ἔργῳ μὲν οὐ
μεγάλην, τῇ δὲ δόξῃ λαμπροτάτην γενομένην.
2 τὰ δ' ἐν Βοιωτίᾳ καὶ Ἁλιάρτῳ δυστυχίᾳ μὲν
ἴσως ἐπράχθη τινί, κακοβουλίᾳ δὲ προσέοικεν
οὐκ ἀναμείναντος ὅσον οὔπω παροῦσαν ἐκ Πλαταιῶν τὴν μεγάλην τοῦ βασιλέως δύναμιν, ἀλλὰ
θυμῷ καὶ φιλοτιμίᾳ παρὰ καιρὸν ὠσαμένου πρὸς
τὸ τεῖχος, ὥστε τοὺς τυχόντας ἀνθρώπους ἐκ-
πηδήσαντας ἐν οὐδενὶ λόγῳ καταβαλεῖν αὐτόν.
οὐ γὰρ ὡς Κλεόμβροτος ἐν Λεύκτροις ἀντερείδων
ἐπικειμένοις τοῖς πολεμίοις, οὐδὲ ὡς Κῦρος οὐδὲ
ὡς Ἐπαμεινώνδας κατέχων ἐγκεκλικότας καὶ τὸ
νίκημα βεβαιούμενος πληγῇ καιρίᾳ περιέπεσεν·
3 ἀλλ' οὗτοι μὲν βασιλέων καὶ στρατηγῶν θάνατον ἀπέθνησκον, Λύσανδρος δὲ πελταστοῦ καὶ
προδρόμου δίκην ἀκλεῶς παραναλώσας ἑαυτόν,
ἐμαρτύρησε τοῖς παλαιοῖς Σπαρτιάταις ὅτι καλῶς
ἐφυλάττοντο τὰς τειχομαχίας, ἐν αἷς οὐχ ὑπ'
ἀνδρὸς μόνον τοῦ τυχόντος, ἀλλὰ καὶ ὑπὸ παιδὸς
καὶ γυναικὸς ἀποθανεῖν ἂν συντύχοι πληγέντα
τὸν κράτιστον, ὥσπερ τὸν Ἀχιλλέα φασὶν ὑπὸ
τοῦ Πάριδος ἐν ταῖς πύλαις ἀναιρεθῆναι.
4 Σύλλας μὲν οὖν ὅσας ἐκ παρατάξεως ἐνίκησε
νίκας καὶ κατέβαλε μυριάδας πολεμίων οὐδὲ
ἀριθμῆσαι ῥᾴδιόν ἐστιν· αὐτὴν δὲ τὴν Ῥώμην δὶς
εἷλε, καὶ τὸν Πειραιᾶ τῶν Ἀθηνῶν οὐ λιμῷ

what he himself had learned not to want. Such was their influence as statesmen.

IV. But as regards contests in war, achievements in generalship, number of trophies, and magnitude of dangers encountered, Sulla is beyond compare. Lysander, it is true, won two victories in as many naval battles; and I will add to his exploits his siege of Athens, which was really not a great affair, although the reputation of it was most brilliant. What occurred in Boeotia and at Haliartus, was due, perhaps, to a certain evil fortune; but it looks as though he was injudicious in not waiting for the large forces of the king, which had all but arrived from Plataea, instead of allowing his resentment and ambition to lead him into an inopportune assault upon the walls, with the result that an inconsiderable and random body of men sallied out and overwhelmed him. For he received his death wound, not as Cleombrotus did, at Leuctra, standing firm against the enemy's onsets, nor as Cyrus did, or Epaminondas, rallying his men and assuring the victory to them; these all died the death of kings and generals. But Lysander threw away his life ingloriously, like a common targeteer or skirmisher, and bore witness to the wisdom of the ancient Spartans in avoiding assaults on walled cities, where not only an ordinary man, but even a child or a woman may chance to smite and slay the mightiest warrior, as Achilles, they say, was slain by Paris at the gates.

In Sulla's case, at any rate, it is no easy matter even to enumerate the pitched battles which he won and the myriads of enemies whom he slew; Rome itself he captured twice, and he took the Piraeus of

453

καθάπερ Λύσανδρος, ἀλλὰ πολλοῖς ἀγῶσι καὶ
μεγάλοις, ἐκβαλὼν Ἀρχέλαον ἐκ τῆς γῆς ἐπὶ τὴν
θάλατταν, κατέσχεν. ἔστι δὲ μέγα καὶ τὸ τῶν
ἀντιστρατήγων. τρυφὴν γὰρ οἶμαι καὶ παιδιὰν
πρὸς Ἀντίοχον διαναυμαχεῖν τὸν Ἀλκιβιάδου
κυβερνήτην, καὶ Φιλοκλέα τὸν Ἀθηναίων ἐξαπατᾶν δημαγωγόν,

Ἄδοξον, ἄκραν γλῶσσαν ἠκονημένον·

οὓς οὐκ ἂν ἱπποκόμῳ Μιθριδάτης οὐδὲ ῥαβδούχῳ
5 Μάριος ἠξίωσε παραβαλεῖν τῶν ἑαυτοῦ. τῶν δὲ
πρὸς Σύλλαν ἀνταραμένων δυναστῶν, ὑπάτων,
στρατηγῶν, δημαγωγῶν, ἵνα τοὺς ἄλλους ἐάσω,
τίς ἦν Ῥωμαίων Μαρίου φοβερώτερος ἢ Μιθριδάτου βασιλέων δυνατώτερος ἢ Λαμπωνίου καὶ
Τελεσίνου τῶν Ἰταλικῶν μαχιμώτερος; ὧν ἐκεῖνος
τὸν μὲν ἐξέβαλε, τὸν δὲ ὑπέταξε, τοὺς δὲ ἀπέ-
κτεινε.

V. Τὸ δὲ πάντων μέγιστον, ὡς ἐγὼ νομίζω,
τῶν εἰρημένων ἐκεῖνό ἐστιν, ὅτι Λύσανδρος μὲν
κατώρθου πάντα τῶν οἴκοι συναγωνιζομένων,
Σύλλας δὲ φυγὰς ὢν καὶ κατεστασιασμένος ὑπὸ
τῶν ἐχθρῶν, καθ' ὃν χρόνον ἠλαύνετο μὲν αὐτοῦ
γυνή, κατεσκάπτετο δὲ οἰκία, φίλοι δὲ ἀπέθνησκον,
αὐτὸς ἐν Βοιωτίᾳ ταῖς ἀναριθμήτοις μυριάσι
παρατασσόμενος καὶ κινδυνεύων ὑπὲρ τῆς πατρί-
2 δος, ἵστη τρόπαιον, καὶ Μιθριδάτῃ συμμαχίαν
διδόντι καὶ δύναμιν ἐπὶ τοὺς ἐχθροὺς οὐδὲν οὐδαμῇ

Athens, not by famine, as Lysander did, but by a
series of great battles, after he had driven Archelaüs
from the land to the sea. It is important, too, that
we consider the character of their antagonists. For
I think it was the merest child's play to win a sea-
fight against Antiochus, Alcibiades' pilot, or to outwit
Philocles, the Athenian demagogue,

> "Inglorious foe, whose only weapon is a sharpened
>   tongue " ; [1]

such men as these Mithridates would not have deigned
to compare with his groom, nor Marius with his lictor.
But of the dynasts, consuls, generals, and demagogues
who lifted themselves against Sulla, to pass by the
rest, who among the Romans was more formidable
than Marius? who among the kings was more powerful than Mithridates? who among the Italians was
more warlike than Lamponius and Telesinus? And
yet Sulla banished the first of these, subdued the
second, and slew the others.

V. But what is of more weight, in my opinion,
than any thing yet mentioned, Lysander achieved
all his successes with the co-operation of the authorities at home; whereas Sulla, though he was overpowered by a hostile faction, and an exile, at a time
when his wife was being driven from home, his house
being demolished, and his friends being slain, when
he himself, too, was confronting countless myriads
of enemies in Boeotia and risking his life for his
country, set up his trophy of victory; and not even
when Mithridates offered him an alliance and forces
to wield against his enemies at Rome, would he make

---

[1] An iambic trimeter of unknown authorship (Nauck,
Trag. Graec. Frag.[2] p. 921).

μαλακὸν ἐνέδωκεν οὐδὲ φιλάνθρωπον, ἀλλ᾽ οὐδὲ
προσεῖπεν οὐδὲ τὴν δεξιὰν ἐνέβαλε πρότερον ἢ
πυθέσθαι παρόντος ὅτι καὶ τὴν Ἀσίαν ἀφίησι
καὶ τὰς ναῦς παραδίδωσι καὶ τοῖς βασιλεῦσιν
3 ἐξίσταται καὶ Βιθυνίας καὶ Καππαδοκίας. ὧν
οὐδὲν ὅλως δοκεῖ Σύλλας κάλλιον ἔργον οὐδὲ
ἀπὸ μείζονος εἰργάσθαι φρονήματος, ὅτι τὸ κοινὸν
τοῦ οἰκείου πρόσθεν θέμενος, καὶ καθάπερ οἱ
γενναῖοι κύνες οὐκ ἀνεὶς τὸ δῆγμα καὶ τὴν λαβὴν
πρότερον ἢ τὸν ἀνταγωνιστὴν ἀπειπεῖν, τότε
4 πρὸς τὴν τῶν ἰδίων ἄμυναν ὥρμησεν. ἐπὶ πᾶσι
δὲ καὶ τὸ περὶ τὰς Ἀθήνας ἔχει τινὰ ῥοπὴν εἰς
ἤθους σύγκρισιν· εἴγε Σύλλας μὲν ὑπὲρ τῆς
Μιθριδάτου δυνάμεως καὶ ἡγεμονίας πολεμή-
σασαν αὐτῷ τὴν πόλιν ἑλὼν ἐλευθέραν ἀφῆκε
καὶ αὐτόνομον, Λύσανδρος δὲ τοσαύτης ἡγεμονίας
καὶ ἀρχῆς ἐκπεσοῦσαν οὐκ ᾤκτειρεν, ἀλλὰ καὶ
τὴν δημοκρατίαν ἀφελόμενος ὠμοτάτους αὐτῇ
καὶ παρανόμους ἀπέδειξε τοὺς τυράννους.

5 Ὥρα δὴ σκοπεῖν, μὴ οὐ πολὺ τἀληθοῦς δι-
αμαρτάνωμεν ἀποφαινόμενοι πλέονα μὲν κατωρ-
θωκέναι Σύλλαν, ἐλάττονα δὲ ἐξημαρτηκέναι
Λύσανδρον, καὶ τῷ μὲν ἐγκρατείας καὶ σωφροσύνης, τῷ δὲ στρατηγίας καὶ ἀνδρείας ἀποδιδόντες
τὸ πρωτεῖον.

any concession whatsoever, or show him kindness even; nay, he would not so much as greet him or give him his hand, until he heard him say personally that he would relinquish Asia, hand over his ships, and restore Bithynia and Cappadocia to their rightful kings. No act of Sulla's whatsoever appears more honourable than this, or due to a loftier spirit, because he set the public interests before his own, and, like dogs of noble breed, did not relax his bite or let go his hold until his adversary had yielded, and then only did he set out to avenge his own private wrongs. And besides all this, their treatment of Athens is of some weight in a comparison of their characters. Sulla, after taking the city, although it had fought against him to support the power and supremacy of Mithridates, restored her to freedom and independence; whereas Lysander, although she had fallen from such a great supremacy and empire, showed her no pity, but took away her democratic form of government, and appointed most savage and lawless men to be her tyrants.

We may now consider whether we shall err very much from the truth in pronouncing our verdict that Sulla won the more successes, while Lysander had the fewer failings; and in giving to the one the preëminence in self-control and moderation, to the other, in generalship and valour.

A PARTIAL DICTIONARY OF
PROPER NAMES

A PARTIAL DICTIONARY OF
PROPER NAMES

A

Abydos, 105, a city of Mysia, on the eastern shore of the Hellespont, nearly opposite Sestos on the European side.

Acastus, 441, mythical king of Iolcus in Thessaly. He was one of the Argonauts, and took part in the Calydonian boar-hunt.

Aedepsus, 409, a town on the N.W. coast of Euboea, nearly opposite Thermopylae on the mainland.

Aegospotami, 107, a stream on the western side of the Hellespont, nearly opposite Lampsacus, with a town of the same name upon it.

Agatharchus, 43, of Samos, prominent at Athens as a theatrical scene-painter, 460–420 B.C.

Alcman, 441, the greatest lyric poet of Sparta, who lived from about 670 to about 630 B.C. He was a Lydian by birth, and was brought to Sparta as a slave.

Alcmene, 313, wife of Amphitryon king of Thebes, and mother of Heracles by Zeus. After the death of Amphitryon she married Rhadamanthus.

Amphictyons, 363, officers of the Amphictyonic League, which comprised the peoples whose common sanctuaries were the temple of Apollo at Delphi and that of Demeter at Anthela, near Thermopylae.

Amphitryon, 313, mythical king of Thebes, and husband of Alcmene.

Anaxagoras, 263, of Clazomenae in Ionian Asia Minor, prominent at Athens as an advanced thinker from about 460–432 B.C., when the enemies of Pericles brought about his banishment.

Anaxandrides, 281, the Delphian, probably of the third century B.C., author of a work on the plundered offerings of Delphi.

Andronicus, 407, the Rhodian, head of the Peripatetic school of philosophy at Rome in the middle of the first century B.C.

Antemnae, 423, an ancient city of Latium, some three miles south of Rome, just below the junction of the Anio with the Tiber.

Anthesterion, 373, the eighth month of the Attic calendar, corresponding to the latter part of February and first part of March.

Antigonus Doson, 143, a grandson of Demetrius Poliorcetes, and king of Macedonia 229–221 B.C.

Antilochus, 283, otherwise unknown.

Antimachus, 283, of Colophon, a celebrated poet of Lysander's time, called " clarus poeta " in Cicero, *Brutus*, 51, 191.

Antisthenes, 3, the Socratic, a pupil of Gorgias and friend of Socrates.

Antium, 149, 163, 167, 171, 181, 215, a city of Latium, on the sea-coast about forty miles south of Rome.

Anytus, 13, 151, an influential politician at Athens, afterwards

DICTIONARY OF PROPER NAMES

famous conspirator in the consulship of Cicero, 63 B.C. (*Cicero*, chapters x.–xxii.).

Censorinus, 337, Caius Marcius, prominent among the leaders of the Marian party and in many conflicts with Sulla. He was finally taken prisoner and put to death by Sulla in 82 B.C. Cicero speaks of him (*Brutus*, 67, 237) as well versed in Greek literature.

Chalcedon, 85, 87, 89, a Greek city in Bithynia, opposite Byzantium.

Chalcis, 389, 391, a city in Euboea, on the strait of Euripus, nearly opposite Chalcis in Boeotia.

Chersonese, 243, 255, 257, 263, the Thracian Chersonese, or peninsula, on the west of the Hellespont.

Choerilus, 281, of Samos, 479–399 B.C., author of an epic poem on the Persian wars.

Cinna, 357, 397, Lucius Cornelius, leader of the Marian party during Sulla's absence in the East (87–84 B.C.). He was consul in 87, 86, 85, and 84. He was slain in a mutiny of his soldiers at Brundisium, where he hoped to prevent the landing of Sulla.

Circeii, 185, a town of Latium, on the sea-coast about eighty miles S.E. of Rome.

Cithaeron, Mt., 311, a range of mountains separating Attica and Boeotia.

Clazomenae, 81, an Ionian city on the southern shore of the bay of Smyrna.

Cleanthes, 15, of Assos, a Stoic philosopher, who succeeded Zeno as head of the school at Athens in 263 B.C. His Hymn to Zeus is still extant.

Cleon, the Halicarnassian, 303, 305, a rhetorician who flourished at the close of the fifth and the beginning of the fourth centuries B.C.

Critias, 97, 113, a brilliant follower of Socrates, like Alcibiades, and later one of the Thirty Tyrants. He was author of tragedies and elegiac poems.

Cyzicus, 67, 81, 83, a Greek city on the Propontis, in Mysia.

D

Daïmachus, 263, 267, perhaps the same person as the Daïmachus of Plataea (*Comparison of Solon and Publicola*, iv. 1), a historian who flourished in the latter part of the fourth century B.C.

Dionysius, 237, the Elder, tyrant of Syracuse from 405 to 367 B.C.

Dodona, 305, a town in Epirus, famous in earlier times for its oracle of Zeus, the influence of which among the Greek states was subsequently assumed by the oracle of Apollo at Delphi.

Dolabella, 415, 421, 449, Cnaeus Cornelius, consul in 81 B.C., and afterwards proconsul of Macedonia. In 77, he was prosecuted by Julius Caesar for maladministration of his province (*Caesar*, iv. 1).

Duris, the Samian, 93, 281, historian and for a time tyrant of Samos, a pupil of Theophrastus. He lived about 350–280 B.C. He was an extravagant and sensational writer.

Dyrrhachium, 409, a city on the coast of Illyricum, known in Greek history as Epidamnus. It was a free state, and sided with the Romans consistently.

E

Ephorus, 95, 277, 291, 305, 319, of Cymé, pupil of Isocrates with Theopompus, and author of a highly rhetorical history of Greece from earliest times down to 340 B.C., in which year he died.

Epidaurus, 363, a city on the east coast of Argolis in Peloponnesus, famous for its shrine and cult of Aesculapius.

Eumolpus, 369, a mythical Thracian bard and warrior, called in to aid Eleusis against Athens, and slain by Erechtheus.

463

DICTIONARY OF PROPER NAMES

Evagoras, 261, king of Salamis in
Cyprus, extravagantly praised,
in the oration of Isocrates bearing
his name, as a mild and just ruler.
He was a constant friend of
Athens from the time here mentioned till his death in 374 B.C.

F

Fenestella, 417, a Roman historian
who flourished during the reign
of Augustus.
Fidentia, 413, a town of Cisalpine
Gaul (now northern Italy), on the
Via Aemilia, south of the Po.

G

Gelo, 155, tyrant of Syracuse 485–
478 B.C., and victor over the
Carthaginians at Himera in 480
B.C.
Glaucia, 447, Caius Servilius, praetor in 100 B.C., a partizan of
Marius, and partner of Saturninus
in the popular tumults of that
year. He perished with Saturninus. Cicero compares him to
the Athenian demagogue Hyperbolus (Brutus, 62, 224).

H

Heraea, 295, a city of northwestern Arcadia in Peloponnesus.

I

Isocrates, 27, the celebrated Attic
orator and rhetorician, 436–338
B.C.

J

Juba, 381, Juba II., king of Mauri-
tania. He lived from 50 B.C. to
about 20 A.D., was educated at
Rome, and became a learned and
voluminous writer. Among his
works was a History of Rome.

Jugurtha, 329, 331, 337, king of
Numidia 112–106 B.C., when
he was brought a prisoner to
Rome, and starved to death in
104.

L

Lamponius, the Lucanian, 419, 455,
one of the principal leaders of the
Italians in the war with Rome
(90–88 B.C.).
Lampsacus, 107, 255, a famous
Greek city on the Asiatic side of
the Hellespont, opposite Aegos-
potami.
Larissa, 401, an important city in
N.E. Thessaly.
Laverna, 341, of unknown site.
Lavicum, 187, an ancient town in
Latium, of uncertain site.
Lavinium, 189, an ancient town of
Latium, near the sea-coast, about
seventeen miles S.E. of Rome.
Lepidus, 435, 437, 443, Marcus
Aemilius, father of the triumvir.
He was driven from Italy by
Pompey in 77 B.C., and died
shortly afterwards in Sardinia.

M

Maedi, 403, a powerful people in
the west of Thrace.
Maeotis, Lake, 359, the modern
Sea of Azov, north of the Black
Sea.
Malea, Cape, 359, the S.E. extremity
of Laconia in Peloponnesus, now
Cape St. Angelo.
Marsi, 331, a warlike nation in
central Italy, often victorious
over the Romans. They were
finally subdued soon after 89 B.C.,
and admitted to Roman citizenship.
Metellus, 341, 343, 419, Quintus
Caecilius, surnamed Pius, consul
with Sulla in 80 B.C., and one of
his most successful generals.
After Sulla's death in 79 B.C., he
went as proconsul to Spain to
prosecute the war against Ser-

torius (*Crassus*, chapter vi.). It has been shown that Metella, the wife of Sulla, was not the daughter of Metellus Pius, but of Metellus Dalmaticus, his uncle.

Metellus, 447, Quintus Caecilius, surnamed Numidicus, consul in 109 B.C., and conqueror of Jugurtha. As censor in 102 B.C., he attempted to expel Saturninus and Glaucia from the senate, but was prevented from doing so and himself expelled and driven into exile for a year (100–99 B.C.).

Meton, 45, the astrologer, the most famous mathematician and astronomer of his time. In 432 B.C., he published a new calendar with a cycle of nineteen years, intended to reconcile the lunar and solar years.

Mithridates, 335, 343, 351, 359, the sixth king of Pontus bearing this name, commonly called Mithridates the Great, 120–63 B.C., the most formidable enemy of the Romans in the East.

Mucius, 441, probably Publius Mucius Scaevola, consul in 133 B.C.

Munychion, 273, the tenth month in the Attic calendar, corresponding to the latter part of April and first part of May.

N

Niceratus of Heracleia, 283, otherwise unknown.

Nicomedes, 399, 405, the third king of Bithynia bearing this name. He was reseated on his throne in 90 and 84 B.C. by the Romans, and reigned ten years after the second restoration till his death in 74 B.C.

Nola, 351, 353, an ancient and important town in Campania, some twenty miles S.E. of Capua.

Norbanus, 411, 413, consul in 83 B.C. After his defeats by Sulla and Metellus, he fled to Rhodes, where he put an end to his life.

P

Panactum, 33, a fortress of Attica on the confines of Boeotia, betrayed to the Thebans in 420 B.C. (Thuc., v. 3, 5).

Pedum, 187, an ancient town of Latium, of uncertain site.

Pergamum, 359, 401, the chief city of Mysia in Asia Minor, from 363 to 133 B.C., the seat of the Attalid dynasty. The last Attalid bequeathed his kingdom to the Romans.

Pharnabazus, 67, 81–89, 111, 113, 115, 285, 287, 289, 301, satrap of the Persian provinces about the Hellespont from 412 till 393.

Pherecydes, 441, of Syros, a writer on cosmogony and mythology who flourished about the middle of the sixth century B.C.

Philippi, 403, a city of Macedonia on the river Strymon, formerly called Crenides, renamed by Philip the father of Alexander the Great.

Phocaea, 243, the most northerly of the Ionian cities in Asia Minor.

Phyle, 291, 311, a fortress on Mt. Parnes commanding the road from Athens and Eleusis to Thebes, some sixteen miles from Athens.

Pompeius, Quintus, 343, 351, surnamed Rufus, tribune in 199, praetor in 91, and consul with Sulla in 88 B.C. Sulla left him in charge of Italy on setting out for the East, but he was murdered by the soldiers of Pompeius Strabo who had been assigned to his command.

Pontus, 305, 359, 397, the district extending along the S.E. shore of the Euxine Sea, the seat of the kingdom of Mithridates.

Praeneste, 417, 499, 423, 429, an ancient city of Latium on a spur of the Apennines about twenty-three miles east of Rome.

Proconnesus, 81, an island in the western part of the Propontis.

Ptolemy, Lathyrus, 143, Ptolemy VIII., king of Egypt 117–81 B.C., surnamed also Soter and Philometor.

DICTIONARY OF PROPER NAMES

R

Rhadamanthus, 313, mythical son of Zeus and Europa, brother of Minos the king of Crete. He fled from Crete to Ocaleia in Boeotia, where he married Alcmene. He became one of the judges in the lower world.

Roscius, 439, a great actor, from whom Cicero learned much, and of whom he often speaks in high terms of praise (cf. *pro Archia*, 8, 17).

S

Sallust, 451, 86–34 B.C., historian of the Conspiracy of Catiline, of the Jugurthine War (111–106 B.C.) and also, in a work that is lost, of portions of the Civil Wars.

Saturninus, 447, Lucius Appuleius, a Roman noble who allied himself with Marius and the popular party, tribune in 102 and 100 B.C., in which year he perished at the hands of a mob.

Selymbria, 87, 89, a Greek city on the northern shore of the Propontis, some forty miles west of Byzantium.

Servilius, 419, Publius Servilius Vatia Isauricus, made consul by Sulla in 79 B.C. In the following year he was sent as proconsul to Cilicia to clear the sea of pirates. He was successful, and received the surname of Isauricus from one of the robber tribes which he subdued.

Sestos, 107, 109, 255, 257, 269, the chief town of the Thracian Chersonese, opposite Abydos on the Asiatic side of the Hellespont.

Signia, 415, an ancient city of Latium, now Segni, some thirty-five miles S.E. of Rome, in the Volscian mountains.

Silvium, 413, a town in the interior of Apulia, of uncertain site.

Sphacteria, 35, an island stretching in front of the harbour of Pylos, on the western coast of Peloponnesus.

T

Tarentum, 411, a great and powerful city in S.E. Italy, at the head of the gulf to which it gave its name.

Taureas, 43, competed with Alcibiades as choregus in a dithyrambic contest at the Greater Dionysia (cf. Demosthenes, *Or.* xxi. 147).

Tectosages, 331, a Celtic people dwelling at the foot of the Pyrenees in Gallia Narbonensis.

Tegea, 319, an ancient and powerful city in southern Arcadia of Peloponnesus.

Theophrastus, 25, 267, 285, 407, the most famous pupil of Aristotle, and his successor as head of the Peripatetic school at Athens. He was born at Eresos in Lesbos, and died at Athens in 287 B.C. at the age of eighty-five.

Theopompus, 95, 277, 319, of Chios, a fellow-pupil of Isocrates with Ephorus, historian of Greece from 411 to 394 B.C., and of Philip of Macedon (360–336 B.C.). He is always censorious of Athens and her popular leaders.

Theopompus, the comic poet, 269, an Athenian poet of the Old and Middle Comedy, who wrote as late as 380 B.C.

Theramenes, 3, 91, 271, a brilliant naval commander who co-operated successfully with Alcibiades in the closing years of the Peloponnesian war. He was one of the Thirty Tyrants and favoured a moderate course, but fell a victim to the jealousy and hatred of Critias.

Thyateira, 405, a large city in the north of Lydia, about forty-five miles S.E. of Pergamum.

Timon, 43, the misanthrope, an Athenian of the time of the Peloponnesian War. He is attacked by the comic poets as a man-hating solitary. Plutarch devotes chapter lxx. of his *Antony* to a sketch of the man. A dialogue of Lucian bears his name.

Timotheus, 339, from 375 to 354 B.C. one of the most popular and successful Athenian commanders.

Tolericum, 187, an ancient town in Latium, of uncertain site.

Torquatus, 421, perhaps the Manlius Torquatus who was propraetor of Africa about 70 B.C.

Troad, 403, a district in the northwestern angle of Mysia, bordering on the Hellespont and the Aegean Sea, named from ancient Troy.

Tyrannio, the grammarian, 407, a native of Amisus in Pontus. He was brought as a captive to Rome by Lucullus in 72 B.C. (*Lucullus*, xix. 7). There he became a teacher, was patronized and praised by Cicero, and amassed wealth.

V

Velitrae, 145, a city of Latium, on the southern slope of the Alban hills, about thirty miles S.E of Rome.

PRINTED IN GREAT BRITAIN BY
RICHARD CLAY & SONS, LIMITED,
BUNGAY, SUFFOLK.